SINGING

IN A STRANGE LAND

SINGING

IN A STRANGE LAND

C. L. Franklin, the Black Church,
and the Transformation of America

NICK SALVATORE

LITTLE, BROWN AND COMPANY

NEW YORK   BOSTON

Little, Brown and Company

Time Warner Book Group

1271 Avenue of the Americas, New York, NY 10020

Visit our Web site at www.twbookmark.com

First Edition: February 2005

Library of Congress Cataloging-in-Publication Data
Salvatore, Nick.
    Singing in a strange land : C. L. Franklin, the black church, and the transformation of America / Nick Salvatore. — 1st ed.
        p. cm.
    Includes bibliographical references and index.
    ISBN 0-316-16037-7
    1. Franklin, C. L. (Clarence LaVaughn), 1915–1984.   2. African American Baptists — Biography. 3. Baptists — United States — Clergy — Biography.   4. African American churches — History.   I. Title.
BX6455.F73S25   2004
286'.1'092 — dc22   2004016658

10 9 8 7 6 5 4 3 2 1

Q-MART

Book design by MADA Design, Inc.

Printed in the United States of America

For _____

Leon F. Litwack

and

Erma V. Franklin

1938–2002

By the rivers of Babylon, there we sat down,
yea, we wept, when we remembered Zion.

We hanged our harps upon the willows
in the midst thereof.

For there they that carried us away captive
required of us a song; and they that
wasted us required of us *mirth,* saying
sing us one of *the songs of Zion.*

How shall we sing the Lord's song in a strange land?

PSALM 137:1–4

CONTENTS

Contents

PREFACE

Born in rural Mississippi early in the twentieth century, a black child who grew up in a land dominated by white men and the white cotton they grew, Clarence LaVaughn Franklin became in time one of black America's most renowned preachers. He never completed grade school, but his intense desire to transcend the limitations Mississippi would impose propelled him. His sermons, compelling original presentations within a deeply familiar preaching tradition, offered new ways of considering the interplay of religious belief, racial identity, and social activism in daily life. His own transitions—from Mississippi to Detroit, from a narrowed understanding to a more complex expression of faith's meanings—served as a model for untold thousands of other black rural southerners as they migrated into the urban industrial world. His musical tastes ranged from the sacred to the secular, reflecting his belief that all forms of music were God's creations. Three of his daughters, all raised in the church, shared this talent and sensibility; one of them, his extraordinarily gifted daughter Aretha, would, in time, transform American music. That, too, he considered fully compatible with his ministry.

There has never been a full study of this remarkable man. This is unfortunate, for to explore Franklin's life is also to examine some of the most important changes in twentieth-century America. The journey that began for Franklin in the Mississippi Delta before World War I was not, in its broad outlines, unique to him. Rather, his effort to project a public voice was part of a multigenerational struggle by African Americans to reinterpret the meaning of American democracy. In that process, a civil rights movement gathered power, patterns of work and community forcefully altered, and an African American musical tradition reconfigured the notes most Americans listened to.

Clarence LaVaughn Franklin was deeply involved in these developments. His sermons, seventy-five of which were recorded live and sold nationally, provided pointed social and political analyses that consciously urged others to discover their voices and to engage the world about them. His Detroit home, moreover, was a crossroads for post–World War II black musical culture. The great jazz and blues artists, gospel singers, rhythm and blues performers, and the enormously talented Detroit youngsters who would so influence popular music mingled at the gatherings he hosted. All of this constituted Franklin's world.

C. L. Franklin was a complicated man, one who knew sin and salvation, one who possessed remarkable strength and painful weakness. A man of the cotton fields and the inner cities, his rise was the crest of a powerful social movement with origins not in the ocean's swell but in the rich loam of the Mississippi Delta. To know him is to understand more fully the complex experiences central to modern American life. And to know that, of course, is to understand more fully ourselves.

SINGING

IN A STRANGE LAND

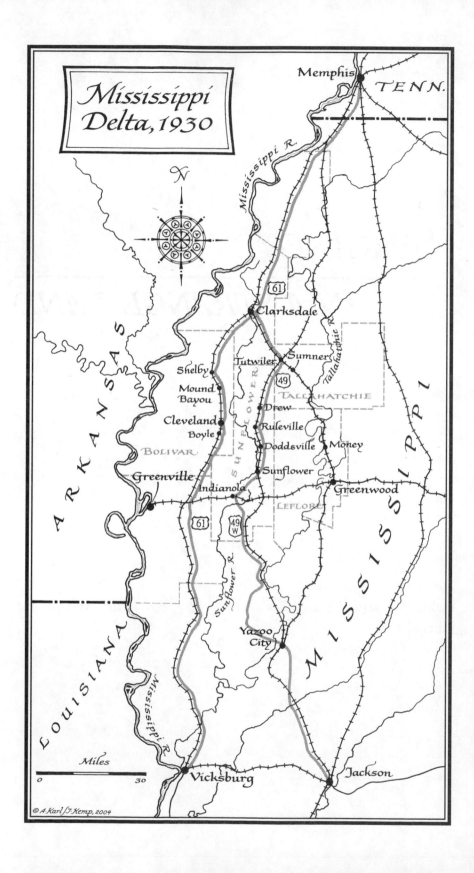

CHAPTER ONE

A DEEP LONGING

"Fa-a-ther," intoned the young teenage soloist from the choir stand at St. Peter's Rock Baptist Church one Sunday morning in the late 1920s. "Fa-a-ther, I Stretch My Hands to Thee." As he sang of the hope that all might yet hear God's "quickening voice and taste [his] pardn'ing grace," the congregation in the small wooden church responded fervently. As Rachel Franklin watched her son and oldest child that morning, a mother's ordinary pride might easily have merged with a growing belief that her boy had been blessed with a special gift. Indeed, Rachel already sensed that her son might well be a messenger of the Lord who would, in time, transform lives. Someday, when people thought of Cleveland, Mississippi, deep in the Delta, they would think first of this young boy with a voice like few others.[1]

*   *   *   *   *

Rachel Franklin was a Pittman, a family with a long history in the Mississippi Delta. Her parents, Elijah J. and Willie Ann Pittman, were both born slaves on cotton plantations. Following freedom, the couple worked the land and raised four children.[2]

It was "directly after" slavery that Elijah Pittman accepted his call to preach the gospel. While no one church had the resources to support him, he preached as a "special pastor" from church to church even as he worked the land, raising cotton for white plantation owners. Rachel was born on March 15, 1897, in Sunflower County, Mississippi, nearby the county seat, at Indianola. At least one of her siblings, her brother, Robert, was older. As a child her family moved to Shaw, in neighboring Bolivar County, and they may have moved back to Sunflower County at a later time. Like many black agricultural workers in the state, the Pittmans would migrate on occasion to adjacent plantations in search of marginal—but, to them, significant—improvements in their working conditions.[3]

Decades later, Rachel recalled little of the daily atmosphere of her early years in Mississippi but the family's religious intensity. "We always have," she commented, "you know, been a Christian family." Whether all of her siblings shared Rachel's commitment is unknown, but her faith deepened through teen years filled with emotional strain, love, and loss. Before she completed her seventeenth year, both of her parents had passed, and she had fallen in love, married, and become a mother. A few short years later, she lost her husband as well. The testing deepened her faith.[4]

Willie Walker, a young Delta man, had met and married Rachel Pittman about 1914. Who his people were, when he was born, where he was raised, the contours of his personality—all remain a mystery. At this distance, it is difficult to have even the barest hint of Walker. He likely courted Rachel while she lived with kin in rural Sunflower County, and theirs was possibly a common-law marriage, as were many among Mississippi blacks at that time.[5] On January 22, 1915, in a farmhouse in the hamlet of Sunflower, just outside Indianola, Rachel delivered her first child, a son the couple named Clarence LaVaughn. She carried her baby with her into the fields as she picked cotton under the intense Mississippi sun.[6]

It is hard to imagine a more hostile environment for a black child to be born into than white-dominated Mississippi during this era. Schools, churches, railroads, hotels, and that then-new phenomenon, the picture show, were all segregated. But those were only the most obvious signs of a racist world. Never would a black child witness whites addressing his older relatives as Mr. or Mrs., regardless of their age or status, and rarely would that child hear his kin use anything but formal titles when addressing whites, no matter how young. Retail stores were not segregated, for the only thing white merchants feared more than taking money touched by "inferior" black hands was to see that same money in the hands of a black mercantile class. But blacks had to wait for service until all whites had been accommodated. On the street, a similar racial etiquette prevailed. Black men were expected to doff their caps to whites; black men and women to step into the street to allow whites to pass. Never would a black adult presume to walk through the front door of a white restaurant or a white private home. The term *nigger* hung in the air, as integral to daily life as the dense humidity of a Mississippi summer day, its purpose to declare irrevocably the narrowed place allowed blacks in public life. Given this, that black adults could neither vote nor serve on juries seemed redundant.[7]

And then there was the violence. In the seventeen counties that comprise the Mississippi Delta, some of the richest alluvial land in all the world, whites lynched a black American more than twice a year between 1900 and 1930, decades that frame the formative years of both Rachel and her son. The "charges" varied. Blacks were accused of "ogling" a white woman, of "sassing" whites, of being "uppity." To forget one's assigned place in this constrained world could result in swift, extralegal punishment, a fact not lost on black parents. A trip to town on Saturday afternoon, anticipated as a break from the exhausting regularity of farm work, brought its own tensions as parents had to train (often harshly, if they would prevent worse harm) their growing children in the cruel realities of that racial code.[8]

This system, self-consciously wrought by generations of Mississippi whites, denied most black residents all civic and political rights, funneled them into a workforce as compliant as the patterns of oppression could achieve, and considered blacks as other than human. The official rationale obscured a far more troubling prospect. In the period following the Civil War, J. C. Crittendon, a Bolivar County black, not only joined with other black men in voting and serving on the county jury, but he was actually elected a county supervisor. In that capacity, he oversaw the construction of the new county courthouse in the county seat at Cleveland in 1872. But Mississippi whites could not accept the possibility of a biracial political culture, and through violence, intimidation, and murder over decades, they worked to return blacks to their "proper" place. In this, they largely succeeded. By the time of Clarence's birth, no blacks had served on juries in Bolivar County for years, and J. C. Crittendon, now a porter, mopped the floors of the very courthouse he once voted to create.[9]

That the racism took its toll on individuals is evident. As the native Mississippian (he was born near Natchez in 1908) and writer Richard Wright recalled, by age ten he had already experienced the murder of two adult male kin by whites: "A dread of white people now came to live permanently in my feelings and imagination. . . . Nothing changed the totality of my personality so much as this pressure of hate and threat that stemmed from the invisible whites." Yet this hatred, which at times seemed to deplete the very oxygen of black Mississippians seeking survival on the wide, flat expanse of the Delta's cotton fields, was not the only reality.[10]

The church, the major black social institution independent enough from white control to nurture children such as Clarence Franklin, provided one such alternative. Egos badly bruised by the week's ugliness could be salved, "niggers" could assume the dignity of a deacon or a mother of the church, and a potent faith that stressed how all of God's children were equally worthy of redemption, both here in Egypt-land and in the afterlife, embraced. Since the days of slavery, the church was also a center of black social life, with picnics, socials, and a pattern of intense Sunday services, revivals, and prayer meetings. Then, too, there were the juke joints or "jook houses," as McKinley Morganfield called them. Born in the Delta the same year as Clarence and, in later years, better known as the blues guitarist and singer Muddy Waters, Morganfield remembered that "everybody went to those places" on Saturday night to dance, listen to the music, and socialize. The following morning found many of the revelers in church as well.[11]

The black family also provided a psychological alternative to racism's searing personal hurts. Here titles of respect and authority whites denied them could be recognized; here adults nurtured children, socialized them, and encouraged them; here the intertwined and thus bittersweet lessons in parental love and racial survival came to be appreciated. While contemporary observers noted that a significant portion (approximately 25 percent in one case) of black families surveyed had single women leading them—

and blues songs frequently extolled the man who rambled, leaving home and family in search of personal independence and human dignity—black family life was always more complex. Many more men remained with their families than left, and the presence of other kin, blood as well as fictive, provided a context that nurtured black children despite the oppressive circumstances that surrounded them.[12]

In the summer of 1916, Rachel gave birth to a second child, a daughter named Louise. Shortly thereafter, following America's entry into World War I in April 1917, Willie Walker entered the army. As far as is known, Rachel remained outside of Indianola, caring for her babies and working the land. She lived close by, if not with, her sister, and both sets of children called her Aunt Rachel.[13] Walker was one of many Mississippi black men drafted (black men accounted for 52 percent of the state's draftees and 56 percent of its actual inductees), and he may have ended up in a service unit, as many black soldiers did. Family lore had him in Paris during the war. How these experiences changed him is lost, but it would not be far-fetched to imagine that in France, if not in the segregated U.S. army, Walker discovered a world where Mississippi's racial codes need not dominate every waking moment. He might have glimpsed, as other African American soldiers did as well, the possibilities of a personal freedom previously unimaginable. If so, how jarring the reentry into Mississippi's reality. The prospect of black soldiers and their kin claiming the rights of citizenship as a consequence of their service infuriated white Mississippians into a panic of violence. Richard Wright, who had largely ignored the war, found that he responded "emotionally to every hint, whisper, word, inflection, news, gossip, and rumor regarding conflicts between the races" as the conflict ended. The reception returning black soldiers encountered was intended to jolt them back into their place. As one Delta veteran explained, his unit had decent treatment until they arrived at their mustering-out base in Mississippi. There they were held, incommunicado, without food, "and forced to break rocks as if we had been sentenced to hard labor until we all banded together, sat down, and went on strike." The courage of that action evoked from white superiors a blunt warning. "We were told by the white officers," Chalmers Archer Jr. remembered, "that we were back in Mississippi now and not some goddamn celebrities in a goddamn ticker tape parade in New York."[14]

"My earliest memory was of my father when he came back from the service," the adult Clarence explained. "That's about as far back as I can go in memory." He was quite young, three, possibly just four: "I recall him coming back in his uniform and playing with us, teaching us how to salute, and things of that sort that had to do with the military." It was a touching recollection, made even more special by the adult son's pride in his father's courage for courting the danger a black veteran risked for wearing his uniform in postwar Mississippi.[15]

But Clarence's memory of his father was painful, too. Shortly after positioning his son's hand against his forehead in an approximation of a smart military salute, Walker was gone, out of Sunflower County, out of the state of Mississippi. Clarence, decades later, sought to explain: after France and the wartime experience, his father "wanted no more of the farm situation, the southern farm situation at least." In the years to come, Rachel almost never talked of Willie Walker. (Clarence, too, was reticent, except with a few close friends such as fellow Mississippian Harry Kincaid, who later reported that he and Clarence talked about "the father-mother thing" throughout their adult lives.) For his son, Willie Walker's abrupt departure was an early, perhaps the most wrenching, hurt Mississippi inflicted.[16]

It was also a difficult moment for Rachel. The separation caused by military service had now become permanent, and if she had benefited from her husband's army pay, that also ended abruptly. A single mother in her twenties, with two children under five and no means of support but her daily labor, she faced a bleak future. Shortly after Willie Walker left for good, she moved her family some seventeen miles north from Indianola to a rural community just outside the town of Doddsville. Within a year, certainly before Clarence's fifth birthday in January 1920, Rachel met and married Henry Franklin, who worked a farm in the Doddsville area.[17]

*   *   *   *   *

The stretch of road that gently bent to the curves of the Sunflower River between Indianola and Doddsville, then curled lazily north and east through Ruleville and Drew, Parchman and on to Tutwiler, a total distance of forty-three miles, pulsated with the tensions and vitality that layered segregated life in Mississippi. Well before that road became State Highway 49W, the frontage acres on either side marked the boundaries of the Delta's largest and wealthiest plantations. This was the classic Mississippi Delta: rich black soil birthing white cotton balls that dotted, pointillist fashion, a landscape stretching flat and motionless to a distant horizon where vision blurred. It was classic Mississippi Delta in another way as well: white folks owned the land and garnered its riches while black folks sweated their days in hard labor and service.

Along this road, for example, in the vicinity of Doddsville, the Eastland family had its vast, 2,300-acre plantation, which served as the base of their political power for generations to come. James O. Eastland, who would become one of the country's most powerful defenders of segregation in the United States Senate, was born into this family in 1904 in circumstances that vividly expressed the area's racial realities. Some months before Eastland's birth, Luther Holbert, a black sharecropper on the family plantation, shot and killed Eastland's Uncle James, who co-owned the family holdings with the future senator's father, W. C. Eastland. Holbert had killed James Eastland and the black tenant farmer accompanying him, when they came to his cabin to threaten him for some unknown conduct involving Holbert's wife. Immediately, both Holberts fled into the swamps, and Delta whites raised a 200-man posse to find them. It took four days. At least three other blacks were murdered in the process, but the Holberts were caught and brought into Doddsville. In a horrific ceremonious burning before an estimated crowd of more than 1,000, each finger was individually chopped off the victims and "distributed as souvenirs" to the assembled white citizens. Eyes were gouged out with sticks. Before the pyre consumed its victims, a large corkscrew "bored into the flesh of the man and woman," tearing out as it was withdrawn by human hands "big pieces of raw, quivering flesh." The moment lived in the memory of Delta blacks for generations.[18]

Six miles north was Ruleville, and then six miles beyond that hamlet was Drew, Mississippi. Including Doddsville, the vicinity around these three small communities was home to many thousands of poor black tenants, increasingly drawn from other parts of the state by the migration northward of Delta blacks and the consequent demand for new workers on these plantations. This large, fluid population, concentrated in so small a region, created as distinctive a cultural expression as the Delta blues. If one could talk of an actual place where such a birth occurred, the Dockery plantation would be as likely a site as any.

Will Dockery established his plantation in 1895, when the Delta was still frontierlike in its natural wilderness. He cleared and planted forty square miles of land five miles west of Ruleville and employed hundreds of black agricultural laborers and sharecroppers. Among them was Henry Sloan, who in the 1890s had begun to experiment with new musical patterns on his guitar. In 1897 the Patton family, including a sixteen-year-old son, Charley, moved to Dockery's. Sloan taught the boy, who shortly became a distinctive musical influence throughout the Delta. Together, they touched an increasingly large number of musicians. Over the next three decades, Howlin' Wolf, Honeyboy Edwards, Roebuck Pops Staples, Tommy Johnson, and Willie Brown were but a few of the blues singers who developed their craft, trading licks and learning new guitar runs from Sloan and Patton and from numerous singers who traveled through Sunflower County, including Robert Johnson and Son House. The space occupied by the Dockery plantation spurred this commingling. Equidistant between Drew and Doddsville, Dockery's sat at the center of Sunflower County's black population, which in 1920 comprised almost 75 percent of the more than forty-six thousand county residents. Just five miles to the west was Cleveland, the seat of Bolivar County, and a bit further were the adjacent communities of Boyle and Shaw. Blues could be heard throughout this whole region. A local railroad, the Pea Vine, immortalized in Patton's "Pea Vine Blues," carried musicians and their audiences between the Dockery plantation and the juke joints in Bolivar County.[19]

Like the religious faith to which it was so intimately linked, the blues affirmed life as found even as the music sought to create new understandings. B. B. King, the blues musician and a Sunflower County native ten years younger than Clarence Franklin, described a Sanctified (i.e., Pentecostal) religious service he attended as a young boy near Indianola. The minister, King explained, "says one thing and the congregation says it back, back and forth, back and forth, until we're rocking together in a rhythm that won't stop. His voice is low and rough and his guitar high and sweet;

they seem to sing to each other, conversing in some heavenly language I need to learn. . . . No room for fear here; no room for doubt; it's a celebration of love."[20]

The mixture of the sacred and secular tones in these songs erased the loneliness and terror, if only for a moment. King and his coworshipers needed the love they sang into being: working conditions may have been better than elsewhere in the state, but by any other criteria, the Delta remained a brutal environment. By the end of the 1920s, almost 12,000 blacks operated farms in Sunflower County but only 194 of them, working less than 3 percent of the cultivated land, actually owned the ground they toiled over. The remaining black farmers, including Henry and Rachel Franklin, were tenants, the minority economically secure enough to supply their family's needs and pay rent in cash to the white owner. Most tenants, however, either sharecropped or worked as day laborers. Sharecroppers depended on the plantation store for their needs in the long stretch between planting the cotton seed in April and the final settlement of accounts in December. Prices were higher at the plantation store than in town—by as much as 10 to 25 percent—but many sharecroppers lived outside of a cash economy and had little choice. The yearly rent usually consumed half the crop, and when the sharecropper brought his cotton to the owner's mill for processing, grading, and sale, the farm and family supplies furnished during the year were deducted as well. Given the 25 percent illiteracy rate among blacks and the near-total powerlessness before a determined white owner, few tenants finished any year with a profit. If they did, they were usually paid in scrip, redeemable only at the plantation store. Vagrancy laws, enforced by the sheriff, and behind him by a posse of white men, prevented many from simply leaving while in "debt."[21]

Even when good fortune prevailed and a sharecropper reinvested his profit in animals and equipment in the hopes of doing even better the following year, trouble often ensued. Fannie Lou Townsend, who four decades later, as Mrs. Fannie Lou Hamer, became a civil rights activist of profound moral courage and strength, recalled a time in the early 1920s, when she was about six or seven and living with her large family on the E. W. Brandon plantation near Ruleville. The year before had been a banner year for her father. He had invested his profits in three mules, two cows, and some new farm tools in an effort to make the leap from share-cropper to cash tenant. On returning home one evening, the family found all the animals dead, poisoned—the work of a local white man. Mrs. Hamer explained: "White people never like to see Negroes get a little success."[22]

*   *   *   *   *

Knowledge of the Franklin family in Sunflower County during the 1920s is sparse. Early in the decade, possibly in 1921 or 1922, Rachel delivered her third child, her first with Henry, a daughter they named Aretha. During this decade as well Henry adopted Clarence and replaced Walker with Franklin as the boy's last name. Not much is known about Henry's personality. In family memory, he is remembered as a hardworking man, perhaps a bit distant, but a good father and a devoted husband. He and Rachel remained together until his death more than three decades later. But whose land they worked in Sunflower County, what church they attended there, how they spent their leisure time, and with whom—all this and more remains unknown. It is not even clear precisely how long the Franklins remained in the Doddsville area. Clarence said he "grew up partially" near Doddsville, and he also recalled that he attended school "in [a] church in Sunflower County." It is likely, then, that the family stayed in the county until Clarence was nine, possibly ten.[23]

On December 14, 1923, when Clarence was but a month shy of his ninth birthday, the molten violence just below the placid formality of the region's enforced racial etiquette erupted once again. Up near Drew, Joe Pullen, a proud black man, a sharecropper, and a World War I veteran got into a dispute with his boss man, W. T. "Tom" Sanders, over the total that was due him on that year's settlement day. Sanders refused to pay what Pullen insisted he was owed and refused as well to give Pullen permission to move off the plantation. Accounts vary at this point; some suggest that Sanders first shot Pullen. But it is clear that Joe Pullen went to his cabin, loaded his gun, returned to the office, and shot Sanders dead. He immediately fled into the swamps east of Drew, carrying with him about seventy-five rounds of ammunition. A posse of more than one thousand white men quickly formed, prominent among them the sheriff of Clarksdale (a town of some ten thousand just northwest of Tutwiler), bearing his department's machine gun. But Pullen knew the terrain and was a sharpshooter to boot. Before he was eventually taken, alive, Pullen killed four posse members and wounded eight others. What then followed was the familiar ritual murder. As Mrs. Fannie Lou Hamer testified: "They dragged him by his heels on the back of a car and paraded about with that man for all the Negroes to see. They cut his ear off and for the longest time it was kept in a jar of alcohol in a showcase in a store window at Drew."[24]

Henry and Rachel may have kept their children from Drew and thus spared them looking at that jar, but there was no way any black parent could isolate their children, especially one as old as Clarence, from the sickening knowledge of the event. The news went up and down the Delta almost immediately, in both the white and black communities. Cautious discussions among black adults took place behind closed doors at home, in church vestibules, and perhaps especially in the barbershops and drinking clubs that peppered the black Delta. After the Pullen murder, Drew and other towns in both Sunflower and neighboring Bolivar County enforced nightly curfews for blacks only. In 1924, the sheriff of Drew shot and killed seven or eight black citizens he deemed too slow in getting off the street shortly after curfew. Thereafter, Drew became known in the black community as a place to avoid.[25]

Sometime in the next year or so, the Franklin family joined the slow but steady exodus of blacks out of Sunflower County. Bluesmen Charley Patton and Willie Brown both left, heading farther north in the Delta. Many others, the less famous, departed for the North, even if it meant risking arrest for a debt yet owed to the landlord. But when Henry and Rachel moved, their steps were less far-reaching, only some fifteen miles north and west of Doddsville, to a farm "about a mile out from Cleveland, Mississippi."[26]

Sharecroppers at Doddsville, the Franklins were cash tenants when they arrived in their new home. (They clearly had been frugal while in Sunflower County.) Although cotton was the major crop, Henry and Rachel also planted a vegetable garden and kept mules, some horses, chickens, milk cows, and hogs.

By Delta standards for blacks, the Franklins were doing relatively well. Yet Henry Franklin was always at a disadvantage, Clarence later explained, both because he was black and because he was "completely illiterate to the point that he couldn't even write [his] name." The family soon moved a few miles south, near Boyle, where the Franklins sharecropped on land rented by the Pennington family. The Penningtons were poor but they were white, part of the 26 percent of Bolivar County that was such. "My daddy," Clarence recalled, made a great crop that year in Boyle, both corn and cotton, "and it was obvious that we were supposed to come out ahead." But at settling time, the Penningtons gathered their male relatives about them, including a son-in-law who "had a reputation for killing blacks." The family patriarch told Henry: "'No, you just didn't make it.' No settlement or anything." Clarence was perhaps eleven, and the weight of Joe Pullen lay heavily on the family.[27]

Deflated, the Franklins returned nearer to Cleveland, this time renting land from "a Mr. Cashbury," a northerner and a local banker who was remembered as "a bit more fair and generous" than the Penningtons.[28] Here the Franklins remained for the following decade, in a four-room, wood-shingled house. The kitchen was the family center, with an open-hearth fireplace and a wood-burning iron stove, dining table and chairs, and a chest "on the wall" to hold flour, sugar, and other staples. There were three bedrooms, each with a bed, dresser, and a mirror. In one of the bedrooms, probably that of Henry and Rachel, stood a "wind-up, floor model" phonograph. There was no parlor, but at the front and back of the hall that divided the rooms, two to a side, were porches that were especially welcome in the heaviness of a summer evening. There was pump water, outhouse, and the commissary store "at the boss's house" for supplies.

Even on Cashbury's land, Henry rarely "came out ahead, despite [the] 20–25 bales of cotton" produced in a given year, and the family always struggled. Clarence remembered that "at Christmas time my mother would cry because the only thing that she could purchase for the children were raisins and oranges and apples and striped candy. I will never forget that striped candy. That's about all. No toys. I never had toys. And that stands out: her crying."[29]

Life for a black youth in the Cleveland area was rigorously circumscribed in the late 1920s. Except when absolutely necessary, most blacks had little to do with whites. Ivory James, a teenager in the countryside some five miles out of Cleveland in the 1920s, recalled of whites at that time: "Well, I have [had] no personal experienced with them, you know." In Cleveland, the young Cleo Myles, born the same year as Clarence, remembered that except for the white family for whom her mother worked, she too had little interaction with whites. As Clarence remembered, life revolved around the family and the farm, church, and "school at the time that schooling was provided."[30]

Farm life was tedious and hard. The Franklins arose by 4:30 in the morning, and from a young age Clarence helped milk the cows and pump water for the mules before hitching them up. He and his stepfather were in the fields by 6:00 A.M. At first, Henry plowed while Clarence chopped cotton, but as he grew into what became his six-foot frame, Clarence too would take a turn behind the mules. About seven they returned to the cabin for breakfast, often ham, rice, gravy, and biscuits. Then Rachel and the two girls joined the men in the fields. When plowing, Clarence would be off alone, preparing a section of the field for planting, and even then, his nascent religious faith and a fierce drive to be someone led him to preach to the birds, his mule, or other animals. When he picked cotton, working with his mother and sisters, they could talk, swap stories, and sing hymns in a manner that alleviated some of the drudgery. Whatever the day's task, however, Clarence and Henry left the fields about noon for dinner; Rachel had prepared it as she made breakfast, and she and the girls went ahead a half hour or so before noon to put it on the table. Black neighbors, their fellow sharecroppers, would sometimes join the Franklins for the midday meal. Presumably, the Franklins would visit in turn as well. But for all, one o'clock marked the time to return to the fields until supper, about six in the evening; kerosene lamps illuminated the house as darkness fell. Following some talk on the porch, the family retired by 9:00 P.M. to recharge their strength for the morrow.[31]

Numerous other black families worked the same plantation and lived within walking distance. As a teen, Clarence played ball, rode horses, shot marbles, and picked berries with other boys. Saturday afternoon was the day to hitch up the mules to the wagon and, with the reins in Henry's hands, ride to Cleveland with legs dangling off the tailboard. There Clarence joined with other boys, and from about age twelve on, he (and they) "began thinking about girls." He could do little more than think, however, for at that time boys and girls tended not to mix in groups once they began noticing each other, at least not when devoutly religious parents were watching. In addition to these Saturday excursions were occasional picnics at one of the local churches, with plentiful supplies of ribs and chicken "provided by whites through certain blacks." (Often these blacks were plantation foremen who supervised black sharecroppers for white owners, but that complicated fact did not always prevent friendship and fellowship from flourishing.) Then, too, nine miles north of Cleveland, was Mound Bayou, an all-black town, an "oasis in the desert," one black journalist referred to it in 1923, whose summer festivals and discreet celebrations of black achievement drew people from throughout the Delta and beyond.[32]

These practices among many Delta blacks—workday dinners shared with family and friends; the easy comraderie of Saturday conversations in town, punctuated by the blue tones of the Delta's itinerant street musicians; the intense fellowship of prolonged Sunday church services; the visiting back and forth—signaled the presence of an intricate black folk culture critical to the maintenance of black sanity in this oppressive world. Yet it was never a smooth process. Richard Wright himself could ask with real bewilderment, decades after leaving Mississippi: "But where had I got this notion of doing something in the future?" For many, the world of the Delta remained so constrained, bound by a narrowed focus of field, faith, and family that turned them inward. But people still dreamed, and even young adolescents sought to give voice to the visions they beheld, even as they worked someone else's cotton. "We had a field," Clarence explained,

> *that ran right up to the railroad track. Just across the railroad track was the 61 highway. And it was meaningful to me, quite an experience as contrasted with my experiences in Sunflower County, to see the trains coming from Memphis enroute to New Orleans and Jackson. The people would be waving out of the windows at us in the field. And the cars going down the highway*

with different license plates from New York and New Jersey and the District of Columbia, Virginia and Connecticut, and whatever. This was quite an interesting thing to me to see that, to observe it. It gave me a deep longing to someday see these places where these cars came from, where the train came from, and where the people on the trains came from.[33]

Highways and railroads—central symbols of the black Delta experience, dominant metaphors in both song and story. They represented the way out of a land of virtual captivity, as the migrants traveling north throughout this decade attested. Black poets teased out the possibilities inherent in those symbols in numerous blues songs with great emphasis on the freedom and dignity a rambling man might encounter when he crossed the Mississippi line.[34]

Without words then to express his thoughts, eleven-year-old Clarence returned to the cotton and, on Sundays, to the choir. But his journey had begun; his imagination was already elsewhere.

CHAPTER TWO

ATTEMPTING HIS IMAGINATION

Clarence would forever be inspired by the longing to be other than the sum of the limitations prescribed for a black youth in the Delta, but how that longing might shape his life remained obscure in the late 1920s. Education, one traditional path to self-definition and fulfillment in American life, was profoundly limited. In Cleveland, he did attend class in an actual school building, as opposed to the well of a church sanctuary. He particularly remembered a teacher who had attended Mississippi's Jackson College, a rarity when most black public school teachers had but a few years of grade-school education themselves. Yet Clarence experienced school as an institution that actually sought to cripple his potential, directly and indirectly. The purpose of the black schools he attended, the adult Clarence thought, was "to keep the blacks backwards." Along with the ill-prepared teachers, the low salaries, and the almost nonexistent supplies was the truncated school term. Black students in the Cleveland area "didn't go to school until after the crops were finished, maybe the 1st of December. And of course you had to come out when farming time started again, in the middle of March." Beyond that were the everyday slights. Black kids walked to school, but white kids rode the school bus, and after a rainstorm, "some of the bigoted drivers . . . would deliberately hit those water puddles to splash water on the blacks." Joining in, the white students on the buses called out "derogatory names like 'nigger, nigger, coon, coon' at the black kids."[1]

One moment in Clarence's boyhood is particularly revealing. When he was about eleven years old, roughly the same age when that inchoate longing triggered by the automobiles on Highway 61 first took remembered form, Clarence's teacher required that he give a speech at an evening school program before parents, community members, and fellow students. He "didn't perform well," he recalled, and expected punishment when he got home. Even decades later, a determined mother's exasperation tinged Rachel Franklin's recollection: "I had done taken time and learned it [the speech] to him and told him just how I wanted him to stand on the stage and how I wanted him to speak up so people could hear him." But Clarence was almost inaudible from the stage. Once home, Rachel demanded that her son change into his pajamas immediately so as to receive a paddling. Clarence lagged and delayed, "because he know what was going to happen, you know."[2]

It is likely that, for this eleven-year-old, the prospect of speaking before an adult audience for the first time simply scared him. But the racial atmosphere he lived with daily affected him as well, poised as he was on the edge of proclaiming a conscious sense of self. Fear of another kind, of not meeting his mother's expectations, may also have constrained his vocal cords. Yet Rachel's tough love had a profound effect. As Franklin noted three decades later, "I've been speaking ever since then! And I mean speaking where folk could hear me." Frightened and defeated that evening in Cleveland, he was on the cusp of a transforming moment.[3]

*   *   *   *   *

St. Peter's Rock Missionary Baptist Church was one of three black Baptist churches in Cleveland during the late 1920s. Founded in 1898, the result of a schism within St. Paul's Missionary Baptist Church, the members of St. Peter's Rock erected a modest building in north Cleveland. The congregation was both small and poor, and completely illiterate. As a result, according to a church history, "a sinner man, Mr. Felix Murray," who could read and write, served as secretary "and worked faithfully at his duty." In 1926, the congregation, under the leadership of Reverend H. Hampton, constructed a compact new building in south Cleveland, at 302 Ruby Street, at a cost of approximately $3,500. Yet another split rent the congregation almost immediately, and Reverend Hampton, carrying a healthy portion of the congregation with him, founded New St. Phillip Baptist Church down the block. For almost two years, St. Peter's Rock lacked all but an occasional visiting minister. Meanwhile St. Paul's, Cleveland's original Afro-Baptist church, grew during these years under the leadership of Reverend J. W. Gayden.[4]

Early in 1928, Reverend John H. Anderson came to St. Peter's Rock as minister. Anderson lived in Shelby, Mississippi, some fifteen miles north on Highway 61, and the Cleveland church was one of four that he ministered to each month. Anderson was both a skillful administrator and a powerful preacher. The congregation of the handsome wooden church soon grew to include nearly five hundred members, the great majority of them tenants and sharecroppers from the surrounding cotton plantations. A piano was added early in his term—an innovation for Baptists—and a variety of committees established to aid the needy, restructure the choirs, and organize separate Sunday school instruction.

The fourth Sunday of the month found Anderson in the pulpit of the Cleveland church. Services usually lasted all day and into the evening. An afternoon meal, served by the churchwomen, provided the needed nourishment and a welcome opportunity for socializing. The program for the other three Sundays of the month varied. On one, the congregation visited a different church. On another, the congregation held Sunday school at St. Peter's, assisted at times by a visiting minister. On the third Sunday, the week preceding Anderson's arrival, they held a testimonial. Led by a deacon, the congregation opened the service with song and then congregants broke into prayer, some chanting with a rhythmic intensity. Personal testimonies followed. Worshipers bore witness to their faith in God, their fidelity to the church, and in confessing their frailties, to the continued power their conversion experience held in their lives. The emotional force of these services and the intimate thoughts and feelings shared in these testimonies bound church members one to another in profound fashion.

Through these communal testimonies, members experienced God as a liberator in this world as in the next: their God had provided them with the strength and courage to sustain in spite of obstacles. He was stern and demanded much, but he was also a God of forgiveness. Their faith in his grace redeemed them time and again. Testifying to this faith forcefully asserted the Almighty's interest in each believer, and that carried with it a sense of personal worth and recognition, of being somebody, that transcended for the moment the ugly realities beyond the church doors.[5]

In August 1929, J. H. Anderson began the yearly revival at St. Peter's Rock. A two-week affair held during the lull just before the cotton harvest, it was a major event in the community. Henry Franklin, who did not share his wife's religious enthusiasm, would not have attended, but many adults did and brought their children as well. The first week consisted of a prolonged prayer meeting under the direction of Reverend Anderson and the more senior deacons. The following week, "preaching week," had Anderson, with no help from other ministers this particular year, preaching daily. He was a powerful, effective speaker, and as his words touched his audience, those considering conversion would move to the front of the church, to the mourner's bench directly beneath the pulpit, where they awaited the movement of the Spirit to lead them to rebirth in Jesus. There a person could languish, waiting for the call to be saved, as night after night Anderson pressed his message home. Those who experienced conversion, who declared themselves touched by divine grace, moved from the bench into the choir stand, facing the congregation from behind the pulpit. There the deacons prepared these prospective church members and the minister examined them, and from that perch the converts continued their revival participation until the baptismal service at the end of the month.[6]

Clarence was there that August for both weeks of the revival. As Anderson preached, Clarence "felt moved. I felt inspired." As he testified in a 1950s sermon, "One Thursday morning, in 1929, I stepped in for myself." He approached the mourner's bench where church members who were already saved engulfed kneeling candidates with their prayers. And when Anderson issued the invitation following his sermon, "I simply got up and went to the altar." After satisfactorily answering questions about the validity of his conversion and the depth of his belief in God, Anderson accepted

Clarence as a baptismal candidate for the service scheduled for the follow-ing week.[7]

On the fourth Sunday of August 1929, Clarence Franklin, Cleo Myles, and approximately twelve to fifteen other converts, many of them youths also, met at the church at 9:00 A.M. Dressed in white robes and white caps, they mounted a flatbed truck for the eight- to ten-mile drive east to the banks of the Sunflower River. Lining the banks as they arrived, their festive-colored clothing radiant against the sloping green limbs of the cy-press trees that hovered over the river's gentle currents, the congregation of St. Peter's Rock greeted the berobed baptismal class with a hymn. Reverend Anderson offered a brief instruction, stressing the validity and necessity of the central tenet of the Baptist faith, "the tradition of [adult] baptism" itself. Then Anderson and two deacons entered the river, and one by one, the newly converted followed. As the minister intoned the words of baptism, "I baptize you, sister [or brother] so-and-so, in the name of the Father and Son and the Holy Ghost," he and one of the deacons would "dip 'em in the water." As the just saved emerged from the river into the morning sunlight, reborn and revived in their Lord, the assembled church greeted them with another hymn. When all had felt the waters flow over them, the by now quite wet new members changed into dry clothes, and the entire congrega-tion returned to Cleveland, where "we were fellowshipped into the church" during the regular service. Young Clarence, who in his fervor had left his dry clothes back at St. Peter's earlier that morning, rode back soaked on the flatbed truck, the wind plastering his wet robe against his body.[8]

In the years to come, many of those converted would recall an over-whelming emotion. "I felt light and like something lifted up off of me," the Delta bluesman Honeyboy Edwards remembered. "You never have that but one time. Once you got it, that's something because God don't give you nothing and take it back." But in contrast, Franklin thought his conversion experience "was more or less typical. . . . It wasn't anything unusual or spectacular." So, too, with the baptismal service, where no overwhelming emotion punctuated his memory. It was not that such feelings embarrassed Franklin or that he had not felt the importance of the moment. Rather, his seemingly flat response is actually a key to understanding the very depth of the religious faith he embraced in 1929.[9]

Theologically, Franklin had understood his sinful, human nature that night on the mourner's bench and thus the need for conversion; but he never saw himself as a sinner bereft of hope. God might be stern and punishment eternal for persistent sinners, "but I never felt really condemned by God," he explained. "I never felt that God had something against me. It seemed to me that God had provided all of these things for me, including his love, and now it was my time to respond." Even after discounting memory's tricks over half a century, it remains evident that this young teenager had grown significantly within the church community since his initial public-speaking failure. His conversion flowed from his emerging sense of worth framed in church and at home, and there were no startling revelations. "Nothing that was sudden: suddenly I understood about the whole thing. No," he later insisted, "I guess the cultivation of that acceptance of the Lord was my continuous participation in the services of the church." Here, in the collective embrace of both family and congregation, was the transforming potential of the black religious tradition, where belief in a God as concerned with this world as with the next provided individuals and communities with an alternative to the demeaning images that surrounded them. The folk story told of a slave preacher addressing the central Christian mystery of Christ's death on Calvary, repeated with variations across generations throughout the black South, signaled the journey Clarence had begun. As the preacher finished the depiction of the pain, the blood, the deep sorrow of Christ's mother and disciples, he paused, "his eyes scrutinizing every face in the congregation, and then he would tell them, 'You are not niggers! You are not slaves! You are God's children!' "[10]

Less than a decade following Clarence's baptismal service, the young Martin Luther King Jr., later a close friend, also experienced conversion in tones that Clarence would easily have recognized. There was no sudden moment of revelation, King wrote in an essay when he was twenty-one, no gathering emotional crisis. He, too, had grown up in the church, and his conversion flowed seemingly effortlessly from the weave of his life. But for both men, for all the remembered lack of drama, their religious conversion and the faith that blossomed from it would largely define their adult engagement with the world around them.[11]

Clarence's conversion came at a moment of transition, even ambiguity, in his life. Neither man nor boy, he nonetheless felt that he was at the "age of accountability" personally and in relation to his church community. Indeed, acceptance of that responsibility in part motivated his conversion. Yet neither he nor his parents considered him an adult. "So far as I was concerned, and so far as they were concerned, I was still a child," he remembered. At the same time, his conversion marked him apart from his father. He "admired" and "loved" Henry Franklin but clearly sought a separate identity "so far as his non-churching going" behavior was concerned. That his biological father had left a decade before complicated these feelings even further. Also, Clarence had started "thinking about girls." While conversion certainly did not diminish that interest, it did channel it in certain ways within the church community. As Cleo Myles recalled, there was a strict moral code expected. At the time of their baptism, she explained, "If you joined the church [and] you went to meeting, you know, dancing was a sin, at that time." How the born-again Clarence navigated these conflicting pressures within and beyond the church community in these years remains unclear. How he would navigate them during the decades to come would be one of the great complications in Clarence Franklin's life.[12]

Then, too, of course, there was the racial atmosphere. Some years before his conversion, Clarence's friendship with "one or two" young white friends ended sharply. In an experience common among southern black youth, Clarence discovered one day that his friends' parents had noticed an unacceptable conversational parity: Clarence was calling his friends by their first names. The parents, Clarence remembered, "would begin telling you to call them 'Mr. Jesse,' call her 'Miss Ann.'" Clarence's response to calling his erstwhile friends by a title? "Did it. I did it. And others did it." Not surprisingly, his white friends' attitudes quickly changed as well. Reflecting as an adult on why he was not "shocked" by the experience, Franklin explained that if from that moment in childhood when "things begin to dawn on you, you're being instructed by your own parents about what the situation is between blacks and whites, and where your place is, as opposed to where his place is . . . [then] when you grow up with that it doesn't shock you." That may well be true but would not therefore negate the presence of a deeper hurt and anger at so dismissive a rejection for being who you were. In Atlanta a few years later, for example, following an identical experience with a white friend, young Martin Luther King Jr. vowed to hate all white people. This anger lasted for years, despite his parents' efforts to encourage in their son a Christian duty to love. Young King's transformation would not come until college.[13]

As he lived with that experience, Clarence at times might have felt that hatred too, as he did the consequent anger over the silence that was survival's price. The reasons seemed unending. In the year of his conversion, a large mob of local whites in Bolivar County lynched Charley Shepard, a black resident, in the classic ceremonial ritual that served to solidify the bonds among whites of all social groups in the Delta. After seven hours of public torture, a fire finally consumed Shepard's still-breathing body.[14]

How Clarence absorbed this horror remains unknown, for he never talked publicly about such emotions. In Mississippi, less than a decade after the Shepard lynching, B. B. King, then thirteen years old, passed the hanging body of another black man lynched "for touching" a white girl. "Deep inside," the man whose voice and music would touch a nation reflected, "I'm hurt, sad and mad. But I stay silent. . . . My anger is a secret that stays away from the light of day because the square is bright with the smiles of white people passing by as they view the dead man on display. I feel disgust and disgrace and rage and every emotion that makes me cry without tears and scream without sound."[15]

The weight of such silence could psychically maim an individual, and some African Americans suffered that fate. But black Mississippians possessed rich resources for creating lives of meaning and purpose despite such horrors. Some found expression and affirmation in the culture of the blues, giving voice in song to ideas that, if said in a public speech, would have brought swift retribution from Delta whites. They also, as Clarence did, looked to the gospel. Following Shepard's murder, he was even more active in the choir. He attended prayer meetings on certain weeknights, as he did testimonial meetings on the third Sunday of the month, although he affirmed that he "didn't do too much testifying." In many Afro-Baptist communities, one or two older church members were assigned to the newly converted, to instruct them in "how to raise a hymn, to pray in public, and to lead a prayer meeting." Between prayer meetings, testimonials, and regular services, Clarence both found the needed tutelage and grew to embrace his new responsibilities. That communal enveloping, framed by faith, provided Clarence and many others with the psychic strength to develop as complete human beings. In the process, he discovered a powerful new timbre to a voice that had only recently been timorous.[16]

*   *   *   *   *

Roebuck Pops Staples, a Delta native and adult friend of Clarence Franklin's, would later sing of the Mississippi of his youth: "Far back as I can remember / Either had to plow or hoe." That, too, was Clarence's world. As was common among Delta blacks, his life was hard and unrelenting, and it became even harder in the 1930s. A national economic depression devastated an already impoverished black workforce, and the possibility of owning the land one worked all but disappeared for African Americans. As the white Delta planter and diarist, Harry Ball, wrote at the time, "The negroes are starving. They throng about us daily, begging for work and food."[17]

None of this encouraged Clarence to stay. He did not consider his father "a successful farmer" and for himself "couldn't see any future in farming. . . . I was good at farming, but I didn't like it after I reached my teenage level and onward." But leaving was easier said than done. Henry Franklin relied on his stepson, now nearly six feet tall and broad shouldered, to do an adult male's work on the farm. Clarence's departure would create additional economic difficulties for his mother and sisters. And what would he do? He was a teenager without specific work skills other than farming. Thus he bided his time, working with his father, unsuccessfully trying to suppress the spits of anger and resentment at his fate.[18]

It was in this mood, after almost two years of sporadic tension with his father as he sought to find a way out of these conflicting emotions, that Clarence attended an evening session of the 1931 annual meeting of the Mississippi State Baptist Convention, hosted by St. Peter's. A division of the National Baptist Convention, the largest African American religious denomination in the nation, the annual meeting drew delegates and preachers from throughout Mississippi. Preaching that night, before a packed crowd, was the legendary president of the state organization, Reverend Benjamin J. Perkins. Perkins was renowned for combining a serious message with a soaring musical delivery as he whooped, or chanted, part of his sermon. Recalled Clarence: "I was standing in the back of the church, with a cap rolled up in my hand," as Perkins preached "on a passage dealing with Thomas, the disciple Thomas, who doubted the resurrection of Jesus. And his sermon was so vivid and so clear to me, and so impressive, that from that night forward, I really felt that I was called to preach." But as with his conversion experience, this call was not a sudden, engulfing metamorphosis. Rather, the initial impulse "gradually mounted, became even more intense as time went on." As this conviction grew in him over a period of months, so too did the tension at home.[19]

As he worked the land in the months following Perkins's sermon, the son must have tried the father sorely. As he plowed, his mother remembered, "he would stop the mule to preach. He couldn't ever do anything steady. He would stop the mule in the middle of the field and the mule would be eating from one row to another while he'd be preaching." Clarence also remembered these incidents, as he did his efforts to preach to the birds and other animals. His teenage intensity, a self-absorption that eclipsed all else, might bring a fond, bemused smile to the faces of some in the family, but one can also imagine Henry Franklin's exasperation as he sought to make a crop with an increasingly distracted stepson.[20]

As spring turned into early summer in 1931, the second year of the devastating Depression, Rachel "had been sick for a good while . . . with malaria." Her son attended services at St. Peter's one evening. That night, Clarence had a vision, the culmination of the months of thinking, praying, and preaching to various animals since Perkins's oratory had moved him. "Yes, yes," Franklin exulted in 1977. "Just in my room, this particular dream I had, that this plank in the wall, and the walls were made of planks, and it seemed that this plank *only* was on fire, but it didn't consume the house." A voice called out from the fire, as his mother remembered the story, telling Clarence "to go preach the gospel to each and every nation." "I don't recall exactly the instructions of the voice," Clarence remarked. "But I do recall having heard a voice." For the sixteen-year-old, this was the proof, the evidence of divine approval, he had been waiting months to receive. The following morning, as Rachel lay in bed resting, he burst into her room and declared: "I was called to preach last night." With a commanding enthusiasm, he announced: "I am going to be a preacher and I am going to take care of you." Armed with his mother's elation ("I was very happy, very happy . . . that he was going to preach the gospel"), Clarence Franklin confronted his father. "'Now you a got to turn me loose because I cannot plow a mule and preach the gospel, so you got to let me go,'" the mother remembered the son telling her husband. Faced with the powerful commingling of family dynamics and divine instruction, the unchurched Henry could only say "Alright . . . you make up your own mind what you want to do. If you want to preach, preach."[21]

And preach he did, though the plow remained, too. Later that summer, with his mother beaming from the first row and his sisters, Louise and Aretha, singing the opening hymn with the choir, Clarence Franklin preached his trial sermon at St. Peter's Rock. He took his text from the New Testament Gospel of John, specifically the verse, "I must work the works of him who sent me, while it is day." There is no record of the points he made or of the emotions he aroused, but it was an apt text for a beginning preacher. The opening verses of the ninth chapter of John's gospel have Jesus meeting a Jewish man, blind from birth, on the Sabbath. Jesus explains that the blindness, which is at its core a spiritual blindness, reflects the absence of a redeeming faith that only a belief in Jesus as the Messiah can rectify. Jesus makes a clay of dirt and spittle, anoints the man's eyes, and restores his sight. Franklin chose as his text the words Jesus spoke to his disciples to explain why traditional strictures against work on the Sabbath had lost their force in light of Jesus' new revelation. In so doing, Franklin was proclaiming publicly a personal decision to put down the plow and instead "work the works of him who sent me."[22]

"I remember delivering it," Franklin would later note. "I imagine it wasn't too well constructed, because I had no training for it. I just spoke about what I felt. . . . I was nervous when I got up before people and began to preach, but after the attempt at delivering the sermon, it was over. Then the people complimented me and encouraged me." Over the years, before he began to pastor his own churches, St. Peter's would call him back to preach, occasionally at "preaching rallies" where "four or five of us would get up and do a short sermon." Franklin carefully studied other preachers:

"Because when you would hear other preachers preach, you would try to determine his course, how he would go about to build his sermon." In part this was to anticipate, to see if you could predict the preacher's mind in advance of the delivery, a way of testing (and eventually asserting) yourself against a more experienced man. But it also had another aspect: "If you did not anticipate, you would simply watch how the structure of the sermon went about. This is the way you improve yourself." Franklin's call to preach, the central experience in his life to date, nourished and provoked his intellectual curiosity at a level unknown in his classroom experience. Here was the boundless sense of the possible every young person can be drawn to, if only they can recognize its first glimmers.[23]

As powerful as was his call to preach, Franklin did not lack other options if he was to escape a life consumed by the plow and the hoe. The blues remained enormously popular throughout the Delta in the years between the two world wars. B. B. King explained that as a child, the "blues meant hope, excitement, pure emotion. Blues were about feelings." Nor was King's appreciation of the blues a generational revolt within the family. His great-aunt Mima (Jemimah) had in her sharecropper's cabin "a crank-up Victrola, a machine that changed my life." Aunt Mima loved music, and it was there that King first heard recordings of both gospel preachers and the blues and jazz of Bessie Smith, Mamie Smith, Lonnie Johnson, Ma Rainey, and Duke Ellington. King declared the legend that had bluesman Robert Johnson selling his soul to the devil for his extraordinary musical talent "bullshit. I would never trade my godly feelings for anything. And in my mind, no blues artist ever has. . . . I believe all musical talent comes from God as a way to express beauty and human emotion." Nor was King unique in this. Muddy Waters's grandmother also had a phonograph on which he first heard both "church songs" and such blues performers as Blind Lemon Jefferson, Charley Patton, and Blind Boy Fuller. As Waters insisted: "As far as music, you get a heck of a sound from the church. . . . I think the best blues singers there are today—even to myself—they came from the church." Perhaps a quarter of Charley Patton's recorded songs were religious. Son House, another influential Delta bluesman, alternated between preaching and playing the blues. Even Cleo Myles, the product of a strict upbringing, recalled that in her teens in

Cleveland her mother allowed her to listen to jazz or blues "as long as . . . it didn't take an effect on you." In short, a devout church member could and did enjoy the music as long as the pleasure did not lead to dancing or sexual experimentation.[24]

The explosive growth of the recording industry during the 1920s enabled black Delta families to explore and enjoy a grand variety of musical forms. No longer limited solely to artists who traveled to their towns, black Mississippians greatly expanded their musical sensibilities with the aid of new technology. Between 1914 and 1919, for example, the three companies that manufactured phonographs had increased their sales nationally almost 500 percent. Releases of blues songs and gospel hymns, primarily sold in black America, likewise grew spectacularly during the 1920s, from fifty records in 1921 to some five hundred six years later. Total record sales of gospel and blues, known in the industry as "race records," topped 10 million in 1927, the equal of the approximate number of blacks in the entire nation. Just as impressive was the growth of recorded sermons. In 1926 only six preachers recorded for commercial labels, although one sold almost 90,000 copies of a single sermon, and religious records far outsold both blues and jazz. Twelve years later, seventy preachers released more than 750 sermons. Prominent among the recorded ministers was Reverend J. M. Gates, pastor of Mount Calvary Church in Atlanta between 1914 and 1941. Gates recorded more than 200 sermons, over a quarter of all released up to 1941, in a distinctive voice that whooped, rasped, and moaned without losing his message. Although not every family owned one, the phonograph became part of the established social pattern of visiting back and forth. Those with a machine shared the music with neighbors and friends; those without nonetheless bought records to play on a friend's machine. A single record thus vibrated in the minds of many. People like Cleo Myles or Clarence Franklin, neither of whom probably went to the juke joints in 1931, nonetheless could enjoy the music and even discreetly tap a foot to it along with family and friends. Little wonder, then, that many blacks fleeing the rising floodwaters of the Mississippi River in 1927 looked first, after family, to save the phonograph.[25]

The Franklins were one of those families with a phonograph, "a wind-up floor model." And they had records to play on it: "We had religious records, we had blues records." Clarence specifically recalled gospel recordings and sides by Texas bluesman Blind Lemon Jefferson, St. Louis's Roosevelt Sykes, and the Delta's Tommy Johnson and Charley Patton. He also remembered playing the records of J. M. Gates, especially his famous "Dead Cat on the Line," a sermon that addressed sexual infidelity and paternity. Like Cleo Myles, he probably did not dance at this point in his life, but he rejected even then the idea that sacred and secular music were in conflict. "Not within me," he later asserted. "I always liked the blues." There were, at St. Peter's Rock, "some church people who didn't approve it, blues, but they didn't understand that it was part of their cultural heritage."[26]

This "cultural heritage" was a thick gumbo of musical and spoken words that conveyed both an ethical dimension and, often, a social commentary as well. Franklin, for example, recalled not only the blues but also stories told throughout the cotton fields of the Delta by some "great storytellers" as they hoed and plowed. A favorite involved Jack Johnson, the first modern African American heavyweight boxing champion, and a trip he took from Chicago to St. Louis in his stylish automobile. Caught after a chase by the police for speeding, Johnson accepted the $200 fine and said: " 'Well, take five [hundred], because I'm coming back the same way.' . . . Well, these black field hands identified with Jack Johnson," Franklin explained. "They identified hopefully with his success and possibly with their own or the success of their children. And therefore they kept these stories alive." Franklin may also have added that these black agricultural workers relished as well the flippant dismissal of white authority Johnson's very success momentarily allowed. In song and story, then, the hurt of a shared oppression found release and even transcendence in the very act of giving it voice.[27]

Where Ellas Bates, the future rock-and-roll star Bo Diddley, quipped about his stern Baptist upbringing in McComb, Mississippi—"Baptist people think *breathin'* is bad, you know"—Franklin came to understand how the musician and the preacher shared a common tradition and, in a certain manner, a common purpose as well. In Charley Patton's music, for example, Franklin might enjoy such songs as "Pea Vine Blues" or "Tom Rushen Blues," the latter about the sheriff in Cleveland, and then listen to the same artist singing "Lord I'm Discouraged" or "Prayer of Death." Each expression—for the Afro-Baptist sermon was, at root, also a musical experience built as much on rhythm as on scripture—sought to touch the audiences they frequently shared, as Saturday night turned into Sunday morning, to spark a release and a regeneration through the power of words. The nature of the performance in each case elicited similar responses. As Thomas A. Dorsey, the most influential composer and performer of gospel blues in the twentieth century, explained, both gospel and the blues have "the same feeling, a grasping of the heart." In church, responding to song or sermon, "they holler out, 'Hallelujah' or 'Amen'. . . . In the theater, they holler 'sing it again' or 'do it again' or something like that." Dorsey, who before his conversion, as Georgia Tom, had played piano for Ma Rainey and Bessie Smith, among other giants of the blues, thought the blues were "as important to a person feeling bad as 'Nearer My God to Thee.' I'm not talking about popularity; I'm talking about inside the individual. This moan gets into a person where there is some secret down there that they didn't bring out. . . . When you cry out, that is something down there that should have come out a long time ago. Whether it's blues or gospel, there is a vehicle that comes along maybe to take it away or push it away." Reverend Emmett Dickinson, in his 1930 recording "Is There Harm in Singing the Blues," sharply criticized those "so-called preachers" who taught that the blues were the devil's work. "You don't know the meaning of the blues," he admonished. "The blues is only an outward voice to that inward feeling."[28]

In an important way, then, Franklin was not forced to make a choice between the church and the surrounding culture that would deny the power of either. Indeed, from the very beginning, he sensed the black sermon's intimate roots in an oral, black folk tradition that, together with blues, tales, and church music, carried the moral and ethical beliefs of a people across generations. B. B. King experienced this as well, struggling with similar feelings to a different end. "Part of me still yearned to serve in the army of the Lord," the blues musician remembered of his teenage years in Sunflower County. "But the truth is that I never got the calling. . . . I never heard that voice. If I had, I wouldn't have argued. But without hearing it, I couldn't fake it."[29]

*   *   *   *   *

Despite his call to preach, Clarence Franklin remained a restless young man. Unable to support himself as a preacher, he had no choice but to continue working the land his family farmed. This did nothing to ease the tension between Clarence and Henry. After a few months Clarence left home—a sudden resolution to a long-simmering friction. His journey was not far, fifteen miles north on Highway 61 to an aunt's house in Shelby, Mississippi. But brief as it was, it did get him out on his own, onto the road that had so stirred his imagination five years earlier. But working his aunt and uncle's farm was as deadening to his spirit as working Henry's land. After a short time, he returned to Cleveland, only to leave again early in 1932, just seventeen, this time as a migrant worker on an extended family trip across the American Midwest.[30]

Paid work was scarce in the Delta during the worst of the Depression, and the price of cotton plummeted as national and international markets collapsed. Hurting, the Franklins, the Pittmans, and portions of this extended family took to the road, as did so many others during those years, in search of work. Clarence's paternal uncle led the expedition, and they set out by car for Caruthersville, Missouri. Travel through Memphis gave Clarence his first view of that complex, pulsating city. The journey also marked his first extended exploration of Highway 61 and the world beyond Cashbury's cotton fields. In Missouri, the group lived in a "tin-top house" and worked cotton; the uncle who led them collected their daily wages and provided for their food and expenses. Clarence recalled getting fired from one job "because occasionally I would just stop the mules and get off the stalk-cutter and go to preaching."

That spring, an agent for a tobacco farmer from Fulton, Kentucky, hired the family to work that harvest and drove them there from Missouri, a journey of more than twelve hours, in an open truck without any provisions. (When Clarence's uncle requested money for food, the white agent laughed.) In Kentucky, the work was hard and the workforce large, culled from migrant workers throughout the South and the Midwest. "All the migrant farm hands lived in tobacco barns, slept on hay," Clarence remembered. That proximity at both work and leisure exposed him to a wider swath of black America than he had ever before encountered.[31]

In Kentucky, as in Missouri, Clarence presented himself forcefully, as a man with a calling:

> *I remember one night when I was in Fulton, Kentucky, in the barn where we were living there were many church people involved. And on Sunday nights they would have services. And one night they asked me to preach. I was frightened and I went out in the back and prayed. Looking toward the stars and prayed for God to help me, give me the strength and encouragement that was necessary for the time. And I did pretty good, pretty good.*[32]

During these months, Clarence lived, worked, and slept with African Americans from many locales other than the Mississippi Delta. Given the rich oral traditions in black culture, he certainly heard new folktales (and new, regional variations of familiar ones) and new songs, sacred and secular, as well as different musical styles in which to play and sing them. And, of course, he encountered preachers, both licensed and "jack-leg," or self-proclaimed, from whom he also learned as he observed. A handsome young man, whose intense vitality animated his broad, dark face, he may also have entered into romantic and sexual relations with women. While Franklin never mentioned this in later interviews, it would be odd if he had not continued to "think about girls" in a more mature manner. Nor would this appear unseemly. For many rural southerners, black and white, premarital sexual experience was common among young people, even expected. This was as true for preachers-in-training as for farmworkers or bluesmen. In these and other ways, then, Franklin's physical journey was psychological and spiritual. His self-consciousness and his self-confidence deepened, and both reconfirmed his calling. His immersion into a broader African American culture widened his vision concerning his coming role, the culture of the people to whom he would minister, and the particular manner in which he would integrate the two into his life.[33]

But in one sense the journey confirmed past experiences rather than opened new vistas. The thread of racial prejudice and segregation wove its way north from Mississippi. Its thickness varied, sometimes nooselike in density, sometimes thinner, as Mississippi physically receded, but it never broke. Young Franklin never spoke of it, but he could hardly have been un-aware of its presence. The memory of the white agent's cavalier attitude concerning food on the trip to Kentucky suggests as much. So did the at-mosphere in Benton Harbor, Michigan, where the Franklins and Pittmans spent between two and three months in the late summer of 1932. Benton Harbor, boasting the nation's largest outdoor fruit market, was an annual destination for migrant workers throughout the first half of the twentieth century. The workers who picked the crops (apples, cherries, peaches, and strawberries, among them) were largely black, and the yearly migration temporarily but dramatically increased the town's black population. White residents took note. In 1923, more than fifteen hundred robed Ku Klux Klan members had stormed Benton Harbor and burned crosses to intimi-date the black workers. Nine years later, the summer Franklin worked in the area, another crowd burned crosses and deported fifty blacks. In the worst of the Depression, those farm jobs were thought to be "white" jobs. This pattern of racial intimidation continued over the following years, as sheriffs' deputies arrested black workers and then exiled them across the county line with orders not to return under threat of a jail sentence or worse. That Mississippi planters still wanted black laborers must have seemed cold comfort.[34]

Yet there was no place else to go. After a brief stop to visit relatives in Arkansas, Franklin returned to Cleveland in late fall of 1932. He was, in his mind, more of a man now than ever before. Ruefully, however, he found himself back in his childhood home, dependent on parents who, however loving, nonetheless still saw him as a child. Even worse, he was back in the fields, sparring with Henry once again, aching for a permanent way out.

Franklin's chance came shortly after he turned eighteen in January 1933. The congregation of County Line Baptist Church in Tutwiler, thirty miles north and east of Cleveland, had need of a preacher and invited Franklin for a trial sermon. He delivered his sermon one Sunday, after taking the bus from Cleveland the night before, and he was accepted as a temporary pastor. This designation was unusual for a Baptist preacher, as a congrega-tion either called a candidate to their pulpit or not. In Franklin's case, there was strong opposition to his youth and lack of experience, but no other candidates were available. Franklin continued in this fashion for some months. One Saturday night he arrived at the deacon's house in Tutwiler with whom he stayed, only to be told that the church had voted him out and invited another minister in his place. Downcast and discouraged, the young preacher prayed most of the night and attended services anyway. When his replacement did not appear, Franklin exultantly assumed the pulpit for both morning and evening services, and the church deacons promptly extended the young preacher's contract for six months. In all the excitement Franklin missed that last bus and had to stay another night in Tutwiler. He arrived back home about 9:00 A.M. on Monday. There he found an angry stepfather already sweaty from two hours of labor in the fields. "Now this going off preaching and coming in this time of day is no good," Clarence remembered Henry shouting, and he demanded his step-son choose once and forever if he would "preach or plow." The young preacher, brimming with enthusiasm over the reprieve the congregation in Tutwiler had just offered, needed no other encouragement for this final confrontation. Claiming the right to determine his life's course, Franklin recalled, that same day "I left home with virtually nothing. And I went down [into the town of Cleveland] and talked with a blind friend of mine, who was very active in our church, a very astute man named Jim. Jim said, 'Well, son, you can stay here with me until you find a place,' and that's where I stayed until I got a little place."[35]

The place Franklin rented was in Cleveland, where he visited parents and sisters with some regularity and began constructing a life for himself as a preacher. While continuing his work at Tutwiler, he also took advantage of any opportunity to preach that came his way. The rallies at St. Peter's Rock were by now comfortable opportunities, and he welcomed invitations from individual churches to take their pulpit on an occasional Sunday.[36] In this regard, Benjamin J. Perkins proved a most welcome sponsor. Perkins, whose powerful sermons had so influenced Franklin, led churches in Clarksdale and Memphis at this time, and he frequently invited young Franklin to take his place in Clarksdale when he was in the Memphis pulpit. As word spread about the power of Franklin's preaching, other churches requested his presence. Franklin shortly established a circuit of four churches between Cleveland and Clarksdale, most of them small plantation churches.[37]

While riding the circuit, Franklin took another traditional step toward claiming adulthood when, on October 16, 1934, three months shy of his twentieth birthday, he married Alene Gaines. Other than that the Reverend E. W. Robert officiated, little is known of the ceremony itself. Nor did Franklin in later years ever mention the marriage publicly or discuss how he met Gaines and who her people were. The length of the marriage also remains a mystery. Whatever their relationship, marriage was an asset for Franklin, offsetting his youth and inexperience in the eyes of suspicious deacons and trustees. As if to underscore this new status, when he gave his name for the marriage license, Franklin exercised the prerogative of southern men, black and white, and gave as his name his initials, C. L.[38]

Once married, Franklin's dissatisfaction with the circuit grew. He wanted the prestige associated with leading one church as the full-time pastor, but his unease went deeper. There was an unsettled quality about him, a sense that his intense drive to define his place in the world lacked a key element. Like the overwhelming majority of rural black ministers, he had not finished grade school, and C. L. hungered for a systematic exposure to books and ideas, to enable him to understand better the new discoveries his inquisitive mind uncovered almost daily. Nor did he want to be like so many others who, between circuit preaching and working cotton, eked out a livelihood that just supported their families on the edge of dire poverty.[39]

Greenville Industrial College, an Afro-Baptist institution, was located in the town of the same name a short sixteen miles south of Cleveland. Greenville in 1935 was a large plantation town of more than fourteen thousand residents. Home to wealthy planters who owned vast amounts of the rich alluvial land beyond the town's limits, Greenville also served as a regional center for ginning, marketing, and financing the yearly cotton crop. The Percy family claimed Greenville as their ancestral home: LeRoy Percy, who had been a kingpin in state politics; his son, William Alexander Percy, a lawyer, financier, and poet famous for the literary gatherings held in his grand residence; and his nephew, Walker Percy, who, in 1935, was just awakening to the power that would make him a brilliant novelist and poet. For Clarence, however, that Greenville was more than 50 percent black was of far greater significance. The town housed at least twenty-eight black churches, with Baptists the largest denomination, and there were many more churches in the surrounding countryside. Since he would have to preach to support his family and pay his tuition, this was of more than passing interest.[40]

Greenville Industrial College promoted the self-help philosophy of Booker T. Washington. The curriculum included theology, literature, and instruction in such trades as brick masonry, carpentry, and mechanics. "It was just a denominational school," Franklin remembered. "It wasn't really accredited." In later years, he characterized his teachers as thoroughly conservative, but at the time, he acknowledged, he embraced what they taught. Beyond instruction in the basic principles of a good sermon (it needed "an introduction, a body, and a climax"), Franklin's teachers stressed the literal truth of the Bible as the bedrock of one's faith. They taught that "man has been on the planet for 6,000 years, stuff like that. . . . They wouldn't dare touch upon anything that dealt with Darwin, anything like that. Evolution, etcetera." Homiletics, the study of preaching, reflected this literal temperament as well. His instructors explained, and Franklin absorbed, that the Holy Spirit actually infused the preacher during the sermon and that the preacher became but a mouthpiece for the Spirit during the sermon's emotional intensity. This Franklin accepted "as a matter of course at that time," as did the majority of his various congregations. In this sense, Franklin's Mississippi ministry was at one with his parishioners; he was, as he acknowledged, a fundamentalist himself. Yet, Franklin rejected one part of his Greenville training, at least in this passive way—a reflection already, perhaps, of a more complex understanding of the cultural sources of the Afro-Baptist faith than his teachers possessed or he could then express. He knew that many in his church audiences smoked, drank, and danced, but he never preached against such habits from the pulpit. With all of its limitations, his college experience proved critical nonetheless. "It was more than I had ever had," a grateful Franklin later noted. "And it kind of challenged me to study." That challenge became a lifelong habit.[41]

During his Greenville days, Franklin preached with conviction and passion, "more or less religiously preoccupied, thinking about the world after," as were most of his ministerial acquaintances. There were a few—"advanced ones," he later called them—who raised ever so gently the question of civil rights, but the typical minister in his Mississippi circle was "more or less indifferent, because of his condition. The white people has taught him that politics had no place in the church, and that religion, in terms of society, was like a departmental thing. You're over here, this is over here, and this is taboo." The omnipresent threat of violence for breaking that taboo secured widespread public acquiescence. Franklin later recalled a story told by Benjamin E. Mays, a leading black scholar and president of Atlanta's Morehouse College, about an alligator placed in a pool surrounded by a fence, where he stayed for years. "And then they removed the fence, but he never came out of that pool."[42]

Franklin's early ministry also taught him other lessons. One Sunday at Macedonia Baptist Church, a small plantation congregation just north of Shelby, Franklin entered the pulpit with news he was leaving. He had just accepted a call "to a much larger church" in Greenville, which would replace Macedonia on his Sunday circuit, Franklin announced before his sermon. Expecting sympathy and even applause at his success, the self-engrossed young preacher discovered instead that "the reverse happened. . . . They got mad. And there was absolutely no response to my sermon." Within the Afro-Baptist tradition, there was no more dismissive conduct possible than to bear silently the minister's words, withholding from him the verbal encouragement that united preacher and listener in a sacred, collective fellowship. C. L. Franklin still had much to learn.[43]

*   *   *   *   *

By 1936, Franklin's marriage to Alene Gaines had ended. Perhaps they shared a mutual recognition of a mistake made; perhaps the driven young husband found her lacking in qualities he thought essential in a pastor's wife; perhaps she died suddenly. No record or memory exists. Whatever the circumstances, marriage remained an important status for the career of this intense, handsome preacher just then twenty-one. In the black church, in Mississippi as elsewhere in the nation, women made up the majority of any given congregation, and it was widely understood that an attractive and effective male preacher might stir multiple emotions in both himself and his majority female congregation. Martin Luther King Sr. recalled that for a young preacher of a marriageable age, there were "plenty of attractive young girls [who] would try to help him make up his mind." Up to a point, this was accepted, but a single preacher who persistently engaged in intense, serial relationships could find his reputation and career seriously undermined. Functionally as well, young preaching men understood the value of a wife as a helpmate in the ministry. Pastors' wives taught Sunday school, directed the choir, played piano, led prayer groups, and often chaired one or more of the various church societies in which women predominated, all the while quietly affirming her husband's moral authority through her conduct as both wife and mother. She was also his eyes and ears among the members. For a driven young preacher such as Franklin, whose aspirations stretched beyond what he could then give full voice to, an ill-considered union might wreak havoc with his future. As King Sr. also noted, once he did marry, increased family responsibilities and the economics of circuit preaching often conspired to undermine the young man's ministry: "Before long, this young fellow might find himself farming right along with someone who was about to become his father-in-law and pretty soon . . . a preacher found he wasn't doing much preaching anymore." Clarence Franklin had no intentions of allowing that to happen to him.[44]

Franklin's preaching duties, family ties, and friendships frequently brought him to Shelby as he traveled his circuit from Greenville to Clarksdale (and occasionally even to Memphis as a guest preacher for Benjamin Perkins). Sometime in 1935, in a Shelby church, he met Barbara Vernice Siggers, who came from a family with deep roots in the area. Although her father, Semial, was born in Kosciusko, Attala County, some 125 miles southeast of Shelby, her mother's people had farmed in the area at least since the 1880s. Clara Lowe Siggers gave birth to seven children. Barbara, her youngest daughter and fourth in the birth order, was born on June 29, 1917, in Shelby. In the early 1920s, the Siggers family relocated to Memphis, part of a migration that more than doubled the city's black population during the decade. In May 1923, Semial died, and Clara, perhaps with the aid of the very oldest children, struggled to provide for the family. Little is known of Barbara's years in Memphis: where family members worked, what churches they attended, or what social activities they engaged in. She was an attractive and talented young woman who enjoyed

reading, playing the piano, and the social activities so much a part of ado-
lescent life. She attended (but probably did not graduate) Memphis's outstanding black high school, Booker T. Washington. The school demanded
intellectual excellence and a strict code of conduct. Each day began with
morning devotions, attended by faculty and students, and concluded with
an in-class devotional service in the afternoon. For Lucie Campbell, who
taught English and American history at the school even as she achieved
national renown as a gospel composer and choir director, Booker T. Wash
ington "was *the* high school" for black Memphis teens. Attending this
school, then, marked Barbara as different from most Memphis black children and from all but a handful of her contemporaries in the Delta.[45]

Nor was it unimportant that Barbara grew into adolescence in Memphis
rather than Shelby. The culture of black Memphis was electric during these
years. Beginning in the 1920s, gospel quartets filled churches, part of a developing gospel blues music that would transform Afro-Baptist religious
expression. Memphians such as William Herbert Brewster and Lucie
Campbell achieved national fame for their work. For those interested in
more secular music (as in the Delta, they were often the same people),
Beale Street was already a mecca, the "Main Street of Negro America," as
George W. Lee called it in 1934. Indeed, few guitar picking black youth
in the deep South did not dream of getting to Memphis. As Muddy Waters recalled of the late 1930s, when he still lived in rural Mississippi near
Clarksdale: "Couple of us what plays, like me and Son Sims, sometimes
we'd go up to Memphis just to come back for the big word, 'We's in Memphis last night.' That was a big word, you see."[46]

Somewhere between ages fifteen and seventeen, however, Barbara and
most of the family returned to Shelby. The depths of the Depression had
finally bested Clara Siggers's efforts to maintain the family in the city, although she left her youngest son, Semial, named after his father, with her
oldest daughter so that he might obtain a better education than was possible in Mississippi. Barbara's circumstances may also have contributed to
the decision to return to the family farm. In March 1934, she had become
pregnant. The biological father wanted nothing to do with mother or son
(who was born on Christmas Eve in Shelby), and the boy, named Vaughn,
did not meet him for more than three decades.[47]

During his time in Shelby, Franklin became friends with Barbara's brothers, Carl, Cecil, and Earl, and would "pal around with them," family lore suggests. But none of the brothers served as matchmakers. Rather, when another Baptist minister invited Franklin to visit his church one evening for fellowship, the guest noticed a young, light-skinned woman at the piano singing in a beautifully clear voice. Another local minister, Reverend Honeywood, introduced them, and the two young people were smitten with each other. For a time they courted, although Franklin's schedule of school and circuit riding often prevented frequent contact. As they discovered similar religious and musical commitments, their relationship grew.[48]

Beyond this, their shared passion for education, for imagining their lives beyond the confines of Mississippi, tied them closer. In Barbara, Clarence found a patient and gifted woman with a level of sophistication that must have been attractive to this yet rough-hewn young man. In Clarence, Barbara found a dynamo whose power and talent, for all the lack of polish, marked him as unusual. Thus, on the rainy evening of June 3, 1936, they married at the home of a deacon of Macedonia Baptist Church. "We had informed the people [in the church] that we wanted to have the ceremony out there," he recalled, and a number of the congregation were in attendance. Reverend W. M. McKennis officiated. Shortly thereafter, in a fashion that echoed his own experience, C. L. legally adopted young Vaughn as his son.[49]

Once again, marriage did not alter Franklin's frenetic pace. While Barbara remained with her family in Shelby, her husband continued both his wide-flung ministry and his efforts to broaden his mind. As he had for a number of years, Benjamin Perkins remained an important, helpful influence. C. L.'s guest appearances in Perkins's Memphis pulpit attracted attention, and sometime in 1937 or 1938, a Memphis church asked him to add their congregation to his monthly circuit.

Established in 1927, First Baptist Bungalow became the second Afro-Baptist church in the North Memphis neighborhood of Douglass Park, named after the nineteenth-century black abolitionist Frederick Douglass. A very poor neighborhood, it paradoxically contained an unusually high percentage of home owners. (These small, "shotgun" houses of two or three rooms off a central hall—down which one could shoot a gun from front to back door without hitting anything—were originally developed in 1900 as a segregated black enclave.) During the 1920s, the community supported an elementary school with a breakfast program and clothes exchange for the poorest children. In 1931, the Parents-Teachers Association established a welfare committee to raise money and other donations "to see that no child had to stay home due to a lack of clothes." Six years later, poverty remained widespread in the neighborhood and residents utilized every available sliver of land to nurture and then preserve fruits and vegetables— more than 100,000 jars—for distribution to the neediest in those troubled times. This self-help effort caught the attention of Eleanor Roosevelt, the First Lady, who visited Douglass Park in November 1937, and later praised the community in her nationally syndicated newspaper column.[50]

While poor, this community possessed an enormous internal cohesion, crafted by men and women of skill and self-confidence, developed in the face of numbing deprivation. For their new preacher, this was a significant turning point. He had gained a foothold in the most dynamic city in the black South and now served a church, albeit for the moment only monthly, that supported the community's social activism. In time, this experience of bringing religion into the congregation's daily life would lead Franklin to reimagine the fundamentalist theological positions that had infused his Mississippi ministry. Still, Shelby remained the center of family life, despite the frequent traveling required of the circuit-riding minister. Barbara was there, and one of C. L.'s churches was Mt. Olive, a plantation congregation just "out from Shelby." While at the church on March 13, 1938, the news reached him that his wife had entered labor with their first child. By the time he got to the house, his daughter, Erma, occupied the rapt attention of both her mother and her brother, Vaughn, who was "looking right down at her" as she nestled in her mother's arms.[51]

With all the joy that Erma's birth brought, it also brought tension. The suggestion of violence that infused the daily exchange of pleasantries between white and black had not lost its power, and the prospect of raising two black children in the heart of the Delta was anything but free of dread and anxiety. As a four-year-old, Vaughn learned that lesson in a fashion that still impressed sixty-one years later. He recalled a Saturday evening, at his Grandmother Siggers's home in Shelby, when *all of a sudden we heard this here noise. I said Grandma, what's that, I heard this noise? And she said, be quiet, hush, and her and her sons and her started running around blowing out candles. And I said, what's wrong? Said shut up, hush, don't say anything. And they were looking out the windows and all these men on horses, I remember looking out, these men on horses with these white robes were going by the house. And I found out that was the Klan, the Ku Klux Klan, passing by the house, it was on a Saturday night. I'll never forget that. But I didn't know what it was all about then.*[52]

The presence of an active Klan organization only reinforced C. L.'s desire to leave the area. His family responsibilities compounded his intent. As Vaughn recalled, his father "was determined by his experiences not to let us [his children] face the same obstacles that he had in order to succeed. He was very rough [adamant] about that." Nor was Franklin alone in this. His Shelby friend and fellow circuit minister, Joseph H. Kyles, the father of four sons, also decided in 1938 to leave the state for Chicago's South Side. Their mutual friend and Delta native, Pops Staples, who removed his family to Chicago in 1936, later captured in a haunting stanza the irreducible reality for black Mississippians that all three men vowed not to subject their children to:

> *They had a hunting season on the rabbit*
> *If you shoot him you go to jail.*
> *The season was always open on me*
> *Nobody needed no bail.*[53]

Within the year the Franklin family followed that well-traveled path carved by thousands of Delta blacks up Highway 61 into Memphis and rented a house at 723 Alston Avenue, in the heart of South Memphis's black neighborhood. Simultaneously, C. L. accepted a full-time position as pastor at New Salem Baptist Church, but a few blocks from the family residence. His circuit-riding days were over—New Salem could pay a living wage—and the family was now both more secure and in a vibrant city. But

C. L. Franklin was not therefore a new man. As Vaughn learned over the years, his father "saw a lot happen in Mississippi, and some of [it] he never forgot." There was a "bitterness" in him, Vaughn thought, a result of the daily oppressiveness in the Delta, that never fully dissipated. "He might have left Mississippi as an individual," Vaughn suggested. "But Mississippi never left him inside, deep down."[54]

How C. L. Franklin handled these and other potentially volatile emotions would define his future career. Most of his ministerial colleagues, even those equally as talented as this young preacher, never left Mississippi. Those who did, moreover, often found disappointment and failure as they discovered that their eagerness for a sophisticated urban congregation exceeded their talent and ability. Against such odds, relatively few might expect "this little black boy from Mississippi" to succeed. But if he did, Cleo Myles later mused, "don't you think that [would be] something to talk about?"[55]

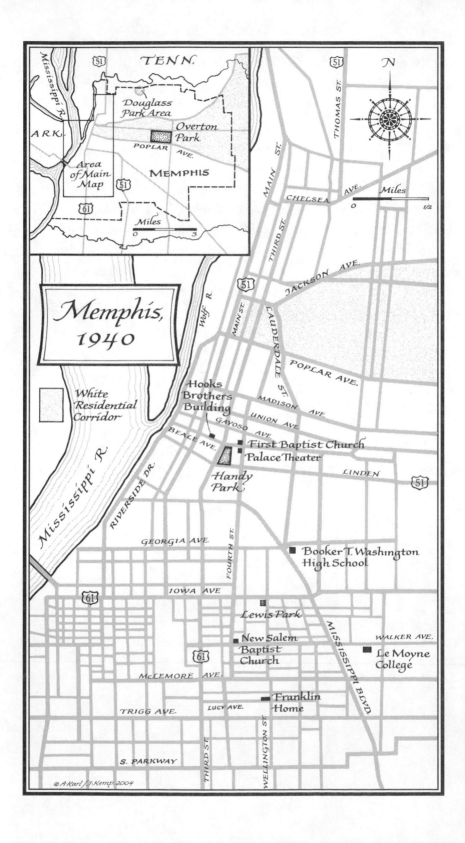

Memphis,
1940

White
Residential
Corridor

TENN.

Douglass
Park Area

Overton
Park

POPLAR AVE.

MEMPHIS

ARK.

Area
of Main
Map

Mississippi R.

Miles
0   3

Miles
0   1/2

N

Hooks
Brothers
Building

First Baptist Church
Palace Theater

Handy
Park

Mississippi R.

Wolf R.

RIVERSIDE DR.

BEALE AVE.

GAYOSO AVE.

MADISON AVE.

UNION AVE.

POPLAR AVE.

LINDEN

MAIN ST.

THIRD ST.

MAIN ST.

LAUDERDALE ST.

JACKSON AVE.

CHELSEA AVE.

THOMAS ST.

Booker T. Washington
High School

Lewis Park

New Salem
Baptist
Church

Franklin
Home

Le Moyne
College

WALKER AVE.

GEORGIA AVE.

IOWA AVE.

McLEMORE AVE.

TRIGG AVE.

LUCY AVE.

S. PARKWAY

FOURTH ST.

THIRD ST.

WELLINGTON ST.

MISSISSIPPI BLVD.

© A.Karl / J.Kemp 2004

CHAPTER THREE

MOVING ON UP

Memphis, then the blackest major city in the United States, with more than 40 percent of its nearly three hundred thousand people of African descent, moved to rhythms more complex and electric than anything found in the Delta. Beale Street, the heart of the black shopping and entertainment district, was the great crossroads. Working men and women shopped there, and filled the clubs on Saturday evenings. Black professionals maintained their offices on the Street as well, even as many showed only disdain for the blues music that flowed from those clubs onto the sidewalks outside, and street intellectuals and political activists debated solutions for the pervasive segregation that crafted social relations.[1]

Beale Street pulsated in the minds of many southern blacks as a symbol of the possibilities that did not exist in the rural South. Yet the Street and its city delivered a far tougher reality than that popular promise often imagined. "I love my whiskey and I love my gin," the Memphis Jug Band sang in its popular "Cocaine Habit Blues" in 1930. "But the way I love my coke is a doggone sin." The large amounts of cocaine and whiskey that fueled the Street's excitement inevitably led to violence. "And the business never closes till somebody gets killed," W. C. Handy sang in his "Beale Street Blues." So renowned was the city's reputation in the 1930s as the murder capital of the nation that the FBI investigated and confirmed Memphis's status for fatal violence as well as its regional preeminence as a drug distribution center. "Cocaine could be bought in stores, like aspirin," one resident remembered. "It came in little flat round containers of wood, known as 'lids,' at fifty cents." With illegal drugs and, until the repeal of Prohibition in 1933, illegal liquor came a perfect opportunity for organized crime to build a sales network through local businesses and black street vendors, bribing politicians and police as needed. The profits of this trade rarely enriched black Memphians. Beale Street, the central artery of black Memphis, was a wide-open venue for pleasures of every description. But there also were consequences, in murdered family members, a reported high rate of venereal diseases, and a wrenching poverty that brought people back to the Street every Saturday night in search of some release from the hardness of the week gone by, whatever the cost.[2]

Scattered among the Beale Street crowds was the city's diverse ministerial community, their clerical black garb distinctive against the kaleidoscope of colors and designs about them. They, too, shopped, stopped to talk, and gathered in regular meetings to discuss themes for the weekly conversations they initiated with their congregations on Sunday morning. And on the Street ministers could, if they chose, mingle with the folks they rarely saw in their church pews. Almost four decades later, the promise of that potential remained vivid. C. L. recalled, "I guess one of the things that I thought about, I thought that Memphis would expand my mind, my experience, expose me to things that I had never been exposed to in Mississippi."[3]

The pulpit C. L. occupied at New Salem Baptist Church, on South Fourth Street just north of Walker Avenue, was at first glance not the most promising. A small congregation in the heart of South Memphis's expanding black residential district, with the majority of members relatively recent migrants much like himself, the church possessed few financial resources. The plain wooden structure, set on a narrow, densely crowded street, announced as much. When C. L. preached his inaugural sermon in 1939, Memphians already boasted of a distinguished group of Afro-Baptist preachers deeply entrenched in the community. Roy Love, president of the Baptist Pastors' Alliance, came to Mt. Nebo Baptist in

1926; S. A. Owen, with a master's degree from Morehouse College, and a leader in the Tennessee Baptist Convention, came to Metropolitan Baptist Church in 1923; T. O. Fuller, a graduate of Shaw University, a major influence among Tennessee Baptists, was the longtime pastor of First Baptist; M. J. Jenkins, a powerful and effective preacher, had sharply increased church membership since arriving at Greater White Stone Baptist in 1924; and W. H. Brewster, the nationally known gospel composer, had been pastor of East Trigg Baptist since 1922. And, of course, Benjamin Perkins, a major figure in the National Baptist Convention, also had his church, which Franklin had visited as a guest. Set against these accomplished and tested preachers, their congregations laced with professional men of means and influence, the young preacher at the small church in South Memphis seemed rather insignificant.[4]

Yet Franklin remained undaunted. Whatever fears he privately held, however inexperienced he felt, no matter how rustic his mannerisms appeared to sophisticated Memphians, he fervently grasped New Salem's pulpit. In the intricate labyrinth that was black Memphis's social order he sensed his relative position, yet he embraced his good fortune. He now looked down Highway 61 into Mississippi, and that changed perspective signaled a major step toward satisfying his old longing.

*　　*　　*　　*　　*

The origins of Memphis's future reputation as an open, bawdy city where violence and guile proved more effective than honest ventures lay in its very formation. In 1819, Andrew Jackson, the hero-general of numerous military campaigns against American Indians, together with two business partners, prepared to sell the land atop the fourth and southernmost of the Chickasaw Bluffs, which run along the eastern bank of the Mississippi in Kentucky and Tennessee. Conveniently, the year before, General Jackson had coerced the Chickasaw tribe to cede the lands to him for a pittance. From these strong armed beginnings, the city grew rapidly. During the 1840s, the population grew by almost 400 percent, and it doubled again in the following decade. Of the more than twenty-two thousand residents in 1860, 30 percent were foreign-born, two thirds of them from Ireland; 17 percent were black. Over these years Memphis became a center of commerce and finance at the western edge of a slave-holding state. The Mississippi River provided immediate access to the commercial markets running north and south through the middle of the emerging nation. Even more important were the agricultural lands immediately south of the city. For Memphians, their city defined less Tennessee's western boundary than it did the northernmost tip of the Mississippi Delta. Money was to be made from the Delta, from the rich, alluvial lands surrounding Memphis and just across the river in Arkansas, from the trade in slaves and the cotton they produced. Plantation owners in turn flocked into the city to conduct business, socialize, and visit the brothels, saloons, and gambling clubs the city was known for even before the Civil War. Many established second homes in the city, and their servants, nannies, valets, mistresses, and laborers sparked the growth of black Memphis.[5]

But then the Civil War came. The Federal victories throughout the Mississippi valley in the latter years of the war put in motion massive movements of black men and women newly freed by Union armies. Some arrived in Memphis and stayed permanently in the city, despite the persistent racial violence and the ultimate withdrawal of the federal government's promise of political and civic equality during Reconstruction. By 1870, black Memphians made up 39 percent of the more than 40,000 residents.[6]

Repeated outbreaks of yellow fever savaged Memphis throughout the 1860s and 1870s. The three episodes in the 1860s were relatively mild. In the worst, in 1867, 550 men and women died of the about 2,500 who were stricken by the fever. The next outbreak, in 1873, devastated the community. Between August and October of that year, yellow fever infected nearly 5,000 Memphians, and approximately 2,000 died. Most of the dead were white residents, as the majority of the city's 15,000 blacks proved not susceptible. More than half of the whites who perished were among the poorest Irish immigrants who lived in "The Pinch," a working-class neighborhood near the waterfront, men and women who lacked the economic resources to flee the city as wealthier whites did. Even worse lay ahead. In 1878, 20,000 Memphians contracted the fever, and almost 6,000 died. So vivid were the fearful memories of 1873 that this time, the exodus began immediately following the reports of the first death on August 13. Ultimately more than 25,000 people, again mostly whites, left the city, searching for cooler and safer climates as far north as St. Louis and into the countryside to the east of Memphis. By year's end, the city's population had fallen to under 20,000, approximately two-thirds of whom were African American. While some whites returned during 1879, a significant portion never did, and this dramatically altered the face of the city. In the 1880 census an overall decline of 17 percent in the city's population was noted, but black residents now composed 44 percent of all Memphians. Twenty years later, the city had regained much of its momentum but the immigrant working people had not returned in numbers. In their place, rural southerners, black and white, streamed into the city. In 1900, twenty years since the last epidemic, the city's population had tripled, while the black portion increased to 48 percent. Only twice between 1880 and 1940 would the city's blacks slip below 40 percent of the population and then only by a sliver each time. Thus, the postwar migrations and the yellow-fever epidemics restructured the city far beyond their immediate impact. Even during the decades of large European immigration throughout the country, Memphis lacked the diverse enclaves of ethnic whites that marked northern and even some other southern cities, with their commingling of work, entrepreneurship, and leisure, in vivid colors and contrasting tones. Instead, the city's African American residents evolved a rich and varied culture that gave Memphis its distinctive renown.[7]

The black world the Franklin family entered in 1939 was relatively youthful—almost 80 percent of black Memphis was younger than forty—and uneducated. The majority of black children under age fourteen attended grade school on average for but six years, and only a small percentage entered one of the two black high schools. The growth of black Memphis during the 1930s—bluesman Leroy Carr exaggerated little when he sang of "All trains going to Memphis town"—had been impressive. Spurred by the hopes of many rural southern blacks to find a paycheck despite the Depression, blacks accounted for 70 percent of the city's new residents between 1930 and 1940, arriving at a rate nearly three times that of whites. Relatively young, without much formal education, the majority from painfully poor rural backgrounds, these migrants lacked the skills attractive to an urban industrial world, even had segregation allowed them to apply.[8]

Most black Memphians lived north of Jackson Avenue or south of Poplar Avenue, in the neighborhoods stretching back from the river where the Irish and other white working people had once lived. While some whites remained in these neighborhoods, federal housing policy in the 1930s quickly altered that pattern. The creation of two whites-only housing projects outside the boundaries of black Memphis, along with the concurrent construction of three other blacks-only housing projects near the river and outside a four-block white business and residential preserve, only intensified the white flight to the underdeveloped eastern areas of the city—following a path first blazed by those whites fleeing the fever. The resulting residential design was unique. The narrowed stem of an imagined white funnel nestled gently against the river, stretching east along the corridor framed by Jackson and Poplar. Included within its span were the riverfront promenade, the cotton exchange, major financial institutions, and the homes of numerous whites. Close by on either side was black Memphis. As the stem continued east toward Overton Park, it widened, reducing sharply the contrasting white and black patterns so evident nearer the river. At East Parkway, the northern boundary of Overton Park, the cup of the funnel arched out in a half circle to the eastern limits of the city, enveloping neighborhoods that were ever more the resting place for whites who traveled daily for work and pleasure into the increasingly black core city. By 1940, 77 percent of the growing black population, forced into confined neighborhoods with inadequate, older residences, lived in substandard housing. This pattern of residential segregation, supported as it was by Memphis officials and federal housing policy, required no race-based local zoning laws to maintain.[9]

Despite these conditions, Memphis provided migrants with jobs which, however low paying, nonetheless positioned black working people within the cash economy—a far cry from the plantation practice of payment in scrip redeemable only at the plantation store. Coupled with the cultural impact of Beale Street and the city's strong church culture, Memphis native Benjamin Hooks thought, there developed a strong alternative to segregation's corrosive power.[10]

*   *   *   *   *

When C. L. Franklin delivered his inaugural sermon at New Salem in 1939, he looked out over a poor congregation that was first organized in 1904 by dissidents from First Baptist on Beale Street. New Salem's membership grew modestly under the leadership of its first pastor, a Reverend Bradshaw, who resigned following the destruction of the church in a 1917 storm. The congregation then called Reverend B. J. Whittaker, who constructed a new, if small, wooden building at 955 South Fourth, a mile south of Beale. In the late 1930s, E. D. Payne held the pulpit. Though the membership had not grown, New Salem attracted attention for its outdoor baptismal pool that was used by many other Baptist congregations.[11]

Situated in the heart of the densely populated, narrow streets of South Memphis, New Salem was one of the many black institutions in the city buffeted by the desperate need of its members. Unemployment in black Memphis still raged at more than 35 percent in 1940. As Honeyboy Edwards remembered of the era: "People walking the streets then was hungry. There wasn't no relief, you'd work all day for nothing" if you could find work at all. Statistics bear Edwards out: the average wage for black men in 1940 in Memphis was between $9 and $12 dollars per week; for black women, a paltry $4 to $7. (The comparable wages for whites were $23 and $15 per week, respectively.) Not surprisingly, the type of work available to blacks was limited. Perhaps the largest group of employed black Memphians were the men (and some women) who gathered early each morning on the street corners in the wholesale cotton district downtown between Jackson and Poplar Streets. There they awaited the open-bed trucks that would take them as day laborers to work the fields of "white gold" on cotton plantations throughout Shelby County and across the Mississippi River in eastern Arkansas. Wages here were as low as 40 cents per hundred pounds of cotton picked—and an efficient worker might pick but two to three hundred pounds daily. The second-largest group of black workers, almost all women, was in service to white families. "Negro women are the main link between the white and black worlds of Memphis," one observer noted of the early 1940s, because every morning thousands of them—"black, and brown and light-tan nurses, cooks, and maids"—made their way from their neighborhoods to the homes of their employers along that white corridor and beyond. There, with long hours, little pay, and the potential for abuse a persistent concern, they worked in support of their own families. Black life in Memphis was harsh, but its very harshness, Honeyboy Edwards thought, posed a peculiar challenge. "If you could make it in Memphis you could make it anywhere."[12]

Franklin was just twenty-four when he arrived at New Salem. Reverend Payne had been dismissed some months before for abusing liquor, and the congregation had invited a series of preachers to give trial sermons. By any standard, Franklin was quite young, lacked the pastoral experience that derived from sustained interaction with one congregation over time, and had "rural" written all over his demeanor. He was attractive: a well-proportioned, dark-complexioned man with a broad, inviting face, close-cropped hair, and rimless glasses that lent an air of solemnity. But his country ambience was sharply noted by more urbane congregants. Alma Hawes Black, reared in Memphis, the daughter of a shipping clerk who had migrated from Mississippi a generation before C. L., recalled vividly her first impressions of her future pastor. She was then sixteen, a church member for four years, and as a student at Booker T. Washington High, influenced by the same stern Lucie Campbell who had taught Barbara Siggers Franklin earlier. Black remembered C. L. Franklin as "poorly dressed" when he first arrived, given to wearing "yellow-type shoes, the kind sold at dry goods stores." His clothes were not only unfashionable in the Memphis context, Black thought, but they were worn, even torn. Yet this young man projected an intense physical magnetism and charisma that many found compelling. When the entire congregation met in a "church business meeting" to decide who would lead them, Franklin was their first choice.[13]

Franklin's country qualities were not necessarily always a drawback. For every family like the Haweses, who had made their migration a generation before, many more in the congregation shared the confusion of C. L.'s far more immediate transition. As he took the pulpit each Sunday morning, they heard in a familiar accent religious themes that echoed childhood experiences. Yet something else occurred as well. Nettie Hubbard, who had first observed C. L. in 1942 and joined New Salem the following year, thought that as their pastor found himself, adjusted to the culture of the city, and deepened the message he delivered, many in the congregation sensed new possibilities for themselves. As his public voice grew, it became a familiar model against which parishioners might test their own voices in new, more assertive ways. "We want to move up a little higher," Julia Ann Carbage explained, reflecting a dominant reaction of the congregation to their pastor. "And so we start at the bottom and climb up, and that's the sort of thing that the preacher, Reverend Franklin, did."[14]

The signal moment in the church week was the Sunday sermon, the most powerful chord that vibrated through the congregation, and Franklin was "the king of the young whoopers," Benjamin Hooks recalled. The whooped sermon's emphasis on the sacred word as performed, as opposed to simply spoken or read, had roots deep in black oral traditions from the slave era that still echoed African influences. Central among these traditions was the need for an active response by the congregation as the preacher delivered his words.[15] In 1940, Hooks was a fifteen-year-old boy who assisted his father and uncle in the family photography business located in the building they owned downtown. In that capacity (the brothers were the primary photographers for black Memphis at this time), the teenager met many black Memphians, including Franklin. "Ben Perkins, of course, was reputed to be the greatest of all [whoopers]," Hooks thought, "but he was middle-aged by that time and Franklin was much younger." Franklin's parishioners shared Hooks's impressions. With Franklin in the pulpit, Ernest Donelson explained, "If you wanted to get a seat for the mid-day service, you had to come to Sunday School [at 8:00 A.M.]. . . . Or stand." New Salem sat approximately four hundred, but Franklin's drawing power from "all over the city" meant that on most Sundays, worshipers "would be lining all around the walls, standing up." Nor was C. L.'s appeal simply emotive. Even early in his Memphis career he began to rethink how he used his sermonic power, specifically how he might span the distance between faith and the daily reality of black life near mid-century.[16]

That gap was substantial. The formal training most southern black ministers gained was minimal, and they as well as their congregations often were uncomfortable with a more literate and sophisticated urban world. George W. Lee, a Mississippi-born Memphis businessman and political activist, argued in 1920 that too many of the local black clergy were "preaching about the glories of the other world and too few [were] pointing out the hell" of this one. A decade later, the *Memphis World*, the local black paper, criticized ministers, along with businessmen and teachers, for their general acquiescence to racism. Ralph J. Bunche, then a young political scientist and later the recipient of the Nobel Peace Prize for international diplomacy, delivered the most damning indictment. Following a research trip to Memphis in 1940, Bunche noted the preponderance of black churches (213 of a total in Memphis of 375) and proceeded to excoriate the black clergy for their timidity and the absence of informed commentary: "The Negro preachers of Memphis as a whole have avoided social questions. They have preached thunder and lightning, fire and brimstone, and Moses out of the bulrushes, but about the economic and political exploitation of local blacks they have remained silent."[17]

In 1939, Franklin fit this stereotype perfectly. As he had noted, he was then a fundamentalist in his theological outlook, one who believed the words of the Bible in literal fashion. His chanting ability, its effectiveness with Mississippi congregations already well known, was used to prepare parishioners for the coming judgment day in a fashion that all but ignored the world they inhabited. From the pulpit, his rich baritone enveloped the listener, lifting individuals and ultimately the congregation. His cadence changed: a tonal center supplanted the earlier conversational pattern, and C. L.'s words now danced, in musical key, to an intense rhythmic beat, marked by vocal crescendos, dramatic pauses, and the bending or lengthening of vowels and word endings. His throat constricted, rasping out a growl that punctuated a line and brought both preacher and listener closer to the spiritual power each evoked.[18]

Franklin's deep longing—what Benjamin Hooks called "an intimate kind of commotion"—drove him still, in a fashion Ralph Bunche never imagined. As in Mississippi, his desire for education remained intense. Almost before his family was even settled in Memphis, C. L. enrolled in Howe Institute. Founded in 1888 as a combined grade school and high school for black children, Howe's seven faculty, under T. O. Fuller's leadership, offered classes in theology, the literature of the Old and New Testaments, and practical instruction in preaching, evangelism, and pastoral work. In addition, Howe offered C. L. an opportunity to make friends with other young ministers also new to the city; there, for example, he first met W. C. Holmes, a fellow Mississippian two years younger, who became a lifelong friend.[19]

As useful as Howe was, it did not sate C. L.'s hunger for education. Although he was "without accreditation," as he put it, lacking the high-school degree, he nonetheless enrolled "as a special student" at LeMoyne College, a historically black school located on Walker Avenue, a short walk from New Salem. Founded in 1871, LeMoyne offered bachelor's degrees to both men and women in the arts and sciences. Here Franklin entered onto a "general study plan" that stressed literature and sociology. This was his first consistent exposure to such subjects, and he reveled in the encounter. He read widely, continued to improve his literacy, and in his sociology classes explored for the first time in a structured fashion the broad outlines of the black American experience. At LeMoyne there "wasn't any heavy emphasis given upon it, but, you know, [we studied] about the equality of men irrespective of their races; differences only where background or environment or education were concerned." In the segregated America of the early 1940s, however, such assertions were significant.[20]

His ministerial career prevented Franklin from completing the degree, though he remained a part-time student at LeMoyne for three years, taking classes in the morning and attending to pastoral duties in the afternoon. Neither the pastors he trained under in Mississippi nor his teachers at Greenville had deviated from a belief in the literal truth of biblical writings. But in Memphis, he recounted, "I began to be exposed to new interpretations, and I started to go to school, and I was exposed to new Biblical views." In addition, he explained decades after, "I started traveling." As his preaching prowess developed, C. L. received invitations to lead revivals throughout the region and beyond, and his conversations with other ministers sharpened his thinking. He also began attending the yearly meetings of the National Baptist Convention held throughout the country, where he listened to famed preachers and shared reactions with other young hopefuls. In the process his ideas changed; they "began to evolve," as he defined himself anew.[21]

While his studies and travels spurred this intellectual bloom, a rather informal weekly meeting in Memphis proved critical in C. L.'s development. On an upper floor in the Hooks Brothers Building, in a former dentist's office, the Baptist Pastors' Alliance gathered each Tuesday for discussion, study, and talk, swapping stories and testing new ideas as they incorporated younger preachers into their fellowship. More experienced ministers guided younger ones, and no less prominent a minister than T. O. Fuller, "as busy as he was," C. L.'s friend W. C. Holmes remembered, "always made that meeting." It was also at these weekly meetings, C. L. explained, that one minister "would review the Sunday school lesson for the other preachers, and one would preach." Both efforts would then be dissected by the assembled preachers, with the occasional joke made at one's rhetorical excesses or another's rustic manners. Within the practical framework of preparing a coming sermon lay the sheer pleasure of exchanging ideas in the company of fellow preaching men. This exhilarating experience C. L. found most important "in terms of cultivating me with Biblical thinking beyond what I'd been exposed to in Mississippi."[22]

Since none of his sermons from his Memphis days (or from his Mississippi preaching either) have survived, it is difficult to say how this experimentation with new ideas actually changed Franklin. C. L. acknowledged that his intellectual growth at first "aroused [in me] some concern in the process of change, but I viewed it more or less as a deepening understanding." However it actually occurred, within a few years that literal rendering of God's written word became more metaphorical, while the here and now became more literal. Like his friend Martin Luther King Jr., who experienced a similar transformation while at Atlanta's Morehouse College a few years later, C. L. remained most profoundly a Baptist preacher. But his faith commitment, like King's, did not require him to confine his intellect. Together with the readings for his

LeMoyne classes, the discussions at those Tuesday meetings challenged Franklin, prodded him to explore even as they provided a context for him to understand those troublesome feelings "aroused . . . in the process of change."[23]

*   *   *   *   *

However he might have appeared in the pulpit on Sunday morning, at home C. L.'s was not the only voice in the family. Barbara Franklin, a talented pianist for the church, possessed as well a superb singing voice. Mahalia Jackson, herself a gospel singer extraordinaire, frequently stated that Barbara "was one of the really great gospel singers" in the nation. During the 1940s, the two women became friends, and Jackson stopped over to visit both Barbara and C. L. when her schedule permitted. Barbara's son, Vaughn, echoed Jackson's evaluation. "Mom had a beautiful voice," he reminisced, decades later. Church members also recalled the power of her voice in the choir as well as her reputation as an effective music teacher. These lessons were few, for however talented she was musically, Barbara gave the major part of her energy to her role as wife and mother.[24]

By all accounts, Barbara's return to Memphis as the wife of a young but promising minister pleased her. The city was attractive, filled with family, friends, and an enormous range of cultural activity. If any feelings remained concerning her departure some years before, her current status calmed them. Despite her talent, she enthusiastically assumed her role as New Salem's first lady and was kindly remembered by church members as "a beautiful personality," "a sweet little woman," and "good looking, too." In Memphis even more so than in Mississippi, however, her public position as a minister's wife was not the easiest of roles. Given that New Salem, like most churches throughout America, was led by a man but was dependent on the dedication and voluntary efforts of churchwomen to function, the possibilities of tension between these women and the new pastor's wife were very real. Years later, C. L. underscored the very problem even as he sought to dismiss it. Speaking directly of Barbara, he explained that he did not recall his wife experiencing any trouble. "I think [a minister's wife] only has difficulties when she goes in and tries to compete with the established leaders there. That might bring about conflict, but she [Barbara] never had any problem like" that. If C. L. was right about the absence of conflicts, he certainly underestimated the degree of tact and diplomacy Barbara employed to steer clear of such tensions.[25]

New Salem, moreover, was only one of many obligations Barbara shouldered in those Memphis years. When she returned to Memphis at age twenty-two in 1939, a handsome, maturing woman about five feet, five inches tall, with a slight frame, her dark hair pulled back to feature her light-complected oval face, she did so with far more complex responsibilities than those carried by the teenage girl who had left some six years earlier. She now had two children, Vaughn, age five, and Erma, just over one year old. By that summer, she carried her third child, Cecil, born the following March. In addition to the demanding task of caring for three young children, she ran the house, cooked and cleaned, and provided her husband with a comfortable refuge from his public life. She also organized the family moves. In their first two years in Tennessee the Franklins lived in at least three different homes in the South Memphis area, all within walking distance of LeMoyne and New Salem. Finally, sometime in 1941, the family settled at 406 Lucy Street, just two blocks south of McLemore Avenue, into a small, two-story wooden house with a cramped front porch on a closely packed, narrow street.[26]

C. L.'s ministerial schedule structured much of their family life. To prepare the sermons each week demanded concentrated periods of time, as did his studies, meetings, and pastoral duties. Sunday, of course, was intensely busy: the 11:00 A.M. service (which might last two or more hours) followed an 8:00 A.M. Sunday school session and preceded the mid-afternoon prayer meeting for youth. Later on Sunday evening, the congregation gathered again for a second service. If there were no guest preachers for one of the services, Franklin preached twice on a given Sunday, introducing his sermons with his signature hymn, Rachel's favorite, "Father, I Stretch My Hands to Thee," all without the benefit of a microphone. As his reputation grew, other ministers called on him as a guest preacher or invited him to preach a week-long revival in another city. Little wonder, then, was Vaughn's recollection through the child's eye: "Mostly, Mother really took care of us because dad was always gone all the time, always going. So, she really raised us." There were some quiet moments, when the frenetic pace eased. Semial, Barbara's younger brother, recalled hearing that after the children were asleep, Barbara and C. L. would read into the night and share their ideas. But certain of C. L.'s activities would fragment even those moments.[27]

On November 17, 1940, Mildred Jennings gave birth to a daughter she named Carl Ellan. Mildred was then a teenager, "a girl, quite young," her daughter recalled, and a member of New Salem, as were her parents. Sometime during her pregnancy or soon after the delivery—the timing is not clear—the new mother told her parents that the baby's father was her twenty-five-year-old pastor, C. L. Franklin. Their response is unknown, but after the birth they sent their daughter away to relatives in Shelby County, outside the city limits, while they kept their granddaughter to raise themselves. Carl Ellan remained in close touch with her mother as she grew up. Franklin visited but a few times when she was an infant, family members later informed her, but she has no memory of him in her youth. It would be eighteen years before father and daughter spent any time together.[28]

At the time, at least a portion of the congregation knew about C. L.'s daughter. As a sixteen-year-old church member in 1940, Alma Hawes Black sharply explained years later, she and her friends not only knew about C. L.'s involvement with Mildred Jennings but heard as well adult church members and her parents at home discuss the issue. Some churchwomen were so upset, Black stated, that for some time afterward, they chaperoned young girls at church functions their pastor attended. This public knowledge of so private a pain would have been deeply troubling to Barbara. Family stories passed down on her mother's side have led Carl Ellan to believe that her birth was the result of a brief sexual encounter and not a sustained affair. If true, and it seems plausible, Barbara might have found over time the will to forgive her husband. But Jennings family traditions speak of separations of unknown intensity and duration between Barbara and C. L. during these Memphis years. There was also talk in the congregation, some church members recalled six decades later, not only about Mildred Jennings but of other affairs as well.[29]

Mildred Jennings suffered, too. Seduced by her pastor, she was in effect banished from her parental home and her church community, from friends and from her child. That her parents may have made those arrangements in an effort to contain the scandal may not always have been a consolation.

Franklin never spoke publicly of the impact of his infidelity on his marriage, nor did he immediately acknowledge his paternity within the family. It was not until 1958 that his other children learned of Carl Ellan's existence. What C. L. did do was to continue to build his career, ever more aware of his magnetic appeal and preaching prowess. He was, of course, not the first Protestant cleric to father a child outside marriage. Baptist ministers had a reputation for affairs with women in the congregation, and Lizzie Moore, a New Salem member at this time, pointedly noted her pastor's appeal to women who were drawn "from far and near" when he preached.[30]

But Franklin seemed to think that the real threat to his ambitious career plans was less the fact of his paternity than open discussion about it. An affair with a consenting, adult woman—while not to be proclaimed publicly—could indeed remain a private matter. For a pastor to press himself on a young congregant, however, violated multiple trusts within the church community. The private sexual lives of public men were rarely acknowledged during the 1940s, save when the inability to maintain surface normality allowed a major scandal to erupt. Franklin, who neither acknowledged Carl Ellan publicly nor requested forgiveness, was not the only pastor to find in the greater good of his divine mission the very grounds to suppress discussion of behavior that would also harm personal ambition. Indeed, he may have reasoned from within his faith that his sins were, in fact, between him and his God alone. More than a decade later, he chanted his cry from the pulpit for a more general forgiveness from his sins that possibly included this moment as well. "O Lord," he began,

> Lord, when I go back through my life,
> I'm doing wrong all the time,
> I bow down and tell him,
> "Lord,
> Would you give me strength/to overcome/my weaknesses."

How he prayed in private in 1940 is not known.[31]

Barbara's options in this difficult moment were profoundly constrained. C. L.'s schedule drove their life in such a way that left limited time for them together. In addition, her relationship with those in the church who knew of these events perhaps now required an additional reserve to protect her own hurt. And yet Barbara persevered, in her own way adding to that impression of normality. She remained C. L.'s wife, bore him two more children, and continued her role in the church, where her support was even more essential for her husband's career. Socially, of course, her choices were sharply limited; for only a few women was divorce a perceived option in that Afro-Baptist world. Practical concerns loomed as well. Barbara was, in effect, an unpaid adjunct in her husband's church. Like many women in that era, Barbara possessed few skills and fewer resources beyond domestic work to enable her to survive with her children apart from her husband. How she or her husband acknowledged this unequal dynamic within their relationship is unknown. But there was another consideration. Barbara's religious faith flowed from a commitment to the central Christian promise of forgiveness and the possibility of redemption for all of humanity's sinners. How could she, a penitent herself before her God, withhold from the man she undoubtedly loved what she herself desired in this world as in the next? So they kept going. Settled in at 406 Lucy Street, Barbara gave birth to her second daughter, Aretha Louise, at home in March 1942. Two years later, Barbara delivered their third daughter and last child, Carolyn.[32]

From a child's perspective, life on Lucy Street was charmed. Vaughn, the only Franklin child old enough to retain strong memories of life during World War II, emphasized that as a ten-year-old, he never knew about segregation because the white world rarely impinged on his childhood activities. He lived in an all-black neighborhood, attended a school with black teachers and administrators, and worshiped in a church that few, if any, whites ever entered. He thought his mother was "a very strict disciplinarian," but so were the neighbors who, if they "saw you do something wrong," Vaughn recalled wryly, "they would whip your tail and then tell your parents." Both sets of grandparents visited, and Vaughn especially remembered the visits of his mother's brothers, who would take him on his "little Schwinn bicycle . . . up and down Beale Street," where he would hear "this blues music coming from these different clubs."[33]

For C. L. and Barbara, the neighborhood also proved attractive. As a circuit preacher in Mississippi, C. L.'s path frequently crossed those of two brothers and fellow Baptist ministers, Jasper and A. R. Williams. C. L. occasionally had preached at Jasper Williams's church in Greenwood, and over time the three men became close friends. The Williams brothers came "out of Mississippi with Reverend Franklin around the same time," Jasper Williams Jr. recollected, and by 1942, they all lived on Lucy Street in Memphis, with A. R. Williams next door to the Franklins, just across the street from Jasper Williams Sr. and his family. If old enough, the children had the run of each other's houses. C. L. was closest with his next-door neighbor, A. R. Williams. The two men played checkers regularly, the games framed by both friendly competitiveness and continuous, prolonged conversation. Williams Sr. was more of a manuscript preacher, one who wrote out his sermon and neither chanted nor evoked intense emotional reactions. C. L. and A. R. shared the whooping style in their preaching.[34]

Increasingly, Franklin's preaching, the foundation of his growing prominence, possessed an undeniable blues sensibility. He "played" his voice, not a guitar, and he prowled the sanctuary as he preached rather than the stage. But for C. L., as for many other ministers nurtured in southern black culture, both expressions addressed the spiritual and physical pain that daily informed life in the segregated world. At the very center of the sacred and secular performances by these talented soloists, an ability to improvise in word and tone allowed each to seek the emotional core in their audience. As performers they stood out from the audiences they addressed, facing them as unique individuals, even celebrities, free to interpret received texts, to reach inward to voice the deepest emotions, and to create new sensibilities. Vocal improvisations dominated: the timbre ranged from falsetto to a full-throated groan within a given song or sermon, and vibrato, the wavering vocal quality that elongated vowels and word endings, raised emotions and signified meaning. For both bluesman and preacher, the intimate pattern of call and response, where audience and artist sought to draw out—to elongate—the essence of the other in a joined search for deliverance, underscored the very communal nature of the performance. The messages offered were not, of course, always identical, but there was a common bond. One Mississippi-born Baptist preacher, who defined the blues as "a worrying mind," thought only someone with a Christian perspective on sin and the soul could sing them.[35]

Surprisingly, Vaughn Franklin has no memory of a record player in the family home on Lucy Street. "We never did hear it" at home, he declared, even on the radio. He did not "have the slightest idea" what music his parents might have listened to at home, but he explicitly remembered the limits on his listening: "'Cause all I was listening to was gospel—and that was it." By the 1940s, a blues influence already infused religious music, a consequence of the innovations of Thomas A. Dorsey and others. Yet the pattern C. L. imposed at home in Memphis (Vaughn remembered him as "a very, a very strict person") may have reflected what he thought fathers with aspirations for themselves and their children should do. Among many black Memphians with aspirations and ambitions there existed a widespread, intensely negative image that connected the music of Beale Street with near-rampant sexual promiscuity, drug use, and the persistent violence that contributed to the city's national reputation. For a young aspiring minister not yet thirty, who had already risked much indulging his sensuality, Beale Street and its images were not associations to cultivate overtly.[36]

Perhaps the key word here is "overtly." Beale Street was, as longtime resident George W. Lee wrote in 1934, "the Main Street of Negro America . . . a place of smoking, red-hot syncopation." W. C. Handy, popularly known as the "father of the blues," helped establish the Street's reputation when, some years before, he played dances in a park on Beale for crowds that approached a thousand people. "I remember the hands in particular—ebony hands, brown hands, yellow hands, ivory hands," he recalled, "all moving in coordination with nimble dancing feet." For all of its mythic power, the heart of the Street's shops and clubs were crowded into the short seven blocks between Fourth and Front Streets. There, for a moment, Handy thought, people "had forgotten yesterday and never heard of tomorrow." Blues artists embellished the Street's image further, and their recordings broadcast the news nationally. For bluesman Hosea Woods, one of the Street's major appeals was obvious:

> *I'm going to Memphis*
> *stop on Fourth and Beale*
> *If I can't find Roberta*
> *I hope to find Lucille.*

The sexual excitement that permeated images of the Street and neighboring Gayoso Avenue, where most of the brothels actually were, touched women as well. Ethel Waters urged her female listeners across the black South that when a "Memphis man comes knocking at the door . . . If you know your business let him in / Because he is so different when loving begins." Bessie Smith turned the image around as her "Beale Street Mama" demanded of her wandering man, "It isn't proper to leave you mama all alone," and threatened, "Beale Street papa, don't mess around with me / There's plenty of petting that I can get in Tennessee." Some perceptive whites caught the excitement as well. Sam Phillips, who would later record many great southern singers—from B. B. King, Howlin' Wolf, and Rufus Thomas to Elvis Presley, Jerry Lee Lewis, and Johnny Cash—on his Sun Record label, first discovered Beale Street as a sixteen-year-old in 1939. He and his friends, all young white Alabamians, "drove down Beale Street in the middle of the night and it was *rockin'!* The street was *busy.* It was so active—musically, socially. God, I loved it!"[37]

Whites were certainly a presence on Beale Street. George Lee's quip that the Street was "owned largely by Jews, policed by the whites, and enjoyed by the Negroes" was a partial truth that reflected a tortured, very American, racial classification.[38] For black Memphis, Beale Street was the crossroads where rural manners and expectations discovered electric, urban possibilities and from that fusion created new visions. Despite a sharply limited black entrepreneurial presence, Beale remained a beacon to black southerners throughout the Mississippi valley. On Saturdays, the "country people" thronged to its shops, coming by wagon, Model-T, and horseback, Lee witnessed, to "bargain with the Jews for clothing, buy groceries at the Piggly-Wiggly, and fish and pork chops of the Greek, and sometimes moonshine in the 'blind pigs'." Children as well reveled in the excitement, enjoying a piece of candy or a small toy as a reward for a week's worth of farm chores. By sundown, most families pointed home-ward. Saturday night, however, was another experience, one that belonged "to the cooks, maids, houseboys and factory hands," Lee noted. "For on this big night of the week . . . the color and tempo of the street reaches its highest point." Here the hands and feet Handy had put in motion moved again to the music, the whiskey, and the promise of sexual adventure. It was a release from the harshness of the week's work, cleaning up after white folk or endlessly picking other people's "white gold." As the blues classic "Stormy Monday" expressed it: "Well, the eagle flies on Friday [payday] / and Saturday I go out to play." White Memphians' experience of the musical culture of Beale Street remained largely limited to Thurs-day nights, when the Palace Theater, in a special whites-only midnight show, headlined that week's black artists in a fashion that allowed whites to listen without violating their commitment to segregation.[39]

Many New Salem members would probably have disavowed Beale Street's enticements, even though more than a few had found their way there the night before. (As the blues song has it, after the eagle flies and you go out to play, "On Sunday I go to church, pretty baby / and I kneel down to pray / 'Lord have mercy / I wish the Lord have mercy on me.'") C. L. was sensitive to this, and that may explain why he never preached on the evils of Beale Street from his New Salem pulpit, just as he had ear-lier refused to criticize directly those in his Mississippi congregations who danced and drank. This intricate balancing spoke to many who navigated between traditional ways and more modern impulses. Lorene Thomas, a devoted New Salem member for almost a decade when C. L. arrived, lived her family life in the space between those two approaches. A woman of deep faith, in 1940 she married Rufus Thomas, a Mississippi born, Memphis-reared young man who already had a career as a blues singer, vaudeville comic, and tap dancer. The same year they married, Rufus took over as emcee of the Palace Amateur Night, the weekly talent contest for young black performers. Rufus (and decades later his daughter, Carla) had a long career performing blues, rhythm and blues, and soul music, all the while married to a deeply religious woman who rarely, if ever, attended his performances. Throughout his marriage, moreover, Rufus Thomas and his children remained active members of St. John Baptist Church, while his wife worshiped at New Salem. As Alma Black explained it: "Everyone knew that Rufus was 'walking the dog'" on Beale Street, but "people wore many hats. When they put their church hat on, different from his Beale Street hat." Muddy Waters, thinking of his first visit to Beale Street in the 1930s, tersely grasped the heart of the Street's cultural power: "Beale Street was the street. Black man's street." All week long, in all its facets, so it was.[40]

Important as they were, however, blues music and church rituals were not the only cultural expressions black Memphians created, as Ralph Ellison put it in 1944, "upon the horns of the white man's dilemma." Among the black elite, literary and dramatic societies, as well as select social clubs, structured life in a rather exclusionary fashion. More inclusive, if not mass organizations, were the black fraternal orders, including the Prince Hall Masons and the Knights of Pythias. C. L., who less than a decade later would hold the highest rank in the Masonic fraternity, in all likelihood joined a Prince Hall Masonic lodge at this time. As throughout the black experience, fraternal lodges in Memphis maintained close ties to the church and included men (and in the auxiliaries, women as well) of varied economic standing committed to the moral code encouraged in church.[41]

A far more populist excursion were the games of the Memphis Red Sox of the Negro Baseball League. Founded in 1919, the Red Sox played at Lewis Park, named after their second owner, R. S. Lewis, a local funeral director. Situated at the corner of Iowa and Wellington in South Memphis, a short four blocks from New Salem, the park and its games were enormously appealing; indeed, if Beale Street could be culturally divisive for some, Lewis Park provided a common meeting place for all of black Memphis. Black churches concluded their services early before a Sunday doubleheader to allow worshipers to get to the park on time. "They put on the best frocks, the best suits, the best of everything they had and went to this ball game," Rufus Thomas, who himself cut quite a figure, observed. These crowds of more than eight thousand were diverse: ministers, businesspeople, and professionals in the crowd sweated cheek by jowl on humid Sunday afternoons with working people who had just come from church or were more slowly recovering from a Saturday night party. Occasionally, someone of the caliber of a Jesse Owens, the 1936 Olympic star, would take on the Red Sox players in a challenge race before the start of a game. This but heightened the feeling of racial pride already evident in the communal celebration the games encouraged.[42]

*   *   *   *   *

In the late nineteenth century, Julia A. Hooks, whose two sons would later run the family's photography business, opened a music school on Beale for both black and white students. She taught classical piano and, with a local reputation as the "black Jenny Lind" (a popular songstress), gave singing lessons as well. That tradition continued among a segment of black Memphis even decades later. With a different purpose, Lucie Campbell organized the Music Club in 1904, attracting members interested primarily in singing, especially sacred works. The growth of gospel music in Memphis and the nation owed much to Campbell, who was the music director of the National Baptist Convention from 1916 to 1963. She advocated for Thomas Dorsey's brand of gospel blues within Baptist circles, and she discovered and trained talented performers, then promoted their careers. Thomas Shelby, for example, a young gifted musician, studied with Campbell and, under her sponsorship, became the pianist for the convention in the 1930s.[43]

But not everyone in the black religious community accepted gospel blues. Many ministers, North and South, banned it from their churches, declaring the incorporation of blues chords and a syncopated beat "sin music." These "mere" singers claimed that their music was a form of preaching, raising many a ministerial hackle at this presumed invasion of ordained prerogative. Echoing the battle lines drawn in their opposition to black secular music in general, these ministers and their supporters ridiculed the gospel blues, insisting that under the guise of faith it simply brought jazz into the sanctuary. Their stubborn position confounded gospel blues advocates. "The European hymns they wanted me to sing," Mahalia Jackson explained, "are beautiful songs, but they're not Negro music. I believe most Negroes—unless they are trained concert artists or so educated they're self-conscious—don't feel at home singing them."[44]

Beginning in the late 1920s in Memphis, the new gospel music sparked the formation of gospel quartets. These all-male groups were community based, drawing members from one or more of the local church choirs or neighborhood organizations and rarely performing as a distinct group during church services. Rather, they expressed their faith in this new style (which, songstress Nina Simone wryly observed, "allow[ed] you to use the same [i.e., forbidden] boogie-woogie *beat* to play a gospel tune"), singing at weekend concerts before local audiences. Through the 1940s, the majority of the Memphis groups were not professionals. Their members were workingmen—porters, laborers, pipefitter's helpers, and the like who maintained their jobs as they polished their performance. Some of these quartets had origins at the workplace: all four members of the I. C. Glee Club, founded in 1927 and active during the following decade, worked for the Illinois Central Railroad and occasionally performed at functions there as well. Other groups such as the Pattersonaires, established at New Salem in 1945, were church based. Ernest Donelson, one of the original Pattersonaires, recalled how each group would have at least one major program yearly, to which they would invite many other groups to perform as well. Coupled with requests from fraternal lodges and community groups for benefit performances, to say nothing of the time spent in practice, quartet members devoted a considerable amount of their nonwork lives to singing their faith. That faith motivated them, as did their place in the local gospel scene. "Well, everybody wanted to out-sing the others, basically," Donelson explained. "There was some competition."[45]

The ability of these quartets to harmonize faith and syncopation proved immensely popular, and it was a clear alternative to Beale Street for those who so desired. But these hymns also carried other meanings. As W. H. Brewster, the pastor of East Trigg Baptist, put it: "I write these songs for the common people who could not understand political language, common people who didn't know anything about economics." With the city's white political machine controlling black access to the voting booth in South Memphis, and with violence against blacks who violated segregation's strictures—to say nothing of directly protesting such conditions—a frequent occurrence, such efforts were anything but insignificant. Brewster's most famous gospel composition, "Move On Up a Little Higher," written in 1946, was not only a hymn about "a Christian climbing the ladder to heaven," but it also urged blacks to "move up" in education, in the professions, in politics, and other aspects of social and political life. Recalled Brewster: "I was trying to inspire Black people to move up higher. Don't be satisfied with the mediocre. Don't be satisfied. That was my doctrine. Before the freedom fights started, before the Martin Luther King days, I had to lead a lot of protest meetings. In order to get my message over, there were things that were almost dangerous to say, but you could sing it." Ernest Donelson concurred. Brewster's hymn, he noted after decades of performing it, is "more of what you call an inspirational song. You listen to it, and you get hope, you see a better day tomorrow." Mahalia Jackson's 1947 rendering of the hymn sold more than 2 million records, when sales of one hundred thousand "constituted the Mt. Everest of the gospel climb."[46]

C. L. never composed a hymn, and there is no direct evidence of his involvement with these gospel groups. But given his attention to the choir at New Salem, to say nothing of his own considerable skill as a singer, he most likely attended occasional gospel concerts and perhaps even sponsored events at New Salem. People like Brewster and Campbell, as well as the blues-drenched gospel quartets in the city, had a profound impact on him in these years. On a personal level, he and Brewster had a good relationship, working well together in various ministerial contexts, and they exchanged pulpits with each other on occasional Sundays. Increasingly, C. L.'s God was both in *and* of this world, as well as beyond it, and he felt the imperative to engage as best he could each aspect of that ineffable continuum. The praise song he presented from the pulpit could extol the spiritual and intellectual richness that infused black cultural life, the sacred as well as the profane. In his sermon "Without A Song," C. L., echoing Brewster, taught: "Some things you can't say, you can sing. Isn't it so?"[47]

*　　*　　*　　*　　*

Perhaps the first quality that attracted the notice of other ministers during C. L.'s early years at New Salem was his ability to regroup the congregation following the departure of the divisive Reverend Payne. As both the crowds at Sunday service and the permanent membership increased, the scope of church activities grew. In addition to church fund-raising dinners that might feature fried chicken, chitlins, or spicy spaghetti and ice cream (the "Heaven and Hell" party), New Salem now boasted a Boy Scout troop; the Red Circle Girls, which taught young girls "to be ladies"; oratory contests for the church's youth; and a revived and enlarged choir. Franklin expanded the deacon board, those men responsible with aiding the pastor in counseling members, and charged them with bringing to his attention families in need for whom he might take up a special collection at services. Franklin undoubtedly saw himself as a preacher first and an administrator a distant second, but he understood that responsibility for the overall condition of the church remained his. In this regard, C. L. proved a good evaluator of others' abilities. James Waller, with assistance from Barbara Franklin and occasionally Thomas Shelby, Lucie Campbell's protégé, proved to be a fine director of music; Reverend Silas J. Patterson was an efficient assistant pastor. Like many pastors, Franklin delegated duties to aides, keeping a sharp eye on church finances himself, while concentrating on preaching and pastoral counseling.[48]

After but a few years under C. L.'s leadership, New Salem had grown considerably larger, achieved institutional stability, and created an intricate pattern of church activities that brought people to the church regularly to discuss issues important to parishioners. This did not go unnoticed by his ministerial colleagues. C. L.'s early involvement with the National Baptist Convention was yet another sign that marked him as a man of ambition and ability. The convention was the largest organization and its leaders among the most influential in black America. Thus attendance at the annual meeting carried both social and career implications. A young minister focused on moving up made friends and contacts with other young pastors; he might also attract the notice of the more famous. As the convention rotated among northern and southern cities annually, regular attendees came to know something of the varied black communities across the nation, and they returned to their congregations with experiences to share and, perhaps, a deeper understanding of their ministry. Attendance also boosted a pastor's standing within the congregation. "That would brighten them up towards me," Reverend Ivory James remembered, "you know, for me to tell that [his conventions experiences], and they could see that maybe I was growing."[49]

C. L. attended his first convention in 1940, in Birmingham, Alabama, and over the next four years attended meetings in Memphis, Chicago, and Dallas, missing only Cleveland in 1941. He gave no sermon nor led a prayer service that was officially noted, but he assuredly made new friends among peers and probably among the more established ministers also. These annual trips introduced Franklin to cities he had never before visited, each with a somewhat different African American cultural expression. The cumulative effect was to impress the possibility that Memphis was not necessarily the terminus of his metaphorical Highway 61. C. L.'s attendance also signaled something about his ongoing relationship with the New Salem congregation. The congregation paid all of his expenses to these gatherings through extra collections taken up specifically for that purpose. This yearly tax, coming on top of weekly contributions and the occasional special collection, so poor a membership would not have levied on itself unwillingly.[50]

The respect C. L. began to garner from his ministerial fellows reflected as well his coolness in a crisis. On a Sunday in mid-May 1943, following a baptismal service in the outdoor pool that brought forty-seven new members into the church, a near-lethal dispute disrupted New Salem services. As the choir reentered the church through the rear door nearest the baptismal pool, gathering before them any stray parishioners not yet back in their pews, a "blood curdling scream" pierced the note Barbara Franklin had just sang. At the rear of the church, a man later identified as J. W. Prophit attacked Mrs. Ocie Tolbert, a church usher, and Willie Lee Anderson, who had been talking to Tolbert in a rear pew. Although married, Ocie Tolbert had carried on an affair with Prophit for some time, until earlier that spring, she expressed her affection for Anderson. (Anderson's stepmother was a church member, as were the Tolberts, and his affair with Mrs. Tolbert, the *Memphis World* ingenuously noted of Anderson, had "led him back to church.") As Prophit saw the couple talking, he left the church for his home a block away and quickly returned with a straight razor, with which he attacked both of them. He "ripped her neck open," Franklin remembered years later. "I don't see how she lived." Anderson, his neck slashed less severely, ran toward the front of the church. Both injured parties lived, and Prophit, who ran from the church, was shortly cornered after having crawled under a white family's house near McLemore Avenue. The commotion within New Salem was riotous, "everybody running and screaming," C. L.'s daughter Erma recalled. As Franklin calmed his members that Sunday, he also sought to direct public discussion of the affair in a manner favorable to New Salem's reputation. In an interview with the *Memphis World* a few days later, he distanced the church from Prophit, claiming he was not a member, and sought to elevate the church and his own pastoral image above the carnage.[51]

Equally important for C. L.'s reputation among his colleagues were the personal qualities he exhibited when confronted with the city's racism. One Sunday in the early 1940s, C. L., Barbara, and Vaughn were driving in the new family car to a church where he was to be the guest preacher. Pulled over by a policeman allegedly for speeding, C. L. told the family to remain quiet while he talked. The policeman accused the "boy" of speeding, Vaughn recalled, and asked for his name, license, and destination. C. L. told him and acknowledged he was speeding. With name and license in hand the policeman then responded, approximately: "Well, ok boy, now you take it easy now." Vaughn looked at his father. "And I could see the expression on Dad's face, he was one angry, angry person." Yet, bitter as C. L. undoubtedly was, his sense of self-worth would not allow the slur to define his response. Nor did he make a public statement about the incident—perhaps because it was such a commonplace form of harassment as to be unremarkable unless more dramatic violence followed.[52]

Deeper than the bitterness, yet driven by it, was the commitment to mobilize others to undo racism's grip. To change the landscape, C. L. took to the airwaves. Radio was not a new technology in black religious life in the 1940s. As early as 1929, Reverend J. C. Austin, then pastor of Pilgrim Baptist Church in Pittsburgh, broadcast Sunday services on a local station; a decade later, such broadcasts could be found nationwide. In a different vein, Elder Lightfoot Solomon Michaux's very successful New York broadcast integrated political commentary with a theological perspective during the depths of the Depression, while in Atlanta in 1940, Reverend William Holmes Borders began a weekly twelve-minute program that stressed social topics "from the distinct viewpoint of the Negro." Gospel quartets and choirs in live performance were another type of religious broadcasting. Memphis, for its part, enjoyed local radio programming of gospel quartets as early as 1929, only six years following radio's beginnings in the city.[53]

C. L. was not the first black Memphian to have a radio program, but he may have been the first pastor to broadcast directly from his church. It was, whatever its precedents, a program that drew considerable attention. Titled *The Shadow of the Cross,* the program began in the summer of 1942 on WMPS, a local affiliate of the Mutual Broadcasting Company. Modeled in part after the popular Cleveland, Ohio-based *Wings over Jordan* program, aired nationally on CBS, C. L.'s broadcast aired each Wednesday evening between ten and ten-thirty. Franklin's purpose was to offer religious inspiration and hymns, provide a moment of unity for "Negroes of the Mid-South," ease interracial tension, and, the Memphis *World* continued, "acquaint white listeners with the Negro's loyalty and accomplishments on behalf of this country." R. S. Lewis, Jr., the son of the former owner of the Memphis Red Sox, who had taken over his father's funeral business, sponsored the show. Invited singers performed, as did the New Salem choir. One of the most popular features was C. L.'s regular performance of a favorite hymn. In addition, C. L. invited speakers to discuss issues of the day—local businessmen, educational leaders, and men and women involved in a variety of religious and social efforts. W. H. Jernagin, a leader in the National Baptist Convention, appeared, as did Shirley Graham, then the southern field organizer for the National Association for the Advancement of Colored People (NAACP). As her inclusion suggests, C. L. looked to air multiple voices, and even in that city's racially tense atmosphere he intended to press against racism's prohibitions whenever he could. In spring 1943, Franklin and Lewis presented a new feature, a weekly news summary of "important happenings of interest primarily to Negroes."[54]

Within months, *The Shadow of the Cross* attracted a wide audience, the

Memphis World describing it as "a veritable 'voice in the wilderness,'" and proclaimed him in "the forefront [of] the growing leadership of young Afro-Americans" locally. C. L. had found the right mix, touching both the hurt and the promise of daily life among black Memphians. As he sought to do from the pulpit, the radio program bridged rural and urban experiences, the hard past with the promise of the future—all in a fashion that underscored the necessity of a more self-conscious individual awareness. The religious component was the wellspring, without which nothing else flowed. But in opening up a broader social and political discussion concerning civil rights, blacks in the war effort, and the opportunities possible even in segregated Memphis, C. L. gave the "colored people of the tri-states new hopes and inspiration" and perhaps even affected some whites. In the Memphis of "Boss" E. H. Crump, the city's political kingpin, where Crump directives forced local black opponents to flee for their lives and prevented labor organizers such as A. Philip Randolph from speaking, this was not insignificant. C. L. Franklin, not yet thirty, roused in others a sense of the future possible as they, too, reclaimed their public voice.[55]

All this was happening only three years removed from his circuit-preaching days in rural Mississippi. His intelligence, magnetism, and hunger to excel in part explain his success. A relentless ambition to be known, honored, and even celebrated for his gifts likewise played a part. Underneath all lay the resolve, born of a near corporeal yet intangible fear first experienced as a youth, never to allow limitations imposed by others to circumscribe his spirit. By 1942, his public position was such that it had been near impossible for the established religious and secular leaders of black Memphis to omit C. L. when they organized the committee that would raise money for the war effort. The committee raised more than $300,000 in 1942, and would raise even more in 1943, when W. C. Handy returned to Memphis to lead a fund drive to replace the bomber—lost in action—black Memphis had earlier funded. The irony of this effort was evident: the money raised would support a segregated military. But C. L. saw his place as in America—a better America, to be sure, but one worth the collective fight to create. This intimate commingling of democratic hopes and racist experience, the essence of black life during this era, was the point of the NAACP's "Double V for Victory" campaign: victory over fascism abroad and over racism at home. This effort was widely supported in black America, and C. L. certainly made his own contribution to it when he invited the NAACP's Shirley Graham on his radio program.[56]

Only twenty-eight in 1943, C. L. Franklin had come a long way rather quickly in the estimation of both fellow preachers and his parishioners. The once-rural newcomer now sported sharply tailored, respectable suits, drove a stylish new car, and carried himself with confidence. His reputation as a preacher of power and substance announced him before he even entered the pulpit, and invitations from near and far landed on his desk in the pastor's small office. He relished the attention, the recognition, the self-confirmation, as William Holmes Borders put it in a widely reproduced January 1943 sermon, that "I Am Somebody." The power that came with such recognition, a heady mix of the sensual and the prophetic in one proclaimed as designated by God to teach and lead, could prove difficult to restrain. And, at times, for C. L. Franklin, it was.[57]

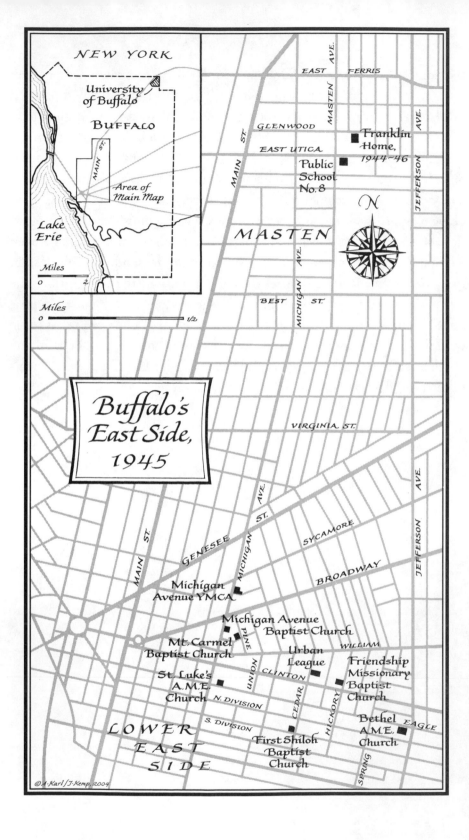

NEW YORK

University
of Buffalo

BUFFALO

Area of
Main Map

Lake
Erie

Miles
0   2

Miles
0   1/2

EAST FERRIS

MASTEN AVE.

GLENWOOD

MAIN ST.

EAST UTICA

Franklin
Home,
1944~46

Public
School
No. 8

JEFFERSON AVE.

MASTEN

N

MICHIGAN AVE.

BEST ST.

VIRGINIA ST.

JEFFERSON AVE.

Buffalo's
East Side,
1945

MAIN ST.

GENESEE ST.

MICHIGAN ST.

SYCAMORE

BROADWAY

Michigan
Avenue YMCA

Michigan Avenue
Baptist Church

WILLIAM

PINE

Mt. Carmel
Baptist Church

Urban
League

Friendship
Missionary
Baptist
Church

UNION

CLINTON

St. Luke's
A.M.E.
Church   N. DIVISION

CEDAR

HICKORY

S. DIVISION

Bethel
A.M.E.
Church

EAGLE

LOWER
EAST
SIDE

First Shiloh
Baptist
Church

SPRING

© A·Karl / J·Kemp, 2004

CHAPTER FOUR

THE EAGLE STIRRETH

Nat D. Williams taught history at Booker T. Washington High, promoted blues music on Beale Street, and wrote a column for the *Memphis World*. He had seen a lot in Memphis, but this was the biggest funeral "ever held in the history of this city." On June 28, 1943, some "four or five thousand persons (chiefly colored)" had crowded the sanctuary and overflowed onto the surrounding streets around Holiness Temple in South Memphis, the preeminent church of the fast-growing black Pentecostal denomination, the Church of God In Christ. The noon services honored a black Baptist minister, not a member of COGIC, as the group was popularly called, but the larger building had been chosen in anticipation of the crowds. In the place of Pentecostal bishop C. H. Mason, C. L. Franklin entered the pulpit to deliver the main eulogy.[1]

The day marked a major turn in C. L.'s life, the first of two over the next few years that signaled the arrival of a mature preacher with credible aspirations for national prominence. Reverend M. J. Jenkins, renowned as a "spectacular, flamboyant preacher" and leader of Memphis's Greater White Stone Baptist Church, had died of acute appendicitis the week before in Buffalo, New York, where he also led Friendship Baptist Church. Although the distance between the cities was great, the arrangement itself was not unprecedented, as the circuit-riding experience throughout the rural South suggested. (B. J. Perkins simultaneously led churches in Memphis and Cleveland, Ohio, and Benjamin Hooks would commute between Memphis and Detroit for more than two decades. Indeed, Jenkins himself led two Memphis churches before accepting the Buffalo pastorate.) Jenkins had led both churches since November 1940, alternating his time between them in two- or three-week cycles. Nat Williams had seen many a southern preacher regard such successful exposure to a northern congregation "as an escape, as an opportunity to leave the environment which nourished him and gave him his training, and as a chance to express himself in a so-called larger sphere." But Jenkins "found it comparatively easy to bridge the gap between the Northern and Southern outlook. No doubt he found that most Northern Negroes are still dyed-in-the-wool Southerners under the skin."[2]

Friendship Baptist held the first funeral on Friday, June 25, with B. J. Perkins delivering the eulogy. The body arrived in Memphis Saturday night, lying in state at Greater White Stone Church Sunday afternoon and evening, as thousands paid their respects. The next day Reverend W. E. Mack, president of the local Baptist Ministers Conference, presented an assistant pastor from Friendship who acknowledged the large number of Buffalo parishioners present, and then Perkins, for a short address. Then Mack introduced the principal speaker.[3]

Franklin took his text from the opening of the Book of Joshua, where the Lord anticipated Joshua's coronation as Moses' successor and Israel's leader. "Moses my servant is dead," C. L. began, citing the biblical verse. "Now therefore arise, go over this Jordan, thou, and all this people, unto the land which I do give to them, *even* to the children of Israel."[4]

The verse he selected remains rich with possible meaning. Within the context of the Afro-Baptist tradition, the biblical citation opening the sermon had a structural significance that could not have escaped C. L.'s or the mourners' attention. The sacred function of such a reading focused the congregation on the broad topic to come, but even more important, it announced (and the congregation's response actively confirmed) the preacher's claim of a divine legitimacy for the words that would follow. Jenkins was one of the experienced ministers who had mentored him when

C. L. came up from Mississippi to preach in the city. Friendship's parishioners knew of this relationship and had themselves appreciated C. L.'s talents, for Jenkins had invited Franklin to preach a very successful ten-day revival at the Buffalo church the year before. The biblical verse C. L. selected suggested more than mourning. It suggested a new anointing: the leader is dead and Yahweh has appointed the successor. With so many Buffalo parishioners in attendance, the command to the successor to "arise, go over this Jordan, thou" into the promised land was Franklin's subtle way to indicate his availability should Friendship Baptist extend its call for a new leader. It was also a signal to Memphis.[5]

* * * * *

There was no immediate call to the pulpit at Friendship Baptist following C. L.'s eulogy; even if considered, the timing would have been inappropriate. But C. L.'s preaching performance again evidenced a prowess impressive for one still not thirty. Weekly, New Salem now strained its narrowed confines when he took the pulpit, and his visits to other churches for guest sermons or week-long revivals only enhanced his reputation. But perhaps the strongest indication of C. L.'s growing preaching presence, in a city filled with well-regarded Baptist preachers, was the young minister's audacious insistence from early in his Memphis ministry that he once a year preach a particular sermon, "The Eagle Stirreth Her Nest." This sermon, along with a few others based on the Book of Ezekiel and Psalm 137, occupied the very apex of the Afro-Baptist preaching canon. Through a century-old folk memory, congregations knew the sermon's dramatic history and held those who attempted it to an exacting standard. Most ministers, if they preached this demanding sermon at all, waited until they had prayed long and deeply over it, until they had garnered the experience needed to explore its meaning for their time, and until they had command of the verbal and musical skills essential to an effective, emotive presentation. C. L., from age twenty-six on, preached that sermon, New Salem's Ernest Donelson explained. When it "became known that he was going to preach that," the crowds came in even greater numbers than usual.[6]

The earliest report of an Afro-Baptist minister preaching "The Eagle

Stirreth Her Nest" predates Franklin's Memphis ministry by almost a century. On January 10, 1846, Sir Charles Lyell, a British traveler, attended services at the First African Church in Savannah, Georgia. The lone white among six hundred black worshipers, Lyell listened as the congregation first offered a hymn, which was then "followed by prayers, not read, but delivered without notes by a Negro of pure African blood . . . with a fine sonorous voice." Rev. Andrew Marshall, the congregation's elected leader, "concluded by addressing them a sermon, also without notes, in good style." Impressed, Lyell recorded the structure of the sermon. Marshall spoke of the human frailty of even a pious man and thus the need for God's grace, comparing the relationship between God and humanity "to an eagle teaching her newly fledged offspring to fly by carrying it up high into the air, then dropping it, and, if she sees it falling to the earth, darting with the speed of lightning to save it before it reaches the ground." In addition to living a moral life, Marshall "told them that they were to look to a future state of rewards and punishments in which God would deal impartially with 'the poor and the rich, the black man and the white.'"[7]

As tantalizingly brief as Lyell's account is, it reveals nonetheless central aspects of an Afro-Baptist preaching tradition that would inform C. L.'s sermons a century later. First is the centrality of song: the service began with a communal hymn, and the preacher's words themselves, delivered in that "fine sonorous voice" were "animated," that is, sung or delivered in a rhythmic pattern. Neither the prayers nor the sermon, moreover, were written down. Reflecting the widespread illiteracy inflicted on southern blacks, the ensuing black oral culture prized improvisation, storytelling, and verbal facility in song, sermon, and speech. This did not therefore mean that these sermons were delivered spontaneously—there was a great deal of careful preparation—but it did mean that the religious service itself, song, prayer, and sermon, constituted a collective moment where all could participate. This call-and-response pattern usually framed the sermon, with parishioners reaching out verbally to the preacher, exhorting him with their vocal improvisations. In the process, worshipers were more than witnesses to a sacred ritual, for jointly, with their preacher, they created the setting where they experienced their God.

Even in the snippets Lyell recorded, the intimate play between the sacred and the secular was evident. The trust in God, and the reliance on God's grace to save humans prone to sin, were familiar signposts in the Christian search for rebirth and redemption. But to assume this sermon concerned only the afterlife was to miss its core complexity. As the final sentences of Lyell's description indicated, this was a sermon of liberation, a sermon that spoke of a spiritual transcendence with a decidedly worldly analogue. What Frederick Douglass said of slave spirituals reflected many a sermon as well: "Every tone was a testimony against slavery, and a prayer to God for deliverance from chains."[8]

As with his eulogy for M. J. Jenkins, no detailed printed reports remain of C. L.'s rendition of "The Eagle Stirreth Her Nest" during these Memphis years. He did record a live performance of the sermon a decade later, however, which is as close to Franklin's themes and his overall approach in Memphis as is possible.[9] Franklin, following a path well worn in the Afro-Baptist preaching tradition, took his text from Deuteronomy, the fifth book of the Hebrew Bible. Moses, told of his pending death and the succession of Joshua, listens as Yahweh foretells of Israel's violation of the covenant and orders Moses to "write ye this song for you, and teach it to the children of Israel: put it in their mouths, that this song may be a witness for me against the children of Israel." It is from the middle of this song, as Moses recounts Jacob's salvation by God—Jacob, too, had wandered into idolatry—that C. L., following tradition, took his text:

> As an eagle stirreth up her nest, fluttereth over her young, spreadeth abroad her wings, taketh them, beareth them on her wings; / So the Lord alone did lead him, and there was no strange god with him.[10]

"The eagle," he began, was a symbol of God, of his "care . . . and concern for his people." History itself, he explained in a conversational tone, was but "one big nest" God stirs "to make man better and to help us achieve world brotherhood." This stirring might cause great pain, he explained slowly, as children cried and some adults shouted out the "Amens," "O Lords," and "All rights" of encouragement. C. L. taught that cataclysmic events such as the Civil War revealed through the pain a larger purpose, for that struggle was "merely the promptings of Providence [the last syllable here elongated three beats for emphasis] to lash men to a point of being brotherly to all men." Daily tribulations carried great positive power: God stirred our individual "nests" in order to "discipline us, help us know ourselves, and help us to love one another, and to help us hasten on the realization of the kingdom of God." Pain was not simply random, cruel, or spiteful, a just desert for sinful humanity; nor was it a justification for alienation, as some blues men and women occasionally suggested. Rather, while pain itself was a universal experience, inherent in the human condition, C. L. preached it had a purpose—it was redemptive. God worked in history, through human beings, and the stirring, at times painful, of "the various nests of circumstances surrounding us" had as their ultimate purpose to activate his people in this world as well as in their preparation for the next.

Still narrating, in a storytelling mode, C. L. returned to the image of the eagle. The eagle was regal, kingly, he declared, "for God is *the* king." Deftly, C. L. drew this heavenly metaphor to earth: "For you see, these little kings that we know, they've got to have a king over them. They've got to account to somebody for the deeds done in their bodies." And the eagle is strong, swooping down to lift up a lamb with just its claws to "fly away to yonder's cliff and devour it." So, too, "our God is strong," a fortress to hide behind when pursued, "a citadel of protection and redemption," "a leaning [again the word stretched out, made animate by Franklin's enunciation] post" for all since the time of Abraham, Moses, and the prophets. As the congregation's response quickened, spurred by the notion of their shared experience with these great biblical figures, C. L. noted God's swiftness in responding to the believer, revisiting the biblical tale of Daniel in the lion's den. "And Daniel rung him on the way to the lion's den," and by the time he arrived, an angel dispatched by God "had changed the nature of lions and made them lay down and act like lambs." With enormous fervor, calling out "my, my, my," and "O Lord," the audience embraced the connection: this strong and regal God would respond, and quickly, as he did to Daniel, even to as poor and unremarkable a group as they were. Finally, C. L. proclaimed, the eagle *has extraordinary sight. Extraordinary sight. Somewhere it is said that he can rise to a lofty height in the air and look in the distance and see a storm hours away. That's extraordinary sight. And sometimes he can stand and gaze right in the sun because he has extraordinary sight. I want to tell you my God has extraordinary sight. He can see every ditch that you have dug for me and guide me around them. God has extraordinary sight. He can look behind that smile on your face and see the frown in your heart. God has extraordinary sight.*

As he reached the word, "frown," he drew it out over three syllables in a tremolo, his deep voice fluttering with emphasis, piercing, as God's messenger, the secrets in individual souls, and the response grew yet more intense. Amid the cries and exclamations of "preach on," "preach heavy," "oh yeah," preacher and parishioners prepared each other for the climactic experience each knew they awaited.

But at that moment Franklin lowered the emotional level slightly, as there was another teaching point he wanted to make. He described how the eagle built the nest, at first softening its surface with down for the eaglets. As they grow, the eagle removed that down, exposing her older offspring to harsher material and a less comfortable nest, and thus propelled them out into the world: "I believe that God has to do that for us sometime," for, as Moses's song prophesied, such interventions recalled the wayward back to faith.

It was at this juncture that C. L. shifted gears. In place of that conversational tone, a musical expressiveness emerged to carry the message forward, as C. L. whooped, or chanted, the remainder of the sermon. He sang in key, modulating his voice from near-falsetto to guttural rasp, creating a rhythmic cadence both with his words and in the interplay created by his voice, the audience's response, and the occasional percussive beat of his hand hitting the pulpit.

"It is said," his rich baritone announced, evoking both biblical and folkloric authority, that a poultry farmer discovered one day "a strange looking bird" in a brood of chickens. The bird grew larger and exhibited decidedly different habits from the chickens, until finally a visitor who knew eagles explained to the farmer what he, in fact, had. The mysterious visitor instructed the farmer to build a cage for, as the eagle got older, "he's going to get tired / of the ground." The farmer did so, and then had to build another, and yet another cage, as the eagle's wing span grew to twelve feet and "he began to get restless / in the cage." One day, when a flock of eagles flew over the farm, this eagle heard their voices and reacted sharply:

> *though he'd never been around eagles,*
> *there was something about that voice*
> *that he heard*
> *that moved*
> *down in him*
> *and made him*
> *dissatisfied.*

Disturbed by the eagle's evident sadness at hearing the other eagles, the farmer opened the cage and set the eagle free. In stages, C. L. preached, the eagle walked hesitantly and tested his wings; circled about a little longer and then flew about the barnyard; and then "He wiggled up a little higher / and flew in yonder's tree." Finally, he wiggled even higher into the mountains.

There was little repetition of phrases, with the important exception of select words and short phrases between the sung stanzas of this sermon. Those words—"and," "O Lord," "why," and "yes he did"—were resting stops for C. L., where he might frame the image for the following lines. But they were also words his voice transformed into emotive signals, announcing that the moment of spiritual elevation was close by. What made C. L. such an extraordinary preacher was that even as he brought the congregation to this peak, he continued to address contemporary issues. As the caged eagle had been touched by the flock above, so too might individuals constrained by segregation find within community self-identity, group cohesiveness, and, ultimately, freedom.[11]

As C. L. brought the sermon to its highest emotional peak, he drew out yet another level of meaning. "One of these days, / one of these days," he repeated, signaling with the repetition the significance of this moment,

my soul
is an eagle
in the cage that the Lord
has made for me.[12]

The cage itself was now C. L.'s own body, "and one of these days" he who made it would open the door "and let my soul / go." Repeating again and again (with an ascending voice in key that approached a scream but for its musicality) the phrase "one of these days," which drove the congregation to its peak, C. L. promised a time "when burdens / are through burdening," and "My soul will take wings, / my soul will take wings."[13]

Ralph Ellison, writing in 1955 of jazz and blues artists, suggested that their fundamental purpose was "to achieve the most eloquent expression of idea-emotions" through "the subtle rhythmical shaping and blending of idea, tone and imagination demanded of group improvisation." The dynamics of Franklin's group improvisation differed from that of a jazz sextet, as did the setting in which such improvised yet patterned performances occurred. In the hands of this masterful preacher, however, each Sunday's sermon arched toward achieving that "most eloquent expression" in a fashion that united preacher and congregation at the moment and beyond. As had many of the artists he appreciated, C. L. had refused to allow the oppressiveness of his Mississippi youth to silence his voice; rather, numerous African American communities, sacred and secular, had nurtured it. This collective strength, self-consciously grasped and fitted to his personality, enabled Franklin to simultaneously preach, teach, and effect the experience of God's presence as few ever had. And for those in Memphis, it was increasingly clear just how rare was the gift this young preacher from Mississippi possessed.[14]

*   *   *   *   *

Though not immediately, it did not take long for the deacons and trustees of Friendship Baptist to act. Soon after Jenkins's funeral, C. L. took New Salem's pulpit one Sunday in stylish fashion, wearing "a kind of Prince Albert outfit . . . tails and all that." The suit, sharply tailored, was a gift from Friendship, probably in appreciation of his eulogy of Jenkins. For a man who but a few years before appeared at New Salem dressed in a worn suit, "tails and all that" symbolized a rather substantial transformation. He now strode through his ministerial responsibilities with an evident self-confidence in his voice, the power it commanded, and the meaning it delivered. That fall, Friendship invited him to give a formal trial sermon, and an offer was extended and accepted. In January 1944, the *Buffalo Criterion*, the city's black newspaper, announced C. L. as Friendship's "newly elected pastor." In his first week the new pastor led a church rally that raised a thousand dollars and, in a sign of pastoral firmness, initiated "a complete overhauling of the church's clubs." His sermon that Sunday drew "a packed house."[15]

Despite his election, C. L. had not completely left Memphis. The same month Friendship announced his appointment, the *Memphis World* referred to Franklin as pastor of New Salem. The following month, the same paper reported, "Rev. C. L. Franklin, pastor, is 100 percent behind the [Boy Scout] Troop" at New Salem. Ernest Donelson recalled his pastor remaining well beyond January. In fact, Franklin never intended to lead both churches, but circumstances delayed his departure. Barbara, then pregnant with Carolyn and responsible for two other children less than four years old, could not orchestrate such a complicated move that spring. In Buffalo, moreover, trouble brewed. In March, just two months following Franklin's election, as he was still splitting his time between New Salem and Friendship, in front of a full Sunday service, C. L. had tendered his resignation, angered over "some discrepancies" that had emerged "between the pastor and his official cabinet of officers." Over the previous four years Friendship had a pastor who was, in effect, part-time. This gave that "official cabinet" of deacons and trustees great leeway in defining church policy. With C. L.'s arrival, however, they discovered they had not just an outstanding, full-time preacher but an "able, competent and active young minister" who allowed no interference with his ministerial prerogatives. A power struggle had quickly commenced. More than once during his long resignation speech, C. L. asserted that "I am not a child and I don't expect to be handled as one."[16] But at a church meeting the evening following his attempted resignation, "the situation was ironed out" and C. L.'s resignation rejected amid protestations of "peace, happiness, and concord to the newly-appointed minister." That settled, Franklin could now make the move from New Salem.[17]

C. L.'s migration north was not an isolated event. Black southerners began leaving the region before World War I, and the pattern intensified in the next decade. World War II brought another major wave of migration, as southern blacks sought the better-paying jobs in the defense industries of Detroit, Chicago, Oakland, California, and elsewhere. So great was this "second 'exodus,'" Nat Williams wrote in the summer of 1943, that he worried that black Memphis would lose its leadership. C. L.'s departure certainly confirmed Williams's fears.[18]

Although a rising figure in black Memphis, Franklin's motivations for leaving the city shared much with those working-class (and to a lesser degree, middle-class) members of church, neighborhood, and work organizations who also sought their future in colder regions. C. L.'s considerable desire for recognition, for a pulpit that might bring him national attention as well as economic gain, made the switch inevitable. In contrast with New Salem, a local reporter explained, Friendship under M. J. Jenkins had doubled its membership to almost two thousand and had retired its $48,000 mortgage, making it one of the few churches in the city "completely owned by Negroes." The economic opportunities for blacks in Buffalo meant that Friendship had many union workers attending, "and they could respond to the church financially better than the people of Memphis could." This translated into concrete improvement for the Franklin family: a higher salary, a comfortable house provided by the congregation, and the prospect of a new model car, much as Jenkins had received from parishioners just months before his death. New Salem, as most Memphis churches, simply could not match these conditions.[19]

Buffalo had the added attraction of not being Memphis when it came to race. How many times in Memphis had Franklin been called "boy"? How many times had he been forced to quiet, or suppress, his own voice at such moments? Black Memphians faced persistent harassment, beatings, and the threat of much worse on the city's segregated buses, when seeking assistance from city and federal offices, and in the city's factories and plants. Buffalo was no paradise, as C. L. would discover, but the city's absence of thoroughly segregated public facilities loomed large from the distance. His congregation there also seemed different. The *Criterion* had praised Jenkins as a "militant and progressive pastor" well before his death, although it provided no details concerning his social or political ideas. That broad political sensibility, perhaps a reflection of the mingling of this new trade union experience with the older collective traditions of the black church, proved highly attractive to C. L.[20]

At New Salem, as expected, members expressed mixed feelings about their pastor's departure. Some were actually "happy to see him go," Nettie Hubbard recalled, a reflection of ongoing church disputes and a lingering resentment over his involvement with Mildred Jennings. Others wanted him to stay but appreciated his opportunity for advancement. "I like to see people advance," Lizzie Moore explained, "'cause, see, most people want to do better." Franklin "got a good start" at New Salem. "We gave him a boost."[21]

On May 24, 1944, Friendship began its five-day celebration of C. L.'s installation. Different Buffalo pastors, accompanied by their choirs and large segments of their congregations, joined with Friendship's congregation in prayer and praise of the new arrival. At each service, ushers formally escorted C. L. to a seat of honor near the pulpit. After the Saturday service, Friendship sponsored "an elaborate banquet" for more than one hundred people. Finally, on Sunday, May 28, before a packed church with hundreds more standing outside the open windows and doors, C. L. took the pulpit at the eleven o'clock service where, before his inaugural sermon, church officers formally installed him as pastor. At seven that evening, before another large crowd, Franklin delivered a second sermon. Over the course of the ceremonies as many as three thousand people participated, though Barbara and the children remained in Memphis. (Barbara gave birth to Carolyn, the Franklins' third daughter and last child, on May 10 and could not attend; in a culture that gave primacy to male activity, neither C. L. nor Friendship's leaders had delayed the ceremony. C. L. indicated his family would join him permanently "as quickly as proper arrangements can be made.")[22]

No record remains of either of C. L.'s sermons that day, but the context of the installation suggested that he would be a force in his new community. The ceremonies themselves were not unique—other Baptist pastors might be similarly feted as well when they arrived at their new church—but the excitement generated in the broader community differed from what most new pastors experienced. The forceful public manner in which he dealt with challenges to his authority and the preaching reputation that preceded him promised a leader of intelligence and strength for the church and, potentially, for the broader African American community as well. Still not thirty, it was hard to believe that only five years separated him from his circuit-preaching days in the Mississippi Delta.

*   *   *   *   *

The "Queen City" was decidedly not Memphis. Its summers could be hot, but rarely did Buffalo experience the humidity that weighted the lungs and made the simplest exertion onerous. Memphians, for their part, might read of violent winter storms that left Buffalo gasping under two or more feet of snow in subfreezing temperatures, but they could no more imagine themselves in such conditions than they could anticipate Rufus Thomas introducing a polka band at the amateur night at the Palace Theater. These regional differences symbolized a different history as well. Buffalo had no tradition of slaveholding, of buying and selling African Americans at public market, and in fact had a strong abolitionist tradition in the nineteenth century. But such historic differences did not prevent sharp racial distinctions from structuring the customs and practices of this manufacturing center at the eastern end of Lake Erie. In 1940, this city in the northwest corner of the state, famous for the nearby Niagara Falls, housed almost two hundred thousand more citizens than did Memphis, but only a bare 3 percent, less than twenty thousand people, were black. As C. L. walked the black commercial section a few blocks from his church, the contrast with Memphis sharply suggested itself. Where Beale Street teemed with black shoppers and music lovers, Buffalo's equivalent, the intersection of Michigan Avenue and William Street in the city's Lower East Side, held but a few shops and clubs. Most of black Buffalo lived in this neighborhood but in a racial configuration quite different from Memphis's pointedly segregated world. As World War II ended, the Lower East Side of Buffalo still remained the enclave of Euro-American immigrants and their children who together accounted for more than 80 percent of the neighborhood's residents. African Americans and these varied groups of white ethnics lived in residential clusters, often adjoining each other; and even when one group gathered on a certain block, a racial and ethnic mix nonetheless earmarked these streets. To be sure, black neighbors would not be welcomed in Eddie Wenzak's bar on Sycamore Street, a Polish enclave that hosted other white ethnics but not blacks. Yet whites and blacks lived near and next to each other, shopped on Broadway, the main business street just south of Sycamore, even as they maintained largely separate cultural and religious lives.[23]

Friendship Baptist Church occupied a double lot at 146–48 Hickory Street, just up from the intersection with Clinton Street, a short walk from the center of black Buffalo at Michigan and William. Reverend R. B. Robinson had founded the church in 1917; under his successor, Twilus Davis, the church had laid its cornerstone with full Masonic ritual in November 1930. In 1939, the congregation removed Davis from the pulpit for "mishandling church funds and conduct 'unbecoming a minister'" and had called M. J. Jenkins to replace him.[24]

The church members who filled Friendship's pews each Sunday were largely working people, mostly southern born. C. L. felt as familiar with them as he had with his Memphis parishioners for, he later recalled, Friendship's members "didn't feel any different about shouting [in services] . . . than they did in Memphis." C. L. also found the Friendship choir quite good, although he thought it lacked an outstanding soloist. Increasingly, music was a central aspect of his ministry, and while at New Salem, he formed a lasting partnership with Thomas Shelby, Lucie Campbell's talented student, whom he had appointed as his minister of music. Franklin invited Shelby, a LeMoyne College graduate and the music director of the National Baptist Convention, to join him in Buffalo. C. L. also hired two assistant pastors. To amass such a professional, full-time support staff, all of whose salaries the congregation supplied, marked a significant change from C. L.'s past experience. The presence of assistants allowed him the needed free time for education and guest-preaching appearances. Young, gifted, and black, Franklin was fortunate to be in one

of the few occupations in America at that moment where that precise combination of qualities was a decided advantage.[25]

Beyond Friendship Baptist's solid economic condition, the continued
growth of better-paid union jobs among black working people in steel,
auto supplies, and other industries reinforced the foundation Franklin inherited. The coming of the union-organizing drives in the late 1930s, coupled with the wartime urgency to maintain high levels of productivity, had
significantly improved the standing of many black families. Yet difficult
economic conditions remained. Two-thirds of blacks employed in industry
in 1940 still held the lowest-paying unskilled jobs. Similarly, Buffalo's significant growth in clerical and sales positions since World War I produced
but 132 black men and women employed in a white-collar workforce of
more than 44,000—a figure that suggested both widespread prejudice and
a profoundly weak black entrepreneurial class. Even more troubling were
the numbers of unemployed in 1940. Citywide, the figure stood at over 17
percent, while within black Buffalo, 26 percent wanted for work. No specific breakdown is available for the employment history of Friendship's
members, but these broader figures suggest a pattern likely found in
Franklin's congregation as well. Employed members, unionized or not,
occupied pews on Sunday cheek by jowl with unemployed relatives,
neighbors, and friends. Add to this mix a small number of professionals—
teachers, doctors, funeral directors, insurance agents, and the like—and
the broad outline of the social structure of Friendship and black Buffalo
emerges more clearly.[26]

Unionized workers created the economic foundation that set Friendship
apart from many other Afro-Baptist churches with a large southern-born
membership, and C. L. respected the attitudes these union members
brought to the congregation. Just as they demanded in the union hall an
emphasis on racial as well as economic justice, so too they returned to the
black community with new ideas for social action. This intermingling was,
however, a complicated process. While no known member of Friendship
Baptist recorded their work history of these years, Olin Wilson, a black
Methodist in the Queen City, explained in an interview decades later how
he navigated the inherent tensions. Born in South Carolina in 1889, during World War I Wilson reluctantly took work on a segregated union job

in Virginia, where he despised the racist atmosphere encouraged by white union workers. In 1923, along with other black southern workers, he arrived in Buffalo, recruited by Bethlehem Steel to break a strike of white workers at the company's Lackawanna plant just outside the city limits. A decade later, still in the plant, he emerged as a key leader with the Steel Workers Organizing Committee, which he joined only after receiving assurances that the new industrial union would reject segregation. Risking his job to organize in an era of continued high unemployment required a certain confidence, if not faith. When later asked if he ever feared for his job during these years, Wilson concisely explained how secular and sacred concerns melded in his mind: "I wouldn't let it worry me at all [at that time]," Wilson replied. He felt that his own union work was "as much my Christian duty" as church attendance. "That [social action] was the part of Christianity we had left off." Wilson's approach resonated among other black working people—he brought many black workers into the union movement—and echoed C. L.'s developing consciousness. In this regard, too, Buffalo held promise for the new pastor of Friendship Baptist.[27]

Although New Salem's and Friendship's members largely consisted of working people, with rural southern roots and relatively new to the urban, industrial world, the contrasting political climates between the two cities created quite different experiences. Working people in both New Salem and Friendship saw in their pastor the embodiment of their hopes for their own slower but inevitable climb. But the significant differences between the two urban economies allowed Friendship's members a grander expression of what concrete form those aspirations might assume.[28]

The different measurements were immediately evident in the parsonage Friendship selected for the Franklin family. In Memphis, the Franklins had rented a number of houses, all in predominately black South Memphis, within walking distance of New Salem. In contrast, as part of the agreement that accompanied C. L.'s call to Friendship's pulpit, the trustees purchased a parsonage for the family's use at 177 Glenwood Avenue, more than two miles north and east of the church and the black residential district. Barbara's brother, Semial, considered the house a "beautiful place, huge," its twelve or more rooms comfortably fitting the Franklins and their five children. Located in the Cold Springs neighborhood in the Masten district, a middle-class neighborhood of more than fifty-five thousand when the Franklins moved in, houses in the area had been available since the 1920s for that small group "of the more prosperous [N]egroes" in Buffalo. In this sense, the distance between church and home signified an important social as well as a spatial distinction. The majority of Friendship's members lived "in the perimeter" at this time, Deacon E. L. Billups noted, referring to the area south of Broadway and east of Main Street that defined the limits of black residences for all but a few. Although C. L. recalled the neighborhood as "a mixed community," in fact, 98 percent of the entire neighborhood's residents were white. In contrast, the streets surrounding Friendship Baptist at the same time were more than 60 percent African American and oppressively poor, with more than a quarter of the adult workforce unemployed. It was the first time that any of the Franklins lived their family life beyond the perimeter.[29]

Racial distinctions seemed not to have been a defining factor in the Franklin children's experience on Glenwood. Just over six years old when she moved, Erma quickly became best friends with the white girl next door and remembered no incidents of prejudice. Her major complaint was Buffalo's climate: "God, it was cold!" It was also during these years on Glenwood that the family sensed that Aretha might possess a special musical talent, her interest in singing and picking at the piano at age three already causing comment within the family. Vaughn, ten years old when the family left Memphis, found in his first "integrated educational system . . . something that was new to me." The teaching level at School No. 8, a few blocks from his house, was "a little bit higher" than in Memphis, and the principal insisted Vaughn repeat a grade. "It was a big change," he recalled without resentment. His Buffalo neighborhood teemed with kids, many more than on Lucy Street in Memphis, and he enjoyed playing with them.[30]

Yet Buffalo at war's end was anything but idyllic for the Franklin family. Relations with neighborhood children may not have been complicated, but Vaughn did have a number of encounters with openly racist teachers who made him "feel like, well, I don't want to go into this classroom, because I know I am not going to pass this here." Similarly, Vaughn and Erma both heard their father mention at dinner-table discussions "obstacles he had run into in Buffalo." But by and large, the children remained isolated from such tensions. When that larger world did intrude upon the family (as with Vaughn's teacher), the response often became Barbara's responsibility. At home, C. L. established rather stern codes of conduct for his children, especially the two oldest, but it was Barbara who reinterpreted them for the children during his frequent absences. His father was "a very strict person," Vaughn explained, who "wouldn't allow us to go to the movies." He never told the older children why. "He would say NO, and that was it." When C. L. was away, however, Barbara "did give us a little bit of leeway." The children were allowed to see a movie, provided they promised not to tell their father. But beyond these and a few other equally frustrating snippets, little is known about the Franklins' family life in Buffalo. Asked years later what his wife felt on leaving Memphis, C. L. quickly claimed that "she expressed appreciation" before exploring in greater detail why the move was important for him. One can imagine the tensions inherent in a relationship strained by five preadolescent children and one very public and frequently absent husband and father. Moreover, what was true for her children with their young playmates may not have been as true for their mother with her adult white neighbors.[31]

The responsibility for five children undoubtedly kept Barbara close to home, at some remove from the daily recognition due the wife of an important minister in the black community. Barbara, however, was not completely isolated. Churchwomen regularly helped her with household chores, babysat for the children, and ran a variety of errands. If she brought the children to the church for a meeting or a choir practice, she had an instant surplus of babysitters from among the women and older girls. Many of these women, moreover, became her friends. In addition, soon after settling into her new home, Barbara's mother, Clara, moved from Shelby, Mississippi, to Buffalo, where she maintained her own residence. Discharged from the military in 1945, Semial, Barbara's brother, joined the Buffalo branch of the Siggers family; that same year, Clara met and married Arthur Press Wofford, an established black Baptist minister in the area.[32]

Barbara and C. L. clearly shared moments together beyond the pressures of the daily schedule. C. L.'s ever-present search for knowledge led him to a literature course at the University of Buffalo "just to acquaint my-self with it. I felt it would widen the horizon of my understanding." In that class he first read Richard Wright's novels and embraced Rudyard Kipling, who became a lifelong favorite. Kipling's poems, meant to be read aloud for their rhythmic cadences, appealed strongly to this developing master of the chanted sermon. In Buffalo as in Memphis, Semial recalled, the couple read after the children were asleep, and these books and articles sparked conversation. There were as well family dinners, often with ministerial guests, with conversation across a wide range of topics. Alternatively, parishioners felt privileged to invite the pastor and his family into their homes. On one such occasion, when the host asked her ministerial guest if he might like a slice of potato pie, Vaughn recalled his father's response: " 'Yes, sister,' he said. 'Just fold it in half!' He loved potato pie." To some ex-tent, then, C. L. incorporated his public world into his family life, and those moments shaped the emotional texture of his marriage and relation-ship with his children.[33]

*   *   *   *   *

C. L.'s appetites, his fundamental drives as well as his more prosaic needs, had always been large. Almost immediately on arriving in the city Franklin sought out "older pastors . . . whom I would call upon and get ad-vice if I did not have any at hand, or did not know who to contact." Among those he met were the two deans of the Afro-Baptist ministry, J. Edward Nash and E. J. Echols Sr., each of whom served as a bridge to a black communal past. Nash, born in Virginia of slave parents in 1868 and college-educated, had led Michigan Avenue Baptist, the city's premier Afro-Baptist church, since 1892. Echols, Mississippi-born and educated at the same Howe School of Religion in Memphis that C. L. attended decades later, took the pulpit at First Shiloh Baptist in 1916. Both churches and the pastors' homes were well within the black perimeter on the city's Lower East Side. Through these and other Baptist ministers, C. L. met prominent black leaders in the local NAACP and the Urban League. He crossed paths with other black residents at the Michigan Av-enue YMCA, which opened in 1925 as a de facto segregated institution.

The Michigan Avenue Y promoted a full program of children's activities, academic and vocational courses, and classes on parenting and other family issues. It also sought to broaden black Buffalo's thinking with a speakers' series that brought to its podium, among others, W. E. B. Du Bois, Nannie H. Burroughs, the leader of the Women's Auxiliary of the National Baptist Convention, and Chicagoan Oscar De Priest, elected in 1928 the first black congressman since Reconstruction. Occasionally, supporters of Buffalo's once-strong nationalist movement affiliated with Marcus Garvey's Universal Negro Improvement Association also addressed audiences at the Y. Franklin had sought similar ends on a smaller scale with his Memphis radio show, but the relative freedom possible in Buffalo marked the Queen City as decidedly different from E. H. Crump's town.[34]

As much as C. L. may have consulted others, he was no longer the relative innocent who had come to New Salem in 1939. Within a month of becoming pastor, he offered his church to A. Philip Randolph for a major mass meeting addressing the condition of black America in a postwar world. Randolph, the son of a minister, was most famous as the leader of the all-black Brotherhood of Sleeping Car Porters, which gained recognition from the American Federation of Labor in 1937 after a twelve-year struggle, and as the organizer of the 1941 March On Washington to demand equality in defense industry hiring. Randolph's presence at Friendship Baptist prominently affirmed the pastor's support of civil rights and trade union activism as a core element of his ministry. A few months later, C. L. and his minister of music, Thomas Shelby, directed a "Battle of Songs" among gospel quartets from Chicago, New York City, and Buffalo. The event was such a success that hundreds were turned away from the packed church. It was, the local paper proclaimed, an "unprecedented vocal program," and it helped C. L. project a presence beyond the walls of Friendship Baptist.[35]

C. L.'s radio program made an even more dramatic impact. In contrast with Memphis, black Buffalo had no radio programming and Franklin's initiative, in late spring 1945, was "rather new to the Negro," the *Buffalo Criterion* noted. Sherman Walker's funeral home sponsored the hour-long weekly program *Voice of Friendship*, which highlighted religious worship (including at times a brief sermon by C. L.), gospel music, and commentary on current events. In an August 1945 radio address, C. L. focused on the profound changes generated by the defeat of Germany and Japan, and then asked of the nation black America's central question. Since it took a combined effort of all races, creeds, colors, and backgrounds in America to win the war, "have we learned the vital necessity of living together in a way where all men . . . are free and equal? Or," he asked ominously, making explicit the central concern he urged his audience to confront, "have we returned to the philosophy of the Bilbos, the Rankins and the Eastlands [all staunch Mississippi segregationist politicians], that of suppressing the minority and denying them the right to free citizenship?" Following his comments came the segment *News about Negroes around the World*, in which C. L. read, much as he had on his Memphis radio program, news briefs about Negroes in the war effort. Given the negative coverage of black nurses and soldiers in the dominant media, Franklin's approach was, said the editors of the *Criterion*, "very uplifting and encouraging" and would, it was hoped, "ultimately lead to better race relations." Friendship and its pastor were to be commended "for [the] responsibility which they have accepted upon behalf of local colored people."[36]

The intense hostility and brutal violence that greeted Willie Walker, C. L.'s biological father, and so many other veterans following the Great War did not occur again in 1945. White attitudes had changed to the extent that the orgy of lynchings was not repeated. Yet the American South remained thoroughly segregated, and race riots in Detroit, New York, and elsewhere against blacks in 1943 clearly indicated the continuing depth of whites' racial hostility. But blacks' attitudes had altered visibly. The "Double-V for Victory" campaign—over fascism abroad and racism at home—sparked a more pointed public debate among African Americans than had existed twenty-five years earlier. Whether returning black veterans migrated North or stayed in the South, as future civil rights leaders Medgar Evers and Amzie Moore did in Mississippi, they shared with their communities a broad commitment that the experience of their father's generation would not be their own. With that resolve, the fight for democracy at home entered a new phase. This intense discussion within black America provided the broader context for C. L.'s own efforts.[37]

The structure of Franklin's radio program, melding sacred and secular themes, prayer and politics, suggested a variety of motivations in this intense, ambitious man. Franklin grasped the simple truth that the larger the audience technology allowed, the greater his potential reach and reputation. He began to use a microphone on Sundays at Friendship. This preserved his voice and allowed him to reach more easily the largest congregation he had ever regularly addressed. C. L. welcomed the extended renown technology made possible, as he did the invitation to give a major sermon at the annual meeting of the National Baptist Convention, held that September in Detroit. That appearance would become the second major turn in his career in as many years.[38]

The National Baptist Convention attracted thousands annually in what was the largest gathering of black religious adherents in the nation. Each convention provided the opportunity to engage in intense socializing, prayer services, and political education. In this regard, the gathering held in Detroit was no different from earlier meetings. At least fifteen thousand Baptists—estimates vary as high as thirty thousand—gathered in Olympia Stadium on West Grand Boulevard for the main sessions, while the Women's Auxiliary, the youth group, and the organization of ministerial wives met at different Detroit churches. Serious tension developed even before the sessions began. It was but two years since a violent, intense race riot had rocked the city, and many white Detroiters adamantly opposed the entry of these Afro-Baptists into a stadium they considered a white public space. A movement to cancel the rental agreement gathered support, and two days before the convention's opening, the nation's black Baptists had no meeting space. In one ironic twist among many in the American racial experience, Reverend D. V. Jemison, president of the National Baptist Convention and a black Alabamian, privately appealed to two white Alabama politicians to intervene. Congressman Sam Hobbs and United States Senator Lister Hill eventually secured Olympia Stadium for the gathering, but racial tension continued. As Reverend J. Pius Barbour, the editor of the *National Baptist Voice*, noted, "We forced our way in that Olympia and the white people took good pains to show us that they did not want us there. There was some kind of crazy union agreement," he explained, "that had white people standing all around there doing nothing and yet getting our money." The situation with the microphone system especially infuriated Barbour. The system required a certain technological expertise, and white union workers simply would not operate it properly, with the result that many a speech or sermon came across as "a growling noise like a hog."[39]

Despite these difficulties, the convention proceeded. Nannie H. Burroughs, the corresponding secretary of the Women's Auxiliary, gave a powerful presentation on the theme that "Christianity must fight for the FIFTH FREEDOM"—that is, amending Franklin Delano Roosevelt's famous 1941 definition of the Allied war aims as the Four Freedoms—the "FREEDOM OF RACE." She decried the continued exploitation of Africa and India by white colonial nations and focused attention on domestic social issues essential to the creation of a more democratic postwar society: the imperative to eliminate urban slums, the southern tenant-farm system, the poll tax, and separate accommodations for the races while providing for the nation's real housing and educational needs. The recommendations from the men's meeting were equally direct, as D. V. Jemison also explored the connection between Christianity properly understood and the promise of American democratic life. He demanded a strengthened Fair Employment Practices Commission to prevent discriminatory actions in the workplace, an end to poll taxes, inequality in public accommodations, and other forms of segregation. Jemison warned that if the world peace now in place took its direction at both home and abroad "from political demagogues" rather than Christianity, the seeds of the next conflagration would already be sown.[40]

While these recommendations would not themselves change national politics, they were not without effect. However many the exact number of delegates present in Detroit, they in turn represented more than 6 million reported members of the organization nationally. These delegates— pastors, deacons, choir directors, church club officers, and church members—all returned to their communities following the six days of the convention with stories, lessons, and understandings of what they heard and whom they met. In this sense, the yearly meeting was a giant turbine, gathering within it varied ideas, experiences, and beliefs within a broad, common framework. When the convention finished, the delegates streamed back to their home territories, electric with new ideas and excited to introduce them. It was, at times, a stunning form of popular democratic social action, a vibrant alternative to the demeaning images of black history and current life that still dominated most white attitudes, elite and popular.

But the main attraction of the convention was always the preaching, the vocal expression of the deepest faith commitments in this communal tradition. At these meetings the great preachers in the tradition exhibited their continued power—or failed to, and dropped a notch in others' eyes. Here, too, newcomers sought to impress and perhaps take advantage of an elder's slippage, elevating themselves closer to the top echelon. Preachers tested themselves against peers (in a manner not totally dissimilar to the after-hours cutting sessions among jazz musicians), and different styles found their exponents. Ministerial contributors to the *National Baptist Voice,* for example, still debated the issue of the whooped or chanted sermon; some thought it bespoke an uneducated, rural people sunk in oppression and poverty. They favored instead the manuscript preacher, who wrote out his sermon in advance in order to incorporate as much book learning as possible. J. Pius Barbour, educated at Morehouse and at Crozier Theological Seminary, where he now trained future generations of black ministers, disagreed. In a 1944 article he distinguished between "the swamp whoop"—the preacher who offers a biblical story "in a sing song fashion, like he has the hiccoughs"—and the "intellectual whoop"—the preacher who "reads a deep essay, which he fools himself into believing is a sermon." Dismissing both, Barbour extolled what he called the "artistic whoop." This required control of a superior musical voice and the ability to "touch any emotion by the cadence of the voice." Such preachers delivered "profound sermons and gradually work the people up" until they reached the spiritual climax where faith, the power of the message, and the emotional openness of the moment prepared all for an experience beyond words. Proponents of one or another approach carried on the debate throughout the convention.[41]

Into this exuberant, complex, and occasionally heated context the preacher from Friendship Baptist, just thirty the preceding January, willingly leaped when he agreed to preach at the Detroit meeting. He had been at numerous conventions before and so understood all too well the defining potential of his first sermon before a national audience. But he was still rather inexperienced. Indeed, Friendship's pastor was not even the most famous C. L. Franklin among Afro-Baptist ministers: Reverend Claude L. Franklin, also known as C. L. and also born in Mississippi, led Great Mt. Lebanon Baptist Church in Brooklyn, New York. The Brooklyn Franklin was college educated, had received an additional divinity degree from Union Theological Seminary in New York, and still whooped part of his sermon. He was the subject of a front-page story in the *National Baptist Voice* just months before the Detroit convention. Yet it was the then less known Franklin from Buffalo who received the invitation to preach. Perhaps one can detect the influence here of B. J. Perkins, in 1945 the national treasurer of the National Baptist Convention, in arranging to give his protégé his moment.[42]

Although already known for the power of his whoop, C. L.'s placement on the program, J. Pius Barbour understood, was but a small act of encouragement to a still-budding preacher whose reach was yet unknown. Given this, Barbour was stunned and upset when he discovered that C. L. intended to preach on the topic of Immortality. "My heart sank!" Barbour recalled, as he considered Franklin's relative inexperience. "How could he handle such a theme?" But to Barbour's astonishment, "The biggest surprise of all was the sermon of C. L. Franklin of Buffalo, New York. . . . He has one of those whoops that comes every fifty years." In the *National Baptist Voice* the following month, he offered the only public report of Franklin's performance:

> *He almost paralyzed the Convention with logic and history and thought. For twenty minutes he preached as if he were in Harvard Chapel and just as the people were gasping at this profound treatment of the subject, he switched gears and threw on that Mississippi whoop and broke up the Convention. There is no doubt about it. He comes nearer to L. K. Williams [a famous preacher and past president of the Convention] than any man I have heard. He is a perfect mixture of profound thought and emotional power.*

Franklin's expectations soared far above former confines, now propelled by public acclaim as never before, and he searched the distant horizon for new possibilities and their challenges.[43]

*   *   *   *   *

Less than six months after the Detroit sermon, C. L. received a call from a Detroit church. Many members of New Bethel Baptist had heard Franklin at the 1945 convention, and when their pastor resigned suddenly in February 1946, they invited C. L. to deliver a trial sermon. Soon after came the call to the pulpit. The reaction at Friendship was explosive. "We felt terrible. We cried. We couldn't understand," congregant Mary Hill remembered. Said E. L. Billups on hearing the news at a church meeting a few days before Franklin left, "It seemed like to me they dropped a bomb."[44]

C. L. later suggested that he would have stayed in Buffalo longer, but he envisioned a different setting for his talents: "I felt Buffalo was an old, staid, conservative, frontier-type of town. I wanted to be in a city where there were crossroads of transportation: trains, planes, where people were coming and going, conventions of all kinds, and migrations. A city that is not static in its growth."[45]

Brief as C. L.'s time in Buffalo was, the experience remained important. He had led his largest church to that time and had his first sustained interaction with black trade unionists. Their demands for justice, grounded in a common prophetic tradition, quickened thought processes already in motion within him. The young boy in Mississippi's cotton fields inventing stories about the passengers on the trains and cars hurtling by had grown into a man no longer caged by Mississippi's strictures or by his own narrowed beliefs. Increasingly, he thought of himself, to the affirming echo of many, as an evolving preacher-prophet with considerable mastery of a complex preaching tradition.

In the short time between June 1943 and September 1945, he had preached at least three commanding sermons: M. J. Jenkins's eulogy, the yearly "The Eagle Stirreth Her Nest," and "Immortality." The power of his spiritual and intellectual offering won him recognition he previously had only hoped for. Now, in moving to Detroit, a city of crossroads and crosscurrents in music, politics, religion, and the people themselves, C. L. eyed with undisguised pleasure that "yonder's mountain" he had long desired.

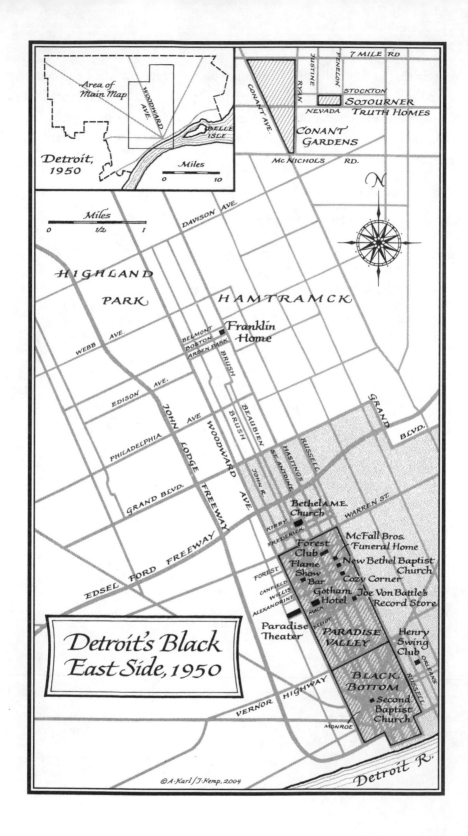

Detroit's Black East Side, 1950

©A·Karl/J·Kemp, 2004

CHAPTER FIVE

HASTINGS STREET

On a summer evening in 1943, a lanky, angular, dark-complected young Mississippian jauntily strolled down Hastings Street, the major artery of Detroit's black neighborhood. This was not the first northern city the twenty-five-year-old had visited, but his nerve endings nonetheless fired at the sensations he took in: the spicy smells of ribs, shrimp, and chicken barbecued over open steel drums on street corners; the fine women with offering eyes working their territory amid the rush of shoppers; the young men, and women too, anticipating the night's excitement, pockets fuller than ever with war-inflated wages. Enticing, too, were the bars and clubs squeezed between other small businesses in this tight urban enclave. But most thrilling of all was the music, blues, jazz, and rhythm and blues (or jump blues, as some called it), streaming live or from jukeboxes out of the clubs and record stores, mingling with the street scenes and smells to create a magical sense of immediate possibilities. As John Lee Hooker, reared near Clarksdale, Mississippi, tried to absorb it all, he thought of his momma, who had not allowed him as a teen "just to stay out all night long, oh Lord!" But he was a man, now, and this was Detroit, Hastings Street— he would "boogie-woogie anyhow."[1]

Hastings was Detroit's Beale Street, the spine of Paradise Valley, the black commercial and entertainment district. "Oh, that was *the street, the street* in town," Hooker declared. "Everything you lookin' for on that street, *everything*. Anything you wanted was on that street. Anything you *didn't* want was on that street." In the 1940s, Paradise Valley had elastic boundaries, depending on whom one asked and where one lived. Warren to the north and Woodward on the west were the generally acknowledged limits, while the eastern edge fluctuated between Hastings and the streets further east over to Riopelle. To the south the Valley ran to the Detroit River, but the lower portion, the streets below Vernor Highway, most older residents still called Black Bottom. Within this narrow space, a little more than sixty acres, almost all of the city's nearly three hundred thousand black residents found homes, schools for their children, and such necessities as food, clothing, and a welcoming church community. Hooker, a budding blues guitarist, knew the neighborhood well. He lived in it, working as a janitor in a series of jobs after 1943, and played rent parties (private dance parties held in individual homes to raise the monthly rent) and the after-hours "blind pigs," where he honed his considerable talents. Gradually making a name for himself—his feet kept an infectious, driving beat under the distinctive blues chords his fingers teased from his guitar—Hooker began to play the smaller bars and occasionally opened for a major act in the larger clubs. In 1948, a producer for the local Sensation record label "discovered" Hooker, and his first recording, "Boogie Chillen," became a national rhythm and blues hit. "When I first came to town, people," Hooker sang,

> *I was walking down Hastings Street.*
> *I heard everybody talking about*
> *   the Henry Swing Club.*
> *I decided to drop in there that night*
> *And when I got there*
> *I said yes people*
> *Yes they were really having a ball!*

That the Henry Swing Club was not on Hastings but at the juncture of Orleans and Madison hurt neither Hooker's success nor the Street's reputation. As one black Detroit woman recalled of the 1940s, reflecting the tales told by husband and brothers who saw service during World War II, most blacks "thought everybody from Detroit was from Hastings Street or Black Bottom."[2]

Hooker was also fortunate to live in the city when its creative musical energy reached a collective peak. More than thirteen new clubs opened in Paradise Valley during the 1940s, and an additional fifteen, also showcasing black musical expression, opened throughout the city, most of them along Woodward or just north of Grand Boulevard and easily accessible to Valley residents. In such clubs as the Flame Show Bar, Sportree's, and Lee's Sensation, local talent such as bluesmen Eddie Burns, Bob "Detroit Count" White, and Eddie Kirkland earned a reputation if not necessarily a living, and jazz musicians Yusef Lateef, Sonny Stitt, and Thomas "Dr. Beans" Bowles developed their styles. This music permeated black Detroit and a small sliver of its white residents as well. WJLB-AM, a major radio station, broadcast bebop jazz live beginning in 1946, and gospel, blues, and R&B were regularly heard on the air despite the absence of a paid black disk jockey. In this atmosphere the audience for nationally known performers was intense. In the five years following the war, musicians as diverse as Josh White, Count Basie, Joe Turner, Dizzy Gillespie, Sarah Vaughn, William "The Lion" Smith, Johnny Otis, T-Bone Walker, Ruth Brown, Nat King Cole, Lionel Hampton, Ella Fitzgerald, Duke Ellington, Cootie Williams, Art Tatum, and Lena Horne—to name but a few—made repeated, well-received appearances at Detroit clubs. So accomplished was Detroit's musical community that visiting regional and national bands recruited its talent repeatedly in the decade after the war. "By 1955 everybody was gone," one jazzman ruefully observed.[3]

Interspersed with the bars and clubs, many actually owned by whites, were the small black-owned businesses that provisioned Valley residents and gave black Detroit its vital if contained entrepreneurial group. If Hooker began his walk down Hastings where it intersected Forest, for example, he might have stopped for a drink at the Forest Club, one of the few black-owned bars in the city. A few doors down, Mrs. Vivian Nash ran a beauty school and salon; while at the corner of Canfield, the McFall brothers, Benjamin, George, and James, operated a well-regarded funeral parlor. At one corner of Willis and Hastings, Turner's grocery store catered to the palates of southern-born migrants. Across the street stood New Bethel Baptist Church, with its interior recently renovated, home to a large and growing congregation. A block farther south, the Cozy Corner welcomed customers, and a few more blocks down, the loudspeakers outside Joe Von Battle's Record Store propelled a constant stream of blues, R&B, and gospel into the street. Tucked in among these establishments up and down Hastings were barbershops, apparel stores, millinery shops, the professional offices of doctors, lawyers, accountants, and insurance agents, furniture and appliance outlets, printing shops, churches, and so much else. The street pulsated with activity, musical and economic, legal and illegal, business and pleasure, sacred and secular. Sunnie Wilson, a fixture in the Valley since the 1930s as a club manager and owner, and for a time the unofficial "mayor" of Paradise Valley, described the neighborhood as "a closely knit community," with relatively little serious violence. The community, Wilson remembered, "had organization." In Erma Franklin's memory, the Valley was "one long stretch of black businesses, successful black businesses. All blacks supported the black businesses. . . . And we enjoyed doing it. It was like everyone knew each other through socializing, church, whatever, school."[4]

Not everyone in black Detroit had as positive memories of Paradise Valley, however. The poet Toi Derrecotte remembered that as a child after the war, her mother and aunt drove with her through the crowded streets on an occasional Saturday night "to laugh at those loud people, to be as close to them as we could allow ourselves, to envy them and to think we were better." Following the spectacle, this family of middling status within black Detroit's social hierarchy drove "through the fancy boulevards, the neighborhoods of those [black] people who sometimes invited my aunt and mother to showers and meetings of the bridge club." Although Berry Gordy, who created Motown Records in 1959, later revised his belief that "all the bad people lived" on the East Side, he retained even as an adult the conviction that as "a place," the West Side—that is, not Paradise Valley—"gave me a sense of right and wrong, a sense of safety in the family, a sense of love and kinship in a community where being good was actually a good thing to be."[5]

The social distinctions Derrecotte and Gordy absorbed as children reflected very real divisions within black Detroit. While the vast majority of black citizens lived in Paradise Valley, selective neighborhoods did exist for the well-to-do. The North End, for example, including Boston Boulevard, Arden Park, and Chicago Boulevard east of Woodward, with capacious homes and well-manicured lawns bordering the wide, tree-lined streets, was one such enclave; so, too, was Conant Gardens, farther northeast. Professional black Detroiters were also clustered to the west of Woodward, especially in the section known as Virginia Park, near Twelfth Street and, farther west, below Tireman (the West Side Gordy referred to). The migration of these wealthier blacks created minimally integrated areas, not unlike the Franklins' experience in Buffalo—at least until the wealthy white residents, disturbed by the slow but continual trickle of even upper-class blacks, moved to the surrounding suburbs of Grosse Pointe or Bloomfield Hills.

Within black Detroit, residential divisions carried social distinctions as well. While some among these elites might of an evening go "down to the Valley . . . dressed to the nines" to catch the acts at the Flame Show Bar, such clubs were not their primary form of social organization. Instead, these men and women belonged to socially powerful organizations such as the Nacirema Club (*American,* spelled backward), the Cotillion Club, and the Detroit branch of the NAACP. College-educated men and women had their own particular groups, where the jocular competition over the relative merits of LeMoyne in Memphis, Fisk in Nashville, or Morehouse and Spellman in Atlanta signified their collective remove from the vast majority of black Detroit—indeed, black America. Upper-class women, most of whom did not work, created their own network as well: groups such as the Modern Matrons Social Club, the Casa Blanca Study Club, and The Poinsettias were exclusive, invitation-only organizations dedicated to self-improvement, the occasional charitable event, and maintaining their identities as groups apart. Not surprisingly, these elites sought their own churches, mostly shunning those where the whooped sermon of the preacher and the gospel rhythms of the choir infused services with the tones of the rural South. Robert Bynum Jr. accurately gauged the intense feeling that fueled this social division when he described the attitudes of elite blacks of the Conant Gardens neighborhood in the 1940s toward Valley blacks moving near the neighborhood: "Basically hoodlums—this was the attitude that they had. The blacks that would come here would be beneath them."[6]

Thus, the black Detroit C. L. Franklin entered when he accepted the call to New Bethel was anything but monolithic. For the next thirty-three years its vitality and its pain, its aspirations and its contradictions, would engage him fully. Here, he would rise to greatness.

*   *   *   *   *

C. L. took the pulpit at New Bethel on the first Sunday of June 1946. He recalled the church, which he had visited months earlier when he gave his trial sermon, as somewhat shabby, "a kind of a storefront," a converted "old bowling alley." In contrast, his Buffalo church was larger and "much nicer." But as he felt "cut off from the onflow of life in this country" in Buffalo, it was decidedly "a step forward to go to Detroit."[7]

In truth, however, New Bethel was not as decrepit as C. L.'s memory suggested. The building was not impressive and the congregation was smaller than at Friendship; but the church had made great strides since its founding in the Depression winter of 1932. Then, a small group of southern-born migrants, members of the Helping Hand Society, a self-help group, had gathered at Eliza Butler's Paradise Valley home to reorganize their religious life. The established Afro-Baptist churches, such as the stately Second Baptist, at 441 Monroe in the heart of Black Bottom, discouraged the emotional tones of rural black working people's religious expression and frowned as well on the spreading use of gospel hymns, with their praise words set to blues rhythms. But those meeting in the Butler home knew that to abandon their familiar religious expression would threaten their very survival in this harsh and strange land. The chanted sermon and the gospel hymns were linchpins to the experience of their faith, and they could not imagine its powerful balm denied them as they adjusted to this northern, urban clime. By March 1932, the small group had numbered more than one hundred and had called a temporary minister to help organize a church. Reverend H. H. Coleman, whose preaching propelled the young Martin Luther King Jr. to accept conversion a few years later, assumed the pulpit that August and remained for more than two years. Following a 1940 split led by Coleman's successor, Reverend N. H. Armstrong, New Bethel's prospects took a new turn when Reverend William E. Ramsey accepted the congregation's call that same year.[8]

Like the majority of the church's members, Ramsey was southern born. The Troy, Alabama, native had "a musical voice" that "stirred the congregation to its depths," as well as an organizational ability and the "quiet, retiring demeanor" that made him, in the words of J. Pius Barbour, "content to remain in the background without any thought of the limelight." This combination of qualities had revived New Bethel. Ramsey had renovated the interior of the old building, begun a building fund to replace it, and built up the membership well beyond anything seen before. Under Ramsey, the membership incorporated black Detroiters of every status and position; while the majority were working people, professionals such as attorney Charles R. Perkins, surgeon V. G. Tolbert, and mortician and church trustee Benjamin J. McFall dotted the congregation. By 1945, reported membership had grown to over twelve hundred. An assistant pastor, Noah G. Cain, had assumed his duties, particularly with the youth, and the church scribe, Mrs. Lucille Marshall, had reported the building fund at over $17,000. More than twelve clubs and departments had channeled members' energy toward aiding the poor and sick, organizing a death-benefit society and numerous self-help clubs, and into the church's nurses corps, usher boards, and choirs—organizations that were the very backbone of New Bethel's institutional presence. Yet dissension had again reared its head in February 1946, and Ramsey, with a core of New Bethel members, left to establish a new church, Gospel Temple Baptist.[9]

C. L. was, to be fair, partly correct in his first impression of New Bethel. When he arrived in June of that year, the church building was inadequate, in need of replacement, and the congregation had been diminished through the schism. But under Ramsey's administration the church had established itself on a secure footing. And prospects were good: between 1930 and 1950, black Detroit grew sixfold, to more than three hundred thousand people, and in that latter year made up more than 16 percent of all city residents. Continued high migration from the South, coupled with a steady birthrate, propelled blacks well beyond the already densely crowded confines of the Valley. Given an effective preacher with sensitivity to the needs of new and recent migrants, the conditions were ripe for church growth.[10]

Franklin had assumed his duties as pastor of New Bethel in June, but his formal installation occurred the following September. A weeklong celebration that involved ministers and congregants from numerous black Baptist churches, the ceremonies also served to introduce C. L. and Barbara formally to the larger community. Visiting ministers extended the fellowship of Detroit's Afro-Baptist world, while other guests reflected C. L.'s earlier career. Juanita Brewster, daughter of W. H. Brewster, the Memphis minister, gospel composer, and Franklin family friend, was the guest soloist. A delegation from Friendship Baptist journeyed to participate in the installation. Mrs. Mary Gaston, that church's corresponding secretary, told the large crowd that "although it is our deepest regret to see him depart from us, we know that God does everything for the best." The festivities ended with a large banquet at the Gotham Hotel, on Orchard Place between Woodward and John R Street, the elite black-owned hotel in Detroit.[11]

In electing the Gotham for his installation dinner, as opposed to the church dining room, C. L. indicated a major tone of his coming ministry. From one perspective the hotel was the perfect choice, as none of the major downtown hotels that served whites in 1946 allowed blacks to enter except through the service entrance. But the choice also introduced Detroit to the personal style, the flair, which would define Franklin's ministry. In 1946, the Gotham symbolized the cultural crossroads. Some nine blocks from New Bethel and just around the corner from the Paradise Theater, the Gotham had been lavishly renovated three years earlier. Most major black entertainers stopped there when they played Detroit, and the hotel became "the place to go and was the major social meeting place" for Detroit blacks with some means. The banquet signaled that proximity to musicians, celebrities, and their culture would be an intrinsic dimension of his ministerial style. Many of Franklin's congregation could not afford tickets for the banquet, yet no one expressed any discomfort about this. It is quite possible that many members saw in C. L.'s choice a positive reflection of their church's coming prominence and, by association, their own as well.[12]

Franklin's primary responsibility, however, was to strengthen and to lead his congregation, and that required the full application of his preaching and administrative skills. Success there, he expected, would create a place for himself in Detroit and, perhaps, beyond as well. Neither goal would come easy.

In certain respects, Detroit was more like Memphis than Buffalo. The "onflow of life" coursed through those two cities, and in each, the black population dwarfed what Franklin had found in upstate New York. While all three communities had established ministerial cultures, the greater variety of religious professions allowed by the larger black population made for a more complex and competitive situation in both Memphis and Detroit. In the Motor City, for example, in addition to the numerous churches associated with the National Baptist Convention, black Detroiters attended regularly other churches affiliated with the three black Methodist national organizations (African Methodist Episcopal, African Methodist Episcopal Zion, and Colored Methodist Episcopal); with the black Pentecostals, the Church of God in Christ; and with such mainline white groups as the Presbyterian, Episcopal, and Congregational denominations, and Roman Catholicism. In addition, there were numerous storefront churches, often established by self-appointed ministers, speaking powerfully to the religious needs of the poor and migratory; it was in Detroit, in the 1930s, that the first mosque of the Nation of Islam took root. There were as well unaffiliated preachers with national reputations such as James F. "Prophet" Jones, who regularly filled his large church on the corner of Linwood and Philadelphia, west of Woodward, with charged sermons extolling individual potential. A vibrant religious culture surged through Detroit, its praise hymns, rhythmic responses, and music streaming into the surrounding streets from worship houses on Sunday in a manner reminiscent of Saturday night on Hastings Street.[13]

Not surprisingly, Detroit's Afro-Baptist ministerial society, C. L.'s immediate professional peers, was enormously complex and varied greatly in its estimation of each other. Some, preachers and congregants alike, gauged a minister's relative standing and position by the size and wealth of the church. Others emphasized even more the level of education attained and the learned quality of the prepared message delivered weekly. A "Morehouse man," for example, or a minister who attended one of the other historic black colleges, possessed both the requisite education and the network of social connections across the nation to mark him apart from the largely untutored rural migrants and, perhaps, recommend him eventually for a leadership position in black Detroit's leading clubs and organizations. Others, however, shunned such criteria, favoring instead a preacher with a charged emotive appeal. Some looked to a minister's social message, urging the congregation to engage political life as a consequence of their faith, as a measuring rod of influence and importance. Nor were these the only distinctions made: one's origins (were you an Alabamian, a Mississippian?) proved important, as did a minister's renown stemming from involvement in Baptist organizational activities at the city, state, or national level.

C. L. was not unaware of this ranking system. Indeed, he utilized his own version of it on occasion. When he arrived in 1946, he later suggested, there were but a handful of Baptist ministers he thought were leaders, and only two were men of his own generation. Like himself, these two were southerners who had assumed their Detroit pulpits in 1946 and 1947, but there were few other obvious similarities.[14]

The son of an evangelist father and a devoutly religious mother, A. A. Banks Jr. was born in Texas in September 1913, sixteen months before Rachel Franklin delivered her son in Mississippi, and attended grade school in Bryan, Texas. His father's ministry took the family to Kansas City and then Pocatello, Idaho, where Banks became "the first Negro male" to graduate from the local high school. The family had some resources, for even in the midst of the Depression, young Banks returned to Texas to attend Bishop College, where he was active in a Christian interracial student organization. Graduating in three years, he then took a master's degree at Howard University and, in 1942, a bachelor of divinity degree, all the while serving as the assistant pastor of Shiloh Baptist church in Washington, D. C. The following year, Reverend Robert L. Bradby, the sixty-six-year-old pastor of Second Baptist, called Banks as his assistant, with the intention of grooming him as a successor. Following Bradby's death in 1946, Second Baptist called Banks. At age thirty-three, Banks led the oldest and most distinguished black church in the city, one founded in 1837, and in recognition of its importance, Reverend D. V. Jemison, president of the National Baptist Convention, himself preached Banks's installation service. The preaching tradition at the church was restrained and intellectual. Since Bradby entered Second's pulpit in 1910, J. Pius Barbour noted, Sunday services were anything but "a knock-down, drag out emotional orgy." Like Bradby, the new minister preached from a prepared manuscript in lecture style. With almost four thousand "audited members" in 1947 and

the funds to maintain the church's stately appearance, Second Baptist offered Banks a natural platform for advancement. A self-contained man
with cautious instincts, his reserved style, administrative capabilities, and
careful encouragement of social change quickly won for him a leadership
position within Detroit's black community.[15]

The second contemporary C. L. noted was Jesse Jai McNeil, born in
Little Rock, Arkansas, in 1913. A powerful intellectual and a manuscript
preacher who avoided the whoop, McNeil held degrees, including the doctorate, from Columbia University. Following a stint at a church in
Nashville and a three-year term as dean of the School of Religion at Marshall College in Texas, McNeil arrived at Tabernacle Baptist Church in
Detroit with a reputation as a "progressive-minded" pastor who emphasized a "strong sociological outlook" in his ministry. Within a year of his
arrival, he constructed a community center adjacent to the church, known
as Neighborhood House, which provided "a day nursery, health center, vocational guidance, and adult education" for anyone in need. In 1949 he in-
stituted a lyceum program, engaging his congregation with a series of
speakers on social, educational, and religious themes. A civil rights activist
whom a local columnist dubbed in 1948 "the preacher who is all out for
N.A.A.C.P., the Committee on Civil Rights, [and] the United Negro College Fund," McNeil described his ministry as bearing "responsibility both
to our congregation and to our community." McNeil quickly assumed a
leadership position in both the black and white religious communities. Active in the World Council of Churches as well as Detroit's Baptist Ministerial Conference, by the mid-1950s he led council delegations to Europe
to study democracy, served on Michigan's State Corrections Commission,
and was active in numerous interracial committees.[16]

As sharply different as the backgrounds of these two men were from
C. L. in education, preaching style, and social connections, the background
and experiences of their wives denoted yet another marked difference. Victoria Banks graduated from Prairie View State University in Texas and received her master's in child development from Iowa State. She assumed
numerous duties at her husband's church and also was the first black in-
structor at the Downtown (i.e., white) YWCA's religious study program.
Pearl McNeil held an undergraduate degree from Howard, a master's from

Fisk, and a doctorate in political science from Columbia University. Deeply involved at Tabernacle Baptist, she also held office in a variety of city and state associations and remained involved with her national sorority, Zeta Phi Beta. More startling, during and long after the House Un-American Activities Committee had scoured Detroit looking for suspected Communist sympathizers, Pearl McNeil continued her work with the Women's International League for Peace and Freedom, one of the very organizations under suspicion by the federal government. Although the Banks, the McNeils, and the Franklins all shared southern roots and were contemporaries of one another, the Franklins would never join the other families at social gatherings among Detroit's elite black professionals, businessmen, and civic leaders. The social distance these differences in education, preaching, and individual style created were not impermeable at all times. Reverend McNeil and a delegation from his church joined in celebrating New Bethel's sixteenth anniversary in 1948, but that significant demarcation line remained throughout C. L.'s career.[17]

As real as these differences were, however, C. L.'s business acumen gained him at least a physical presence among this more elite cohort. In negotiating the terms of his contract with New Bethel in 1946, he had insisted the church purchase a parsonage for his family's use. Whether he or the trustees selected the neighborhood remains unclear, but when the Franklins arrived in Detroit, they moved into an elegant mansion at 649 East Boston Boulevard worth an estimated $17,000. Nestled in among the equally expensive homes of other black professionals and ministers in the city's North End, some three miles north of his church, C. L. happily found himself in a rather rarefied atmosphere. As in Buffalo, many wealthy whites resided in the neighborhood, and his fellow black residents reflected a particular economic and social standing. Toi Derrecotte remembered that in the 1940s, when most blacks still lived in Paradise Valley, "many of the cream-colored had floated away to mansions on Arden Park and Boston Boulevard." C. L.'s dark-chocolate skin distinguished him in that company, as did his relative lack of wealth. Nevertheless, with the financial help of New Bethel's working people, C. L. and Barbara grew into a style the equal of any in the neighborhood, and then some. William Robinson first entered the six-bedroom Franklin home in the winter of 1946–47, when he became friendly with Cecil, the Franklins' six-year-old son. Robinson lived one street over, on Belmont, and was a regular in the Franklin home throughout the 1950s. He remembered it as "a huge house," "a beautiful mansion," and recalled vividly the impression the interior made on his young mind: "Once inside, I'm awestruck—oil paintings, velvet tapestries, silk curtains, mahogany cabinets filled with ornate objects of silver and gold. Man, I've never seen nothing like that before!"

There was as well impressive furniture, including "an elaborate Emerson TV," and a grand piano that Smokey Robinson remembered Aretha, not yet five years old, playing on one of his first visits.[18]

With his family settled and comfortable, C. L. addressed the administration of New Bethel. As often occurred in Baptist polity, where congregations frequently dismiss their pastors and call another, one of the trustees at New Bethel had assumed the leadership role in all but name after Ramsey left. Echoing C. L.'s experience in Buffalo, this man "more or less controlled the church," had significant trustee support, and resisted C. L.'s immediate efforts to assert his authority. Eventually, C. L. "turned him out" without splitting the church, using patience, a crafty intelligence, and an iron determination grounded in the sure knowledge of the hold his preaching exerted on the members. The new pastor did not "jump on [the trustee] prematurely"; rather, he waited until the man's growing resistance to, and resentment of, his rulings led members themselves to complain about the trustee's obstructionism. Quickly, he outflanked the trustees who opposed him. When they left New Bethel, he was free to replace them with his supporters.[19]

In other ways as well Franklin imposed his will on the church. During his trial sermon, he had carefully watched the collection baskets and calculated that there was but $40 from a crowd of some five hundred that Sunday. At that moment he "made a decision that if I became pastor I would change that, and I did." He increased church membership dues and instituted multiple collections each Sunday: one for the building fund, one for the poor and destitute, and one for church expenses, including his salary and upkeep. Secure in his appeal as a preacher, C. L. encouraged in members "over the years" the necessary "loyalties and discipline about giving."[20]

This aspect of the Afro-Baptist ministry has long been scorned by critics as exploitative, as these clerical leaders secured their economic standing on the offerings of their largely poor members. There is some truth in this, and one could find parallel situations among the numerous parishes of Detroit's Catholic working class. But the members of New Bethel and other religious communities offered their hard-earned dollars freely each Sunday as they thought reasonable, given their individual circumstances. They also gave in direct relationship to what they understood their pastor gave them, and in C. L. Franklin they had a superior preacher whose weekly sermons engaged their intellect and their spirit. The Baptist minister, moreover, had little choice but to raise the weekly collections. Unlike such Protestant denominations as Methodists and Episcopalians, or Roman Catholics, Baptist churches had no ecclesiastical structure to dispense funds in a financial crisis. Each Baptist church stood on its own foundation, each congregation the final arbiter of the individual institution's leadership. In this most American of circumstances, minister and members had only each other to assure their continued collective presence. The majority of the congregants at New Bethel, poor as they were, repeatedly affirmed the value they placed on their church and their pastor. They understood, as did C. L., that part of the role they required of the pastor was to raise from them each week the necessary funds to keep the entire enterprise solvent and growing.

In the first two years of his ministry in Detroit, C. L. focused considerable attention on establishing a reputation. This required the help of ministerial colleagues and a number of them, along with their parishioners, joined in celebrating the anniversaries of New Bethel's founding and his own second anniversary as pastor during 1947 and 1948. Coupled with his appearance, accompanied by his members, at other churches on similar occasions, New Bethel's people proudly appreciated their pastor's stature among his peers, the majority of whom also lacked the advanced degrees of the elite. The fundraising, of course, continued. At the church's fifteenth anniversary in 1947, members raised almost $8,000 for the building fund, then the most successful single drive in New Bethel's history. A year later, additional drives retired all but $3,000 of the mortgage on the parsonage on East Boston Boulevard and raised an additional $5,000 for the poor.[21]

Milton Hall was but one of the thousands of New Bethel members whom C. L. touched. Seventeen years old in 1948, Hall arrived in Detroit fresh from rural Arkansas. Within a few months he found New Bethel, heard C. L. preach, and "I joined up with that church family the second Sunday in March in 1948, and I've been there ever since." C. L. impressed him deeply: "I could see that he was a God-sent man and he had a sermon, a song, and prayer . . . [and] he wasn't short on none of them." A church member for more than half a century and a deacon for more than three decades, Hall supported his family through working at Ford Motor Company, where he was a union member for over thirty-five years. "See," he exclaimed, "Reverend Franklin spoke for me when I couldn't speak for myself. I was with the church. I was with the crowd. He [C. L.] on front. He did the preaching, he did the speaking. I didn't have nothing to do, but I was recognized. I had somebody to speak for me."[22]

For Deacon Hall, the New Bethel congregation became an extended family and its pastor, whose faith was palpable to the young man, a rock in a time of awkward transition. Inexperienced, without formal education, overwhelmed by the very intensity of the city, his sense of self was yet understated, his confidence weak. The company of those who had themselves undergone similar transitions—his pastor, too, had once been unable to speak—was a comfort. Critical, however, was the opportunity to gather self-knowledge and awareness in the shadow of a preacher with an uncanny ability to address the deepest recesses of another's soul. Through his faith and through his pastor's influence, Milton Hall came to exult in the knowledge that he was, indeed, somebody, that he possessed a unique voice with which he might leave his mark on the world. In the years to come he would counsel church members in spiritual difficulty, raise his voice against racist practices within his union, and participate in civil rights activities. He was but one of a thousand men and women who joined New Bethel in 1947 and 1948, drawn by this preacher who, from the wellspring of his faith, framed a ritual space each Sunday that allowed them to glory in his voice as they discovered new dimensions in their own.[23]

*   *   *   *   *

In the summer of 1948, workers tore down the former bowling alley C. L. disliked so much and began construction of a larger, modern facility on the same site. The congregation prepared for a season wandering to different venues for services: trustee Bernard McFall's funeral home, the Music Hall in Paradise Valley, and at other churches on Sunday afternoons following their host's traditional morning services. Most frequently, New Bethel gathered at Brewster Center, a city-run facility in the publicly funded Brewster Homes, a few blocks from New Bethel, but even there they could be preempted, and the center was never available for Sunday evening services. C. L. was quite aware of the inherent danger that members would find other churches, the congregation weaken, and fundraising decline. This last was most serious, since New Bethel's building fund could not cover the full cost of the construction project. That continued pressure led C. L. to ignore his initial misgivings and accept an offer, supported by his trustees, from a black minister who doubled as an insurance agent to underwrite the additional financing. The trustees "had a blind confidence" in the man, Franklin thought, and they dismissed his insistence that the insurance agent sign a written contract. Hesitant of crossing his trustees when he had no personal knowledge of the would-be financier, C. L. agreed, against his better judgment. New Bethel's funds covered the demolition, and the framing and roofing of the new building. But when Franklin and his trustees looked for their financial backer, he never came through, kept whatever retainer he had received, and New Bethel faced a severe crisis. Prepared for a nomadic existence for a number of months, they now faced a prolonged dislocation. Franklin watched with dismay as members "drifted away" and desperately sought a radio program to keep his and New Bethel's name before the city. But no station was interested in a pastor without a church building. Even the *Michigan Chronicle*, the Detroit black weekly that had given him good coverage since his arrival, seemed to forget he existed, as the paper went for nearly a year without any mention of him.[24]

Franklin ultimately found the financing to complete the building, but the new church would not be ready for services until the fall of 1951. As difficult as this transition proved to be, the personal tensions C. L. simultaneously confronted were far more troubling for him and his family.

Sometime in 1948, exactly when remains unclear, Barbara Franklin separated from her husband of twelve years and returned to Buffalo, where her mother still resided. The four children C. L. fathered with her remained with him in Detroit. Their brother, Vaughn, accompanied his mother. Neither C. L. nor Barbara left any testimony concerning the end of their marriage; Vaughn, at age fourteen the oldest child in the family when they separated, preferred not to discuss his reflections on his parents' relationship.[25]

Barbara's two years in Detroit had generated little public attention. Unlike Victoria Banks or Pearl McNeil, she never was the subject of a feature story in the local or national black papers. Yet to the extent that Barbara's life was private, her husband's became even more public. What had been true in Memphis and Buffalo was now even more pronounced. Vaughn remembered that in Detroit, "Dad . . . wasn't home that much," and child-rearing was, again, his mother's domain. Barbara's departure was a split, but it was not the abandonment of her children that journalists and authors later claimed. Barbara's second daughter, Aretha, is emphatic that "despite the fact that it has been written innumerable times, it is an absolute lie that my mother abandoned us. In no way, shape, form, or fashion did our mother desert us." The children who remained on Boston Boulevard with their father stayed with Barbara during the summer in Buffalo, and she visited them in Detroit occasionally throughout the school year. Brenda Corbett, C. L.'s niece, recalled her grandmother Rachel attributing the separation to Franklin's schedule, especially C. L.'s traveling to give guest sermons, and the resulting strains on the marriage. Although too young to have known Barbara herself, Brenda also suggested that, given human nature, the causes of the separation "could've been a whole lot of other things, you know." In fact, the absence of any credible evidence as to the emotional state of either Barbara or C. L. (the separation never proceeded to divorce and thus no legal testimony exists) leaves much obscured by time and reticence. That so devoted a mother left her children with her estranged husband, however, in an era when wives regularly received custody, hints at the tension and the unequal power that existed between husband and wife.[26]

In Buffalo, Barbara reconstructed her life. She lived in her mother's home, worked at a music store, and later trained as a nurse's aide. Almost immediately, she rejoined Friendship, where she assisted in children's pageants and gave private music lessons. Although Friendship's former first lady, Barbara easily reentered the congregation as a regular member, resumed her friendships, and as was widely known in the church, entered into a serious relationship with the aptly named Trustee Young, who served as both a deacon and a trustee. Vaughn, too, returned to the congregation, and he entered high school in 1948. He would finally be told that C. L. was not his biological father in 1951.[27]

C. L. faced a different dilemma as a single parent of four children aged ten or younger. From Erma's birth in 1938 on, C. L.'s approach to fathering his young children reflected a love that found its expression through the prism of three formative relationships. The first, of course, was the absence of his own father, a rambling man who never returned after teaching his son to salute. The distance that defined his relationship with Henry Franklin did little to encourage in C. L. an appreciation of the effect paternal nurturing could have. Looming over the absent males was his mother, Rachel, both disciplinarian and nurturer, the steady force in his life. But his image of her, reinforced by broader cultural attitudes, framed his expectations of any woman he would take as a wife. In his mind, he never subordinated family concerns to his career; his very success provided the family with its foundation. Some woman would be around to take care of domestic needs.

As Barbara's departure did not substantially alter C. L.'s patterns within the home, of necessity he sought other solutions. Some New Bethel women, Myra Perkins recalled, "made ourselves available to look after the children," but this was a temporary solution. A more satisfactory approach brought in housekeepers from outside the congregation to cook, clean, and take care of the children. Sylvia Penn, another New Bethel member, interviewed these women for the position in the decade after the separation. There were occasional visits from Mahalia Jackson, gospel singer Clara Ward, and two of her backup group, Frances Steadman and Marion Williams, all of whom were devoted to the family, but these arrangements lacked a steady familial presence. Soon Rachel and Henry Franklin arrived from Mississippi. Henry, taken sick, was unable to continue farming, and both Rachel (whom the children would call "Big Momma") and her son understood the multiple advantages of the senior Franklins' move to Detroit. In their first years, they did not live in the house on Boston Boulevard but in a home C. L. provided. Nonetheless, Rachel was a constant presence, extending her maternal care to her grandchildren as well as her son. As Brenda Corbett noted, throughout her decades in Detroit, "she pushed him and she was right there for him." For his part "Son," as his mother called him, fulfilled the promise he made her when, at sixteen, he vowed to both preach and "take care of you."[28]

Rachel Franklin's love, belief in discipline, and deep religious faith stabilized the daily life of the children in Detroit. But in a few short years, all five of the children experienced another crushing blow. Walking home from his Buffalo high school one day in the spring of 1952, Vaughn, by then a junior, "stopped at this little canteen place" near his house for a soda. He and a friend saw an ambulance speeding down the street but thought nothing of it. Twenty minutes later he opened the door to his house, yelled out "hello!" to his mother—only to be told by his grandmother that Barbara had just succumbed to a heart attack. "She was sick on and off" for some time, he remembered, but he "never did know what was really wrong with her." Vaughn's brothers and sisters came out from Detroit for the funeral service, accompanied by two or three adults. Their father did not attend.[29]

After Barbara died, Mahalia Jackson noted that "the whole family wanted for love." The children in Detroit were still very young, and the dual shock of separation and death within four years inevitably hurt deeply. They sought comfort from both father and grandmother, members of New Bethel, and visiting adult friends, and they forged tight bonds among themselves. In Buffalo, an older Vaughn of necessity handled his losses differently. He lived with his maternal grandmother as he finished high school and then attended the University of Buffalo for a year. In 1954, he enlisted in the Air Force, where he remained twenty years, and only infrequently had contact with his family in Detroit.[30]

C. L., thirty-three when he and Barbara separated, a vitally handsome man with an ever-growing reputation as a compelling preacher, continued with his life much as he had before.

*   *   *   *   *

Without a church building, a radio presence, or much press attention, Franklin sought other ways to retain his members and to keep his name before the larger public. Positive notice in the national Baptist press for his preaching at the annual convention was useful, but C. L. also needed attention closer to home. Not surprisingly, music provided him the necessary venue. Franklin's enthusiasm for a strong musical presence in his church was not necessarily the norm among Afro-Baptist ministers in 1950. Many preachers, especially those lacking outstanding musical ability themselves, saw church singers as rivals and the music as a necessary but threatening accompaniment to their sermon. To the question of which—sermon or hymn—would have prominence, most would answer the sermon, but many a preacher harbored the suspicion that a significant number of his congregation actually felt differently. Secure in his ability as a singer and a preacher, C. L. proved a most generous supporter of talented gospel performers, the famous as well as the beginners.[31]

C. L. had a powerful singing voice and, a friend explained, "a real affinity to singers." As in his churches in Buffalo and Memphis, Franklin stressed the need for a strong choir at New Bethel and brought with him from Buffalo Thomas A. Shelby, the Lucie Campbell protégé, to serve once again as his minister of music. Both C. L. and Shelby were close with Thomas Dorsey, and Dorsey's influence was especially evident at New Bethel in the person of James Cleveland, who arrived as choir director after Barbara's return to Buffalo. Born in Chicago in 1931, and raised up at Pilgrim Baptist, where at age eight he was a soloist in Dorsey's junior choir, Cleveland possessed a prodigious musical talent that would shortly earn him national renown as the "Crown Prince of Gospel." He and C. L. were close friends. The younger man stayed with Franklin and his family on Boston Boulevard for a number of years, exerting a tremendous musical influence on the children, especially Aretha. Together with Shelby, Cleveland built the temporarily nomadic choir into a powerful instrument for giving praise. Singers such as Grace Cobb, the diminutive Sammy Bryant, and Willie Todd, whom C. L. regarded "as one of the best singers that I've ever heard," were but a few of the enormously talented, if largely unknown, choir members.[32]

Reverend Samuel Billy Kyles, who was a Chicago teenager in the early 1950s, had known Franklin all of his life, as C. L. and his father, Joseph Kyles, were friends, fellow Mississippians, and ministers who frequently preached from each other's pulpits. Chicago was the "mecca of gospel singing" at this time, with Roberta Martin, Mahalia Jackson, Sally Martin, and Thomas Dorsey among the nationally prominent and most influential Chicagoans. But C. L., the younger Kyles explained, "was trying to move as much of that [as possible] to Detroit where he was. . . . I mean, he'd always have the best choir directors and nothing was too good for the choir." It was anything but unusual, then, in February 1949, for C.L. to attend a gospel competition held on a Sunday afternoon at the Forest Club on Hastings. A Detroit group, The Flying Clouds, had invited the Harmony Kings from St. Louis and the Highway Q.C.'s from Chicago to share the billing with them. The Chicago quartet impressed C. L. and particularly the lead singer, an eighteen-year-old from Mississippi by the name of Sam Cooke. Cooke possessed a compellingly clear tenor voice and an uncanny ability to improvise within the gospel tradition. C. L. immediately invited the quartet to stay in Detroit and, when they explained the need to return home, invited them back to perform on gospel programs he organized.[33]

The Highway Q.C.'s were, in effect, the apprentice group for the Soul Stirrers, one of the nation's most famous gospel groups. Based in Chicago, and under the leadership of tenor Rebert H. Harris, the Soul Stirrers tutored the Q.C.'s between their road trips, and when an opening occurred in 1950, they elevated Cooke to fill the spot. Before Cooke joined the Soul Stirrers, audiences had responded intensely to the group within a religious context; under Harris's leadership, the Soul Stirrers remained relatively immobile as they performed, focusing attention less on themselves than on the hymn and its Christian purpose. Cooke's presence fundamentally transformed the particular grace of that delivery. His handsome good looks accentuated the irrepressible rhythmic motion of his body as it moved to the beat, and his voice's passion, phrasing, and tonal quality gave a joy to these hymns that few could resist. Women especially responded viscerally, as much to Cooke's prayerful words as to the alluring singer who delivered them. The two oldest Franklin daughters understood Cooke's appeal immediately. "When I first saw him," Aretha recalled, "all I could do was sigh. . . . Sam was love on first hearing, love at first sight." "He use to pat us on our heads," Erma expressed with delight decades later, referring to Cooke's visits to her home. "Call us little 'Curly Tops'. . . . Aretha and I had the biggest crushes on Sam Cooke." The two young girls were anything but alone in these feelings. Wilson Pickett, a Detroit-reared rhythm and blues singer whose concerts proclaimed an exuberant sexuality, described Cooke's 1950s gospel performances: "Them sisters fell like dominoes when Sam took the lead. Bang. Flat-out. Piled three deep in the aisles." So intense was the public reaction, so pointed at the Soul Stirrers' newest member, that it soon became evident that Cooke himself and only secondarily the sacredness of the music was increasingly the main attraction for many in the audience. It was precisely this tone in gospel music that discouraged the more traditional Harris and led him to retire from the Soul Stirrers in 1950. Under Cooke's leadership, the group promptly developed a distinctly pop-derived orientation. Musical accompaniment replaced Harris's a cappella sound, and the new lead singer quickly became a celebrity in his own right, much as such secular performers as T-Bone Walker, B. B. King, and Wynonie Harris. It was little comfort to Rebert Harris that what he objected to in his former group was, in fact, but a small part of a more far-reaching cultural transition.[34]

Franklin, of course, reacted quite differently. From the first time he heard Cooke until long after the completion of the new church building, he brought Cooke and the Soul Stirrers back to Detroit and to New Bethel. In its way, C. L.'s preaching galvanized audiences much as Cooke's singing did, and he appreciated empathetically the young man's desire for celebrity status. Franklin realized now, more than ever before, how permeable were those borders between sacred and secular, how he might create a compelling public persona in the space where the religious and the social, the gospel hymn and the blues, mingled. The prospect that fame—being recognized as somebody—might follow, was not, he thought, disturbing.

His house on Boston Boulevard could not have been better located to support this expectation. The young local talent alone was astounding. Whether they lived in the neighborhood or first connected with family members at school or church, an impressive group of future national artists who would transform popular American musical culture came through Franklin's home. Smokey Robinson, soon to be the lead singer of the Miracles, lived nearby, as did Diana Ross, the future lead singer of the Supremes. Mary Wilson, another founding member of that group, first met the Franklin children at New Bethel, where her family worshiped, and then later became Carolyn's classmate in elementary school. Other friends were Jackie Wilson, the future rhythm and blues star, and most of the youngsters who a few years later would form the Miracles, the Four Tops, the Temptations, and the Spinners. And then, of course, there were the Franklin children. All three daughters had piano lessons, and music of every description—from the young pianists and singers, from brother Cecil's growing record collection, and from the radio—permeated the Franklin home. All three daughters would become outstanding writers and interpreters of songs, and Aretha would become, in time, one of the most creative inventors of a distinctly American musical style. But for C. L., the new popular music already evident in the enthusiasms of his children and their friends was not the cultural force he had felt so absent during his Buffalo years.[35]

One afternoon in the early 1950s, Aretha came home from school and heard "an especially brilliant style of music" coming from the grand piano in the living room. A heavyset man, head tilted to avoid the smoke of the cigarette dangling from his lips, sat at the piano. At a break, C. L. introduced his daughter to his friend, Art Tatum, a jazz pianist so respected that trumpeter Dizzy Gillespie once said of him: "First you speak of Art Tatum, then take a deep long breath, and you speak of the other pianists." Tatum spent considerable time in Detroit in the early 1950s, playing regularly at Baker's Keyboard Lounge at Livernois and Eight Mile, and was a frequent visitor to the Franklin home. He was, however, only one of many musicians and singers to enjoy C. L.'s friendship and hospitality during these years. The great blues singer Dinah Washington was a close friend who stayed at the Franklin home, cooking meals and coaching the older daughters in their singing. Sarah Vaughn, Oscar Peterson, Nat "King" Cole, Dorothy Dandridge, and many other black performers regularly found a welcome and often a party on Boston Boulevard when they played Detroit. Arthur Prysock, the jazz singer, a professed Christian and a close friend to C. L., was a frequent guest. The pastor usually brought him to New Bethel on Sunday morning to sing during services. Jazz great Lionel Hampton also was a particularly good friend and, when in town, a New Bethel regular. Two gospel women became like family to C. L. and his children. Clara

Ward, the lead singer of the Ward Singers, was quite close to C. L. and immensely comfortable in the house. Along with James Cleveland and Mahalia Jackson, Ward had the most profound musical influence on Aretha, but her relationship with C. L. and her engaging personality won her the affection of the other children as well. Smokey Robinson recalled that when he came into the Franklin house to play "with Cecil or [flirt] with Aretha, I might actually hear Clara Ward herself singing in their kitchen" as she prepared a meal. Then, of course, there was Mahalia Jackson. A family friend since Memphis days, she remained close with C. L. through his separation from Barbara and his involvement in the more secular world. Jackson herself refused to sing blues or, in nightclubs, even gospel, despite offers of enormous amounts of money. In 1958, she recorded the song "I'm Going to Live the Life I Sing about in My Song," which affirmed her faith commitment for all to hear. C. L. had already chosen a different approach in understanding his faith's relation to the secular world, yet he and Mahalia remained very close, "like sisters and brothers," Erma remembered. A visitor to the house whenever in Detroit, within a short time after arriving Jackson would enter the kitchen, put a pot of collard greens on the stove, and prepare dinner.[36]

The numerous parties C. L. hosted when these entertainers played Detroit were selectively planned. Sylvia Penn, who organized many of them, suggested that the guest list included only "four or five people in the church." Since Penn and her husband counted for almost half of that number, few New Bethel people were invited. Franklin did not socialize with church members when, enjoying a drink and a wide-ranging conversation, his house pulsated with impromptu live performances. Many in the congregation would have been scandalized had they known, a fact C. L. clearly understood.[37]

From conviction rather than caution, however, Franklin sought to narrow the presumed divide. Through his sacred role as a preacher, he explored in his sermons what was to many an apparent contradiction: rather than a source of evil, the space where the sacred and the secular mingled was the very source of his strength, the wellspring from which the core of his message flowed. That space was, in fact, humanity's central experience, its grounding, for Franklin preached that his God acted through human beings living in this world. There was no idealized spiritual space free of taint and temptation.[38]

As Franklin integrated these multiple influences in his life into even more compelling preaching performances, he still faced the practical problem of preserving a wandering congregation. The absence of a radio program did not help. In Memphis and again in Buffalo, C. L.'s radio programs attracted new members to his church and spread his reputation, although the two consequences were not necessarily identical. The programs had proven of interest to many who felt drawn less by a desire to join C. L.'s church than by the preacher's pointed socioreligious analysis of contemporary events. In any case, what struck Franklin was how his exposure in that medium spread his name across the community. "I knew [that] by reaching the whole city," he later explained of radio's significance, "it was much better than just preaching to the people who just came into the church."[39]

Without a radio show, Franklin turned to other means. In 1950, he recorded a gospel hymn, "I Am Climbing High Mountains," for Philadelphia's Gotham label. One of four sides he recorded that fall, the appearance of the two 78 records underscored C. L.'s continued willingness to explore new technological possibilities to promote his message and his reputation. Most likely Joe Von Battle, whose record shop at 3530 Hastings was just down the street from New Bethel, made the recordings. Deeply a part of the Hastings Street music scene, Von Battle held the key to potential success for many local artists. He recorded them both for his own label, JVB, and sold their tapes to larger record companies. Eddie Burns, a Detroit bluesman who backed John Lee Hooker on many of his recordings, depicted Von Battle as "a kind of big-shot guy. Mouth full'a gold, rode around in Lincolns. He was a hot shot and he was cuttin' just about everything that walked up and down Hastings Street. He'd just go out there and flag 'em in because he has a studio at the back." The industry in Detroit was chaotic and competitive, with paper-thin profit margins encouraging questionable practices, in part because the industry was itself but a minor adjunct to the larger scenes in Chicago, Cincinnati, Los Angeles, and elsewhere. In 1950, for example, Von Battle recorded four sides with Hooker using an alias to avoid legal action from another local company with exclusive right to Hooker's music. C. L.'s financial arrangements with Von Battle for his gospel hymns remain unknown, but not unlike any other aspiring musician on that street, C. L. also found through Von Battle the opportunity to reach a broader audience. At first, that may have seemed like enough.[40]

Cutting that gospel record also marked Franklin as different from the majority of other ministers. It was one thing for him to bring his choir to Sacred Cross Baptist to engage in "another preaching and singing battle" with his good friend, Reverend M. L. Franklin, and his choirs. That was, in the words of Horace White, an older, culturally conservative Detroit minister, a "private" affair.[41] But if only a very small percentage of African American ministers had radio programs in the city at this time, the number of those who recorded hymns was negligible. In a community where the gospel blues were still not welcome in many congregations, C. L.'s recording set him apart in a public fashion. He possessed real talent and was anything but bashful about expressing it. What he first began in Memphis when he shed his literalism and explored a new relationship between faith and the world about him, he now proclaimed with a maturity and a confidence as never before.[42]

*   *   *   *   *

On Sunday, October 14, 1951, New Bethel's long exodus finally ended, and the congregation processed into their new church. They had more than survived their wandering; like the Israelites of old, they had grown through the tribulations. Church membership increased as the new building neared completion, and the pastor's openness to the Hastings Street community generated some rather unusual support. After the original fiasco, C. L. had secured the needed loan from a "downtown broker," which allowed major construction to continue. What was more noteworthy, Bill Lane, the *Chronicle*'s entertainment reporter, wrote in 1953, was that during the construction "night club owners, beauty and barber shop operators, numbers bankers, professional and business people, and plain citizens were all donating money to start a new building for the young minister they heavily admired." C. L. was unique among his fellow ministers in that he welcomed all of the residents of Hastings Street—prostitutes, drug dealers, and pimps as well as the businessmen, professionals, and the devout working classes. Since 1946, he had greeted on the street those usually shunned by church people, talked to them with respect, remembered their names, and invited them to Sunday services. C. L. believed, Charlie Thompson explained, "that if anybody needed redemption, it was the unsaved," and that could not be achieved by "running from these people." Responding to such unexpected kindness from a Baptist minister, these men and women embraced Franklin in turn. As Sylvia Penn noted, prostitutes, jazz musicians, drug dealers, and "every pimp in the city liked him. . . . They would give him money and I'd go to them and sell tickets for him too."[43]

Even more unusual was Franklin's ability to retain the support of his conventional parishioners as he opened the church doors to the Hastings Street habitués. Teachers, lawyers, and insurance agents mingled each Sunday with working people, some with well-paying union jobs but the majority far poorer. Among them were sprinkled musicians and other Hastings Street regulars. Franklin had an ability to cross social lines, to draw from the more respectable in his flock a sense of compassion for those less so. "Reverend Franklin taught me how to love people," Robbie McCoy, a religiously devout friend and admirer explained. He taught me how "to respect people. How to do for those persons who needed help." Franklin drew from people a better sense of themselves than they often thought possible. This Christian vision, together with his profound preaching power and charismatic appeal, stretched outward from the church sanctuary to create the possibility of a broad, inclusive community. Perhaps the deep impact of this power explains the extraordinary step taken by New Bethel in December 1950. Contrary to the Baptist tradition, which cherished each church's ability to call and to dismiss pastors from their pulpit, the congregation accepted C. L. Franklin "as a life time pastor of New Bethel Baptist Church by a majority vote (84–15)." For his part, the church minutes stated, C. L. agreed he would resign as pastor if two-thirds of the paid-up members voted him out or "at anytime that he became an open and public shame to the church." A lifetime contract at a major Afro-Baptist church, at age thirty-five—with little more than a decade of major church preaching behind him and only four years at New Bethel—was unusual among his peers. To have received it even as he prodded his members, at times to their discomfort, to expand the parameters of their faith's meaning in the world was extraordinary.[44]

The opening of New Bethel ten months later was a glorious affair, with festivities filling the week preceding the formal entrance into the church. On Tuesday, October 9, W. E. Ramsey and his congregation presented a program especially prepared for the "county, state, and city politicians" in attendance that evening. That Wednesday, New Bethel's Thomas Shelby directed a gospel celebration that featured Mahalia Jackson and Robert Anderson and his Chicago choir. Thursday brought M. L. Franklin to the pulpit, with a program emphasizing the involvement of business and professional people in the church. At all of these events large audiences, including people from throughout Detroit and even a delegation from Friendship Baptist in Buffalo, enthusiastically participated. Finally, on Sunday morning, October 14, a "massive parade," reminiscent "of huge religious crusades of the past," one reporter enthused, joyously made its way to the church. They gathered first at the Brewster Center and then processed throughout Paradise Valley: east to Hastings and then up Hastings to Alexandrine, a left to St. Antoine, a right onto Willis, then another right one block to Hastings before the marchers beheld the new stone-and-steel church. As they entered the building cries of surprise broke through the decorum. The interior was enormous, capable of seating twenty-five hundred people, and possessed a choir loft behind the pulpit with room for two hundred singers. Five murals dominated the sanctuary's high walls: three depicting the central mysteries of the Christian faith ("The Last Supper," "Jesus in Gethsemane," and "The Resurrection") "and two professional paintings of the admired pastor himself." Knotty-pine joists supported the ceiling, as they did the enormous balcony. Three floor-to-balcony windows on each side allowed ventilation and, in good weather, a position for the overflow crowd to witness services. Although incomplete (funds for office space, new pews, and the baptismal pool were yet to be raised), the $225,000 building was a stunning change from the former bowling alley.[45]

As the enormous crowd filled the church and settled in, the choir offered a hymn, and one of New Bethel's assistant ministers, Reverend J. T. Furcron, led a devotional service. More hymns followed, and then C. L. Franklin approached his new pulpit for the first time. His text that day was from the Book of Joshua, which recounts the Israelite conquest of the Promised Land in the decades following Moses' death. Specifically, Franklin selected the twelfth verse of the fourteenth chapter, where Caleb, now eighty-five, reminds Joshua of his efforts as a military scout forty-five years earlier against the Canaanites. Although the rest of his group betrayed their mission, Caleb persevered, and Moses promised him "the land whereon thy feet have trodden" after the Israelite conquest. "Now therefore give me this mountain," Caleb demanded of Joshua, who then awarded him Hebron.[46]

Franklin read the biblical text and then announced the sermon's central theme: "a man of high objective." He began with a detailed discussion of Caleb's history, emphasizing how Caleb had come through the Egyptian bondage, the exodus, and subsequent wanderings, and had always remained faithful to the goal of freedom for his people. In contrast, many of the Israelites lacked the will to follow their God's commands; resisted and even sought to harm their leader, Moses; and were willing to settle for bondage in Egypt. In a direct, bracing comment, he reminded his congregation on that joyous occasion that so many in biblical Israel "were willing to satisfy themselves with a second or third class citizenship in Egypt rather than face head-on the inevitable difficulties that one must encounter on the high road of adventure." Biblical Israel at this time was "so overcome with the slave psychology of Egypt that had been imposed upon them that they were willing to conspire against and even murder, the man who was leading them to that freedom."[47]

Certainly, the phrase "second or third class citizenship" had a contemporary rather than a purely biblical ring. Citizenship within Egypt was never a central issue for the Israelites in bondage, but that concept possessed vital meaning for blacks in postwar America. So, too, with his discussion of "the slave psychology of Egypt." While that had a clear biblical reference, it also carried a potent corollary within African American life: the portrait of Caleb whose faithfulness to his divine mission distinguished him from those who had internalized the oppressor's image of themselves. Here, in this new building, C. L. took a great step forward, using for the first known time the ritual of the sermon to challenge his people to free themselves. And as Franklin talked of that man of high objective, the parallel with New Bethel's pastor was not lost on many in the congregation. More than a building had risen.[48]

CHAPTER SIX

THOUGHTS OF LIBERATION

Just before ten o'clock in the morning on Thursday, February 28, 1952, Coleman Young, a thirty-four-year-old World War II veteran, settled into his chair in room 740 of the United States Federal Building in downtown Detroit. His was not a voluntary appearance, and his lawyer, George W. Crockett Jr., accompanied him. Together, these two black men observed Congressman John S. Wood, Democrat of Georgia and chair of the Un-American Activities Committee of the United States House of Representatives, gather his notes and hold a final brief consultation with his counsel. Then in its fourth day of public hearings investigating the threat of Communist subversion in the auto industry, the committee had already cleansed one local media outlet of a presumed traitor: Joseph Bernstein, labeled a Communist official in the hearings on Tuesday, found himself fired from his position as a layout artist for the *Detroit News* the following day. But three days earlier, as all in that room well knew, a federal appellate court had upheld the conviction of Julius and Ethel Rosenberg for revealing atomic secrets to the Soviet Union. As the chairman gaveled the session to order, a bevy of regional and national print journalists quickened their attention, and the technicians opened the radio microphones that would broadcast the hearing live throughout the Detroit region.[1]

Young's examination began innocently enough. Responding to the committee counsel's queries, Young explained his background—Alabama born but reared in Detroit's Black Bottom after his parents migrated in the 1920s—and employment history since graduating high school in 1937, much of which involved positions within various trade unions in the city. But very quickly, the battle was engaged. Frank Tavenner, counsel for the committee, lectured Young that he expected cooperation in uncovering the threat of Communist infiltration in the numerous organizations the witness had joined. Young bristled. He informed Tavenner that he would not "react only in such a manner that this committee may desire me. In other words, I might have answers you might not like." Tavenner immediately followed with, "Are you now a member of the Communist Party?" Young refused to answer, citing the Fifth Amendment's constitutional guarantee against self-incrimination, as well as "my rights under the first amendment, which provides for freedom of speech, sanctity and privacy of political beliefs and associates, and, further, since I have no purpose of being here as a stool pigeon, I am not prepared to give any information on any of my associates or [their] political thoughts." Undeterred, Tavenner then asked Young about his involvement in the National Negro Congress—"That word is 'Negro', not 'Niggra,'" Young interrupted. Admonished by the chair not to argue with counsel, Young retorted: "It isn't my purpose to argue. As a Negro, I resent the slurring of the name of my race."[2]

Accused of being uncooperative, Young responded sharply. "I consider the denial of the right to vote to large numbers of people all over the South un-American, and I consider"—he was cut off but quickly regained the initiative—"I consider the activities of this committee, as it cites people for allegedly being a Communist, as un-American activities." In a direct exchange with Chairman Wood, who proudly informed the witness that he had received all of the "112 Negro votes cast" in his Georgia district in the last election, Young's anger was barely containable. "I happen to know," he informed the Congressman, that "in Georgia, Negro people are prevented from voting by virtue of terror, intimidation, and lynchings. It is my contention you would not be in Congress today if it were not for the legal restrictions on voting on the part of my people."[3]

Added Young: "I can assure you I have had no part in the hanging or bombing of Negroes in the South. I have not been responsible for firing a person from his job for what I think are his beliefs, or what somebody thinks he believes in, and things of that sort. That is the hysteria that has been swept up by this committee." Young's testimony revealed a verbal style deeply grounded in African American oral traditions, reflecting the creative use of language heard daily on Hastings Street's corners, in Mississippi's juke joints, in Sunday sermons, and in beauty shops and barbershops across black America.[4]

Coleman Young, all too aware of the broader political climate, never thought his testimony would have any effect on the committee itself. Pugnacious by nature, he simply would not—perhaps could not—let statements he so deeply disagreed with pass unchallenged. But the tone and texture of his testimony had another intended purpose. Since the late 1930s, Young's political activity sought every opportunity to challenge attitudes of both blacks and whites concerning the place of blacks in American life. He knew that the dimensions of room 740 were limited, but he was acutely conscious of the radio microphones. Unwittingly, the congressman had given Young a platform far broader than he had ever had before, and unlike some witnesses, he grasped it enthusiastically. His vision of justice and democracy, lofted across the airwaves, infiltrated the homes, shops, and workplaces of Detroiters, black and white. Many in both communities sharply disagreed with him, as the helpful testimony of black leaders Edward N. Turner and Shelton Tappes before the committee indicated. But Young's words and uncompromising demeanor challenged many, in black Detroit particularly, to question accepted categories and beliefs. In this way the unwilling, and by inference, un-American witness and the self-righteous, and by their very definition, American committee members oddly joined together to further the political education of black Detroit.[5]

Harry Kincaid was one of many who listened. Twenty-six at the time, born and raised in the small town of Ruby, in Leflore County, Mississippi, Kincaid had arrived in Detroit after finishing high school in 1945. Staying with an uncle until drafted into the military, he served two years in the Army and then returned to Detroit. An intelligent and curious man who possessed ambitious visions of future possibilities for himself and his people, he returned south in 1948 to attend Southern University in Louisiana. Three semesters later he was back in Detroit, a member of Second Baptist and, as a worker at the Packard Motor Car plant, a member of the United Auto Workers as well. By 1951, he began attending New Bethel's services after Second Baptist had finished, where he heard something in C. L. Franklin's preaching he found sorely lacking in Λ. Λ. Banks's sermons. With the same restless curiosity an inspired Kincaid listened to the broadcasts of Young's testimony the following February. That was the moment, he thought, "when a lot of people [first] were attracted to him . . . [and] along the way a lot of us respected him for his standing up and learned more about his past activities." Later in 1952, when Harry Kincaid left Second Baptist and formally joined New Bethel, his curiosity and emerging political consciousness found a nurturing political home.[6]

Others had similar reactions. Marc Stepp, a Kentucky native who joined the United Auto Workers at a Detroit Chrysler plant in 1942, pointed to the hearings as the source of the respect he held for Young, despite their many political disagreements. Grace Lee Boggs, an Asian American woman married to a black man, understood from her new friends and neighbors when she arrived in Detroit in 1953 that "Coleman Young had just become a hero in the black community." For many black Detroiters, Young's challenge proclaimed at its core that "if being for human rights makes me a Communist, then I'm a Communist."[7]

They were far from alone, though a quick investigation by a visitor to Detroit about this time might have reported that blacks had little interest in political issues. There were no elected black officials; political commentators in the Michigan *Chronicle* might be dismissed as self-interested elites; and the majority of residents appeared resigned to long work weeks punctuated by Saturday night revels and Sunday morning atonements. But that would be misleading. Just below the surface skimmed by such a hasty inspection surged varied black voices struggling to integrate the rural southern tones of their first language with the staccato, machine-driven rhythms they experienced daily on the Motor City's streets and in its gritty workplaces. Recalled Boggs: "In barber shops, on front porches, at funerals and weddings, folks testified from their own personal experience, wondering collectively why white folks were so inhuman and usually concluding that it was because they were more interested in material gain than in human relations." Opinions varied and sharp debates, often accompanied by ritualistic insults ("the dozens") delivered with an improvisational verbal skill that belied the lack of formal education, were the norm. Such exchanges were a form of entertainment, to be sure, but they also encouraged exploration of ideas that could transform individuals.[8]

*　　*　　*　　*　　*

Black southern migrants swelled Detroit's African American population by more than 600 percent between 1920 and 1950, and most arrived with their hopes for industrial jobs etched on their farm-weathered faces. At its best, migration initially shocked one's sensibilities. "Chicago, here I come," Muddy Waters remembered anticipating as he left Mississippi. But his initial reaction to the city emerged in a much lower register: "That big empty city, here I am, little lost black boy in it." Margaret Branch, at a far younger age, experienced her own confusion. She came to Detroit at age eleven from the same North Memphis neighborhood where C. L. had preached monthly during the late 1930s. North Memphis had no sidewalks, indoor plumbing had just recently been made mandatory for new construction, and she had never bathed in anything but a portable tin tub. Outside, the family's chickens patrolled the backyard. Detroit was so strange, even when the difference was most welcome. As she met other youngsters, the concern with style stunned her. "Everybody laughed at me" at first, thought her "a country looking bumpkin." Down home, she had one pair of shoes for the year; in Detroit, all but the most poor usually did better than that.[9]

As impressive as the black percentile increase was, the actual number of whites who migrated was nearly double that of African Americans. Whites of every background, heavily from the South and from small, midwestern towns, accounted for 70 percent of the city's population increase during these decades. These men and women brought with them dominant American attitudes about race, including a fierce commitment to segregation in both public and private life, and their attitudes resonated with those of many native-born white Detroiters at every economic level. Despite the numerical disparity, whites' anxieties mushroomed in the face of the continued black migration. For their part, blacks watched with anger and dread as more and more white southern men patrolled their neighborhoods in the blue police uniforms that all too often provided the officers a license to act beyond the law. Detroit's police "had always been cruel" toward blacks, hotelier Sunnie Wilson wrote of this era. Their overt "racial animosity" he thought a consequence "of a leftover Southern hatred for blacks" that the many southern-born patrolmen "were raised on . . . and they fought to maintain a sense of superiority."[10]

Detroit was not the Deep South, but it was also anything but a promised land for its black residents. Arthur Johnson, the southern-born executive secretary of the Detroit NAACP, recalled on arriving in Detroit in 1950 that "I felt, number one, that the air was a bit freer in Detroit. . . . But I soon came to realize that this was only a kind of surface thing, that race was as much a daily factor in the lives of African Americans here in Detroit as in Alabama, Georgia, Mississippi." The culture of race played out differently in each region, but in both, the majority of whites found it inconceivable that black people had any demands on the democratic process worthy of attention.[11]

Two events occurred in Detroit during the war years that took the measure of the white majority's attitudes. In 1942, city and federal authorities had restricted the new federal housing project, the Sojourner Truth Homes, for black occupancy only. Situated in northeast Detroit, close by the black middle-class enclave of Conant Gardens, the Sojourner Truth buildings sat amid a large Polish Catholic parish, St. Louis the King. From the initial discussions of the project, the parish pastor, Father Constantine Djiuk, had organized resistance to any thought of black residents in the neighborhood. On many a Sunday he preached of how "we have the Jews and Niggers making a combination [in the city elections]," even as those same Jews "cheat the Niggers worse than they used to cheat the Polish peasants who trusted them." On February 28, moving-in day at the Sojourner Truth Homes, members of St. Louis the King, augmented by irate whites from other areas and armed with bats, clubs, pipes, and some firearms, had attacked the first trucks to arrive that morning, packed with the new residents' worldly possessions. Over the next two days, police had largely watched as whites attacked blacks; but when blacks massed to retaliate, the police had moved in force against them. Of the 220 people arrested, 109 were held for trial—all but three of them African Americans. By May, black residents assigned to apartments were finally able to occupy their homes, but the pattern of events in 1942 would be repeated across the next decades in numerous Detroit neighborhoods. Black Detroit's need for additional housing beyond Paradise Valley encountered intense violence from whites adamant in defense of their neighborhood. Often, as at St. Louis the King, they invoked divine law as justification. The police, unless directly ordered by superiors, usually intervened to support white protesters.[12]

A year later, well into spring 1943, "hate strikes"—work stoppages by unionized white workers who refused to work alongside unionized black workers in the auto industry—had continued to exacerbate racial tensions already rubbed raw in the intense struggle for housing in this crowded, rigidly segregated city. These feelings erupted at the one place in the city where large groups of blacks and whites jostled shoulder-to-shoulder seeking amusement and relief from the summer heat. On Sunday, June 20, a fight had broken out between black and white youth at Belle Isle, an island in the Detroit River accessible by a footbridge from Grand Boulevard East. White sailors had joined the fray, and within hours rumors spread through both races of a black woman and her baby thrown off the bridge and of white girls raped by black youth. The city had imploded, and over the following two days thirty-five people died, among them twenty-five blacks and a white policeman. Nearly seven hundred were injured, and more than $2 million of property damage had occurred. State and federal troops had occupied the city. Black soldiers in a segregated unit at a nearby Army base, armed and concerned for their families and friends, had commandeered trucks to take them to Detroit. They were stopped at the gates of the base, their five leaders arrested by military police, and the city had slowly simmered down to its normal levels of segregation and its attendant tension.[13]

The 1943 riot taught different lessons to different groups within Detroit. While the presence of white southerners on the police force was troublesome for blacks, the efforts by some post-riot commentators to blame the violence on recent white southern migrants, the "hillbillies," created a convenient scapegoat to obscure just how widely accepted racist attitudes were within white Detroit. More than 65 percent of Detroit's police force was from the Midwest, not the South, and the persistent resistance to black neighbors came from almost every Euro-American ethnic group. With some important exceptions, the June riots had brought a rededication to segregation in neighborhoods and in public areas such as restaurants, hotels, and Olympia Stadium, a rededication that had the support, active or implicit, of clergy, businessmen, elected politicians, and most congregants of white Protestant and Catholic parishes. Those with means continued to flee to the surrounding suburbs. Those whites without such means, or just stubborn, remained to fight black expansion politically and in the streets as well.[14]

Black Detroiters, however, had learned a different lesson from the experience. Most realized that to organize armed resistance, other than in self-defense, was near suicidal. Even when defending themselves, the costs would be high. Some, including those involved in the union movement or with the local NAACP, appreciated the power of government action. The hate strikes, for example, had ceased as the result of joint action by the national office of the United Auto Workers and the federal government. To force public debate over equal treatment in employment, housing, schools, and public safety, however, would require the political mobilization of a black population that was ever remaking itself through continued migration.[15]

Some black Detroiters had been active in electoral politics since the 1920s, with but limited success. Then, the legacy of Abraham Lincoln's Emancipation Proclamation remained strong and bound most black voters to the Republican Party. The alternative, a national Democratic Party controlled to a large extent by the same white southern racists black migrants had left behind gladly, offered little. During the 1930s, however, that began to change as the social programs enacted by the New Deal under Roosevelt won over many whites and blacks alike. Locally, three black political activists—lawyers Henry Bledsoe and Joseph Craigen and mortician Charles C. Diggs Sr.—organized black voters for the Democrats in 1932. Attracted to Roosevelt's policies, these men also opposed the Republican governor's defense of state contractors who refused to hire African Americans. Diggs was elected as a Democrat to the Michigan Senate in 1936, as was Reverend Horace White a few years later. Although the Democratic Party now drew more strength from black voters, Republicans still garnered significant black votes, particularly in city elections, into the 1940s. Anti-Democratic sentiment remained strong, and many blacks had profoundly ambiguous feelings about the United Auto Workers' presence in local Democratic politics. Racism by rank-and-file white unionists, and the relegation of those blacks hired to the most dangerous and least remunerative jobs, affected the political thinking of many.[16]

The 1945 municipal elections for mayor and Common (City) Council marked a new turn in black electoral activity. In the months preceding the primary that August, white neighborhood associations throughout the city organized home owners to sign restrictive covenants, agreeing never to sell to blacks. The well-organized white residents of Detroit's Southwest neighborhood, near Ford's Rouge River plant, arrived thirty-five hundred strong at City Hall in March and successfully prevailed upon the Common Council to reject plans for a black housing project in their area. In this atmosphere, African American leaders and activists joined with UAW leaders to create a slate of candidates for the coming election. Meeting at the Lucy Thurman YWCA in Paradise Valley, they selected Richard Frankensteen, a UAW vice president, as their candidate for mayor and endorsed three men for Common Council, one of whom was Reverend Charles A. Hill, pastor of Hartford Avenue Baptist Church. No black American had been elected to the city's governing body since 1918, when the system of citywide elections for each council seat replaced the more decentralized, district-based selection process. African American political and religious leaders had earlier agreed to sponsor but one nominee—Hill—in a concerted effort to break the council's all-white composition.[17]

Both Frankensteen and Hill did well in the light voter turnout for the August primary. Frankensteen outpolled the incumbent mayor, Edward Jeffries, by some fourteen thousand votes, and Hill placed ninth among eighteen finalists chosen to contest for the nine council seats in the November election. But the primary proved to be the high point of their campaigns. The election's dominant issues revolved around race and the control of neighborhoods, and white Detroit organized effectively at the polls to defeat any candidate deemed sympathetic to black needs. A low black turnout hurt too, and both Frankensteen and Hill lost decisively. Renewed efforts nonetheless followed. In 1947, Hill ran again, with Coleman Young as his campaign manager, as did three other black candidates. All four lost. The following year, Hill ran once more, managed this time by George W. Crockett, the Florida-born, University of Michigan–trained lawyer who settled in Detroit in 1943. Running as a Democrat who supported Henry Wallace, Roosevelt's former vice president and then a third-party presidential candidate, Hill faced fierce attacks for alleged Communist leanings. He lost yet again, as he would in 1949 as well. No black candidates for council won election during these years, regardless of their political positions.[18]

By 1951, when Hill ran and lost for the fifth time, Charles J. Wartman, then the city editor of the Michigan *Chronicle*, published a two-part series on the question: "Can Negroes Gain Seats in Common Council?" Wartman understood the racism at work in the city, as he did the barrier created by the citywide electoral system. He recognized as well how a black candidate's identification with white union leadership often generated opposition, even among black union members. Yet these were not in themselves the crux of the persistent electoral failures. "Hundreds of thousands of eligible Negro voters are still staying away from the polls in droves," he argued, and most of them were not even registered to vote. Wartman blamed the leadership "of the Negro community [that] has not stimulated the Negro sufficiently where politics are concerned." The destructive competition between Detroit whites and blacks, he continued, where one group fears "that the presence of another group threatens them," could not be overcome by a complacent black electorate.[19]

However instructive the articles were, Wartman's focus on the role of black elites blinded him to the swirling crosscurrents that coursed through black Detroit. Southern migrants arrived in successive waves, and it proved difficult to weave a collective political consciousness quickly amid the unceasing motion of migration. White Detroit's violent reactions made it only more so. Complicating this process even further were the multiple allegiances black Detroiters held. Church membership alone, the focal point for so many, itself offered a series of options, with competing denominational affiliations, preaching styles, worship rituals, and understandings. As the one institution that collectively celebrated fundamental elements of African American culture, however, the church remained, with all its variations, the closest thing the city had to a mass black organization, complete with an interdenominational ministerial alliance. Certainly, far fewer blacks were in the union movement, although their influence within their own community exceeded their numbers. In the union hall, they learned important skills for organizing people, making public presentations, and calling and running meetings. They also learned to be artful navigators, maneuvering among white union members, the more liberal national leadership, and other blacks who, because of the prevalent racism, doubted the entire undertaking. In these and other groups, moreover, there were as well veterans, men who had risked their lives for American democracy and who were determined "not to be second class citizens." These veterans, Marc Stepp recalled of his and his friends' attitudes, returned to the Motor City, saying: "No, we aren't going to do that anymore, that's all. You screwed up my dad [following World War I], you aren't going to screw me up."[20]

Arguably, a significant portion of nonelite black Detroit in the early 1950s were less like Coleman Young or Marc Stepp. Generations of oppressive conditions in their home states had subverted the belief that they possessed the right to a public voice or to the political power necessary to alter the conditions that so viciously structured their lives. William Bundy's experience in 1946 reflected this dilemma. A graduate of Morgan State College, Bundy lived on Cherrylawn Avenue near Seven Mile Drive, in the small black community in the northwest section of the city. Unable to find a job in a postwar economy flooded with returning veterans, Bundy became a "cadet clerk" in a program initiated by the local Urban League to obtain black men and women positions, even menial ones, among the city's major employers. The city's water board hired him as a meter reader for residential neighborhoods. Quickly, white homeowners protested, finding the presence of a black man in uniform on their property a threat, and city officials banned Bundy from his job. The incident itself is far less dramatic than other racial assaults the city's black citizens experienced, but it was also a common occurrence. Black municipal workers were overwhelmingly grouped among the unskilled and most seasonal employees, an experience not dissimilar to that of black auto workers. No black resident, regardless of occupation, could eat in downtown restaurants, try on clothes at Hudson's, the major department store, or if they had the disposable cash, hail a cab home from downtown. The unexceptional nature of these insults, relentlessly flowing through the course of one's daily life, sapped the spirit and quieted the voice of many in patterns long familiar from past southern exposure. In a city many black migrants still viewed through prepolitical lenses, calls to electoral combat could easily seem irrelevant to those preoccupied with daily survival.[21]

To move large numbers toward the public engagement Charles Wartman advocated required the full resources of black Detroit across all social and economic divides. In the intertwined associations of kin, friendship, and membership in a bewildering variety of organizations grew the links that might bind black Detroit. But during the 1950s, by far the most common gathering place for blacks of every description was the black church, the community's core institution. This was C. L. Franklin's domain.[22]

*   *   *   *   *

When Franklin led New Bethel into its new building in October 1951, the structure's impressive design and spacious interior signified the expectation of even greater prominence to come. Rooted again at the corner of Hastings and Willis, the congregation grew quickly and claimed seventy-eight hundred members by October 1953. Although membership records are not available, the recollections of numerous congregants suggest a church population primarily of southern origins, the vast majority of whom had migrated in numerous cycles since the 1920s. Alabama and Mississippi backgrounds predominated, and the vast majority of parishioners were working people, day laborers, maids, janitors, and the like. Most were not union members. There were as well numerous small-business people, a slice of Paradise Valley's prostitutes, gamblers, and pimps, and a self-selected layer of the professionals Charles Wartman considered a world apart from the majority. Many parishioners, like their pastor, had not finished grade school, and relatively few had any college training.[23]

Franklin was not the only minister in the city to preach to so varied an audience, nor was his the only church that experienced so dramatic an increase in its members. But his reputation both as a preacher and as a compassionate pastor raced through and beyond Detroit. Repeatedly during the 1950s, southern black migrants arrived in Detroit with only Franklin's name as their final destination. Whether they appeared at the church or at his front door on Boston Boulevard, C. L. swung into action, calling on a network of New Bethel activists organized into the church's various departments and boards. Recalled Sylvia Penn, calls from the pastor along the lines of "'I got to get these folks a place to stay, they're here on my porch,'" were not infrequent. "'I've got to get them some food, they got three children with them, they got two children, and we've got to help find them a job,'" C. L. would say. "And," Penn proudly stated, "he never turned anybody down."[24]

Franklin's compassion infused his sermons, but he also used his pulpit to discomfort his audience, to challenge those still at ease with a "slave psychology." For C. L., the essential starting point was not politics, however, but the deeper realm of individual personality.

In "Moses at the Red Sea," delivered in the mid-1950s, C. L. began by identifying the day's text—Exodus, chapter 14—but did not cite those comforting lines that recounted the Red Sea parting, the Israelites escaping, and the closing water engulfing Pharaoh's pursuing army. Instead, C. L. directed his audience to earlier verses, where the Lord chastised a Moses who beseeched for help rather than lead his people. God demanded Moses to "lift thou up thy rod, and stretch out thine hand over the seas, and divide it," allowing the Israelites safe passage. C. L. then announced the theme of the sermon: "Facing a crisis with God. Facing a crisis with God."[25]

Franklin began, as always, in a narrative voice. Israel's liberation was part of her "marching toward nationhood," but that goal reflected more than simply a political purpose. "God had a destiny for Israel, God had a role in history for Israel to play." Nor was this solely a metaphor. This biblical God—C. L.'s personal God as well—intervened in history, in the daily affairs of humanity. In the hands of some, the promise of God's intervention could encourage quiescence, a passive reading of the familiar phrase, "God will provide." But Franklin taught that God acted through individuals in

Picking "white gold," near Memphis, c. 1930s.

(Courtesy of Mississippi Valley Collection, University of Memphis)

Expectations for the future, late 1930s: moving day into public housing (Foote Homes), Memphis.

(Courtesy of Memphis and Shelby County Room, Memphis Public Library)

First Baptist Church Bungalow, Memphis, 1930s.

(Courtesy of Margaret Branch and the Douglass Alumni Association)

*C. L. Franklin, pastor, New Salem
Missionary Baptist Church, early 1940s.*
(Courtesy of Reverend Mary Moore, pastor, New Salem Missionary
Baptist Church, Memphis)

*Barbara Siggers Franklin (1917–1952),
1940s.*
(Courtesy of Erma Franklin)

*Rufus Thomas (1917–2001), Beale Street
regular, church member, and soul singer
extraordinaire, c. 1954.*
(Courtesy of Mississippi Valley Collection, University of Memphis)

*Mrs. Lorene Thomas (1919–2000), New
Salem church member for almost sixty years,
married to Rufus Thomas.*
(Courtesy of Reverend Mary Moore, pastor, New Salem Missionary
Baptist Church, Memphis)

Sold Two Millions In Bonds

THE COLORED DIVISION OF THE WEST TENNESSEE WAR FINANCE COMMITTEE

Who Were Responsible for the Sale of Over One Million Dollars of Bonds Last April.

GEO. W. LEE
Director, Manager of Atlanta Life Insurance Company

BLAIR T. HUNT
Principal, Booker T. Washington High School

L. C. SHARPE
Principal, Douglas School

J. ASHTON HAYES
Principal, Manassas High School

O. T. WESTBROOKS
District Manager, Union Protective Assurance Company

JOHN ARNOLD
Executive Secretary, Friendly Clinic President Junior Negro Chamber of Commerce

H. D. WHALUM
President, Union Protective Assurance Company

REV. W. H. BREWSTER
Pastor East Trigg Baptist Church

REV. J. L. CAMPBELL
Pastor St. Stephens Church

DOCTOR W. A. BISSON
President, Bluff City Medical Association

S. W. QUALLS
President S. W. Qualls & Son

J. H. JOHNSON
Pastor Morning View, Little Rock Churches

REV. ARTHUR W. WOMACK
Pastor Collins Chapel C. M. E. Church

EDDIE HAYES
President Negro Chamber Commerce

DOCTOR S. B. HICKMAN
Exalted Ruler, Beale St. Elks

DOCTOR U. S. WALTON

REV. D. L. GARRETT
Warner Temple Church

ROBERT JONES
Business Manager Colored Carpenters Union

MATTHEW THORNTON
Mayor of Beale St.

MRS. MARY MURPHY
President of City Federated Clubs

MISS LUCY CAMPBELL
Teacher Booker T. Washington High School

MISS ALICE DEAN
Cashier Atlanta Life Insurance Company

MRS. ROBERT JACKSON
Daughter Ruler of Elks

T. H. HAYES
President T. H. Hayes & Sons

MRS. ADDIE DANDRIDGE JONES
Teacher at Manassas High School

REV. W. E. MACK
President Pastor Alliance

REV. L. C. FRANKLIN
Pastor New Salem Baptist Church

R. S. LEWIS, JR.
Manager R. S. Lewis Funeral Home

W. F. NABORS
Manager Dixie Homes

DOCTOR A. N. KITTRELLE

DOCTOR W. O. SPEIGHT
Director Union Protective Assurance Co.

J. A. SWAYZE
Vice President Universal Life Insurance Company

M. S. STUART
Vice President Universal Life Insurance Company

H. E. OATES
Manager Foote Home

ROBERT WRIGHT

ALONZO LOCKE
Head Waiter Peabody Hotel

NAHANIEL (NAT) WILLIAMS
Professor History, Booker T. Washington High School

REV. ROY LOVE
President Ministers Alliance

REV. H. B. BRUNSON
Pastor Mt. Moriah Baptist Church

REV. FLOYD DANIELS
Pastor Progressive Baptist Church

C.L. (front row, second from left), 1943, among the leaders of the war bond drive in black Memphis. His name is incorrectly given as L.C.

(Courtesy of Mississippi Valley Collection, University of Memphis)

Advertising poster for one of Memphis's most famous gospel quartets, c. 1945.

(Courtesy of Mississippi Valley Collection, University of Memphis)

Reverend and Mrs. C. L. Franklin in a formal pose, c. 1945–1946.

(Courtesy of Reverend E. L. Branch)

Laying the cornerstone for New Bethel, Hastings Street, 1951, with full Masonic rites by the Prince Hall Masons. C.L., facing camera, is wearing his Masonic apron.
(Courtesy of Erma Franklin)

C.L. and his new Cadillac in the driveway of his home on Boston Boulevard, 1952.
(Courtesy of Erma Franklin and Sabrina Garrett-Owens)

The Franklins, August 1952, at first pastor's anniversary following Barbara's death. From left: Cecil (12), Erma (14), C.L. (37), Carolyn (8), Aretha (10).
(Courtesy of Erma Franklin)

Clara Ward, inscribed to C.L., c. 1950.

(Courtesy of Erma Franklin)

Part of Franklin's touring group, on Hastings Street, 1950s. From left: Thomas Shelby, minister of music; Little Sammy Bryant, soloist; others unidentified. New Bethel's dining room is visible in upper right.

(Courtesy of Erma Franklin and Sabrina Garrett-Owens)

Sunday night, New Bethel, Hastings Street, "the common frame of reference for the black church prototype," c. 1953. (Courtesy of Myra Perkins)

Reverend David Hudson in front of Joe Von Battle's Record Store on Hastings Street, c. 1954. Permanent advertising for C.L.'s records is partly visible on window to right.

(Courtesy of Reverend E. L. Branch)

Clara Ward, C.L., and unidentified man, relaxing in a nightclub, 1950s.
(Courtesy of Erma Franklin and Sabrina Garrett-Owens)

Men's Day, New Bethel, 1950s. From right: Judge Wade McCree, future Common Council member William T. Patrick, unknown, C.L., Congressman Charles Diggs Jr., Charles Diggs Sr., Congressman Adam Clayton Powell, unknown.
(Courtesy of Brenda Corbett)

In front of the pulpit at New Bethel, Hastings Street, c. 1955. From left: Cecil, Rachel, C.L., Erma, and Brenda Corbett.
(Courtesy of Brenda Corbett)

Part of the overflow crowd at Bethel AME Church, Frederick and St. Antoine Streets,
straining to hear the speeches at the mass meeting protesting the verdict in the trial
of Emmett Till's murderers.

(Courtesy of Walter P. Reuther Library, Wayne State University)

Women's Day,
New Bethel, 1950s.
From left:
Daisy Williams,
Catherine Pearson,
Bertha Bobo,
Eliza Butler, C.L.,
Sank Austin (chair,
Deacon's Board),
Dorothy Robinson,
Lobelia Moose,
Marguarette Martin,
Doris Gordon.

(Courtesy of Brenda Corbett)

Clara Ward, inscribed but unsigned (from the 1955 trip to Europe?).
(Courtesy of Erma Franklin and Sabrina Garrett-Owens)

The Franklins, late 1950s. Back: Erma, Aretha; front: Carolyn, C.L. (in silk smoking jacket), Cecil.
(Courtesy of Erma Franklin)

Eleventh anniversary as pastor, Gotham Hotel, 1957. Ben Kosins, of Kosins Clothiers, C.L.'s outfitter, presents gifts.
(Courtesy of Brenda Corbett)

C.L., undated (late 1950s?).
(Courtesy of Reverend E. L. Branch)

Aretha and her father, before their joint appearance at the W. C. Handy Music Festival in Memphis, 1961. The picture on the wall is of Handy.
(Courtesy of Mississippi Valley Collection, University of Memphis)

Pastor's anniversary, 1960. Front: Lucille Marshall, C.L.; back: Aretha, Cecil, Erma.
(Courtesy of Erma Franklin)

"March for Freedom," Woodward Avenue, June 23, 1963: Martin Luther King Jr., center, hand raised; to right, C.L.; to left, Benjamin McFall, Walter Reuther.

(Courtesy of Erma Franklin and Sabrina Garrett-Owens)

Expectations for the future, June 23, 1963.

. (Courtesy of Erma Franklin)

*Reverend Albert
Cleage addressing the
rally at Cobo Hall
that concluded the
March for Freedom
on June 23, 1963*
(Courtesy of Walter P. Reuther
Library, Wayne State University)

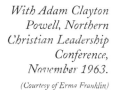

*With Adam Clayton
Powell, Northern
Christian Leadership
Conference,
November 1963.*
(Courtesy of Erma Franklin)

*C.L. with
Fannie Tyler,
his private
secretary, 1960s.*
(Courtesy of Fannie Tyler)

Rachel Franklin ("Big Moma"), C.L.
("Son"), and Carolyn, 1960s.
(Courtesy of Erma Franklin)

C.L., smartly dressed in a double-breasted
suit, cufflinks flashing, gesturing during a
press conference, March 31, 1969, as he
questions police conduct in the aftermath of
the New Bethel "shootout."
(Courtesy of Walter P. Reuther Library, Wayne State University)

C.L., ministerial cross
and chain prominently visible,
with attorney Nick Arvan,
leaving court following the
dismissal of charges against
C.L. for possessing marijuana,
May 29, 1969.

(Courtesy of Walter P. Reuther Library,
Wayne State University)

The Franklins at one of Aretha's concerts, c. late 1960s (New York City?). From left: Earline (Cecil's wife), Brenda Corbett, Carolyn, Cecil, C.L., Aretha, Erma.

(Courtesy of Erma Franklin)

In pastor's office at New Bethel, following a revival service, late 1960s. From left: Mel Hatcher, Reverend Leroy Jenkins (evangelist), Beverli Greenleaf, Janet Gelyard, C.L., and Ben Washington (chair, Trustee Board).

(Courtesy of Beverli Greenleaf)

C.L. with friends, 1970s.
From left: O'Neil Swanson,
C.L., Ben Washington,
Mayor Coleman Young,
Mr. Waterman,
Dr. Claud Young.
(Courtesy of Brenda Corbett)

With Coretta Scott King, Atlanta, early 1970s.
(Courtesy of Erma Franklin)

Waiting for the congregation's
response from New Bethel's pulpit,
on Linwood, August 22, 1977.
(Courtesy of Walter P. Reuther Library,
Wayne State University)

order to bring his ultimate plans to fruition. In this fashion, human concerns were central matters of faith. God inspired, and those so uplifted changed not only their lives, but the world, on his behalf. In short, God wanted you to find your voice and use it. Indeed, the very trials and pains endured during captivity in Egypt prepared the Israelites for freedom. Teaching as he preached, C. L. held that this was not an accident, for "in every crisis, God raises up a Moses. . . . His name may be Moses or his name may be Joshua or his name may be David, or his name, you understand, may be Abraham Lincoln or Frederick Douglass or George Washington Carver, but in every crisis God raises up a Moses, especially where the destiny of his people is concerned."

It was not always easy. Moses struggled to lead his people toward freedom, but the difficulties he and they encountered came not just from Pharaoh. As harsh as those trials were, "sometimes some people can become so adjusted to slavery and oppression that they are not willing to give it up." C. L. reminded his audience that even as they left their Egyptian bondage, joyously "singing Moses' praises" and projecting "visions of prosperity," the Israelites did not grasp the basic reality "that any people who traveled the high road to security, to justice, to all the privileges that come to citizens, must pay the price. . . . Everybody wants justice." The preacher pointedly informed the audience, "Everybody wants freedom, everybody wants what's coming to them, but very few of us take the time to think about the price that must be paid for these things and the responsibility that goes along with the achievement of them."

With that admonition still reverberating, Franklin brought his listeners back to "the brink of the Red Sea" where the Israelites could hear "the rattling of the chariot wheels of Pharaoh" coming up fast. Some criticized Moses publicly for leading the freedom movement and agitated for a surrender that would avoid a battle even as it would "lead them back into the oppression of Egypt." It was at this point that C. L.—still in his narrative voice, his teaching voice, although he had already musically tuned, in key, certain words and phrases—embodied the voice of God chastising a Moses who stood confused before his people's anger. "The instrument of deliverance is within your hands," Franklin's God insisted. "It's within your possession. The way out, the powers that need to be brought into exertion, is within you. . . . What are you crying about, Moses? What are you look-ing for? What do you think that you want? . . . Stretch out the rod that's in your hands. I don't have a new instrument to give you, I don't have a new suggestion for you, I do not have a new plan. Your course has already been charted by destiny. Stretch out the rod that's in your hand."

As C. L. preached it, to trust in the Lord was no otherworldly escape. Instead, it was an enormously difficult task that required, in faith, an indi-vidual transformation of consciousness that could only be achieved through an intimate grappling with deeply embedded fears. But the possi-ble rewards, too, were great, in the promise of a reconstituted vision of self and, in time, as a transformed community, a better world:

> *What am I saying? I'm saying that sometimes in the midst of our own crises, in the midst of our own life-problems, in the midst of the things that we find ourselves involved in, sometimes the power of our deliverance is in our own power and in our own possession. What you need, my brothers and sisters, is within you. First of all, it's faith in God, and second, faith in yourself, and thirdly, the will and determination to put these into practice. The man who stands and simply cries will never go over his Red Seas. The man who stands or the woman who simply stands and com-plains, stands before your Red Seas or your own problems, and simply cries, will never find the way out.*

A complex transformation had just occurred. What had begun with an emphasis on the role of leaders in freedom movements, which would have been familiar to Charles Wartman, had evolved into an insistence that in-dividuals, regardless of social standing or education, had within themselves the power to be a Moses, a Lincoln, or a Douglass in their own personal and social context. They were, in fact, *already* somebody; they need but rec-ognize that. The idea that one could postpone deliverance until the ap-pearance of an extraordinary leader was, C. L. made clear, false comfort. Many had so internalized the pain of migration, the deep hurt of racism that they had, for solace, only an idealized, otherworldly Jesus or the at-tractions of Hastings Street's drugs and alcohol. The goal of Franklin's ministry was to reach these people, to help them find the source within themselves to reinvigorate their lives. In this sense, C. L.'s version of Moses in this moment of crisis was not overtly political; it was far more important than that. John Lewis, who avidly studied Franklin's sermons while a student at Nashville's American Baptist Theological Seminary in the late 1950s, caught this quality succinctly. A Franklin sermon is "good for the people on a Sunday morning," Lewis noted. "But it is also good for you Monday and Tuesday, and the rest of the week and for days and years to come."[26]

As he began to whoop, Franklin's message remained consistent, but he brought that modern message home in tones redolent of the rural South:

And now the Lord said,
"Hold out your rod
over the sea."
O Lord.
And listen!
When you exert the powers
that God has given you,
when you go to your extremity
you'll find God waiting for you.

C. L. also offered a caution: human suffering, and thus evil, was all too real, and the desired transformation may yet require patience. "Don't lose faith," his rhythmic voice insisted, "and don't give up courage. Oh, wait on the Lord."[27]

As always in C. L.'s sermons, the qualities he infused his biblical actors with were to a degree autobiographical. Traditional Christian analysis informed his preaching, as did his continued voracious reading in theology, history, and literature, and frequent discussions, at times seminarlike in their intensity, with other ministers. But the message he preached reflected those influences through the prism of his heightened self-consciousness. As a youth in Mississippi, C. L. had struggled with self-doubts similar to many his audiences knew. Yet through faith, reason, and the support of others, he had found a way to stretch out his hands, to trust in himself and in his God. From Mississippi, Jasper Williams Jr., the son and nephew of Franklin's close friends, reflected that C. L. "brought with him . . . [the idea] that he could be who he wanted to be, do what he wanted to do, have what he wanted to have." Charlie Thompson, who came up from Mississippi in the 1950s, emphasized that C. L. touched especially those with a "lower reputation" of themselves because the sermons let them know "that he see[s] them as having self-worth, they was put here for a purpose." Strengthened by his pastor's powerful efforts "in building confidence," Thompson quit his menial job, signed on as a vacuum-cleaner salesman, "and I went in there on fire. I had developed, just listening to him . . . good work ethics, good work habits." Harry Kincaid offered similar testimony. C. L.'s influence on his family, he deeply believed, resulted in all six children attending college and succeeding in the world. His friend and pastor preached "about religion and the total man. . . . Not just in church service, but during the week when you are out there, as the common street term is, 'hustling,' trying to make ends meet." Franklin's ability to address both his faith and the world about him touched Kincaid profoundly: "That's what I meant by total religion, religion covering the total man." That, too, is what C. L. Franklin meant.[28]

*   *   *   *   *

C. L. had never given up on a radio program, and even before the euphoria at taking possession of the new church building ebbed, he got it. Within weeks he initiated broadcasts of the 10:00 P.M. Sunday evening service over a Dearborn radio station. The situation was not ideal. Although physically adjacent to Detroit's western boundary, the station's weak signal could not reach all the neighborhoods east of Woodward. While the agent with whom C. L. worked promised to move him to a Detroit station at the first opportunity, the continued spotty reception created a growing financial deficit for the program. There were no sponsors to cover production costs, and the poor signal limited the pool of potential new church attendees and their contributions. Quickly, a $900 debt accumulated. Worried church officers approached their minister, concerned that the debt could only grow and threaten New Bethel's financial stability, and they requested that their pastor terminate the broadcast. Their concern was real, but C. L. saw in it a potential opportunity. Irked at the "constant grumbling and complaining" he heard throughout the congregation and possessed of a supreme confidence in his abilities, C. L. countered the delegation's request with an offer of his own. "You just turn Sunday night over to me," he paraphrased his words twenty-five years later. "I will liquidate the indebtedness, and the church will be relieved of any responsibility for this deficit, or any responsibility involving the broadcast." As Deacon Willie Todd, a soloist in the Radio Choir in 1951, remembered: "So they granted him, told him he could have the broadcast and all the proceeds."[29]

Whether he knew what was to come next or not, C. L.'s assumption of all responsibility came at a most opportune time. A week later, the agent moved the program to Detroit's WJLB, at the time the major transmitter of black music in the city. Since 1946, it offered programs of jazz, gospel, blues, and rhythm and blues; since 1950, the station's enormously popular disc jockey, Leroy (Rocking with Leroy) White, dominated the black music market. Immediately, Franklin was a hit. "I started preaching, and the people seemed as it were to come up out of the ground," he remembered. Many who listened were stunned. The radio service—broadcast live from New Bethel, complete with a narrator, announcements of interest, and a 150-voice choir including, for a time, the talented gospel singer and future popular performer Wynona Carr—"was an outright production," said Samuel Billy Kyles, the then-teenage son of C. L.'s Mississippi friend, appreciated as much for its entertainment as its spiritual value. Franklin's sermon, usually between twenty-six and twenty-eight minutes long, was the centerpiece, but solos by Little Sammy Bryant, Lucy Branch, Willie Todd, and the preacher himself, backed by the extremely talented choir, were greatly anticipated. This presentation captivated Detroit, Benjamin Hooks explained: "Nobody . . . commanded the number of people he commanded on his Sunday night broadcast." The impact on church attendance was electric. Some, like Dr. Claud Young, cousin to Coleman and the future personal physician to C. L., tuned his car radio one night while driving about Detroit, encountered Franklin in mid-sermon, and found his way to New Bethel the following Sunday evening. Others who first heard

C. L. in their cars immediately drove to New Bethel, radio pulsating with Franklin's rhythms, to catch the conclusion in person. Yet others, listening at home, resolved to attend in person another Sunday. C. L.'s sermons sometimes went beyond the program's allotted time because, Kyles thought, "he wanted to go off the air while he was still preaching." That may have reflected C. L.'s sense of style—a disdain for leaving the audience with silence—but, whatever its design, it was very effective. "And that would make somebody say," Kyles remarked wryly, " 'I gotta go over there next Sunday or something.' "[30]

"Folks came from all over Detroit to attend church services," Willa Ward, a member of the famous gospel group the Clara Ward Singers, observed. "Even nonmembers really piled in on those days" when C. L. preached. So large were the crowds, Willie Todd noted, that the police "cut the traffic off," routing it "around another way. And the people would be standing in the streets just to hear him preach." While the enthusiastic response was perhaps more than at first expected, the strategy to attract nonmembers from throughout the city—one C. L. first devised at New Salem in Memphis—was quite conscious.[31]

Franklin was by no means the first Afro-Baptist minister in Detroit to use the radio, but he was the first to create an hour-long program specifically intended for the listening audience. And his sermons were such that Sunday evening at New Bethel quickly became an event to be seen at, a place where the faithful and the famous gathered. Over the next twenty years, pastors of other churches rescheduled their evening services so as not to conflict with those at New Bethel. Benjamin Hooks, pastor of Mt. Moriah Baptist in the 1960s, did this so that both he and his members might attend New Bethel's evening service themselves; Reverend James Holley at Little Rock Baptist did the same. Indeed, for those ministers not put off by C. L.'s chanted, rhythmic delivery, Sunday evening at New Bethel was a special moment. Depending on the weather, they milled about before services in the church vestibule or on the sidewalk outside, the regulars as well as out-of-town visitors, greeting each other, swapping stories, and acknowledging the appreciative nods of the congregation as they filed by. "There was a fellowship," Holley explained. "It was a coming together of a family." When C. L. arrived in his late-model Cadillac, driven by a deacon, the ministers relished the greeting, the broad smile, the shared joke as this commanding preacher ("Big Daddy," Holley affectionately called him) moved through them toward a hallway that led to a side entrance to the sanctuary. The ministers then processed down the center aisle to the pews at the front reserved for them. From the pulpit, C. L. would call out their names, recognizing them as he would select others in the audience. This quality endeared Franklin to many, and if it was calculated, the calculation reflected C. L.'s belief that all human beings "are imbued with the instinct or the desire for recognition."[32]

Franklin's success with the radio program did create some tension within the congregation. The quickness with which he liquidated the debt led some of the same church officers and members "to grumble again," Franklin remarked with laughter, "because any monies above the expenses became mine." C. L. "was a very mean person when he wanted to be," Sylvia Penn acknowledged of her close friend and pastor. "He could be pretty treacherous, you know, when you crossed him." He dismissed the complaint bluntly ("It didn't move me at all"), and he paid himself and his musical directors, program narrator, and choir soloists a weekly stipend from the profits. Thirty seven years old, with a lifetime contract as minister of New Bethel, this determined, self-confident, and driven man could respond fiercely when he thought his prerogatives questioned.[33]

In 1953, C. L. entered into another business arrangement, also beyond the provenance of the church, one whose impact would shortly secure his reputation as a preacher beyond compare, a national celebrity within black America on the level of a Sam Cooke, a Mahalia Jackson, or a Little Richard. A talent scout for a recording company approached Wynona Carr about signing a contract; at her suggestion, he also talked with C. L. Nothing came of the conversation. Soon after, Joe Von Battle, the Hastings Street entrepreneur, approached Franklin after a Sunday evening sermon and raised the idea again. "'Reverend,'" C. L. approximated Von Battle's words years later, "'the thing that you're talking about and the way you're saying it, people will buy that. It's just like all these people that are here tonight, they'll buy it.'" This time, Franklin was convinced, the welcome prospect of additional income and the greater recognition that would follow if the sermons caught the public's fancy proving too enticing. Success was not guaranteed. Franklin had, of course, recorded in 1950, but that was music, gospel hymns. Preachers simply did not make spoken recordings in the early 1950s, and sales were poor for the few who tried. Earlier, in the 1920s and 1930s, an Atlanta minister, J. M. Gates, had sold hundreds of thousands of recordings of his sermons, when the then-current technology limited his selections to approximately three minutes. Von Battle and Franklin proposed to press on vinyl nearly an entire half-hour sermon, including C. L.'s introductory rendition of "Father, I Stretch My Hand to Thee." Technological innovation over a quarter century allowed this greater length, but the success of the project remained questionable. No minister in the black church experience to that moment had ever dared to record the main body of his sermons and offer them for sale. Most preachers, if they thought at all about such a possibility, worried that repeated listening would reveal the weakness of the message, the forced emotional appeal intended to camouflage that very problem, or, even worse, both. Undaunted, C. L. Franklin welcomed Von Battle's taping equipment to his pulpit alongside WJLB's microphone.[34]

The recordings were an immediate sensation. Detroiters bought them in large numbers, and Von Battle distributed them on his JVB label to other record shops in the Midwest and the South. Von Battle's operation was small, and he could neither press enough records nor handle the bookkeeping and advertising to take full advantage of the opportunity. But there was no question that Franklin was a major success. When Von Battle put a new sermon on his sound system, flooding the Hastings Street sidewalk with the mellifluous power of that voice, crowds frequently gathered to listen. "More than once," Marsha L. Mickens, Von Battle's daughter, remembered her father saying, he "had to call the police to break up the crowds that would gather to hear" the recorded sermon.[35]

All this attention made C. L. an even more attractive figure as he leaned across the pulpit or sauntered down Hastings Street during the course of a day's business. This handsome, virile man, in effect single since 1948, had never been bashful about his sexuality, which he considered, along with the desire for recognition, "one of the great psychological needs" all humans experience. That some women, in and outside the church community, responded with a matching passion, C. L. considered one of life's great delights. Kathryn Curry, a young Detroit woman, had an affair with C. L. over two years in the early 1950s. Her awe was palpable: "There is only one Lord Jesus in my life and that's you." She wrote "Dearest Frank" about 1953, in her handmade book, "Memories." Curry reveled in the memory of their recently concluded relationship, which C. L. had gently ended. "Continue to have it your own way," she chided him, "but I couldn't wait to tell you about remembrance of things past." There was also a handsomely dressed, beautiful, light-skinned woman, known now only as Evelyn, whose photo revealed a longing expression that belied her demurely posed hands atop crossed, well-covered knees. Her inscription was to the point: "My love for you is now and forever, my darling Frank." Sylvia Penn, who had originally introduced Kathryn Curry to her pastor, noted that New Bethel attracted many "pretty girls 'cause he was single." Often, she would call C. L., only to be told, " 'I got some company,' " to which she knowingly replied, "Who is it this time?"[36]

Talk about C. L.'s involvements with women provided his critics, particularly those in the ministry, with additional cause to dismiss him. The critics were not necessarily innocents themselves, but the open, public manner in which C. L. squired his women about town upset them. From their perspective, C. L. was not exploring the boundary of the sacred and the secular—he had, rather, fallen over into the abyss. This, in turn, reinforced criticism of his preaching style and doubts about his recording career. Even before his appearance on the JVB label, many had dismissed him as a mere entertainer, a panderer to popular emotions, a preacher who lacked an intellectual core to his sermon. More so in 1953, following C. L.'s carefully produced radio program, his record sales, and New Bethel's mushrooming membership rolls, these critics—with not a little jealousy—regarded C. L. as a celebrity hound, an embarrassment to the ministry they sought to serve. Were these charges accurate, C. L.'s stretch toward national fame would quickly falter, for no sermon so empty of meaning could withstand repeated scrutiny by the insightful if often unschooled people whose perceptive folk commentary on preachers and their messages was a staple of the black oral tradition.[37]

*　　*　　*　　*　　*

In the three years between 1953 and 1955, JVB Records released at least sixteen sermons from among the approximately one hundred C. L. preached at New Bethel. Von Battle recorded many more, and why these sixteen were selected for distribution, and by whom, remains unclear. Also unknown is the precise date of the original delivery of any of them. Two additional major sermons, recorded on the JVB label by 1955, complete the broad framework of his thinking and public teaching at mid-decade.

"Dry Bones in the Valley" became enormously successful, selling widely and frequently requested by promoters of gospel programs. Like "The Eagle Stirreth Her Nest," this sermon was among the most challenging a black preacher could deliver, and its roots also reached back to the slave experience. Some ministers shied away from it throughout their careers, unwilling to take on its complex mix of deep faith, collective self-criticism, and existential doubt in the context of their own era. C. L.'s version of "Dry Bones," recorded when he was nearly forty years old, was a mature version of a sermon he had given before but delivered now by a man in full possession of his preaching powers.

Where "Moses at the Red Sea" explored the issue of individual responsibility in the context of faith, the centrality of a faith that transcended the boundaries of human knowledge and reason framed "Dry Bones." Franklin began by reading Ezekiel 37:1-4, where the Lord placed the prophet Ezekiel in a valley full of dry bones and, after surveying the valley, asked, "Son of man, can these bones live?" Ezekiel responded, "O, Lord God, thou knoweth," to which the Lord demanded, "Prophesy from these bones, and say unto them, 'O ye dry bones, hear the word of the Lord.'" As an anticipatory murmuring snaked through the pews, C. L. announced his theme: "the prophet and the valley of dry bones."[38]

Introducing Ezekiel, a young man trained as a priest of Israel, C. L. stressed that the meaning of Ezekiel's vision was to convince Israel that "her God had not fallen, and her God was not dead." Encouraged by the cries and shouts of affirmation from an already aroused audience, he painted with words Ezekiel's vision for his people: the prophet saw "the vague outlines of a man sitting upon a chariot throne engulfed in a cloud," with "priestly functionaries" bustling about. As Franklin told it, Ezekiel's vision depicted "wheels that he saw in the middle of wheels," guarded by angels, and "these wheels had eyes, and . . . did not deviate from their course." C. L. explained that the prophet's purpose in retelling the vision was to remind Israel of "the overruling Providence and power of God," that God's plans included them. The first, innermost wheel represented Israel and was ever moving. Superimposed on that was Babylon's wheel, also in constant motion, its positioning reflective of Israel's captivity within Babylon. A third wheel, encompassing the others, represented "God's universal wheel and God's universal plan." All the wheels were in motion simultaneously, and an Israelite or a Babylonian might imagine that one or the other of their wheels dominated at a given moment; but the movement of all the wheels reflected the deeper truth that "all of God's plans are always moving," for "God's plans *never* stand still." The congregation cried out yet again, and C. L., tempering their emotion while drawing them yet closer, calmly asked them to "pray with me if you please," as he shifted into his next section.

In Ezekiel's vision, "Babylon was a desolate place." Considered in its day one of the world's great cities, Babylon was to a captive Israel nothing but "a valley of depravity . . . of disfranchisement . . . of hopelessness, a valley of dry bones, a valley of lifelessness." Amid cries from the deacons in the chairs behind the pulpit to "take your time" and pace the delivery, C. L. asked how a city as proclaimed as Babylon could yet be perceived as a valley. "Well," he began,

> you see, a city may be one thing to one people, or a country may mean one thing to one people, and altogether another thing to another people. When the white Europeans came to this country, embarked upon these shores, America to them was a land of promise, was a mountaintop of possibilities, was a mountaintop of adventure. But to the Negro, when he embarked upon these shores, America to him was a valley: a valley of slave huts, a valley of slavery and oppression, a valley of sorrow; so that often we had to sing: "One of these days, I'm going to eat at the feasting table"; "One of these days, the chariot of God will swing low."

Barely five minutes into the sermon, C. L. had already presented two central, interwoven themes: the force of God's providential plans (Israel's "God had not fallen . . .") and the incorporation into those plans of the African American historical experience ("One of these days . . ."). He did something else as well. In contrasting the experiences of European and African Americans in the American promised land, C. L. sketched the outlines of an alternative historical vision that acknowledged the fundamentally different histories of blacks and whites on these shores. One person's bondage was, in fact, the basis of another person's freedom. Although the contexts were quite different, Franklin's sermon and Coleman Young's testimony each proclaimed this alternative understanding of history.

Then C. L. suddenly seemed to be reminded of some unfinished business before the congregation that demanded attention. "What is a prophet anyway," he asked, and responded that the terms *prophet* and *preacher* are interchangeable, "for a prophet is a preacher, and a preacher ought to be a prophet." A prophet, he was quick to say, was "not a funny person . . . selling luck or anything like that," a reference undoubtedly to one Detroit religious figure whom C. L. had publicly criticized, the self-appointed Prophet (James) Jones.[39] The prophet he had in mind instead was sent from God and possessed "sight, insight, and foresight." What began as a sidebar and just skirted claiming for himself a prophet's status, now brought C. L. back to his theme, for when considering "a real prophet . . . such a man was Ezekiel."

The valley of "Israel's Babylonian situation" was a symbol, he explained, a metaphor. A valley is, by definition, "a low place between mountains." In this case, those mountains represented the various barriers—economic, social, political, and religious—to freedom. But C. L.'s point was not a crude application of a sacred text to a secular context. The prophet was "in the Spirit," possessed by God, when he envisioned the valley; the prophet remained in the Spirit as the Lord "led him to the midst of the valley and sat him down" to ponder "the heart of Israel's problems, and Israel's situation in Babylon." When the survey of Israel's problems, that "valley of dry bones," was complete, "the Lord posed a question" to the prophet. "'Son of man,'" the preacher intoned, thumping his hand rhythmically on the pulpit and stretching out his words as he incanted, "I wish you could hear him say that. '*So-on of ma-an, ca-an the-ese bo-ones live?*'" A controlled pande-monium engulfed the pews, people shouting out "Amen" and "Yes, sir!" Deep, appreciative laughter—the result, perhaps, of a sharp recognition of the challenge, the immediacy in Franklin's words—broke out near the mi-crophone, and cries of anticipation for what was yet to come traveled down from the balcony to the main floor and back. Simultaneously, one could hear again from the deacon's chairs behind the preacher the caution, re-flecting a desire to prolong the moment as well as the preacher's energy, to "Take your time, sir."

As he waited for the emotion to pass, Franklin turned his attention to a fundamental problem of human existence. That phrase, "son of man," he told his audience, ached with the weight of humanity's limitations. Any "son of man" might be a scholar, a doctor, a psychologist, or a psychiatrist, well versed in human "drives and reactions and responses and tendencies," Franklin suggested, with a melodic emphasis on certain words anticipating the whoop yet to come. Human knowledge has explored the physical and psychological world, achieving much good in the process. But the central question remained: "I want to know, with all of this knowledge, can you tell me: *Can the-ese bo-ones live? Can these bo-o-nes live?*" With all of human knowledge at hand, neither the prophet nor humanity, past nor present, could respond, and the prophet "had to give up." Before the presence of evil, embedded deep in the human soul and reflected here in the image of Babylon as a valley of death and desiccation, mankind was powerless to do more than diagnose the case. "What we can't do is write a prescription," the preacher taught by familiar analogy. "So the prophet had to say, 'Lord, thou knoweth. Lord, thou knoweth,'" and trust that "ultimately, if we have faith, he'll give us the answer."

That power and pervasiveness of evil, the human suffering it entails, and mankind's blindness in the face of it raised fundamental questions for those in the pews. If God's providence toward his people was real, how could he allow such suffering? There was no simple answer. As he transitioned into his whoop, Franklin recalled his thinking regarding the starkness of the prophet's existential dread: "The loneliness of it. The frustration of it."[40]

"If you want the answer," God told the prophet, the answer to the multiple aspects of the "Babylonian problem," then "you go out . . . and preach to those dry bones." C. L., with droplets of sweat glimmering against his dark face, shaped the prophet's protestations to convey his own experience: "Some of the living souls that I preach to don't respond to me, and what could I expect from dry bones?" "What can I preach to dry bones about," Ezekiel implored his God from the depths of his fear and isolation. "What kind of text can I use?" The answer was immediate: "Tell those dry bones / to hear the word of the Lord, / to hear the word of the Lord." The prophet preached day and night in the valley, growing increasingly discouraged and despondent as the bones remained inert. Through that central paradox that wrests salvation from suffering, the faith of Franklin's Old Testament prophet grew stronger from the very pain he bore. Thus the prophet preached again and yet again, although "not able to see what the results would be." But then:

> *One morning,*
> *the valley began to rumble,*
> *yes it did.*
> *One morning*
> *the valley began to shake,*
> *and*
> *there was a mighty*
> *moving around.*

On that morning, Franklin sang, Ezekiel "saw the old dry bones / in motion," and the New Bethel congregation exploded with a joyous exultation of faith rewarded. C. L., in full whoop, in key, with his message focused, chanted the skeletal bones back toward wholeness, much as the prophet had. The foot bone searched out an ankle, which in turn found the knee bone, and then the thigh and the hip bones, "moving toward back bones," to the shoulder, the neck, and finally the head, redeeming the bones from desolation, creating from a fractured hopelessness the possibility of human wholeness. All the while this prophet's voice "kept on preaching, / 'O ye dry bones / hear the word of the Lord.'"

With the congregation nearly overcome by the hurt of the joy within, Franklin explained what happened next. As God created the flesh to cover the bones that were, as yet, but lifeless corpses, he ordered the prophet to

> *Turn now*
> *and preach to the wind.*
> *Tell the wind*
> *that God wants the wind to blow,*
> *. . . and blow breath into these bodies.*

Twenty-nine times in his conclusion, Franklin chanted of God's "words" or his "Word," the ultimate protection against the wrenching despair Ezekiel suffered. Human efforts were important, C. L. reiterated, but they may pass away while "his word will always stand." And when these earthly trials are over, "when I get on to the [River] Jordan, / I want his Word right there":

> *I want him to let his Word*
> *be shaped like a vessel*
> *and let my so-o-ul*
> *o-o-o-ohh, step on over.*

This was the faith that could transform a valley of dry bones—indeed, transform anything.[41]

Beatrice Buck, the secretary to the owner of the Gotham Hotel before she became C. L.'s secretary in 1956, poignantly described her reaction to Franklin's sacred performance. C. L.'s message "gave me something to think about . . . to strive for, it gave me new, renewed faith in God, and I do believe in God." The biblical stories themselves, interpreted through the voice of this majestic preacher, told "of the struggles that somebody had been into or some biblical person, and how they came out of it. It also taught me how prayer changes things." Reverend Jerome Kirby, who joined New Bethel as a child in the late 1940s, soon after his family arrived from Arkansas, emphasized as well that Franklin's message emboldened many southern migrants. His proclamation of faith's meaning in human history and his pointed avowal of an alternative understanding of the black experience in America, made Franklin, Kirby thought, "a link to the [civil rights] movement." Here, in the joined power of his ideas and their delivery, men and women rose to new life.[42]

All of Franklin's efforts at self-education (he was again taking college classes in Detroit, at Wayne State) never erased his poignant awareness of the command of words and ideas regularly exhibited by an A. A. Banks or a Jesse Jai McNeil. Franklin did not doubt his power from the pulpit; he was just too smart a man not to know his weaknesses. As a result, he sought out Reuben Gayden, a boyhood acquaintance (and now a good friend) from Cleveland, Mississippi. Gayden's father, J. W. Gayden, had led St. Paul's Missionary Church in Cleveland between 1926 and 1935, when Rachel and C. L. attended St. Peter's Rock. The younger Gayden also became a minister and dean of the School of Religion at Natchez College, where he developed a reputation as a brilliant interpreter of theology and biblical studies. Never able to retain a pulpit for long—his rather dry preaching style disappointed, and even when married, he enjoyed other women and his liquor too much for most congregations—Gayden focused on his intellectual work. That occupation also led to difficulties as he veered sharply from Baptist orthodoxy, questioning literalism at every turn, so much so that even some theologically liberal ministers thought him suspect.[43]

Franklin organized an ongoing study group in his home during the 1950s that lasted more than a decade and invited Gayden to lead the weekly seminar. Gayden was in constant need of money, and the collection Franklin raised from the ministers who attended provided some steady income. For C. L., this seminar was not unlike the Tuesday ministers' meetings in Memphis. These Detroit preachers shared ideas, discussed effective techniques for presenting a sermon, and enjoyed one another's company. As in Memphis, these meetings were well known to both other ministers and parishioners, and many ministers desperately hoped for an invitation. But now one man guided the discussions. Gayden usually presented a biblical text, examined its historical setting, and explored its theological meaning from a variety of viewpoints, as a prelude to a general discussion. Gayden gave his students "nuggets for sermons," Jasper Williams noted, which they individually developed. When Franklin entered the pulpit, then, working from a brief outline rather than a prepared manuscript, someone who knew Gayden might well have recognized aspects of his thinking in Franklin's words, though the sermon itself was distinctly C. L. in its narrative structure, style of delivery, and message.[44]

This was indeed the case with "Without a Song," which completes the central group of sermons that contain the major themes in C. L.'s preaching in this era. In this sermon he took for his text the opening four verses of the 137th Psalm, where the Israelites, sitting "by the rivers of Babylon . . . wept when we remembered Zion." The Babylonians desired an amusement from their captives, to have them perform "one of the songs of Zion" as a diversion to pass the time. Captive and despondent, with their sacred songs mocked, Israel uttered the pained cry of the oppressed down through the millennia: "How shall we sing the Lord's song in a strange land?"[45]

The subject that evening, C. L. announced, was "Without a Song." "These proud Hebrews in Babylon" were teachers, scholars, government officials, and rabbis, Franklin explained, and the Babylonians required of them a song as an amusement, an entertainment for their captors. Given that context, the Israelites refused, thinking the request "untimely" and "out of place. . . . Said they, 'How *can* we sing the songs of Zion in a strange land?'"

Franklin disagreed. The Israelites should have sung, he argued, perhaps especially Zion's songs, for song has a universal appeal that can convey "many messages." C. L. turned then to the first of three interrelated historical sketches that explored the promise and potency of song. He talked of the West Indies, probably of Jamaica, where "some of the inhabitants of the country," colonial subjects of a European power, used song in electoral campaign rallies to raise issues concerning independence they could not discuss openly from the platform. He recalled a favorite saying of his, paraphrasing W. H. Brewster, "Some things you can't say, you can sing. Isn't that so?" and called on the congregation to affirm in their response one of the deepest truths in African American folk culture.

His second vignette shifted the focus to Europe. Some time before the Nazi assumption of power in Germany in 1933, Roland Hayes, the

Georgia-born African American tenor, walked onto a stage in one of Berlin's opulent concert halls. Infuriated at the presence of this non-Aryan, Nazis and their sympathizers in the audience "went into howls and hisses to make it impossible for him to sing." Hayes stood there, "with his eyes closed and his arms folded," the dissonance intensifying until, finally, arms still folded and eyes still shut, he began to sing, "Lord, thou art my peace, thou art my peace." In C. L.'s retelling, this "great voice" soared above the insults, quieted the raucous hall, and Hayes completed his concert. "I'm trying to tell you," C. L. stressed again, "what can be done in a song."

He drove his message home, drawing directly on his people's experience in the United States. Slaves were frequently "called upon to sing" by masters, and despite the conditions they endured, they "never missed a chance to sing." This was not simply a reflection of the white master's power, nor was it confirmation of the master's image of the purported childlike innocence of "their" slaves. Rather, Franklin taught, finger jabbing at the podium as the congregation responded fervently, the slave sang "because it was his songs and the gospel he heard by those ancient ministers that kept hope alive in his heart." Under the very eyes of their captors, the slaves sang for themselves, of their fundamental commitment to survive, expressing as they did an alternative vision of Christianity, its relationship to slavery, and the meaning of the term *master*. "I think they should have sung," C. L. reiterated.[46]

Franklin then called by name the work of the African American folklorist Miles Mark Fisher, who recorded the tale told from one generation to the next of an "old woman," a slave named Mary, "in the Carolinas or in Georgia," who attended a revival during the eighteenth century's major religious awakening preached by Charles Wesley, the English Methodist preacher. So many whites had crowded into the small chapel that slaves were barred from their traditional place in the balcony and listened from outside, through open windows. When Wesley finished and the call went out for those ready to accept Jesus to come forward, Mary "walked in the front door . . . down the aisle, and took a seat to join the church." The local pastor confronted her: "Lady, you can't join this church." Perplexed, but trusting the spirit of her conversion, Franklin's Mary responded: "But sir, I got 'eligion. I've been converted. I felt the power of God here today while the man preached, and I want to jine the church." The pastor remained adamant, and as Mary returned down the aisle, tears streaming across her cheeks, she mumbled to herself, "'I'm going to tell God one of these days how you treat me.'" At this point her fellow slaves, still at the windows, created a song that centuries later still carried one of the deepest expressions of hope in African American culture:

> *Oh Mary, don't weep, don't mourn;*
> **Pharaoh***'s army got drownded;*
> *Mary, don't weep, and then don't mourn.*

That God's providence would in time drown even as powerful an opponent as the Egyptian army on behalf of one as seemingly insignificant as Mary was the psychological foundation of a sense of self profoundly different from what the dominant society expected from its slaves. "Think of the message that is wrapped up in that song," Franklin exhorted. "I think that everybody ought to have a song. I think that Israel should have sung down in Babylon."[47]

Captivity can be oppressive, C. L. preached, but even the worst oppressor "can't keep me from dreaming . . . [or] from singing." The young boy who did just that as he worked the cotton fields close by Highway 61 now affirmed, with his mature voice, a future where "one of these days, a chariot is going to swing low for me." Lest anyone confuse that enigmatic phrase, "one of these days," with passivity, C. L. immediately reminded the congregation that slaves had gathered illegally, outside the presence of whites, for their own religious services. White masters opposed such gatherings, C. L. instructed, not because they were antireligious or because they wished to deny to slaves religious expression. Rather, the masters "feared that this congregating would create unity and give rise to thoughts of liberation, and so they forbade them, in many cases, to congregate."[48]

Among the colonial people of the Afro-Caribbean world, as for African Americans confronting the stark evil of European or American racism, to sing a song through the darkness, the trials, and the tribulations was simultaneously a spiritual and a political act—one that trusted, Franklin thought, in the providence of God acting through individuals to effect their salvation *and* their liberation. The portraits he painted—the Moses in each individual; the courage of Roland Hayes; the sustaining faith of Ezekiel; the eagle soaring toward freedom; and Mary, the black everywoman, before whom even Pharaoh's armies ultimately faltered—were calculated to call individuals, preoccupied with daily affairs or floundering under racism's pervasive impact, to a new, more self-conscious expression and engagement. Hinken Perry, another Mississippi native, a New Bethel member for half a century, a deacon for almost four decades, and an autoworker and union member for thirty-four years, was one of many for whom Franklin's message reverberated. "Well," Deacon Perry explained, Reverend Franklin would "often talk about the importance of the political. We can't live without politics, so he kind of brought politics right along with religion, because both of 'em was important. We live in a political world. We have to be involved."[49]

To Franklin, this was biblical Israel's mistake. In not singing, in not giving voice to their vision even in captivity, Israel remained "hampered by her nationalistic thinking . . . by many inhibitions that were inherent in [her] culture." Their intent was nationhood, in a promised land beyond the boundaries of their captors. Thus the Israelites could refuse to sing before their captors because their covenant with God foretold of their deliverance into the Promised Land. They were sojourners in Babylon, atoning perhaps for a lack of past faith but assured that Yahweh their God would deliver them. Inclusion into Babylonian political life, even if possible, was not the goal.[50]

Like the Israelites, African Americans were a covenanted people, chosen by their God and weighted with the responsibilities of that relationship, and they did inhabit a strange land. But the circumstances of their involuntary migration into another's promised land created a different historical experience. For African Americans, their passage from Africa to the proclaimed New Israel of America was a passage *into* Egypt, into oppression, into captivity. The exodus theme remained central; but as both enslaved and free men and women, black Americans identified deeply with pre-deliverance Israel. In song and folktale, as in sermons and public speeches, the sharpness of this difference cut to the very core of their judgment on the American experiment. To the degree that the nation curtailed blacks' freedom, it violated its own covenant.

African Americans were, in a profound manner, also home, even in their captivity. The identification with the Israelites of old aided immeasurably in the development of a sense of peoplehood, but for most, that collective consciousness was not tied to the creation of an independent nation state. There was no realization of another promised land akin to the sustained Zionist movement among Jews; nor, except for a small group, was a biblical text such as the 137th Psalm the foundation for a religio-political imperative to remove to Africa, as it was among Rastafarians throughout Afro-Caribbean culture. In C. L.'s vision, African Americans were not dispossessed wanderers and therefore could not afford the luxury of remaining silent. So they should sing—to recognize themselves as a group, to develop perspective, to organize to change the very society that oppressed and, just maybe, the oppressor. It was a strange land, but it was their land nonetheless. He knew that to sing of what might not yet be possible to say would bring the day much closer when that metaphorical chariot of many meanings would, indeed, "swing low for me."[51]

*   *   *   *   *

Most who heard him live or on records, Franklin reflected later in his career, knew little about the Bible beyond "limited excerpts." His detailed biblical descriptions were the gateway through which audiences could place themselves in a historical continuum. In the face of persistent criticism from some members that he had strayed from the traditional emphasis on Jesus as personal savior, Franklin maintained his approach. "You just preach about Jesus sometimes," he said. "But then you preach about some other things." He had "one foot in that older tradition," Reverend Bernard Lafayette thought. But he possessed as well "a black consciousness" of his people's history. He was "the apex of the bridge" between the two traditions.[52]

Franklin's efforts did not cease when he left the pulpit, sermon finished. On a Sunday afternoon in the fall of 1954, for example, James and Grace Lee Boggs, two self-described Marxist revolutionaries, ascended to the pulpit at New Bethel Baptist Church. C. L. R. James, the West Indian Marxist theoretician, had emphasized the critical importance of the

African independence struggles then in progress, and the Boggs's small Detroit group concurred. They produced a booklet on the struggle in Kenya and sought to have churches sponsor "Kenya Sundays" to discuss the issue. C. L. was the only Baptist minister and one of only three black ministers of any denomination whom the Boggses approached who welcomed their effort. This was but two years after the House Un-American Activities Committee hearings in Detroit, and the nation remained obsessed by a fierce campaign to root out Communists. The Mau Mau, Kenya's revolutionary guerrilla soldiers and the image of armed, successful black African soldiers, touched a fear deeply imbedded in an American racialized consciousness. Franklin was not a political comrade of the Boggses. But he appreciated the importance of African independence and its meaning for black Americans, and he welcomed the couple to his church. Grace Lee Boggs recalled Franklin as one "of the most politically conscious preachers in Detroit" and remembered that she and her husband "sold more than four hundred copies of the Kenya booklet to members of New Bethel from the pulpit."[53]

Franklin was not a political innocent, open to any and all winds that swirled about the corner of Hastings and Willis seeking a church welcome. But he gave his pulpit to anyone whom he thought had the best interests of his people at heart, regardless of whether he agreed with their analysis, and he almost never critiqued an individual by name from his pulpit, regardless of what he thought of their program. Still, he did not shy away from all debate. The first major issue he raised, in the mid-1950s, concerned the relationship between the Communist Party's political vision and his analysis of human rights. C. L. framed the issue as a matter of faith. The question asked of the Pharisees in Jesus' time was relevant "tonight, [for] New Bethel and Detroit" as well: "What do you think of Jesus?" Where the biblical question concerned whether the ancient Jews perceived Jesus' lineage from the line of David (therefore making him human) or as "the Christ of God," a central question before Franklin's congregation that night "in this so-called Atomic Age" was, "What is your idea of a loyal citizen of America?" Since "Communism looms menacingly upon the horizons of these troubled times," to define the meaning of loyalty "folk must take a stand, either for or against" Communism. There was as well another critical question that required attention, namely, one's position on "human rights, not racial rights, human rights." In contrast with Communism, which he treated as a domestic question, human rights were of international concern, as people throughout the world, regardless of "race, creed, or color," demanded answers.[54]

While noting that these two issues "challenge our times," C. L. insisted that "the great question must be settled first." Whether the issue is democracy, Communism, human rights, or social justice, each must first answer the question "What think ye of Christ?" If one accepts Christ as savior, then "the question of Communism is settled." Communism is "atheistic and ungodly," with "no place in it for God." Certainly, then, C. L. emphasized, "There's no place in it for me, for I'll take my stand with God." That same embrace of Christ determined one's stance on human rights. In many churches in the United States and throughout the world, racial and class distinctions, enforced by those "that pose as worshippers and followers of Christ," bar many from the sanctuary. But "if you get straight on Christ, my brothers and sisters, you believe in equality and you believe in the justice of all men." To follow Christ is to set out "upon the highway of justice . . . the highway of peace . . . the highway of brotherhood," for Jesus "does not trod any other highway." As he concluded this sermon, chanting with passion, C. L. depicted contemporary injustices as reenactments of the crucifixion perpetrated by people, church members among them, who "have Jesus shoved / out of your whole week / except on Sundays." This was indeed the core of Franklin's political vision, one that integrated personal salvation and social awareness in the symbolic language of a common faith. The arena in which Franklin preached that vision was about to get even larger.[55]

CHAPTER SEVEN

FAME

By the mid-1950s, Paradise Valley hailed C. L. Franklin on the street with the enthusiasm usually accorded a headliner at the Flame Show Bar. As this handsome, charismatic minister strolled down Hastings, consciously extending New Bethel's sanctuary into that secular space, he gathered people to him for a word, a request, a shared quip, advice. The markers of his local success—the sharp increase in the New Bethel congregation, the ecstatic crowds swaying to his voice over Joe Von Battle's loudspeakers on Hastings—preceded him, and his expansive smile and focused eyes welcomed even before he spoke.

Franklin reveled in this adulation, sensing in it a promise for the future that knew no bounds. Nor was he intimidated when certain New Bethel members wagged their heads reproachfully in the church vestibule before services, whispering of the scandal they thought their pastor's friendship with the Hastings Street prostitutes, gamblers, drug dealers, and club operators brought on the church community. Boldly, with an attitude one younger ministerial colleague later described as "all lion," C. L. confronted these concerns directly from the pulpit. One who has "found Jesus can see something good in everybody's life," he instructed, or at least "can see the potentialities." "When did you get so good that you can't be seen in certain districts?" he goaded his critics. "Jesus didn't declare any district off limit" or declare any group not to "have the opportunity to come to him." Just the opposite was the case: Jesus "was a friend to sinners." In another sermon a short time later, C. L. switched perspective as his criticism became even more pointed: "Some folk would make us think that Satan is only in Paradise Valley or that Satan is only on Hastings Street, but we have found that Satan is in any community." Like the good evangelical that he was, C. L. rejected as false comfort church membership, regular attendance, and other outward signs as predictors of salvation: "Satan is on all the boulevards. Satan is in all of the fashionable communities. Wherever men live, Satan is there."[1]

C. L.'s enthusiasm for his work stemmed in good part from the same compelling need for recognition he accorded the Hastings Street regulars. Mississippi's scars still marked him, from the faint, if intense, memory of his wraithlike father to his experience of "segregation in the raw," as he termed it, which fueled his ambitions even decades later. "My greatest personal achievement," he commented in 1977, "is that I had the guts and the initiative to extricate myself from a life that was a one-way road leading nowhere." Here was the source of his dual emphasis on faith in God and self, and the corresponding will to act on both. Here, too, in this private cauldron, he tempered his profound affirmation that such wounds would not define his humanity. His fellow Mississippian, Muddy Waters, knew the feeling as well: "I wanted to be a known person. All my life that's what I worked for." It was precisely this vulnerability in C. L. and his ability to share occasional hints of it in public that gained for him the desired acclaim.[2]

Franklin understood the hurt inside only imperfectly. The crosscurrents of his private tensions created at times a self-doubt that redoubled that need for recognition. A man of large and exuberant appetites, the other needs (he had noted sex, sustenance, and security) were also passionately acknowledged— and indulged. A complex, very human man, on the brink of national fame and celebrity, Franklin increasingly found his public career and personal conduct reflected in the glare of the spotlights that fame generated.[3]

*   *   *   *   *

Despite his call to integrate sacred and secular commitments into one powerful voice, Franklin had yet to develop a political presence in Detroit. True, he had a lifetime membership in the NAACP branch and undoubtedly applauded the decision of the United States Supreme Court in *Brown v. Board of Education*. Under the direction of NAACP lead counsel Thurgood Marshall, plaintiffs from five school districts filed suit against the Supreme Court's ruling, delivered in *Plessy v. Ferguson* in 1896, that accepted the fiction that "separate but equal" facilities met the constitutional standard of equal opportunity for all citizens. The decision in *Brown v. Board of Education*, announced on May 17, 1954, unanimously overturned *Plessy*, toppling this racist premise of American civic life.[4] Yet racial tensions in Detroit remained much as they had been. Three weeks before the court's decision, Richard Henry, a black reporter with the *Chronicle*, had entered Bankes' Bar in a white West Side neighborhood to investigate a claim that a black woman had been denied service. Attacked by the white patrons at the bar for his curiosity, Henry pressed assault charges against one man in particular. Two weeks later, a local judge found the accused not guilty and admonished the reporter: "You do not live in that neighborhood. You went into that bar looking for something and got more than you bargained for. I am going to leave it at that!" Three months later, jazz great Lionel Hampton and a party of friends were denied service at a downtown bar. And as C. L. still sought a more public political voice, Mississippi inflicted another painful lesson on black America.[5]

In August 1955, Emmett Till, a fourteen-year-old Chicago boy, visited relatives in LeFlore County, Mississippi. On a sweltering day late that month, he and a group of other black youngsters traveled three miles from his uncle's cabin into the little town of Money. There this exuberant teenager, alive with South Side Chicago's street slang, allegedly violated white Mississippi's rules of racial etiquette when he entered the small grocery store and flippantly addressed Carolyn Bryant, the white clerk whose husband, Roy, owned the store. A few days later, on Sunday, August 28, at two o'clock in the morning, Roy Bryant, his half-brother J. W. Milam, and possibly a third person banged on the door of Mose Wright's cabin, demanding his nephew, the "boy" who had so insulted Carolyn Bryant. Three days later, Till's body, his face all but unrecognizable from the brutal beating he had absorbed, partly surfaced in the Tallahatchie River when it caught on a snag. Around his neck, secured with barbed wire, was a 125-pound cotton-gin fan. So badly had he been tortured before his death that Till at first was identified only by the ring on his finger, a keepsake from his father.[6]

As brutal as this murder was, it was not the only one that spring and summer in Mississippi. Three months earlier, "persons unknown" fired three shotgun blasts at Rev. George Lee, killing him instantly as he drove in Belzoni, the seat of Humphreys County, some fifty miles south and west of Money. In a predominately black county, Lee's public advocacy of voter registration—he was an NAACP activist—had brought repeated threats. But unlike the reaction to Lee's murder, which remained more local than national, Till's death mobilized a national protest movement that marked a turning point for black Americans. The courage of two of Emmett Till's relatives played a major role. The decision of Till's mother, Mamie E. Bradley, to wake her son in an open coffin and to allow photographers from the black magazine, *Jet,* to publish the pictures, stirred an intense re-action among African Americans nationally. Massive numbers of people moved in slow procession past Till's coffin in Chicago, and rallies of be-tween ten thousand and fifty thousand protesters took place in Chicago, Detroit, New York, and elsewhere. Individuals previously apolitical were transformed by the news and especially by the pictures; then-youngsters such as Kareem Abdul-Jabbar, Anne Moody, Cleveland Sellers, and Diana Ross were jarred as never before in their young lives. "I began to think of myself as a black person for the first time, not just [as] a person," Abdul-Jabbar (in 1955 the twelve-year-old Lewis Alcindor) recalled. He, like so many other black youth, "lost my childish innocence" as he viewed the photographic image of Till's ravaged face. "I will never forget Emmett Till," Diana Ross stated, assessing years later the impact these events had during her eleventh summer. As Mrs. Bradley intended, the reactions to those photographs ensured that her son's life had "been sacrificed for something."[7]

The courage of Till's uncle, Mose Wright, also politicized many. An eyewitness to the abduction, he received numerous death threats warning him not to testify at the trial of Bryant and Milam in Sumner, Tallahatchie

County. Nonetheless, on an intensely hot September day, in a packed, tension-filled courtroom where few Mississippi whites ever expected a black to testify against one of them even in a minor civil proceeding, Mose Wright drew up all of his five feet, three inches, pointed what journalist Murray Kempton called "his black, workworn finger" directly at J. W. Milam and exclaimed, "Thar he." With Milam's eyes burning like "coals of hatred" at him, Wright then turned and identified Roy Bryant as his nephew's second abductor. For good measure, when interrogated by the defendants' attorney, this sixty-four-year-old tenant farmer and circuit preacher pointedly refused to add the honorific, "sir," when addressing the white man. Mose Wright became a symbol of that deep wellspring of black resistance that was again coming to the surface. As Kempton reported from the trial that September, it was this man, "condemned to bow all his life," who made the trial even possible, for "he had enough left to raise his head and look the enemy in those terrible eyes when he was 64."[8]

The acquittal verdict for the two defendants, delivered on September 23 by the all-white, all-male jury after sixty-seven minutes of deliberation, surprised only the willfully innocent. In Detroit, for example, *Chronicle* reporter Richard Henry asked fellow blacks on the street about the prospects of justice, and none expected "southern justice" to be anything other than just that. Black novelist Chester Himes, speaking as "a Negro in New York" who read of the lynching and trial "in impotent fury," spoke for many who also awakened to the "real horror [that] comes when your dead brain must face the fact that we as a nation don't want to stop [such violence]. If we wanted to, we would." In a controlled fury, Himes urged Americans to "take the burden of all this guilt from these two pitiful crackers. They are but the guns we hired." Coming as it did a decade after the successful conclusion of a war for democracy, the murder of Emmett Till became a horrific benchmark of just how far black Americans had yet to travel toward equality.[9]

On October 6, 1955, just two weeks after the verdict in the Mississippi trial, C. L. Franklin wrote a public letter to the Detroit NAACP that was published in the Michigan *Chronicle*. Franklin's announced recipient was attorney Edward Turner, a former president of the Michigan NAACP, the current president of the Detroit branch, and a southern-born migrant with impeccable, upper-middle-class credentials. The intended audience was far broader. C. L. began by praising as "very impressive" the public rally the organization had held in late September at Bethel A. M. E. Church to protest the verdict in the Till case. An enormous crowd overflowed the large Paradise Valley church, and the address by Medgar Evers, state president of the Mississippi NAACP, stirred all.[10] However, despite the crowds, Franklin now suggested, the organization's impact on black Detroit remained sharply limited. He evoked the image of "a local barber shop," that central gathering place for black working-class men, where hair was cut and the foibles of white folks and snobbish, "dicty," elite blacks alike were skewered for hours on a Saturday morning. Franklin explained that the "barber-shop-talk" he heard recently had disturbed him. In a prolonged discussion with more than a dozen men, all "expressed almost complete ignorance of what the NAACP had done, or was doing, for Negroes." He had rushed to fill the gap, Franklin explained, his subtle sarcasm just barely contained, recalling "to the best of my remembrance, and in chronological order" the organization's achievements, but to little avail. To these men, working people for whom the Hastings Street neighborhood was home, the activities of the NAACP simply did not affect their lives. The organization "was doing little for racial progress," they told Franklin. C. L. deftly turned back on itself the anticipated black middle-class reaction to the message of this male, barbershop chorus: "Nothing is to be gained from merely 'bemoaning' . . . such un-informed attitudes" in the "very people for whom the N.A.A.C.P. is so dedicated . . . [and] from whom the organization should reasonably expect support."

Franklin did offer readers one solution. With feigned innocence, he asked whether it would "be at all possible . . . to compile a single, easy to understand pamphlet for mass distribution" that would convey "the purpose, program and achievements" of the organization. If that were "at all feasible," he urged it be distributed to all organizations "to which Negroes belong" for "person-to-person distribution." Churches, he noted, would be particularly helpful in this task, and he ingenuously pledged New Bethel's help in a mass distribution of "a copy [of the pamphlet] plus sermons on the subject." Franklin extended to his erstwhile addressee the "kindest personal regards" and, in a summary conclusion of his veiled critique, expressed "best wishes for increased success through a 'grass roots' educational program."[11]

Franklin meant his letter to mobilize the pain of Till's death toward political engagement. This poised, urbane preacher had once been a fourteen-year-old black boy in Mississippi; his own son, Cecil, was but a year older than Till had been. And, of course, Franklin as well as his barbershop companions, like so many southern-raised black Detroiters, must have experienced Till's death through the tortured memories of childhood violence. Franklin knew that many black Detroiters pressed, however slowly, beyond that fear, and he thought that the people along Hastings Street were ripe for collective action. Annual black-tie dinners celebrating the largest branch in the nation might raise needed funds for the NAACP's important legal challenges, but these same dinners did little to attract the Hastings Street regulars. Black working people, particularly the majority who were not union members, remained largely an afterthought as the leadership simply assumed that their programs and policies spoke for them. As a lifetime member of the organization, C. L.'s point was not to end such banquets (although he attended infrequently) but rather to expand the organizational vision. If this "grass roots" orientation could emerge, it would be further proof that Emmett Till had not died in vain.[12]

Franklin's letter proclaimed his assumption of a new public role, and in it he offered his ministry at New Bethel as an example for the secular NAACP. Indeed, C. L. projected himself as a proxy for the people he claimed to understand and represent. Whose sermons, after all, would be included in the proposed handout?[13]

In this bloodied season of Emmett Till's death, Franklin aided efforts to raise funds to send Detroit's first black congressman, Charles Diggs, Jr., to Sumner, Mississippi, to observe and report on the trial. In this same season New Bethel's Political Action Guild also began its activity. Occasional meetings such as "Kenya Sunday" were important, but C. L. wanted a more continuous effort. To that end, with the assistance of New Bethel stalwarts Harry Kincaid and Sylvia Penn, he organized the guild in 1955 as one of the recognized departments of the church. The guild sponsored local and national speakers on Sunday afternoons, organized support for sympathetic political candidates, and staffed a voter-registration table in the church foyer before services during election season. The guild also performed another role. When members came to their pastor, complaining about difficulties they encountered with the police, city services, or the schools, "Frank," as C. L.'s close friends called him in his Detroit days, "would in turn get Kincaid and other folks to look at the complaint and then would carry it" to a conclusion. Set against the impact of C. L.'s sermons, the guild allowed members to organize with others to protest racially discriminatory city services, attempt to elect a responsive candidate, or sponsor talks on national issues. In all of these activities and more, political action made concrete the new thinking encouraged by sermons heard on repeated Sundays.[14]

On one level, Franklin's intent was educational. Harry Kincaid remembered C. L. saying that the congregation would benefit from hearing candidates for local or state office because if they won, New Bethel's people "would understand what they wanted from the candidates themselves." As always, though, there were other purposes. The guild provided Franklin with a secular platform deeply grounded in church culture from which to exert leadership and support suitable candidates for office. His goal was not political office. Rather, in a fashion consistent with his use of radio technology in his ministry, the guild allowed C. L. to project himself as a leader of a grassroots movement. Arthur Johnson, for one, thought this was the central purpose of the guild. Franklin intended "to give recognition to other leadership," as Johnson, a Morehouse College graduate, classmate of Martin Luther King Jr., and executive director of Detroit's NAACP branch during the 1950s, recalled his reaction at the time, "to develop some new strategies of organization. And, quite frankly, to get around the discipline of the N.A.A.C.P." In this respect, Johnson considered Franklin similar to Martin Luther King Jr., who had encouraged the formation of a social and political action committee in his Montgomery, Alabama, church the year before Till's lynching. Both men, Johnson remarked, refused to be burdened "with a constitution, with bylaws and all of that, with the disciplines that make for good organization" as represented by the NAACP. Johnson was the very essence of an organization man, and he recognized the potential threat such freelance leaders as King and Franklin presented to the NAACP's position.[15]

Yet, regardless of what the educated black elite thought of him person-ally, C. L. knew they in fact needed him, for he and others like him pro-vided access to the black church — the one truly mass organization in black America. Some among that elite did appreciate Franklin's considerable skills. Johnson particularly underscored Franklin's "conscience" as ex-pressed in his preaching. He considered the minister "to be a person of strong intellect," who possessed a "thinking ability" and "the capacity for vision." During this time, Johnson thought, Franklin first distinguished himself, "stood above the pack" as "a leader of extraordinary ability . . . al-ways willing to come to the front line, who brought the issues and chal-lenges of our struggle to the center of the pulpit." This was high praise, even in retrospect, from one whose organization C. L. had scolded so pub-licly.[16]

In the decade following Till's death, Franklin intensified his political ac-tivities. He opened New Bethel's doors to any group or political candidate he considered seriously engaged with social problems. He rarely criticized a candidate from the pulpit and strove to present a range of opinions. But he did damn with silence those with whom he deeply disagreed. C. L. was a liberal Democrat in his political affiliation, which for a black Detroit res-ident in the postwar decades meant advocacy for civil rights legislation, support for the labor movement to the extent it practiced equality within its ranks, and a demand that the government at every level create equitable socioeconomic conditions for all citizens. To those who would carp that he strayed from the faith, he retorted that even "religious people gotta walk on sidewalks, use electricity and drink water too — to say nothing of having a job." C. L. had made these points before 1955, but in the aftermath of the Emmett Till protests, he desired to create an institutional presence to em-body his call, one simultaneously distanced from the NAACP and from the well-educated, Afro-Baptist church leadership.[17]

For all of his public engagement, however, Franklin's challenge to estab-lished groups remained limited. He sought to involve more black working people in politics, and gladly offered himself as their representative. To this extent, Franklin threatened the established leadership's singular control. He lacked, however, the self-effacement and patience required for actual grassroots organizing, for building slowly over time an institutional expression of the changed consciousness his sermons sought. Nor was his political analysis fundamentally different from that of the established leadership.

Franklin's involvement in the 1956 presidential campaign revealed the parameters of his political thinking. In October of that year, the guild and the Progressive Civic League, a West Side group of black professionals, cosponsored a talk by Adam Clayton Powell. The Harlem congressman had been a frequent visitor in recent years, and Sylvia Penn credited Powell with encouraging C. L. toward political action a few years before. But the late October talk proved troublesome. Shortly before it, Powell, a lifelong Democrat, endorsed publicly for reelection the incumbent Republican president, Dwight David Eisenhower. So intent was Adlai Stevenson, the Democratic challenger, on retaining the support of southern Democratic segregationists in the Congress, Powell and many African Americans thought, that his commitment to enforce *Brown v. Board of Education* seemed hesitant at best. Although Powell made it clear that he supported Democratic candidates for all other offices, his announcement for Eisenhower caused an uproar, especially as the congressman claimed that during a meeting in the White House, he received from Eisenhower "his promise to prove [if reelected] that he is not a captive of the south."[18]

Powell, who besides being a congressman was pastor of Abyssinian Baptist, Harlem's largest and most influential church, had agreed to deliver a nonpartisan address from Franklin's pulpit on Sunday evening, October 21. Like Franklin's sermons, it was to be carried live over WJLB. Looking to capitalize on Powell's endorsement of Eisenhower, the local Republican Party purchased the opening fifteen minutes of the hour-long program for a paid political message—in effect, preventing Franklin from introducing Powell—and selected attorney Willis Ward to deliver the speech that would. It was a move guaranteed to infuriate Franklin and many in his congregation, sensitive as they were to the political and social distinctions within black Detroit. Ward himself was a Republican candidate for Congress, running against the popular incumbent, Charles Diggs, Jr. He was also a lifelong member of the elite Second Baptist, where his father had been a deacon for more than twenty-five years. Since declaring his candidacy the previous July, Ward had enjoyed the full public support of his pastor, the influential Republican minister A. A. Banks. Ward's partisan opening remarks further angered many listeners, and the Republicans ultimately appeared foolish when Powell took the pulpit and endorsed Diggs and the entire Democratic ballot with the exception of its presidential candidate.[19]

Franklin, present that evening, was sharply critical of Ward's address, perhaps seeing in it the influential hand of Second Baptist's minister, who thought Franklin somewhat crude and never accorded him any trace of public recognition. When pressed, C. L. explained that the Federal Communications Commission's rules concerning the purchase of radio time for political announcements had bound the management of WJLB to grant Ward airtime.

Eisenhower won reelection with nearly 40 percent of the black vote nationally, while Diggs easily won his Detroit district, but the tumult had significantly raised black Detroit's—and Franklin's—political temperature. Angry at what the Republicans had done—it was his voice, after all, they had silenced—Franklin demanded the resignation of the New Bethel trustee who had supported Ward. Such public opposition Franklin would not let pass.[20]

*   *   *   *   *

In 1956, Franklin's fame as a gospel preacher far exceeded his reputation as a political strategist. He had joined the gospel tour three years earlier and crisscrossed the country preaching the sermons Joe Von Battle had already sold. Quickly, a distinctive pattern emerged. A local promoter, often a minister, organized a program, signed local and national gospel groups to appear, and arranged for a local radio station to air repeatedly in advance the particular sermon Franklin would preach. C. L. inevitably arrived with what he called "my group": a driver, his current personal secretary, two New Bethel vocalists, and a pianist. Following the event, Franklin's entourage moved on to another city or returned to Detroit, the tour completed.[21]

The gospel tour was already a well-established feature of black public life when Franklin joined it. In cities across the country, local gospel groups performed year round in area churches. Some of these local groups, such as the Pattersonaires from Memphis and Detroit's Meditations, with Della

Reese singing second lead, achieved a limited national acclaim, but all of them hungered to open for the more famous national singers when they appeared nearby. The Dixie Hummingbirds, the Clara Ward Singers, Sister Rosetta Tharpe, the Soul Stirrers, Mahalia Jackson, to name but a few, drew large crowds to the biggest churches or, when a number of them appeared together on a program, to a local auditorium. Gospel programs drew a mixed crowd. African American businessmen and professionals often were in attendance, although the majority of these audiences were relatively poor workingmen and working women. There was as well a scattering of whites. The blues-inflected gospel of Sister Rosetta Tharpe or the clarity and depth of Sam Cooke's vocal anticipation of soul music attracted fans both churched and not. A bevy of small, independent music labels promoted the groups' recordings while a few performers, Mahalia Jackson, for example, signed with major recording companies. Whether nationally famous or locally known, these gospel singers provided black America, north and south, with a major form of public religious testimony and, although religious traditionalists would reject the very idea, an enjoyable form of entertainment as well.[22]

What was remarkable about the gospel tour before Franklin's presence transformed it was the dramatic absence of preachers in this sacred event. Ministers might urge their congregations to attend and, if they promoted the program, might also gain financially from it. Rarely, however, did they offer more than a prayer and usually only very early in the program, well before the main act closed the evening. This arrangement reflected a deeper tension in the Afro-Baptist community. Many ministers regarded music as of secondary importance in their service, but parishioners often responded more enthusiastically to the incessant blues beat backing the gospel message of gifted singers. At times, to a minister's profound chagrin, the contrast with the reception given his sermon proved embarrassing.[23]

Franklin rendered this pattern of the gospel tour obsolete. He welcomed gospel singers, not least because, as Jasper Williams observed, "he was a preacher who could sing! And, you know . . . you didn't find that every day." Indeed, supremely confident of his talent, already known as the "Black Prince," the "Jitterbug Preacher," "the preacher with the golden voice," Franklin regularly and enthusiastically appeared with some of the best singers in the country. Promoters quickly positioned C. L. Franklin last on the program, which was usually held not in a local church, as had been customary, but in the largest auditorium available. Like the white evangelical Billy Graham, C. L. began to reach mass audiences never before thought possible.[24]

In 1956, C. L. appeared on a gospel program in Jackson, Mississippi, organized by a local minister, L. H. Newsome. As he usually did, Franklin arrived that afternoon with his group and settled into a segregated hotel. After having his shoes shined and his clothes cleaned, he visited with Newsome, who was also a gospel DJ on a local radio station. As Newsome played the sermon the audience would hear that evening, Charlie Thompson, a teenager living in Jackson who knew Newsome, came by the station and met the famous Detroit preacher for the first time. More than forty years later, the power of that experience impressed him yet. Franklin, he remarked, "had an elegant appearance," his clothes were impeccably stylish, and he possessed something even "regal about him." He was younger in appearance than Thompson expected and carried himself with "a certain little strut . . . a certain walk about him," erect, square-shouldered, even "ram-rod," yet with a rhythm to his gait. Even with an overwhelmed teenager, Franklin offered recognition and respect. He "would look you right in your eyes with a smile," Thompson remembered, and when he shook hands, he wasn't distracted or focused on someone else: "He gave you his total attention." S. L. Jones, then twelve, also attended the evening program at the large Masonic Temple in Jackson and approached Franklin at its conclusion. Decades later, he remembered the man with profound appreciation: "And he took the time to talk to me and I told him who I was."[25]

The program itself was staggering, including the Maceo Wood Singers, with whom the young minister Samuel Billy Kyles then performed, and Roberta Martin and her singers. The Clara Ward Singers were then at the height of their fame, with the powerful voices of Henrietta Waddy and Marion Williams backing the incomparably talented Ward herself. Also there was Little Sammy Bryant, a dwarf and one of the major soloists in the New Bethel choir, who projected her powerful voice across large halls in a fashion that made audiences gasp. Finally, the preacher's fourteen-year-old daughter, Aretha, approached the microphone. She had recently recorded her first gospel songs live, before an open microphone, during services at New Bethel and had only recently begun touring with her father. For all the polish and mature command she would later possess, the raw power and passion in her voice at this time still mark her first gospel recordings as among her best work. Only after her performance, which the preacher witnessed from his seat on the platform facing an audience already nearing its emotional peak, did Clarence LaVaughn Franklin move to center stage.[26]

Incredibly enough, given what had just occurred, he began with a hymn, with "his prayer song," Charlie Thompson remembered, "Father, I Stretch My Hand to Thee." Thompson could not recall how many verses the preacher sang that night, but when Franklin felt the hymn had worked its power, he moved into his sermon, citing the Apostle Paul's letter to the Philippians 3:13–14 as his text. In the sermon, recorded the year before as *Pressing On,* C. L. stressed Paul's humility rather than his well-known insistence on ascetic virtues, asserting that Paul would take credit for but one virtue, namely, his dedication to press toward salvation despite whatever may have occurred in the past. Then, after all of the emotion of the gospel music, his whoop electrified the audience, matching, indeed surpassing, the earlier gospel tones as he brought his message home. "But I never heard anything or anybody move a crowd of people the way Reverend moved those people that night," Thompson later mused, still in the wonder of it. "I was sixteen years old and I was, and I ain't never [been] moved to that extent."[27]

Charlie Thompson was not the only person beyond New Bethel who reacted to C. L. that way. Franklin's preaching, projected through radio speakers by local DJs and from record players, flooded living rooms across the nation and made him almost a familiar presence to thousands upon thousands of listeners. S. L. Jones, who later led Detroit's Mt. Zion Baptist Church, where to Jones's delight, C. L. attended his 1970 installation, marveled at how many people in his own ministry had never met Franklin yet "felt like they knew him . . . [and called] him Frank." He saw this particularly in preachers in small towns and smaller churches who regularly said, almost matter-of-factly, "I was listening to Frank last night." They thought of C. L. as "one of the guys" whom they knew from his records, Jones thought, "because he made them feel a part of what he was doing." Others were struck by different qualities. His reputation as a chanting preacher drew those who found gospel music a touch too secular and, perhaps more surprisingly, those who might like gospel but rejected church itself. Such was his influence that black ministers and lay people alike, churched or not, critics as well as supporters of his theology and lifestyle, flocked to any program he graced.[28]

C. L.'s sermons on tour echoed those he delivered from New Bethel's pulpit. In many ways, the very technology that spread his fame constrained this revival preaching. Audiences wanted to hear the recorded sermons they already knew; they wanted to see this man in full delivery, to feel God's power work on them through him—viscerally, physically, spiritually. While there "may be some deviations," some moments where "you can improvise," Franklin later reflected, "you generally stay within the same theme." At first, he resented this limitation on his ministerial prerogative to preach as he pleased, especially as the most recently released sermon was usually in demand. Franklin felt that the promoter's insistence that audiences "want to hear what they have been hearing" truncated his need "to express myself in other sermons." But he adjusted, and especially as the total of sermons Franklin released reached seventy-five, he had a greater leeway with producers and audiences alike.[29]

The fundamental purpose of his preaching, however, was no different on tour than at New Bethel. As was true for the gospel singers in their fashion, the goal of C. L.'s efforts was to evangelize, to bring people to Jesus, by moving audiences "in more ways than just the emotional," to "impart some thoughtfulness and inspiration in them." At every stop, local ministers counseled those who had accepted the call and, not insignificantly, sought to enroll the newly converted in their congregations. Franklin did not think it disrespectful if he and the gospel groups practiced their ministry in a manner that simultaneously entertained and made money. As tensions grew during the 1950s over changes in the religious culture— Could ministers be celebrities in their own right and still preach Jesus? Could the Ward Singers and other groups perform gospel in Las Vegas nightclubs and still live out their Christian ministry?—Franklin remained unperturbed. In church or on tour, he held that the black religious community wanted the experience to be "entertaining as well as enlightening." To Reverend Kyles, "Frank did something that no one had ever done with the spoken word" in the 1950s. He popularized the sermon well beyond the church sanctuary "and strangely enough it did *not* lose its sacredness. I mean, [audiences] never saw him as a pop [artist]. . . . He was Reverend Franklin. He was deeply religious."[30]

Between his duties at New Bethel, his incessant touring, and his responsibilities in the Baptist Convention, C. L.'s schedule grew immensely complicated. In part because of this, C. L. flew to his engagements while his "group," leaving a day or two earlier, drove his car, usually a new Lincoln or a Cadillac Eldorado. This arrangement conserved the harried pastor's time, but it also limited his exposure to a part of America that fiercely defended segregation. The black-only boarding houses and hotels they regularly stayed in were particularly comforting, but C. L. narrowed the time spent traveling the roads of the South to a minimum. His anger at the indignities already suffered in his life remained palpable, and although he diverted his fury at racist insults away from open confrontations with whites, he occasionally did so in ways potentially dangerous. Reverend Kyles recalled C. L. telling him of a trip through one southern city when his car broke down. A mechanic was not immediately available or simply would not work on the car, and a crowd of whites encircled this fashionably dressed, handsome black man, calling him "boy," laughing, seeking to provoke. Franklin contained himself, as he had that day a decade earlier when confronted with the commonplace taunts of a Memphis policeman. Instead of responding, he walked through the mocking crowd to an auto dealership "and bought a brand new car and paid cash for it on the spot. . . . Just pulled his money out, bought a car on the spot." For a well-attired black man, with an entourage in a late-model, expensive car (no matter its mechanical difficulties) and a money clip bursting with large bills, to thwart so publicly the pretensions to superiority of that white crowd, in a manner reminiscent of a Jack Johnson folktale, was both daring and dangerous. Black males during the 1950s had been lynched and murdered for far less.[31]

Despite his efforts to limit his absences, C. L. left New Bethel in the hands of assistant ministers on more Sundays than many in the congregation desired. He tried to get back for Sunday services, flying in on Saturday, preaching Sunday morning with perhaps a guest preacher for the evening radio service, if he had to leave for his next engagement that afternoon. Some in the congregation grew restive with this, and attendance did drop in his absence. Margaret Branch, whose mother, Lucy Branch Layten, often traveled with the Franklin group in the 1950s, heard parishioners complain to the pastor about his frequent absences. His response, as blunt as his earlier confrontation with his deacons over his Detroit radio show, was brief. "But he'd turn around and tell them this, simply this," Branch remembered. " 'Ya'll don't pay me enough money to sit here every Sunday. I have to go elsewhere and make money.' " This flippant dismissal of his pastoral duties reflected the appeal of a celebrity culture that increasingly drew C. L. closer. And make money he did. In his early years on tour, C. L. might command a guarantee as high as $700 for an appearance, though the figure more often was closer to $500. But as his fame grew and the crowds increased, he wondered whether promoters might not be taking advantage of him. In Houston in 1955, for example, Gertrude Ward, Clara's mother and a gospel promoter known for her sharp financial dealings, promised C. L. $500 to preach at the city auditorium. When he got to Houston, a local preacher and disk jockey commented that ticket sales had been enormous "because we've been really burning your records up down here." He joked with C. L. that his fee must be "a bundle." The next morning at the hotel, the maids gathered at his door to meet him and confirmed that before he joined the program the Ward Singers had always sung at churches with far less capacity. Franklin confronted Gertrude Ward backstage, demanded $1,500, and when she resisted, pulled out his plane ticket and told her he would return home immediately. He got his fee that day, and he understood more clearly from then on just how much of a celebrity he was among African Americans. Shortly after this experience, he commanded $4,000 for each appearance, an enormous sum at the time for one gospel performer. (Elvis Presley received $7,500 for one television appearance in 1956.) But promoters were only too happy to pay C. L.[32]

In 1956, two technological developments catapulted C. L. into an unrivaled position among Afro-Baptist and, indeed, all black preachers, regardless of denomination. Joe Von Battle initiated the first event that spring when he approached his friend Leonard Chess with a business proposal. Chess and his brother, Phil, who were white and ran Chicago's independent rhythm-and-blues record label, Chess Records, had signed such blues artists as Muddy Waters, Howlin' Wolf, Junior Wells, Buddy Guy, Etta James, and John Lee Hooker. Leonard Chess had long desired to expand into the potentially highly profitable, black religious market. Von Battle, who owned the recording rights to the sermons of the nation's premier black preacher, anticipated a financial windfall by leasing those rights to Chess. C. L., for his part, welcomed the greater recognition the Chess label allowed, as he did the 6–8 percent return anticipated on each album. Using JVB's master tapes, Chess pressed new recordings for nationwide distribution, and the company's distribution network brought C. L.'s voice to hundreds of record stores across the nation Von Battle could never reach. This alone multiplied the potential audience for the touring gospel programs. Chess also dramatically improved the technical quality of the recordings. C. L.'s first sermons on JVB had appeared on 78-rpm records, with a cumbersome technology that required three or four records to present a half-hour sermon. Chess issued the new sermons on a forty-minute LP with much improved technical sound. Beyond the enhanced audience, Franklin's association with Chess revealed a preacher standing alone atop the mountain, without any serious ministerial competition for national, popular prominence. Most preachers who recorded sermons between 1945 and 1970—far fewer than before the war—usually released but a handful, many only one or two. C. L. was the preeminent exception. He continued to record new sermons into the 1970s, while Chess reissued additional original JVB recordings in a more technologically advanced format. Franklin's success in this medium was without parallel, at that time or in the history of preachers, black or white.[33]

One consequence of the arrangement with Chess records was that C. L.'s radio presence also took a dramatic turn. In 1956, a creative Nashville disc jockey paired with an enterprising record-store owner and sponsor in Gallatin, Tennessee, just outside the city, created an even wider audience when they began airing a Franklin sermon every Sunday evening at ten o'clock. While most radio stations not affiliated with a national network had a broadcast radius of less than fifty miles, Nashville's WLAC, a 50,000-watt, clear-signal station, had a range closer to 1,000 miles. And after nine in the evening, when most other stations went off the air, WLAC's reach stretched nationwide and then some. John Lewis heard it in Troy, Alabama; the aspiring singer James Brown heard it in Augusta, Georgia; the poet Al Young caught it on the Mississippi Gulf; and Ruth Brown, already a star on the rhythm-and-blues circuit on her way to international acclaim, listened to it "all the way from California to Virginia." Some even claimed that the signal reached Korea, Iceland, and Australia when the atmospherics were just right. What made WLAC special was what the station programmed with the power it possessed. Three white deejays—Bill "Hoss" Allen, Gene Nobles, and John "John R." Richbourg—who programmed rhythm and blues and gospel for African American audiences, were wildly successful with blacks and young whites during the 1940s and 1950s. B. B. King sat, "enthralled," listening to blues over the station in the late 1940s, when he was on the cusp of beginning his own career; Al Young tagged Gene Nobles an "Afro-Caucasian," for the "vein of patter," the verbal improvisation, that flooded the airwaves on his program. Bernie Besman, John Lee Hooker's first producer, credited Nobles with turning Hooker's "Boogie Chillen" into an overnight national hit. Nobles had turned to programming for black audiences originally at the request of a group of African American college students in Nashville and proved so successful that his fellow disc jockeys soon followed his lead. Nobles had needed a financial backer, however, for the station managers remained dubious. He had asked a friend, Randy Wood, who owned a record shop and the small independent label Dot Records, to underwrite these shows at a cost of $6 per night. It was, perhaps, the savviest investment Wood ever made.[34]

The purpose of the show was to sell records, and Randy's Record Mart developed into one of music radio's most successful mail-order businesses, a model of aggressive entrepreneurship. Randy's sold a large volume of blues, gospel, and rhythm-and-blues recordings, in addition to C. L.'s sermons. The recording companies and, to a lesser extent, the artists received their share from the sales. Perhaps even more important for Franklin and for such recording artists as T-Bone Walker, Bobby Blue Bland, and the young Etta James, the exposure drew listeners nationwide to their live performances. WLAC's programming also influenced popular musical culture, when black American music, especially rhythm and blues, increasingly appealed to white audiences in the form of rock and roll. "Can't tell you how many white people have told me," B. B. King stated, "they got hip to black music 'cause of Randy's." That dynamic, as much sociological as musical, caught even the Chess family by surprise. On a 1953 trip to Gallatin, Marshall Chess, Leonard's eleven-year-old son, and his father both exclaimed in surprise as they watched white teens buying rhythm-and-blues records at Randy's. It was a glimpse of a potential new audience for the records they then marketed almost exclusively to black audiences.[35]

Soon, Sunday evening at ten o'clock on WLAC was a profound religious moment, anticipated during the week by a vast radio audience. The devoutly faithful, such as John Lewis and his family, filled church pews Sunday mornings and afternoons, "and then you come home on Sunday night and it's radio worship" on WLAC, with gospel hymns and C. L.'s powerful preaching. Others less devout also found welcome inspiration and uplift. These weekly, recorded sermons led preachers to think of C. L. as a friend, a confidant, to talk of "Frank" in a fashion that joined them to him in their common, sacred task. John Lewis and Jasper Williams were only two of an unknown number of teenage boys, intent on a ministerial career, who huddled around the radio Sunday evening to hear the most accomplished preacher in the African American tradition. In his room at his parents' house in Memphis, Williams would surreptitiously get "under the bed" with his radio when C. L. came on, "because I didn't want to offend my father." Williams's father and C. L.'s friend, Jasper Williams, Sr., did not whoop, preaching instead from a manuscript. But preachers young and old studied Franklin's sermons, imitating his pacing, his growls, and his cadence so obviously that the standing joke among ministers and laity alike was that C. L. had brought more preachers to perdition than Satan himself, in despair at their inability to emulate the New Bethel master. C. L. himself never foresaw such a response: "I had thought of [the initial JVB records] in terms of recording on the spot, recording live at the church, right out of a regular service, and the record sales more or less for people to hear them. I didn't know that they would respond the way they did." This was only twelve years since Franklin had ascended the pulpit at Friendship Baptist, where he first used a microphone regularly. His voice and its message, amplified by modern technology, now reached from sea to sea.[36]

Himself a product of this transformation from a southern, rural world, Franklin's amplified voice and the congregation's responses continued to encourage others to find theirs. As he did from his New Bethel pulpit, Franklin projected on national radio a model of black religious commitment that engaged the secular world, his faith resonating deeply within the collective, cultural experience of African American people. With no exaggeration Reverend Jesse Jackson once asked: "Did not our ears perk up for years before we had a television or an elected official in America, if we could just hear WLAC, Nashville, Tennessee, Randy's, on a Sunday night? Sunday night, New Bethel, Hastings Street, was the common frame of reference for the black church prototype."[37]

*　　*　　*　　*　　*

C. L.'s effort to insert himself into the political life of black Detroit while touring incessantly—a near-impossible task in itself—was strained further by a growing tension within the National Baptist Convention. Struggle for control of the organization turned ugly in 1956–57, and the growing prominence of C. L.'s friend Martin Luther King Jr. became the flashpoint of a more complex battle that demanded Franklin's attention.

Formed in 1894 by a merger of three black Baptist organizations, the National Baptist Convention, Incorporated, USA, as it was formally known, claimed a membership of nearly 3 million members in 1916. Forty years later, that figure surpassed 4.5 million. Whatever the precise accuracy of the reported numbers, two points were clear to all observers. The National Baptist Convention represented a significant majority of all black Americans who reported religious membership, and it was the largest mass organization, sacred or secular, black Americans possessed. The presidency of the convention was an office highly sought and fiercely defended, for in a thoroughly segregated America, its leader was among the most influential public men in the black world. Elias Camp Morris, born to slave parents in Georgia in 1855, held the office between 1894 and his death in 1921. His successor, Lacy Kirk Williams, held power from 1922 until 1940, when an accident took his life. D. V. Jemison followed in 1941. It was widely understood that all three of these men would serve for life and resign only for health reasons. Open challenges such as the one Chicago's J. C. Austin organized against Williams in 1930 were rare. Centralization of power in the hands of the president limited the possibility of a serious challenge, and the promise of patronage kept most national and state officials well within the incumbent's realm.[38]

A momentary breakdown of this autocratic system made the convention's 1953 election unusual. Postwar expectations had created restlessness in this institution as in other areas of African American life, and more ministers bristled at the prospect of continued one-man rule than ever before. At the 1952 convention, a coalition of primarily younger ministers spearheaded a successful reform of the constitution to limit the president's tenure to no more than four consecutive one-year terms and mandated the selection of an executive secretary to share some of the president's duties. These changes would open the way, as Reverends Marshall L. Shephard and Gardner C. Taylor enthusiastically proclaimed in their reform journal, *Baptist Layman,* "for bringing to the front young men of merit." As D. V. Jemison announced his health-related retirement effective with the conclusion of the 1953 meeting, the presidential election that year in Miami proved the most fiercely contested in decades. Five candidates presented themselves, all professing allegiance to the recent reforms, and Joseph H. Jackson, pastor of Chicago's Mt. Olivet Baptist, won decisively.[39]

Born in Mississippi in 1900, Jackson received his license to preach at age fourteen, attended Jackson College (now Jackson State University) while he rode a rural Mississippi circuit of four churches, and in 1927 accepted a call from Bethel Baptist Church in Omaha, Nebraska. In 1932, he received his bachelor of divinity degree from Colgate Rochester Divinity School in upstate New York. Like so many other ministers, this smart, intense, and ambitious man regarded the convention as the organizational expression of his faith and as the vehicle for his advancement. As he became more and more involved in convention politics, he simultaneously accepted calls from ever more prestigious churches: Philadelphia's Monumental Baptist Church in 1934 and, seven years later, Mt. Olivet Baptist in Chicago. Jackson had never been a civil rights activist. During the 1930s, as William Holmes Borders and Martin Luther King Sr. led their congregations in demonstrations for racial equality in Atlanta, Jackson exhibited the caution that marked many Afro-Baptist ministers at that time. In an interview in 1932, while still a student in Rochester, Jackson stated proudly that in the area of race progress, whatever "we have achieved has been done under the protection of the Stars and Stripes." Jackson took a critical approach to the culture of his people. "As a group," he insisted, "we must develop a higher standard of culture." Literacy was necessary but by no means sufficient, he explained. "We must know how to appreciate the finer things of life such as those in which they [i.e., white people] have attained distinction." Two decades later, Jackson merged his concerns with black patriotism and cultural progress with a general commitment to work for equality. The new tone owed more to timing than to transformed conviction.[40]

By 1956, the emerging civil rights movement had captured the imagination of many. As a national leader, Jackson had to reflect a sensitivity to these trends—he sent a contribution to King to aid the Montgomery boycott—even if he sought to direct them toward a more cautious goal. What propelled Jackson's particular urgency, however, was the manner in which a boycott of the segregated public buses in Montgomery, Alabama, elevated a new contender for national black leadership. Martin Luther King Jr. was only twenty-seven in 1956, but his distinctive public voice, grounded in a familiar biblical expression, touched large crowds at nightly mass meetings and soon won him national recognition. Jackson did not fear an immediate challenge from the young minister. King Sr. was a Jackson supporter, for one, and Jackson considered the son too young, too inexperienced in the convention's byzantine politics, to mount a successful challenge. The rise to prominence of the younger King was a threat nonetheless, for it challenged Jackson's position as the preeminent black spokesman. To complicate matters further, King's emergence in the national spotlight in spring 1956 came only a year before Jackson's tenure as president was to end. Jackson had no intention of ceding power, and the preelection maneuvering already generated bitter debate over whether the 1952 reforms were valid. His critics saw an attempt to reinstate the pattern of lifetime tenure. In the maneuvering at the 1956 Denver convention, Martin Luther King Sr., William H. Brewster of Memphis, and C. L. Franklin all took the floor to argue against tenure limitations on behalf of President Jackson.[41]

As many of the reform-minded ministers were also civil rights activists, Jackson planned a convention program that gave them public prominence in an effort to win their support in his 1957 reelection. To this end, Jackson arranged for a series of ministers to speak on civil rights, sponsored a symposium on the issue of gradualism in demanding full rights, and invited Roy Wilkins, the executive secretary of the NAACP, and Howard Thurman, the liberal theologian, to address the convention. The crowning moment in Jackson's effort to reposition himself came when he escorted the young leader of the Montgomery movement to the podium. King's speech, not surprisingly, electrified the delegates. But King was so effective that Jackson now feared that this young minister less than half his age stole not only the day but perhaps the convention itself. From this moment, Jackson resolved to contain King and the activist ministers drawn to him. The first step in that struggle would be to retain his office at the 1957 meeting in Louisville, Kentucky.[42]

Intense organizing and bitter acrimony filled the year between conventions. Jackson's opponents, led by William Holmes Borders of Atlanta, gathered in St. Louis in December 1956 to develop strategy and draft a form letter to fellow ministers. A month later, the convention's board of directors, meeting in Hot Springs, Arkansas, passed a resolution, seconded by King Sr., to declare the St. Louis delegates "an independent organization with rights and privileges of their own" and, therefore, no claim on the membership or resources of the National Baptist Convention. C. L. Franklin, present at the meeting, did not dissent from this first step toward expulsion. Privately, the tension rose even higher. Reports surfaced that H. H. Humes, the extremely conservative leader of the Mississippi State Convention and a staunch Jackson supporter, had accepted funds from white segregationists to be "the paid stool pigeon of Senator Eastland and his gang." Gardner C. Taylor, pastor of Concord Baptist Church in Brooklyn, New York, told a black reporter a month before the 1957 convention that a lifetime president in command of the reins of power could never be "cooperative" and thus never work to mobilize the political consciousness essential to furthering the civil rights movement. From the opposite position, W. H. Brewster wrote Jackson in August 1957 to assure him that he had already prepared "a special group to serve as our cheering squad in Louisville." He also arranged for a "behind closed doors" meeting place for Jackson forces before the convention opened, to ensure "perfect coordination in our on-the-spot action."[43]

The tensions accompanying these plots and counterplots grew to a fury that shook the Louisville convention. At a prearranged moment, Brewster's "special . . . cheering squad" burst onto the convention floor, shouting slogans and waving banners. In the chaos that followed, Jackson supporters suspended the rules and reelected Mt. Olivet's pastor to a fifth consecutive term. Quickly, ministerial tempers erupted, fistfights broke out on the floor, the Louisville police occupied the building and arrested four delegates, and the convention's printed program became irrelevant. Jackson supporters won election to every position, and the president immediately dismissed J. Pius Barbour—a critic—as editor of the *National Baptist Voice.* Legal challenges to the election soon were filed, charging that Jackson unconstitutionally "usurped" the office of the presidency.[44]

Given Franklin's national fame and influence, both sides desired his support. Reformers were disappointed when he supported Jackson publicly, and some questioned his recent commitment to political action. But C. L. understood the dispute differently. For him, the National Baptist Convention was the most important organization in black America, a vehicle for both individual and collective advance. To run the risk of damaging it by a schism (when Jackson held the majority of the delegates) was inconceivable. C. L. did not then interpret the tension as primarily concerned with the organization's stance toward the civil rights movement. King Sr., of course, had remained as strong a public advocate of J. H. Jackson's reelection as had Franklin. Instead, hoping that the decisions reached in Louisville resolved the tension, Franklin turned again toward his burgeoning public career.

*   *   *   *   *

Franklin was now a star, and although he did not sacrifice his sacred artistry, this status brought with it new possibilities and challenges. Wealthier than ever before, Franklin faced the demands of family and career, New Bethel's desire for a pastor and the call of the road, additional business opportunities, and political involvements, all vying for his attention. A very human man, whose expressed needs at times reflected but dimly the hurts in his soul, discovered that people whom he had never met discussed his personal life in intimate detail. It was a heady time and one fraught with tension, as Franklin learned there was a price to be paid for this fame.

C. L.'s distinctive presence was not a role he stepped into each Sunday. His was a performance, to be sure, but even in its sacred dimension it was a performance that reflected openly, boldly, with joy and at times with pain, Franklin the man. His sermons, alternately exuberant and inclusive and, in turn, direct or even abrasive, flowed from the core of his intense, complex personality. His preaching revealed his persistent intellectual hunger, his deep delight in and involvement with music, musicians, and their world, and a need for affirmation—divine as well as human—that was so profoundly a part of his spirit. Predictably, he welcomed the attention national renown brought and approached it in a manner distinctly his own.

The first thing that struck an audience was C. L.'s sartorial style. Long discarded were the torn, worn, and outdated suits, accented with those "yellow-type shoes, the kind sold at dry goods stores," which had draped his solid frame when he arrived in Memphis in 1939. He now preferred expensive wool and silk suits, in shades of gray, brown, cream, and white, as well as the more traditional dark blue. Alligator-skin shoes, diamond stickpins, flashy rings, watches, and ministerial crosses complemented his colorful neckties. While he occasionally bought clothes on the road, his regular haberdasher was a downtown Detroit firm, Kosins. He was, New Bethel member Carolyn King thought, "a snazzy dresser." Even on an ordinary weekday, "He always was matching from head to toe." By the mid-1950s, his sense of style and fashion was well known. Mahalia Jackson, no insignificant figure herself, once kept C. L. waiting to leave for a Christmas party as she "finished dressing with care. Can't look just anyway going to a party with Rev. C. L.—man has 35 suits."[45]

C. L.'s fashionable appearance and obvious material success reflected a broader cultural transformation. In 1950, religious traditionalists had banned the Ward Singers from a National Baptist Convention meeting with objections to "their flamboyant dress and mannerisms." They were overruled—the group had a runaway national gospel hit, "Surely God Is Able," at that time—but resistance to the presentation of the sacred in a more secular fashion continued. Franklin's public style and demeanor irritated some, even as it opened new vistas for others. His example "took the preachers out of the . . . white Panama hat, the high-top shoes, and the blue suede suits," Claud Young thought. As preachers imitated his voice, or tried to, so did they follow "his dress, his mannerisms," S. L. Jones recalled. "I mean, C. L. Franklin was heard and seen and felt in preachers everywhere."[46]

If C. L.'s clothes, jewelry, and penchant for top-of-the-line Cadillacs caused traditionalists concern as they struggled against a broader transformation of religious culture in postwar America, it was a rather simple change in his hairstyle that truly scandalized many more. Sometime before 1954, Franklin exchanged his close-cropped, natural hairstyle for processed hair, known on the street corners of black America as the "conk." The process itself was rather simple, if at times painful: a barber or a beautician used various chemicals, including lye, to straighten the naturally curly hair of the client and then proceeded to form the hair into any one of a number of styles. The process took much longer than the traditional haircut, cost significantly more, and lasted perhaps a few weeks or a month before a return to the barber was needed—but none of these factors caused the intense reaction to the conk. Rather, in black men particularly, the conk projected a cultural meaning that traditionalists found offensive in church members, to say nothing of ministers.[47]

To have a process suggested a man sympathetic to if not a participant in the black entertainment world, where blues and jazz musicians mingled with gamblers, drug dealers, pimps and prostitutes, racketeers, and other members of what some called the demimonde, or the sporting life. Duke Ellington, Jimmy Lunceford, Nat "King" Cole, and boxing champion

Sugar Ray Robinson, as well as large numbers of young black men in Paradise Valley, all sported variants of the look: the "New Yorker," with its wave undulating across the head, or perhaps the "Tony Curtis" where, with a curl over the forehead, the processed hair on the front and sides was swept back into a "DA" (literally, an approximation of a duck's ass) at the back of the head. Otis Williams, a Detroit teenager in the 1950s who would soon form the singing group the Temptations, captured well the significance of the style: "As I got more serious about my singing group, I became more interested in perfecting my image. I had to be cool, and back in the mid-fifties that required a process." A decade earlier Malcolm Little, later famous as Malcolm X, and B. B. King both wore the conk out of a similar desire "to be cool." This phenomenon disturbed many. In a four-part series in the Michigan *Chronicle* in 1958, a concerned Ofield Dukes argued that the conk reflected poorly on black Americans. While he thought the chemical process required to straighten hair, especially the lye, was particularly dangerous, he underscored a more worrisome cultural danger. He attributed the popularity of the style to "psychological factor[s]—those of identification and association" and implied that the conk reflected blacks' desire to mimic white characteristics. However, like Charles Wartman's earlier writing on politics in the same paper, Dukes understood only a portion of a more complex phenomenon. As the novelist Albert Murray suggested, for "most Negroes . . . the process goes with certain manners in clothes, speech, music, and even movement, which are anything but ofay [i.e., white] orientated." For some, the conk was a statement of youthful rebellion, a critique of the more reserved, middle-class cultural norms offered as the singular model of proper behavior for all African Americans by elite blacks such as Dukes, a newspaper editor and leader in the Detroit branch of the NAACP.[48]

C. L. Franklin, with his modified New Yorker process—a series of discrete waves rippling back across his head—distilled through his public style the essence of this larger cultural tension. He was a respected preacher who dressed well, if a bit too flashily for some, and who lived among the black elite, first on Boston Boulevard and then, in the late 1950s, on the even more exclusive LaSalle Boulevard, west of Woodward and north of Grand Boulevard. His sermons proclaimed such virtues as self-help, self-respect, individual initiative, and political engagement which, in themselves, would have been warmly received at NAACP meetings—if only offered by someone else. But the image C. L. presented increasingly offended secular elites and religious conservatives alike. It was disturbing enough that a preacher of his standing frequently reminded audiences that church membership in itself meant little ("I see mean, evil, lowdown people in the church," he told New Bethel one Sunday), that before God there was no essential difference between the churched and the denizens of Hastings Street. But the conk, that symbol of the street hustler making his way in a shady, sinful, and usually illegal subculture, especially grated.[49]

Some traditionalists wondered, given C. L.'s flaunting of their sense of the sacred, whether he had not slipped off the thin-edged boundary where he defined his faith. The eleventh anniversary celebration of his leadership of New Bethel was a case in point. Such celebrations were common among Afro-Baptist congregations, as church members honored their pastor and offered a monetary gift, a new car, and sometimes both, to express that appreciation. A week of evening services, sermons, and singing by visiting clergy and choirs from near and far marked the occasion, which usually culminated with a banquet in the church dining room prepared by the women of the congregation. C. L.'s 1957 celebration followed this pattern, but only to a point. Various Baptist ministers led the services during the week of July 7, but C. L. also asked his friend, Bishop Theodoshia Hooks, of Everybody's Temple of Holiness, a local Pentecostal congregation, to lead one night's service. For traditionalists, the fact that Bishop Hooks was female and in the pulpit offended just as much as the fact that she was Pentecostal, a sect many Baptists disdained. Departing yet further from the norm, C. L. held the banquet not in the church dining room but rather in the Ebony Room of the Gotham Hotel. This was not the first time he had used the Gotham since his 1946 installation dinner; his 1954 banquet was in the same room. But the 1957 affair held a different surprise. Seated at the head table, along with Judge Wade McCree, attorney and candidate for Common Council, William T. Patrick, Jr., and other dignitaries were "Mr. and Mrs. T-Bone Walker." Placing the popular Texas blues artist at the head table was classic Franklin. The two men knew each other, C. L. loved his music, and the guitarist played Detroit that week. It was, however, "probably a little bit different" from what most other ministers would do, Bea Buck, C. L.'s former secretary, conceded. While some thought Walker's blues sounded almost like a sermon, many others were more likely to remember his 1948 Detroit arrest on drug charges or the skimpily clad woman who joined him nightly on stage for certain songs. C. L. never gave such comments recognition. "He was not intimidated by public criticism," Reverend Jerome Kirby explained. If Franklin intended to act in a certain way, "he was going to do it whether you thought he should do it or not." He was, Gardner C. Taylor emphasized, "quite an amalgam."[50]

Walker was not the only artist Franklin socialized with. B. B. King considered C. L. "my main minister." Regardless of what time King closed his Detroit set the night before, he was in a front pew for morning services at New Bethel, and when King remarried in 1958, he and his fiancée flew to Detroit so that C. L. could perform the ceremony at the Gotham. If Franklin provided King with a religious approach he could embrace (the singer carried C. L.'s recordings on tour), Franklin exerted a direct professional influence on another blues singer, Bobby "Blue" Bland. Bland had "lost the high falsetto" that had made his voice so recognizable and needed another sound to distinguish his approach from others. He listened to "'The Eagle Stirreth in [sic] Her Nest' over and over and over," practicing C. L.'s "squall," the climax of his whoop when the eagle is released from his cage, until he "got it to perfection." Bland's version of the "squall" became his trademark.[51]

In other ways as well, C. L. lived unconventionally. He was, to be sure, a preeminent Baptist minister, but he was also a relatively young, handsome single man, on the road many days a year. Segregation forced all black performers to gather together in the hotels and rooming houses that would accept them, with the result that traveling preachers and gospel groups lived cheek by jowl with blues, pop, and rhythm-and-blues performers. They might be at the same hotel on Tuesday evening in Shreveport, Louisiana, then again on Thursday in Baton Rouge, and Saturday in Little Rock, Arkansas. It was in the very nature of the circuit, Erma Franklin explained of her experiences traveling with her father during school vacations, that "we would run up on Sam Cooke and Dinah Washington and Lionel Hampton and, oh my God, all the gospel singers." Present, too, might be some of the great black comedians, such as Redd Foxx, Pigmeat Markham, or Moms Mabley, and singers B. B. King, Bobby Bland, Ruth Brown, Wynonie Harris, Little Richard, and Chuck Berry. The star quality audiences bestowed on these secular artists proved attractive to many gospel performers. Traditionalists might grumble, and Mahalia Jackson sang her beautiful and somewhat reproachful hymn, "I'm Going to Live the Life I Sing about in My Song," but the transformation of the religious culture continued apace.[52]

The strains of being on the road were quite real. Promoters frequently reneged on the agreed fee, the whites-only restaurants refused food and the gas stations restrooms, and the threat of violence hung as a constant reminder of the dangers of black performers becoming too visible to the white world. In Birmingham, Alabama, for example, a group of white racists, opposed to the presumed "savage" sexual influence black music had on white audiences, violently broke up a Nat King Cole concert before an all-white audience. The beaten and shaken performer canceled his southern tour and returned to Chicago. Such tensions intensified as the civil rights movement grew and heightened the very human needs performers experienced as they balanced alternating bouts of exhilaration, fear, and decompression that were the emotional essence of tour life, even in good times. As Ruth Brown put it, the "final compensation" after the applause faded and the promoter hopefully paid in full "lay in the comraderie among the artists on these tours." Performers might tour for as much as three months at a time, and daily they "told jokes, played games, laughed, cheated, shot the bull and made love. That last was inevitable," Brown noted, explaining the obvious, "for we were all flung in at the deep end of the adrenalin tank. . . . It seldom got to the point of 'Let's get married,' it was just being natural and keeping your business within your business, but these 'tingums' [affairs] could be hot stuff while they lasted."[53]

Gospel performers were as human as anyone else and did not live apart from any aspect of this performance culture. While not all had affairs with other performers or with fans—the Dixie Hummingbirds, for example, enforced a very strict code of behavior for group members—many did. As a teenager in the 1950s, Etta James toured with Little Richard (Richard Penniman) and recalled it as "a time of crazy orgies, and Richard, along with nearly everyone else, was a willing participant." One of the "wildest parties" she attended occurred in Philadelphia, where, among others, gospel singer Alex Bradford's sexual appetites stood out in the young singer's memory. "When it came to partying," James commented in a more general vein, "the gospel gang could swing all night." Willa Ward, Clara's sister, recalled a particular evening following an annual Baptist convention in Chicago in which Bradford also figured prominently. Ministers and gospel singers, some of them bisexual, gathered and after earlier leading delegates "to holy dancing and shouting [they] were now doing their own inspired thing," Willa archly commented. At this party she first discovered her sister's bisexuality, when one of the hosts approached Clara to apologize for not inviting a woman for her that evening. Questioned by her sister, Clara explained, as Willa remembered, that while "my thing is men," her mother's controlling protectiveness and intrusive spying "gets between me and any man I decide to get tight with." It was a painful, awkward moment for the sisters and a complicated one for the revelers who, the next morning, donned their clerical collars and tuned their voices for the convention's morning session.[54]

This, too, was part of the world C. L. inhabited. His road tours were usually not as long as those of many groups, but he often went for two weeks or more. Frequently accompanying him on these tours, beginning in 1956, was his daughter Aretha. She had already gained a reputation in church circles as a phenomenal singer, and she also had talent with the piano. In 1956, she had recorded her first gospel hymns. One can hear the powerful influence of Clara Ward in the young Aretha's versions of "Precious Lord" and "Never Grow Old," but there was another quality as well. Jerry Wexler, who produced some of Aretha Franklin's greatest songs on Atlantic Records in the late 1960s, commented of those first gospel sides that the "voice was not that of a child but rather of an ecstatic hierophant," that is, of a gifted priestess possessed of the Spirit.[55]

On March 25, 1956, Aretha turned fourteen and, shortly after, gave birth to her first son, whom she named Clarence, after her father. Lurid and unsubstantiated rumors as to who was the baby's father spread almost immediately, ranging from various performers who frequented the house to C. L. himself.[56] Aretha stated that her baby's father was a local Detroit youth who was not involved after the baby's birth, and the Franklin family, she continued, was very supportive. C. L. was not judgmental, Aretha recalled, but he did impress on her the new responsibilities she now carried. C. L.'s other decisions that spring, however, suggested a rather peculiar understanding of what those responsibilities might entail. Aretha had withdrawn from school by the sixth month of her pregnancy, and her father never insisted that she return. Instead, by early summer, he added his daughter to his gospel program, along with Sammy Bryant, the Clara Ward Singers, and Alex Bradford and his group. They drew enormous crowds at almost every performance, and young Aretha gained a new standing among her friends. Smoky Robinson was dumbfounded when "Ree" returned from one tour to announce that she had actually met Fats Domino. While Aretha was away, Rachel, "Big Mama," cared for young Clarence.[57]

C. L.'s inclusion of his daughter, a vulnerable woman-child, on the tour all but demanded that she grow up fast. In that intensely emotional, sexually charged adult context, she was at once a starstruck kid, a mother still discovering the meaning of those emotions, and an attractive female with a young teenager's profoundly uneven self-confidence. What arrangements C. L. made to shield her from the tour's nocturnal activities are not known, but her very presence unavoidably exposed her to experiences well beyond her years. What further strained the credibility of C. L.'s pronouncements on maternal responsibilities were the persistent rumors, percolating beneath the public acclaim, indicating that Frank, too, participated in what Ruth Brown called the "final compensation." There are few specifics, however, and no eyewitness accounts available, only numerous references to his love of nightlife and the company of women. But it seems probable that Franklin enjoyed the company of women on the road as much as he did in Detroit.[58]

Since C. L. and Barbara separated in 1948, Franklin probably only rarely wanted for female companionship. He never remarried but opportunities presented themselves at almost every turn. Ruth Brown, for one, always went to C. L.'s for dinner when she played Detroit, for "he had a thing for me for quite a while," she discreetly recalled, and she was clearly taken with him. "This man's cloth was silk, and I mean made to measure. He sported a 'konk,' and was tall, fine-looking, and very, very suave." Anna Gordy, an executive in her brother's Motown Records, had a serious relationship with C. L. some years before she married singer Marvin Gaye. Poet Al Young saw C. L. so frequently with his mother in his Detroit home that Young assumed they would marry. Lola Moore, whom Aretha called "Daddy's lady friend," had a somewhat different relationship: she lived for a number of years in C. L.'s home. There were undoubtedly other women as well. C. L. projected a compelling sensual presence, and he had never been particularly committed to monogamy. By 1956 it was public knowledge that C. L. was "a popular man-about-town," the African American magazine *Color* reported in January 1957. He was "often seen escorting some of the city's most attractive women. But he always tells news reporters (even in the presence of the women) that he is not altar-bound."[59]

Churchwomen also reached for him. Mary Wilson, a New Bethel member between 1956 and 1963, and an original member of Motown's most famous group, the Supremes, understood this power as a teenager. C. L.'s charisma, as she referred to it, was so vibrant "that everyone was fascinated by him. Women absolutely loved him. He was a ladies' man! My mother adored him." Not every woman who expressed such feelings became intimate with C. L. But some did.[60]

The flow of women through C. L.'s life reflected both a highly sensual nature and his decision, made after his separation, to forgo a permanent, exclusive relationship with any woman. This pattern, which led to a series of simultaneous relationships of different depth and duration, reflected something else as well. C. L.'s multiple involvements satisfied his powerful sexual appetite and he undoubtedly enjoyed the social company of these women, but the relationships had sharply defined limits. It was nearly impossible for any one of the women rotating through his life at any one time to become truly intimate with this public man. He arrived, left, and then returned, regularly, in a manner that suggested a sustained effort, if not necessarily a fully conscious one, to forestall an intimacy that might breach the barrier he had constructed around his vulnerable private self. C. L. had learned a most profound lesson about manliness about age four, in the wake of his father's departure: men left relationships. C. L.'s protectiveness toward his mother flowed from this, an idealized response of an only son to replace his father, and from childhood on, he tried at times to explore that loss, particularly with Harry Kincaid. But the incessant stream of female partners, part of a broader pattern of living a largely public role even in his private life, suggested that much remained unresolved. In his head he understood the weight of abandonment, but in his heart he felt a fear of entanglement. Beyond the gifts of friendship and sensual pleasure, the women he dated played a role in his life not unlike his audiences throughout the country. He kept most at a distance, his most serious tensions and emotions beyond their reach, leaving them all too often able only to offer adulation.

That many at New Bethel considered sex outside of marriage a sin caused C. L. no hesitation. He rarely preached on sexual morality and freely went to whatever club featured the musician he wanted to hear. These evenings often concluded with an impromptu party with the musician and assorted friends, either at his house or at the home of Sylvia and William Penn, less than a mile north of his church. But, as before, Franklin was careful about whom he partied with. C. L. enjoyed himself largely with a set of friends who, whether they attended his services or not, lived well beyond the accepted parameters of New Bethel's dominant culture. Some church people joined him—the Penns, Ralph Williams, Melvin Wrencher (who toured with him), Claud Young, but only a few others. C. L. "treated [church members] nice as Christians," Sylvia Penn explained. "He treated them right but he didn't . . . he did not get personal with [them], and he did not socialize with them. So then he kept them away from him where they couldn't meddle in his business." "I have to be careful," C. L. told one of his deacons in the early 1960s. "I can stumble here and fall and the news be in California before sun go down."[61]

Despite his apparent resolve to avoid permanent romantic entanglements, the spectrum of Franklin's relationships included at least one, with Clara Ward, that was prolonged and intense. Born in Anderson, South Carolina, in 1924, the youngest of three children, Clara Ward moved with her family to Philadelphia when a child. At age eleven, together with her thirteen-year-old sister, Willa, and her mother, Gertrude, Clara began her career with the Ward Singers. Before she had barely started, however, Gertrude fell seriously ill, and the two girls stayed with relatives in

Philadelphia. During this time the sisters were repeatedly sexually abused, together, by a male cousin. Eventually, Willa overcame her fear (the onset of menstruation scared her more than the cousin's threats: "I was convinced I was having a baby," she wrote) and told her mother and her aunt, the mother of the abuser. Clara, in Willa's account at least, suffered the abuse in numbed silence. The emotional violence, however, reverberated deep in her being. Three years later, at Willa's sixteenth birthday party, crowded with teenage friends and relatives, the often titillating game of "Post Office," where the "mailman" delivers kisses to a member of the opposite sex, turned into a nightmare for the fourteen-year-old Clara when a boy inserted his tongue in her mouth. Her terrified screams immediately brought Gertrude, who quickly sent the friends home. Willa recalls no comforting words between mother and younger daughter concerning the horrific memories the young boy's kiss had triggered. Rather, Gertrude proceeded to beat Willa for allowing the game in the first place, a practice the Ward parents subjected their daughters to regularly for the slightest expression of interest in boys.[62]

During the next decade, the Ward Singers' fame spread widely. Gertrude's distinctive voice lost its power, and a series of female vocalists joined the two sisters. Clara emerged as the more powerful and compelling singer, the one who could bring the crowd to its feet begging for but another sound of her voice. In 1943, the group's career took a major leap when, at the Baptist convention, Clara's lead vocals and piano accompaniment captivated the thousands in attendance. From that moment on, bookings for the Ward Singers came easily, as word of the performance spread across the national Baptist network. Although no longer performing, Gertrude Ward remained a central force in her children's lives, especially that of her younger daughter. She dominated Clara's emotional life and with a hawk's eye sought to outwit her daughter's efforts to form relationships with men. She also exerted control over the considerable money Clara's talents garnered. Gertrude would approve spending for the lavish costumes, wigs, and the lavender Cadillac touring cars Clara so desired, but her reputation as a controlling, even devious, presence extended well beyond her family. C. L. ran up against her manipulations early in the tour, and Mahalia Jackson once reduced a somewhat tense photo shoot of a number of gospel groups to gales of laughter (and great pictures) when she sang out to an impassive Gertrude: "Mother Ward, do you still owe me any money?" Willa left the group in 1947, after she had managed to marry and already had children. The Ward Singers were reorganized with the addition of Henrietta Waddy and the incomparable soprano Marion Williams. But Clara remained, ever more famous and yet a captive of her mother's commanding presence.[63]

C. L. met Clara in the late 1940s. It was obvious that he felt deeply for her, but whether these feelings were the final fracture that splintered his marriage remains speculative. Willa first noted a change in her sister's relationship with C. L. in 1949, the year after Barbara returned to Buffalo. That year, the Ward Singers headlined a large gospel program that included Mahalia Jackson, Sammy Bryant, and C. L. at Philadelphia's Metropolitan Opera House. In the wake of the enormous success of their "Surely God Is Able" record, the Ward Singers attracted thousands of adoring fans. C. L. and Clara "seemed to share the Holy Spirit intermingled with the human spirit," Willa thought. For long after, she considered that moment "the start of my sister's one and only heart, soul, and flesh real romance."[64]

In 1949 she was a grown woman of twenty-five, but Clara Ward's emotional life remained dominated by a childlike compulsion to heed her mother's imperious demands, even as she regularly demeaned her adult self in order to sneak around them. The tour, in this regard, could be a nightmare, as Gertrude stalked the halls, ever alert for the slightest impropriety in her daughter's conduct. Frustrated by what Willa called "Mom's sensitive nose" where "the sweet aroma of *amour*" involved her daughter, C. L. and Clara devised a cover story in which Clara came to Detroit for a week or more to help a harried pastor and single father by babysitting C. L.'s children. Predictably, Gertrude complained that Clara sang for free at New Bethel on these visits but never seemed to have grasped, as Willa put it, "that the good Reverend was doing most of the sitting—and more—with my sister." Even more contorted preparations went into the planning for the couple to attend the World Baptist Alliance in London in 1955. Both Ward sisters encouraged their mother not to attend, and C. L. and Clara carefully cleared their schedules to allow for an extended tour of Europe and the Holy Land after the London meeting. Surprisingly, when Clara informed her mother after all the plans were in place, Gertrude's resistance was less than expected: "I guess it was time to bend a little," Willa surmised, "or lose Clara completely to the rest of the world—C. L. Franklin's world."[65]

What C. L. thought of all this remains unclear. As all who knew him well might attest, he could be direct, blunt, and demanding. Yet he was very gentle with Clara. During the anxious months preparing for their European trip, Willa witnessed moments when C. L. "reinforced Clara's spirits when she became weak and held her up when fear just about collapsed her." In public, of course, he revealed nothing of his relationship with Clara, only noting that "it so happened" they found themselves with the same itinerary from London to Paris, Rome, Athens, Damascus, Beirut, Cairo, Jerusalem, "and other places of interest." A decade later, when Clara suffered a stroke, his gentle protectiveness encouraged her again. When he visited, he sang to her of the love they had yet to experience and the places yet to see, and urged her to recover.[66]

As attached to Clara Ward as he was, C. L. Franklin nonetheless defined a distance. He never committed solely to her, saw other women during their long relationship, and, in all probability, expected similar conduct from Clara as well. In different ways, they were both haunted people, driven by forces they incompletely understood. By choosing so troubled a lover—Clara Ward lacked the emotional resources to match C. L.'s forceful personality—C. L. all but guaranteed there would be no breach of his inner wall of privacy. But while Clara loved him, a number of C. L.'s closest friends suggested that deep feeling was not reciprocated. Claud Young called Clara's declaration "extremely one sided," while Bea Buck simply stated, "Reverend Franklin was not in love with her." Although it is possible that there was an instance when C. L. actually considered marriage to Clara, that might have reflected a moment's particular passion.[67] Emotionally drained, "whipped to shreds, completely shorn of self-control," Clara's main solace during the late 1950s and after, her sister said, was "singing the Gospel and slurping the booze." Sylvia Penn thought Clara had become "more or less like a drunk" who "lived a miserable life." Once she stayed with her tormented friend at the Gotham Hotel for two weeks, getting her sober and emotionally strong enough to leave Detroit. In all likelihood, this was the Clara that C. L. could not abide at close range for prolonged periods. Penn, one of the few churchwomen whose thirty-year friendship with C. L. encompassed his private social life, recalled C. L. up-braiding Clara in her presence "many times," saying, "You don't even have a life of your own. No man's going to have you and your mother's running your life."[68]

For a man whose public standing, financial position, and sense of purpose derived from a religious calling, Franklin's public style and rumored conduct caused particular concern among church people. How could a professed man of God so blur the distinctions between the sacred and the secular that his faith appeared to justify conduct most of the faithful would deem immoral? This was in part the issue Al Young's mother, Mary, raised when, as C. L. left her bedroom one Sunday morning, the son asked his mother whether they would marry. "All right, you asked, so I'll tell you. You're old enough now," she responded. "I couldn't marry anybody like that," for C. L. "would spend Saturday night with me. Then, at the crack of dawn, he would hop up out of bed, shove his little bottle of whiskey in his coat jacket and say, 'Oh, Mary, I have to preach.' Al, I just couldn't marry anybody like that."[69]

Undoubtedly others, even though lacking the specific knowledge Al Young's mother possessed, felt similarly, perhaps even more strongly. The strain in the Afro-Baptist faith tradition that demanded an iron curtain between the sacred rituals and secular temptations remained real enough for many. The popular gospel quartet the Dixie Hummingbirds, for example, were famous for the stylish clothes they wore while performing but felt deeply that "life in the sanctified lane demanded more" of its performers. Similarly, Mahalia Jackson rebuked the Ward Singers when that group began singing gospel in Las Vegas nightclubs. Where Clara Ward insisted she was doing the Lord's work among the unchurched, Mahalia remained dismissive: "It is blasphemous to sing the Lord's music in taverns."[70]

There was yet another tradition within the Afro-Baptist world, a tradition of forgiveness that emphasized the power of that same sacred ritual to offer "a balm in Gilead / that makes the wounded whole." C. L. taught that, of course, from the pulpit, and he was not the first preacher in American religious history who found a pointed personal meaning in his public words. That quality of forgiveness, moreover, came in many ways. For Bea Buck, that her friend "was kind of a womanizer, anyhow," was not surprising. Black Baptist ministers, she thought it widely understood, had a reputation for intimate relations with the female members of their congregations, as blues artists had long sarcastically attested. What she thought different for C. L. was his "being in the [national] spotlight." Others were deeply troubled but found in his very manliness a cause to forgive. "Reverend Franklin was a man," Robbie McCoy explained with wonderful juxtaposition. "But we surely, truly, did love him." Willie Todd, the devout choir soloist, heard the rumors and at first thought that C. L. did "just what any man, a natural man, would do." On reflection, he considered that such an explanation might not "cover the territory" for a minister, and he was very clear that as a leading deacon in New Bethel, he demanded a different moral standard for himself and his fellow deacons. Yet his very faith propelled him to extend a forgiving hand. "Every man is a man," he mused. "And a man will do a man's thing, you know. Now that's something him and God would have to work out." Others such as Deacon Wallace Malone and C. L.'s former associate pastor, E. L. Branch, also acknowledged his faults, his "personal struggles," and his troubled "inner issues" but stressed a forgiveness of these human faults, especially in light of his unquestioned positive religious and social impact.[71]

Carolyn King, the daughter of an early New Bethel member, grew up in the church during the 1960s and served for a time as church secretary while in high school. Without any impropriety intended or implied by her words, she unabashedly admitted that she had idolized him. Some in the congregation, including at least one church trustee, had criticized her for being an uncritical "C. L. Franklin lover," who dismissed in a gush of religious emotionalism what others considered were debilitating faults. But King understood her pastor and her faith at a deeper level. She, too, acknowledged that C. L. "wasn't a God, he was a man," and that there were "things that he did that I didn't like." But her deep respect for him, grounded in the power of his sermons and his counsel, created her own moral calculus. She might not tell Franklin what conduct of his she deplored, "but I had enough sense to know the difference between right and wrong."[72]

As with many others, Carolyn King's understanding came only with a struggle over several fundamental questions. Can imperfect people perform good deeds? Can a flawed minister lead others to salvation? C. L. certainly thought so, urging his parishioners to follow his words and not necessarily his actions. As he preached one Sunday in the 1950s, "every now and then" he had to pray over his own conduct. Nor was C. L. the only one so troubled. The extramarital affairs of another Afro-Baptist minister, Martin Luther King Jr., are well known from illegal tapings of them made by the government. Less well known is the deep interest in pornography and promiscuous behavior exhibited throughout his adult life by Paul Tillich, possibly the most influential Protestant theologian and thinker in the twentieth century. This human frailty, even among those anointed to illuminate the path of faith, led Reverend Gardner C. Taylor, a preacher of great renown who knew C. L., to recognize in Franklin an "irreducible core of faith" that coexisted with his deep "secular attachments." The "magnificent anomaly of preaching," even the "audacity of preaching," Taylor once wrote, he found "in the fact that the person who preaches is in need himself or herself of the message which the preacher believes he or she is ordained to utter."[73]

This all too human Franklin, with rumors humming sotto voce just beneath the public acclaim, turned his attention back toward politics. It was a sign of the changing consciousness he had partly encouraged, however, that where his public letter following the Emmett Till memorial two years before had positioned him as a critic of established organizations, new voices had emerged that would include C. L. himself as part of the problem he had once criticized.

CHAPTER EIGHT

NEW VOICES

When C. L. had held his eleventh anniversary celebration at the Gotham Hotel in July 1957, T-Bone Walker was a major attraction, but another guest commanded the audience's full attention. William T. Patrick, a successful lawyer and the child of an upper-middle-class black Detroit family, was a candidate for Detroit's Common Council. In contrast with Reverend Charles Hill in earlier campaigns, Patrick enjoyed the full support of a more politically engaged black Detroit, the elite organizations as well as the less prominent groups such as New Bethel's Political Action Guild. Franklin had already endorsed Patrick from the pulpit and had invited the candidate to give the keynote speech at his celebration. Government, Patrick had insisted, required "Christian leadership" in responsible positions to ensure an active moral vision in its deliberations. Patrick's point was not to create a theocracy, with conversion as the litmus test for election, but rather to insist that the more universal principles of Christianity be applied consistently, particularly concerning civil and human rights. The audience of some two hundred enthusiastically applauded his words.[1]

Certainly, those in the audience understood Patrick's meaning within the context of black Detroit's continuing difficulties. Relations between black residents and the police remained tense, for example, and many

African Americans considered the police aggressively hostile toward black residents in almost any interaction. Ethel Watkins's experience the preceding winter was a recent case in point. The thirty-year-old black seamstress had purchased a home on Cherrylawn Street, in northwest Detroit, an area distinctive for the row after row of workingmen's cottages that fulfilled many of their owners' dreams. It was a neighborhood of white working people—good union men and women, church members, too—and the Cherrylawn residents fiercely resisted the prospect of black neighbors. When Watkins moved in that February, she faced howling mobs, vandalism, and threats of further violence for more than a month—all despite a near-constant police presence. The dominant union in Detroit, the United Auto Workers, and particularly its national president, Walter Reuther, had earned a national reputation as advocates of racial equality. The UAW's support of civil rights nationally, however, did not necessarily mean much in Detroit. One survey of white union members a few years earlier found only a small distinction separating Detroit union members from the 80 percent of whites who opposed or were "neutral, ambiguous" to ending segregation in housing, schools, or jobs. "The slight difference that does appear," the poll reported, "shows the union people less favorable than others toward accepting Negroes."[2]

Although the prospect of Patrick's victory in November was most welcome, the structure of Common Council—Patrick would be one of nine members—tempered expectations. If elected, Patrick could give voice to black grievances, but regarding the depressed economic condition of many, he would be almost powerless. The days of the hate strikes had passed, but the attitudes held by a majority of whites still presented serious obstacles to workplace equality. In auto plants, for example, the city's largest industry, African Americans remained concentrated in the worst jobs, few held even minor positions in their local union, and none held national office. A 1960 government investigation found that black workers totaled 38 percent of the UAW Local 228 in Detroit but only 2 percent of its skilled workers. At the enormous Ford Local 600, which carried a heroic reputation in union circles for its militancy during the struggle to establish the union in the 1930s, blacks comprised more than 41 percent of the nearly thirty thousand members but only 3 percent of its skilled workforce. The exclusion at General Motors was even more thorough: of the more than eleven thousand skilled union workers throughout that giant corporation, only sixty-seven were black, as were barely 1 percent of the more than one thousand apprentices in the system. At the hearings of the U.S. Commission on Civil Rights in Detroit in 1960, Horace Sheffield pointed out that African American apprentices in the skilled trades "are not even sufficient in number to replace Negro skilled workers already employed."[3]

These patterns were not accidental. Since 1945, black workers had demanded the union support an antidiscrimination clause in its contract proposals. In an era when no federal law effectively prevented discriminatory treatment, such a clause was essential if equality were to be attained. Wary of the expected resistance from white members and committed to the position that hiring matters remained management's prerogative, UAW officials refused. The result left these decisions in the hands of a decentralized managerial structure, spanning the social distance from shop-floor foremen to white-collar personnel directors, which proved highly susceptible to the wishes of the majority-white workforce. Asked just before the war to explain why black workers were so disproportionately concentrated in the most onerous and lowest-paying positions, one management official stated: "Yes, some jobs white folks will not do; so they have to take niggers in, particularly in duco work, spraying paint on car bodies. This soon kills a white man." He then added of black workers: "It shortens their lives, it cuts them down but they're just niggers."[4]

Disenchanted with their union's tepid approach, a group of dissident black union members challenged this inaction. Led by Robert "Buddy" Battle, Horace Sheffield, Marc Stepp, Nelson Jack Edwards, and others, they founded in 1957 a black caucus within the UAW, the Trade Union Leadership Council. TULC was not antiunion: despite the racism in the union, supporter Milton Hall explained, "You needs a union. You needs a backup." Rather, these black working people demanded the union bring black workers into leadership positions and open training programs to allow more blacks into the skilled positions on the shop floor. The formation of TULC, with its more aggressive public demands, marked another turning point in black Detroit's mobilization. The caucus introduced a more militant tone into the debate within the black community and with the politicians who ran the city. It was another sign that the era when one organization's vision and resources dominated black protest in Detroit was fast coming to a close. Franklin, a strong union supporter and still a critic of the NAACP's approach, publicly encouraged his trustee and TULC cofounder, Nelson Jack Edwards.[5]

Predictably, the creation of TULC produced an immediate backlash in the larger union. Carl Stellato, president of Ford Local 600, publicly attacked Sheffield as being antiwhite and, along with a majority of white union officers in locals and at international headquarters, demanded that Sheffield and other union staff members involved with TULC be fired. There was "significant opposition from white trade unionists" at all levels throughout the union, Douglas Fraser remembered, and Reuther's initial support was lukewarm at best. Emil Mazey, the union's national secretary-treasurer, publicly denounced the group and its NAACP allies for "its criticism of labor for actions which were obviously the sins of management." (And this from someone who represented a progressive, at times militant, tendency within the union, one that supported civil rights in other contexts beyond the union hall.) Resistance by white unionists remained strong. Many of these men and women were the same people who, joining with family, neighbors, and friends, defended by force if necessary the whiteness of their parishes, schools, and residential communities.[6]

As summer edged toward fall that year, Reverend Albert B. Cleage Jr. took possession of his new church on the city's West Side, giving black Detroit yet another alternative to the voices of the community's traditional leaders. Cleage came from a privileged northern background. The oldest of seven children, he was born in 1911 in Indianapolis, while his father was completing his medical training at Indiana University. The family moved to Kalamazoo and then Detroit when he was still a toddler. In Detroit, they lived on the West Side, in the Tireman area, the elite enclave of black businessmen and professionals where Berry Gordy's family also had their home. The Cleage family prided itself on its nearly white complexion and worshiped at Horace White's Plymouth Congregational Church, where church culture valued lighter skin as a social marker for entrée into elite circles. Educated at Wayne State and then at Oberlin's School of Theology, Cleage became an ordained Congregational minister and, in 1946, accepted a position at the racially mixed St. John's Congregational Church in Springfield, Massachusetts. Five years later, he returned to Detroit as the new pastor with St. Mark's United Presbyterian Community Church, at Twelfth Street and Atkinson on the city's West Side. In accepting the position, Cleage agreed to abide by the discipline of the Presbyterian tradition.[7]

Two years later, however, resistance to Cleage's emphasis on social problems led to his removal from the pulpit. Undaunted, Cleage returned to his original denominational affiliation, formed Central Congregational Church, and reaffirmed his mixture of faith and social activism. Although C. L. Franklin professed a similar vision, the two ministers had at best a passing relationship at this time. It was in 1957 that Cleage's congregation moved into a large, well-appointed building at Linwood and Hogarth, on the West Side.[8]

Shortly after taking possession of the new building, Cleage organized a special service to pray for "the People of Little Rock," Arkansas, a city occupied by federal troops that September to force compliance with the Supreme Court's decision mandating school integration. He was by no means the only black pastor who so prayed, but the tone of his service touched a different chord than the one usually heard in public. The violence, "the obscene racial hatred" shown by white Little Rock toward the nine black high school students, we would like to call "unbelievable," Cleage began. "But we are not surprised . . . because all of us, in one way or another, wherever we live, experience this same fear, hatred and contempt every day of our lives." Those "hate filled [white] faces which line the streets of Little Rock" are very familiar to black Americans. "We've seen them in employment offices when we search for work in New York City," on teachers' faces in Detroit schools, and "everywhere" on politicians, policemen, and common pedestrians alike. "Little Rock," he insisted, in a tone as hard as it was realistic, "is the face and heart of a nation unmasked." Cleage expressed hope in the democratic potential of the white majority but warned that a "new Negro" was now emerging, conscious of rights, steeled against white intimidation, and willing to accept nothing "less than complete citizenship." It was this "new Negro" that the Little Rock "mob in its insane frenzy" sensed and whose very presence fueled "in some measure a part of its frustrated anger." Cleage's blunt analysis, delivered with an unmistakably militant edge, appealed to many already weary of the slow tempo of change. His church's membership grew quickly, attracting those already in motion politically, and provided Cleage with an increasingly viable base for political activities.[9]

William Patrick won election that November and assumed his seat on Common Council the following January. It was a decided victory for black Detroit, but by no stretch of the imagination did anyone think that New Bethel's Guild, its pastor, or even TULC brokered Patrick's election. Rather, Patrick's candidacy joined together the city's black electorate under the leadership of traditionally powerful organizations such as the NAACP, the Urban League, the Nacirema and Cotillion Clubs, and the United Auto Workers, the dominant liberal political power group in the city, to forge a winning alliance. Despite a black population approaching 30 percent of the city's total, an African American candidate could only be elected in 1957 with progressive white support. The newer voices heard in union halls and church pulpits were then but modest pieces of the coalition. In the excitement over Patrick's election, few paused over the news that Louis C. Miriani, the UAW-backed mayoralty candidate, had also won.[10]

*   *   *   *   *

Franklin was one of those alternative voices, but he had achieved little success in translating the power of his sermons into effective political action. In part his pastoral duties, combined with incessant travel and continued concern with the tensions still swirling about the National Baptist Convention, demanded his time. New Bethel's Political Action Guild had proved quite important for his congregants in their reach toward a more public voice but was not the vehicle to carry C. L. to citywide political prominence. Neither the guild's institutional reach nor its titular leader's interest in actual political organizing were sufficient to achieve such a goal. C. L. continued to relish the spotlight that followed his every move, an attraction that largely precluded the unspectacular, sustained effort essential to organizing. There was as well another demand on his time that he could no longer put off: he was the single father of a very complex family whom he reared largely in the glare thrown by that spotlight.

And his family was often on his mind. In a late 1950s sermon, "Hannah, the Ideal Mother," concerned that contemporary parents were "detouring from the path of the traditional patterns of motherhood," C. L. charged that "the twentieth-century mothers," these "atomic age mothers . . . are not acting like mothers." Divorce was prevalent, marriage taken too lightly, and "some people" would have done better "if they did not have children." Echoing attitudes broadly held throughout American society across racial, economic, and cultural divides, Franklin preached that in the act of giving birth, women "are performing thereby a divine duty and responsibility," one that comes with additional "responsibilities and obligations. Whether you like it or not, God has so endowed you and has enabled you to bring forth children into the world, and you become the steward, the God-appointed guardian over those children." Reflecting a nineteenth-century code of female domesticity, C. L. emphasized the mother's role in teaching the child language and, through words and example, "the first things that they know about God." Lest anyone misunderstand, Franklin stated clearly that a woman's role was indeed special, for mothers were "a little bit closer than father" to their children. He urged his congregants to reject the modern trend of limiting family size to one or two children and underscored his belief in the necessity of discipline. He then retold the story of his mother (who was in the congregation that Mother's Day) punishing him for the poor speech he had delivered three decades earlier in Mississippi. Rachel, he inferred, was the contemporary embodiment of the biblical Hannah.[11]

During the generally expansive economic conditions in Detroit in the 1950s, black men had better opportunities for higher-paying jobs in auto and other manufacturing concerns than did black women, and thus Franklin's assignment of traditional roles within the family economy made a certain economic as well as cultural sense. But it was also during this decade that black women's earning power began a significant rise, while that of black men slowed, if it did not yet decline. This combination of a potentially new economic role for women, coupled with the slow stirrings of new attitudes toward divorce and family limitation, challenged traditional practice. C. L.'s sermon, then, was intended as a counterstatement. Growing up in an agricultural society, he insightfully exaggerated in another sermon, "We didn't have hardly anywhere else to go but to church. But the young folk who are coming up today are faced with all kinds of resultant problems emanating from a complex urban society." With two working parents, Franklin reiterated even years later, his thinking constant, the children "spend many hours alone" or with other unsupervised children, and "there's no telling what they might get into." The solution, in short, was for women to remain in the home.[12]

Thus, the essence of "Hannah, the Ideal Mother," for all the power of its delivery and the enthusiasm that greeted its repeated presentation over the years, remained mired in an earlier cultural moment. Franklin—who encouraged silenced southerners to find their voice, to envision a new political presence, and to explore various forms of cultural expression, all the while gently but insistently prodding them to transform their initial fundamentalist perspective—could not harness that creativity to present a revised understanding of the interior landscape of family life. Had Franklin been able to use his personal history as a resource in this regard, as he had in so many other contexts, he might have explored the changing nature of marriage so as to allow a more compelling presentation of even his traditional ideas. But that would have required a willingness to acknowledge, however obliquely, his feelings about his father, his marriage, about relations between men and women, about his experience of migration, and about that deeply American belief that often equated a rise from poverty with the essence of fathering. Such thoughts, however, he rarely allowed himself to express; never once in a sermon did he ever mention Willie Walker or Henry Franklin. Instead, as in "Hannah," he constructed an ideal to cover his actual, if imperfect, human experience.

C. L. always managed to have a woman at the helm at home who accepted her role as mother in a fashion that, not unlike the idealized Hannah, allowed him his freedom. Before 1948, it was Barbara, and following their separation, it had been his mother and a series of housekeepers and friends. These arrangements allowed him unquestioned access to the traditional male role despite the absence of a permanent mate.

Over the years since Barbara's death, the composition of the family had changed in certain important ways. Vaughn, after graduation from high school, entered the U.S. Air Force. Tragedy brought another kind of change when, in January 1954, C. L.'s younger sister, Louise, died of cancer. She had been living in Detroit, and her funeral at New Bethel was large. The official participants signified the family's stature in the community. Two former New Bethel pastors, H. H. Coleman, who delivered the eulogy, and W. R. Ramsey, attended, as did A. R. Williams, of Memphis, along with other Detroit preachers; Mahalia Jackson, Clara Ward, and Sammy Bryant soloed with the New Bethel choir. C. L. and his mother enfolded Louise's daughter, Brenda, then age seven, into his family, where she was raised with the other children "like brother and sisters [as] opposed to first cousins."[13]

By the time the family moved to the large, well-appointed house at 7415 LaSalle Boulevard, "an estate home," Aretha remembered, on "an exclusive residential street with enormous lush trees and manicured lawns," Henry Franklin had died and Rachel lived with Brenda in the carriage house just behind the main building. That same year, 1958, the family grew yet again in a rather dramatic and, for the children living in Detroit, initially a shocking manner. Carl Ellan Kelley, C. L.'s natural daughter with Mildred Jennings from his Memphis days, contacted her father by letter. She knew from her mother's family he was her biological father, and as she approached her eighteenth birthday, she felt compelled to contact him in order to know "who I am," she explained years later. Carl Ellan and her mother were members of A. R. Williams's Memphis church, and the daughter knew that her pastor and C. L. were "like brothers." She talked with Williams at some length and then, with his encouragement, "wrote dad." C. L. did not respond directly to her but rather called his close friend. What transpired between the two preachers remains unknown, but Carl Ellan sensed that her pastor forced C. L. to acknowledge her existence. It was not something that C. L. would have at first approached enthusiastically. The rumors of his personal life were widespread, and Carl Ellan's reemergence would only intensify interest in them. Far more profoundly troubling was the meaning of his daughter's incorporation within the family. None of the children in Detroit, from the oldest, Erma, to the youngest, Brenda, knew of Carl Ellan's existence. To them, her very presence questioned the depictions of their parents' relationship they had previously learned.[14]

Whatever precisely passed between A. R. Williams and C. L. Franklin in that or subsequent phone calls, the result was that Carl Ellan visited Detroit a few months later. Under considerable pressure, C. L. nonetheless did for his child what his father had never done for him. To acknowledge the child he had walked away from was a significant act, one that may have eased the memory of his childhood pain. Carl Ellan experienced it differently. She thought that he had been "painted into a corner to acknowledge what happened." Regardless, she welcomed the opportunity. On that first visit, Carl Ellan spent part of the time at a hotel and then came to the Franklin home, where she met all of the other children but Carolyn. In a very real way, an earthquake had shaken the children's familial foundation. Yet, over time, a real closeness developed between some of the children, probably encouraged initially by Rachel Franklin's example, as "Big Mama" embraced Carl Ellan as one of her own.[15]

With her father, there was a different pattern. C. L. never acknowledged Carl Ellan's presence from the pulpit, as he might other family members; nor did he ever publicly ask for God's forgiveness before congregations in Memphis or Detroit—a not-uncommon ritual for clergy and laity alike in the Afro-Baptist tradition. Yet, as Carl Ellan occasionally visited Detroit over the next five years, she felt her father's initial awkwardness diminishing. In 1964, after she moved from Memphis to New Orleans, their relationship grew closer. When C. L. came to New Orleans, he usually found time to visit with her and once sat her in a deacon's chair behind his pulpit, a seat of honor, as he preached. A few years later, after she moved to Seattle, she and her father were close enough that he gave Clara Ward, then touring, her phone number. The two women met, and after the concert, Carl Ellan brought Clara and a group of friends back to her place for "an all-night girl talking party" that largely focused on C. L.[16]

Rachel Franklin, however, preserved the emotional balance in the family. She was a slight woman, perhaps a little over five feet, but she possessed an unrivaled emotional power. Without exception the grandchildren, whatever the specifics of their biological relation, returned the unquestioned love they received from her and relied on her for needs both pragmatic and emotional. She was a source of support and encouragement, a stern disciplinarian, and she touched them deeply through the force of her religious faith. Mother Rachel also occupied an important role in New Bethel where, given the absence of a pastor's wife, she was the de facto first lady of the congregation. But it was on her son that she had the greatest impact. Her presence allowed him to maintain his traditional attitudes toward family life (and the traditional male freedom from it), since she now played the role Son had projected onto Hannah. It was one she accepted smoothly.[17]

While C. L. was on the road, surrounded by music and friends, his children stepped forth into Detroit. Al Young recalled his teen years in 1950s Detroit, a city so saturated with music that people "walked and talked and thought and fought to it." Its power was infectious: "Smokey-throated kids on playgrounds and street corners harmonized in counterpoint and weren't even studying about cutting a demo or getting discovered." The Franklin children relished the excitement. Cecil, sixteen in 1956, remained close with Smokey Robinson, who, in turn, introduced the Franklins to his new friend, Diane Ross. Shortly later, Ross moved to the Brewster Housing projects, where she formed a singing group with Mary Wilson and Florence Ballard. Mary Wilson was a member of New Bethel as, less regularly, was Diane Ross. A few years later, Diane became Diana and the group, the Supremes, one of the most successful groups ever recorded by Motown Records. As a teenager on a Saturday afternoon, Mary Wilson relished joining with the Franklin girls and other teens at the movies, rollerskating at the Arcadia rink, or playing the pinball machines at a neighboring arcade. Aretha, whose singing stunned Wilson in church, would "whiz by" on her skates, attuned to the music over the loudspeakers: "She didn't just skate; she bopped." Wilson's classmates at Algers Elementary School in 1956, the first year of school integration in Detroit, included Carolyn Franklin, who was already forming a singing group and arranging its material. Within a few years, Ross and Ballard also became high-school classmates, and Otis Williams, soon of the Temptations, asked Carolyn for a date.[18]

C. L.'s children were the brightest stars in this extraordinary cluster. Erma and Aretha soloed with the New Bethel choir from an early age, and when Carolyn and Brenda began singing in church when they were "the littlest things," they skipped the children's choir and immediately "got to sing with the grown folks." The "Franklin girls," Mary Wilson remembered of these years, were already "local celebrities." After finishing high school, Erma sought a career in music. Her fine voice attracted the attention of Berry Gordy, also an occasional member of the New Bethel congregation and an aspiring record producer then. In 1959, Gordy offered her "All I Could Do Was Cry," but Erma would not record it, as she was then more interested in jazz. Etta James did, and it became a signature song for her. Carolyn, still in high school in 1960, possessed a fine voice and a magnificent ability at writing and arranging songs. Unlike his three sisters, Cecil was not a particularly good singer.[19]

Without question, the most famous of the Franklin children, even in the 1950s, was Aretha. Her extraordinary voice drew both adults and her fellow teens to New Bethel and to concerts on her father's tours. She was but sixteen and already a rising star in the gospel world. In the same year that witnessed Carl Ellan's entry into the family, Aretha gave birth to her second son, whom she named Eddie, after his father, a Detroit teen. How C. L. reacted to Aretha's pregnancy or to Erma's, who had a baby boy and soon after separated from her husband, remains unknown. Aretha stated that his "concern and participation in the lives of his children were exemplary" and insisted that, with all of the demands his career imposed, "he still performed the duties of a dad with patient love on the road and at home." That C. L. might have desired to do this, after his own fashion, is possible, but that he could do that for all of his children, "on the road and at home," remains improbable. He was gone often, whether it was out at the Gotham or the Flame Show Bar of an evening, or on the road near and far from Detroit. There were private moments, such as Aretha's fond memories of watching the prizefights on television with her dad, "with popcorn and hot dogs and screaming and cheering." But often the house was filled with people, with singers and musicians eating, drinking, and partying; with church people at more sedate teas; and with a close group of ministerial friends for late night discussions. Recalled Sylvia Penn, Franklin was "very, very good to his kids. He gave them anything, those kids never had to wash, iron, or do anything. He had people there to wait on them." But this path was actually the easier for C. L., an approach to parenting that remained a far cry from the stern Mother Rachel he evoked in his sermons, whose disciplinary hand left the distinct feeling of being loved long after the sting of the spanking subsided.[20]

It was not that C. L. did not care for his children. Erma, for example, remembered numerous lectures the children received concerning behavior and especially emphasizing the importance of education. Like parents the world over, C. L. delivered criticism of a specific act and then, for emphasis, drew on his own, less-privileged childhood to drive the point home. "Then you'd get that sermon," Erma laughingly recounted. "Oh, and then how they used to [have] to go on the truck and sharecrop, you know, in the fields. Which was to make us feel guilty," she quipped. Clearly, C. L. cared for his children, but his expression of that caring came on terms comfortable for him emotionally and for his career rather than necessarily in ways the children might have needed. He was "a man, not a water walker," Carl Ellan suggested of her father. "Just a man."[21]

*   *   *   *   *

Despite the pressure of his schedule, Franklin tried again in 1959 to build a citywide organization that would offer him a secular platform comparable to his pulpit. The Metropolitan Civic League for Legal Action began with another critique of established black organizations whose efforts to curtail police brutality and job discrimination, Franklin thought, were never aggressive enough. Since Mayor Louis Miriani won election two years earlier, relations between the police and black Detroit, never very good, had deteriorated further. Franklin's league appealed to those who so often were on the receiving end of the police club or the indiscriminate police raid: the league announced it would provide legal and medical assistance for victims and hold a series of public meetings to protest the mayor's public support of current police practice. C. L. was the founding president, but as before, neither his travel schedule nor his personality particularly recommended him for organizational leadership. Instead, two other Detroit Baptist clergy, William J. Bishop and J. H. Bruce, actually ran the group. The league's achievements remain obscure, as there is no evidence it represented any victim of police actions. Although it claimed seven hundred members in 1961, the league soon disbanded in an acrimonious public dispute when it supported the reelection of the Wayne County prosecutor, Samuel H. Olsen, who was widely perceived as hostile to black defendants. By that time, Franklin was no longer associated with it.[22]

The league was "a flower that want[ed] to bloom," Arthur Johnson thought, but even had C. L. devoted his considerable energy to the organization, it is doubtful that a different outcome would have emerged. The league offered no compelling alternative politics to distinguish itself, and C. L.'s power, always more prophetic than programmatic, was less suited to developing sustained political programs. He was also away even more than usual in the years following the league's founding. Urban renewal claimed his church in 1960, as it did Hastings Street itself, replacing the vibrant cultural crossroads with the Chrysler Freeway. Dispossessed a second time in a decade, the congregation wandered again and often had to make do without their famous pastor's presence. Franklin accepted a call to lead a large new church in Los Angeles, attracted by the weather and the opportunities in the entertainment industry, and he simply stayed in Los Angeles as long as he desired at any one time, without ever resigning his position at New Bethel. So dominant was his control of New Bethel's governing bodies, and so anxious were members to retain their pastor at whatever cost, that C. L. "just [came] back to New Bethel whenever he got ready," his friend, Jasper Williams, observed. With a foot in two cities, it would be nearly impossible for Franklin to create a forceful political presence in either.[23]

Of course, in contrast to Martin Luther King Jr., who by now had implemented an alternative politics constructed around nonviolent civil disobedience—or to less famous ministers, such as Samuel Kyles in Memphis, Kelly Miller Smith in Nashville, or Fred Shuttlesworth in Birmingham, who led protest movements in their cities—Franklin devoted relatively little energy to building a movement. Even when he did focus on the league, he shared much with the approach favored by the very groups he criticized. Franklin welcomed into the league ministers such as Albert B. Cleage Jr., of Central Congregational Church, who was consciously building a church community focused on social and political action. But he rejected the active involvement of two of Cleage's leading members, the brothers Richard and Milton Henry, on grounds that they had once been accused of Communist sympathies and therefore, Charlie Thompson surmised, "could be a liability to the organization." This attitude aligned Franklin with his erstwhile NAACP opponents and distanced him sharply from Coleman Young's earlier tradition of activism.[24]

Franklin remained able to connect his faith's powerful stories to the emergence of a more historically grounded, self-conscious identity among African Americans in the urban, industrial world they now largely inhabited. But beyond his dedication to his ministry and to using the pulpit to encourage others to give voice to an expanded consciousness, his efforts lacked focus, divided as they were between two cities, two congregations, and the continuing allure of the celebrity recognition his talents brought him. He had come a long way from the plow, and he meant to enjoy it. As his record sales and appearance fees rose, he reveled in the celebrity culture his new base in Los Angeles made even more attractive. In 1962, C. L. even assured a Los Angeles entertainment management firm that were the parties to agree to terms, he would promise "to at all times devote myself to my career." As the specific contractual terms defined only recording royalties and appearance fees, it is hard to gauge precisely how C. L. envisioned this new balance between faith and fortune.[25]

While Franklin's energies were spread thin, others in the Motor City focused more concretely. TULC strove to improve the situation of black workers in both the UAW and other area unions and encourage a more aggressive black political presence in future elections. But conditions within the union movement remained difficult for black working people. Four years after the 1955 merger of the American Federation of Labor and the Congress of Industrial Organizations, which had generated significant hopes for change, there remained at least thirteen national unions operating in Detroit that did not accept black members, that segregated them into separate, powerless locals or denied them access to apprenticeship programs. Of the 134 unions in the merged AFL-CIO, only 5 had any black representatives on their national board. Two of the unions were predominately black, and the other three were decidedly left-wing in their politics. The United Auto Workers, its progressive reputation notwithstanding, had none. Trade-union interracial committees, Horace Sheffield judged, had "become nothing more than public relations agencies" intent on creating "a good image as far as the union is concerned."[26]

At the United Auto Workers' national convention in Atlantic City in October 1959, TULC members regrouped to demand again representation on the International Executive Board. At a meeting with TULC members the evening before the convention opened, Walter Reuther pleaded the weakest of excuses in refusing to support a black candidate. The union was bound by American social conventions on race issues, he stated. He then added insult and insensitivity to temerity by claiming that the time was not yet but would come, he assured the black delegates, when "a Negro will be qualified" for the position. Still, Horace Sheffield spoke during the convention and placed in nomination for the position Willouby Abner, a Chicago organizer for the UAW, a lawyer, and an NAACP activist. The convention received Sheffield's nominating speech in near silence. Abner then stood and, as decided beforehand, declined; there was absolutely no support from the white delegates, Reuther supporters all. Buddy Battle led some forty-five black delegates in a walkout on the last day of the convention less to influence policy—decisions had already been made and many delegates had left—than to demonstrate their commitment to continuing the fight. It had some effect: at the next convention, Nelson Jack Edwards, a TULC founder, a New Bethel congregant and trustee, and a longtime UAW member, became the first African American elected as an international representative.[27]

Although C. L.'s attention to secular politics drifted at times, he remained deeply involved, if most often in a quiet way, in the effort to control the National Baptist Convention. It was with this organization, and not the Metropolitan League or the NAACP, that Franklin maintained his most consistent institutional commitment. Three years after the tense 1957 meeting, the ferocious struggle again dominated the national convention. The reform forces gathered in Philadelphia to challenge Jackson's bid for another term. Once more, police were called to maintain order, as supporters of Jackson and Gardner Taylor each claimed victory for their presidential candidate. Legal battles followed, and at the following year's convention in Kansas City, delegates participated in the closest approximation to open warfare ever witnessed in the convention's long history.

Physical struggles between opposing forces broke out for control of the microphones, for the aisles through which speakers approached the podium, and for the podium itself. In the melee, Jackson supporter A. G. Wright, pastor of Detroit's New Harmony Baptist Church, fell to his death from the dais. Twenty-five police cars responded, and police officers secured the building. Jackson again claimed victory while the reformers despaired of ever changing the National Baptist Convention. Instead, many, among them Charles Hill, A. A. Banks, and H. H. Coleman of Detroit, and C. L.'s friend from Memphis, W. C. Holmes, left to form the Progressive National Baptist Convention.[28]

As one of the most influential ministers in the convention, C. L. commanded considerable attention. Many expected him to support the reformers and even to align with the Progressives. Franklin advocated civil rights, had long been friendly with both Martin Luther Kings, father and son, and sought in his sermons to activate that yet-silent voice in others. All of these positions conflicted sharply with Jackson's lifelong conservatism. In July 1961, just before the tragic Kansas City convention, King and Jackson argued over the merits of the recent "freedom rides," where integrated teams of activists risked their lives to end segregation on interstate buses and public accommodations. While King thought the tactics used by John Lewis and his comrades absolutely appropriate, Jackson argued that "Negroes going to jail won't touch the conscience of the segregationists. Their moral sensitivity is not that tender." The Baptist leader condemned civil disobedience as a tactic, insisting that any protest must obey even an obviously immoral law. Jackson offered an alternative approach to King's, one he called "from protest to production," which emphasized the responsibility black Americans had "to invest what we have in order to help produce the things we need and the things that will enrich our community and our nation." This argument, with its separatist, self-help tones reminiscent of Booker T. Washington's thinking and the contemporary approach of the Nation of Islam, rejected the goal of desegregating public buses in favor of creating investment and job opportunities for African Americans that would enable them to buy their own cars. As Bernard Lafayette remembered: "He [Jackson] would say, 'That should be your goal, not to waste your energy trying to see if you could sit next to a white person on a bus.'"[29]

Following the 1961 convention, Jackson had stripped both Kings of their official positions within the organization, a move tantamount to expulsion. A week later, when he preached the Detroit funeral of A. G. Wright, Jackson had delivered a furious public attack on the "freedom movement" and, by implication, the younger King. "The disrespect for law in the move for freedom has opened the way for criminals to come into our midst," Jackson had decried, proclaiming his ministerial enemies as the "hoodlums and crooks" who occupy "the pulpits today. They are not men who have God on their side."[30]

Franklin faced a complicated situation. He respected J. H. Jackson personally, admired him, and even before this crisis freely discussed policy differences with him. But while the public attacks on King undoubtedly ired Franklin, he never resigned from the convention: he was one of a cohort of ministers far more activist and militant than Jackson, who remained within the fold despite deep disagreements. To Franklin, as to ministers Clay Evans of Chicago and Sandy Ray of Brooklyn, the convention represented the most significant mass organization in black America. In its programs and from its pulpits, these activists thought, a message went out that could—and did—mobilize black consciousness.[31]

But if Franklin stayed, he did so on his own terms. His concluding sermon at the yearly gathering was an event anticipated by thousands of delegates, whose offerings provided the preacher a handsome fee and the convention a sizable contribution. (As chair of the Evangelistic Board, the committee charged with encouraging effective preaching and revivals nationwide, Franklin devoted to his duties the most energy of all the leadership posts he ever held. In all of these commitments to the convention, however, Franklin remained his own person.) In the aftermath of the schism, he praised publicly the freedom movement and King's leadership, and the relationship between these two men remained quite close. C. L. was King's "favorite preacher," one of the civil rights leader's closest aides noted. Many a Sunday evening during a strategy meeting, when sleep was often scarce and tempers short, Bernard Lafayette recalled, King would "stop the meeting, you know, in time for Franklin to come on" over WLAC radio. "Martin loved C. L.," Samuel Kyles affirmed, and that feeling was mutual. For his part, Jackson, who could be a vicious political infighter when necessary, had few options. As Jasper Williams understood the dynamic between them, Jackson "could not afford to be mad" with Franklin "because Reverend Franklin wouldn't care what Dr. Jackson thought. And Dr. Jackson knew that and he needed him." Franklin's ability to embrace both J. H. Jackson and Martin Luther King created a space for less famous Baptists to follow his lead, participate in the freedom movement, and retain allegiance to the institution that nurtured their spiritual and psychological growth.[32]

In Detroit, meanwhile, other new voices emerged in response to changing conditions. Prominent among them were the Henry brothers, Milton and Richard, whom C. L. had rejected for membership in the league. In tandem with their very close friend Albert Cleage, the Henry brothers would develop an intricate, if conflicted, relationship with Franklin across the coming decade.

The brothers, like Cleage, were also northerners, two of the eleven children born in Philadelphia to Walter and Vera Henry between 1914 and 1935. Walter Henry was a postal worker, holding a steady job at good pay that placed the family high in economic standing among the city's non-professional black families. The parents were "strivers," one childhood friend of Milton's noted, who stressed the importance of education, devout faith, and respectable conduct as the keys to success. They led their children to public libraries weekly, insisted that they read widely, and, Vera Henry explained, consciously sought to "teach our children to love God and respect themselves as decent human beings and good Americans." Milton, born in 1920, absorbed these lessons in his own fashion. An Army Air pilot during World War II, a member of the all-black Ninety-ninth Pursuit Squadron stationed in Montgomery, Alabama, Henry refused to adapt to southern racial etiquette, much as Jackie Robinson, Coleman Young, and countless other black soldiers had done during their military service. As a result, he did not receive an honorable discharge from the service, a mark that would lead Temple University's law school to reject his application. Although Yale did accept him, these experiences radicalized him. In 1948, while still a student in New Haven, Henry organized in black Philadelphia on behalf of the League for Non-Violent Civil Disobedience to a Segregated Army, urging young black men to refuse to register for the military draft with the Selective Service System. The league, led by A. Philip Randolph and his assistant, Bayard Rustin, sat Henry in a sound truck, where he discussed these issues over the loudspeaker as the vehicle traveled through black Philadelphia. Ernest Dunbar, then a young man, heard Henry's words. "In the world of 1948," he recalled, " it seemed like a shocking heresy even to blacks." It also shocked the city's legal establishment. His Yale law degree notwithstanding, Milton "failed" the Pennsylvania entrance exam to practice law when, during the obligatory interview, he refused to accept as a condition of passing the restriction that he not defend any civil rights cases in the city.[33]

In 1950, Milton moved to Pontiac, Michigan, a city thirty-one miles north of Detroit, where he quickly challenged the de facto segregation of the city's public schools. Shortly after, his younger brother, Richard, who as an eighteen-year-old had helped on the sound truck, arrived and soon became an occasional reporter for the Michigan *Chronicle*. Richard did not have the same formal education as Milton, but he became an avaricious reader and critical thinker committed to the education of his people. In his role as a public intellectual, he published an eleven-part series in the *Chronicle* between April and June, 1954, which discussed in accessible language the relationship between historical memory and contemporary black consciousness. Titled "Conspiracy of Silence," the articles ran as the Supreme Court's desegregation order in *Brown v. Board of Education* appeared and offered a quite different perspective. Henry began with the assertion that the "single evil in American life" that fostered bigotry was, in fact, a conspiracy of silence concerning "the true story of the Negro's past." Whites and blacks both believed in "Negro inferiority," he argued, for both groups held that "the Negro lived in savagery and darkness until brought into contact with the white man."[34] Most blacks internalized this assumption, knew no other history to correct it, and thus "constantly feel they must 'prove' themselves to whites." Whites, on the other hand, "constantly expect that feeling from Negroes." This explained the infuriating pace of change, as majorities in both groups thought that black people "must, therefore, 'work up' to equality with the white." In a wide-ranging analysis based on the premise that history is important because "the past is eternally joined to the present," Henry discussed the achievements of African culture north and south of the Sahara Desert. He drew on the work of American scholars such as the historians W. E. B. Du Bois and Carter G. Woodson, the anthropologist Melvin J. Herskovits, as well as El Edrisi, "a Moslem historian," and R. E. G. Armattoe, a Ghanian poet and critic, to stress African achievements in government, the arts, science, and literature that were never taught in U.S. schools. Africa was the source of humanity, its very birthplace, and in Egypt he found a distinctively black people whose cultural achievements, he asserted, became the foundation of Western civilization.[35]

Importantly, Richard Henry examined the use of cultural difference in creating race-specific evaluations of worth. Human sacrifice in an African country like Dahomey (now Benin), a religious practice whose shock value long bolstered white convictions of black inferiority, "was no more barbarous than watching a neighbor burn at the stake was to a citizen of Massachusetts." Some months later, in a new introduction to the reissue of the articles, Henry continued the discussion. The "history professor [who] prates glibly of Greece and Rome" but remains silent about Africa, India, China, and the Middle East is bad enough; but "equally as bad . . . if not worse" was the highly selective analysis of European history usually offered. The emphasis on Greece and Rome all but demanded historical silence concerning other progenitors of Western civilization who, as Rome reached its height, "were living in comparative barbarism at the same time." Rejecting this approach as a "perversion of history," Henry argued that "different groups of people," framed by different historical and cultural experiences, arrive "at different answers to the same problems." Thus, the determination of any society's "'worth'" has nothing to do with race or with difference but with whether the sociocultural solution "has met the problems" specific to that context. In this manner, Henry concluded with acute insight, "the real obligation in the teaching of Negro history involves not so much an appraisal of Negro history alone as a reappraisal of World history in general."[36]

Albert Cleage's background was even more elite than that of the Henry brothers, but his thinking had developed in similar fashion. From his pulpit at Central Congregational and from podiums across Detroit, he delivered public lectures venomously critical of the social pretensions and apolitical stance of the black elite he knew so well. Weaned on the promise of American democracy presented as fact, the Henry brothers and Albert Cleage developed their critical vision together, becoming part of a deep, subterranean current in black America whose lived experience caused them to loosen the traditional intellectual pilings that had long anchored the community. C. L. shared the broad outlines of this critique but the contours of his self-education, framed within a decidedly nonelite, southern-reared mentality, marked a significant difference between him and this impressive activist trio. Still, early in the new decade, a political kinship bound these varied approaches. From a pulpit such as Franklin's, from Richard Henry's articles, from mobilized black autoworkers in TULC, from Detroit crowds defending street-corner orators from police harassment, and from such examples as offered by the year-long struggle of the Montgomery boycotters came the demand to create a more critical understanding that better reflected the actual distance between the promise and the experience of American democracy. Evident in the campaign to elect William Patrick to City Council in 1957, these currents coalesced with even greater force in the 1961 Detroit mayoralty campaign.[37]

The underlying issues in the 1961 campaign had changed little since the 1943 riot. In his detailed series on race in Detroit that appeared in 1960, Charles Wartman emphasized four critical areas: the "ascribed status" (the very phrase an echo of South African apartheid policy) that maintained segregated patterns in housing throughout the city; the hostility exhibited by a police force with only 150 black officers out of more than 4,000, in a city where blacks approached 30 percent of the population; the limited job opportunities that still prevailed for many; and the segregated nature and poor facilities of the schools for black children. (These same issues had dominated Wartman's 1953 analysis of the city.) There had been some progress to be sure. Black judges such as Wade McCree had been elected, as was a councilman, and there had been an increase of 49 police officers since 1953—but few in black Detroit believed fundamental change had occurred.[38]

The record of the incumbent Democratic mayor also was an issue throughout black Detroit. Louis C. Miriani had been elected with the support of every major group in Detroit. Labor hailed him, as did executives in the auto industry and the leaders of the chamber of commerce. The newspapers provided favorable coverage, and black voters voted for him as well. But under the rubric of "cracking down on crime," Miriani had ordered his police chief to organize widespread stop-and-search operations in black neighborhoods. In one such sweep over a period of days, a search for two accused murderers resulted in the detention of more than 1,500 African Americans, held in police station cells for various lengths of time and eventually released without any charges being pressed. When police chief Herbert W. Hart then attacked publicly the black press and the NAACP for their criticism of these tactics, the mayor supported him. Under Miriani, integration of the police proceeded only imperceptibly, and his opposition helped defeat Councilman Patrick's resolution to strengthen the city's Commission on Community Relations, the purported municipal protector of civil rights.[39]

While black voters were ready to reject Miriani, a familiar electoral problem remained. The UAW, still assuming its central role in progressive politics, backed Miriani and inferred that black voters would just have to accept its decision as the price of coalition politics. But few whites understood how blacks' attitudes had changed since 1957, or how the TULC might mobilize black Detroit for a campaign beyond the limited concerns of trade unionism. With the labor movement, the police department, the citywide white homeowners' association, and the business community all arrayed against them, TULC leaders Horace Sheffield and Buddy Battle, working closely with Reverend Stephen Spottswood of Metropolitan A. M. E. Zion Church, devised a "Five Plus 1" electoral strategy. The plan advocated support of the four incumbent Common Council members who supported Patrick's resolution to strengthen the city's Commission on Community Relations, as well as Melvin Ravitz, a liberal professor of sociology at Wayne State who was running for council for the first time. The "1" in the slogan referred to the young, liberal Democratic challenger to Miriani, Jerome Cavanaugh, a lawyer. Sheffield and Spottswood had been impressed by one of Cavanaugh's early television appearances and, after further investigation and discussions with him, decided to organize support for him throughout black Detroit. TULC brought together in working harmony the other major black organizations (the Urban League, the NAACP, the Nacirema and Cotillion Clubs). They, in turn, reached out to the church community through the Interdenominational Ministerial Alliance, a citywide organization of white and black ministers. As the possibility of victory seeped deeper in the community, touching members of New Bethel's Political Action Guild and other similar groups throughout the city, TULC made another critical decision: they organized church members, trade unionists, and volunteers into a massive door-to-door campaign that registered individuals to vote the suggested slate. The election results astounded everyone: Cavanaugh easily defeated Miriani, and the five council candidates all won their seats. It stood as a transforming moment for black Detroit, an election that marked the public recognition of the very real political power they possessed. Coalitions would be necessary in the future, but what exhilarated black voters was their success against both the established union movement and the business community. The era of dependence on white trade-union leaders appeared over, and a more demanding black voice, unified for the moment, celebrated its coming out in this urban, industrial world.[40]

*   *   *   *   *

C. L. Franklin also celebrated this signal moment in Detroit's history. Through the Metropolitan Civic League for Legal Action, Franklin had participated in the political mobilization to the extent his schedule allowed. As the founding president, he welcomed mayor-elect Cavanaugh when he addressed the league's victory meeting following the election. But how much time he personally devoted to the campaign remains unclear. His touring continued, Los Angeles remained attractive, and familial and ministerial concerns demanded his attention as well.[41]

As his children, except for Carolyn, the youngest, reached college age, C. L. actively looked to guide them toward careers. This was consistent with his belief that a father's role, while less central than a mother's, had a certain primacy regarding the external world. Vaughn, of course, already had a career in the Air Force. C. L.'s relationship with Carl Ellan was yet too new for him to play a forceful role, though he did insist that his son Cecil attend college. Accepted at Morehouse College in Atlanta, Cecil balked, unwilling to leave friends in Detroit and unsure of what he might study. C. L., who had made all the arrangements for his admission, confronted his son. He would personally put the son on the plane, Franklin announced, but if Cecil elected not to attend classes, "then just remember don't come back here." C. L.'s expression was harsh but, after the fashion of his mother, quite to the point. Years later, after Cecil had graduated cum laude and had become the successful business manager for Aretha, he thanked his father for the tough choice he had presented.[42]

Erma, too, felt her father's concern that she attend college. Following the birth of her second child, she went to Clark University, also in Atlanta, where she stayed for two years. In 1962, during her sophomore year, musicians she knew from Detroit, who toured with the popular R&B band led by Lloyd Price, played a club in Atlanta and urged her to audition for the band. She did, Price made an offer, and the combination of the salary proposed and the excitement promised led Erma to accept immediately. Erma had been interested in a music career ever since Berry Gordy had approached her, and Lloyd Price's band proved to be a wonderful musical fit. Her biggest record was the original version of "Piece of My Heart," which rose into the top ten on the national rhythm-and-blues charts in 1967. Erma's mother-in-law, Ollie Patterson, cared for her children, Thomas and Sabrina, while she was touring.[43]

Aretha's situation proved more complicated. Eighteen in 1960, she already had two children and had left high school before graduating. She also possessed a considerable reputation from her gospel recordings and tour appearances. Her musical abilities were exceptional, and when she told her father of her desire to record popular music, the preacher father and this talented gospel-performing daughter became the talk of the church world.

The most dramatic example of a revered gospel performer "going pop" during the 1950s was Sam Cooke. The gospel star released his first secular recording, "Loveable," in 1957, under an alias, Dale Cooke, in an ineffective effort to avoid a negative reaction from his gospel fans. Cooke had a reason to be worried. When his crossover became public (no name change could mask his voice), many of his gospel supporters felt angry, even be-trayed, by their musical minister's embrace of the secular. Even before Cooke's celebrated crossover, Ray Charles had infused his popular music with the harmonies and inflections of the black church. In the wake of Charles's enormous influence, many gospel quartets, the famous as well as those more obscure, delivered popular lyrics set to sacred harmonies, while the music of those groups who remained within the gospel tradition in-creasingly reflected popular trends.[44]

Precisely because church traditionalists sensed the inevitability of this sea change, many reacted strongly when the daughter of the nation's fore-most black preacher followed Sam Cooke and others into popular music. Some in New Bethel were openly critical of Aretha and even more so of her father for allowing her to record rhythm and blues. "Can't serve two masters," Hulah Gene Hurley said, summing up the feeling of many. The criticism spread well beyond Detroit. Throughout the South, ministers and parishioners alike were openly critical, and Jasper Williams thought "it was a very traumatic time for the church" nationally as well as in Detroit.[45]

C. L.'s defense of Aretha was immediate and public. In an interview with the Michigan *Chronicle*'s entertainment reporter in March 1960, shortly after he accompanied Aretha to New York to initiate discussions about recording contracts, he confirmed directly that her "switching to the popular field [is] with my permission." He dismissed the argument that, as a minister, he should "frown upon popular or jazz music," because "good Christian people can be involved in the popular field," as were many of his "respected personal friends." C. L. extolled a musical diversity that incor-porated "all kinds of music as long as it is good." He acknowledged that Aretha may have left the gospel field but "she has not left the church nor turned her back on the religious training she received in her home." The following year, C. L. and Aretha appeared jointly in Memphis's Ellis Au-ditorium at the first Handy Festival of Music. Advance billing pitted the "Hallelujah Street" hymns of the father against the "Beale Street" songs of the daughter, but the actual performance underscored the multilayered cul-tural vision each possessed. Aretha took the stage first and sang gospel se-lections before C. L. preached to the large crowd. The service concluded, C. L. had the doors of the church thrown open as he announced that

Aretha would now sing R&B and whoever wanted to stay or leave could do just that. Relatively few left. As Jasper Williams, present in the audience that day, recalled with a bemused chuckle, in this father's fierce defense of his young daughter's career "he never backed down from that and it was very, very hard to do that in that day. But people, because it was him, accepted it. They accepted it. It was like taboo, it was the worst thing in the world that a gospel preacher should do or could do, but he didn't care."[46]

By November 1960, Aretha's record, "Today I Sing the Blues," landed on Detroit's Top Ten list, along with songs by such local friends as Jackie Wilson, the Miracles (with Smokey Robinson), and her longtime favorite, Dinah Washington. Within two years, hometown enthusiasts were calling her "the female 'Ray Charles'" and the "New Queen of the Blues" (to distinguish her from *the* queen, Bessie Smith). But in fact her career sputtered during these early years, as producers at Columbia Records never quite allowed her to record material that touched her soul. In her performance style, however, Aretha captured the very essence of black church worship service. For her brother, Cecil, Aretha did "with her voice exactly what a preacher does with his when he moans to a congregation." For Ray Charles, Aretha "always sang from her inners," from the deepest source within. "In many ways she's got her father's feeling and passion," for when C. L. "—one of the last great preachers—delivers a sermon, he builds his case so beautifully you can't help but see the light. Same when Aretha sings." But C. L. himself had the last word for those critics who trembled for shame over his support of his daughter. "Aretha is just a *stone* singer," Franklin declared. "If you want to know the truth, she has never left the church."[47]

But the church itself changed, as did political debate and musical expression as the 1960s progressed. A new generation, one born and reared to the rhythmic cacophony of urban Detroit, drove this transformation, and in the process challenged ministers as diverse as C. L. Franklin and A. A. Banks, to say nothing of Detroit and the nation itself.

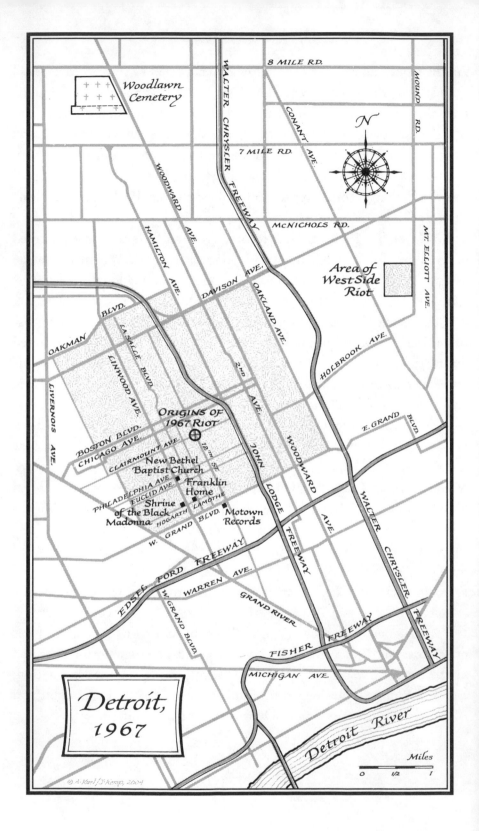

Chapter Nine

A RISING WIND

The continued police dragnets, a familiar daily violence on the streets, and the deterioration of those schools that had "tipped" predominantly black infuriated Milton and Richard Henry and their pastor, Albert Cleage. Too many failures by politicians to deliver on campaign promises, too many empty avowals of racial democracy by union leaders together produced a deep suspicion of liberal solutions. They had supported Jerome Cavanaugh's candidacy but never expected freedom to flow from the mayor's hands. Instead, Milton Henry later recalled, this trio supported political coalitions they thought potentially beneficial while simultaneously looking "to be more overt and to be sort of the devil in the pot." Early in the 1960s, being "the devil" meant to increase militancy and aggressiveness in demanding full rights in a city that still had segregated restaurants and hotels, to say nothing of residential and occupational discrimination. Inevitably, this approach brought them into direct conflict with the established civil rights groups in the city.[1]

In late November 1961, the first issue of their new weekly, the *Illustrated News*, appeared. Edited by Henry Cleage, Albert's attorney brother, the paper's intent was to create "the kind of newsletter that you need to build a grassroots movement," said Grace Boggs, a political ally. The first four issues featured a series by Albert Cleage, "The Negro in Detroit," geared to challenge conventional thinking. These articles were a fiercely critical analysis of the local black elite who so desperately "wanted to get along—to be like their white neighbors . . . [that they] consciously and deliberately sacrificed every racial characteristic and stereotype for the cause of acceptance." The elite, Cleage suggested, had been largely successful but for one major problem: their acceptance by white Detroit would not survive as the "slums spilled over" and the growing black population's need for housing shattered white liberals' confidence in integration.

What made Cleage's thinking especially different from others' was that he did not condemn the "slum hoodlum with his hostility and violence." Rather, he found the reasons for the hoodlum's actions in the "anger at *the world* which has rejected him," as evidenced in the social conditions that structured daily life. An inner sense of "*worthlessness*" motivated this person and the admittedly destructive behavior was, in its "own peculiar way," a fight "for *recognition* and *acceptance*." In a conclusion guaranteed to generate an intense reaction, Cleage suggested that both the "teenage hoodlum" in a "black leather jacket and tight blue jeans" and the "middle class person" concerned "with the 'right people'" and "a house on the 'right street'" shared an identical insecurity. Each lacked a sense of self and—to borrow a metaphor from Ralph Ellison's 1952 novel—each remained invisible to themselves. Neither thought themselves somebody.[2]

Very few people in Detroit at this time spoke publicly as Cleage did. C. L. Franklin certainly addressed the issue of self-worth among African Americans of all ages, but he neither bestowed semi-approval on that "slum hoodlum" nor ridiculed the prospects of integration. Quickly, however, the group around Cleage and the Henry brothers committed itself to a political strategy that kept "moving the ante up," pushing beyond "where we were" so as "to be the catalyst down in there, creating the change."[3]

Early in 1962, they went public as the Group on Advanced Leadership (GOAL), its very name a critique of the well-known civil rights organizations. Richard Henry presided over a membership composed primarily, his brother Milton noted, "of professionals and educators, people who were professors in the universities here." In its first months, GOAL attacked the segregated nature of the city's schools, as well as the biased textbooks used in them, and threatened a lawsuit over the city's singular focus for urban renewal (i.e., destroying housing to make room for commercial development or freeways) in black neighborhoods such as Paradise Valley. The group also called on black voters to support only black congressional candidates in the 1962 primary.[4] In all of these activities, Cleage and GOAL followed their dual strategy of seeking alliances even as they roiled the pot. Cleage, for example, became a member of the executive board of the Detroit NAACP in late 1962, while he regularly delivered withering public criticism of what he considered its conservative inaction. In a speech at a luncheon of the Booker T. Washington Business Association, a politically conservative group of elite black businessmen and professionals (many of whom Cleage had known since childhood), he directly held them responsible for making his militant approach necessary. The "sickness of frustration, anger and hatred among Negroes," he argued, was the result of a weak black leadership "pussy-footing with discrimination." He accused the elite of being primarily concerned with bias in their professional worlds. Until the appearance of GOAL, he challenged, the city had lacked the "militant, vocal leadership . . . of the type that gives a point and direction in the life of Detroit Negroes."[5]

Although Cleage and the Henry brothers often made uninformed and ill-considered attacks on others, their criticisms of education policy and urban renewal attracted considerable support. As Cleage argued at a socialist forum in Detroit's Eugene V. Debs Hall in September 1962, "a militant and independent Negro leadership" focused on the needs "of the total Negro community" just might mobilize large numbers of previously inactive black citizens. The apathy so often noted was not inherent in these men and women, he insisted, but rather grew from their exclusion from civic life by both white society and elite blacks. Cleage argued that racism was not an episodic social illness but a structural consequence of America's social and political culture, and he therefore demanded a thorough, indeed a revolutionary, cure. His approach increasingly found an audience. Even the *Detroit News* felt compelled to include Cleage in its 1962 discussion of the city's black leadership. "He is a militant and a nationalist," the paper explained, "but not a fakir nor a wild-eyed visionary."[6]

That same year, Cleage brought jazz drummer Max Roach and his wife, singer Abbey Lincoln, to the church to discuss "Black Nationalism in Jazz." Lincoln's natural hair—what would in a few years be called an Afro—caused much comment among the hundred people present, and the couples' discussion of nationalism ranged well beyond the world of jazz. Cleage gently criticized the couple for several "questionable arguments and conclusions" and upheld the possibility (which Roach ignored) that whites committed to a radical transformation of America could be allies. He also wondered at the simplistic economic thinking at the core of the couple's philosophy of racial uplift. Although not yet a nationalist himself, Cleage applauded the speakers for the courage to speak their minds and proclaimed the evening "an exhilarating experience" that made "a genuine contribution" to political debate.[7]

No one could confuse the tone and substance of Franklin's 1955 public criticism of the NAACP with Cleage's acidic dismissal of contemporary black leaders. But each man shared a conviction in the potential of the individuals in the pews before them, and as they continued to evolve, each realized the need for a more aggressive approach to the city's problems. By June 1963, they would join forces to pose the greatest threat to date to Detroit's established civil rights leadership.

*   *   *   *   *

On March 10, 1963, New Bethel's second exodus ended as an exuberant C. L. Franklin led a caravan of three hundred cars from the church's temporary quarters to a newly renovated structure on Linwood and Philadelphia, on Detroit's West Side. An all-black construction company had transformed the former theater into a church with a seating capacity of over twenty-five hundred. Some furnishings and many decorative touches still awaited completion, but taking possession ended a difficult period for Franklin and the congregation. They had survived two years of wandering as the city refashioned the Hastings Street corridor and weathered a legal challenge by three disgruntled members over the pastor's management of construction funds. Franklin himself had wandered in more ways than one. In contrast to his practice during the construction of the new Hastings Street church a decade earlier, he traveled extensively during this second dislocation, treating Los Angeles as his second home. But now, standing in the new pulpit for the first time, his gaze flitting from the packed floor to the equally crowded curved balcony, Franklin's joy burst forth. "This is a day of victory, triumph and achievement," he exulted, "and we are happy." C. L. praised the faith and the commitment of the congregation, and he proudly offered the beautiful structure created by skilled black workers as proof not of "reverse racism," but of what "as a race we can do for ourselves if we take advantage of opportunities to qualify ourselves." Telegrams poured in from President John F. Kennedy, J. H. Jackson, Martin Luther King Jr., and many others. It was a special moment. "On this particular occasion," Charlie Thompson recalled, laughing at the memory, "you just couldn't shut him [Franklin] up. He was kind [of] like Muhammad Ali! You couldn't shut him up, I tell you. . . . Everybody could feel it. Peoples just applauding and crying and it was really something to celebrate for." Not insignificantly, walking into New Bethel's new sanctuary ended Franklin's dalliance with Los Angeles. Within the bounds of his customary travels, he was home to stay.[8]

Despite his time away from Detroit, Franklin had followed the political upheavals created by GOAL and the direct-action tactics, including sit-ins and group arrests, practiced by the young militants in the Detroit chapter of the Congress of Racial Equality (CORE). It was, however, a struggle seven hundred miles to the south, led by his good friend, Martin, that provided him reentry into the highly contentious freedom movement in the Motor City.[9]

After the Montgomery bus boycott, Martin Luther King Jr. had become the nation's most recognized civil rights activist. As the leader of the Southern Christian Leadership Conference (SCLC), King and his allies raised considerable funds to finance direct challenges to the systematic segregation of the Deep South. Early in 1963, King and SCLC turned their attention to Birmingham, Alabama. The state of Alabama, perhaps second only to Mississippi, was a center of white resistance to civil rights. That January, the newly elected governor, George C. Wallace, declared in his inaugural address that his administration would "draw a line in the dust and toss the gauntlet before the feet of tyranny. And I say, 'Segregation now! Segregation tomorrow! Segregation forever!'" Birmingham's Commissioner of Public Safety, Eugene "Bull" Connor, fervently supported the governor's sentiments, which he had long enforced by any means necessary. On Wednesday, April 3, the first demonstrators marched downtown to face arrest at the hands of Connor's police. Over the next week, the mass demonstrations continued, but as white resistance intensified, fewer black demonstrators willingly offered themselves for arrest and possible beatings. King, worried that serious defeat for the movement was imminent, sought new tactics to rejuvenate the Birmingham movement. On April 12, Good Friday in the Christian calendar, King, his chief assistant, Ralph Abernathy, and the city's longtime leader of the Alabama Christian Movement for Human Rights, Fred Shuttlesworth—ministers all—led a group of demonstrators who were arrested and then jailed.[10] But even that potent symbolism failed to generate more protesters. By Thursday, May 2, SCLC implemented another tactic long debated and discussed: More than one thousand young people, students in the black grade schools and high schools of the city, streamed out of the Sixteenth Street Baptist Church in waves of fifty at a time, into Kelly Ingram Park, which marked the divide between black and white Birmingham. There, a phalanx of police met them, arrested them, and carted them to jail in police wagons. The following day, Connor ordered his fire department to turn water hoses on a second massing of young protesters and his police to use their snarling guard dogs to contain the demonstrators. By Saturday morning, newspapers around the world reproduced the horrifying pictures of teenagers and children under brutal attack by the city's forces of public safety.[11]

Despite the international press attention, the cost of the demonstrations, including bail money, fines, legal fees, and daily sustenance for demonstrators, drained SCLC's treasury, and King and his advisers had to raise more money immediately. They turned to three nationally known supporters who were also gifted fundraisers: Mahalia Jackson, Harry Belafonte, and C. L. Franklin. Jackson responded with plans for a program in Chicago, held on May 27, which C. L. helped to organize. The writer and radio commentator Studs Terkel emceed the event, introducing in turn Dinah Washington, Eartha Kitt, and Aretha Franklin, whose rendition of "Precious Lord," Thomas Dorsey's famous gospel hymn, "turned church out," in the words of one eyewitness. King then spoke, and the event raised more than $50,000 for SCLC.[12]

Efforts in Detroit proved more complicated. As in black communities across the nation, the visual images from Birmingham fueled both comments and protest. One ill-planned protest meeting early in May attracted only fifty people—enough, however, for Albert Cleage's supporters to demand he speak to the group. TULC announced that same week plans to participate in a national march on Washington for May 30, Memorial Day, to protest the "ghastly events" in Birmingham. On Friday, May 10, Franklin and New Bethel trustee Benjamin McFall asked forty people to an invitation-only meeting to support Mahalia Jackson's effort in Chicago. Some thirty attended, but the five major civil rights organizations in the city ignored the invitation. Significantly, Franklin did not invite Cleage. He may have reasoned that while Cleage's continuing public attacks on other black leaders attracted some, they made coalition-building immensely difficult. Franklin may also have noticed how Cleage's supporters worked to dominate every event they attended.[13]

The meeting elected officers for an organization whose purpose was already reaching beyond simply a support role. Franklin became chairman, McFall co-chairman. The board of directors and committee chairs included Thomas Shelby, Jackie Vaughn III, James Del Rio, Nelson Jack Edwards, and John Burns, all men close to Franklin. In acknowledgment of his public stature, the absent Cleage was later asked to become one of the fourteen directors. C. L.'s leadership position remained intact—but only for the moment.[14]

The traditional black leadership, who had largely ignored the May 10 meeting, convened five days later. This time, Franklin was not invited. Disturbed at Franklin's prominence at the first meeting, the assembled leaders requested a private meeting with Franklin the following day to ask him to step down as chair of the new group. Pressed by George Crockett, then a leading member of the Cotillion Club, who "insisted [Franklin] had no leadership image or experience for this sort of thing," Franklin refused. He had been duly elected and "would continue to serve until removed by a proper vote." The exchange sparked a public conflict with the black elite that C. L. had long anticipated. Two days later on May 17, the ninth anniversary of the *Brown* decision, a large crowd came to New Bethel in a heavy rain for the group's second meeting. All of the major organizations had sent representatives. The new organization adopted the name Detroit Council for Human Rights (DCHR), and its committee structure expanded. The traditional leadership angled to have two of its supporters appointed to head the planning committee, with power to speak for the council—a move that would have made Franklin's position honorific rather than substantive. C. L. refused to step aside, and the two designated spokesmen, Dr. D. T. Burton and the young lawyer John Conyers Jr., resigned instead. Franklin's supporters applauded, and those who had previously dismissed him had no choice at the moment but to accept his authority.[15]

By the May 17 meeting, Franklin's plans had progressed well beyond a simple supporting role for the Chicago rally. The group announced a major march in Detroit, with King as the main speaker, with a dual goal of supporting SCLC and focusing attention on racial issues in Detroit. On May 20, Franklin asked Councilman William Patrick to sponsor his application for a permit for a march, then set for June 11, of some one hundred thousand people down Woodward Avenue. As was his style, Cleage supported the march but saw in the DCHR an opportunity to supplant the old leaders who, he argued, spoke on behalf of "white 'Liberals' rather than for the Negro masses." If Franklin could "avoid being boxed in by the old guard leaders," Cleage argued, ". . . we may see a complete change in the Detroit picture, and soon." Such words did not sit well with the Baptist Ministerial Alliance, which had initially supported the march but now rescinded its approval. Some of their opposition was personal: resentment of C. L.'s stature and success, and the fact that until now he had rarely been active in any of the community activities the Alliance sponsored. When Franklin appeared at an Alliance meeting on May 28 to discuss the reversal, a fight nearly broke out. Reverend A. L. Merritt, president of the Alliance, denied Franklin speaking privileges, as his dues were not yet paid. New Bethel's minister exploded, denouncing the decision and demanding the floor based on his seventeen-year membership in the group. Merritt refused, and C. L. "angrily went after" him but was restrained by other ministers. As C. L. later told a Detroit reporter, "I temporarily lost my temper," but he refused to be dissuaded by such opposition.[16]

What enabled Franklin to retain his leadership position—for his opponents were correct: he had rarely volunteered, nor had he been asked to involve himself in their public activities—was his close friendship with King. The civil rights leader had asked him for help, and King's wife, Coretta Scott King, reinforced that connection with a well-publicized telegram prior to the May 17 meeting that praised Franklin on behalf of her husband for "sparking a city-wide fund drive" for SCLC. As potent as that endorsement was, Franklin's opponents persisted in efforts to unseat him. Just before May 30, Crockett and TULC's Horace Sheffield called SCLC's Atlanta office to inform King's staff of what they considered a disastrous situation in the making. In a long discussion with Rev. Wyatt T. Walker, one of King's main assistants, the two men explained their inability to remove Franklin and urged SCLC either to withdraw King's participation for the march now planned for Sunday June 23, or have SCLC publicly appoint Charles W. Butler, pastor of New Calvary Baptist Church, as SCLC's Detroit coordinator. Hoping for a compromise—perhaps because there was no way to convince King to withdraw support from his friend—Walker, impressed by the critique of Franklin, chose the second option. Butler, an active member of the Baptist Ministerial Alliance, which had just denied Franklin speaking privileges, announced his own appointment at a meeting at New Bethel on May 30. Neither Franklin nor anyone else objected, but they also ceded no ground in leading the fundraising or the coming demonstration.[17]

Of course, the open tension between Franklin and Detroit's entrenched black leadership, religious and secular, had deep roots. But there was as well a personal dimension that drove both sides in this dispute. Men like Edward Turner, A. A. Banks, and their colleagues had long dismissed Franklin as a mere preacher. They abhorred his public style and denigrated his political analysis. Yet, in this moment of crisis, King had reached out not for Arthur Johnson, his Morehouse College classmate, nor other close acquaintances among the black social elite, but for the Mississippi-born migrant.

It was not just Franklin who worried the entrenched black leadership. Cleage's considerable organizational and oratorical skills, coupled with Franklin's ability to move crowds, posed a substantial threat to their position. But the politics of the two men were not, in fact, interchangeable.

Both were committed to integration at this time as were the other leaders, but Cleage's persistent critique of American liberalism's systematic inability to solve African American problems distinguished him from Franklin, who remained a liberal Democrat. Traditional leaders feared Cleage's influence on Franklin (whose intellect they belittled privately); they worried that together, the potential effectiveness of these two men might mobilize those whom these elite leaders had always presumed to represent. Arthur Johnson of the NAACP caught well their mood of apprehension. The march "was the first major challenge to the leadership of the NAACP" during his tenure in Detroit. With the increasingly militant language finding stronger echoes on Detroit's streets in anticipation of the coming march, "none of us knew exactly where things were going."[18]

In early May, before the march had received much public attention, Mose Atkins, "a colored citizen" of Detroit, wrote the NAACP to suggest a new tactic. In an effort to force the Kennedy administration to intervene in Birmingham, the group should have "our colored bus drivers go on strike and tie up Detroit bus service. This will learn the Kennedys to keep their word." A few weeks later, an anonymous letter to Detroit's Urban League struck an angrier tone. Reflecting perhaps Cleage's rhetorical influence, the writer warned "you old Uncle Toms" to "move and move right or we are going to move you out and no one will listen to you." Insisting that the established leaders must "stop pleasing these white people," the writer added: "We are watching you and if you don't go right you won't have anyone to lead and then the white man won't need you either." Even longtime NAACP supporters waved caution signs. One such local activist, known only as Patterson, castigated the organization for its refusal to publicly support Franklin and the DCHR's march. He predicted the demonstration would be a success "beyond all expectations because the *PEOPLE* will be participating . . . not the $100.00 plate dinner members but the *little people*." And he warned that "a 'rising wind' of resentment and bewilderment on the part of the community" toward the NAACP would grow even more forceful. "You will have an open revolt on your hands soon within the organization. Believe this please," Patterson pleaded. "I'd be *with you*—But you make it difficult."[19]

On June 7, in a last effort to control the march, a committee chaired by

A. A. Banks that included Arthur Johnson and Charles W. Butler met with Franklin and other officials of the Detroit Council for Human Rights. Incredibly, Banks insisted that all funds raised be split equally between SCLC and the Detroit branch of the NAACP. Franklin rejected this immediately. Only days before, his hand had been strengthened when, in a conference call with King, Wyatt Walker, Charles Butler, and himself, King requested Detroit ministers to send telegrams affirming their support for the June 23 march directly to Franklin, who would then transmit them to Atlanta. As Arthur Johnson well understood, King's support trumped all arguments.[20]

Franklin's understanding of black Detroit's history infused his call to join the march. Alone among the city's leaders, C. L. emphasized in a newspaper interview that the coming march would mark—almost to the day—the twentieth anniversary of the 1943 riots. The "same basic, underlying causes" for that disturbance "are still present," he explained, as are the "fear and frustration" so evident in 1943 as well. "We comprise nearly 30 per cent of the population, for example, but 70 per cent of us live in substandard housing. Our demonstration," he declared in his own blunt way, reflecting his evolution since his 1955 public letter, "will serve as a warning to the city that what has transpired in the past is no longer acceptable to the Negro community. We want complete amelioration of all injustices. This is a new leadership."[21]

As the march grew closer, the back-room maneuvering intensified. A spokesman for the Baptist Ministerial Alliance criticized Franklin's and Cleage's insistence on black leadership of the march, while black leaders in the UAW (particularly Sheffield, Buddy Battle, Nelson Jack Edwards, and Marc Stepp) negotiated with Franklin over Walter Reuther's role in the event. Marc Stepp, who attended the meeting, recalled that Franklin and other unnamed DCHR leaders demanded an all-black leadership because they "didn't want Walter to take it over." The negotiations resulted in a role for Reuther that did not challenge DCHR's control, but the deep suspicion of the powerful union's assumption of primacy regarding black Detroit's interests remained. The NAACP also worked to outflank the march leaders, secretly printing a thousand picket signs with the group's name prominently displayed. "I was trying to keep the NAACP from being smothered," Arthur Johnson explained, decades later.[22]

However important the political maneuvering was to those involved, it played itself out against a somber backdrop. Early in the morning of Wednesday, June 12, a sniper, hiding in nearby bushes, shot dead Medgar Evers, the World War II veteran and head of the Mississippi NAACP, as he crossed from his car to the front door of his home in Jackson, Mississippi. Evers had given the powerful speech at Detroit's demonstration and memorial commemoration of Emmett Till's murder in September 1955. On Saturday, June 22, on the eve of the Detroit march, police arrested Byron de La Beckwith, a former United States Marine, in his home in Greenwood, Mississippi, and charged him with the murder. De La Beckwith proudly affirmed his membership in the White Citizens Council of Mississippi, and Greenwood's elected city attorney volunteered his legal expertise to the accused.[23]

Sunday, June 23, broke clear in Detroit, the temperature warm but not excessive, the bright sunshine an encouraging welcome for the day to come. By noon, people began massing along Woodward Avenue for the 4 P.M. start, and the crowd grew enormously as the churches let out in the early afternoon. The marchers, *Chronicle* reporter Ofield Dukes later wrote, were diverse: "Negroes of all classes—street walkers, doctors, school children, senior citizens, drunks, clergymen and their congregations, etc.— came from near and far to 'walk for freedom.'" It was, in so many ways, a C. L. Franklin crowd. As the numbers surged to somewhere between 125,000 and 200,000 people, the joyous marchers took possession of the streets in the city's main shopping and entertainment district where, until recently, they had been denied equal service. Significantly, the march was a black affair. White marchers never appeared in appreciable numbers— "masses of brown and black people punctuated by sympathetic whites" was *Chronicle* columnist Broadus N. Butler's impression. Some black unionists expressed disappointment at the noticeable absence of most of their white coworkers.

Though an omen of further difficulties to come, the absence of many whites did not dampen the enthusiasm of the day. As the fifty-seven-year-old Mrs. Ethel Cherise well understood, the cause of the joy lay in the seriousness of the moment. "I am here to walk for our rights," she told a reporter, "and nothing could keep me away." The march celebrated publicly an emerging black consciousness, one long in the making through migration and adjustment to this urban world, a consciousness nurtured in the attitudes of returning veterans, discussions over the *Brown* decision, Emmett Till's open casket, and the example of the people of Montgomery, Alabama. C. L. Franklin had every right to feel proud of his role in this. Well before 1963, his Sunday sermons and pointed public letter encouraged the new tone now so evident on Woodward Avenue, as the largest civil rights demonstration ever held in the nation began.[24]

As a small percentage of the marchers eventually squeezed into their seats at Cobo Hall, filling the arena to capacity, Ramsey Lewis, Dinah Washington, Jimmy McGriff, Erma Franklin, and the Four Tops entertained. The formal program began with C. L.'s mentor, Reuben Gayden, offering the scriptural reading. Then the entire assembly rose to join in James Weldon Johnson's "Lift Every Voice and Sing," the song widely recognized as the Negro national anthem. The mayor briefly greeted the crowd, as did Walter Reuther and other officials. DCHR leaders were then introduced. A mass choir sang the civil rights standard "We Shall Overcome," and Lillian Hatcher, the black UAW official, spoke of the role of black women in the freedom struggle. Three speakers, among them Albert Cleage, spoke of Detroit's civil rights problems, and C. L. Franklin raised the offering as the choir sang a selection from Rossini. Only then did Congressman Charles C. Diggs Jr. approach the microphone to introduce the main speaker.[25]

King thanked C. L. Franklin, "my good friend," and the council for organizing the demonstration and applauded the marchers for their evident "discipline" and "commitment to non-violence." He reminded the audience of the promise of Lincoln's Emancipation Proclamation, which took effect on January 1, 1863, and that a century later, "the Negro . . . is still not free" in what was yet "an anemic democracy" in America. "Segregation is a cancer in the body politic," he intoned, and with a quickened rhythmic cadence, the Baptist preacher responded directly to the Alabama governor's recent inaugural speech. "In a sense," King exhorted, "we are through with segregation now, henceforth, and forever more." African American people had changed dramatically in recent decades. "A new sense of dignity and . . . self-respect" were obvious. "The Negro came to feel that he was somebody." Rejecting calls for gradualism, King stressed "the urgency of the moment" in this ongoing "social revolution": "We want all our rights, we want them here and we want them now." Embracing this "magnificent new militancy," King nonetheless warned against racial separatism. He understood the psychological frustration many felt but insisted that "black supremacy is as dangerous as white supremacy."

"This afternoon I have a dream," King then announced with heightened emphasis. "It is a dream deeply rooted in the American dream." His dream foretold of a time when "the sons of former slaves and the sons of former slaveholders will be able to live together as brothers. I have a dream," he called out, reaching higher, the fervent audience response encouraging him, that "little white children and little Negro children" will be "as brothers and sisters. I have a dream this afternoon," he prayed again, that "one day" homes and churches will not be burned to the ground "because people want to be free. I have a dream this afternoon," he declared, his rhythmic tones setting the audience to clapping and swaying, that "there will be a day we will no longer face the atrocities that Emmett Till and Medgar Evers had to face. That all men can live in dignity. I have a dream this afternoon," he reiterated, at one with the audience now, that "my four little children" will not have to suffer "the same young days" of discrimination "that I had to come up in. They will be judged by the content of their character and not the color of their skin." He shared with the ecstatic congregation—for they had church that afternoon in Cobo Hall—his vision of a world where the words of the prophet Amos were a lived experience, where "justice will roll down like water and righteousness like a mighty stream." "One day," he even dared, "we will recognize the words of Jefferson that all men are created equal . . . endowed by their Creator with certain inalienable rights, that among these are life, liberty, and the pursuit of happiness—Yes—I have a dream this afternoon."[26]

As the throng eased back into their seats, the combined choirs offered a musical selection in memory of Medgar Evers, and a special offering collected a scholarship fund for his children. C. L. Franklin then introduced other dignitaries as the crowd slowly moved toward the doors.

*   *   *   *   *

In the immediate aftermath of the march, a euphoric mood captivated much of black Detroit. Pickets appeared at breweries that had never hired black workers—their contract with the Brewery Workers union prohibited such action—and at local grocery-store chains that collectively employed less than a handful of blacks in senior staff positions. Within days, black workers, salesmen, and managers received new promotions. Letters also came into civil rights offices applauding the march. Mrs. E. Backer, a self-described "negro mother without a diploma or a job," wrote Arthur Johnson, telling him how "proud I am to be a negro." In her "most humble manner," fully aware that she and her friends, lacking education, "are not qualified [and] have only you to rely on," she pleaded for black leaders to "please hold on to this beautiful unity" achieved on June 23. She then offered the suggestion that all of the groups unite into one organization "according to parlimentary [sic] procedures, and please don't let hunger for power or the desire to make individual history mar this wonderful goal."[27] By mid-July, it appeared that Mrs. Backer's hopes were answered as some thirty Detroit organizations, from the Cotillion Club, the Trade Union Leadership Council, and the NAACP to GOAL and the DCHR, formed a new coordinating group, Operation Negro Equality (ONE), with an emphasis on obtaining equal economic opportunity.[28]

But appearances deceived. Behind the scenes, vicious infighting persisted. In city government, allies of the traditional leadership advised that to control Franklin's group, it was necessary to control Albert Cleage. "This man's star is on the ascendancy in this city," an unsigned report suggested. "Anybody who wants to destroy the Council must contend with him. His position is pivotal." A significant portion of ONE's steering committee, along with leaders of TULC and the Baptist Ministerial Alliance, sought to do just that. Two days after the march, another dispute erupted that worried Franklin, as he, too, now strove for unity. James Del Rio, a wealthy realtor long active in the NAACP, a New Bethel trustee, and a close friend and coworker in organizing the march with C. L., stated on June 25 that the success of the demonstration was "a direct repudiation of the NAACP." At the national convention of the NAACP in Chicago over the July 4 holiday, the Detroit chapter led a walkout when Del Rio appeared as a panelist to discuss housing issues. Franklin quickly sought to play down the tension.[29]

C. L. Franklin observed the jostling egos, competing political positions, and public posturing with some dismay. He was certainly capable of similar conduct, but in the months following the march, he took a different path. For the first time in his career, he actively led a secular, political organization to which he committed his considerable abilities. He chaired mass meetings at New Bethel and elsewhere of five hundred and more; oversaw the creation of a program that focused on equality in jobs, housing, and schools; conferred with other leaders repeatedly to iron out differences and form a common approach; and met with the mayor to obtain his active, public support. It was, nonetheless, a complicated dance choreographed against the swirling forces of protest that formed what Albert Cleage called a "summer hurricane."[30]

At three o'clock in the morning on Friday, July 5, a twenty-four-year-old black woman walked with a friend near the intersection of John R Street and Watson, in the area known before urban renewal as Paradise Valley. Two white officers stopped the black couple, confiscated a pocketknife from Cynthia Scott's friend, Charles Marshall, and interrogated the pair. Police later claimed that the couple acted suspiciously, incongruously explaining that Scott brandished "'several bills of currency' in her hand" as they approached. The police also claimed that Scott had yet another pocketknife and slashed at Patrolman Theodore Spicher as he tried to put her in the squad car. Marshall stated that Scott possessed no knife, told the officer that because she had done nothing wrong she would not get in the car, and began to walk across the street. Both Marshall and Spicher agreed on what happened next: the patrolman drew his gun and, as Scott reached the opposite curb, fired twice, hitting her in the back with each bullet. As she turned, he fired a third shot, striking her this time "in the lower right stomach."[31] Scott fell dead.

City prosecutor Samuel H. Olsen quickly exonerated Spicher solely on the testimony of the two policemen. Olsen, whose reputation was already dismal among black residents, refused to credit the statements of other eyewitnesses, all of whom were African Americans, because he considered their accounts "too biased." That Scott was "an admitted prostitute," familiar to the two officers as such, was widely known among black East Side residents, as was Spicher's reputation for excessive violence toward African

American suspects in his custody. Immediately following Olsen's ruling, Richard Henry called a demonstration for Saturday, July 13, at police headquarters. The small protest attracted activists from the DCHR and GOAL, as well as from Uhuru, a black-only youth group founded the previous March by students at Detroit's Wayne State University. Led by Luke Tripp, a twenty-two-year-old senior majoring in mathematics and physics, Uhuru (which means *freedom*, in Swahili) positioned itself rhetorically as even more militant than Cleage and the Henry brothers. Cleage found himself in the odd position of criticizing the angry crowd inflamed by Tripp for its "simple thinking" about violence as he worked to calm the protesters. No city official heeded the call for a full investigation of Spicher's actions. In late July, attorney Milton Henry, representing Scott's mother in an unsuccessful $5 million damage suit, cross-examined Spicher for more than two hours in court. Henry depicted Spicher's strained, inconsistent testimony as "conclusive evidence that the killing was a plain case of murder." Yet despite the outcry—even highly respectable ministers wrote angry, anguished letters to city officials—no other groups but DCHR and Uhuru joined GOAL in the demonstrations.[32]

The fury that followed the killing of Cynthia Scott indicated the emergence of a new tone in black protest. Much had changed in a very short time. The public voice of the migrants had been hard won, their determination fierce and their commitment deep. It was in this context that the deeply talented C. L. Franklin proved so effective. But these rural influences had not framed this new consciousness. Rather, Detroit's crowded concrete neighborhoods, patrolled by "brutes in blue," as Luke Tripp called the police, had fueled it. This new expression accepted as a given the foundation already established but took its tone from thwarted expectations. The difference was not simply generational: the northern-born and -raised trio of Cleage and the Henry brothers were decades older than Tripp and his fellow students, all of whom moved toward greater militancy that summer. The reactions to the lynching of Emmett Till had marked a significant moment in this process, but it was now, when continued horrors tore at the rising expectations generated by the civil rights movement, that this angry new voice found broader expression.

The most astute leaders recognized the depth of the problem. As an internal analysis by Detroit's Urban League acknowledged honestly, what gave the militants their credibility was the critical fact that the civil rights movement in Detroit, as in most northern cities, "has been of greatest benefit to a very small segment of Negroes." College graduates and some with high school degrees fared well, positioned as they were to take advantage of new opportunities. But for the majority of black, working-class Detroit, lacking marketable skills, education, and a union card, the freedom movement remained "of negligible good." These were the "masses" both the new and the traditional leadership claimed to speak for, although even Albert Cleage quaked before their actual fury. In reality, no one spoke for them.[33]

This militancy, of course, was not totally new. Detroit had long been the center of black nationalist thinking, and Marcus Garvey's black nationalist philosophy remained evident in the city long after its national strength ebbed in the 1920s. The Nation of Islam, a separatist African American religious movement, had its origins in Detroit in the early 1930s and grew in succeeding decades. If the Garvey movement was largely dormant in the 1960s, its remaining members honored for their longevity rather than their contemporary impact, the opposite was the case with the Nation. Under Elijah Muhammad, the organization had grown significantly in the 1950s, particularly as the result of the missionary work of a recently released prison convert, Malcolm Little. Known by his Muslim name, Malcolm X, compelling and charismatic, preached a version of Islamic faith (Christianity, he exhorted, was the slaveholders' religion), black pride and self-dignity, and an implacable opposition to racists, among whom he publicly included all white Americans. His biological brother, Wilfred X, led Detroit's Mosque No. 1. By 1963, Malcolm's message exerted a powerful, influential appeal. He spoke truths, however simplistically framed at times, "like thunder beginning to gather its strength," and his uncompromising militant perspective that famously demanded black liberation by any means necessary filtered into neighborhood debates throughout black America. Some welcomed his influence with a wry smile, as if they had been waiting for some time. The "one thing I loved about our group," Milton Henry recalled of his comrades in GOAL, was that we "wanted to [do] whatever was necessary, before Malcolm even said that, by any means. [We] wanted to do what was necessary to become human."[34]

As Cynthia Scott's murder suppressed the euphoria that followed King's June speech, so too another tortured cycle of uplift and disillusionment drew national attention. On August 28, King delivered a magnificent address before 250,000 people, largely black, at the Lincoln Memorial in the nation's capitol. It became known internationally as the "I Have a Dream Speech," and it borrowed some of the phrasing, ideas, and tones he had explored in Detroit two months earlier. Following King's speech, New York attorney Conrad J. Lynn, with the support of Cleage and the Henrys, released a statement to the press announcing the formation of the Freedom Now Party. Unrealistically predicting 1 million votes for the new party in the 1964 elections, Lynn, a longtime political activist influenced by Marxism and, at the time, counsel for an integrated group of demonstrators arrested while protesting New York's segregated building-trades unions, suggested the various African independence movements as models for "American Negroes." He also insisted that the party was not "anti-white": "Our banner is not racism, but self-reliance." Within a week of Lynn's announcement, LaMar Barron, an unemployed twenty-nine-year-old Uhuru member, wrote the *Chronicle* in his capacity as the acting chair of the Detroit branch of the party. He attacked gradualism, derided black dependency on elected "white liberals . . . who are responsible for whitewashing the murderer of Cynthia Scott," and endorsed an all-black party as the best means to end the political paralysis inherent in "alternating between a Democratic Lucifer and a Republican Satan."[35]

On Sunday, September 15, slightly more than three weeks later, a bomb exploded at the Sixteenth Street Baptist Church in Birmingham, the center of the city's civil rights movement, where waves of young people had excitedly left for Bull Connor's jails only months before. The explosion killed four young girls as they left Sunday school. On Tuesday, September 17, Reverend Fred Shuttlesworth eulogized Carole Robertson. The next day, Reverend King struggled with the darkness that permeated his dream as he eulogized Addie Mae Collins, Denise McNair, and Cynthia Wesley. It was the twenty-ninth bombing of African American structures in Birmingham since 1951. Little wonder, then, that increasing numbers of African Americans questioned a belief that direct, nonviolent resistance to evil would both release the oppressed and transform the oppressor.[36]

In this charged atmosphere C. L. Franklin and Albert Cleage planned for a national conference of black civil rights leaders that November in Detroit. Although Cleage maintained his public criticism of established black leaders, to most observers the two men appeared to work well together. By mid-October, the DCHR released the conference schedule: Saturday's panels would discuss topics including jobs and black political action, as well as plans for "direct action programs relative to these topics"; Sunday, November 11, Adam Clayton Powell and Mahalia Jackson would headline a massive rally at Cobo Hall. An impressive list of civil rights leaders and activists indicated they would attend, including Reverend Kelly Miller Smith who, along with John Lewis, had led the student civil rights movement in Nashville in 1959; three members of King's staff; and William Worthy, the left-wing correspondent of the *Baltimore Afro-American*. As late as Sunday, October 27, Detroit's leading newspaper ran a major story on the Northern Negro Leadership Conference, in which C. L. noted that the new group he expected to emerge from the gathering "has not been clearly defined and won't be until after this meeting." But Cleage and the Henry brothers had developed a clear agenda for the proposed new group well before October. Less than twenty-four hours later, Cleage attacked Franklin in print, resigned from the DCHR, and announced his own conference to be held that same weekend. Even in these mercurial times, the news stunned onlookers.[37]

As Franklin debated how to respond, a preoccupied Martin Luther King arrived in Detroit the following week for a speech to the Michigan Education Association. When pressed by reporters to comment on the new party, King generalized, indicating that he knew little about the specifics. Discouraged by the Democratic Party's capitulation "to the undemocratic ideals of the southern Dixiecrats" as well as by the Republicans' willingness to "too often accept the blatant hypocrisy of the right-wing Northerners," King allowed that he "would favor something like this if it would increase the Negro's voice in politics." King and Franklin huddled for a brief discussion during that busy day. King subsequently endorsed publicly the originally scheduled conference and announced that he would send representatives to discuss a merger between Franklin's new group and SCLC, with the intent of creating a new national civil rights group with a presence in northern cities.[38]

Though King had again lent his considerable prestige to his friend, this time the effort failed. Franklin was caught between two opposing forces: Detroit's traditional civil rights leaders bristled at the proposed new competition and redoubled their efforts to undermine Franklin and the DCHR. They almost need not have worried, however, as the tension between Franklin and Cleage precluded further joint efforts. Cleage had filled the conference's panels with his ideological supporters and had inferred that the meeting would ultimately endorse the Freedom Now Party. New Bethel's preacher had either ignored or not fully understood Cleage's organizational efforts, forgetting the adage that the devil was in the details. Franklin fought back, objecting to the political slant of the invited guests, but it was too late to salvage even a shaky unity. Certain that the black revolution was imminent, Cleage considered it his political responsibility as a self-proclaimed leader to achieve that goal by any means he possessed. He had little choice but to resign from the council, as the majority of its directors were Franklin supporters, but he did so with dramatic effect, declaring that the Franklin group "lacked the vision necessary" to maintain the momentum of the June march which, he somewhat contradictorily now pronounced, was "essentially . . . a hollow thing without substance." With an eye to the masses he momentarily expected to rise in support of his program, this elite-reared son of Detroit's African American aristocracy grandly proclaimed that in "renouncing the independent black political action represented by the FREEDOM NOW PARTY, and the new Negro image which is called 'black nationalism,' the DCHR has renounced any reason for its existence."[39]

In his response to Cleage, Franklin delivered the clearest analysis of his political philosophy he ever gave outside the pulpit. In two press conferences, he rejected gradualism in achieving black freedom, deplored the glorification of violence and the embrace of separatism, and reiterated that nonviolence was the "only sane means" to achieve "political power, economic security, and human dignity for all people." Like his friend King, C. L. reaffirmed his opposition to nationalism: "Neither white nor black segregation is the desired end." He reminded all of black participation "in the American struggle" over the centuries. The very difficulty of that history as lived by generations past demanded that it "cannot now become negated and determined as futile attempts. Those who are interested in an American Indian reservation-type segregation," he fiercely argued, "surely are welcome to it." The history of third parties in America, moreover, "seemingly lead . . . nowhere." He cited former President Theodore Roosevelt's 1912 campaign for the presidency on a third-party ticket, as well as the campaigns of Wisconsin senator Robert La Follette in 1924 and former vice president Henry Wallace in 1948. The prospect was even more discouraging for an independent black party, for "the mathematics of such a proposition, a black minority lining up in a political warfare against a white majority is not practical at all." In line with his commitment for his people to take their rightful place in the society Franklin considered their home, however problematic that claim remained, he also strongly objected to the involvement of "subversive or Communistic elements" or militant nationalists alike.[40]

Franklin's political affirmations reflected the message offered in his Detroit sermons across more than a decade of Sundays. He understood the growing frustration and was perhaps the local public figure with the strongest connections, personally and culturally, to those masses others evoked. The complexity of that understanding led him to insist, as he had in the past and would in the future, that revolutionary romances from the political left or separatist dreams from the right must be rejected outright. Freedom could come—indeed, must come—in the fulfillment of America's democratic promise, however difficult that task. This was a fundamental difference between Franklin and Cleage, and it could not be resolved. As a consequence, Detroit hosted two conferences that second weekend of November. The DCHR gathering was poorly attended and lacked many of the prominent speakers advertised earlier. Spokesmen, saving face, blamed misleading directions for the small numbers even as they asserted that significant decisions had nonetheless taken place. Cleage's conference, hastily named the Northern Negro Grass Roots Leadership Conference, had slightly larger if still disappointing attendance, but it featured Malcolm X at its Sunday evening rally.

Malcolm's address, recorded by Milton Henry and widely distributed as "Message to the Grass Roots," became one of his more popular speeches. Its approach could not have been more different from a Franklin sermon.

In a talk rent with contradictions, Malcolm X reduced his political analysis—in itself a departure from the traditional message of Elijah Muhammad—to a simplistic assertion of the power of skin pigmentation to determine destiny. He proclaimed a 1955 international conference of unaligned Asian and African nations as a model for black Americans. The conference, Malcolm exaggerated, recognized in the white man "a common enemy" and barred all whites from their deliberations; thus delegates were able to "talk shop" and achieve unity. The actual history of relations among these erstwhile allies, to say nothing of the fierce political struggles within many of these nations despite shared skin tones, was far different than what Malcolm projected. This idealization of revolutionaries of color led Malcolm into one of the more horrific morality tales of this or any other speech he gave. Recalling a picture he had seen in *Life* magazine, he praised "a little Chinese girl, nine years old," as an example black American revolutionaries would do well to consider. The magazine picture caught the child just before she pulled the trigger that killed her kneeling father "because he was an Uncle Tom Chinaman."

In this speech as well Malcolm developed a soon-to-be-popular distinction, if one without clear programmatic meaning, between "the black revolution and the Negro revolution." In his wildly misleading narrative, the "house Negroes" predictably catered to the white master and were reputedly rewarded for it, while the "field Negroes—those were the masses" who "in the field caught hell." Malcolm proclaimed that it was the "house Negroes," now "twentieth-century Uncle Toms" in the guise of civil rights leaders, that continue "to keep you and me in check . . . to keep us passive and peaceful and nonviolent." Given that the echo of that little girl's pistol shot yet reverberated in the audience and was an object lesson for dealing with "Uncle Toms," the speech, geared to touch raw feelings, offered little more than murderous incitement by way of rhetorical exaggeration.[41]

"Message to the Grass Roots" did possess some nuance, however, particularly when heard. Malcolm's intonation could generate gales of laughter that softened a stark moment. His exaggerated pronunciation of the term *Negro*, as "Knee-gro-ow," mocked equally southern segregationists and traditional leaders shy of the term *black*. Similarly, his depiction of the "house Negro" who proudly announced, as the master explained he was not feeling well, "*We's sick,*" inevitably brought down the house. Malcolm's truth here resided not in his history but in the public recognition of the psychological impact of slavery and the ensuing century of harsh exclusion. For many who heard him, laced between the peals of laughter was a more painful confrontation with self. He might stride the stage like "a conqueror," possessing "a fearless tongue," as one reporter wrote, yet contradictions persisted. His pungent criticism of black men who allowed their women and children to suffer nonviolently in demonstrations while they willingly served in America's wars never comprehended the deep pride of many black veterans. Instead, Malcolm saw their service as but another example of the black masses' false consciousness, much as he saw their love of pork, blues, soul music, and Christianity as further evidence of the power others exerted over blacks. Many in Detroit and across the nation listened, and many were moved. Relatively few, however, came forth to join the movement Malcolm promoted.[42]

*   *   *   *   *

The debacle of that second weekend in November 1963, with its dual meetings both poorly attended, marked C. L. Franklin's last effort to lead a secular political movement. His opponents among the traditional leadership proved far savvier than he in their political maneuvering, as did the allies he thought he had found. But amid the swirl of ideas, debates, and demonstrations that intensified that fall and into 1964, Franklin, without a platform other than his pulpit, still remained a serious public presence in the city.

Only two weeks after the failed conferences, reporters found their way to Franklin's New Bethel office for his reaction to the assassination of John F. Kennedy. It was "a tragic blow," a saddened Franklin declared, as tragic as the one that "felled President Abraham Lincoln" a century before. He insisted that the assassination was not isolated from other recent events: the "sniper did not pull his trigger alone." Franklin accused Alabama's governor George Wallace, Mississippi's governor Ross Barnett, "and all the forces of hate and evil" who were "as surely in Dallas with the sniper as they were in Jackson, Mississippi when Medgar Evers was felled." A month later, he presided over the New Bethel funeral of Dinah Washington, the outstanding blues singer and friend who had participated enthusiastically in the June march. In February 1964, in an obvious effort to revive his role as a political leader, Franklin announced plans (ill-fated, he would discover) for a Freedom Jubilee on the anniversary of the 1963 march. That same month, the Michigan *Chronicle,* whose editors were deeply tied to the traditional black leadership in the city, named Franklin as one of eight outstanding Detroit religious leaders working on behalf of human rights. Stunned, perhaps, when first informed privately, he was quick to capitalize on the honor. Friends sponsored a major testimonial dinner at Cobo Hall the week of the *Chronicle*'s announcement. Some two thousand people attended, a Who's Who of black Detroit's younger political, religious, and entertainment worlds. Elected state representatives served on the ticket committee, as did such aspiring politicians such as John Conyers Jr., and William T. Patrick emceed the three-hour-long program. Four of C. L.'s favorite church singers—Willie Todd, Grace Cobb, Lucy Branch, and William Penn—offered solos. It was a striking public moment. Not present were most of the "old guard" leaders, although by now it was clear that the differences between C. L. and those leaders were more about style and tempo, important as those issues might be, than fundamental political philosophy. None of them, nor most of the dinner guests, embraced Milton Henry's declaration, delivered two weeks earlier over Detroit radio, that black Americans should reject integration as the central goal of the freedom struggle.[43]

Later that fall, after a month's vacation in Los Angeles, Franklin joined with the "young Turks" to endorse John Conyers Jr. for a new congressional seat that opened in a largely black district in the city. The year before, Conyers had joined the effort to unseat Franklin as chairman of the "March to Freedom." A year later, Franklin recognized the potential benefit for his people in a Conyers victory and held no grudges against the ambitious young lawyer. Conyers's opponent in the primary was Richard Austin, a candidate clearly aligned with the older black leadership. At stake was not only the race itself but the direction of black electoral politics in Detroit. Horace Sheffield, the TULC founder now thought by many as indistinguishable from the elites he once criticized, backed Austin, as did the established civil rights organizations. Nelson Jack Edwards, New Bethel trustee, member of the UAW's executive board, and TULC member now sharply critical of its current political direction, supported Conyers. The intense primary fight, a continuation of the struggle against the Reuther administration's support of Louis C. Miriani in the 1961 mayoralty race, was so fierce that the UAW forbade all staff people from campaigning for Conyers on pain of losing their jobs. That edict proscribed John Conyers Sr., the candidate's father and a UAW activist since the original organizing drives in the late 1930s, from supporting his son publicly. Franklin was one of the first ministers to endorse Conyers, and he used his Sunday evening radio program to bolster Conyers's appeal. Ultimately, the UAW's arrogance turned even some established leaders toward the candidate, who won the primary in a very close race and the subsequent general election in a landslide. Garnering more than 138,000 votes, he overwhelmed black Republican Robert Blackwell's 25,589 and Milton Henry's 1, 504 votes.[44]

Henry's poor showing was by now a surprise to only a few. Malcolm's presence had boosted Albert Cleage's prominence in some circles, but Cleage found it difficult to build a coherent political movement upon the new attention. The Freedom Now Party did field candidates in the November 1964 elections and collected more than twenty-two thousand signatures across Michigan to gain access to the ballot. Supporters predicted the party would attract at least one hundred thousand votes. Cleage stood for governor, Milton Henry challenged Conyers Jr., and attorney Henry W. Cleage opposed incumbent prosecutor Samuel H. Olsen. The results were discouraging. Cleage obtained less than twenty thousand votes statewide, and no other party candidate posed even a minor threat. Unable to convince the very people he claimed to represent, Cleage followed the example of the other self-appointed leaders he had long criticized. In denying that his party had been repudiated by black voters, he blamed the black masses instead. "Negroes lack the indignation that people should have in the face of injustice," he stated, gliding over the inherent contradiction with his earlier harangues. Within two weeks of the election, Cleage and Grace Boggs resigned from the Freedom Now Party, having lost the power to set postelection strategy to the Henry brothers and their supporters.[45]

C. L. continued in this public vein in succeeding years. He sponsored visits to Detroit and New Bethel by Coretta Scott King in 1965 (and her husband in 1966); raised money for SCLC's massive campaign in Selma, Alabama, in 1965; and served on that organization's national board. He also cofounded the Christian Evangelistic Crusaders, a church-based organization of nine pastors and their congregations intent on rescuing "our young people who have inherited our frustrations and hopelessness" from finding their solutions solely in "secularism and materialism." These efforts at outreach reflected his belief, affirmed repeatedly in his sermons, that faith and social responsibility were intertwined strands of the same mission.[46]

Fifty years old in 1965, and in relatively good health, Franklin still cut a trim figure in his stylish suits and glistening hair, his jewelry flashing as he talked. But the young minister he once was had become an energetic, solidly middle-aged man. Unlike many other men of his generation, whose daily life involved limited travels to and from familiar destinations such as work, shopping, church, and friends' homes, C. L. had spent much of the last decade and more on the gospel tour, crisscrossing the nation in what was, cumulatively, an exhausting set of sacred performances. The physical toll was perhaps most obvious. The flights, the long car rides between tour stops, the friends, the parties, the late-night sessions weighed on him more as the years passed. Each day of the tour was a day spent largely in the public eye, responding to demands from others for his attention, for a word, an autograph, an interview. Each encounter, no matter how enjoyable, drew on his emotional reserve. Franklin was gregarious, outgoing, and possessed reservoirs of energy, but after fifteen years he was exhausted. Beyond the near-continuous motion, the very act of preaching night after night drained him even as it exhilarated. "People expect a lot out of the black preacher," C. L. once explained, and feel disappointed "unless you extend yourself and expend a lot of energy." The structure of the tours, moreover, added to the toll. C. L. traveled with a small entourage, and when the car broke down or some other difficulty occurred, it was usually Franklin who dealt with the problem. C. L. "would have done better [on tour] as a Billy Graham," his friend Billy Kyles pointed out, with "an organization sponsoring what he was doing." But Franklin rarely operated as an organization man.[47]

Beneath the physical tiredness and the expenditure of emotion lay even more complicated issues. The glory and honor of being C. L. Franklin was but the flip side of being so famous that there were very few people in whom you could confide. "Who does a C. L. Franklin talk to, you know," James Holley asked. "Who does C. L. Franklin use as a mentor?" There were some, to be sure, such as Reuben Gayden, Claud Young, Mahalia Jackson, the Dallas preacher Caesar Clark, and possibly others, though C. L. never directly identified people in this way. What was clear, however, was that their numbers were far fewer than those who sought him out. There was as well a more pressing issue. His gradual recognition of his diminishing inner drive, what Benjamin Hooks had recognized long before as the "intimate kind of commotion" that powered him out of Mississippi and sustained his career, collided with a demanding ego still desirous of the affirmation long offered by the audience's wave of adulation. "Reverend Franklin's biggest competitor," Jasper Williams sharply intuited, "was his past, his youthfulness, and the older you get the less you're able to compete with yourself." This recognition was evident in the gradual easing of activities after 1965.[48]

Being on the road less meant that Franklin was at New Bethel more, and this was good for the church. For numerous reasons, membership had slowly begun to dip after the move to Linwood in 1963. Urban renewal meant the displacement of residents as well as buildings, and for some, New Bethel was no longer as convenient a stop. Those who still resided in Paradise Valley but lacked cars found the city's limited bus schedule an obstacle. Some had found another congregation to their liking in the years without a permanent structure. The number of young people who remained active in church beyond their teen years also declined noticeably. The new neighborhood, too, may have played a role. The area around New Bethel deteriorated sharply in the years after the church opened, and the crossroads of Linwood and Philadelphia marked an increasingly impoverished spot with both high unemployment and high crime rates. C. L.'s children, concerned over the social deterioration—the family home on nearby LaSalle Boulevard had been ransacked one summer evening in 1962, while C. L. preached a few blocks away—pressed their father again to move the church farther out toward the suburbs beyond Eight Mile Road. He refused, as he did their subsequent request that he move his residence to a better, safer neighborhood downtown. "No, that's where they need me," his daughter Erma remembered him insisting, speaking of the neighborhood of both his church and home. "No, this is where I live. This is where I am going to stay." And that he did, even as the Sunday attendance continued to slip into the 1970s.[49]

His daily activities at New Bethel were not dramatically different from the years when he traveled so extensively. He was just able to do more with less strain. He counseled parishioners, oversaw church committees (although he generally gave the person he appointed to head a group significant latitude), and presided over the monthly meetings of the trustee and deacon boards. His power to touch individuals even in common interactions continued to astonish. Charlie Thompson marveled that when he sat down with you, C. L. "could make you feel like you was somebody that he cared about. He could make you feel that" because "he was very emotional himself, strong feelings and he demonstrated those feelings." Margaret Branch, who worked in the church office in the 1960s, had similar experiences. In daily exchanges with C. L., discussing her schoolwork or her plans for the future, she remembered that "he'd always give you recognition for what you were doing. . . . Everybody got praised . . . and identified." Beverli Greenleaf, who joined New Bethel in the mid-1960s, as a young woman fresh from the small hamlet of McCurry, Arkansas, always thought of C.L. first as the pastor who counseled her and, second, as the preacher who moved her, so touched was she by his evident concern for her and other parishioners. This concern extended to younger ministers as well. James Holley, Samuel Billy Kyles, and associate pastors Leonard Flowers, E. L. Branch, and C. L. Moore were but a few of those C. L. influenced over his career. Kyles remembered when, as a young minister without a pulpit, C. L. paid him "as much as a pastor" for a guest sermon. Jesse Jackson, too, felt Franklin's warm embrace. Jackson's mentor, Rev. Clay Evans of Chicago, and C. L. were good friends, and C. L. undoubtedly met the young divinity student through Evans. Franklin and Jackson became close, and Franklin brought him into the New Bethel pulpit, invited him to his 1967 anniversary celebration, and together with Evans, preached Jackson's

1968 ordination service. All this occurred well before the young minister became a national figure.[50]

Precisely because C. L. Franklin knew intimately the demands of his chosen profession, his counsel could be quite hard on young men considering the ministry. Jerome Kirby's parents, migrants from Arkansas, had joined New Bethel in the late 1940s, but they entered another congregation nearer their new home when their son was a young boy. A little more than a decade later, Kirby approached his first pastor for guidance. This seventeen-year-old had struggled for some time over whether he was called to preach. He lacked a sign such as the burning plank C. L. envisioned at age sixteen, and he remained racked by doubt and confusion. Apprehensively, he climbed the concrete stairway, with dull, grayish walls, to the pastor's office on the second floor, above and to the right of New Bethel's sanctuary. He knocked and entered on C. L.'s cue. Kirby began to explain his concerns, only to be told by the great preacher that he was too busy to see him now. Over the following weeks this scene occurred again and again, with Kirby becoming more and more distraught. Finally, Franklin asked him in, told him to hang up his hat and coat, and take a seat. This very young man sat before Franklin's desk and responded as best he could to the few questions C. L. posed. Rather quickly, Franklin dismissed him, told him to get his hat and coat and to leave. The stunned teenager did as he was told. As he reached the door, C. L. stopped him with words that seared themselves into Kirby's consciousness: "But wait now a minute, let me tell you this. If you can keep from doing it, then don't." To Kirby, "that one saying had so much in it." It was just a sentence, and yet through it C. L. gave the young minister-to-be a guideline for his struggle. Kirby would realize he could not "keep from doing it" and, in time, led his own congregation, yet another minister touched by the powerful legacy of C. L.'s own struggles in Mississippi decades earlier.[51]

Free of "that steady grind" of the gospel tour, Franklin relished even more the fetes and celebrations that came his way. Both Adam Clayton Powell and John Conyers invited C. L. as their guest to Lyndon Baines Johnson's inaugural ceremonies in January 1965, following the president's landslide victory over Republican Barry Goldwater the previous November. Franklin thoroughly enjoyed his place among the celebrities and the pomp in the nation's capital. At home, New Bethel and his friends honored him yearly, marking his anniversary as pastor of New Bethel with major banquets at downtown hotels. The guest list for each approached a thousand people, and the style he introduced at his first banquet in 1946, at the long-demolished Gotham Hotel, continued on an even grander scale. Beyond the celebratory aspect, these gatherings were also fundraisers. Each year on the anniversary, the congregation raised a cash purse for their pastor or bought him a new car, and sometimes both.[52]

Franklin considered these gifts donations from a thankful congregation and, therefore, not income. The Internal Revenue Service, however, had some questions. During the 1960s, Franklin reported a salary from New Bethel of approximately $13,600 yearly, and he noted occasional additional income but never more than $1,000. Once, in 1968, he acknowledged anniversary gifts of almost $10,000 but claimed that as a gift "without prior prompting . . . and not for services," it was nontaxable. This was legal at the time. However, the income he did declare rarely included his significant fees from the gospel tour or royalties received from the sales of his recorded sermons. Thus, after deducting expenses and the exemptions for his mother, youngest daughter, and himself, he never reported more than $8,600 in taxable income. The government objected and, focusing on the years between 1959 and 1962, charged that Franklin failed to report more than $75,000 in income, the equivalent of a $10,000 tax obligation.[53]

A furious Franklin looked for culprits. Dissidents in the congregation, he suggested in 1965, upset with his handling of the city funds awarded when the Hastings Street church was condemned, were in part responsible. His daughter Aretha put it more bluntly: "Someone from New Bethel had dropped a dime on my father, telling the IRS that he was earning billions." In another mood, however, C. L. drafted a letter to Lyndon Johnson just five months after attending the president's inauguration, claiming a peculiar kind of ignorance for so proud a man. "I am originally from Mississippi," he informed Johnson, a Texan, "where preachers were not required to pay income tax, at least Negro preachers." He first understood this obligation in Memphis, went to the local IRS office, only to be ordered by the agent "to go home and forget about it"—his $35-a-week salary was deemed insignificant. C. L. implored Johnson to influence the IRS to settle with him, to "lay out a program of payment with which I can comply." His claims to the president seem improbable. Franklin's yearly salary in 1940, although he was anything but wealthy, was still significant. More pertinent was the question of whether this sophisticated man, who regularly called on a small group of attorneys for advice, had learned anything about federal tax law in the intervening twenty-five years. But C. L. was not thinking clearly. He faced serious charges and deeply resented the government's approach to the investigation. In Los Angeles, he complained to an IRS official in Washington, "agents have inquired indiscriminately among nurses, musicians, and just regular working people . . . [who] have never had any business relations with me whatsoever." They asked Mrs. Mabel Chapman, for example, "if I gambled or sold narcotics." Such "indiscriminate inquiries" far afield from the actual charges were, C. L. insisted rightly, only "designed to impugn my character and create an unpleasant situation [for me] all over the country." Although he did not make the argument publicly at the time, privately Franklin felt that his prominence as a social activist, particularly regarding the June 1963 march, "put me in the spotlight and prompted the government to investigate my finances."[54]

In April 1966, the U.S. attorney presented a grand jury indictment before a federal judge in Detroit. Each of the four counts in the charge carried a maximum sentence of a year in prison and a $10,000 fine. Immediately, C. L.'s friends and supporters moved to help. Robbie McCoy, one of the Chronicle's religion reporters, publicized plans for a benefit fundraiser, and many wrote her of their prayers and support for the embattled minister. "The Rev. Mr. Franklin has supported a large number of known persons who needed assistance financially" over the years, McCoy wrote, and she urged all to return that support when he needed it now. In this way the anniversary banquets between 1965 and 1967 became the occasion of black Detroit's public embrace of and practical support for C. L. Franklin. Eventually, in fall 1967, Franklin pleaded no contest to the charge of underreporting his income between 1959 and 1962. The judge fined him $2,500, ordered him to pay the delinquent taxes, and placed the preacher on probation.[55]

Despite Franklin's evident culpability, many perceived him as a victim.

Well before he argued it publicly, parishioners and friends thought the investigation was punishment for his leadership of the march, and they concurred with Franklin when he termed the government's investigation sensational and intentionally destructive. When Franklin's sentence had yet to be announced, Charles Simmons wrote the *Chronicle* to remind readers of the charges against former mayor and current city councilman Louis C. Miriani. Against Franklin's figure of $75,000 in unreported income, Miriani failed to pay taxes for those same years on $258,000, much of which he made while serving as mayor at $25,000 a year. In contrast to Franklin, however, Miriani claimed he was too ill to stand trial, and the judge agreed. "This is the type of inequality," Simmons concluded his letter, "multiplied by the thousands where Negroes are concerned, that 'tries men's souls' and provokes them to violence. Justice seems to bury its head in the sand on some occasions."[56]

Although without a political organization to lead, C. L.'s public reputation grew significantly during these years. He was, of course, the father of Aretha who, by 1967, had achieved the acclamation of both white and black audiences with a talent deeply affected by the black church tradition. While C. L. never achieved a comparable level of fame, certainly not in white America, he recognized in his daughter's performances that mixture of the sacred and secular that had long informed his preaching. And as African American expression in politics, popular culture, and religion underwent an exhilarating, at times explosive, development in the 1960s, Franklin's well-known affinities drew considerable attention again. It surprised few, for example, in October 1966, when Franklin buried from New Bethel one of the city's most prominent black gangsters and reputed drug dealers, Sanders Mallory Jr., better known as "Nick the Greek." Mallory died of cocaine poisoning while in prison and was, for some, a folk hero. (His funeral attracted an estimated fifty law enforcement officers, who snapped photographs of the mourners.) C. L. not only led the service and eulogized Mallory, a "flamboyant character" of Detroit's nightlife, but welcomed to the pulpit Milton Henry for a second eulogy.[57]

This inclusion of Milton Henry suggested another aspect of C. L.'s integration of politics, culture, and religion. In the few years since the bitter public split left the DCHR in tatters, ideological differences had ever more sharply separated Franklin, Cleage, and the Henry brothers. Cleage remained a nationalist, incessantly active and vocal, who developed a distinct religious approach, what he called "Black Christian Nationalism," to American racial issues. He transformed his church on Linwood into the Shrine of the Black Madonna, with a portrait of the black Christ's black mother the dominant icon. The Henry brothers moved in a different direction. Milton, ever more committed to a secular black-nationalist revolution, accompanied Malcolm X to Africa in 1964. On this trip Malcolm made his celebrated hadj to Mecca and returned to revise publicly the simple racial dualities he had once preached. Milton and Richard embraced the now independent leader—Malcolm had broken with the Nation of Islam—and invited him to speak at the inaugural dinner sponsored by the Afro-American Broadcast Company. Milton had formed the company to promote black culture and to honor individuals and companies, including Berry Gordy's Motown Records, for their efforts to present "the Negro to the total society as a being of inherent dignity." Malcolm X, whose Queens, New York, home had been firebombed the night before while he and his family slept, addressed the sparse audience at Detroit's Ford Auditorium on Sunday, February 14, 1965. He denounced nonviolence, appealed to black male pride to resist racists who threatened black women and children, and predicted that 1965 would be the "longest, bloodiest, hottest year of them all." Two days before Malcolm's next scheduled talk, at New York's Audubon Ballroom, his home base, on Sunday, February 21, he gave an interview to Gordon Parks, the black photographer and reporter. Malcolm rejected his past denunciations of all whites (numerous African leaders had "awakened me to the dangers of racism"); described himself during his twelve years in the Nation of Islam as "a zombie then"; and predicted that if he was to be a martyr, "it will be in the cause of brotherhood." It was his last public discussion. That following Sunday afternoon, before a large crowd that included his wife and four children, three assassins, later identified as members of the Nation of Islam, murdered Malcolm before he could finish greeting the audience.[58]

In the aftermath of Malcolm's death, the Henry brothers, including Laurence, a writer and photographer, published *NOW!*, a magazine edited by Richard advocating a black American revolution, and formed an alliance with Robert F. Williams, the former NAACP leader from Monroe, North Carolina, then in exile in Cuba. The brothers also embraced the Cuban revolution as the optimal model for would-be black American revolutionaries. Their planned trip to Cuba in January 1966 to visit Williams, whom they already touted as a prospective leader of the American revolution, proved a dismal failure. Cuban authorities, acting on the requests of the U.S. Communist Party, refused visas. The party, as did its political guides in the Soviet Union, opposed black nationalism, seeing in it a threat to their emphasis on class conflict as the singular catalyst for social change. The finale of the Henrys' effort to influence international politics approached a classical farce. Milton and Laurence typed a single-spaced, seven-page letter to the Cuban leader that pronounced their revolutionary credentials and instructed Castro on the revolutionary potential of the "black masses." In clipped, contradictory sentences, the brothers warned that a rebuff would be considered "as a repudiation of every black militant in the U.S."; promised security for Castro or his representative to visit the United States to meet with the "grass roots revolutionaries who struggle and dream by themselves"; and threatened that if a satisfactory reply did not come within two weeks, they would "publish throughout the Negro press our account of what has transpired. We owe nothing less," they grandly concluded, "to our people." Castro's answer came a few months later, when he rather unceremoniously shipped off Robert F. Williams to the People's Republic of China, then the ideological alternative to the Soviets within international Communism.[59]

None of this global revolutionary posturing attracted Franklin, whose vision remained framed by the power of black political and cultural expression to create a fuller American democracy. But when nationalists addressed concerns grounded in black Detroit's actual experience, Franklin participated without hesitation. He had done this when he included Milton Henry in Mallory's funeral just months after the Cuban debacle and again when informed of a proposed nationwide strike of African Americans called for February 13, 1967. The strike was to protest the removal of Adam Clayton Powell from his congressional seat on charges, among others, that he misused congressional funds. In Washington, Congressman John Conyers sat on the subcommittee investigating Powell's fitness to serve, and his support of the subcommittee's "stringent recommendations" outraged many in his district. C. L. spoke at a meeting that January at Cleage's church and at a second meeting at New Bethel a few weeks later. At both events, C. L. rebuffed critics who worried about a negative white reaction, arguing that in Detroit as elsewhere, "anti-Negro reaction had already reached the 'oppressive' stage."[60]

Unfortunately for Franklin and other strike leaders (Grace Boggs, comedian Dick Gregory, and the new president of the Detroit NAACP, Reverend James Wadsworth, among them), the strike was a near total failure, even in Detroit. Planning for the event was too hasty and the announced goal too removed from individuals' daily experience to justify the forfeit of a day's pay. Undaunted, the organizers came together again in late June for the second Black Arts Convention in Detroit. Franklin joined with Milton Henry and Albert Cleage on a panel discussing black religion and black nationalism; poet Nikki Giovanni, novelist John O. Killens, and Dudley Randall, publisher of the recently formed Broadside Press, discussed black literature; while Ed Vaughn, owner of a nationalist-orientated bookstore and the driving force behind the conference, led a discussion on economic self-help.[61]

For some, Franklin's involvement in such activities was confusing. His defense of nonviolence as a tactic and of integration as a goal were well known, as were the sharp-edged comments Cleage and the Henry brothers delivered about him in public. Within New Bethel, where nationalist sentiment was not popular, few if any found Cleage's amalgamation of nationalism and Christianity attractive. Yet Milton Henry thought he understood Franklin's motivation. Decades later, Henry suggested that Franklin "was a lover of his people too." The freedom struggle ultimately demanded that individuals transcend personal differences to work together whenever possible.[62]

Also true was that Franklin himself had more complex attitudes than he necessarily revealed in every public debate. He loved Martin Luther King and supported his friend's program without question. Like King, however, Franklin possessed a layered understanding of that plastic term *integration*. For Franklin, his friend and proud pupil Jasper Williams understood, integration meant "that every man ought to have the right to be treated like all men. But in terms of him just loving to be in the white world," he remarked, "he never came across to any of us as that being his desire." Black church culture, for example, would—and should—remain black.[63]

C. L.'s commitment to nonviolence was similarly complicated. He did nothing in public to challenge King and thought that notions of armed revolutionaries attacking white American institutions were worse than an infantile fantasy—they were suicidal. Yet his commitment was not philosophical, and his specific Mississippi experience led him to doubt nonviolence's universal transformative power. Franklin carried a pistol at times, and he never joined confrontational, nonviolent civil rights demonstrations in either Detroit or the South but once, and then at King's specific request. For Franklin, integration was not a political metaphor for the elimination of a strong black cultural identity, any more than tactical nonviolence required that he relinquish his proclaimed American right to bear arms in self-defense.[64]

Following his appearance at the Black Arts Convention early in July, Franklin left for a European vacation, his congregation's anniversary offering temporarily quelling concerns about his tax liabilities. He returned a few weeks later, just before the most destructive domestic upheaval in American history transformed Detroit into a war zone.

It began on Twelfth and Clairmont, just a few blocks from New Bethel, early on Sunday morning, July 23, when police raided a "blind pig," or after-hours club. By that afternoon, the fury that had accumulated over so many years—spurred by police violence, random murders of unarmed black residents, high unemployment, deteriorated housing—broke the last restraining barrier. By Sunday afternoon, crowds controlled many of the streets in the riot area and physically threatened John Conyers when he tried to calm them. Looting and burning began, and local and state police, the National Guard, and then federal troops occupied the city. Both blacks and whites engaged in armed assaults. In the intense roaming battles that lasted until Thursday, July 27, more than 7,200 were arrested and 27 charged with sniping (although most of these charges would be dismissed); 43 were killed—thirty-three black, ten white. Approximately $40 million in damage rained down on buildings, homes, and other property. It was a horrific experience. Recalling, with poetic license, his formative years in Detroit, the hard tone of John Lee Hooker's voice strained to grasp the enormity of what had happened: "My hometown is burning to the ground / worster than Vietnam." Large sections of black Detroit lay in ruins, block after block of fire-gutted buildings with exterior walls yet standing, supporting invisible floors and roofs. The firebombing of Dresden during World War II became the immediate journalistic metaphor. Decades later, in the neighborhoods to the east and to the west of Woodward, that image remained.[65]

As was true for every other pastor, politician, and celebrity in Detroit that week, C. L. Franklin could, with Hooker, only cry. Those in the streets responded only to superior force, and the armed troops enforcing martial law discouraged community peacemakers from even trying. The weight of that week in July 1967 bore down heavily on the city for the remainder of C. L.'s life, and beyond. It was not, however, the only tragedy that would befall Franklin in the coming decade.[66]

CHAPTER TEN

NOW HE IS DOWN

In the months after the July 1967 riot, a violence-laden rhetoric increasingly dominated Detroit's political climate. Business and trade-union leaders, in alliance as before with the traditional black civil rights organizations, sought to direct Detroit's post-1967 recovery through New Detroit, Inc., which had at its disposal significant private and public funding to revive the economy and repair the city's neighborhoods. But militants of various tendencies could no longer be excluded from such organizations. Shaken elites, white and black, hoped their inclusion might protect the city from the fury that no one, in fact, controlled. Some activists found seats on New Detroit's board. Others, such as the small League of Revolutionary Workers, a Marxist-influenced organization of black workers within the UAW, remained outside. Not surprisingly, Albert Cleage managed to do both. Now a weekly columnist for the *Chronicle*, Cleage created the City-Wide Citizens Action Committee to vie with New Detroit to determine policy and obtain public funds. Together with Karl Gregory, an economics professor at Wayne State, and Milton Henry, Cleage created a People's Tribunal in August 1967, to try the policemen accused of murdering three black men at the Algiers Hotel during the riot. The grand jury's actions in releasing one officer and holding the other on reduced charges had incensed the three organizers. They expected the tribunal would turn equally angry observers into committed activists. Some close to Cleage went further. James and Grace Boggs argued that the violence of July 1967 created "the intense emotional unity that is necessary to a national movement." Terming the events of July a rebellion and not a riot, they foresaw a black revolutionary movement rising from Detroit's ashes, the forerunner of a new nation.[1]

At times that "emotional unity" seemed in scarce supply during the winter and spring of 1968. Milton Henry's call for all blacks to declare February 21, the third anniversary of Malcolm X's death, a national holiday met with little response even from Detroit's schoolchildren. Undaunted, Henry convened a convention in March at Cleage's church to create an independent black nation. (Although he lent his church, Cleage himself rejected the idea of a separate national territory, as did James and Grace Boggs.) On Saturday, March 30, at Cleage's Shrine of the Black Madonna, two hundred delegates from several states willed the new nation into existence. They called it the Republic of New Africa and pledged their "total devotion" to work "for the fruition of black power, for the fruition of black nationhood." In their Declaration of Independence, they declared themselves "forever free and independent of the jurisdiction of the United States of America." In this "revolution against oppression," they presented the new nation's goals: to achieve freedom for black people in America, to support world revolution, and to "build a New Society that is better than what we now know and as perfect as man can make it." The convention elected Robert F. Williams, whom the Henrys continued to promote as the American revolutionary leader although in exile in the People's Republic of China, president; Milton Henry, who now often responded to the name Brother Gaidi Obadele, first vice-president; Betty Shabbazz, Malcolm X's widow, second vice-president; and Brother Imari Obadele, formerly Richard Henry, Minister of Information.[2]

At the heart of the founders' revolutionary faith was a self-grandeur that edged toward the delusional. Two weeks before the convention, Milton Henry wrote Mao Tse-tung, leader of the Chinese Communist government, announcing the coming meeting because "our lack of land and sovereignty and the racism of the United States make it appear impossible for you to attend or to send a representative to be with us." Henry's presumption, recalling his earlier approach to Fidel Castro, must have left the Chinese revolutionary baffled.[3]

*　　*　　*　　*　　*

On Wednesday, March 27, 1968, C. L. Franklin arrived in Memphis. King and the staff of the Southern Christian Leadership Conference, stretched to their very limits, were orchestrating two major campaigns simultaneously. The previous December, SCLC had announced plans for the Poor People's Campaign, a national effort to focus attention on issues of poverty and economic injustice for all Americans. Three months later, without a national staff or the local leadership essential for that grassroots campaign in place, King found it impossible to refuse the call for help from Memphis's all-black sanitation workers union. They had been on strike since February 13, and their condition was dire. In their racially segregated city job, wages and working conditions were abysmal, and Mayor Henry Loeb adamantly refused to recognize their union. As he had in other crises, King asked for help. To his relief, Franklin was one of many who responded. King knew that Franklin's skills and reputation as a preacher familiar with street life and the forgotten could be effective with Memphis's angry, often unchurched young blacks, who did not easily warm to nonviolence as a tactic.[4]

Franklin arrived very late that evening and did not attend the march on Thursday morning, in keeping with his long practice of limiting his exposure, whenever possible, to white southern anger and violence. He left word for his friend that he would be ready to speak that evening, as planned. But that was too late. Young black Memphians, some affiliated with local gangs, looted stores along the line of march, and the police responded fiercely and indiscriminately. SCLC cancelled the rally, Franklin returned to Detroit, and a shaken King left for Atlanta.[5]

Increasingly worried about the impact of violence on the movement, King committed himself to march again on April 5 but included in the preparations leaders of the Invaders, a prominent local black gang. King and his staff arrived on the third for strategy meetings. As always when he arrived in

Memphis, a white limousine and driver were placed at his disposal, courtesy of the R. S. Lewis and Sons Funeral Home—the same family who had sponsored C. L.'s Memphis radio program a quarter of a century earlier.

After a series of meetings into the early evening, one at which the Invaders agreed to act as marshals at the Friday march, King asked his close friend and assistant, Ralph D. Abernathy, to speak at a pre-march rally that night. Tired and overwhelmed with unfinished tasks, King intended to work on the massive demonstration the Poor People's Campaign scheduled for May in the nation's capital. When Abernathy, Billy Kyles, and others arrived at the church, however, they understood immediately that the crowd, smaller than normal due to a fierce storm due that evening, expected King, as did the bank of national television and radio reporters arrayed about the sanctuary. Abernathy called King at the room they shared at the Lorraine Motel, a black-owed facility at 406 Mulberry Street, five blocks south of Beale, the Memphis oasis for black artists on both the gospel and the R&B tours. King came immediately and waited pensively as Abernathy gave an uncharacteristically long biographical introduction.[6]

A tired, subdued King took the pulpit on the evening of what was the fifty-second day of the strike. He joked about his friend's excessive words, welcomed the audience, and then entered into a long explanation of why, of all the eras of history, he was most happy to be alive at this moment. At this time, he felt, the central moral and political issues that had troubled humanity since Moses led the Israelites out of Egypt had come to a crisis so severe that survival itself was at stake. The Memphis struggle for justice was part of that larger "human rights revolution." As his voice gathered force, he reminded his people of the 1963 Birmingham campaign. There, too, the opposition was fierce, and Bull Connor's fire hoses reflected "a kind of physics," the force of which Connor fully expected would sweep the demonstrators from the street as just so much debris. But King proclaimed amid cries from the audience, Connor's "physics . . . somehow didn't relate to the transphysics that we knew about. And that was the fact that there was a certain kind of fire that no water could put out." So, too, would it be in Memphis, where it was necessary to embrace "a kind of dangerous unselfishness," to place the needs of the sanitation men and the cause of justice above personal self-interest.

Shifting focus, King turned to the topic of death, his own death. He reminded the audience of when, a decade before, he had been stabbed by a deranged woman in New York City. So close was the tip of the blade to his aorta that had he sneezed, he would have died. But he did not sneeze—a sign, listeners might infer, of his divinely appointed role—and he since had participated in the efforts of the civil rights movement to resuscitate American democracy. But new threats now loomed. Only that morning, the plane bringing him to Memphis had been delayed by bomb threats, and the question was asked: "What would happen to me from some of our sick white brothers?" King acknowledged that he did not know what was ahead, although he knew it would be difficult. "But that doesn't matter with me now." Like Moses just before his death, "I've been to the mountaintop." The prospect of a long life pleased him, he confessed, but his main charge was "to do God's will," to hold faith with the God who had brought him higher: "And I've seen the promised land. I may not get there with you. But I want you to know tonight that we, as a people, will get to the promised land. And I'm happy tonight. I'm not worried about anything. I'm not fearing any man. Mine eyes have seen the glory of the coming of the Lord."[7]

None of his staff had ever heard him speak so intimately in public about his confrontation with death. "We were all awed and shaken by Martin's speech," Andrew Young recalled. "But Martin seemed buoyed by inspiration."[8]

The next day, April 4, King and his staff had a series of meetings. A harried King looked forward to a soul-food dinner at Billy Kyles's house, prepared by Kyles's wife, Gwen, and a group of women from his Monumental Baptist Church. Kyles arrived at room 306 in the Lorraine Motel about five. King, Abernathy, and Kyles talked and joked as Kyles hurried them along. Abernathy picked out a shirt and Kyles a tie for King to wear. About quarter to six, as Abernathy returned to the bathroom to apply aftershave, Kyles, and then King, walked out onto the little balcony off the room. In the courtyard below, SCLC staff members Andrew Young, James Bevel, Jesse Jackson, the musician Ben Branch, and limousine driver Solomon Jones, among others, milled about. King leaned over the railing, teased Jackson about not having the proper attire for dinner, and asked Branch, whose trumpet rendition of "Precious Lord, Take My Hand" had delighted him at an earlier mass meeting, to play it that night. As Jones called up to remind King to bring a coat, because it would be cool that evening, Kyles took a few steps away from King, toward the door to the room. At that moment, a shot rang out. Martin Luther King Jr. fell to the balcony floor, one foot thrust through the railing, a gaping wound to his head. He would die within the hour.[9]

As with so many others across the nation and the world, it took C. L. Franklin "quite a while before I got over the experience." Like other close friends, C. L. had been warned by King. Recalled Franklin, "He sat right in my basement, one Sunday night," after he had spoken at New Bethel, "and he said, 'Frank,' he said, 'I will never live to see 40.' He said, 'Some of our white brothers are very, very sick, and they are dangerous. I'll never see 40.' And he was 39 when he was killed." Franklin had lost a dear friend as well as a leader whom he profoundly admired. The depth of C. L.'s grief remained private; his saddened public comments struck the correct, official tone. But he probably knew, as many worried, that more had died than just one man.[10]

*   *   *   *   *

King's assassination that April only reinforced the Republic of New Africa's convictions. A month later, Brother Imari arrived in Washington to deliver a formal diplomatic note to the "representatives" (actually two security guards) of U.S. Secretary of State Dean Rusk. The communiqué officially requested the start of negotiations between the two nations and demanded that the U.S. government cede five southern states and pay $200 million in compensation for the expropriation of black labor during and after slavery. By June, citing the absence of an American response as a provocation, the Republic announced the formation of the Black Legion, "a black army to fight for black rights." In its nationalist rhetoric, militant posturing, and infatuation with armed struggle, if not in its diplomatic approach, the Republic reflected a growing tone in public political debate.[11]

Cecil Franklin found these attitudes simply wrong, perhaps even suicidal. Twenty-eight in 1968, the Morehouse graduate and Air Force veteran was now married and an ordained minister who served as an assistant pastor at his father's church. He also chaired the Detroit branch of the Poor People's Campaign. In a wide-ranging interview in the *Chronicle* that February, he scoffed at the embrace of violence currently fashionable: "Do you think 190 million whites will allow 45 million, at most, blacks to burn down their country? We're heading for genocide." "Just set up a picket line," he advised, when confronted by a businessman's refusal to integrate. "You don't have to burn them out, they're not going to stay unless they're making a profit."[12]

On Monday, May 13, the Midwest contingent of the campaign, approximately six hundred strong, arrived in Detroit for a rally. Some four thousand local supporters marched down Woodward to Cobo Hall, many wearing the "uniform" of the campaign, denim jackets and bib overalls. That evening, the police and demonstrators argued over an illegally parked sound car. Something was thrown, and the police responded with force: mounted officers wielding batons rained down blows on unarmed people. The Franklins, father and son, quickly shifted the remaining crowd toward New Bethel, where Claud Young and church nurses provided medical services, and cots and blankets were set up. C. L. criticized the police in a press conference, and Ralph Abernathy arrived to demand a full investigation. The police violence was part of a larger national pattern intended, he argued, to discourage marchers. A few days later, with no resolution in sight, the Midwest contingent that now included Detroit's group continued its march to Washington.[13]

SCLC named the Washington encampment (erected in West Potomac Park, between the Washington and Lincoln memorials) Resurrection City, an open call for a new life for the nation and its oppressed citizens. However well-intended such expressions were, the reality proved far more discouraging. Lyndon Johnson, who had stunned the nation on March 31, when he announced he would not stand for reelection that November, placed federal troops and Washington security forces on alert before the first demonstrators arrived on May 11. In effect, this cordoned off the United States Congress, the intended object of the demonstration, from the marchers. Despite the efforts of national director Reverend Bernard Lafayette and his staff, SCLC's planning suffered even greater delays in the wake of King's death. The first of the wooden shanties intended to house participants was not constructed until two days after the first group arrived. Organized youth gangs from Memphis, Chicago, and elsewhere added to the tension, and by May 22, the organizers demanded that two hundred gang members leave the campgrounds. Not all did. The weather also contributed to the chaos, as heavy rains turned the grass into a slippery, muddy slop. The number of protesters peaked at about twenty-five hundred on Sunday, May 26, and dropped to barely five hundred eleven days later, the day following the assassination of New York senator Robert Kennedy, after his triumph in California's Democratic presidential primary. The often-postponed Solidarity Day, meant to boost morale and increase attendance, was finally held on June 19, with addresses by Reverend Benjamin E. Mays, Coretta Scott King, Walter Reuther, and the remaining Democratic presidential candidates, Senator Eugene McCarthy of Minnesota and Vice President Hubert H. Humphrey. After the speeches, even more people left for home.[14]

C. L. Franklin had not accompanied his son in mid-May, when the Detroit participants left for Washington. But he did go to Washington in June, for Solidarity Day, and he preached two days later at St. Stephen's Baptist Church. There Franklin took his text from the book of Daniel, particularly the account of three Israelites, Shadrach, Meshach, and Abednego, who refused to worship Babylon's gods. C. L. had given the sermon many times before, and it served his political purposes well that evening. The three men were willing participants in the Babylonian government, Franklin preached, for there is nothing wrong with political engagement even in a strange land. But their refusal to worship false gods underscored his central message that "there are *higher* laws" than those of a mere king. The men's proud affirmation before the king, reasserting their refusal to bow, led to their confinement in a fiery furnace. At this point, with the audience aware of the Lord's coming intervention that would save these dissenters, Franklin turned the sermon directly toward the present. America, "our *republic*," he argued, is putting law above justice here in Washington: "I feel like if the state was as concerned about justice as they are about law and order—there wouldn't be any need for Resurrection City." He warned of yet more dangers to come, of continued poverty, jailings, humiliations, murders, and asked of the audience but "one *firm* resolution today: *we're not goin' bow!*"[15]

*   *   *   *   *

Some weeks later C. L., accompanied by his daughter Aretha, attended the somber SCLC convention, the first since King's death. The gathering in Memphis, held in the wake of a depressing conclusion to the Poor People's Campaign, painfully underscored the consequences of King's absence. The speeches, including one by C. L., and the hymns, including selections by Aretha, could not lift the gloom. Back in Detroit, Franklin involved himself at New Bethel; traveled a little—he was still the chair of the Evangelistic Board of the NBC; and continued an active social life that included visits with Clara Ward. But his powers continued to recede.[16]

That fall, he supported the Democratic presidential candidate, Hubert Humphrey, in his race with Republican Richard Nixon and the segregationist, third-party candidate, George Wallace. The Wallace phenomenon was disturbing, as the Alabama governor appealed to a significant minority of white working people in Detroit. Wallace Malone, a UAW member since 1949 and a New Bethel trustee, recalled heated discussions in the plants that revealed the profound limits of the union's official stance on integration among many rank-and-file members. That same campaign saw the return of Coleman Young to a larger public spotlight. Publicly a Democrat now, if still with a biting critique of that party's policies (he had been elected to the Michigan State Senate during the 1960s), Young supported the national ticket. After Nixon won the election in a very close race, C. L. turned his attention more fully to his pastoral activities. On New Year's Eve, he joined other ministers as one of the major preachers at the "Watch" meeting, "an old form of expressing thanks to God" for past blessings and future hopes. Franklin and his colleagues began services at ten o'clock in the evening and preached into the new year.[17]

During the fall's presidential campaign, Franklin had labored to create a new, hopefully for-profit organization that would promote the cultural contributions of black peoples throughout the world. At a Chicago press conference early in the new year, he announced the formation of the International Afro Musical and Cultural Festival, Inc., an enormously ambitious undertaking with a projected board of directors of forty-four people serving on nearly twenty separate committees. The board's composition indicated that the chairman had learned well some lessons from his long association with Albert Cleage. C. L. surrounded himself with old friends and appended an "honored guests" list of famous black performers, an effort to call in favors from members of the entertainment community he had so long befriended. The Astrodome in Houston, Texas, would host the inaugural event that June.[18]

Well before Houston, C. L. delivered three sermons at New Bethel that revealed the explicit importance of traditional and contemporary black cultural expression to his sacred performances. He had long drawn on the rich oral traditions of black song and folklore, integrated within a black preaching legacy passed down by example and reborn in the voices of successive generations. As this preaching tradition had directed, he always began his sermons with a biblical text, to affirm God's blessing on the preacher and the words to come. Now, however, Franklin altered that customary practice. In the sermons he gave during Negro History Month in February 1969, his central texts were not biblical, even when he read a passage from the Bible. In yet another departure, he did not deliver these sermons from his accustomed outline—a series of phrases usually, which allowed his talents, experience, and preparation to mix with the spirit at that moment to breathe a transcendent meaning into his words—but instead from prepared manuscripts written in advance that incorporated long, precise quotations from a variety of authors. The results were mixed. His delivery was at times stilted, the power of his rhythmic pacing often absent, and his message occasionally wandered.

Franklin took as his first authority the "godfather of soul," James Brown. Adapting the title of Brown's enormously popular song, "Say It Loud, I Am Black and I Am Proud," as his sermon's title, Franklin extolled the growth of pride among African Americans in recent times. Neither "exaggerated self-esteem" nor "haughtiness or arrogance," this pride was instead a testimony to "one's own dignity, self-respect," and to "one's own racial identity." Martin Luther King had done much to arouse these feelings, for in the mass act of saying "no" to oppressive power there developed "a sense of wholesome pride, a sense of dignity, and a sense of somebodiness never witnessed before." But, Franklin offered, King was not alone. Brown, too, encouraged "a new sense of dignity and somebodiness." He cited at length poems by both Langston Hughes and Countee Cullen to illustrate the deeper history of the simple sentence "I am black and beautiful." To prevent any ambiguity, Franklin then turned to address a pressing contemporary issue: "We as Christians do not agree with those who preach black supremacy and separatism." Integration and nonviolence melded black political and cultural traditions into a race pride "with malice toward none and charity toward all." That complex union of protest politics, the "somebodiness" rooted in the slave spirituals (famously proclaimed by William Holmes Borders on national radio in 1943, and the core of C. L.'s preaching), the potential still vital in Abraham Lincoln's vision of the possible all these continued to frame C. L.'s central vision. But this intermingling of the martyred hero and the musician may still have scandalized some of New Bethel's more conservative parishioners.[19]

The next week C. L. delivered a meandering sermon in a stilted voice. His text was from the prophet Jeremiah, particularly the phrase in the first chapter, "to whom the word of the Lord came." Immediately, however, he explained that the sermon's subject was the then-popular song, "Heard It through the Grapevine."[20] A tortured effort led Franklin to the theme that, as American history schoolbooks all but ignored black people, most of what "we have received" about that history has come "as it were through the grapevine." He singled out in this regard Carter G. Woodson's efforts from the 1920s to build Negro History Week and also offered a long list of black men and women whose achievements were notable. The grapevine was, in fact, the alternative vision embedded deep within African American culture, "the grapevine of history, authentic history" essential for self-knowledge, survival, and race pride in this strange land. Properly understood, the grapevine revealed that despite superficial appearances, "the Negro in one way or another has been the central thread of American history." He explained: "I'm saying that men like Bilbo and Rankin [Mississippi segregationist politicians] and men like [George] Wallace and all of these kinds of people went into office because they happened to hate Negroes." Now, however, the mobilization of the black community inverted that dynamic, and it represents "a concrete challenge [to] and the severest test of the world's boasted democracies." But his reading voice lacked its normal rhythmic pacing, and the tuning of words was minimal. The congregation's response, with but a few exceptions, was subdued as well, a sharp reminder, by contrast, of the intimate partnership that structured his preaching.[21]

The third leg of Franklin's trilogy was strongest both in theme and presentation, even approaching the power of his more familiar sermons. He opened "The Meaning of Black Power" with a long citation from King's *Where Do We Go From Here*, which traced the origins of the slogan to a 1966 demonstration in Mississippi. The notion of black power was then new to the civil rights movement, C. L. reminded his people, but novelist Richard Wright and others had long ago used the term. As the phrase was an "essentially emotional concept," it carried different meanings. In an effort to go beyond the "verbal flourishes and the hysteria of the mass media," Franklin announced that the sermon would "assess its values, its assets and its liabilities, honestly."

Black power was, at root, "a cry of disappointment," Franklin told a packed New Bethel that Sunday evening, "born from the wombs of despair and disappointment . . . a cry of daily hurts and persistent pain." In a fundamental way, black power is "a reaction to the failure of white power" to act justly. Like Malcolm X, but in a very different fashion, C. L. recognized the legacy of slavery and racism, of forced lessons that blackness was "a sign of biological depravity," that "his whole history has been soiled with the filth of worthlessness." Like Malcolm, too, Franklin castigated his people for frequently lacking the self-awareness to grasp "how slavery and segregation have scarred the soul and wounded the spirit of the black man." But unlike Malcolm, C. L. turned to the "grapevine of history, authentic history" he had learned as a boy in church, in Mississippi. There, "the old Negro preacher" countered such bleakness by reaching toward his people with a fierce admonition: "You are not *n i g g e r s*." C. L. restated this legacy, now in a higher vocal register and with an elongated, lilting delivery. "You are not *s l a v e s*, you are not hewers of wood and drawers of water; you are God's children." This, then, was another meaning of black power, to think of oneself "as a child of God and a member of the human family." Again, in contrast to Malcolm and to Albert Cleage, C. L. rejected efforts to tie black power to black nationalism, "for that means pro-black," a term he rejected because it "means the same thing that the southern white man means. His nationalism is pro-white."

Franklin emphasized the need for African Americans to build political and economic strength in order to break down "the iron curtain of racial exclusion" that still framed the policies of "so many companies and industries in our city and country." No longer reading from his text, Franklin now preached of the need to "control our own destiny," to own rather than rent homes, and to support black businesses for the jobs they create for "your sons and daughters." School boards, financial institutions, jobs, and above all the police—in the city now more than 40 percent African American, all must truly serve the people they represent. As he moved into his chant, Franklin decried the fear and distrust blacks held of each other, a residue of what the "white folk taught us" in slavery. As the prolonged shouts and pitched cries from the pews urged him on, he professed to understand men who "dedicated themselves" to achieving this vision. Jesus, he proclaimed, as his palm kept the beat on the pulpit, suffering in the garden was such a man, and so too were Gandhi, Marcus Garvey, and Martin Luther King. The gap between these leaders and the people in New Bethel that night was all too real, yet C. L. sought in abbreviated form a transformation similar to what he had once achieved in the magnificent sermons of his prime. He would "go on anyhow," despite his unworthiness. Those in the pews could as well "keep on marching, keep on believing, keep on suffering," for "O-o-h-h! one of these days / my master / will say, 'Well done.'"[22]

*   *   *   *   *

Barely had New Bethel absorbed Franklin's sermon on black power when the volatile public tensions that idea evoked engulfed the church in a firestorm of bullets. On March 29, 1969, on a bitterly cold Saturday evening, nearly 150 black men, women, and children came through the doors into New Bethel's welcome warmth. Many dressed in bright, multicolored African-style robes. A small group, perhaps ten, wore the military fatigues, black jump boots, and black berets that identified them as members of the Black Legion, the Republic of New Africa's military wing. As the crowd settled in, RNA leaders Imari and Gaidi Obadele (Richard and Milton Henry) spoke briefly with Ralph Williams, a New Bethel trustee responsible that evening for preparing the church for Sunday's services after the meeting. Originally scheduled to meet in another church, the RNA approached C. L. Franklin a few days before their convention, when the original pastor withdrew his offer in the face of criticism. Franklin, who of course knew the Henrys quite well, readily agreed.[23]

The first sign of trouble came when Milton Henry began his opening remarks. Ralph Williams looked on, horrified, as Henry spoke while flanked by two uniformed Legionnaires, "standing there like soldiers with [loaded] rifles." Other armed men stood guard at the front and side doors of the church. Williams immediately called his pastor, who uttered a stunned "No!" when informed of the presence of guns within the church sanctuary. Pastor and trustee agreed that nothing could be done immediately that would not worsen the situation but that Williams should tell RNA leaders that he had to close the church at 11:00 P.M. As that time approached, however, Milton Henry was yet in the middle of his major speech. Other RNA officials told Williams to "just be calm," because the meeting was almost over.

When Henry finished, he lingered in the well of the sanctuary, talking with supporters. Williams cut some of the lights to encourage the crowd to leave. A large group had moved into the foyer at the rear of the church, preparing to exit onto Philadelphia Street. A smaller group, including children, gathered by the church kitchen, whose side doors opened onto Linwood. Williams hesitated to turn off more lights; he did not want anyone to hurt themselves in the dark. Accompanied by a guard, Milton Henry left through the kitchen for his car parked outside just as a police car traveling north on Linwood, staffed with two rookie officers, screeched to a halt parallel with the kitchen door. Officers Michael J. Czapski and Richard E. Worobec thought they saw a group of perhaps ten or twelve armed men milling about south of the door. On foot, they approached a single armed man near the door. Shots rang out, Czapski fell dead, and Worobec, seriously wounded, crawled back to the patrol car. As Henry and his driver quickly left the scene, only to be apprehended ten minutes later, the wounded officer called in a plea for help at 11:43 P.M. Although the only uninvolved eyewitness to the shooting remembered seeing one armed man that evening, Worobec's repeated message, "They're shooting at us," raised other fears in the minds of the police. Within minutes, a large police force arrived, convinced it was at war with black-power insurrectionists thought to be barricaded in the church. At 11:50 P.M., police stormed the church entrance on Philadelphia.[24]

Within New Bethel, bedlam erupted. Although the police later claimed that they encountered "a hail of gunfire" when they approached the church, the physical evidence examined the following day proved definitively, in the words of the official report of the Detroit Commission on Community Relations, "that the firing came from the outside." As the police opened fire, shattering the glass doors and windows, those in the foyer, screaming with fear, first ran and then fell to the floor, crawling in every direction, seeking safety from the barrage. Ralph Williams, who had tried to lock the front doors after the first shot, found himself crawling down the right aisle toward the piano just by the pulpit, along with approximately twenty other people. As the police, now in the rear of the church under the balcony overhang, continued their fire, Williams led his group through the kitchen to the steps that led to the basement and, ultimately, a subbasement. At that point, "no one knew what this was all about." The police soon followed. As Williams recalled:

> So then in a few minutes they found out that we were down in the basement and they told us, say, all right, you all come out of the basement. And one police said, "Well, we're gonna kill all of you down there." And I just know then, you know, I wouldn't come out alive. So when we come around them back steps and looked up, we, they told us all to put our hands high up over our heads and when we looked, when we looked up like that, I guess there must been about fifteen shotgun barrels sticking down in there. Now, suppose somebody had pulled the trigger? And I think the only reason that they didn't kill us down there, it was two black police that come on the scene.

Led back into the church, Williams's group joined the others prostrate on the floor, under armed guard, until handcuffed, when they were allowed to stand. White male police officers intimately searched cuffed black women in front of family and friends, denied arrested people access to toilets, and refused them permission to call a lawyer. Frequent police use of the crudest racial epithets exacerbated the fear prisoners already felt.[25]

At 5:00 A.M. on March 30, Franklin and James Del Rio arrived at the home of George Crockett, the lawyer once jailed for contempt of court who was now a judge himself. Elected in 1966 to the city's Recorder's Court, he was the jurist on duty that Sunday. Reports had already reached Franklin and Del Rio, then a state representative, that the 142 people arrested were detained incommunicado at the main police garage, subjected to continued verbal threats and physical abuse. When Crockett arrived at police headquarters, no one would provide him with even a partial list of the detainees. Quickly, he established a temporary courtroom on the first floor of the police building, opened it to the press, and when Jay Nolan, the assistant prosecutor, arrived, began processing those in custody in small groups of ten. After four groups had come before the court, William Cahalan, the Wayne County prosecutor, arrived. In open court, Cahalan ignored the judge and ordered the police not to bring any additional prisoners before Crockett. When the court resumed at noon that Sunday, the prosecutor himself had to agree that 130 of the detainees were free of suspicion of murder and moved to release them. Of the twelve who remained in custody, Crockett demanded that prosecutors provide probable cause to keep them jailed. Based on the evidence offered, Crockett ordered two held without bail and released another, on a $1,000 bond, in the custody of his attorney. He ruled that the evidence offered concerning the other nine was neither compelling nor obtained in a constitutional manner. No one would ever be convicted for the killing of Officer Czapski.[26]

Later that Sunday, when C. L. returned to New Bethel for the morning service, his parishioners arrived to discover their church had become a war zone. Many immediately criticized their pastor for renting it to the Republic, a group most thought was deeply wrongheaded. Franklin found his long-time friend and minister of music, Thomas Shelby, in the pastor's office, bemoaning whoever "let those people have the church. Oh my God."

C. L. mimicked Shelby some years later, "They torn up our church." Franklin remembered chastising him: "I said, 'Shelby, we are in the throes of a revolution, a social revolution. Some people have lost their lives in this revolution. And we have lost a little glass. So I think we got out cheap.'" In a newspaper interview that same day, Franklin defended the rental of the church as "routine," criticized the Republic for its use of guns, and affirmed his long relationship with the Henry brothers. "I do not denounce these people," he asserted. "Their goals are the same as ours, only they approach them from different directions." Beneath the "cry of daily hurts and persistent pain" that followed "the failure of white power," deeper than the very serious disagreements over strategy and tactics with groups such as the Republic, there was at root a common pursuit of freedom.[27]

Over the following week, the battle begun that Saturday night continued in the political arena. On Monday, March 31, a demonstration of three hundred police and policemen's wives, entirely white, protested Crockett's actions in front of Recorder's Court on St. Antoine, just south of Clinton, in the heart of the old Black Bottom neighborhood. Fueled by misleading, lurid headlines, particularly in the *Detroit News*, they denounced Crockett's presumed release of possible murderers and began circulating a petition to impeach the judge.[28] That same day, Franklin called a press conference. He regretted the death of a police officer in this incident, but he reminded all of the social geography of what was already being called the "New Bethel Shootout"—it occurred in the heart of the neighborhood "where the 1967 riot began." C. L. criticized the police for their overreaction, the indiscriminate shooting into the church, and for their "abusive handling" of those arrested. The organ, the pulpit, and the second-floor pastor's study all bore bullet holes, and church records and funds were arbitrarily confiscated. These actions, along with the "biased and slanted" press coverage of the event, could only widen the gap between white and black in Detroit "and add to the many bruttle [*sic:* brutal] experiences that the black community has suffered in the past." On Wednesday, Ralph Abernathy held a press conference at New Bethel, reiterating many of the charges Franklin had made, and C. L. led a meeting of white and black religious, political, and community leaders in support of the statement. On Thursday, perhaps as many as two thousand African Americans, led by

Detroit's black police officers and sheriff's deputies, demonstrated in support of Judge Crockett in front of the court building.[29]

The Detroit Police Officers Association, much of the press, and the majority of whites in the city and its surrounding counties attacked Crockett severely, accusing him of releasing murderers because they were black. In contrast, the legal profession applauded his defense of constitutional liberties in a period of crisis, and the presidents of the American, Michigan, and Detroit bar associations, as well as his friend William Patrick, president of New Detroit, Inc., all endorsed Crockett's conduct strongly. It was the judge, however, who most eloquently explained the central issue. In a statement issued on Thursday, April 3, Crockett reviewed the issues in the case in some detail before approaching the "racial overtones" at the heart of the matter: "Can any of you imagine the Detroit Police invading an all-white church and rounding up everyone in sight to be bussed to a wholesale lockup in a police garage? Can any of you imagine a [white] church group . . . being held incommunicado for seven hours, without being allowed to telephone relatives and without their constitutional rights to counsel? . . . Can anyone explain in other than racist terms the shooting by police into a closed and surrounded church?" For Crockett and for many in black Detroit, whatever they thought of the Republic of New Africa, the answer was a consistent "no."[30]

George Crockett stated later that the New Bethel incident represented the "coming of age" of black Detroit. The 1967 riot was "the wrong way" to achieve that objective, he thought. So destructive was the riot, so violent its effect on both body and spirit, that it could not provide a broad common goal for future political action. Nor did groups such as the Republic or the League of Revolutionary Workers receive any notice, their marginal influence all too obvious. Instead, Crockett pointed to the events of March 29 and their aftermath as central. "I think blacks really got a sense of solidarity as a result of the protest following the New Bethel case," he suggested in 1984. At the middle of all this was C. L. Franklin. His forceful public statements and his willingness to confront his more conservative parishioners and colleagues again distinguished him from many city leaders. Skeptical of revolutionary projections and deeply committed to creating a society of democratic equality despite the barriers yet in place,

Franklin nonetheless understood the need for solidarity that would allow discussion of differences and keep vital progress toward that social revolution.[31]

*   *   *   *   *

The New Bethel incident marked C. L.'s last major political role in Detroit. He remained active in encouraging a black presence in local politics and used his pulpit to call out those he especially desired to recognize. As militants increasingly ran for office and channeled their thinking within the electoral system, the solidarity Crockett identified built bridges across factions previously at odds. C. L. supported these efforts, but a younger generation increasingly assumed leadership roles. C. L.'s relative quiescence had other causes as well. By the early summer of 1969, two different charges against him turned his attention to the legal system in a far more personal manner than his defense of George Crockett had required.

In May, on a return trip from Dallas, the new venue of the cultural extravaganza planned by the International Afro Musical and Cultural Festival, American Airlines lost Franklin's bags for more than twenty-four hours. Before they finally turned up in the company's lost and found department in Detroit, police searched the bags and discovered a "small quantity of marijuana." Franklin may have been on a suspects' list, for this was not the first time officials had investigated him for alleged drug use. A year earlier, Franklin had suddenly left the winter meetings of the National Baptist Convention, canceling a highly anticipated sermon, when rumors "spread across the nation" that his luggage had been confiscated on suspicion of drugs when he had deplaned in Little Rock. He denied any wrongdoing then, and no charges were filed.[32] In 1969, Franklin angrily suggested that marijuana had been planted in his bags and claimed that the press in Detroit and elsewhere immediately "tried and condemned" him: "From one end of the country to the other stories implied that I was a dope addict, irresponsible as a pastor and administrator, and that myself and my children were loose morally." C. L. defended himself as best he could, denied he was an "irresponsible parent," and applauded when, in June, the judge dropped the charges, noting that the bags had been outside his possession for a significant period. But his troubles persisted. C. L. claimed that as a consequence of his arrest, negotiations for the Dallas auditorium had collapsed, and a number of the prominent stars had withdrawn. He had no choice but to cancel the newly named "Soul Bowl." Facing serious financial loss, especially as C. L. vowed to reimburse funds invested by friends such as Jasper Williams, he announced a $10 million suit against the airline to compensate him for his actual loss and the "irreparable damage to his prestige as a Christian leader" the ensuing publicity caused. The suit never reached court, partly because a week following that announcement, yet more troubles surfaced. Franklin's creative financial accounting again caught the attention of the authorities, this time Michigan's tax officials. In time, that case would—like his earlier tax run-in—be settled by Franklin's payment.[33]

All this was part of C. L.'s life unraveling in the years following the New Bethel shootout. The powerful vision that marked his 1950s sermons still framed his public image and preceded him into every pulpit he ascended. Increasingly, however, fatigue and illness occupied him. High blood pressure kept him from New Bethel's pulpit for some weeks that fall, and even when in the pulpit, his power continued its inevitable decline. The drug charges particularly rankled. The stories told in public were but echoes of what had been rumored in private. Fellow ministers and New Bethel members later claimed to know of the preacher's occasional marijuana use. Given the customs of the entertainment world he so enjoyed, this might not be surprising. Yet the press coverage of his various difficulties did not alone mark his slippage. Despite the posturing he performed for the media when announcing the legal suit, C. L. never worried seriously about what others thought of him—perhaps with the exception of his mother. Rather, his travels, partying, and preaching all contributed to an aging process that grew progressively more obvious. At times, his sermons must have been painful to hear, as the manuscript text of a mid-1970s version of his incomparable "Without a Song" indicated. On other occasions, friends had to rescue him from the pulpit, because whatever drink he had used to gird himself against his declining powers controlled rather than calmed him at that moment. Still, occasional brilliant bursts of light, once a near-daily experience, illuminated a world much grayer. Such a moment occurred in

January 1972, when C. L. basked in the power of his daughter's gift and the embrace of a packed church that made no demands on him. In Los Angeles, at James Cleveland's church, this proud father beamed as Aretha recorded *Amazing Grace,* her powerful gospel album. And New Bethel still loved him, although, perhaps especially there, in the pulpit that embodied the power of his voice, he often could not help but imagine himself as he once was, and that could not but pain him.[34]

Franklin was not the only activist involved in the New Bethel incident and its aftermath for whom that event marked a turning point. Change was perhaps most noticeable within the Republic of New Africa. By November 1969, Imari Obadele had resigned from the cabinet after losing a struggle with his brother. For Imari, the lesson from the New Bethel shootout revealed the need for one hundred thousand armed black troops to protect the new nation. Milton Henry thought this foolhardy. The following month, Robert F. Williams, back from exile, resigned as president of the Republic. After eight years abroad, it had taken Williams just a few months to grasp the dismal reality lurking beneath the exaggerated rhetoric. He rejected separatism and armed conflict except as a last resort, and he considered integration a "more desirable" tactic to achieve "self-determination for black people." The more fervent supporters, few as they may have been, were stunned, but the Republic's limited moment was in fact over. Robert Williams resolved his legal difficulties and lived a private life, working at the University of Michigan library in the 1970s. Imari Obadele led his remnant to Hinds County, Mississippi, where they purchased the natal site of the Kush District, the name given the five states Obadele and his followers yet expected the U.S. government to cede to them. In 1975, the Republic held national elections to select the "*Provisional Government* for the subjugated Black Nation." Some seven thousand African Americans voted, primarily in Mississippi.[35]

Milton Henry traveled a different path. His horror over the "very traumatic experience" that March evening at New Bethel led him to reject armed struggle and to reconsider the consequences even a self-professed "devil" need consider when stirring the pot. Following the split, Milton turned his attention to his law practice and searched for more viable ways to remain active politically. While his brother settled in Mississippi, Milton became counsel to a group of African American businessmen exploring investment opportunities in Africa. Intrigued by their announced goal of developing Africa for the Africans, Henry soon found himself in Ghana advising the group in their negotiations. Disillusionment was immediate. The businessmen, many of whom he had known for years, wanted him to "help them steal, in essence, these people's [diamond and gold] leases and mahogany, and this and that, you know." In this troubled mood, a despondent Henry hired a car one morning to take him into the country where he might walk and think: "And I was walking and I came upon this old English church and they had a weather beaten sign out in front of it with the words of Paul on it, said, 'Know ye not but you are not your own, you have been born with a price, even the blood of our Lord Jesus Christ.' And, boy, it was an existential moment for me."

He was in his early fifties at the time, and his conversion experience as he told it paralleled the biblical Saul's on the road to Damascus but with an ironic twist. Saul, after three days of blindness, saw again when he discarded his Judaic faith to embrace the religion of Jesus. Milton Henry, blinded as well in his mind for a far longer period, regained his vision only when he returned to the core religious tradition he thought he had left long before. That same day, he called his wife in Pontiac and made plans to return home immediately. Shortly thereafter, he entered a seminary to prepare for ordination. He remained a lawyer and served as pastor at Christ Presbyterian Church, in Southfield, a Detroit suburb, for decades, where he preached a message of faith and social engagement.[36]

Albert Cleage had already distanced himself from the Republic. He remained committed to his version of black Christian nationalism, preaching of a black revolutionary Jesus whom whites had expropriated for their own ends. In the early 1970s, he traveled widely, wrote numerous articles and books, and remained active politically, supporting militant black candidates through networks of citizens he had spurred into action over the past decades. By the mid-1970s, Cleage, then known as Jaramogi Abebe Agyeman, limited broader political involvements to focus on his church. James and Grace Lee Boggs, Albert Cleage's close comrades over many decades, continued to stress the complex interplay of class and race within industrial capitalism as their major political issue. As they struggled with the relevance of Marxism for an

American movement, they also created grass-roots coalitions around specific issues. The various revolutionary goals they promoted never came to fruition, but their actions did bring many people from their porches into the broader community to press for change.[37]

Paradoxically, it was two former radicals among this older generation of activists who, as Democratic Party candidates, most immediately benefited from the militants' turn toward electoral politics. Coleman Young, whose 1952 congressional testimony aired over Detroit radio altered the perspectives of many, had been reelected to the state senate numerous times. Claud Young, first cousin to Coleman and C. L.'s physician, recalled that, at the time of Coleman's testimony before the House Un-American Activities Committee in 1952, "Frank knew Coleman. I mean *knew* Coleman!" But that was a public awareness of the other's reputation, and it is likely that a more personal connection evolved only after the events at New Bethel in 1969. The preacher and the politician spent considerable time together at the meetings and protest rallies that followed the shootout, and they discovered in each other kindred spirits. Both were quick-witted men who dressed well, enjoyed the full range of life's pleasures, and in their different ways professed a deep commitment to their people's future. With Claud Young, they spent many evenings at one another's houses, sipping Scotch, telling stories, and discussing politics. When Young announced his candidacy for mayor in 1973, C. L. was an early supporter. In that year's Democratic primary, Franklin ignored Mel Ravitz, the liberal white UAW-endorsed candidate whom he had supported in earlier elections, seeing in Ravitz' candidacy yet another attempt by a white-led labor movement to salvage its former dominance of black political life. Instead, standing behind the pulpit on a Sunday evening, the radio microphones broadcasting every syllable to a large Detroit audience, C. L declared his personal support for his friend. Young's subsequent election brought ecstatic joy to black Detroit but evoked fear and loathing from the majority of the city's dwindling white population. On election night, a small group of Young's friends celebrated giddily into the early morning. As the mayor-elect pronounced that phrase, "my police department," referring to the same department that had "been hitting you upside your damn head" for years, Claud Young remembered, "we fell out laughing."[38]

The election in Detroit of an African American mayor did mark a coming of age. Through Young, black Detroit now directed the very institutions that had systematically discriminated against them, and worse, for so long. Reelected in 1977, Young remained in office until 1993, presiding over an increasingly ravaged local economy. George Crockett, Young's counsel at those 1952 hearings, remained a judge at Recorder's Court until his retirement in 1978. Two years later, at age seventy-one, he won election to Congress, where he served for a decade. Like his comrade Coleman Young, Crockett had also traversed successfully the social space that separated outsiders from members of the city's black inner elite. In their way, Young, Crockett, and Franklin, among others, had journeyed far beyond their Mississippis, real and metaphorical. For C. L., since the days he first longed to explore Highway 61, he had grown into a public role far different than the one prescribed for most young Mississippi black boys.[39]

*   *   *   *   *

Franklin experienced no radical transformation in the aftermath of the New Bethel shootout. In a basic way, the lessons of that event required no break with his past. He remained the militant integrationist and committed Christian who searched for the best in an American democratic tradition he insisted his people must claim as their own. As black Detroit largely turned its collective face away from separatist or revolutionary solutions, activists of nearly every tendency, from NAACP supporters to disillusioned separatists, funneled that assertiveness into a continuing transformation of the city's political structure. Franklin again assumed a role, if now a minor one, in this transformation even as he husbanded ever more closely his waning energies.

Old habits brought renewed public notoriety. In 1972, Detroit police arrested Franklin on drunk-driving charges after his new Cadillac collided with another car as he left "an alley adjacent to the Rio Grande Motel" a few blocks from his home, at five-thirty on a Saturday morning. Neither he nor his passenger, a twenty-six-year-old woman, were injured, but the court did require C. L. to post a $1,600 bond, due to an outstanding traffic warrant already issued for another accident. After some hours in custody, he stood silently as his lawyer posted the bond. Decades before, Franklin had a firmer control over his impulses, seeing them perhaps as the "final compensation," in Ruth Brown's phrase, for his extraordinary sacred performances. Increasingly during the 1970s, however, one senses a more desperate quality. Fatigue, age, polyps on his throat, high blood pressure— the causes varied, but C. L. felt his energy wane. Not surprisingly, funerals, especially of close friends, also took a toll. In 1973 he preached and his daughter Aretha sang at the Philadelphia funeral of Clara Ward. Although not as close as they once were, C. L. nonetheless had lost a dear friend. Other funerals inevitably followed. The 1976 service for Florence Ballard, an original member of the famous Motown group the Supremes, provided C. L. with another dramatic moment reminiscent of his prime, as he preached to an overflow congregation packed with entertainment celebrities. Back in New Bethel a few months later, his mood was more somber, his conduct ever more typical. C. L. sat on the dais during the funeral of Benjamin McFall, the mortician, confidant, and friend, a co-planner of the 1963 march and a New Bethel trustee for thirty-five years. Illness prevented Franklin from delivering the eulogy, and he sat mute in the pastor's chair behind and to the side of the pulpit.[40]

The jarring presence of C. L. Franklin, seated, his voice silenced as others preached, soon became all too common. In part, his absence from the pulpit precipitated the sharp decline in New Bethel's membership during the decade, but C. L. was powerless to change. Whether visiting another Detroit church or at the yearly Baptist convention, an announcement that C. L. Franklin would preach drew crowds that listened, with disappointment, as the famous preacher introduced a substitute, often an assistant minister, in his place. The letter of a Los Angeles minister in fall 1977 was typical. Reverend J. W. Evans asked C. L. to extend his stay at his church's twentieth anniversary by a few days, with a solicitous concern that reflected a broader awareness. "Please don't think that I am trying to be too strenuous upon you," he wrote Franklin, "because I realize that you are not Preaching as long as you once have." Evans offered the still-famous preacher $1,000 to preside over another's sermon and give a brief closing message.[41]

While his muted voice left audiences disappointed, Franklin's recordings from years past continued to sell well throughout the decade, and African American divinity students still studied his sermons. In contrast, however, with John Lewis's experience two decades earlier, when he huddled around the radio with fellow students, straining to catch every Franklin tone and rhythm, fewer young people did so in the 1970s. The political and cultural upheavals that followed in the wake of the protests Lewis and many others led encouraged different sensibilities in a generation now twice removed from Franklin's formative experiences in the Mississippi Delta. Church attendance among young people, as Franklin well knew, had dropped considerably. Even among divinity students, the chanted sermon seemed to many as old fashioned as the blues themselves, and the less emotive, more purely intellectual approach of a Gardner C. Taylor or a Howard Thurman vied with the new militant themes of the Black Theology movement as more suitable approaches for an increasingly sophisticated, urban black audience.

Despite the changes that accompanied aging, Franklin was not despondent. Sixty-two in 1977, he was neither elderly nor incapacitated. Within the new limits he had to acknowledge, he continued an intensely active life. He mentored young preachers such as Jerome Kirby, much as J. H. Anderson and B. J. Perkins had served as his models decades before. He was attentive to his assistant ministers, particularly C. L. Moore, Leonard Flowers, and E. L. Branch, younger men whose careers he advanced. He continued to collect money for charity and, reflecting the changing era, raised considerable amounts through talks and benefits to establish a C. L. Franklin Scholarship fund for the college expenses of New Bethel's young members. He also took great pride in his family. Rachel, his mother, remained his fervent advocate and was present for the 11:00 A.M. service at New Bethel every Sunday her health allowed. His children, too, gathered. Vaughn, forty years old when he left the military in 1974, reentered Franklin family life, and Carl Ellan Kelley's relationship with her father continued to grow during the 1970s. By the mid-1970s, Erma's singing career had ended, and she returned to live in Detroit. Carolyn wrote and arranged music and lived in Detroit, as did Brenda Corbett, their cousin. Together, this trio often provided backup vocals for Aretha. Accompanied by her brother Cecil, who had left the ministry to manage her career,

Aretha was on the road frequently, performing and recording, living in that world of celebrity that her father had explored before her. From all of them, Franklin took deep pleasure in their presence and in their achievements, for whatever his deficiencies as a parent when they were younger, his adult relationships with them were strong and mutually rewarding.[42]

His curtailed activity encouraged reflection. In the fall and winter of 1977–78, he welcomed a young blues musician and musicologist, Jeff Todd Titon, into his home for a series of long, revealing interviews. C. L. allowed Titon to videotape six of his sermons. Franklin also shared his reflections with a local reporter. He and the church had experienced many "trying times" since 1946, he explained to the *Detroit News* interviewer, and he touched on his efforts through his sermons and other activities to affect the thinking of his audiences. The results, he thought, were positive: "My church is not as narrow minded as it was, when I became its pastor. It's gratifying to look back at the way things were and to see how far we've come and to know my leadership had an impact on the revolution." Protest, he commented, was "necessary . . . as a first step in the movement." But now, with political avenues open and the community more actively engaged, elected black politicians such as Coleman Young had the opportunity to enact laws "to insure equality of opportunity." In both protest and politics, Franklin explained, he had tried to make a difference.[43]

Perhaps it was simply hard to explain in only a few words what he had done. For decades, C. L. Franklin had preached to raise self-consciousness, to compel his audiences to shed a "slave psychology," to find the courage to stretch out their hands and allow their God to act in and through them. At the center of that struggle he stressed the necessity to sing *because of* the pain; to nurture one's voice in a strange land was in fact to develop a vision of the possible that countered the debilitating limits others imposed. Various infirmities increasingly stilled his voice, yet as often was the case with celebrities, the accolades continued. In May 1979, smiling, eyes crinkled with pleasure, his broad face a warm, inviting welcome, Franklin beamed from the inaugural cover of *Church Magazine*. His perfectly styled conk, touched to avoid even the hint of gray, and his thin, trimmed mustache evoked a certain worldly confidence. His three-piece, cream-colored suit perfectly complemented his coloring, with further accents from the light shirt, paisley tie, and pendant around the neck. The well-tailored outfit emphasized his square, broad shoulders, and there was only the slightest hint of added weight. The photographs were proof that, on some days, he could still project a charismatic aura the near equal of any in his prime.[44]

Some weeks later, on the first weekend in June, New Bethel celebrated their pastor's thirty-third anniversary in their pulpit with a full program of sermons, hymns, and gifts. A week later, on Friday evening, June 8, C. L. attended the first anniversary celebration of his former assistant, E. L. Branch, at Detroit's Third New Hope Baptist Church. He brought with him a current assistant, R. W. Wright, and following a genial discussion in the pastor's office, the three men entered the sanctuary. There, in a pattern by now almost expected, the advertised preacher introduced the assistant who would deliver the sermon while the more famous man sat in a deacon's chair. Franklin did "make some strong remarks that night," Branch remembered, and as always, whether he preached or not, Franklin "received the offering." His comments that Friday night at Third New Hope was the last time his voice carried from the pulpit into the pews.[45]

As his children had insisted for some time, the near West Side neighborhood surrounding his church and home had become increasingly dangerous. Franklin knew the danger for, just a week earlier while he enjoyed his celebration at New Bethel, a burglar had broken into the well-kept LaSalle Boulevard house, only to be scared off by the alarm. That concern weighed on him following the services at Branch's church. Rather than joining Branch and Wright for a late meal, Franklin told the young ministers he had to return home, where he had people working on the house. "If they don't take something," he wryly told Branch, "they will leave the door open so somebody else can." Nothing was disturbed, however.[46]

Just after midnight, early on June 10, C. L. relaxed, alone in his upstairs bedroom, watching television. Outside, a group of burglars, four men and two women, attracted by the antique stained glass in the windows they hoped to detach and sell, prepared to enter the house. Earlier that evening, this makeshift group of thieves had tried unsuccessfully to break into several other homes in the neighborhood. In something of a random decision born of their frustration, they decided the glass warranted a final effort.

None of the robbers had any idea whose residence it was, nor was it clear that would have made any difference to them. Patrick Watson Thompson, age twenty-three, climbed up the back porch and pried open a screen on a second-floor window as the others waited below. Franklin heard a noise, probably when Thompson removed the screen, and retrieved the loaded pistol he always kept in the house. Thompson came through the window, crept down the hall, and thrust his head into the bedroom, only to find that Franklin "was laying for me." Franklin fired two shots. Thompson returned fire with his semi-automatic handgun. It was about one o'clock that morning, neighbors later testified, when they heard the four distinct shots from the house. Sometime after, neighbors investigated and discovered Franklin unconscious, crumpled over, one bullet in his right knee and another, rupturing the femoral artery, in his right groin area. His gun and two of its spent shells lay strewn about. There was no evidence that Thompson had been hit. In their panic, Thompson and the others fled, leaving behind the glass and almost $30,000 in cash and checks, the wounded pastor's anniversary gifts.[47]

By the time the ambulance arrived, Franklin had lost an enormous amount of blood. He went into cardiac arrest on the way to Ford Hospital's emergency room and was resuscitated by the paramedics, only to suffer another arrest at the hospital. Given the blood loss, his unconscious state, and successive heart stoppages, the attending doctors decided to accept "the fact that he was gone." Some minutes later, someone in the room exclaimed that the patient was "Aretha Franklin's father," and with great effort they resuscitated Franklin once again. Claud Young, who was not in the room but who talked at length with the doctors who were, estimated that Franklin's brain was without oxygen from nineteen to twenty-nine minutes. Whatever the precise time, that interval determined the quality of Clarence LaVaughn Franklin's remaining life.[48]

Aretha, accompanied by Carolyn, Cecil, and Brenda, was performing in Las Vegas when Brenda received the phone call. The four immediately rushed back to Detroit, where Erma was already at the hospital, along with her grandmother, Claud Young, and other close family friends. The prognosis was not encouraging. C. L. remained on the critical list, in a coma, "unresponsive, comatose." By the start of his third week in the hospital,

C. L.'s conditioned worsened, and a hospital spokeswoman indicated new "complications as a result of the prolonged coma." As the family prayed, the police arrested the six individuals who were present when he was shot. All were young, residents of Detroit, and African American. One of the men received immunity in exchange for his testimony against Thompson, and two others pleaded guilty to burglary and assault with intent to murder. The two women pleaded guilty to reduced charges of breaking and entering, a plea bargain that infuriated the more than twenty thousand delegates attending the NBC's Christian Education meeting in Pittsburgh. A jury found Thompson not guilty of attempted murder; his lawyer convinced the jury that the testimony against him was tainted by self-interest. He did receive a ten-year sentence for the break-in. Two others, brothers Jerome and Howard Woodward, received long sentences for reneging on their agreement to testify, but their sentences would be sharply reduced a year later, on a technicality. In an irony that revealed yet again the intimate, if often tortured, intertwining of black and white lives in Detroit, the county prosecutor who tried the burglars was the same William Cahalan who had defied Judge George Crockett a decade before. Even odder, the judge who sentenced the Woodward brothers was Samuel H. Olsen, the former county prosecutor who had refused to investigate the Detroit policeman who killed Cynthia Scott.[49]

A past of a different kind trailed the news of the shooting across black America. C. L.'s well-known penchant for the nightlife and his well-publicized 1968 drug trial spawned a storm of rumors and innuendoes. In one rendering repeated widely, embellished with a bewildering array of imagined details, Thompson and Franklin were principals in "a drug deal that went bad or something." The money found in the bedroom only spurred such speculation, as in some versions, Franklin became the dealer and not the buyer. Given his continuing income-tax difficulties, however, it should not have surprised anyone that he operated with cash whenever he could. Billy Kyles heard the rumors, too, and stressed that he never saw any "factual evidence" to support them. His friend had no need for money, he noted, and was not addicted to any drug. The conduct of the police and the burglars alike further undermined the credibility of these legends. Given his continued public stature, to say nothing of his well-known drug arrest, it was inconceivable that C. L. could operate as a serious drug dealer without attracting the attention of the police, many of whom would have been only too happy to embarrass Mayor Young and black Detroit with such a spectacular arrest. Three of the six burglars who were given full or partial immunity, moreover, never raised the issue of drugs with police or prosecutors, despite the potential benefit in such revelations for them.[50]

Prayer vigils and fundraisers dominated the months and years that followed. Still in a coma that December, Franklin came home from the hospital. He had survived a series of infections, could breathe without life support, and hospital costs were mounting. There was also the hope that a return home to familiar surroundings would aid his recovery. The search for signs became an exhausting emotional effort for family members. Aretha worriedly told Erma some months after their father returned home that C. L. was "less responsive" than two months ago, although he "seemed to brighten up when Cecil visited last night." Friends and parishioners came to the house daily, offering prayers, food, and a quick visit to tell Reverend of their love. Ralph Williams and Harry Kincaid came daily to carry their pastor from the bed to a chair, to improve his circulation. Fannie Tyler, C. L.'s private secretary and trusted aide, came nearly every day as well, as did Mother Rachel. E. L. Branch played tapes of C. L.'s sermons on his afternoon visits, praying for a spark of recognition to light up his mentor's eyes. At times, the unconscious Franklin startled visitors. When Margaret Branch entered the bedroom one evening, "he raised up on that bed." Frightened, "scared to death," she nonetheless glimpsed hope: "but he was trying to talk to me." It was an involuntary rather than a willed movement, however, and he did not regain consciousness. Cneri Jenkins and his wife also visited occasionally, and he was certain on one visit that his pastor "was trying to tell me something, but, he just, spit was flying everyplace."[51]

Although he remained at home, the costs for Franklin's twenty-four-hour care remained high. New Bethel established a trust fund that had reached $32,000 by January 1980. As appreciable as it was, that amount covered less than four months' care; his approximate monthly expenses came close to $9,000. That April, thirteen thousand people jammed into Cobo Hall to hear Aretha, James Cleveland, Pop Staples and his daughters, Mavis and Cleo, Jesse Jackson, and others perform in a concert that raised some $50,000 for expenses. In both 1982 and 1983, major benefits were held at the church, organized by Fannie Tyler, Harry Kincaid, Carolyn King and others, but the financial drain persisted. Claud Young eased it to a degree, for he never submitted a bill for his medical services. But the family's decision not to apply for available government benefits (the idea of this proud man relying on government benefits grated on the family) necessitated constant fundraising to relieve Aretha of some of the financial burden. These bursts of organizational activity, not unlike Franklin's own involuntary reactions, raised expectations and momentarily lifted the shroud of sadness. But family, close friends, and well-wishers alike were forced to return to a more depressing reality. The medical log book kept by his nursing staff for almost three years after his release from Ford Hospital left little room for sustained optimism. Amid the notations of visitors arriving, various involuntary motions by the patient, and the instructions from doctors lay the stark, unforgiving data, recorded multiple times each eight-hour shift, of a person approaching his final journey. Everything ingested—he was fed intravenously and, at times, could swallow baby food—and everything eliminated was weighed, measured, and examined. And always, always, with the measured solemnity of a muffled drum in a memorial march, the entry with its unchanging message was inscribed by the shift nurse: "Neuro status remains unchanged."[52]

On Easter Sunday morning, 1981, nurse M. Woodall came on duty at seven. She noted that her patient was "comfortable listening to the radio." In years past, C. L. would have already led a sunrise service, preaching a sermon with power and insight on the multiple meanings of his Lord's resurrection. That morning, as he lay comatose, his nurse offered a poignant prayer: "Happy Easter Rev. May your resurrection back fully with us be very very soon."[53]

As C. L. lay unconscious, powerless, the church and the congregation he had led for so long underwent a painful, angry struggle over his succession. The battle left New Bethel almost as disabled as its pastor. At issue were the terms of the lifetime contract he signed early in his tenure at New Bethel. The key clause in the document provided that C. L. would remain pastor, absent a commanding majority of the membership voting to remove him, "as long as breath was in his body." He remained breathing, without life support, but clearly could no longer lead the church. Within ten hours of the 1979 shooting, the trustees and deacons named Franklin's longtime senior assistant, the blind preacher C. (Clinton) L. Moore, as minister-in-charge until the pastor recovered fully. At first, the arrangement worked well. The shock of the shooting, the concern for his recovery, and the sadness for the family and for the congregation as a whole held in check the varied, normal tensions inherent in an organization as complex and important in its members' lives. But as 1980 gave way to 1981 and their pastor remained unavailable, some began to question the arrangement. At the center of this was Moore. An electrifying preacher in the Franklin tradition, Moore was both popular and ambitious. Moore let it be known that he wished to be named pastor, with Franklin named pastor emeritus, as he was, in fact, performing that position anyway. But Moore's visible ambition angered different leadership groups within the church. His open desire to replace C. L. stunned the stricken pastor's most fervent supporters. Fannie Tyler, Carolyn King, Willie Todd, Beverli Greenleaf, Wallace Malone, Harry Kincaid—personal and church secretaries, choir soloists, deacons, and trustees—among others were particularly appalled, because they well knew how Franklin had encouraged and supported Moore for more than a decade.[54]

Moore's bluntness precipitated the crisis. "No one can operate anything from a sick bed," he stated frankly. "Nobody can lead if he doesn't know what he is leading." To those like Carolyn King, praying that Franklin would return but committed to honoring his position until "the inevitable," Moore's position amounted to backstabbing by an intimate family member. For Deacon Milton Hall, his support for his pastor also transcended contractual obligations. "See," he told C. L. Moore directly, "Reverend Franklin spoke for me when I couldn't speak for myself. I said, now he is down, I'll speak for him." On October 3, the deacons and trustees of New Bethel gathered and, after much discussion, voted to remove Moore from his temporary position. A strong minority opposed the decision. Moore claimed irregularities in the vote and called a membership meeting for October 20, under his leadership, to place the decision before the entire membership. So important was this congregation to Afro-Baptist Detroit, however, that William Holly, president of the Council of Baptist Pastors, stepped in to preside. Some fifteen hundred voting members attended and, "by a large percentage," supported Moore's removal. Moore led a walkout, court suits followed when he tried to retain the New Bethel name, and he quickly established a new church, Enon Baptist.[55]

New Bethel was devastated. Longtime friends and parishioners hurled epithets at one another, and the Franklin family felt an overwhelming sense of betrayal. The church also suffered a grievous institutional loss. Many left with Moore for Enon; another significant number withdrew from both churches. By spring 1982, New Bethel still had no permanent pastor, had but 105 paying members, and faced the awkward task of celebrating the church's fiftieth anniversary. Joseph H. Jackson, president of the NBC, preached the anniversary sermon in recognition of New Bethel's central role in the city's black religious life. C. L.'s most famous daughter and many other family members stayed away. The emotions would be too painful, an unnamed relative told a reporter. "Things have not been happy for her since her father was hurt and things haven't been well at the church." Away from the public eye, however, the remaining deacons and trustees were at work, and on Sunday, July 11, following a series of trial sermons that spring, they installed Robert Smith, Jr., a thirty-year-old pastor from Pratt City, Alabama, as co-pastor, with the understanding that he would automatically succeed Franklin upon his death. Once again, a southerner had come north to lead New Bethel. But it could not be the same.[56]

EPILOGUE

On Friday, July 27, 1984, at 10:30 A.M., more than five years since he was shot, Clarence LaVaughn Franklin died. He never regained consciousness. The coroner listed homicide as the cause of death. He was sixty-nine years old.[1]

On Wednesday, August 1, 1984, at two o'clock in the afternoon, the doors of Swanson's Funeral Home opened. Inside, the body of C. L. Franklin lay in state. It was appropriate that his final rites began there. C. L. had been friends with the Swanson family for many years, and the funeral home itself was on Grand Boulevard East, on the northern edge of the old Paradise Valley area, midway between C. L.'s former home on Boston Boulevard and the site of the New Bethel pulpit he first ascended in 1946. Late into Wednesday night and all day Thursday, and again on Friday morning, the crowds came in the wilting heat to see his face once more, to pay their respects one last time. On Friday afternoon, August 3, O'Neil Swanson temporarily closed the casket, and assistants wheeled it to a resplendent 1940 black LaSalle hearse, with spotless whitewall tires, highly polished finish, and gleaming chrome trim the equal of the stylish man it transported. C. L. Franklin was coming home to New Bethel for the last time.[2]

That evening, August 3, the family and the congregation held the first of two services to mark C. L.'s passing. With Robert Smith and James Holley the officiating ministers, an overflowing New Bethel joined in a memorial service for this preacher and pastor who lay before them in an open casket. Ward Lott, a New Bethel trustee and Worthy Master of the city's Prince Hall Masonic Lodge 10, offered condolences on behalf of C. L.'s Masonic brethren. Tributes also came from pastors, including E. L. Branch, and from Mrs. Robbie McCoy, a longtime friend and religion editor for the Michigan *Chronicle*. New Bethel's mass choir offered hymns, as did gospel singer Delores Barrett Campbell. Herbert Pickard, one of C. L.'s favorite pianists, accompanied these sacred performances. As moving as the memorial was, it was but a prelude for the service the following day. That same evening, busloads of ministers and mourners continued to arrive in the city from Birmingham, Buffalo, Chicago, and elsewhere. Even more ministers, the prominent as well as those far less famous, arrived by plane.[3]

Saturday morning, August 4, at eleven o'clock, at New Bethel—that was the major remembrance, the final farewell. The weather that morning was oppressive, as "a searing heat" gripped the city from daybreak and only intensified as the sun inched towards its apex. By nine o'clock, the nonreserved seats in the church were nearly full, and ushers brought out additional folding chairs to fill the side aisles on the main floor and the nooks and crevices in the corners there and in the balcony. Already the temperature inside matched the 90-plus degrees outside, and a sea of white fans moving "in cadence," some thought, as in "the old time revival," sought in vain to circulate the dank, laden air. By eleven o'clock, nearly three thousand people had squeezed within the church, and an estimated six or seven thousand more crowded the streets outside, listening to the choir over loudspeakers. At the front of the church, in the well of the sanctuary, directly below the pulpit, lay Franklin's open casket, his full body visible. To either side were richly colored wreaths of flowers, into some of which had been braided a recording of one of Franklin's sermons. Behind the pulpit, the pastor's chair and portrait were draped in black, and above the choir loft the neon sign proclaimed, as it had for decades, the church's essential act of faith: "One Lord, One Faith, One Baptism."[4]

Sometime after eleven o'clock—the crowds outside forced innumerable delays—the procession into the church for C. L.'s "transitorial services" to the next life began. Adorned in white, symbolizing hope despite their loss, the family marched slowly down the center aisle, led by Franklin's eighty-seven-year-old mother, his six children, his niece, and followed by a large group of relatives and close friends. Each stopped before the open casket for a prayer and a final sad goodbye, before turning to their right to fill the thirteen reserved pews in the center section. Next came the pallbearers, followed by the deacons, trustees, and the members of various church boards and committees. Like the family, many wore white. Throughout, the choir sang. The program that morning listed forty-three speakers and eleven different musical offerings. But even if each speaker honored the time limitation Fannie Tyler, his private secretary and organizer of the service, had established, it would have been impossible that day to have heard all. The air was so thick within the church, the crush of people in the pews so intense, that one inadvertently pinned another's arms in the massed crowd, and many gasped for breath. After consulting with the family and his doctor cousin, Coleman Young announced that conditions would force an alteration of the program. With apologies, some thirty speakers were eliminated and the schedule readjusted to reach more quickly the two main speakers. The first of these called to the pulpit was Rev. Jesse Jackson of Chicago.[5]

Jackson had spent the spring of 1984 as a candidate for the presidency of the United States in the Democratic Party's primaries. As he told the crowd, C. L., whom he "affectionately called the Rabbi, the Learned One," had preached his ordination service in 1968 and, even before that, had brought the young seminary student into this very pulpit. As was evident to many as he processed, holding Aretha's arm, Jackson had grown close to the Franklin children as well: "Erma and Cecil and Carolyn and Aretha—we're family."

C. L., Jackson declared, "was a prophet . . . [a] rare, not just [a] unique" man. His reach stretched beyond New Bethel into the heart of black America: "Did not our ears perk up for years before we had a television or an elected official in America, if we could just hear WLAC, Nashville, Tennessee, Randy's on a Sunday night? Sunday night, New Bethel, Hastings Street, was the common frame of reference for the black church prototype. The soul of Motown was Hastings Street before Grand Boulevard."[6] A commanding presence in black America, Franklin touched singers and musicians, ministers, and untold numbers in his audiences with his "substance and sweetness," with his challenge that the church "be relevant and ask the Lord to give us *this* day, our daily bread." This he accomplished despite being born half a century "before we had the right to vote. Born in poverty—poverty could not stop him. He was born in segregation. It was illegal for a black man to get an education. No public accommodations. No right to vote."

Nonetheless, Jackson exclaimed, C. L.'s "flower did blossom. That's why we're here today to say thank you for a petal, for an insight, for a song, for a sermon." But now, like Moses and Joshua, Isaiah and Daniel, like his friend Martin, like Jesus himself, C. L. "had to go home." Their common faith, Jackson reminded all, found the joy amid the pain, a joy Aretha sang of in one of her first gospel recordings decades before. "There is a land," he intoned, evoking in the church's memory her incomparable talent even as a fourteen-year-old, "where we shall never grow old," where pain and sorrow are no more. That was the land to which C. L. went ahead of us.[7]

Tributes followed, layered between musical selections from Johnny Taylor, one of C. L.'s favorite singers, Samuel Billy Kyles, and Arthur Prysock, the jazz singer and close friend. Then Jasper Williams, pastor of Atlanta's Salem Baptist Church and long a protégé in Franklin's preaching tradition, came to the pulpit. The eulogist, he grasped the microphone in his hands, and with a power and tonality that eerily recalled C. L. himself, he sang: "Fa-a-ther, I stretch my hands to thee." For a moment, as Williams rendered the various stanzas, it was possible to imagine C. L. himself in the pulpit. As he finished the hymn, Williams moved into his sermon, centered on the theme that C. L. was "a good soldier of Jesus Christ." Some twenty-five minutes later, with the audience on the brink of physical and emotional exhaustion, Jasper Williams concluded this "extraordinary service," perhaps the largest ever held in Detroit.[8]

The cavalcade of hearses, limousines, and private cars stretched twenty city blocks along Linwood, from Grand Boulevard West to Joy Road. Slowly, the cars proceeded to his interment at Woodlawn Cemetery, on Woodward Avenue, where it met Detroit's city limits.[9]

So ended C. L. Franklin's journey, nearly nine hundred miles to the north and east of the tiny Mississippi Delta hamlet where it had begun. But as befits one who rose so far, his influence struck deep and remains even today. C. L.'s complex personality often generated contradictory actions. His sensuous nature led him at times into situations that hurt others deeply. Yet that passionate engagement, when channeled from the pulpit, allowed him to touch many. His faith itself was anything but simplistic. Its biblical roots remained even as he moved away from a fundamentalist approach, and his insistence on faith's place in the world helped other recent migrants in urban America to define a more assertive place for themselves. He was indeed just a man, and his faults were writ large, one consequence of his fame. But withal, he defined for himself an inner sense of freedom against a harsh American backdrop and communicated that possibility to others in ways that changed lives.

Franklin preached to raise consciousness—of self and of one's relation to society. His faith encouraged individuals in his audiences to assert in private and in public that they were, in fact, somebody. This was Franklin's power. It remains his legacy. Even today, one cannot listen to a Franklin sermon without recognizing his effort to draw out each listener, to lift up each voice to new levels. C. L. Franklin understood the necessity for African Americans to sing in this strange land, despite the reaction that caused in many quarters. The act of singing laid claim to the land in the face of the very hostility that made it so strange. The result, a communal song of dissent and of affirmation, encouraged Babylonian and Israelite, black and white, to transform that land, and in the process to explore more fully the intimate ties of their common humanity.

More than a quarter of a century after bullets stilled his voice, C. L. Franklin's sermons continue to speak to us. Like people the world over, many Americans discover and define their political and social beliefs in their hallowed sites of worship. Franklin preached a particularly powerful version of this intermingling of the sacred and the secular, one deeply rooted in the African American church tradition. He spoke of tolerance as well as justice, of the centrality of faith as well as the specific responsibility of each individual to live those commitments in this world. He acknowledged reason's limits but never thought his faith required a rejection of his intellect. If his faith propelled him into the world, he never assumed it provided him with a blueprint for action; rather, his faith led him to explore in public the promise of an American democratic tradition. During his lifetime, C. L. of necessity shared his thoughts primarily with black Americans, so complete was the segregation in law and culture that then enveloped the American imagination. That specific time, thankfully, has passed, and as Americans continue to explore the boundaries between faith and political life, the career of this Mississippi-born preacher speaks powerfully to contemporary debates. C. L. Franklin's message soared above the limitations of his era, giving voice to the universal meaning at the center of the black church tradition. The overarching themes of his life's work remain relevant to even broader audiences decades later.

Acknowledgments

I have been enormously enriched by the warmth, friendship, and generosity of many in the Franklin family. Erma Franklin, C. L.'s oldest daughter, was enthusiastic about this book from the time we met, and that feeling deepened as we traversed together the complicated issues inherent in the relationship between the biographer and the subject's loved ones. Her sister Aretha did not sit for an interview; her autobiography, which appeared in late 1999, remains her account of her extraordinary family. She has been aware of my work, however, since my earliest visits to Detroit in 1998. Vaughn Franklin and his family were supportive and helpful, as was Carl Ellan Kelley. Brenda Corbett, a niece raised as a sister within the family, warmly welcomed me. Her insights and advice, in a formal interview and in innumerable conversations, were of great benefit, as was her constant encouragement. Together with her husband, James Corbett, they helped make my research trips to Detroit ever more enjoyable. Central also to this reception within the family has been Sabrina Garrett-Owens, Erma's daughter, and her husband, Oliver Owens. During my first extended research trip in Detroit, Sabrina sensed that I might be in need of a home-cooked meal and invited me to accompany her mother for Sunday dinner. She, too, has been tremendously supportive of my work and, with her husband, the Corbetts, and Erma while she lived, has welcomed me and my family into their lives.

I am also deeply appreciative of the support and encouragement of Jeff Todd Titon, an ethnomusicologist at Brown University. That he introduced me to Erma Franklin would have been enough to win my gratitude, but Jeff did much more. Years before I began my work, Jeff had conducted one long interview, in thirteen sessions between October 1977 and May 1978, with C. L., without question the most detailed and informative interview Franklin ever gave. Early on, Jeff provided me with a transcript of the interview and permission to use it in my book. Nor did he stop there. From his own collection he provided me with tapes (and his own transcriptions of them) of more than seventy of C. L.'s sermons. These acts of generosity by someone whose deep involvement with C. L. Franklin has produced articles and a book-length collection of sermons went far beyond scholarly collegiality. Jeff is a generous spirit, an insightful scholar, and a kind man whose support transcends anything I might have imagined. His compilation (in progress, in DVD format) of video- and audiotapes of Franklin sermons, interviews, and other material will be enormously useful for teaching as well as scholarship.

I have also been most fortunate in the institutional assistance I have received. Both the School of Industrial and Labor Relations and the American Studies Program at Cornell University have exceeded expectations time and again. Edward Lawler, Dean of the ILR School, and Frances Blau and Martin Wells, successive Directors of Research at the School, were consistently supportive, as has been R. Laurence Moore, director of the American Studies Program. A Mark C. Stevens travel grant from The Bentley Library at the University of Michigan was most helpful. Support of another kind came from the Advanced Institute for the Study of Religion at Yale University, where I had the good fortune to spend the academic year 1999–2000 as a senior fellow. Under the direction of Jon Butler and Harry Stout, the Institute did everything in its power to allow its fellows to devote their full attention to exploring Yale's rich library collections. It was a foundational year for me in understanding the task on which

I had embarked. That year was enhanced yet further by my colleagues at the Institute. Spending an academic year in an adjoining office to Cheryl Townsend Gilkes and Judith Weisenfeld was a gift. It was also at Yale that I first met Barbara Savage, a wonderful scholar whose comments on my work-in-progress have been invaluable. The kindness and encouragement of Reverend Frederick "Jerry" Streets, the University Chaplain at Yale, was a constant, but one event particularly stands out. Jerry and his wife, Annette, invited me to their home one evening where they had gathered seven African American ministers of various denominations, with a combined preaching experience that approached two hundred years. We listened together to a Franklin sermon, and then I listened, taking notes, with the occasional question, as these preachers talked for more than four hours about that sermon, their understanding of Franklin's preaching, and of his place in the broader African American religious tradition. It was an extraordinary evening, one that influenced my work deeply. My profound thanks to the Streets, and to their guests, for that opportunity.

Critical support of another kind came from those who invited me to speak about this project as it evolved. Within the Afro-Baptist community, I have been privileged to deliver talks and exchange ideas at the three most important churches Franklin himself led. Reverend Robert Smith Jr., the pastor of New Bethel Baptist Church since Franklin's death, has welcomed me to his pulpit three times for talks. On one occasion New Bethel sponsored, with the Cornell Alumni Club of Michigan, a social following the talk that allowed me to listen to audience reactions at greater length. He and his wife, Cynthia, have also been most welcoming to me and my family whenever we attended Sunday services at the church. The congregation of New Bethel has also been very supportive, and I deeply appreciate their welcoming spirit. I would particularly like to thank Mrs. Beverli Greenleaf, Deacon Milton Hall, Ms. Carolyn King, Deacon and Mrs. Wallace Malone, Deacon Hinken Perry, Mrs. Myra Perkins, and Mrs. Fannie Tyler. Reverends E. L. Branch, James Holley, Jerome Kirby, Samuel Billy Kyles, and Jasper Williams, all with deep connections to New Bethel even as they lead their own churches, took the time to instruct this novice in the richness of the Afro-Baptist tradition. My deep thanks to these men and women, and to all who allowed me to talk with them about C. L. Franklin.

In Buffalo, New York, Reverend William S. Wilson Jr., pastor of Friendship Baptist Church, twice invited me to speak before a combined audience of church members and Cornell University alumni. He, too, sponsored a social after the first talk, which allowed me to learn as he and others discussed my comments about their former pastor. In Memphis, Tennessee, Reverend Mary Moore, pastor of New Salem Baptist Church, and her husband, Ronald, were very generous. They made it possible for me to meet and interview seven men and women who had been church members during Franklin's tenure. Conversations with the Moores on the church's history were very informative and helpful.

Reverend Robert L. Johnson, director emeritus of the Cornell United Religious Work, and his successor, Reverend Kenneth I. Clarke Sr. and his wife, Reverend Yolanda Clarke, welcomed this project, discussed it with me, and brought me into the pulpit at Cornell's Sage Chapel three times in recent years for talks. Bob also made the initial contact for me that led to interviews with Reverend Bernard Lafayette and Congressman John Lewis.

Academic colleagues were also important. I was fortunate in having the chance to try out ideas before demanding audiences at Emory University; The College of the Holy Cross; Vanderbilt University; the Charles H. Wright Museum of African American History, Detroit; Yale University; University of Massachusetts, Amherst; New York University; Princeton University; Universita di Torino, Italy; and University of California, Berkeley. My Cornell colleagues endured me twice, first before a joint audience of faculty and alumni of the School of Industrial and Labor Relations and then when I gave the inaugural Rabinor Lecture in American Studies. Still others shared their insights on draft chapters or papers delivered at various conferences. I am most grateful to Robert Bussel, Jon Butler, Jacqueline Goldsby, Kenneth Clarke, Yolanda Clarke, Jefferson Cowie, Cheryl Townsend Gilkes, Leon F. Litwack, David O'Brien, Steven Pond, Albert Raboteau, Barbara Savage, Valerie Smith, Harry Stout, Frederick Streets, Clarence Walker, and Judith Weisenfeld. Ann Sullivan's insights on an early draft were enormously helpful. Professor Odie H. Tolbert of the University of Memphis shared with me a portion of his wide knowledge of the gospel tradition, and Ernestina Snead and Christopher Loy helped me think about the blues tones in Franklin's sermons. The archivists and librarians at the research libraries listed in the notes were unfailingly helpful. I would especially thank Julie Copenhagen, the head of interlibrary loan services at Cornell's magnificent Olin Library, and Mike Smith, director of the Walter P. Reuther Library at Wayne State University, and his staff, for their assistance. I benefited more than they may have realized from the work of my undergraduate research assistants in the School of Industrial and Labor Relations, and I am very grateful to William Adams, Palak Shah, Kevin Sills, Gayraud Townsend, and Kristina Yost.

The penultimate draft of this book received a thorough read from a group of friends in different scholarly disciplines. Their engagement with my work was humbling, their comments incisive and thought-provoking. If I have not taken all their suggestions, thinking through them has made this book immeasurably better. My sincere thanks to Glenn Altschuler, Jon Butler, Robert Hutchens, Harry Katz, Barbara Savage, Frederick Streets, and Jeff Todd Titon. This is now the second occasion I have had the privilege of working with Geoff Shandler in bringing a manuscript into book form. Now editor-in-chief and vice-president at Little, Brown, he remains, preeminently, a superb editor. His incisive questions and comments always demand attention. Working through them, even when I do not follow them, invariably sharpens my consciousness of my own efforts. That Geoff achieves this without ever forgetting whose book it is suggests another dimension of his skill and tact.

I have dedicated this book to two people who have had an enormous impact on me as well as the project. I only met Erma Franklin in January 1998, and less than five short years later, in September 2002, she passed, after a hard struggle with cancer. She possessed an intelligence that was matched only by her sharp wit, and her infectious embrace of life framed both. There was much that could have distanced us: experience and background, to be sure, but even more delicate was my role as the inquisitive biographer. That we overcame these complications at all was due to Erma. She acknowledged more than once that a biography that portrayed her father as a saint would lack all credibility, even as she probed to be certain that there was not lurking in me a sensationalist intent on vivid headlines. I have tried to keep faith with our conversations. Beyond this, we became good friends, and she became an important teacher of mine. At one level, of course, she was a source of information about her father, but she also prodded to be sure I understood him and his career within the broader African American context. Yet for all the importance of these discussions, her friendship gave me yet another gift in the last year of her life. To talk with her frequently, usually by phone, as she struggled with her own mortality was to witness a courageous human being. Her wit, her realism, and her commitment to live life until she could no more gave a definition to the terms *spirit* and *courage* that touched my very soul.

I have known Leon F. Litwack since September 1968, when I entered his graduate seminar in American history at the University of California, Berkeley. He was from the first an outstanding teacher and mentor, who urged me to push beyond where I then thought I could go. Within a few years we became friends as well, and that friendship has deepened across the decades. Leon is for me an exemplary model of the committed historian. His intellectual work, in a career that explores the centrality of race in American life, is deeply researched, carefully narrated, and beautifully written—and he has remained a bastion of thoughtful consistency against the cycles of enthusiasms that have swept through the academy in recent decades. My enduring image of Leon will always be of him at a podium, a black leather jacket framing him as a Jerry Garcia necktie sways to his motion, speaking from his mind, with his heart, seeking, like the good preacher he is, to raise our consciousness, to call us to a higher sense of our collective American possibilities. Words fail to convey his impact on me. I can say that I love him and thank him.

Finally, as has been true now for more than three decades, Ann's presence informs every page of this book, and my life.

NOTES

For publication facts of books and articles cited in the notes, see the bibliography.

The following abbreviations are used in the notes:

ACLU   American Civil Liberties Union of Michigan, Metropolitan Detroit Branch, Archives of Labor and Urban Affairs, Walter P. Reuther Library, Wayne State University, Detroit

ALUA   Archives of Labor and Urban Affairs, Walter P. Reuther Library, Wayne State University, Detroit

CAB   Claude A. Barnett Papers, Chicago Historical Society, Chicago

CCO   Circuit Clerk's Office, Bolivar County Courthouse, Cleveland, MS

CLF   Clarence LaVaughn Franklin

CLFP   Clarence LaVaughn Franklin Papers, in the personal possession of Erma Franklin and Sabrina Garrett-Owens

DCCR   Detroit Commission on Community Relations/Human Rights Department Collection, Archives of Labor and Urban Affairs, Walter P. Reuther Library, Wayne State University, Detroit

DUL   Detroit Urban League Papers, Bentley Historical Library, University of Michigan, Ann Arbor

EF   Erma Franklin

FAK   Francis A. Korngay Papers, Bentley Historical Library, University of Michigan, Ann Arbor

FBI   Federal Bureau of Investigation, C. L. Franklin File, Department of Justice, Washington, DC

GB   Gloria Brown Papers, Bentley Historical Library, University of Michigan, Ann Arbor

JHJ   Reverend Joseph H. Jackson Papers, Chicago Historical Society, Chicago

JPC   Jerome P. Cavanagh Collection, Archives of Labor and Urban Affairs, Walter P. Reuther Library, Wayne State University, Detroit

KJV   King James Version of the Bible

KMS   Kelly Miller Smith Papers, Vanderbilt University Special Collections, University Archives, Nashville

MDCC Metropolitan Detroit Council of Churches Collection, Archives of Labor and Urban Affairs, Walter P. Reuther Library, Wayne State University, Detroit

MHC   Michigan Historical Collection, Bentley Historical Library, University of Michigan, Ann Arbor

NAACP National Association for the Advancement of Colored People, Detroit Branch, Archives of Labor and Urban Affairs, Walter P. Reuther Library, Wayne State University, Detroit

NDI   New Detroit, Inc. Collection, Archives of Labor and Urban Affairs, Walter P. Reuther Library, Wayne State University, Detroit

NHB   Nannie H. Burroughs Papers, Library of Congress, Washington, DC

PRB   St. Peter's Rock Baptist Church File, Bolivar County Library, Cleveland, MS

RF   Rachel Franklin

RFW   Robert F. Williams Papers, Bentley Historical Library, University of Michigan, Ann Arbor

RRC   Robert R. Church Family Papers, Special Collections, Mississippi Valley Collection, University of Memphis Libraries, Memphis

SAO   Samuel Augustus Owen Papers, Special Collections, Mississippi Valley Collection, University of Memphis Libraries, Memphis

SEC   Second Baptist Church [Detroit] Papers, Bentley Historical Library, University of Michigan, Ann Arbor

UAW   United Automobile Workers of America

URL   Una Roberts Lawrence Collection, Southern Baptist Historical Library and Archives, Nashville

VF   Vaughn Franklin

WPR   Walter P. Reuther Collection, UAW President's Office, Archives of Labor and Urban Affairs, Walter P. Reuther Library, Wayne State University, Detroit

1. A Deep Longing

1. On CLF's role as a soloist at St. Peter's Rock, see interview with Reverend C. L. Franklin by Jeff Todd Titon, October 5, 1977, 8 (hereafter cited as CLF Interview). The full text of the hymn can be found in Bailey, "The Lined-Hymn Tradition in Black Mississippi Churches," 13–14. CLF's adult rendering of this hymn can be found on his Jewel album *The Eagle Stirs Her Nest;* another powerful version can be heard on Marion Williams, "The Moan," on her album *My Soul Looks Back.* On the tradition of lining out hymns, see Lincoln and Mamiya, *The Black Church in the African American Experience,* 354–56.

2.   The specific circumstances of the working lives are unknown; for a detailed description
      of the economic conditions facing black Mississippians in this era, see McMillen, *Dark
      Journey*, 111–94.

3.   Rachel Franklin, Certificate of Death, State of Michigan, recorded December 7, 1988,
      CLFP (copy); interview with Rachel Franklin by Jeff Todd Titon, 2–4 (hereafter cited
      as RF Interview); CLF Interview, October 5, 1977, 1; interview with Brenda Corbett
      by author, 1–2 (hereafter cited as Corbett Interview). Corbett, a granddaughter of
      Rachel and a niece of CLF who was reared with the Franklin family in Detroit after
      her mother died, noted that Rachel Franklin had an elder brother, Robert, who died in
      the 1960s in his sixties. See Corbett Interview, 10; see also Robbie McCoy, "The
      Church World," *Michigan Chronicle*, March 16, 1968, for a brief account of the death
      of another of Rachel's brothers, Alonzo Pittman

4.   RF Interview, 14; Corbett Interview, 12, 36.

5.   On marriage patterns in the Delta and in the rural South in general, see Powdermaker,
      After Freedom, 68, 143, 157, 197–205. Charles S. Johnson discusses the manner in
      which "stolen children," that is, children from premarital sexual relations, were incor-
      porated within existing families in Alabama. See Johnson, *Shadow of the Plantation*,
      66–68. Bluesman David "Honeyboy" Edwards recalled that, in 1927, while his mother
      raised a crop near Shaw, Mississippi, his father worked land further south in the Delta:
      "And my mother was pregnant when my daddy come home, pregnant by another man.
      But my daddy accepted her." Edwards, *The World Don't Owe Me Nothing*, 13, 18. In
      other cases, as many a blues song tells, a less understanding and more violent reaction
      ensued.

6.   CLF Interview, October 5, 1977, 1; Corbett Interview, 13.

7.   See Powdermaker, *After Freedom*, 43–55; McMillen, *Dark Journey, passim;* Grossman,
      Land of Hope, passim.

8.   Cobb, *The Most Southern Place on Earth*, 113–14; Morant, *Mississippi Minister,* 43–44;
      Harris, "Etiquette, Lynching, and Racial Boundaries in Southern History," 388 ff. For
      a comprehensive survey of racial violence and lynching throughout Mississippi, see
      McMillen, *Dark Journey*, 224–53.

9.   Cobb, *The Most Southern Place on Earth*, 90. On this process throughout the South see
      Litwack, *Been in the Storm So Long;* Litwack, *Trouble in Mind;* Foner, *Reconstruction.*

10.   Wright, *Black Boy (American Hunger)*, 70–71. In Ralph Ellison's novel *Invisible Man,*
      the narrator recalls an English professor who had explained, with references to James
      Joyce and William Butler Yeats, that "[w]e create the race by creating ourselves and
      then to our great astonishment we will have created something far more important: We
      will have created a culture" (354).

11.   Welding, "An Interview with Muddy Waters," 4–5; Gilkes, "The Black Church as a
      Therapeutic Community." For an excellent discussion of the relationship between blues
      and church cultures, see Titon, *Early Downhome Blues,* 17–20, 31–32.

12.   Powdermaker, *After Freedom*, 143–64; Johnson, *Shadow of the Plantation*, 33.

13.   CLF Interview, October 5, 1977, 2; telephone interview with Brenda Corbett by au-
      thor (hereafter cited as Corbett Interview (telephone)); RF Interview, 12; interview
      with Carl Ellan Kelley by author, 2 (hereafter cited as Kelley Interview).

14.   McMillen, *Dark Journey*, 302–3; CLF Interview, October 5, 1977, 1; Harris, "Eti-

quette, Lynching, and Racial Boundaries in Southern History," *passim;* Wright, *Black Boy (American Hunger),* 71; Archer, *Growing Up Black in Rural Mississippi,* 19, 25–26. Some twenty million U.S. Army personnel records for soldiers who served between 1912 and 1959 were lost in a fire at the St. Louis branch of the National Archives in 1973. No index exists for the records that survived. The Mississippi State Archives in Jackson has index cards for men who served in the World War I era, but they contain no personal or family data other than names and places of enlistment. Telephone conversation with Ms. Viv Barrett, St. Louis National Archives, by author, October 4, 2000; telephone conversation with reference librarian, Mississippi State Archives, by author, October 4, 2000.

15.   CLF Interview, October 5, 1977, 3–4.

16.   Ibid., 1; interview with Harry Kincaid by author, 4 (hereafter cited as Kincaid Interview). Mr. Kincaid refused to be drawn out in more specific detail. On RF's reluctance to talk about Willie Walker, see RF Interview, 14; Corbett Interview, 3–4.

17.   CLF Interview, October 5, 1977, 1; RF Interview, 15. Office of the Director, United States Bureau of the Census to the Social Security Administration, Re: Clarence LaVaughn Franklin to Erma Franklin, October 26, 1979, Detroit (copy), CLFP, officially attests that in the manuscript schedules for the census in Sunflower County, Mississippi, as of January 1920, Clarence Walker, age four, is listed as a stepson in the family of Henry and Rachel Franklin.

18.   Cobb, *The Most Southern Place on Earth,* 113–14; Mills, *This Little Light of Mine,* 29–31. The quotes are from the *Vicksburg Evening Post* as cited in Mills.

19.   Evans, *Big Road Blues,* 169–70, 175–76, 194; Cobb, *The Most Southern Place on Earth,* 280–81, 291; Barry, *Rising Tide,* 101–2; Edwards, *The World Don't Owe Me Nothing,* 3–4, 245, 252; U.S. Bureau of the Census, *Negroes in the United States, 1920–1932,* 74–76; U.S. Bureau of the Census, *Fourteenth Census of the United States, 1920,* vol. 3, *Population,* 533–40. For lyrics of "Pea Vine Blues," see Taft, *Blues Lyric Poetry,* 211–12; Palmer, *Deep Blues,* 53–54; Patton can be heard singing the song on his album *King of the Delta Blues.* On Patton's influence on the Delta blues, see Evans, *Big Road Blues,* 176 ff.; Titon, *Early Downhome Blues, passim;* Palmer, *Deep Blues,* 48–92; Pareles, "Pops Staples, Patriarch of the Staples Singers, Dies at 85"; Nager, *Memphis Beat,* 73; Stephen Calt and Don Kent, liner notes to Patton, *King of the Delta Blues.*

20.   King, *Blues All Around Me,* 17. Robert Palmer wrote in *Deep Blues,* "Only a man who understands his worth and believes in his freedom sings as if nothing else matters" (75). On the blues in broad perspective, see Ellison, *Shadow and Act;* Murray, *Stomping the Blues;* Jones, *Blues People.* For an important discussion of the relationship within African American culture between sacred and secular music in the 1920s, see Higginbotham, "Rethinking Vernacular Culture."

21.   U.S. Bureau of the Census, *Negroes in the United States, 1920–1932,* 238, 592, 650; Powdermaker, *After Freedom,* 81–92; Cobb, *The Most Southern Place on Earth,* 98–112; Oshinsky, *"Worse Than Slavery,"* 114–21; Edwards, *The World Don't Owe Me Nothing,* 7–8.

22.   Hamer, "To Praise Our Bridges," 21; see also Mills, *This Little Light of Mine,* 7–9. For a similar sentiment from an Alabama black sharecropper, see Rosengarten, *All God's Dangers,* 26–27.

23. For evidence of adoption see Office of the Director, United States Bureau of the Census to Social Security Administration, Re: Clarence LaVaughn Franklin to Erma Franklin, October 26, 1979, Detroit (copy), CLFP, which affirms that in the manuscript census for Bolivar County, MS, as of April 1, 1930, Clarence E.[sic] Franklin, age fourteen [sic] is listed as a stepson in the family of Henry and Rachel Franklin; CLF Interview, October 5, 1977, 1–2; CLF Interview, October 7, 1977, 38. For contemporary information on the disastrous state of education for blacks in the county, see Powdermaker, After Freedom, 307–17; for Fannie Lou Hamer's memories of her parents' efforts to educate their children, despite the truncated school semester and the fact that "most of the time we didn't have clothes to wear," see Hamer, "To Praise Our Bridges," 323; see also Marsh, God's Long Summer, 11.

24. Hamer, "To Praise Our Bridges," 322–23; Mills, This Little Light of Mine, 11–12; Evans, Big Road Blues, 190–92. On Clarksdale see U.S. Bureau of the Census, Fifteenth Census of the United States: 1930, vol. 3, pt. 1, Population, 1281.

25. Grossman, Land of Hope, pt. 1; Evans, Big Road Blues, 193.

26. Evans, Big Road Blues, 193; RF Interview, 15.

27. CLF Interview, October 5, 1977, 2–6; U.S. Bureau of the Census, Fifteenth Census of the United States: 1930, vol. 3, pt. 1, Population, 1282–83; Sillers, History of Bolivar County, Mississippi, 9.

28. Rachel Franklin stated that she and her husband owned some forty acres of land in Mississippi, and that may be accurate, but there is no evidence to support it. Her son mentioned his family's sharecropping and renting and explicitly stated that his stepfather never owned land. See RF Interview, 20; CLF Interview, October 5, 1977, 17–18.

29. CLF Interview, October 5, 1977, 4, 6, 18; CLF Interview, October 7, 1977, 34–35, 37.

30. Interview with Reverend Ivory James by author, 2–4 (hereafter cited as James Interview); interview with Cleo Myles by author, 15–16 (hereafter cited as Myles Interview); CLF Interview, October 7, 1977, 20.

31. CLF Interview, October 5, 1977, 14–17. On CLF's preaching in the fields as a boy, see CLF Interview, November 15, 1977, 156; RF Interview, 6; Corbett Interview, 14–15; interview with Erma Franklin by author, 6 (hereafter cited as EF Interview).

32. Lawrence Lightfoot, Balm in Gilead, 202; CLF Interview, October 5, 1977, 7–8, 12, 17; Myles Interview, 10–11; Cobb, The Most Southern Place on Earth, 80–81; Thompson, "Mississippi," 200–201, n. 17. The reference to Mound Bayou is from J. Egert Allen, "Mississippi—Home of the 'Sun-Kissed' Folks," The Messenger 5, no. 9 (September 1923), as reprinted in Lutz and Ashton, These "Colored" United States, 177.

33. CLF Interview, October 5, 1977, 10, 16; Wright, Black Boy (American Hunger), 75–79, 161–62. See Palmer, Deep Blues, 86, for an account of blacks in Cleveland, Mississippi, on a Saturday in 1930.

34. On these images in blues songs see Oliver, The Meaning of the Blues; Jones, Blues People; Palmer, Deep Blues. The history of the automobile in Mississippi, and the development of the state's highway system during this decade can be followed in Hataway, "The Development of the Mississippi State Highway System," esp. 286, 294; Weeks, Cleveland, 122–23, 129; Lessig, "'Out of the Mud,'" 56–59; Ownby, American Dreams in Mississippi, 85–86.

2. ATTEMPTING HIS IMAGINATION

1. CLF Interview, October 5, 1977, 2–3, 10–11; CLF Interview, October 7, 1977, 38. On the segregated schools in Bolivar County in the 1920s and the 1927 decision of the United States Supreme Court [*Gong Lum v. Rice*] that upheld the practice, see Kluger, *Simple Justice*, 120–21.

2. CLF Interview, October 5, 1977, 11; RF Interview, 10–11.

3. CLF, *Hannah, The Ideal Mother*. See Kluger, *Simple Justice*, chapter 14, for a discussion of psychologist Kenneth Clark's famous experiments with dolls in determining the impact of segregation on black children in the context of the Supreme Court's 1954 decision *Brown v. Board of Education*. A contemporary critique of those experiments can be found in Scott, *Contempt and Pity*, esp. chaps. 6, 7.

4. *Souvenir Booklet of the 82nd Anniversary and Homecoming of the St. Peter's Rock Baptist Church*, n.p.; St. Paul's Missionary Church, *A Century with Christ*, 1.

5. *Souvenir Booklet of the 82nd Anniversary and Homecoming of the St. Peter's Rock Baptist Church*; untitled typescript (a brief history of St. Peter's Rock), n.p., PRB; Myles Interview, 18–19; CLF Interview, October 7, 1977, 31–33. For a discussion of church as "the highlight of the week [because] it was where the music got all over my body and made me wanna jump," see King, *Blues All Around Me*, 15–16. King attended the Church of God in Christ, a Sanctified denomination, as a youth in Indianola.

6. Myles Interview, 2–5; CLF Interview, October 5, 1977, 11; CLF Interview, October 7, 1977, 26, 29.

7. CLF Interview, October 7, 1977, 22, 26; CLF, "Jesus at Bethesda."

8. Myles Interview, 4, 7–8; CLF Interview, October 7, 1977, 27–28. For a similar description of an Afro-Baptist service in Florida a decade earlier, see Thurman, *With Head and Heart*, 18–19.

9. Edwards, *The World Don't Owe Me Nothing*, 12; CLF Interview, October 7, 1977, 22.

10. CLF Interview, October 7, 1977, 22, 27–28; Thurman, *With Head and Heart*, 21. Recalling her Mississippi youth, Margaret Morgan Lawrence wrote in 1975 that "in the crisis of death, adolescence, or when a husband ran away, the black people I know in the urban and rural Mississippi of fifty years ago turned to religion for comfort in the literal sense of the word; that is through religion they 'joined' their strength, body, mind, and soul." Cited in Lawrence Lightfoot, *Balm in Gilead*, 13–14. For a broader discussion of African American religious cosmology, see Mitchell, *Black Belief*, 125 ff. Fluker, "The Failure of Ethical Leadership," 11–12, explores the meaning of the oral tradition within a religious framework.

11. Martin Luther King Jr., "An Autobiography of Religious Development" (1950), in Carson, *The Papers of Martin Luther King, Jr.*, 1:361. See also Reverend Fred Shuttlesworth's account of his "gradual conversion" within family and church communities in Manis, *A Fire You Can't Put Out*, 27–28.

12. CLF Interview, October 7, 1977, 27, 29; Myles Interview, 10–11.

13. CLF Interview, October 5, 1977, 12, 13, 14; King, "An Autobiography of Religious Development," in Carson, *The Papers of Martin Luther King, Jr.*, 1:362. Bluesman John Lee Hooker, who grew up near Clarksdale during the 1920s, remembered a more turbulent message instilled by his ministerial father. *"[Y]ou just got to stay in your place,"* he

said, recalling his father's tone. "You can't do *that*, you can't do *that*. I can't tell you just what he said—this word and that word—but he said, 'You can *not* mess with these people.' He kept pounding it into our heads." See Murray, *Boogie Man*, 21–22.

14. Cobb, *The Most Southern Place on Earth*, 114.

15. King, *Blues All Around Me*, 51. As a young boy in Georgia, Martin Luther King Sr. also witnessed a lynching that left him with "terrible dreams" and, for a time, a ferocious hatred of whites. See King, *Daddy King*, 30–31.

16. CLF Interview, October 7, 1977, 28, 38; James Interview, 18–19, 26; *Souvenir Booklet of the 82nd Anniversary and Homecoming of the St. Peter's Rock Baptist Church*, n.p.; Thurman, *With Head and Heart*, 18–19.

17. Pops Staples, "Down in Mississippi," *Peace to the Neighborhood*. On the change in landowning patterns among Delta blacks, see McMillen, *Dark Journey*, chap. 4, esp. 113–15; Ownby, *American Dreams in Mississippi*, 77; Cobb, *The Most Southern Place on Earth*, 112, 186; Barry, *Rising Tide*, 123. Ball is cited in Cobb, *The Most Southern Place on Earth*, 185–86. For a contemporary account of the hard times blacks endured across the South, see Nannie H. Burroughs to Una Roberts Lawrence, July 2, 1934, Washington, DC, URL.

18. CLF Interview, October 5, 1977, 17–18.

19. In Mississippi in 1936, of a total of 3,638 black churches of all denominations, 2,391 (66 percent) were Baptists; of the 415,182 black Mississippians reported as church members, 322,362 (78 percent) were Baptists. See U.S. Bureau of the Census, *Religious Bodies: 1936*, 1:83. National figures for denomination can be found in ibid., vol. 2, pt. 1, 144. The National Baptist Convention's own figures for members in 1940 are broadly consistent with these numbers. See National Baptist Convention, *Proceedings of the Sixtieth Annual Session of the National Baptist Convention, 1940*, 135. On Reverend Perkins see Myles Interview, 13; James Interview, 2; CLF Interview, October 7, 1977, 39–40, 42; CLF Interview, November 15, 1977, 159; interview with Reverend Benjamin Hooks by author, 13 (hereafter cited as Hooks Interview). Erma Franklin recalls her father discussing Perkins's "interpretation of the Bible and his willingness to share his spiritual or religious knowledge with my dad. And just the way he carried himself as a minister. And he was one of the ones that encouraged my dad." See EF Interview, 7.

20. RF Interview, 6, 17; CLF Interview, November 15, 1977, 156–57. Corroboration of these memories from stories told throughout her childhood can be found in EF Interview, 6; Corbett Interview, 14–15.

21. RF Interview, 9, 17; CLF Interview, October 7, 1977, 39; CLF Interview, November 15, 1977, 159–60; Corbett Interview, 13–14.

22. RF Interview, 20; CLF Interview, October 7, 1977, 39, 40; John 9:1–5 (KJV).

23. CLF Interview, October 7, 1977, 40, 43; CLF Interview, November 15, 1977, 157. In contrast his proud mother thought the sermon was "very good" and remembered that during it she "[s]houted out, you know, when the spirit strike me, I got to shout." RF Interview, 7.

24. Cobb, *The Most Southern Place on Earth*, 281; King, *Blues All Around Me*, 20–22, 23, 33, 77; Harrell, *Varieties of Southern Evangelicism*, 241; Welding, "An Interview with Muddy Waters," 4–5; Myles Interview, 22. The rich mix of sacred and secular blues recorded by Patton between 1929 and 1934 can be heard on Patton, *King of the Delta*

Blues. For an insightful discussion of the social context of the phonograph in the Delta, see Titon, *Early Downhome Blues,* 281–86. Many blacks from varied social backgrounds staunchly opposed the intermingling of sacred and secular music. See David Evans's discussion in *Big Road Blues,* 106–8, and James Interview, *passim.* In their liner notes to Patton, *King of the Delta Blues,* Stephen Calt and Don Kent note that "some blues musicians spoke of being wary of performing gospel songs that were counter to the life they were leading. Son House reports Willie Brown was afraid of being struck by lightning if he performed a religious piece. Patton had no problem getting 'in the spirit' and often performs with more conviction than other guitar-evangelists."

25. Newman, "Entrepreneurs of Profits and Pride," 207; Titon, *Early Downhome Blues,* 200, 281–86; Oliver, *Songsters and Saints,* 140, 145, 160; Wolff et al., *You Send Me,* 20; Murray, *Boogie Man,* 24–25; Cobb, *The Most Southern Place on Earth,* 281. For an important, perceptive analysis of African American music and class affiliations, see Higginbotham, "Rethinking Vernacular Culture." There was some suspicion of the phonograph, however. Bluesman Jasper Love remembered that in the Delta of the 1920s, "Some black listeners felt that they [phonograph machines] were the white man's way of spying on blacks in their homes and refused to talk when a record was playing." Cited in Ferris, *Blues from the Delta,* 8–9.

26. CLF Interview, October 7, 1977, 35–6; CLF Interview, October 12, 1977, 55. CLF's eldest daughter, Erma, has said of her father's attitudes toward sacred and secular music, "Yes, he thought that God blessed you with this talent, you know, he didn't say you had to use it in a certain capacity." EF Interview, 30. A selection of Gates's first recorded sermons can be heard on Gates, *Complete Recorded Works in Chronological Order.* Margaret Morgan Lawrence also recalled that her relatives in Mississippi during the 1920s had an "extensive collection of records for that time and place, a collection that embraced the field from Mamie Smith's blues to Enrico Caruso." See Lawrence Lightfoot, *Balm in Gilead,* 131–32.

27. CLF Interview, November 1, 1977, 97–98. See, for example, Blind Lemon Jefferson, "Match Box Blues" (1927) and Roosevelt Sykes, "Skeet and Garret" (1929), which can be found in Taft, *Blues Lyric Poetry,* 128, 262, respectively. For other examples of the power of folk tales concerning boxers such as Joe Louis, see Remnick, *King of the World,* 227; interview with Robbie McCoy by author, 6–7 (hereafter cited as McCoy Interview).

28. Bo Diddley is quoted in Collis, *The Story of Chess Records,* 112–13. Pops Staples recalled similar tensions at home as well, see ibid., 53. The range of Patton's music can be heard on Patton, *King of the Delta Blues.* For discussions of the interconnection between the blues and religious experience, see Harris, *The Rise of Gospel Blues,* esp. 154–55; McCarthy, "The Afro-American Sermon and the Blues"; Edwards, *The World Don't Owe Me Nothing, passim;* Rosenberg, *Can These Bones Live?* esp. 62; Mitchell, *Black Belief,* 145–46. Dorsey is quoted in Harris, *The Rise of Gospel Blues,* 96–97, 98–99. Dorsey as Georgia Tom can he heard backing Ma Rainey on nine 1925 recordings on Ma Rainey, *The Paramounts Chronologically;* he can be heard with Tampa Red on eight sides recorded between 1928 and 1934 on Tampa Red, *The Guitar Wizard.* Dickinson is quoted in Titon, *Early Downhome Blues,* 287.

29. RF Interview, 7–8; King, *Blues All Around Me,* 58. Works that have been particularly

helpful in considering the complex commingling of sacred and secular expressions include Harris, *The Rise of Gospel Blues;* Higginbotham, "Rethinking Vernacular Culture"; Murray, *Stomping the Blues;* Ellison, *Shadow and Act;* and the letters of Ellison and Murray collected in Murray and Callahan, *Trading Twelves,* esp. 166.

30. CLF Interview, October 5, 1977, 17–18. Franklin's memory for dates of events that occurred decades earlier is not always precise. While the length of time he spent in Shelby, for example, may be in question, the order of his travels and experiences between ages 16 and 22 is fairly certain, even if the exact timing is still in question, when his interviews of October 5, 7, and 21, 1977, are read together. He made a generally successful effort to order the experiences in his interview of October 7, 1977, 19–20.

31. CLF Interview, October 5, 1977, 18–19; CLF Interview, May 17, 1978, 254.

32. CLF Interview, October 7, 1977, 40–41. Dorothy Swan recalls the power of CLF's early preaching in Mississippi in Titon, "Reverend C. L. Franklin," 94.

33. CLF Interview, October 5, 1977, 19. See also Powdermaker, *After Freedom, passim;* Johnson, *Shadow of the Plantation, passim;* Johnson, *Growing Up in the Black Belt,* 224–41.

34. Kotlowitz, *The Other Side of the River,* 229, 260–70; Dawson, *Negro Folktales in Michigan,* 7. In 1934 Marcus Cooley, a black migrant from Iowa, was said to have hung himself in jail after being arrested by Benton Harbor police for parole violation, an incident many African Americans considered murder. See Kotlowitz, *The Other Side of the River,* 263.

35. CLF Interview, October 21, 1977, 84–85; CLF Interview, November 15, 1977, 156; "The Preacher with the Golden Voice," 41; Nelis J. Saunders, "A Born Leader," *Michigan Chronicle,* May 22, 1965. Some of the dates in the Saunders article are not correct.

36. See James Interview, 5, for a discussion of his experiences as a local preacher in Bolivar County in the 1920s and 1930s.

37. CLF Interview, October 21, 1977, 85; CLF Interview, October 12, 1977, 43–44, 52. On the continued impact of Perkins on CLF, see EF Interview, 7; Hooks Interview, 13; interview with Reverend E. L. Branch by author, 27–28 (hereafter cited as E. L. Branch Interview).

38. M. K. Young to Erma Franklin, October 5, 1979, CLFP. Young, an employee of the Social Security Administration, a division of the federal Department of Health, Education, and Welfare, sent Erma Franklin at her request a Certificate of Contents of Document(s) or Record(s) affirming CLF's marriage to Alene Gaines. The information Young provided lists Gaines as twenty-five but erroneously gives CLF's age as twenty-one, when he would have been still three months shy of his twentieth birthday. See also the couple's marriage license in Marriage Record Book, Bolivar County, Mississippi, 2d District, Book 44, 474, CCO. I want to express my appreciation to a Bolivar County clerk, known to me only as Barbara, who confirmed this information for me during a phone conversation July 2, 2003.

39. See Lincoln and Mamiya, *The Black Church in the African American Experience,* 98, and Reid, *The Negro Baptist Ministry, passim,* for a discussion of the education level of rural black ministers.

40. Federal Writers Project, *Mississippi,* 351–53. On the Percy family see Cobb, *The Most Southern Place on Earth, passim.*

41. CLF Interview, October 7, 1977, 20; CLF Interview, October 12, 1977, 46–48, 52. Richard Wright recalled of his Mississippi youth a similar intensity: "I hungered for books, new ways of looking and seeing. It was not a matter of believing or disbelieving what I read, but of feeling something new, of being affected by something that made the look of the world different." Cited in Wilson, *Judgment and Grace in Dixie*, 124.

42. CLF Interview, October 12, 1977, 53–55. For a different perception of this relation between religion and politics in the black South in 1935, see the report of Noble Y. Beall, a white minister affiliated with the Southern Baptist Convention. After spending a year visiting and interviewing black Baptists throughout the South, Beall concluded that "the American Negroes are keenly conscious of their slavery, emancipation, suppression, and disfranchisement, [and] they are putting forth every effort to bring themselves up to equality with White Americans." Beall complained that they were confusing social themes and a faith-based message and thus were "prostituting the churches and their organizations for illegitimate ends." See Beall, "Real Dangers of the American Baptist Negroes," June 15, 1935, 1, Box 1, folder 9, 1, URL.

43. CLF Interview, May 17, 1978, 253; CLF Interview, October 12, 1977, 44, 51.

44. In black Mississippi churches in 1936, there were ten women for every six men. That ratio is based on all black worshipers in the state; since Afro-Baptists comprised 77 percent of that total, their ratio may have been even higher. See U.S. Bureau of the Census, *Religious Bodies: 1936*, 1:83, 864–65; King, *Daddy King*, 53–54.

45. Telephone interview with Semial Siggers by author (hereafter cited as Siggers Interview); Silver and Moeser, *The Separate City*, 52. For a brief biography of Nat D. Williams, one of Booker T. Washington High School's outstanding teachers between 1930 and 1972, see Cantor, *Wheelin' on Beale*, 34–35. Lucie Campbell's career at the school is discussed in Walker, "Lucie E. Campbell Williams," 59–60. In 1933 only 18 percent of black children enrolled in Memphis schools attended either of the high schools; see Memphis, *Benefits and Opportunities for Colored Citizens of Memphis*, 16.

46. On the city's black culture at this time see Lornell, *"Happy in the Service of the Lord,"* 123–5; Lee, *Beale Street*, 13, and *passim*; and below, chapter 3. Muddy Waters is quoted in McKee and Chisenhall, *Beale Black and Blue*, 233. John Lee Hooker, who grew up in the Clarksdale area to become a famous Detroit-based bluesman in the late 1940s, expressed similar attitudes about Memphis; see Murray, *Boogie Man*, 24, 31.

47. Siggers Interview; interview with Vaughn Franklin by author, 1–3, 5–6 (hereafter cited as VF Interview). On black Memphis during the 1930s see Biles, *Memphis in the Great Depression*, chap. 5.

48. RF Interview, 19; CLF Interview, October 12, 1977, 56; CLF Interview, November 8, 1977, 142.

49. Marriage Record Book, Bolivar County, Mississippi, 2d District, Book 47, 473, CCO. There was some question about Barbara Siggers's actual age. Her eldest daughter, Erma Franklin, in a telephone communication with me on August 15, 2000, gave her birth date as 1917, which corresponds with the date of birth (June 29, 1917) given on her death certificate. This would have made her just shy of nineteen when she married; CLF, forty-one years later, remembered his wife as twenty when they married; the marriage license lists her as twenty-five. The license does list CLF's age accurately, how-

ever. See CLF Interview, November 8, 1977, 142; Barbara Franklin, Certificate of Death, New York State Department of Health, March 7, 1952 (copy), CLFP.

50. Douglass Alumni Association, *Douglass Heritage*, 6–7, 17, 19, 21–27. C. L. Franklin (misnamed Charles L.) was also listed as pastor of First Baptist Bungalow in "Directory of Churches, Missions, and Religious Institutions of Shelby County, National Baptist Convention U.S.A. Inc. Bodies (Colored)," June 25, 1940, typescript, n.p., Box 11-A, SAO.

51. CLF Interview, November 8, 1977, 141; EF Interview, 1; VF Interview, 27, 42.

52. VF Interview, 43.

53. Interview with Reverend Samuel Billy Kyles by author, 1 (hereafter cited as Kyles Interview); Pareles, "Pops Staples"; Pops Staples, "Down in Mississippi," *Peace to the Neighborhood.*

54. *Polk's Memphis (Shelby County, Tenn.), City Directory, 1939*, 330, 1484, 1487; Biles, *Memphis in the Great Depression*, 91; CLF Interview, October 12, 1977, 53; VF Interview, 27–28.

55. Myles Interview, 29.

3. Moving On Up

1. U.S. Bureau of the Census, *A Statistical Abstract Supplement: City and County Data Book, 1949*, 351, 375. Blacks in Memphis numbered more than 121,000 individuals out of a total population of 292,942. In contrast, New York, with a population (7,454,995 in 1940) more than twenty-five times that of Memphis, had a black population (477,119) just less than four times as large; Chicago's total population (3,396,808) was more than eleven times that of Memphis while the black population (278,532) was just over twice as large. Savannah, Georgia, had a total population of 95,996, 45 percent of whom were black. Ibid., 351, 363.

2. Memphis Jug Band, "Cocaine Habit Blues" (1930), on the collection *Walk Right In: The Essential Recordings of Memphis Blues;* Taft, *Blues Lyric Poetry*, 223; Handy as cited in Nager, *Memphis Beat*, 29. On Memphis jug bands at this time see Cohen, *Nothing But the Blues*, 64–65. The full lyrics to Handy's song can be found on the American Memory Web site, www.memory.loc.gov, as of October 15, 2001. On Memphis and crime see Dickerson, *Goin' Back to Memphis*, 51, 58; Nager, *Memphis Beat*, 25–29; Coppock, *Memphis Memoirs*, 101; McIlwaine, *Memphis*, 313. For an account of the rise in the city's murder rate during the first decades of the twentieth century, see Miller, *Memphis during the Progressive Era*, 92–93.

3. CLF Interview, October 12, 1977, 53.

4. On Love see *Memphis World*, July 9, 1943, and May 12, 1944; on Owen see Thurman, *With Head and Heart*, 17, 57; Williams, *Biographical Directory of Negro Ministers*, 390; on Fuller see *National Baptist Voice*, January 15, 1942, 6; Walker, "Dialectic Tensions in T. O. Fuller's Historical Writings," 21–22; interview with Reverend W. C. Holmes by Reverend Randolph Meade Walker, McWherter Library Special Collections, 1–6 (hereafter cited as Holmes Interview); on Jenkins see *Memphis World*, June 25, 1943; Johnson, *1943 Year Book and Directory*, 136–37; on Brewster see Boyer, "William Her-

bert Brewster," *passim;* Boyer, "Contemporary Gospel," 140–43; on Perkins in Memphis see Perkins, *Rev. Benjamin J. Perkins Answers the Erroneous Statement;* Lee, *Beale Street,* 163–64; interview with Reverend Joseph Lee Burkley by Charles W. Crawford, McWherter Library Special Collections, 1, 7 (hereafter cited as Burkley Interview); Hooks Interview, 13–14.

5.   Capers, *The Biography of a River Town,* 5, 22–23, 107–9, 164; Brock, "Memphis's Nymphs Du Pave," 58; Berkeley, *"Like a Plague of Locusts,"* chap.1.

6.   Johnson and Russell, *Memphis,* 1; Federal Writers Project, *Tennessee,* 51–52, 210; Capers, *The Biography of a River Town,* 36, 164; Corlew, *Tennessee, a Short History,* 149, 157, 325, 366–68; Berkeley, *"Like a Plague of Locusts,"* 16, 21, 103–6.

7.   Young, *Standard History of Memphis, Tennessee,* 170–84 ; Capers, *The Biography of a River Town,* 107–9, 164, 183–205; Nager, *Memphis Beat,* 18–25.

8.   See McKee and Chisenhall, *Beale Black and Blue,* 74; McIlwaine, *Memphis,* 319; Murray, *The Negro Handbook, 1944,* 19; Johnson, *1943 Year Book and Directory,* 9, 11; Sigafoos, *Cotton Row to Beale Street,* 140; Capers, *The Biography of a River Town,* 164; U.S. Bureau of the Census, *Sixteenth Census of the United States: 1940,* vol. 2, pt. 6, *Population: Characteristics,* 689, 709–12; Leroy Carr, "Memphis Town" (1930), in Taft, *Blues Lyric Poetry,* 46. Memphis in 1940 was the eighth largest urban black population; in comparison Detroit, ranked sixth, had 149,119 black residents, who comprised only 9.2 percent of that city's total population. See Murray, *The Negro Handbook, 1944,* 19.

9.   Biles, *Memphis in the Great Depression,* 90, 94–95; Daniel, *Lost Revolutions,* 123; Silver and Moeser, *The Separate City,* 31–33, 38–39, 131–32; Sigafoos, *Cotton Row to Beale Street,* 172. In the postwar years the still segregated Lauderdale Houses became the home of a poor white family from Tupelo, Mississippi, Vernon and Gladys Presley, and their young son, Elvis. See Guralnick, *Last Train to Memphis,* 33–34. On the creation of Memphis through annexation of adjoining lands, see Capers, *The Biography of a River Town,* 125.

10.   Hooks as quoted in McBee, "The Memphis Red Sox Stadium," 162.

11.   Interview with Alma Hawes Black by author, 41, 42 (hereafter cited as Black Interview); telephone interview with Alma Hawes Black by author (hereafter cited as Black Interview (telephone)); [Reverend Mary Moore], "History of New Salem Baptist Church from 1904 to the 1980s," (typescript in author's possession), 1.

12.   Edwards, *The World Don't Owe Me Nothing,* 59–60; Biles, *Memphis in the Great Depression,* 92–93; McIlwaine, *Memphis,* 312; Sigafoos, *Cotton Row to Beale Street,* 192, 195. According to the 1940 federal census, among employed black men, 58 percent occupied unskilled or service jobs; another 24 percent were listed in a broad, semiskilled category ("operatives and kindred works"); and 9.4 percent were craftsmen. Among black women, 83.7 percent were recorded as unskilled or service workers. See U.S. Bureau of the Census, *Sixteenth Census of the United States: 1940,* vol. 3, pt. 5, *Population: The Labor Force,* 374–80.

13.   Black Interview, 6, 41; interview with Julia Ann Carbage by author, 14 (hereafter cited as Carbage Interview); Black Interview (telephone).

14.   Interview with Lizzie Moore by author, 14 (hereafter cited as Lizzie Moore Interview); Black Interview (telephone); interview with Nettie Hubbard by author, 15 (hereafter

cited as Hubbard Interview); Carbage Interview, 14, 44; CLF Interview, October 12, 1977, 53.

15. For a concise, illuminating discussion of the chanted sermon, see Raboteau, *A Fire in the Bones*, 141–51.

16. Hooks Interview, 9–10; interview with Ernest Donelson by author, 8–9, 15 (hereafter cited as Donelson Interview); interview with Catherine Hawes Rogers by author, 11 (hereafter cited as Rogers Interview).

17. On the educational level of black southern clergy see Una Roberts Lawrence, "General Statistics Concerning Negroes in SBC Territory," typescript (copy), 1937, in Box 4, folder 15, URL; Reid, *The Negro Baptist Ministry*, 71, 94 and *passim;* Mays and Nicholson, *The Negro's Church*, 249 and *passim*. Lee is quoted in Harkins, *Metropolis of the American Nile*, 125. On the *Memphis World* see Shannon, "Tennessee," 341; Bunche, *The Political Status of the Negro in the Age of FDR*, 501. Martin Luther King Sr. recounts a painful experience as a young rural preacher new to Atlanta when a congregation refused to offer him any encouragement, so dismayed were they by his rural expressions and manners; see King, *Daddy King*, 55–57.

18. CLF Interview, May 3, 1978, 204.

19. Hooks Interview, 31. On CLF's intellectual drive, see EF Interview, 12; Kincaid Interview, 28; for comments by New Salem members see Donelson Interview, 15; Black Interview (telephone). On Howe see Howe Institute School of Religion, *Commencement Program* (1944); Howe Institute, "Announcements," (typescript, 1945), Box 9, SAO; Howe Institute, *Announcements* (Memphis, 1948); *National Baptist Voice,* January 15, 1942. On Holmes see Holmes Interview, esp. 1–6; Williams, *Biographical Directory of Negro Ministers*, 246.

20. CLF Interview, October 7, 1977, 20; CLF Interview, October 14, 1977, 57, 59. On LeMoyne see Federal Writers Project, *Tennessee*, 227.

21. CLF Interview, May 3, 1978, 204–5.

22. CLF Interview, October 12, 1977, 53; Hooks Interview, 2. The comment about Fuller is from Holmes Interview, 2, 3. On the Baptist Ministers Alliance and the tension with the competing Baptist Ministers Union, see Baptist Ministers Union, *Facts Truthfully Presented, passim;* Perkins, *Rev. Benjamin J. Perkins Answers the Erroneous Statement, passim;* letter to the editor, *Memphis Commercial Appeal,* May 8, 1933.

23. CLF Interview, May 3, 1978, 205; Hooks Interview, 14–15, 28–29. Hooks insisted that CLF remained a fundamentalist in his literal interpretation of the Bible, a point for which I find little evidence. See the discussion of the self-professed fundamentalist E. E. Cleveland, a black clergyman who specifically rejected a belief in the inerrancy of the Bible, in Davis, *I Got the Word in Me*, 2. On Martin Luther King Jr. see Baldwin, *There Is a Balm in Gilead*, 166–67. On fundamentalism in general, see Marsden, *Fundamentalism and American Culture*.

24. Mahalia Jackson is quoted in Bego, *Aretha Franklin*, 12; John Hammond, liner notes to Franklin, *Amazing Grace*. See also VF Interview, 8–9; EF Interview, 15; Garland, "The Lady Who's the Soul of Soul," 26; Donelson Interview, 9, 10; Black Interview, 10; interview with Willie Mae Moseley by author, 10 (hereafter cited as Moseley Interview).

25. CLF Interview, October 14, 1977, 68–69; Black Interview, 10; Carbage Interview, 10.

On the role of women in the black church see Higginbotham, *Righteous Discontent;* Gilkes, "The Politics of 'Silence.'"

26. The residences were all within the area bound by Iowa and McLemore Avenues on the north and south and Mississippi Boulevard and South Third Street on the east and west. The various Franklin residences are noted in *Polk's Memphis (Shelby County, Tenn.) City Directory, 1939,* 330; "Contributors to Baptist Missionary & Evangelical Convention," Memphis (typescript, n.d.), Box 3, SAO; *Polk's Memphis (Shelby County, Tenn.) City Directory, 1941,* 384; National Baptist Convention, *Proceedings of the Sixty-first Annual Session of the National Baptist Convention, 1941,* 192; *Polk's Memphis (Shelby County) City Directory, 1943,* 383.

27. VF Interview, 6; Siggers Interview.

28. Kelley Interview. I want to express my profound appreciation to Carl Ellan Kelley for discussing her father with me; to Erma Franklin for agreeing to help me contact Ms. Kelley; and to Brenda Corbett, CLF's niece, for calling Ms. Kelley before I did to introduce me to her on behalf of the family. The actions of these three Franklin family women typify the type of access and support I have been given by the Franklin family in the research for this book. Their commitment to an honest and thorough study of their exceptional father's (or uncle's) life and career has moved me personally and greatly aided my historical work.

29. Kelley Interview; Hubbard Interview, 36; Black Interview (telephone). Mrs. Black was the only church member I found who was active in New Salem in 1940 and old enough to understand such events.

30. Lizzie Moore Interview, 14.

31. CLF, *The Inner Conflict.*

32. Erma Franklin, "Memories of the Franklin Family," 1, CLFP.

33. Corbett Interview, 6–7; VF Interview, 4–5, 11, 12, 18, 42; Franklin, *Aretha,* 3–4; RF Interview, 18.

34. Interview with Reverend B. T. Moore Sr. by author, 13–14 (hereafter cited as B. T. Moore Interview); VF Interview, 4; Hooks Interview, 4, 32; interview with Reverend Jasper Williams Jr. by author, 1–3 (hereafter cited as Jasper Williams Interview).

35. For more discussion of this point see Boyer, "Contemporary Gospel," 23–27; Harris, *The Rise of Gospel Blues,* 154–55, and *passim;* Werner, *A Change Is Gonna Come,* 31; Jones, "An Interview with Henry H. Mitchell," 92; Walker, *"Somebody's Calling My Name," passim;* Spencer, *Sing a New Song;* Neal, "Any Day Now," 151–52. Neal writes: "At the pulsating core of their emotional center, the blues are the spiritual and ritual energy of the church thrust into eyes of life's raw realities. [T]hey are, in fact, extensions of the deepest, most pragmatic spiritual and moral realities." "Any Day Now," 152. Reverend Rubin Lucy is quoted in Rosenberg, *Can These Bones Live?* 62.

36. VF Interview, 13–14, 38; Black Interview (telephone); Rogers Interview, 27.

37. Hosea Woods, "Fourth and Beale" (1929), in Taft, *Blues Lyric Poetry,* 320; Waters, "Memphis Man" (1923), in Taft, *Blues Lyric Poetry,* 288; Bessie Smith, "Beale Street Mama" (1923), on Smith, *The Complete Recordings, Vol. 1;* Handy, *Father of the Blues,* 101; Lee, *Beale Street,* 13; Escott, *Good Rockin' Tonight,* preface (n.p.), 1.

38. For a more detailed analysis of the complex racial classification of Jews and other European immigrants in America, see Jacobson, *Whiteness of a Different Color.*

39. Lee, *Beale Street*, 13, 62–3; Capers, *The Biography of a River Town*, 231–32; Frank Stokes, "South Memphis Blues" (1929), in Taft, *Blues Lyric Poetry*, 259. T-Bone Walker wrote "Stormy Monday" and first recorded it in 1942; it has since been covered by most major blues and blues-influenced rock artists. See Dance, *Stormy Monday*, 62, 90, 156–58, and the artist himself on Walker, *Stormy Monday*. For an account by a white Memphian of the midnight shows at the Palace, see Coppock, *Memphis Memoirs*, 211–15.

40. Donelson Interview, 26; Black Interview (telephone); Guralnick, *Lost Highways*, 57, 60; Jon Pareles, "Rufus Thomas Dies at 84, Patriarch of Memphis Soul," *New York Times*, December 19, 2001. Waters is quoted in McKee and Chisenhall, *Beale Black and Blue*, 233.

41. In the early 1950s CLF had achieved the rank of a thirty-third degree Mason, the highest possible and one that took considerable time to reach. See CLF's Masonic membership cards, CLFP. On the origins of the black Masons and Odd Fellows, see Salvatore, *We All Got History*, *passim*. Ellison's comment is from a review of Gunnar Myrdal's *An American Dilemma*; the review was written in 1944 but not published until Ellison included it in *Shadow and Act*, 315–16, twenty years later.

42. Donelson Interview, 28; McKee and Chisenhall, *Beale Black and Blue*, 68; McBee, "The Memphis Red Sox Stadium," 153–57, 159–60, 162.

43. Lee, *Beale Street*, 153–54, 157; Nager, *Memphis Beat*, 178–79; George, "Lucie E. Campbell: Baptist Composer and Educator," 40.

44. Mahalia Jackson, *Movin' On Up*, 60–63; Duckett, "An Interview with Thomas A. Dorsey," 5; Harris, *The Rise of Gospel Blues*, 197–98 and *passim*; Ward-Royster, *How I Got Over*, 62–63, for a discussion of gospel guitarist Rosetta Tharpe. See also Boyer, "William Herbert Brewster," 213–14, who stresses the "similarities," but not a "real relationship," between the musical structures of classic blues and gospel.

45. Lornell, *"Happy in the Service of the Lord,"* 12–13, 43–44, 123–25; Donelson Interview, 20–22; Simone is quoted in Levine, *Black Culture and Black Consciousness*, 200. The core group of the original Pattersonairs can be heard on their 1984 recording *Book of the Seven Seals*.

46. Brewster, "Rememberings," 201, 209; Donelson Interview, 20. A few years later, Brewster recalled, "Elvis Presley came here [to East Trigg Baptist], a truck driver," to absorb the gospel beat, "and now he is the greatest thing." Brewster, "Remembering," 112. On Mahalia Jackson's recording see Goreau, *Just Mahalia, Baby*, 112, and Jackson, *The Apollo Sessions, 1946–1951*. On the politics of Memphis see Bunche, *The Political Status of the Negro in the Age of FDR;* Doyle, "Gestapo in Memphis"; Jasper, "Minority Vote Helped Ruin 'Crump Machine'"; Biles, *Memphis in the Great Depression, passim;* Silver and Moeser, *The Separate City*, 48–49. Concerning segregation and violence toward blacks, see Miller, *Memphis during the Progressive Era*, 191–94; Johnson and associates, *To Stem This Tide*, 33, 70, 73; and the 1940 commentary of Benjamin E. Mays, president of Atlanta University, quoted in Silver and Moeser, *The Separate City*, 15.

47. Donelson Interview, 19; CLF, *Without a Song*. Donelson knew Brewster "well" across four decades.

48. Hubbard Interview, 28–29; Black Interview (telephone); *Memphis World*, February 25, 1944; Carbage Interview, 30; Donelson Interview, 20–21. On the role of the minister

as a preacher in contrast with other duties, see Rooks, "Toward the Promised Land," 27.

49. James Interview, 10.

50. National Baptist Convention, *Proceedings of the Sixtieth Annual Session of the National Baptist Convention, 1940,* 166. The wife of Reverend William Holmes Borders, pastor of Atlanta's Wheat Street Baptist Church, implored her husband to use church funds for a round-the-world trip in the late 1950s with a self-serving argument that nonetheless contained a kernel of truth about the relationship between pastor and congregation: "Holmes, our people know they'll never make such a trip themselves. Now, you came out of the same red gumbo Georgia clay that most of them did. You'll be making this trip for them." Quote attributed to Mrs. Holmes in English, *Handyman of the Lord,* 82–83.

51. Telephone interview with Erma Franklin by author, November 9, 2001; *Memphis World,* May 21 and 25, 1943; Donelson Interview, 16–17; Rogers Interview, 16–17; CLF Interview, October 12, 1977, 44–46. CLF's memory about this event is not fully accurate. While he recalls the horror of the incident clearly, he mistakes the names of some of those involved and places the event as much as a year later. For the basic story I have followed the more contemporary newspaper accounts.

52. VF Interview, 28. On the issue of the streetcars and the protest against, and enforcement of, segregation, see *National Baptist Voice,* June 15, 1943; *Memphis World,* July 28, 1944; Johnson and associates, *To Stem This Tide,* 33.

53. Clipping, Box 386–1, CAB; Webb, "Michaux as Prophet," 3–4; English, *Handyman of the Lord,* 56–57. On gospel groups see *Memphis World,* April 16, 1943; Lornell, *"Happy in the Service of the Lord,"* 177. CLF Interview, November 8, 1977, 140–41, and May 3, 1978, 204, contain his recollections of the program. For a broader discussion of black radio during these years, see Savage, *Broadcasting Freedom.*

54. *Memphis World,* August 20, 1943. On Shirley Graham's politics at this time see Lewis, *W. E. B. DuBois,* 385, 498, 526. Within a few years Graham would marry DuBois.

55. *Memphis World,* August 20, 1943. Even a decade later, the radio program continued from New Salem; see Daniel, *Lost Revolutions,* 130–31. In 1940 a prominent druggist, J. B. Martin, was forced to leave Memphis for fear of his life because of his opposition to E. H. Crump's political machine. See J. B. Martin to R. R. Church, March 20, 1941, Box 7, folder 12 (copy) and Claude A. Barnett to Wendell Wilkie, January 11, 1941, Box 7, folder 15 (copy), RRC; *Memphis Commercial Appeal,* November 13, 23, 1940. In 1943 Crump denied A. Phillip Randolph, the civil rights activist and trade unionist, permission to speak at Reverend Roy Love's Mt. Nebo Baptist Church, under threats of wholesale arrest of the city's black leaders especially. See "Randolph Denounces Crump Machine in Memphis," special press release, Box 7, folder 1; and unsigned [Robert R. Church] to Honorable James B. Wright, November 18, 1943 (copy), Box 7, folder 27, RRC; *Memphis World,* November 5 and 12, 1943. On the fear generated among many black Memphians, see Donelson Interview, 31; Black Interview, 31–32.

56. Johnson, *1943 Year Book and Directory,* 10. On the War Bond Committee's activities see *Memphis World,* February 23, 1943, and January 21, 1944; McKee and Chisenhall, *Beale Black and Blue,* 85; W. C. Handy to "Dear Friend Still" [William Grant Still],

September 20, 1943, New York City, as reprinted in Southern, "In Retrospect," 212. On the NAACP activities see *Memphis World,* April 13, 1943; on the "Double V" campaign see Sullivan, *Days of Hope,* 134–37.

57. On Borders's sermon see *National Baptist Voice,* April 1, 1943; Lischer, *The Preacher King,* 49. Borders's "I Am Somebody" sermon generated a deluge of requests for transcripts. The sermon was adapted and later used by Reverends Martin Luther King Jr. and Jesse Jackson and by the soul singer James Brown.

4. THE EAGLE STIRRETH

1. Nat D. Williams, Focussing [*sic*] the News, *Memphis World,* July 2, 1943; Johnson, *1943 Year Book and Directory,* 137.

2. Hooks Interview, 5–6, 16; *Appreciation Day Honoring Benjamin Lawson Hooks, Minister and Judge Appointee* (Memphis, 1965), n.p.; Nat D. Williams, Focussing [*sic*] the News, *Memphis World,* June 29, 1943; Hattie Glenn, "Friendship Baptist Church," *Buffalo Criterion,* May 22, 1943.

3. *Memphis World,* June 29, July 2, 1943.

4. Joshua 1:2 (KJV)

5. Laymon, *The Interpreter's One-Volume Commentary on the Bible,* 122–25. (This was one of the biblical commentaries, in its two-volume edition, that CLF used during his career; see CLF Interview, May 10, 1978, 242.) CLF notes his experience with the revival at Friendship in CLF Interview, November 30, 1977, 173. On the meaning of invoking the biblical text within the unfolding experience between preacher and congregation weekly, see Raboteau, *A Fire in the Bones,* 142; Mitchell, *Black Preaching,* 56; Davis, *I Got the Word in Me,* 67–68.

6. *Memphis World,* July 2, 1943; interview with Charlie Thompson by author, 7 (hereafter cited as Thompson Interview); Donelson Interview, 6. On the place of this sermon in the Afro-Baptist tradition, see Spillers, "Fabrics of History," 84 n. 3, 107; Bengston, "The Eagle Stirreth Her Nest," *passim.*

7. Lyell, *A Second Visit to North America,* 2:2–4. For a more detailed discussion of Marshall and his church, see Raboteau, *Slave Religion,* 189–94, 198–99.

8. Douglass, *My Bondage and My Freedom,* 99; Mays, *The Negro's God as Reflected in His Literature,* 59. For a powerful and thoughtful analysis of this spiritual experience among Afro-Americans throughout the western hemisphere, see Marks, "Uncovering Ritual Structures in Afro-American Music."

9. CLF did offer another version of this sermon in 1963, one that was dramatically different, both longer and more historically oriented. It was not received as well as the 1953 version and, significantly, it was one of the few sermons CLF actually wrote down before delivering. See CLF's Jewel version of *The Eagle Stirs Her Nest.*

10. See Exodus chaps. 20–23; Deuteronomy 31:19 and 32:11–12 (KJV). The text of this sermon is the last citation.

11. John Lewis's description of whooping is useful here: "Ah, it's not just the minister speaking to the congregation but it's also the congregation speaking to the minister and

together they're reaching to a much higher level. Something is happening there." Interview with John Lewis by author, 5 (hereafter cited as Lewis Interview).

12. I follow here Jeff Todd Titon's presentation of the whooped sermon in poetic form; see Titon, *Give Me This Mountain*, 41–45.

13. CLF, *The Eagle Stirreth Her Nest* (Chess version). Years later CLF recalled that a LeMoyne College professor once preached this sermon at New Salem, using the eagle as a symbol of freedom, and suggested that Frederick Douglass and Booker T. Washington "and all of the well-known blacks that had succeeded" followed in the path of that symbol. See CLF Interview, November 1, 1977, 96–97. What record producer Jerry Wexler once said of the rhythm and blues star Wilson Pickett applied to CLF as well: "Wilson would scream notes where other screamers just scream sound." Quoted in Guralnick, *Sweet Soul Music*, 214. For analyses of the chanted sermon and its ritual context, see Marks, "Uncovering Ritual Structures in Afro-American Music," 64–67; Mitchell, *Black Preaching*, 120–21; Raboteau, *A Fire in the Bones, passim;* Rosenberg, "The Psychology of the Spiritual Sermon," 137–38; Lischer, *The Preacher King*, 114. On CLF's performance of his sermons see Kyles Interview, 34; Jasper Williams Interview, 10.

14. Ralph Ellison, "Living with Music" (1955), in Ellison, *Living with Music*, 5–6. See also Henry H. Mitchell's insightful discussion of the "common characteristics between black preaching and jazz improvisation" in Jones, "An Interview with Henry H. Mitchell," 92.

15. CLF Interview, October 12, 1977, 44; *Buffalo Criterion*, January 15, 1944. CLF mistakenly dates the gift of the suit to a time before Jenkins's death.

16. *Memphis World*, January 28, February 25, 1944; Mission Board of the B. M. and E. Convention of Tennessee, *First Inspirational and Evangelistic Regional Meeting*, n.p.; Donelson Interview, 33.

17. *Buffalo Criterion*, March 25, 1944. CLF remembered this moment differently, and erroneously, decades later. He recalled that some at Friendship "opposed me in ways, or my methods, but they were not overt." Most in the congregation, he accurately recounted, "liked me as a preacher but they also had to feel that I was an asset to the church." CLF Interview, November 30, 1977, 172–74.

18. Nat D. Williams, "Focussing [*sic*] the News," *Memphis World*, July 9, 1943. On black migration see Grossman, *Land of Hope;* Sernett, *Bound for the Promised Land;* Trotter, *The Great Migration in Historical Perspective.*

19. On Friendship see *Buffalo Criterion*, April 10, 1943; *Memphis World*, February 26, 1943; CLF Interview, October 14, 1977, 60–61; CLF Interview, November 30, 1977, 170–71. Jenkins's ministry in Buffalo is recounted in the *Buffalo Criterion*, January 16, January 23, February 13, February 20, March 27, April 10 and 17, May 22, and June 12, 1943. See also *Memphis World*, February 26, 1943.

20. On the harassment of blacks during World War II, see Johnson and associates, *To Stem This Tide*, 33, 73; *Memphis World*, July 28, 1944. On Randolph in Memphis see Robert R. Church Jr. (unsigned copy) to Honorable James Wright, November 18, 1943, n.p., Box 7, folder 27, RRC; A. Philip Randolph, "Speech at Memphis, Tennessee, First Baptist Church," and A. Philip Randolph, "An Open Letter to E. H. Crump," April 6, 1944 (copy), Box 4, folder 44, RRC; *Memphis World*, November 5 and 12, 1943; March

28 and April 4, 1944; Tucker, *Black Pastors and Leaders,* 135–43; Black Interview, 31. On Jenkins see *Buffalo Criterion,* February 26, 1943.

21. Carbage Interview, 9; Hubbard Interview, 36–37; Lizzie Moore Interview, 14.

22. *Buffalo Criterion,* June 3, 1944. Placing the demands of career over family was anything but unusual among ministers. Thomas A. Dorsey, the famous gospel blues composer and performer, left his wife near childbirth in Chicago to preach a revival in St. Louis. The indescribable pain he endured following the death of both wife and child while still in St. Louis he ultimately transformed into the haunting power of his well-known hymn "Precious Lord, Take My Hand." See Dorsey's introduction to his and Marion Williams's version of the hymn on Dorsey, *Precious Lord.*

23. The population of Buffalo in 1940 was 575,901, of whom 17,694 (3.1 percent) were black. Of these African Americans, about 88 percent (15,549) lived in the Lower East Side neighborhood. See U.S. Bureau of the Census, *Sixteenth Census of the United States: 1940,* vol. 2, pt. 5, *Population: Characteristics,* 136–37; Childs, *The Political Black Minister,* 52; Kraus, *Race, Neighborhoods, and Community Power,* 43–48. A decade later, the city's population had increased minimally to 580,132, but black residents had more than doubled to 36,645, of whom some 79 percent (29,127) lived in the neighborhood. Despite the increase, black residents still accounted for only 6.3 percent of the city's population. See U.S. Bureau of the Census, *Seventeenth Decennial Census of the United States, 1950,* vol. 2, pt. 32, *Population: Characteristics,* 32–52; Imse, *Metropolitan Buffalo Perspectives,* 7; Reid, *The Negro Baptist Ministry,* 3; Kraus, *Race, Neighborhoods, and Community Power,* 44. The social and cultural milieu of Eddie Wenzak's bar is sensitively evoked in Klinkenborg, *The Last Fine Time.*

24. See *Buffalo News,* November 10, 1930, and March 20, 1939; *Buffalo Courier-Express,* January 18, 1947.

25. CLF Interview, November 30, 1977, 170–71, 175–76; VF Interview, 17; interview with Edward Lee Billups by author, 13–14 (hereafter cited as Billups Interview); *Michigan Chronicle,* September 5, 1964; National Baptist Convention, *Proceedings of the Sixty-fifth Annual Session of the National Baptist Convention, 1945,* 240.

26. *Buffalo Star,* August 16, 1940; Carpenter, *Nationality, Color, and Economic Opportunity in the City of Buffalo,* 139–40; Butler, Taylor, and Ryu, "Work and Black Neighborhood Life in Buffalo, 1930–1980," 114–15. For the employment figures see U.S. Bureau of the Census, *Sixteenth Census of the United States: 1940,* vol. 3, pt. 4, *Population: The Labor Force,* 391–96. By 1950 at least one important change had occurred, indicating the potential power of the union to aid black progress: two-thirds of black industrial workers now held jobs above the unskilled level. Still, both the clerical and professional/proprietary groups among blacks remained insignificant, with less than 1 percent of the citywide total in each group. See U.S. Bureau of the Census, *Seventeenth Decennial Census of the United States, 1950,* vol. 2, pt. 32, *Population: Characteristics,* table 77. (The 1950 figures use the Standard Metropolitan Area, which includes surrounding suburbs, for the first time in calculating urban data.) Unemployment in black Buffalo in 1950 remained abnormally high: 15.6 percent against a citywide average of 6.8 percent. See Butler, Taylor, and Ryu, "Work and Black Neighborhood Life in Buffalo, 1930–1980," 115–16.

27. Billups Interview, 15–16; interview with Mary Hill by author, 15 (hereafter cited as

Hill Interview). For contemporary discussions of changes in black job prospects during the war, see *Buffalo Courier-Express,* October 13, 1942; May 9 and June 5, 1943. On Wilson see McDonald, "Interview with Olin Wilson," 90–91; Williams, *Strangers in the Land of Paradise,* 71. See Sernett, *Bound for the Promised Land, passim,* for an important discussion of the impact on religious faith of black migration to northern cities. For a broader analysis of black workers in these industries in Buffalo, see Northrup, *Negro Employment in Basic Industry,* pt. 4, *passim;* Weaver, *Negro Labor,* 33–34, 122.

28. Lizzie Moore Interview, 14, 36. E. L. Billups is an Alabama-born working man who joined Friendship Baptist in March 1945 at age eighteen. That same week he began work at the Dunlop Tire and Rubber Company in Buffalo, where he worked until November 1998. Throughout his working career he was a member of Local 135, United Auto Workers Union, where he served as a shop steward and was deeply involved in Friendship as well. He became a deacon in 1948, served as a church trustee, and for more than two decades was the Superintendent of Friendship's Sunday School, in charge of organizing the religious and cultural education of the church's children through their teen years. See Billups Interview, 2–3, 14, 16.

29. Billups Interview, 6; CLF Interview, October 14, 1977, 59; VF Interview, 16; Siggers Interview; Carpenter, *Nationality, Color, and Economic Opportunity in the City of Buffalo,* 160; Buffalo, City Planning Commission, *Buffalo's Population in 1975,* 19; Butler, Taylor, and Ryu, "Work and Black Neighborhood Life in Buffalo, 1930–1980," 115–16; Graebner, *Coming of Age in Buffalo,* 82; Kraus, *Race, Neighborhoods, and Community Power,* 52. For a comparison of both neighborhoods in 1940, see Taylor, "The Theories of William Julius Wilson and the Black Experience in Buffalo, New York," 68; Butler, Taylor, and Ryu, "Work and Black Neighborhood Life in Buffalo, 1930–1980," 114–15. There is some discrepancy as to the Franklins' correct address: *Polk's Buffalo (Erie County, N.Y.) City Directory, 1946,* 328, lists it as 177 Glenwood; it is listed as 179 Glenwood in National Baptist Convention, *Proceedings of the Sixty-fifth Annual Session of the National Baptist Convention, 1945,* 240.

30. VF Interview, 14–17; EF Interview, 11; Erma Franklin, "Memories of the Franklin Family, 1, CLFP.

31. VF Interview, 15, 26, 29, 38–39; EF Interview, 11; Siggers Interview.

32. CLF Interview, November 30, 1977, 173, 185; Hill Interview, 9; Siggers Interview; VF Interview, 18, 21, 23; RF Interview, 19.

33. CLF Interview, November 30, 1977, 173; CLF Interview, May 17, 1978, 249–50; Siggers Interview; VF Interview, 34.

34. CLF Interview, November 30, 1977, 168; Williams, *Strangers in the Land of Paradise,* 103, 104, 105, 120, 123–78; Yearwood, "First Shiloh Baptist Church of Buffalo, New York," 81–84. On the Garvey movement in Buffalo see Williams, *Strangers in the Land of Paradise,* 105, 178–80; Watkins, "The Marcus Garvey Movement in Buffalo, New York," 40–44. The history of the Michigan Avenue Y before 1940 is told in Williams, *Strangers in the Land of Paradise,* 100–122.

35. *Buffalo Criterion,* February 5 and 19 and May 6, 1944. The debate over the structure of the postwar world can be followed in *Buffalo Criterion,* February 5, March 18, May 27, and December 9, 1944; November 10, 1945; *Buffalo Courier-Express,* June 27 and August 3 and 5, 1943.

36. Hill Interview, 4; *Buffalo Criterion*, August 25, 1945.

37. On black veterans and the civil rights movement see Dittmer, *Local People*, 1–18; Dalfiume, *Desegregation of the U.S. Armed Forces*, 122–23, 132–33.

38. CLF Interview, May 3, 1978, 204.

39. *National Baptist Voice*, October 1, 1945; Wilson, *Toast of the Town*, 95.

40. Nannie H. Burroughs, "Report of the Corresponding Secretary," National Baptist Convention, *Proceedings of the Sixty-fifth Annual Session of the National Baptist Convention, 1945,* 343–51; *Michigan Chronicle*, September 15, 1945. On the Fair Employment Practices Commission see Reed, *Seedtime for the Modern Civil Rights Movement*.

41. *National Baptist Voice,* April 15, 1940, and October 1, 1944. For continued discussions of whooping, see ibid., June 15, 1951, and January 1953; on Barbour see Williams, *Biographical Directory of Negro Ministers,* 34.

42. *National Baptist Voice,* December 15, 1944; *Michigan Chronicle,* September 15, 1945.

43. *National Baptist Voice,* October 1, 1945. Franklin took his text from 2 Corinthians 5:1–2; see National Baptist Convention, *Proceedings of the Sixty-fifth Annual Session of the National Baptist Convention, 1945, 57.*

44. Hill Interview, 12, 18; Billups Interview, 8. Both Mary Hill and E. L. Billups remarked that the church meeting called to discuss CLF's leaving was explosive. Deacon Billups, who attended the 1946 meeting but did not speak at it, stated that older members "discussed about some things that I definitely wouldn't want to be, to be a part of this [interview], and, but, I'll tell you this, we were here that night until quarter to three in the morning." Both agreed that they heard no stories of Franklin engaging in relations with women in or out of the congregation. See Hill Interview, 17, 19; Billups Interview, 18.

45. CLF Interview, October 14, 1977, 60.

5. Hastings Street

1. John Lee Hooker, "Boogie Chillen," in Hooker, *The Legendary Modern Recordings;* Wilson, *Toast of the Town,* 64, 101–2; Derricotte, *The Black Notebooks,* 94.

2. Hooker quoted in Murray, *Boogie Man,* 103. On the boundaries of Paradise Valley see Wilson, *Toast of the Town,* 43; Bjorn, *Before Motown,* 39; Murray, *Boogie Man,* 97; interview with Sheldon Tappes and with Richard L. King in Moon, *Untold Tales, Unsung Heroes,* 105, 161–62, respectively. On the city's growing black population see Detroit Urban League, *A Profile of the Detroit Negro, 1959–1967,* 21; also of interest for the Hastings Street neighborhood is a report by the Detroit City Planning Commission, "Population Change by Census Tracts and Tract Areas, City of Detroit, 1930, 1940, 1950, 1960," (mimeo., n.p., 1963), Box 71, DUL. On Hooker's early career, rent parties, and the Henry Swing Club, see Mike Rowe, liner notes to Hooker, *Detroit Blues,* and Hooker's version of "House Rent Boogie" on the same album; Edwards, *The World Don't Owe Me Nothing,* 240; Collis, *The Story of Chess Records,* 30; Murray, *Boogie Man, passim;* Bjorn, *Before Motown,* 66. Hastings Street's reputation during and after World War II is recalled in the interview with Dorothy Elizabeth Lawson in Moon, *Untold Tales, Unsung Heroes,* 118.

3. On the growth of Detroit's musical scene see Russ J. Cowans, "Those Roaring 20's

Were Haphy [*sic*] Days!" *Michigan Chronicle*, April 11, 1964; Lt. Fred L. Williams, "When Detroit Was a Really Jazzy Site," *Michigan Chronicle*, February 21, 1981; Bjorn, *Before Motown*, 61–104, esp. 64, 74, 77, 90; John Cohassey, liner notes to *Hastings Street Grease*, vol. 1; John Sinclair, liner notes to *Hastings Street Grease*, vol. 2. The emergence of black DJs is discussed by Bill Lane, untitled clipping [*Detroit Tribune*], n.d. [1952], Box 5, FAK. On the appearances of nationally famous acts in these clubs, see the advertisements in the entertainment section of the *Michigan Chronicle*, 1945–1950; on the decline of Paradise Valley's music scene by the mid-1950s, see the interview with Earl Van Dyke in Moon, *Untold Tales, Unsung Heroes*, 242; *Michigan Chronicle*, April 10 and October 9, 1954; April 14, 1956. Gerald Early provides an insightful analysis of the city's musical foundations in his *One Nation Under a Groove*.

4.   For descriptions of Hastings Street establishments see Bjorn, *Before Motown*, 43; Wilson, *Toast of the Town*, 104–5. On the social texture of the Valley see Wilson, *Toast of the Town*, 64–65; EF Interview, 44–45; interview with Karl Gregory by author, 8–11 (hereafter cited as Gregory Interview).

5.   Derricotte, *The Black Notebooks*, 94; Gordy, *To Be Loved*, 16, 22–23.

6.   Sugrue, *The Origins of the Urban Crisis*, 197–207; Bauer, *Open the Door*, 17; interview with Norman McRae and with Robert Bynum Jr. in Moon, *Untold Tales, Unsung Heroes*, 185, 199, respectively. The activities of the myriad social clubs among black elites can be followed in the society pages of the *Michigan Chronicle*; see, for example, the issues of January 11 and 25 and April 19, 1947; March 19, 1949.

7.   CLF Interview, October 7, 1977, 21; CLF Interview, October 14, 1977, 60–61; CLF Interview, November 30, 1977, 193.

8.   *National Baptist Voice*, June 15, 1944; New Bethel Baptist Church, *"Gospel Tribute" for Reverend Clarence LaVaughn Franklin, December 10, 1979*, n.p.; interview with Willie Todd by author, 7 (hereafter cited as Todd Interview); Clayborne, *The Papers of Martin Luther King, Jr.*, 1:361 n. 4. On the rise of gospel music see Harris, *The Rise of Gospel Blues, passim;* on the social and psychological importance of these churches within a faith context, see Sernett, *Bound for the Promised Land;* Gilkes, "The Black Church as a Therapeutic Community"; Paris, "Moral Development for African-American Leadership," 24; Trulear, "The Lord Will Make a Way Somehow," 89–97; King, *Daddy King*, 93.

9.   *National Baptist Voice*, June 1 and November 11, 1941; June 15, 1944; March 1 and December 15, 1945; *Michigan Chronicle*, April 6, 1946.

10.   Stovall, *The Growth of Black Elected Officials in the City of Detroit, 1870–1973*, 6. In the 1950s Detroit as a whole lost population for the first time in its history (–9.7 percent) due largely to whites leaving for the suburbs, and the resulting racial density in neighborhoods intensified significantly. See Detroit Urban League, *A Profile of the Detroit Negro, 1959–1967*, 23. This transformation occurred with much political conflict, violence, and destruction of property as racial tensions were fought out block by block, neighborhood by neighborhood. See Sugrue, *The Origins of the Urban Crisis*, pt. 3.

11.   *Michigan Chronicle*, September 14, 1946; Billups Interview, 20. On the Gotham see Wilson, *Toast of the Town*, 154–55; Dancy, *Sand against the Wind*, 113–14; interview with Beatrice M. Buck in Moon, *Untold Tales, Unsung Heroes*, 188. Buck worked at the hotel between 1951 and 1955.

12. Interview with Kermit G. Bailer in Moon, *Untold Tales, Unsung Heroes*, 179.

13. For a broad overview of black religion and black church organizations in this era of migration, see Lincoln and Mamiya, *The Black Church in the African American Experience;* Sernett, *Bound for the Promised Land.*

14. CLF Interview, October 14, 1977, 65. He also noted Reverends H. H. Coleman, William Haney, Horace White, and "the minister Bishop" of the African Methodist Episcopal denomination whose name he did not recall.

15. On A[llen] A. Banks and Second Baptist see *Detroit Free Press*, March 16 and 19, 1936; *National Baptist Voice*, February 15, 1947; May 1, 1950; February 15, 1951; May 1953; *Michigan Chronicle*, December 29, 1945; June 8 and 15, 1946; January 11, May 3, and November 15, 1947; A. A. Banks to Nannie H. Burroughs, January 7, 1947, Box 3, NHB; Williams, *Biographical Directory of Negro Ministers*, 32. Harry Kincaid migrated from the Mississippi Delta to Detroit in 1949. A war veteran and a "Southern University man," Kincaid joined Second Baptist, a church that epitomized his aspirations for social and economic mobility. The sermons left something to be desired, he felt, and, after meeting CLF and discovering their common Delta roots, Kincaid began attending New Bethel following Second's services and soon joined CLF's church. In this case, common experiences and the draw of the rural-inflected church services proved critical, and his new affiliation did not deter Kincaid from achieving his economic goals. See Kincaid Interview, 2, 4, 13.

16. On McNeil see *National Baptist Voice*, February 1, 1944; *Michigan Chronicle*, September 4 and December 18, 1948; June 10, 1950; May 12, 1951; J. J. McNeil to Nannie H. Burroughs, January 24, 1944, Nashville; McNeil to Burroughs, April 12, 1945, Marshall, TX; McNeil to Burroughs, June 26, 1948, Detroit, all in Box 20, NHB.

17. On Victoria Banks see *National Baptist Voice*, February 15, 1947, and May 1953; *Michigan Chronicle*, January 11, 1947; on Pearl McNeil see *Michigan Chronicle*, June 10, 1950 (Bill Lane's column), and June 5, 1954.

18. New Bethel Baptist Church, *The Sixteenth Anniversary Program*, n.p.; EF Interview, 24, 36, 45; interview with Myra Perkins by author, 39 (hereafter cited as Perkins Interview); Derricotte, *The Black Notebooks*, 94. Barbour depicted the paradoxical situation with pointed humor: "The Detroit preachers ought to be on the back row in heaven," he proclaimed. "It would not be fair to the rest of us who live in humble homes for those fellows to have all those fine mansions on Arden Park and Boston Boulevard and then reside on Hallelujah boulevard in Heaven." *National Baptist Voice*, February 15, 1951. On CLF's house see Robinson, *Smokey*, 28, 29.

19. CLF Interview, October 14, 1977, 69–70; CLF Interview, November 30, 1977, 174–75.

20. For a detailed discussion of this from the ministerial perspective, one that CLF may well have read, see S. L. Morgan Sr., "The Economic Struggle between Pastors and Churches," *National Baptist Voice*, December 15, 1947.

21. *Michigan Chronicle*, May 10, 1947; March 13 and May 29, 1948; New Bethel Baptist Church, *The Fifteenth Anniversary Program*, n.p.; New Bethel Baptist Church, *The Sixteenth Anniversary Program*, n.p.

22. Interview with Milton Hall by author, 1, 2, 5, 10, 17, 23 (hereafter cited as Hall Interview).

23. On this increase in New Bethel's membership see New Bethel Baptist Church, *The Sixteenth Anniversary Program*, n.p.

24. Brewster Homes, built in 1937, held 941 units in eight 14-story buildings between Hastings and Beaubien, two blocks west, and a few blocks south of Willis. See Boykin, *A Handbook on the Detroit Negro*, 53–54; *Michigan Chronicle*, October 25, 1947, and November 3, 1948; Wilson, *Dreamgirl*, 21; Gordy, *To Be Loved*, 43; Stovall, *The Growth of Black Elected Officials in the City of Detroit*, 61. On CLF at this time see New Bethel Baptist Church, *"Gospel Tribute" for Reverend Clarence LaVaughn Franklin*, 2; CLF Interview, October 14, 1977, 63–64; CLF Interview, November 2, 1977, 104; "The Preacher with the Golden Voice," 42. CLF incorporated the church's struggles into a sermon a decade later; see his recording *The Devil Tempts Jesus*.

25. VF Interview, 21. In her book Aretha Franklin explains that at that time, "adults did not discuss their affairs with children" and thus she and her siblings had no idea then (and by implication now) of the causes of the separation. See Franklin, *Aretha*, 5.

26. Perkins Interview, 8, 9; EF Interview, 15; Siggers Interview; VF Interview, 10; Corbett Interview, 7–8; Todd Interview, 14–15. On Barbara's alleged desertion see "Lady Soul: Singing It Like It Is," *Time*, June 28, 1968, 63; Farley, "Soul Sister 2000," 78; Franklin, *Aretha*, 5–7; VF Interview, 22–23; interview with Sylvia Penn by author, 1, 2 (hereafter cited as Penn Interview). For other uses of that term see Wexler, *Rhythm and the Blues*, 205–6; Broughton, *Black Gospel*, 98; Garland, "The Lady Who's the Soul of Soul," 26; Heilbut, *The Gospel Sound*, 276.

27. Franklin, *Aretha*, 6–7; VF Interview, 5–6; Billups Interview, 21, 24–25; Hill Interview, 21–25.

28. Perkins Interview, 17; Penn Interview, 1, 2, 4. On Rachel Franklin see VF Interview, 35; RF Interview, 19; Todd Interview, 14; interview with Carolyn King by author, 15 (hereafter cited as King Interview); Corbett Interview, 12, 13–14.

29. VF Interview, 22–23; Franklin, *Aretha*, 20; Billups Interview, 25; Todd Interview, 14–15; Penn Interview, 2.

30. Mahalia Jackson is quoted in Broughton, *Black Gospel*, 98. See also VF Interview, 23–25, 32.

31. *National Baptist Voice*, October 1, 1948.

32. CLF Interview, November 2, 112–13, 1977; CLF Interview, November 30, 1977, 186; Kyles Interview, 13, 14; Todd Interview, 9–10; George, "Lucie E. Campbell" (1987), 38, 39; Boyer, *The Golden Age of Gospel*, 247–49, 257–58; Franklin, *Aretha*, 52; "James Cleveland: King of Gospel," *passim*. On the rivalry between preachers and sacred singers see Kyles Interview, 13, 14; Lincoln and Mamiya, *The Black Church in the African American Experience*, 346; Harris, *The Rise of Gospel Blues*, 184–85. Grace Cobb was a member of New Light Baptist Church but frequently sang with the New Bethel choir. Sammy Bryant can be heard singing "The Angels Keep Watching over Me" on the album *None but the Righteous: Chess Gospel Greats*.

33. *Michigan Chronicle*, February 19, 1949; Kyles Interview, 10, 13–14; Franklin, *Aretha*, 44; Hirshey, *Nowhere to Run*, 47–48; Wilson, *Toast of the Town*, 157; Wolff, *You Send Me*, 52–54. Kyles was born in 1934 in Shelby, Mississippi, where his father, also a minister, was friends with CLF. The family moved to Chicago in 1938. See chapter 2 above.

34. Franklin, *Aretha*, 49, 52; EF Interview, 37; Todd Interview, 9–10; Boyer, *The Golden Age of Gospel*, 196–99; Wolff, *You Send Me*, 84, 142; Pickett is quoted in Hirshey, *Nowhere to Run*, 47. When Cooke left the Highway Q.C.'s, Lou Rawls took his place; he left in 1953–54 to join the Chosen Gospel Singers, and Johnnie Taylor replaced him. In 1957, when Cooke left the Soul Stirrers to become a pop singer, Taylor became that group's lead singer. In time all three of these extraordinary lead singers for the Highway Q.C.'s would have successful careers in pop, soul, and rhythm and blues. See Brother John, liner notes to Highway Q.C.'s, *Count Your Blessings*.

35. EF Interview, 49, 66; Corbett Interview, 16; Ross, *Secrets of a Sparrow*, 92; Wilson, *Dreamgirl*, 22–23, 26–27; Franklin, *Aretha*, 36; Bego, *Aretha Franklin*, 15.

36. Franklin, *Aretha*, 10, 43, 49; Gillespie is quoted in Lester, *Too Marvelous for Words*, 165; Bjorn, *Before Motown*, 117. See also Bego, *Aretha Franklin*, 35–36; interview with Beatrice Buck by author, 7, 36 (hereafter cited as Buck Interview); Jasper Williams Interview, 23; "Preacher with a Golden Voice," 42; Robinson, *Smokey*, 25–30; Corbett Interview, 17; EF Interview, 25, 49, 50, 57, 58; Mahalia Jackson, "I'm Going to Live the Life I Sing about in My Song," on Jackson, *Gospels, Spirituals, and Hymns*.

37. Franklin, *Aretha*, 40, 43; EF Interview, 2; Penn Interview, 12.

38. For other expressions of this idea see Thompson Interview, 31; Duckett, "An Interview with Thomas A. Dorsey," 11.

39. CLF Interview, October 14, 1977, 64–65.

40. *Michigan Chronicle*, January 13, 1951. (I have been unable to find a copy of this recording; in Hayes and Laughton, *Gospel Records, 1943–1969*, vol. 1, n.p. (CLF entry), it is identified as Gotham G682.) On Joe Von Battle see *Michigan Chronicle*, October 16, 1948, and July 3, 1954; Bjorn, *Before Motown*, 173; O'Neal and van Singel, *The Voice of the Blues*, 214; Murray, *Boogie Man*, 168, 271. Eddie Burns is quoted in Murray, *Boogie Man*, 142. On the conditions in Detroit's recording industry at this time, see Mike Rowe, liner notes to Hooker, *Detroit Blues;* Dave Sax, liner notes to Hooker, *The Legendary Modern Recordings;* Murray, *Boogie Man*, 107–8, 111, 117.

41. White's cultural conservatism regarding the whooped sermon, gospel blues, and decorum for religious services, particularly when the services are broadcast, can be followed in *Michigan Chronicle*, March 4, 11, and 18 and April 1, 1950; his strong public support for black workers and the UAW during the 1941 Ford strike is discussed in Bontemps and Conroy, *They Seek a City*, 223; Meier and Rudwick, *Black Detroit and the Rise of the UAW*, 32–33, 55–60, 69–70, and *passim*.

42. *Michigan Chronicle*, October 10, 1953.

43. Ibid.; Thompson Interview, 22; Penn Interview, 17; see also E. L. Branch Interview, 21.

44. McCoy Interview, 33; "Minutes of New Bethel Baptist Church, 4210 Hastings Street, December 5, 1950, held at Sacred Cross Baptist Church," typescript, n.p., CLFP.

45. *Michigan Chronicle*, October 13 and 20, 1951; October 10, 1953.

46. Joshua 14:6–15 (KJV).

47. *Michigan Chronicle*, October 20, 1951.

48. For a recording of this sermon from the late 1950s, see CLF, *Give Me This Mountain*.

6. Thoughts of Liberation

1. *New York Times,* February 26, 27, 28, 29, 1952; House Committee on Un-American Activities, *Hearings: Communism in the Detroit Area,* pt. 1, 2877–78, 2892; Kochman, *Rappin' and Stylin' Out,* 234–35; Gale Group, Inc., "George W. Crockett, Jr., 1909–1997"; interview with George W. Crockett in Mast, *Detroit Lives,* 168–69. The most complete discussion of the Rosenberg case, which argues convincingly that Julius Rosenberg was in fact guilty as charged and that the trial judge violated numerous constitutional rights, is Radosh and Milton, *The Rosenberg File.*
2. House Committee on Un-American Activities, *Hearings: Communism in the Detroit Area,* pt. 1, 2878–79, 2880–82, 2885, 2886.
3. Ibid., 2884–85.
4. Ibid., 2887.
5. For the testimony of Turner, president of the Detroit branch of the NAACP, see ibid., 2811–17; for the testimony of Tappes, an international representative of the UAW, see ibid., pt. 2, 3117–44.
6. Kincaid Interview, 1–4, 13, 29, 31.
7. Interview with Marc Stepp by author, June 2, 1999, 12, 40–41 (hereafter cited as Stepp Interview (1999)); interview with Marc Stepp by author, April 12, 2000, 12–14 (hereafter cited as Stepp Interview (2000)); Boggs, *Living for Change,* 86, 96.
8. Boggs, *Living for Change,* 86.
9. Interview with Margaret Branch by author, 1, 27, 29–30 (hereafter cited as Margaret Branch Interview). Muddy Waters is quoted in McKee and Chisenhall, *Beale Black and Blue,* 236.
10. On the growth in population see Stovall, *The Growth of Black Elected Officials in the City of Detroit,* 6; Sugrue, *The Origins of the Urban Crisis,* 23. On black–police relations in Detroit into the 1930s, see Wilson, *Toast of the Town,* 114; Dancy, *Sand against the Wind,* 291; Stovall, *The Growth of Black Elected Officials in the City of Detroit,* 47–48; Robert W. Bagnall, "Michigan—The Land of Many Waters" (1926), in Lutz and Ashton, *These "Colored" United States,* 163–64; Thomas, *Life for Us Is What We Make It,* 164–66, 229–35; Young, *Hard Stuff,* 36; Boykin, *A Handbook on the Detroit Negro,* 23; Dillard, "From the Reverend Charles A. Hill to the Reverend Albert B. Cleage, Jr.," 102–4. On white southerners in Detroit see Hartigan, *Racial Situations.* For an extraordinary fictional account of small-town white Midwestern migration into Detroit, see Oates, *them.*
11. Interview with Arthur Johnson by author, 4–5 (hereafter cited as Johnson Interview).
12. See Capeci, *Race Relations in Wartime Detroit,* chaps. 5–7; McGreevy, *Parish Boundaries,* 72–76, 77; Sugrue, *The Origins of the Urban Crisis,* 73–75; Thomas, *Redevelopment and Race,* 23–26; Thomas, *Life for Us Is What We Make It,* 143–48. Djiuk is quoted in McGreevy, *Parish Boundaries,* 75. For a sensitive discussion of the use of religious faith in defense of racism, see Marsh, *God's Long Summer,* chaps. 2, 3.
13. On hate strikes see Capeci and Wilkerson, *Layered Violence,* 184–85; Meier and Rudwick, *Black Detroit and the Rise of the UAW,* 162–74. On the 1943 riot see Capeci and Wilkerson, *Layered Violence, passim;* Lee and Daymond, *Race Riot,* 74 and *passim;* Thomas, *Life for Us Is What We Make It,* 166–72.

14. Capeci and Wilkerson, *Layered Violence*, esp. chap. 4; Hartigan, *Racial Situations*, 50–69, 88–107; McGreevy, *Parish Boundaries, passim;* Sugrue, *The Origins of the Urban Crisis*, 76–77, 193–94, 245–46.

15. For black responses see Meier and Rudwick, *Black Detroit and the Rise of the UAW, passim;* Thomas, *Life for Us Is What We Make It*, chap. 7.

16. See Lenore Wilson, "Three Angry Men Led Bloodless Revolution," *Michigan Chronicle*, February 25, 1956; Thomas, *Life for Us Is What We Make It*, 257–70; Elizabeth L. Gulley to Nannie Helen Burroughs, October 24, 1925, Detroit, Box 9, NHB; Stepp Interview (1999), 36–37; Stovall, *The Growth of Black Elected Officials in the City of Detroit*, 8–9, 70–73; Bunche, *The Political Status of the Negro in the Age of FDR*, 590, 591; Boykin, *A Handbook on the Detroit Negro*, 87, 90.

17. *Michigan Chronicle*, January 20, February 3, and March 10, 1945; Sugrue, *The Origins of the Urban Crisis*, 77–81. On the 1945 primary campaign see *Michigan Chronicle*, March 31, June 2, July 28, and August 4, 1945; Stovall, *The Growth of Black Elected Officials in the City of Detroit*, 110–16; Dillard, "From the Reverend Charles A. Hill to the Reverend Albert B. Cleage, Jr.," 175–82. On Hill's career see *Michigan Chronicle*, November 3, 1945; November 11, 1947; November 14, 1959, November 18, 1967.

18. See *Michigan Chronicle*, August 11 and 18 and November 3, 1945; June 7, August 30, September 13, October 4 and 11 and November 8, 1947; August 21 and September 4, 1948; *Ebony*, August 1969, 118; Young, *Hard Stuff*, 90, 91, 106–7; Stovall, *The Growth of Black Elected Officials in the City of Detroit*, 120–22; Jacoby, *Someone Else's House*, 235; Frank A. Nolan, Chairman [Wallace rally Committee] to "Dear Friend," May 25, 1947, Detroit, reel 3, SEC.

19. For Wartman's articles see *Michigan Chronicle*, November 17 and 24, 1951.

20. Stepp Interview (2000), 25.

21. *Michigan Chronicle*, November 2, 1946. On the employment conditions for blacks in both city government and among major employers, see Fransic [*sic*] A. Kornegay, "Employment Survey of Negroes in City Departments as of February 15, 1946" (typescript), Box 4, folder 132, FAK; Sugrue, *The Origins of the Urban Crisis*, 91–123. For an illuminating analysis of Detroit's black elite, see the anonymous three-part series on black society in the *Michigan Chronicle*, January 12 and 19 and February 2, 1952; see also Dancy, *Sand against the Wind, passim.*

22. For a different analysis of the black church and politics from a more recent perspective, see Reed, *The Jesse Jackson Phenomenon.*

23. On New Bethel's membership see *Michigan Chronicle*, October 10, 1953. Even allowing for exaggeration, it is clear the church's membership grew significantly. For discussions of the social composition of New Bethel, see interview with Hicken Perry by author, 4, 43 (hereafter cited as Perry Interview); Todd Interview, 6, 32; interview with Ralph Williams by author, 21 (hereafter cited as Ralph Williams Interview); Stepp Interview (1999), 42; Perkins Interview, 4, 55; Margaret Branch Interview, 33; interview with Wallace Malone by author, 8, 9, 14 (hereafter cited as Malone Interview); Thompson Interview, 20; McCoy Interview, 5, 6; interview with Cneri Jenkins by author, 4 (hereafter cited as Jenkins Interview); EF Interview, 12–13.

24. Penn Interview, 44. Penn's recollection was confirmed in independent interviews with Patricia Rodgers, a former church secretary at New Bethel, and longtime church mem-

ber and activist Myra Perkins. See interview with Patricia Rodgers by author, 8 (hereafter cited as Rodgers Interview): Perkins Interview, 13.

25. Exodus 14:15–16 (KJV); CLF, *Moses at the Red Sea*.

26. Lewis Interview, 7–8; see also B. T. Moore Interview, 26–27.

27. For discussion of the text and the ideas in the sermon, see Laymon, *The Interpreter's One-Volume Commentary on the Bible*, 47–48; Lischer, *The Preacher King*, 56–57, 127; Roberts, *The Prophethood of Black Believers*, 37–38; Spillers, "Fabrics of History," 169 ff. On the concept of providence in African American theology, see Mitchell, *Black Belief*, 132–35.

28. Jasper Williams Interview, 14; Thompson Interview, 24–25; Kincaid Interview, 28–29, 31; interview with Reverend Jerome Kirby by author, 5–6 (hereafter cited as Kirby Interview). Harry Kincaid's son gave a moving confirmation of his father's views at a celebration of Franklin's career held at New Bethel on July 29, 2001 (author's notes).

29. *Michigan Chronicle*, December 1, 1951. For his early experience on Detroit radio see *Michigan Chronicle*, July 23, 1955, and May 22, 1965; CLF Interview, October 14, 1977, 64–65; Todd Interview, 10–11.

30. On WJLB and Leroy White see *Michigan Chronicle*, May 24, 1952; Bjorn, *Before Motown*, 90; Franklin, *Aretha*, 50; CLF Interview, October 14, 1977, 64–65; CLF Interview, November 2, 1977, 122; CLF Interview, November 30, 1977, 193; Kyles Interview, 18, 19–20, 51; Hooks Interview, 22–23; interview with Claud Young by author, 2–3 (transcript in possession of author; hereafter cited as Young Interview); Todd Interview, 3–4, 11. On Wynona Carr at New Bethel see Boyer, *How Sweet the Sound*, 130–32; CLF, *The Barren Fig Tree*.

31. Ward-Royster, *How I Got Over*, 118; Todd Interview, 3–4. On the evening program and Wynona Carr see Lee Hildenbrand and Opal Nations, liner notes to Carr, *Dragnet for Jesus*.

32. Hooks Interview, 22–23; Ralph Williams Interview, 56; interview with James Holley by author, 2, 16 (hereafter cited as Holley Interview); Kyles Interview, 18; CLF Interview, November 2, 1977, 108–9; CLF Interview, May 10, 1978, 225–26.

33. CLF Interview, October 14, 1977, 64–65; Todd Interview, 10–11; Penn Interview, 31.

34. CLF Interview, October 12, 1977, 48; Oliver, *Songsters and Saints*, 145; Young, *Woke Me Up This Morning*, 191–94.

35. Interview with Marsha L. Mickens in Moon, *Untold Tales, Unsung Heroes*, 361–62; Smith, *Dancing in the Street*, 42.

36. Kathryn Curry, "Memories," n.p., CLFP; "Evelyn," photo and inscription, CLFP; Penn Interview, 13.

37. Three Baptist ministers discussed this ministerial critique of their friend's preaching style; see Jasper Williams Interview, 5–6; E. L. Branch Interview, 12–13; interview with Reverend Bernard Lafayette by author, 23 (hereafter cited as Lafayette Interview). See also "The Preacher with the Golden Voice," 41.

38. CLF, *Dry Bones in the Valley*.

39. See *Michigan Chronicle*, June 18, 1955; for a brief discussion of the Jones–CLF relation, see Todd Interview, 12. On Jones's career in Detroit before this see *Michigan Chronicle*, July 12, 1947; November 19, 1949; December 9, 1950; July 16, 1966; and the

unsigned interpretative series which appeared on January 17, 24 and 31 and February 7, 1953; *Ebony,* April 1950, 67–69.

40. CLF Interview, October 14, 1977, 81. For an insightful analysis of this sermon see Taylor, *How Shall They Preach,* 54–55; also of interest is Thomas, *Biblical Faith and the Black American,* 82. On CLF's version of this sermon see Lafayette Interview, 17–18. For a contemporary, critical view of this suffering motif in the African American tradition, see Pinn, *Why, Lord?* Albert J. Raboteau's analysis, however, remains compelling; see Raboteau, *A Fire in the Bones.*

41. I have benefited greatly from Horace A. Porter's reflections on CLF's version of this sermon, which he compares and contrasts with Ralph Ellison's fictional Reverend A. Z. Hickman's preaching of the same sermon. See Porter, *Jazz Country,* esp. 115–18; Ellison, *Juneteenth,* esp. 125–28.

42. Buck Interview, 1–2, 37, 39; Franklin, *Aretha,* 31; Kirby Interview, 1–3, 5–6, 27, 38; Kincaid Interview, 31.

43. Kirby Interview, 5; Kincaid Interview, 27–28. On Reuben Gayden see St. Paul's Missionary Church, "*A Century with Christ,*" 1; *National Baptist Voice,* June 1972, 7; *Michigan Chronicle,* August 21, 1954; Georgia L. Gayden to Nannie Helen Burroughs, December 27, 1947; June 16, 1948; February 2 and May 9, 1952; February 11 and August 24, 1955; November 16, 1956, Box 10, NHB; CLF Interview, October 14, 1977, 68; CLF Interview, November 2, 1977, 108–9; interview with Reverend David Matthews by author, 5–6, 13–18 (hereafter cited as Matthews Interview); B. T. Moore Interview, 15, 23; Hooks Interview, 14; Holley Interview, 9–10, 18–19; Young Interview, 7–9; interview with Reverend S. L. Jones by author, 11 (hereafter cited as Jones Interview); Thompson Interview, 7–8; Corbett Interview, 26–27; EF Interview, 27. At least once CLF asked for specific help when preparing a major sermon; see R. B. Gayden to "Dear Dr. Franklin," August 20, 1964, Greenwood, MS, CLFP. Occasionally CLF noted in his sermons readings that provided material for his narrative, ranging from Robert Ingersoll, the nineteenth-century American freethinker, to the "great Protestant magazine" the *Christian Century,* to *Time* magazine and various Christian writers. See the following CLF sermons: *The Twenty-third Psalm; The Barren Fig Tree; Silver and Gold I Have None; All Things Work Together for Good to Them That Love God; Why Are Ye So Afraid, O Ye of So Little Faith?; The Rich Man and the Beggar; Fret Not Thyself.*

44. Jasper Williams Interview, 8; Young Interview, 9; Kyles Interview, 30–31; E. L. Branch Interview, 14–16; Penn Interview, 27–28; "Featured Minister of the Month," 5.

45. CLF, *Without a Song;* Psalm 137 (KJV). Verses 5–9 of this psalm exhibit an intensely nationalistic and militaristic urging of Israel to destroy her enemies, even to dashing "thy little ones against the stones." CLF never referred publicly to them.

46. On the meaning of song in the slave experience, see Levine, *Black Culture and Black Consciousness;* Raboteau, *Slave Religion;* Raboteau, "African-Americans, Exodus, and the American Israel," 8–9; Long, "Perspectives for a Study of Afro-American Religion in the United States," 59–60.

47. Thurman, *With Head and Heart,* 18; Raboteau, "'The Blood of the Martyrs Is the Seed of Faith,'" 33–34; Mitchell, *Black Preaching,* 15–16; Cone, "The Servant Church," 73; Paris, *The Social Teaching of the Black Churches,* xi–xv.

48. For discussions of the relationship between faith and social action, see Smith, *Social Crisis Preaching*, 3, 17; Proctor, *The Substance of Things Hoped For*, 12–13; Fluker, "The Failure of Ethical Leadership and the Challenge of Hope," 6, 11–12; Fauntroy, "Black Religion and Politics," 49; Roberts, *The Prophethood of Black Believers*, 22–23; Lewis Interview, 11–12. A particularly compelling analysis can be found in Thurman, *Jesus and the Disinherited*.

49. Perry Interview, 10.

50. For further development of his critique of Israel's nationalism, see CLF, "Behold, I Send You Like Sheep Into a Pack of Wolves" and *What Think Ye of Jesus?*; CLF Interview, November 1, 1977, 99–101.

51. Raboteau, "African-Americans, Exodus, and the American Israel," *passim*, esp. 9, 13–15; Raboteau, "'The Blood of the Martyrs Is the Seed of Faith,'" 32; Mabee, "African Americans and American Biblical Hermeneutics," 104; Bennett, "Black Experience and the Bible," 129 ff. On the Rastafarian use of Psalm 137 see Werner, *A Change Is Gonna Come*, 233; Davis, *Bob Marley*, 63–64; Stephens, *On Racial Frontiers*, 213. One of the leading Rastafarian singers, Bob Marley, was tagged as "the psalmist of Jamaican reggae;" quoted in Davis, *Bob Marley*, 192. Performances of this psalm in this reggae-Rastafarian tradition include The Melodians, "Rivers of Babylon," on Cliff, *The Harder They Come*, and Steel Pulse, "Worth His Weight in Gold (Rally Round)," on their album *True Democracy*. The psalm was also used in relation to Italian unification in the late nineteenth century; see Giuseppe Verdi's opera *Nabucco*. Clearly not all African Americans agreed with CLF; for different approaches see Reed, *The Jesse Jackson Phenomenon*, and Michael C. Dawson's analysis in *Black Visions*.

52. CLF Interview, November 30, 1977, 171–72; Lafayette Interview, 36–38. See also E. L. Branch Interview, 28–29; Spillers, "Fabrics of History," 167–68, 169–76.

53. Boggs, *Living for Change*, 69, 91, 121. That James Boggs's cousin Irene was a New Bethel member active on the Usher Board suggests the intricate weave that bound this community. For a discussion of Robert Ruark's commercially successful 1955 novel, *Something of Value*, with its depiction of African independence fighters in general, and the Mau Mau in particular, as barbaric and beyond efforts at "civilizing," see Hickey and Wylie, *An Enchanting Darkness*, 194–97.

54. CLF, *What Think Ye of Jesus?*; the text is from Matthew 22:41–42 (KJV).

55. See Fauntroy, "Black Religion and Politics," 49, for a brief discussion of the adaptability of that symbolic language. For a broader discussion of the power of a dissent grounded in the very expectations of the political culture it would transform, see Walzer, *The Company of Critics*, and Salvatore, *Eugene V. Debs*.

7. FAME

1. CLF, *Following Jesus*; CLF, *The Story of Job*; Kirby Interview, 21–22. Kirby observed that CLF "was all lion and he presented and delivered his messages that way."

2. VF Interview, 27–28; *Detroit News*, September 26, 1977; CLF, *The Eagle Stirreth Her Nest*; CLF, *Fret Not Thyself*; Kincaid Interview, 28. Muddy Waters is cited in Tooze, *Muddy Waters*, 85.

3. CLF Interview, May 10, 1978, 225.

4. On *Brown* and other court cases that dismantled legal segregation, see Kluger, *Simple Justice.*

5. *Michigan Chronicle,* April 3 and 17 and July 7, 1954.

6. Metress, *The Lynching of Emmett Till,* 14–43, *passim; Michigan Chronicle,* September 17, 1955. Till's father, Louis, served as an army private in the European theater during the war. In February 1945 he was found guilty in a military trial of the "premeditated murder" of one Italian woman and the rape of two others. On July 2, 1945, he was executed by hanging at the American military base in Leghorn, Italy. See *Michigan Chronicle,* October 22, 1955.

7. *Michigan Chronicle,* May 28, 1955; Metress, *The Lynching of Emmett Till,* 25; Wolff, *You Send Me,* 123–24; Ross, *Secrets of a Sparrow,* 81; Moody, *Coming of Age in Mississippi,* 121–26; Sellers, *The River of No Return,* 14–15. Abdul-Jabbar is quoted in Metress, *The Lynching of Emmett Till,* 277.

8. *Michigan Chronicle,* September 17 and October 15, 1955. The Murray Kempton article is reprinted in Metress, *The Lynching of Emmett Till,* 65–67. The precise wording used by Mose Wright can be found in the caption to a *Life* magazine sketch of the trial reprinted in Metress, *The Lynching of Emmett Till,* immediately preceding 153.

9. *Michigan Chronicle,* September 24, 1955; Chester Himes is quoted in Metress, *The Lynching of Emmett Till,* 117.

10. On Edward Turner see U.S. House of Representatives, Committee on Un-American Activities, *Hearings: Communism in the Detroit Area,* 1:2811–12. On the protest meeting see *Michigan Chronicle,* September 24, 1955; Johnson Interview, 18–19.

11. *Michigan Chronicle,* October 22, 1955.

12. In May 1956 the Detroit NAACP reported more than fourteen thousand members; see *Michigan Chronicle,* May 26, 1956, and, for earlier figures, *Michigan Chronicle,* June 6, 1953, and July 2, 1955. For an analysis of earlier challenges to the leadership of the Detroit NAACP, see Bates, "A New Crowd Challenges the Agenda of the Old Guard." CLF left no record of his personal reactions to the Till lynching, but in an interview forty-four years later, his close friend Harry Kincaid pointedly, with felt emotion, and without any prompting informed an interviewer of his origins near the town where Till was murdered. Mr. Kincaid did this within two minutes of the start of the interview. See Kincaid Interview, 1.

13. For one parishioner's experience of this, see Thompson Interview, 26.

14. On the Political Action Guild see Kincaid Interview, 9–10; Penn Interview, 23; Young Interview, 15–16; Johnson Interview, 22–23; *Michigan Chronicle,* October 9, 1954; New Bethel Baptist Church and the Progressive Civic League, *Program: Adam Clayton Powell at New Bethel Baptist Church,* n.p.; Progressive Civic League, *Program: 10th Anniversary Meeting,* n.p.; New Bethel Baptist Church, *8th Annual Radio Broadcast Program,* n.p.

15. Kincaid Interview, 10; Carson, *The Papers of Martin Luther King, Jr.,* 2:290; Johnson Interview, 22–23.

16. Interview with Arthur Featherstone by author, 7 (hereafter cited as Featherstone Interview); Johnson Interview, 19–21. For a perceptive 1952 analysis of the relationship between secular black elites in the urban North and the ministerial leaders of churches

with large migrant populations, see Reid, *The Negro Baptist Ministry*, 12 and *passim*. CLF also commented that the black church was "uniquely situated" to encourage political action. CLF Interview, November 2, 1977, 118.

17. CLF quoted in *Detroit News*, September 26, 1977. See also Kincaid Interview, 7, 8, 10; E. L. Branch Interview, 22; EF Interview, 40–41; Stepp Interview (2000), 20, 21; Ralph Williams Interview, 39, 40; CLF Interview, November 2, 1977, 118. For the presentation of these ideas in CLF's sermons at this time, see *Counting the Cost, The Fiery Furnace, Ye Are the Salt of the Earth, The Foolish and the Wise Builders,* and *The Project of Making Man.*

18. On Powell's earlier visits to New Bethel see *Michigan Chronicle*, October 9, 1954; New Bethel Baptist Church and the Progressive Civic League, *Program: Adam Clayton Powell at New Bethel Baptist Church*, n.p.; Progressive Civic League, *Program: 10th Anniversary Meeting*, n.p.; Penn Interview, 23. On the 1956 presidential race see *Michigan Chronicle*, October 27, 1956; Lichtenstein, *The Most Dangerous Man in Detroit*, 371–72.

19. On the 1956 Powell affair see *Michigan Chronicle*, July 28, October 20 and 27, and November 3 and 10, 1956. Powell is quoted in *Michigan Chronicle*, October 27, 1956. For a contemporary analysis of the black Republican vote that November, see *Michigan Chronicle*, November 17, 1956. Although cosponsored by New Bethel and featuring CLF's radio hour on WJLB, the event was held at the larger King Solomon Baptist Church.

20. *Michigan Chronicle*, November 3 and 10, 1956.

21. CLF Interview, May 3, 1978, 219.

22. Horace Clarence Boyer, *How Sweet the Sound*, 127–28. (Reese's given name was Delloreese Patricia Early.) On the gospel tour see ibid., 55–57; Heilbut, *The Gospel Sound, passim;* interview with Hulah Gene Hurley by author, 17, 19–20 (hereafter cited as Hurley Interview); *Baltimore Afro-American*, August 31, 1957. On Sam Cooke, who became the lead singer of the Soul Stirrers in 1951, see the insightful discussion in Guralnick, *Sweet Soul Music*, 32–36. On Tharpe, see Heilbut, *The Gospel Sound*, 189–96. CLF comments on whites in the audiences on tours in CLF Interview, May 3, 1978, 224.

23. Kyles Interview, 15–16; Boyer, "Contemporary Gospel," 23–27; Davis, *I Got the Word in Me*, 78–79; Lincoln and Mamiya, *The Black Church in the African American Experience*, 346; Walker, *"Somebody's Calling My Name,"* 22; Harris, *The Rise of Gospel Blues*, 184–89, 202.

24. Jasper Williams Interview, 33; CLF Interview, May 3, 1978, 203; Matthews Interview, 2–3; Smith, *Dancing in the Street*, 42.

25. Thompson Interview, 10–16; Jones Interview, 1–2.

26. Kyles Interview, 15; Boyer, *How Sweet the Sound*, 105–6, 111; CLF Interview, May 3, 1978, 221; "The Preacher with the Golden Voice," 40. On Little Sammy Bryant see Ray Funk, liner notes to *None but the Righteous*, 4–5. For Aretha's first known public performance, see Isaac Jones, "In Detroit Churches," *Michigan Chronicle*, August 23, 1952. "Oretha," as Jones referred to her, sang "God Will Take Care of You." Her earliest gospel recordings are available on Franklin, *Aretha Gospel*. For the list of gospel performers that evening in Jackson, Mississippi, see Thompson Interview, 10–11.

27. CLF, *Pressing On;* Thompson Interview, 13–14.

28. Jones Interview, 1–2, 17–18; Jasper Williams Interview, 35; Kyles Interview, 15–16; E. L. Branch Interview, 11.

29. CLF Interview, November 30, 1977, 183, 184; CLF Interview, May 3, 1978, 199, 200, 219, 222, 223; CLF Interview, May 10, 1978, 229; Ralph Williams Interview, 15, 58, 59.

30. CLF Interview, November 2, 1977, 13; CLF Interview, May 3, 1978, 222, 223; Kyles Interview, 36; E. L. Branch Interview, 11. For similar testimony on CLF's faith see telephone interview with Reverend Gardner C. Taylor by author (hereafter cited as Taylor Interview).

31. Jenkins Interview, 10; Ralph Williams Interview, 9–10; Buck Interview, 12–17; Kyles Interview, 43.

32. Perkins Interview, 24; Margaret Branch Interview, 15; CLF Interview, October 14, 1977, 70–71; CLF Interview, October 21, 1977, 87–88; Heilbut, *The Gospel Sound,* 276; Guralnick, *Last Train to Memphis,* 287. On Gertrude Ward see also Buck Interview, 15; Goreau, *Just Mahalia, Baby,* 233.

33. Cohodas, *Spinning Blues into Gold,* 135; Collis, *The Story of Chess Records,* 149; CLF Interview, November 15, 1977, 152; Funk, liner notes to *None but the Righteous,* 4–5; Young, *Woke Me Up This Morning,* 193–95; Hayes and Laughton, *Gospel Records, 1943–1969,* vol. 1, n.p. (CLF entry). Don D. Robey, founder of Peacock Records, had approached Franklin in 1954 after Clara Ward informed him that the preacher was "interested in recording, at this time, for a reputable Company." A contract was never signed. See Robey to "Dear Reverend Franklin," February 15, 1954, Houston, CLFP.

34. Thompson Interview, 9–10; Hayes and Laughton, *Gospel Records, 1943–1969,* vol. 1, n.p. (CLF entry); Heilbut, *The Gospel Sound,* 273–74; Guralnick, *Sweet Soul Music,* 138; Ward, *Just My Soul Responding,* 139; Brown, *Miss Rhythm,* 142; EF Interview, 4; Boyer, *How Sweet the Sound,* 53; King, *Blues All Around Me,* 50; Maultsby, "The Impact of Gospel Music on the Secular Music Industry," 24–26; Young, *Woke Me Up This Morning,* 40; Murray, *Boogie Man,* 132, 133–34; Cohodas, *Spinning Blues into Gold,* 61. On Dot Records see Cohodas, 128–29, 211; Escott, *Good Rockin' Tonight,* 6; Ward, *Just My Soul Responding,* 44.

35. Cohodas, *Spinning Blues into Gold,* 61, 76; Young, *Woke Me Up This Morning,* 40; Ferris, *Blues from the Delta,* 96; King, *Blues All Around Me,* 184; Brown, *Miss Rhythm,* 142; Lewis Interview, 2.

36. Lewis Interview, 1; Lewis, *Walking with the Wind,* 73–74; Jasper Williams Interview, 9; CLF Interview, October 14, 1977, 71–72.

37. Reverend Jesse Jackson, remarks given at CLF memorial service, August 3, 1984, CLFP (tape; transcript in possession of author).

38. McBeth, *The Baptist Heritage,* 782–86; U.S. Bureau of the Census, *Religious Bodies: 1936,* vol. 2, pt. 1, 144; Smith, *The National Baptist Bulletin, 1946,* 37; Smith, *The National Baptist Bulletin, 1948,* 7; National Baptist Convention, *The Record of the 76th Annual Session of the National Baptist Convention, 1956,* 243. On the first three presidents see Fitts, *A History of Black Baptists,* 81; Jackson, *A Story of Christian Activism,* 78–79, 127, 218; National Baptist Convention, *Proceedings of the Sixty-ninth Annual Session of the National Baptist Convention, 1949,* 9; McBeth, *The Baptist Heritage,* 787.

39. Hamilton, *The Black Preacher in America*, 159–60; Jackson, *A Story of Christian Activism*, 223; *Baptist Layman*, May–June 1953. The other candidates were Sandy Ray, Brooklyn; E. W. Perry, Oklahoma City; Marshall Shephard, Philadelphia; and Raymond J. Henderson, Los Angeles. For accounts of the lead-up to the convention and the election, see Nannie Helen Burroughs to "Dear Rev. [Joseph H.] Jackson," April 16, 1953, Box 38, NHB; *National Baptist Voice*, April, May, June, July, August, September, and October 1953. J. Pius Barbour's account in the September issue credits Jackson's victory to his command of the majority of the state presidents and their organizations, a political force far more formidable than that of the national office under an ailing and organizationally weak President Jemison.

40. Jackson, *Unholy Shadows and Freedom's Holy Light*, 69; Williams, *Biographical Directory of Negro Ministers*, 264; McBeth, *The Baptist Heritage*, 787; untitled clipping, February 15, 1932, Box 68, folder 1930s, JHJ. On Jackson's "Declaration of Negro Intentions" see *Michigan Chronicle*, May 5 and 19, 1956.

41. On the Montgomery boycott see Garrow, *Bearing the Cross*, 11–82. On the tensions surrounding the 1956 convention see National Baptist Convention, *The Record of the 76th Annual Session of the National Baptist Convention, 1956*, 58–59, 62; "Banksie" [Mrs. A. A. Banks, Jr.] to Nannie Helen Burroughs, March 22, 1956, Detroit, Box 3, NHB, for her discussion of Martin Luther King Sr.; and the columns of Nelis J. Saunders, The Stained Glass Window, in *Michigan Chronicle*, September 15 and 22, 1956. On King Jr. as a threat to Jackson, see Kyles Interview, 24.

42. On the program see National Baptist Convention, *The Record of the 76th Annual Session of the National Baptist Convention, 1956*, 52–57, 63–65; Jackson, *A Story of Christian Activism*, 312–16. Jackson's reaction to King is discussed in Lewis V. Baldwin, *There Is a Balm in Gilead*, 209–24; Lincoln and Mamiya, *The Black Church in the African American Experience*, 31.

43. On the St. Louis meeting and its aftermath see *Pittsburgh Courier*, December 29, 1956; "Dear Pastor and Co-Worker," n.d. [1956], mimeo. letter of St. Louis reformers, in Box 73, folder NBC, USA, Inc, 1953–1982, JHJ; National Baptist Convention, *The Record of the 76th Annual Session of the National Baptist Convention, 1956*, 158–60; Nelis J. Saunders, The Stained Glass Window, *Michigan Chronicle*, February 2, 1957. The preconvention infighting can be followed in J. Pius Barbour to Nannie Helen Burroughs, July 26, 1957, Chester, PA, Box 3, NHB; Gardner Taylor to Claude A. Barnett, August 23, 1957, Brooklyn, Box 386–2, CAB; W. Herbert Brewster to Joseph H. Jackson, August 1, 1957, Memphis, Box 73, folder N.B.C. National: Notes for N.B.C. Exec. Board, JHJ. The broad public discussion can be found in the *Michigan Chronicle*, February 23, May 11, June 8, and September 7, 1957, and in the wide-ranging interviews on tenure with ministers from across the country published in the paper's issues of June 29, July 6, 13, and 20, and August 10, 1957.

44. On the Louisville meeting and its legal aftermath see *Michigan Chronicle*, September 14 and 21, October 5, November 23, December 21, 1957; January 4 and 18, 1958.

45. On CLF's sartorial style in Detroit see Jenkins Interview, 19; Penn Interview, 11; Jasper Williams Interview, 4–5; Franklin, *Aretha*, 12; Broughton, *Black Gospel*, 97; McGraw, "Style to Spare," 72; King Interview, 14–15; Goreau, *Just Mahalia, Baby*, 225; George, "Lucie E. Campbell" (1987), 40.

46. Young Interview, 48; Jones Interview, 48.

47. The eminently respectable Mahalia Jackson was a beautician who processed black women's hair regularly and without public comment. Her "croconoling," a form of the process, "was absolutely the best we had seen anywhere," Willa Ward-Royster stated. "Those hairdos lasted three times longer than when anyone else did them." Ward-Royster, *How I Got Over*, 67. On the procedure for the conk see *Michigan Chronicle*, January 23, 1955, and May 10, 1958.

48. *Michigan Chronicle*, January 23, 1955; April 26 and May 3, 10, and 17, 1958; DeCaro, *On the Side of My People*, 55; King, *Blues All Around Me*, 143; Williams, *Temptations*, 27–28; Murray, *The Omni-Americans*, 50–51. As a young teen in the 1950s Cecil Franklin and a friend processed their schoolmates' hair in the Franklins' downstairs bathroom for years. Their skill and cheaper fees than the traditional barbershop attracted numerous clients, and when Cecil left for Morehouse College, he turned the business over to his close friend Smokey Robinson. See Robinson, *Smokey*, 58; Franklin, *Aretha*, 48. The opening chapters of Aretha Franklin's autobiography also suggest how multiple cultural influences could be framed within a dominant African American cultural experience even by a young teenager and her friends. See Franklin, *Aretha*, esp. 3–62.

49. McGraw, "Style to Spare," 72; Franklin, *Aretha*, 72; Smith, *Dancing in the Street*, 42; EF Interview, 45; Lewis Interview, 20. Sylvia Penn is cited in Franklin, *Aretha*, 12. For CLF's critique of the pretensions of church members, see CLF, *The King, Lord of Hosts*. In his 1954 sermon *The Prodigal Son*, CLF stressed that the elder brother who stayed in his father's house "was too selfish to come in and join in the banquet" celebrating the return of the younger, prodigal son: " So that Jesus intends for us to learn in this that it is dangerous to stay in the Church and be selfish as it is to go out but finally come back."

50. On CLF's anniversaries in general see Perkins Interview, 39–41; interview with Beverli Greenleaf by author, 34 (hereafter cited as Greenleaf Interview); King Interview, 19; *Michigan Chronicle*, August 16, 23, 1952; June 5, 12, and 19, 1954; June 18, 1955. On the 1957 celebration see *Michigan Chronicle*, July 6 and 27, 1957. On T-Bone Walker see *Michigan Chronicle*, March 6, 1948; Pete Welding, liner notes to Walker, *The Complete Imperial Recordings, 1950–1954*; Levine, *Black Culture and Black Consciousness*, 236, 237; Buck Interview, 6, 8; Hurley Interview, 13, 15; Kirby Interview, 23; Taylor Interview.

51. King, *Blues All Around Me*, 193–94, 197; Gordon, "Bobby 'Blue' Bland," n.p.; Elder, "Bobby 'Blue' Bland," 3; Guralnick, *Lost Highways*, 77.

52. EF Interview, 2; Ralph Williams Interview, 11; Bego, *Aretha Franklin*, 20–21; King, *Blues All Around Me*, 150; Brown, *Miss Rhythm*, 120–21; Heilbut, *The Gospel Sound*, 75–76, 85, 261–63; Mahalia Jackson sings this on *Gospels, Spirituals, and Hymns*.

53. Boyer, *How Sweet the Sound*, 55–57; Brown, *Miss Rhythm*, 121–22. On Nat King Cole see *Detroit Free Press*, April 12, 1956; Zolten, *Great God A'Mighty!* 204. Ruth Brown's early career is discussed in *Ebony*, May 1952, 53–56; *Michigan Chronicle*, January 5, 1963.

54. Zolten, *Great God A'Mighty!* 40–42; James, *Rage to Survive*, 75–76; Ward-Royster, *How I Got Over*, 68–69; Brown, *Miss Rhythm*, 127. Willa Ward-Royster dates this party to 1943 but it more likely occurred during the 1952 NBC convention in Chicago.

Alex Bradford (1927–1978) would have been an unknown sixteen-year-old in 1943, almost a decade away from the release of his first gospel recording in 1951. See Young, *Woke Me Up This Morning,* xxiv.

55.   Bego, *Aretha Franklin,* 24; Robinson, *Smokey,* 37, 47; Heilbut, *The Gospel Sound,* 106; Wexler, *Rhythm and the Blues,* 203; Collis, *The History of Chess,* 149.

56.   In recent years a number of academics, writers on popular music, historians and theologians, and ministers sensitive to the African American religious experience have told me categorically that CLF was the father of Aretha's first child. All "heard it" from somebody else: ministerial talk, blues and R&B singers, gospel performers. To each I asked the same question: What verifiable evidence, however limited, is there that might support such a claim? No one had any. In all the research for this book, I did not find any evidence to support this assertion. Given the absence of credible documentation, one could hope that those who, for whatever reason, relish the tale might cease its retelling.

57.   Robinson, *Smokey,* 37, 47; Franklin, *Aretha,* 62.

58.   On CLF's tours, see *Michigan Chronicle,* September 17, 1955; October 13, 1956; March 28 and September 25, 1959; April 8, 1961; CLF Interview, May 3, 1978, 201; Buck Interview, 2; interview with Beatrice Buck in Moon, *Untold Tales, Unsung Heroes,* 188; Roebuck Staples to CLF, January 5, 1961, Chicago, CLFP. Typical is the statement by Jerry Wexler that CLF "reputedly took a walk on the wild side." He undoubtedly did, but without more specific information, the broader meaning is hard to discern. See Wexler, *Rhythm and the Blues,* 205–6.

59.   Brown, *Miss Rhythm,* 131; Kathryn Curry, "Memories," CLFP; "Evelyn," photo and inscription, CLFP; Franklin, *Aretha,* 9, 11, 26, 27, 53; Young, "Aretha Franklin," 3; Goreau, *Just Mahalia, Baby,* 185–86; Buck Interview, 24; Williams, *Temptations,* 62; "The Preacher with the Golden Voice, 42.

60.   Penn Interview, 12, 13, 31; Kathryn Curry, "Memories," n.p., CLFP; Wilson is quoted in Bego, *Aretha Franklin,* 25. See also Rose "Venus" Searcy to CLF, n.d. [November 26, 1956, postmark], Detroit, CLFP.

61.   Penn Interview, 8, 9, 12, 13, 31; Ralph Williams Interview, 19–21; Perry Interview, 53.

62.   Ward-Royster, *How I Got Over,* 3–35, 50–52. The quote is on p. 34.

63.   Ibid., 56–68; Boyer, *How Sweet the Sound,* 104–7; Buck Interview, 20; Goreau, *Just Mahalia, Baby,* 233. See also Mary Katherine Aldin, liner notes to The Clara Ward Singers, *Meetin' Tonight!*

64.   Ward-Royster, *How I Got Over,* 100, 117–20.

65.   Ibid., 117; Heilbut, *The Gospel Sound,* 276. On the meeting of the World Baptist Alliance see the eyewitness reports of the Detroit Urban League leader and Afro-Baptist Francis A. Korngay dated July 16, 19, 20, 1955 (carbon copies), Box 4, FAK. The report of July 19, after devoting most of its space to a discussion of A. A. Banks and Jesse Jai McNeil, states that "[o]ne of the striking personalities of this conference is the dynamic radio preacher, C. L. Franklin."

66.   Ward-Royster, *How I Got Over,* 119, 169; CLF Interview, October 21, 1977, 85–87; *Michigan Chronicle,* July 9 and August 27, 1955; CLF's passport (issued June 13, 1955), CLFP; Kelley Interview. In his sermon *The Rich Man and the Beggar,* CLF briefly mentioned "the displaced and [the] refugee camps" he had seen the year before in Jordan and Lebanon.

67. Kyles Interview, 37. Kyles suggests that CLF actually proposed to Ward but that she refused him since she did not think they could maintain dual careers as a couple.

68. Kincaid Interview, 4; Young Interview, 38; Buck Interview, 19–20; Ward-Royster, *How I Got Over*, 122–23; Penn Interview, 20–22.

69. Young, "Aretha Franklin," 3.

70. Zolten, *Great God A'Mighty!* 40–41; *Michigan Chronicle*, September 28, 1963. For further exchanges on this issue of gospel in nightclubs, see *Michigan Chronicle*, October 13, 1962; June 22 and August 17, 1963. For a popular treatment of Clara Ward that emphasizes her lavish style and presentation, see *Ebony*, October 1957, 24–27.

71. Buck Interview, 24; McCoy Interview, 10; Todd Interview, 31; Malone Interview, 33; E. L. Branch Interview, 29. For blues artists' commentary on preachers see Son House, "Preachin' Blues," on Son House, *Father of the Delta Blues*; Hi Henry Brown, "Preacher Blues," and Joe McCoy, "Preachers Blues," reprinted in Taft, *Blues Lyric Poetry*, 41, 181, respectively.

72. King Interview, 24.

73. Buck Interview, 8; CLF, *The Inner Conflict* (see also CLF, *Following Jesus* and *The King of the Jews*); Taylor Interview; Taylor, *How Shall They Preach*, 27. On Martin Luther King Jr. see Dyson, "A Useful Hero," 13–14; on Tillich see Tillich, *From Time to Time*, 175, 183–91, 241–42.

8. NEW VOICES

1. *Michigan Chronicle*, July 27, 1957.

2. On the UAW see Meier and Rudwick, *Black Detroit and the Rise of the UAW, passim.* On Ethel Watkins see *Detroit News*, February 22 and 24 and March 8 and 18, 1957; *Detroit Free Press*, February 24 and March 13, 1957. On violence over housing in the 1950s, see Sugrue, *The Origins of the Urban Crisis*, 246–58. The poll results are reported in Kornhauser, *Detroit as the People See It*, 84, 91, 100.

3. See the testimonies and statements of Walter Reuther and Horace Sheffield in U.S. Commission on Civil Rights, *Hearings Held in Detroit, Michigan*, 38–66 (esp. 63–65) and 77–94 (esp. 87), respectively; Sugrue, *The Origins of the Urban Crisis*, 95–105. See *Michigan Chronicle*, December 24, 1960, for a contemporary reaction to the hearings.

4. Boyle, "The Kiss"; Sugrue, *The Origins of the Urban Crisis*, 101–2; Widick, *Detroit*, 92–93. The auto industry official quoted is cited by Widick, "Black Workers," 54. For a sharply different view see Horace White, "Democracy a Reality at UAW-CIO," in *Michigan Chronicle*, September 4, 1954. For a study of efforts during the war to ensure fair employment practices nationally, see Reed, *Seedtime for the Modern Civil Rights Movement*. In 1954 Charles Wartman wrote a detailed analysis of the unions affiliated with the American Federation of Labor and their relations, often quite hostile, with black Detroit. See *Michigan Chronicle*, March 20 and 27, April 3, 10, 17, and 24, and May 1, 1954.

5. For assessments of TULC see Stepp Interview (1999), 6–7; Lichtenstein, *The Most Dangerous Man in Detroit*, 375–81; Sugrue, *The Origins of the Urban Crisis*, 174–77; Babson, *Working Detroit*, 165–66.

6.   Hall Interview, 20–21. For earlier African American caucuses within the UAW see interview with Joseph Billups by Herbert Hill, Shelton Tappes, and Roberta McBride, ALUA; Stevenson, "African Americans and Jews in Organized Labor," 252. On the economic conditions of black Detroiters during these years, see Detroit Urban League, *A Profile of the Detroit Negro, 1959–1967*, 33; Sugrue, *The Origins of the Urban Crisis*, 125–52. For the reaction of UAW officials see *Detroit Times*, January 20, 1960; interview with Douglas Fraser by author, 14–15 (hereafter cited as Fraser Interview); Lichtenstein, *The Most Dangerous Man in Detroit*, 379 (Mazey quote).

7.   On Cleage and his family history see *Michigan Chronicle*, February 26, 1949, and April 12, 1952; obituary of Albert B. Cleage Jr., *New York Times*, February 27, 2000; Ward, *Prophet of the Black Nation, passim;* Williams, *Biographical Directory of Negro Ministers*, 111. On the importance of skin color in the family, see Buck Interview, 33; Young Interview, 20; Boggs, *Living for Change*, 118–19.

8.   On Cleage's years at St. Mark's, and particularly the development of his perspective from one that stressed a "high intellectual and cultural level" to social activism, see *Michigan Chronicle*, May 12 and November 17, 1951; March 21 and 28, 1953. On Cleage's new church see *Michigan Chronicle*, September 28, 1957. The theologian Reinhold Niebuhr influenced him as well; see Ward, *Prophet of the Black Nation*, 102.

9.   *Michigan Chronicle*, October 19 and 26, 1957.

10.   On the 1957 election see *Michigan Chronicle*, February 16, July 13, August 3 and 17, September 7 and 21 and October 12 and 19, 1957; January 11, 1958; *Detroit Times*, June 7, 1957; Stovall, *The Growth of Black Elected Officials in the City of Detroit*, 6, 119, 129–33. "[W]e were the moving force" in the Patrick election, Douglas Fraser of the UAW recalled decades later, but given the union's long resistance to endorsing black candidates, "we haven't got too much to brag about." Fraser Interview, 23.

11.   CLF, *Hannah, The Ideal Mother.* CLF took his text from 1 Samuel 1:4–11. On Victorian domestic thinking see Sklar, *Catherine Beecher.*

12.   Farley, Danziger, and Holzer, *Detroit Divided*, 74–75, 103–6; CLF, *Study to Show Thyself to God.* For CLF's analysis of the problems confronting black youth in the city, see also CLF, *The Inner Conflict* and *Counting the Cost;* CLF Interview, October 5, 1977, 15–16; CLF Interview, October 14, 1977, 58.

13.   VF Interview, 23–25, 32; Corbett Interview, 5, 11, 22. On Louise (Franklin) Bryant's death see *Michigan Chronicle*, December 19, 1953; January 23 and February 6, 1954; Perkins Interview, 38.

14.   Kelley Interview; Franklin, *Aretha*, 72. There is no mention of Kelley in Aretha Franklin's autobiography.

15.   Kelley Interview.

16.   See also Carl Ellan to "Dear Daddy," December 15, 1970, CLFP, where Carl Ellan regrets she cannot afford to come to Detroit for the holidays and concludes, "Of course, the high spirits of my love are always present. Take care, and be a good boy."

17.   EF Interview, 2; Corbett Interview, 12.

18.   Young, *Bodies and Soul*, 20; Robinson, *Smokey*, 109, 137; Wilson, *Dreamgirl*, 22, 23–24, 26–27; Ross, *Secrets of a Sparrow*, 1, 26–27, 90–93; Williams, *Temptations*, 44. A vivid description of Detroit's 1950s black youth culture is in King, "Searching for Brothers

Kindred," 21–29; for an insightful analysis of key aspects of this culture and its impact on American culture in the 1960s, see Early, *One Nation under a Groove.*

19. Corbett Interview, 19–20; Wilson, *Dreamgirl,* 23, 73–74; Cohodas, *Spinning Blues into Gold,* 186–87. On Carolyn Franklin see EF Interview, 30–31. On Cecil Franklin see anonymous [EF?], "Biography of Cecil LaRone Franklin," n.d., n.p. (transcript), CLFP; Corbett Interview, 38–39. Cecil later would become his sister Aretha's business manager between 1969 and 1989.

20. Franklin, *Aretha,* 42, 59, 70–71; Penn Interview, 2.

21. EF Interview, 8, 12; Kyles Interview, 51, Kelley Interview.

22. Metropolitan Civic League for Legal Action, "Constitution," (typed original, n.p.), CLFP. On police actions under Mirani see *Michigan Chronicle,* May 17 and 24 and November 29, 1958; February 17, March 7, July 25, September 5, 1959; December 16, 1961; Johnson Interview, 6; Thompson Interview, 40. For a fuller presentation of Johnson's views of the Detroit police, see his 1960 testimony in U.S. Commission on Civil Rights, *Hearings Held in Detroit, Michigan,* 302–20. On the dispute over the reelection of prosecutor Samuel H. Olsen, see *Michigan Chronicle,* July 28, 1962; Olsen offered his perspective on these issues two years earlier; see U.S. Commission on Civil Rights, *Hearings Held in Detroit, Michigan,* 500–503.

23. Johnson Interview, 25; Thompson Interview, 40. On the "urban renewal" of the Hastings Street area see *Michigan Chronicle,* October 27, 1951; July 24, 1954; April 6, 1957; April 9, 1960. On CLF in Los Angeles see *Michigan Chronicle,* September 25, 1959; Jasper Williams Interview, 24; B. T. Moore Interview, 21–22; Hurley Interview, 20–21; Hooks Interview, 19. Hooks places this a few years later, suggesting that CLF's involvement may have continued in some fashion into the mid-1960s.

24. Thompson Interview, 49. Ironically, Young was simultaneously beginning to reposition himself as a decidedly liberal, yet mainstream politician. On Young's political career in the early 1960s see *Michigan Chronicle,* July 23 and 30, 1960; May 12, 1962; Rich, *Coleman Young and Detroit Politics,* 61–90.

25. On CLF and the entertainment industry see CLF to Donroyal Enterprises, Los Angeles, February 23, 1962, Detroit, and H. Cohen, Ass't Trust Officer, Bank of America to CLF, July 19, 1963, Los Angeles, both in CLFP. At times his ministerial and celebrity roles might merge, as when he appeared at the bedside of Etta James, his daughter Aretha's friend, as she was coming out of "a nod" from too much heroin in the early 1960s. CLF was friendly with her doctor as well, a somewhat dubious medical advisor to musicians and singers. James described Franklin sitting "by the side of my bed, where he prayed for me and kept reassuring me I'd be all right." James, *Rage to Survive,* 121.

26. The unions that discriminated are named in George Weaver to Walter P. Reuther, January 27, 1960, WPR. See also Sheffield's testimony in U.S. Commission on Civil Rights, *Hearings Held in Detroit, Michigan,* 79–80.

27. On the 1959 UAW convention see *Michigan Chronicle,* October 24, 1959; Stepp Interview (1999), 15; interview with Horace Sheffield by Herbert Hill and Roberta McBride, 17–19, ALUA; interview with Robert Battle by Herbert Hill, 36–37, ALUA; Lichtenstein, *The Most Dangerous Man in Detroit,* 376–77. The following year Randolph and others founded the Detroit-based Negro American Labor Council to fight segregation within labor; see *Detroit Free Press,* May 27, 1960. On Nelson Jack Edwards see *Michigan Chron-*

icle, May 26, 1962; March 14, 1964; October 15, 1966; *Illustrated News,* May 14, 1962; interview with Horace Sheffield, 21–23, ALUA; Young Interview, 32–33.

28. On the 1960 convention and its aftermath see *Michigan Chronicle,* September 17 and 24 and October 1 and 8, 1960; *Philadelphia Evening Bulletin,* September 9, 1960; *Philadelphia Inquirer,* September 10, 1960; Caesar Clark, "The True Philadelphia Story," *National Baptist Voice,* October 1960; A. A. Banks to "Dr. Gardner Taylor," November 1, 1960, Detroit, reel 4, SEC. On the 1961 meeting and the planning for the Progressive Convention see Gardner Taylor to A. A. Banks, August 2, 1961, Brooklyn; A. A. Banks to "Dear Dr. Taylor," August 10, 1961, Detroit; A. A. Banks to Reverend Marvin T. Robinson, August 17, 1961, Detroit; and A. A. Banks to "Dear Friend Taylor," September 27, 1961, Detroit, all on reel 4, SEC; Haizlip, *The Sweeter the Juice,* 197–98; Progressive National Baptist Convention, *Minutes of the First Annual Session of the Progressive National Baptist Convention, 1962,* 57–64; *Michigan Chronicle,* September 9, 16, and 23, 1961. Jackson's position can be found in *National Baptist Voice,* June, July, and August, 1961; Jackson, *Unholy Shadows and Freedom's Holy Light,* 117–30. For useful discussions of the Progressive National Baptist Convention see Lincoln and Mamiya, *The Black Church in the African American Experience,* 36–38; McBeth, *The Baptist Heritage,* 787–88; Fitts, *A History of Black Baptists,* 100–102.

29. McCoy Interview, 29; *Michigan Chronicle,* July 1, 1961; Jackson, *Unholy Shadows and Freedom's Holy Light,* 184 and *passim;* Lafayette Interview, 33–34. Jackson's opposition to the civil rights movement had support within the Convention. See, for example, Matthews Interview, 26–29, in which this staunch supporter of, and successor to, H. H. Hume as leader of the Mississippi Baptist Convention discussed his opposition to movement activists in Mississippi. Similar ideas were expressed by Ivory James, a Baptist minister who actively opposed the movement. See James Interview, 13–17.

30. Martin Luther King Jr. had been elected vice president of the Sunday School and Baptist Training Union Congress between 1958 and 1961. See *Michigan Chronicle,* June 28, 1958; July 25, 1959; February 2 and July 2, 1960. On King's removal see *Michigan Chronicle,* September 23, 1961; A. A. Banks to "Dear Friend Gardner [C. Taylor]," September 27, 1961, Detroit, reel 4, SEC; Hooks Interview, 33; Lincoln and Mamiya, *The Black Church in the African American Experience,* 36–37.

31. EF Interview, 27–28, 29; Matthews Interview, 23; Kyles Interview, 24, 27. On the positions CLF held within the Convention, see National Baptist Convention, *Proceedings of the Sixty-eighth Annual Session of the National Baptist Convention, 1948,* 13; National Baptist Convention, *Proceedings of the Sixty-ninth Annual Session of the National Baptist Convention, 1949,* 14; National Baptist Convention, *The Record of the Seventy-third Annual Session of the National Baptist Convention, 1953,* 32; National Baptist Convention, *The Record of the Seventy-fourth Annual Session of the National Baptist Convention, 1954,* 40; National Baptist Convention, *The Record of the Seventy-fifth Annual Session of the National Baptist Convention, 1955,* 40; Rev. Charles W. Alexander to Bd. of Directors, NBC, August 28, 1964, CLFP.

32. McCoy Interview, 11, 30; Rev. Charles W. Alexander to Bd. of Directors, NBC, August 28, 1964, CLFP. On Martin Luther King's tuning in CLF see Lafayette Interview, 18, and the confirmation of it by two others who also witnessed it at different times: Lewis Interview, 16; Kyles Interview, 22. On the closeness of King to CLF see Kyles Interview, 22;

Hooks Interview, 22; Lewis Interview, 14; Ralph Williams Interview, 31; EF Interview, 5; Corbett Interview, 22; Baldwin, *There Is a Balm in Gilead*, 299 n. 88, 302; Bego, *Aretha Franklin*, 109, citing Aretha Franklin. CLF refers to his friendship with King in CLF Interview, November 8, 1977, 148. For Williams's assessment see Jasper Williams Interview, 15; he notes his support of J. H. Jackson's policies in Jasper Williams Interview, 11.

33. *Michigan Chronicle*, September 3, 1966; interview with Reverend Milton Henry by author, 1, 9, 10 (hereafter cited as Henry Interview); Dunbar, "The Making of a Militant," 27–28; Boggs, *Living for Change*, 119–20. On Jackie Robinson's wartime experience see Rampersand, *Jackie Robinson*, 99–109; for Coleman Young's see Young, *Hard Stuff*, 67–75.

34. For the history of this idea and the debate over it, see Phillips, *American Negro Slavery;* Stampp, *The Peculiar Institution;* and Fredrickson, *The Black Image in the White Mind.*

35. The series "Conspiracy of Silence" ran in the *Michigan Chronicle* April 10, 17, and 24, May 1, 8, 15, and 22, and June 5, 12, 19, and 26, 1954. Henry's analysis of inferiority is in the April 10 article; he discussed Egypt in the issue of April 24. For a passionate contemporary debate on the role of Africa, and especially Egypt, in African American consciousness, see Bernal, *Black Athena* and *Black Athena Writes Back;* Lefkowitz and Rogers, *Black Athena Revisited;* Walker, *We Can't Go Home Again.*

36. Richard Henry tried his hand at irony as well, in a manner that reflected the influence (but not the comedic timing) of Langston Hughes's nationally known fictional character, Jesse Simple. See Henry, "Is the White Race Vanishing?" *Michigan Chronicle*, November 27, 1954.

37. Henry Interview, 7–8; on the defense of street corner speakers see untitled clipping [*Detroit News*], July 8, 1957. Cleage's critique is in *Michigan Chronicle*, August 1, 1959.

38. Charles J. Wartman, "Race Relations—1960!" *Michigan Chronicle*, January 9, 16, 23, and 30 and February 6, 13, 20, and 27, 1960. Wartman's analysis in 1960 can be compared with his earlier series, "Detroit—The Years After" (*Michigan Chronicle*, February 21 and 28 and March 7, 14, 21, and 28, 1953), and with the far more optimistic and, to that extent, misleading analysis by a local reporter, "This Is City of Promise to Negro," in the *Detroit Free Press*, June 16, 17, 18, 19, 21, 23, 24, 25, 26, and 27, 1957.

39. Stovall, *The Growth of Black Elected Officials in the City of Detroit*, 136–37; *Michigan Chronicle*, January 7 and 14, 1961; *Detroit Free Press*, January 4, 1961. See also Patrick's letter to Miriani concerning integrating the police force in *Detroit Free Press*, March 7, 1959. For details on the relations between Miriani and black Detroit see *Detroit Free Press*, May 17 and 24 and November 29, 1958; February 17, July 25, and September 5, 26, 1959. A detailed analysis of the highly biased process that resulted in seventy-one white and two black Detroit police officer candidates in 1959 is available in Staff Report, Detroit Commission on Community Relations, "A Synopsis of Background, Findings, Conclusions, and Recommendations of a Study of Detroit Police Department Personnel Selection Practices," January 15, 1962, Box 59, folder 11, JPC.

40. On the 1961 election see *Michigan Chronicle*, October 21 and November 18, 1961; January 6, 1962. Stovall, *The Growth of Black Elected Officials in the City of Detroit*, 138; Young, *Hard Stuff*, 156; interview with George W. Crockett by Herbert Hill, 35–36, ALUA; interview with Mel Ravitz by Sidney Fine, 18, MHC; Dillard, "From the Reverend Charles A. Hill to the Reverend Albert B. Cleage, Jr.," 244–45.

41. *Michigan Chronicle*, December 16, 1961.

42. On Cecil see CLF Interview, October 14, 1977, 58–59.

43. On Erma see *Michigan Chronicle*, February 9, 1963; December 19, 1964; June 12, 1965; Sabrina Garrett-Owens (Erma Franklin's daughter) to author, e-mail, July 17, 2003. Erma Franklin's recording of "Piece of My Heart," is on Franklin, *Golden Classics*. Some months after the record was released, Janis Joplin's subsequent cover version became a national hit.

44. Ward, *Just My Soul Responding*, 189–92; Lornell, *"Happy in the Service of the Lord,"* 35–37; *Michigan Chronicle*, April 19, 1958; Giddens, *Riding on a Blue Note*, 278; Hirshey, *Nowhere to Run*, 26–27; Nager, *Memphis Beat*, 179–80; Wolff, *You Send Me*, 86–87; Robinson, *Smokey*, 213–16; Maultsby, "The Impact of Gospel Music on the Secular Music Industry," 28. Thomas Dorsey criticized those who crossed over (see Wolff, *You Send Me*, 87); so did Martin Luther King Jr. (see Ward, *Just My Soul Responding*, 189).

45. Hurley Interview, 21–22; Todd Interview, 18; Corbett Interview, 17–18; Penn Interview, 12–13; Margaret Branch Interview, 11; Lewis Interview, 18; Jasper Williams Interview, 22; Matthews Interview, 42; Kimble Interview, 42.

46. *Michigan Chronicle*, March 5, 1960; Jasper Williams Interview, 22; Corbett Interview, 17–18; *Memphis Press-Scimitar*, December 14 and 19, 1961. On Aretha's first years in the record business see CLF Interview, October 14, 1977, 59; EF Interview, 30; Kyles Interview, 50; and the following letters: Aretha Franklin to "Miss Jo Basil King," August 30, 1960, Detroit; unsigned [President, Columbia Records] to "Miss Aretha Franklin, c/o Rev. C. L. Franklin," June 25, 1960, New York (draft of proposed contract); Hobart Taylor Jr. to "Dear Frank," n.d. [January 27, 1961], Detroit, all in CLFP.

47. *Michigan Chronicle*, November 5, 1960; August 8 and September 1, 1962. On the course of her career, see Franklin, *Aretha*, 84–127; Guralnick, *Sweet Soul Music*, 332–52; Wexler, *Rhythm and the Blues*, 215, 245, and *passim;* Broughton, *Black Gospel*, 100; Ward, *Just My Soul Responding, passim.* Cecil Franklin is quoted in Maultsby, "The Impact of Gospel Music on the Secular Music Industry," 28; Ray Charles in Charles, *Brother Ray*, 269; CLF on Aretha Franklin's album *Amazing Grace*. The power of this sacred tradition on a spectacular, live, "secular" performance can be vividly experienced with the Aretha Franklin and Ray Charles duet "Spirit in the Dark" on *Aretha Franklin Live at Fillmore West*. The four-disc collection *Queen of Soul: The Atlantic Recordings* gathers together Franklin's most influential recordings.

9. A Rising Wind

1. Henry Interview, 4.

2. *Illustrated News*, November 27 and December 4, 11, and 18, 1961. The quotes are taken from the issue of December 11, 4–6; Boggs, *Living for Change*, 121. For a popular discussion of the economic difficulties in urban, black communities during the 1950s, see J. B. Lenoir, "Eisenhower Blues," on Lenoir, *The Parrot Sessions*, 1954–5.

3. Henry Interview, 19.

4. For GOAL's activities in 1962 see, concerning education, *Michigan Chronicle*, February 3 and 10, April 14, June 16, and December 29, 1962; *Illustrated News*, April 2, 1962; Ward, *Prophet of the Black Nation*, 80–81; Boggs, *Living for Change*, 20; concerning

urban renewal, Richard B. Henry to Edward M. Turner, January 12, 1962, Detroit, Part 1, Box 2, NAACP; *Michigan Chronicle,* May 5, 1962; concerning an all-black vote, Reverend Nicholas Hood to Henry Cleage, April 16, 1962 (copy), Detroit, Box 13, folder 12, DCCR; *Michigan Chronicle,* June 30, July 7, and August 4, 11, and 18, 1962; *Illustrated News,* April 2 and July 2 and 23, 1962; *Detroit Free Press,* August 4, 1962; *Detroit News,* August 4, 1962.

5. Henry Interview, 2–3; Fine, *Violence in the Model City,* 26; *Michigan Chronicle,* February 3 and 10 and April 21, 1962.

6. *Michigan Chronicle,* September 15, 1962; *Detroit News,* October 16 and 18, 1962 (the quote is in the issue of October 18). See also *Business Week,* July 20, 1963, 32, 34, for a slightly later assessment of Cleage's tactical abilities in negotiating antidiscrimination policies with major corporations in Detroit.

7. *Illustrated News,* March 5 and December 3, 1962.

8. For New Bethel's experience with urban renewal and its search for a new site, see New Bethel Baptist Church, "Church Resolutions," (typed), November 23, 1959; New Bethel Baptist Church, "Agreement with lawyer Kenneth N. Hylton" (copy, unsigned), n.d. [August 1960], both in CLFP; CLF Interview, October 14, 1977, 66; *Michigan Chronicle,* January 16 and March 12, 1960; January 21, September 9 and 23 and November 11, 1961; April 14, 1962; *National Baptist Voice,* April 1962. On taking possession of the new building see *Michigan Chronicle,* February 2 and 16 and March 9 and 16, 1963; Thompson Interview, 37–38; King Interview, 3; Francis A. Korngay to "The Reverend C. L. Franklin," March 8, 1963, Detroit, Box 12, FAK.

9. On CORE in Detroit see interview with Grace Bazemore by author, 2–7, 11–18; interview with Ray Bazemore by author, 11–18; interview with Clyde Cleveland by author, 3 ff. (hereafter cited as Cleveland Interview); *Michigan Chronicle,* June 27, 1964. A useful history of the national organization is Meier and Rudwick, *CORE: A Study in the Civil Rights Movement, 1942–1968, passim.*

10. It was while in jail at this time that King wrote his "Letter from a Birmingham Jail," which became famous only later. The document is reprinted in Washington, *A Testament of Hope,* 289–302.

11. Branch, *Pillar of Fire,* 41–49, 75–81; Manis, *A Fire You Can't Put Out,* 344–390.

12. Goreau, *Just Mahalia, Baby,* 348–51; EF Interview, 50; unsigned report, "The March," n.d. [June 1963], typed, closed files, DCCR.

13. The meeting where GOAL supporters demanded Cleage speak is recounted by James Boggs in Nicholas, *Questions of the American Revolution,* 11; on TULC's call (which never materialized that May) see *Michigan Chronicle,* May 11, 1963. The Nicholas article gave rise to the legend that Cleage was the singular leader of the ensuing Detroit mobilization. "Through his [Cleage's] influence, preachers all over the city began holding nightly meetings in their churches, building up momentum for the march," Boggs told Xavier Nicholas in *Questions of the American Revolution.* These meetings simply did not occur, in part because by May 1963 Cleage was persona non grata to many ministers who had a year earlier withdrawn permission for GOAL to distribute the *Illustrated News* in their churches. See Reverend Nicholas Hood to Attorney Henry Cleage, April 6, 1962 (copy), Detroit, Box 13, folder 12, DCCR; *Michigan Chronicle,* August 4, 1962. For Cleage's equally harsh assessment of all other black leaders closer

to this event, see his "Notes for a Conference on Uncle Tomism," *Illustrated News*, February 18, 1963. Both Boggs, *Living for Change*, 124, and Smith, *Dancing in the Street*, 26–27, follow James Boggs's account uncritically.

14. For a discussion of the May 10 meeting see unsigned report, "The March," n.d. [June 1963], closed files, DCCR; *Michigan Chronicle*, May 18, 1963.

15. See unsigned report, "The March," n.d. [June 1963], closed files, DCCR; Joseph E. Coles to Richard V. Marks, memorandum, "Negro Leaders Meeting on Birmingham, Alabama," May 22, 1963; Coles to Marks, memorandum, "Detroit Council for Human Rights," May 22, 1963; Coles to Marks, memorandum, "Third Meeting of the Detroit Council of Human Rights," June 4, 1963, all in Part 3, Box 19, folder 6, DCCR; *Michigan Chronicle*, May 18 and 25, 1963. For a list of officers of the DCHR see "Letterhead," n.d. [May 1963], Series 11, Box 16, folder: "Detroit Council for Human Rights," ACLU.

16. On the permit for the march (originally called for June 11), see CLF to William Patrick, May 20, 1963 (copy), Detroit, CLFP; Albert B. Cleage, "100,000 Negroes to Protest Birmingham Brutality," *Illustrated News*, May 27, 1963. On the tensions within the Baptist Ministerial Alliance see *Michigan Chronicle*, June 1, 1963; *Detroit Free Press*, June 12, 1963; untitled, undated clipping, "Preachers Nearly Come to Blows," Box 19, folder 6, DCCR; McCoy Interview, 16–17.

17. *Michigan Chronicle*, May 18, 1963. On the continued opposition to CLF see unsigned report, "The March," n.d. [June 1963], closed files, DCCR; *Michigan Chronicle*, June 1 and 8, 1963.

18. Johnson Interview, 29–32. In an anonymous, handwritten evaluation of the DCHR leadership, a staff member of the Detroit Commission on Community Relations, a city department with close ties to the established black leadership, wrote of Franklin that he was "congenial" and "Democratically orientated" but lacked the desire for personal advancement through his political activities. "At a distance he looks weak," the evaluator continued, "but perhaps apparent weakness means strength." The final comment sharply caught Franklin's lasting image among black elites: "Hair do: conk." Cleage was described as a consistent supporter of Franklin, who nonetheless "feels a bit threatened by Cleage." The DCCR writer estimated Cleage's influence within the community "at a high point" that spring and noted that Cleage "has insistently argued for maintenance of Negro leadership of the DCHR." Unsigned evaluation of DCHR leadership, handwritten, n.d. [spring/summer 1963], Box 12, folder 12, DCCR. For a sympathetic, historical overview of black Detroit's traditional leaders and organizations, see Ofield Dukes's eleven-part series in *Michigan Chronicle*, September 14, 21, and 28, October 5, 12, 19, and 26, and November 2, 9, 16, and 30, 1963.

19. Johnson Interview, 32–33; interview with Arthur Johnson by Sidney Fine, MHC, 11–12 (hereafter cited as Johnson Interview (MHC)); Mose Atkins to "President Naacp [*sic*]," May 7, 1963, Detroit, Part I, Box 6, folder: Correspondence May 1963, Incoming, NAACP; Patterson to "Hi" [Arthur Johnson], n.d. [received June 10, 1963], Detroit, and Patterson to "hi" [Arthur Johnson], "Wednesday Morning" [June 19, 1963], Detroit, Part I, Box 6, folder: Correspondence June 1963 Incoming, NAACP (the quotes are from the second letter); anonymous to [Detroit Urban League], June 19, 1963, Detroit, Box 3, FAK. See also Cleage, "Notes for a Conference on Uncle Tomism."

20. A. A. Banks to "Detroit Council of Human Rights," June 5, 1963 (copy), Detroit, Part

I, Box 6, folder: Correspondence June 1963 Incoming, NAACP; unsigned report, "The March," n.d. [June 1963], closed files, DCCR; Johnson Interview (MHC), 11–12.

21. *Detroit News,* June 8, 1963.

22. *Detroit Free Press,* June 12, 1963; Stepp Interview (1999), 7–8, 9; Stepp Interview (2000), 16–19; Johnson Interview, 32–33. See also CLF to Richard V. Marks, Secretary/Director, Detroit Commission on Community Relations, June 8, 1963, Detroit, and Marks to James Trainor, Mayor's Office, June 10, 1963, Detroit, both in Box 4, folder 8, DCCR; and Arthur L. Johnson to Garrison Clayton, Chief of Police, Dearborn, MI, June 19, 1963, Detroit, Part I, Box 6, folder: Correspondence June 1963 Outgoing, NAACP, for that organization's efforts to hold a march through heavily segregated Dearborn on June 22, 1963.

23. *New York Times,* June 24, 1963. De La Beckwith would not be convicted of the murder of Evers until three trials had occurred and thirty-one years had passed.

24. Ofield Dukes, "Walk for Freedom Drew Many Types," and Reverend Malcolm Boyd, "It's Everyone's Struggle," both in *Michigan Chronicle,* June 29, 1963; Broadus N. Butler, "Freedom March in Perspective," *Michigan Chronicle,* July 6, 1963; *Detroit Free Press,* June 24, 1963; *Detroit News,* June 24, 1963.

25. Detroit Council for Human Rights, *Official Program,* n.p.

26. *Michigan Chronicle,* June 29, 1963 (not the complete text of King's speech).

27. There were also letters critical of the march from Detroit-area blacks, usually citing the hostile reaction of white employers to the march and, as a consequence, to the writer as well. See anonymous to "NAACP," postcard, n.d. [postmarked July 21, 1963], Part I, Box 6, folder: Correspondence June 1963 Incoming, NAACP; "Cora to N.A.A.C.P.," postcard, n.d. [postmarked August 4, 1963], Part I, Box 7, folder: Correspondence August 1963 Incoming, NAACP.

28. On the movement for equal employment see *Detroit Free Press,* June 25, 1963; *Michigan Chronicle,* July 6, 13, and 20 and August 10, 1963. On unity efforts see Patterson to "Hy" [Arthur Johnson], June 25 [1963], Part I, Box 6, folder: Correspondence June 1963 Incoming, NAACP; Mrs. E. Backer to "Leaders of Negro Equality," July 7, 1963, Part I, Box 6, folder: Correspondence July 1963 Incoming, NAACP; "Minutes, Metropolitan Detroit Conference on Religion and Race," July 12, 1963, Box 8, MDCC. On discrimination against black professionals see Richard S. McGhee, M.D. to Arthur L. Johnson, August 10, 1963, Detroit, Part I, Box 7, folder: Correspondence August 1963 Incoming, NAACP. On ONE see *Michigan Chronicle,* July 20 and August 3, 1963; *Detroit Free Press,* July 1, 1963; Richard H. Austin [chairman of ONE], "Greetings," August 15, 1963, Detroit, Part I, Box 7, folder: Correspondence August 1963 Incoming, NAACP. For a prescient analysis of the need for, and the pitfalls associated with, such unity, see Dan Burley, "Why Negroes Don't Get Ahead," *Michigan Chronicle,* July 15, 1961.

29. On Cleage see *Michigan Chronicle,* July 6, 13, 1963; unsigned evaluation of DCHR leadership, handwritten, n.d. [spring/summer 1963], Box 12, folder 12, DCCR. On ONE see unsigned, "Report on the TULC Meeting of July 11, 1963 concerning ONE (Operation Negro Unity)," July 12, 1963, Detroit, Box 4, folder 1, DCCR. Concerning Del Rio see *Michigan Chronicle,* July 13, 1963; James Del Rio to "The Board of Directors, Detroit Branch of the NAACP," July 17, 1963, Detroit, Part I, Box 6, folder: Correspondence July 1963 Incoming, NAACP; Arthur L. Johnson to James Del Rio,

July 29, 1963, Detroit, Part I, Box 6, folder: Correspondence July 1963 Outgoing, NAACP. For CLF's reaction to Del Rio's charges see Raymond McCann, "Man of Many Moods," *Michigan Chronicle*, July 6, 1963.

30. *Detroit News*, June 25 and July 3 and 21, 1963; *Detroit Free Press*, July 10, 1963; *Michigan Chronicle*, August 3, 1963; Albert Cleage, "Detroit Feels Brunt of Negro Pressure," *Illustrated News*, July 8, 1963 (reprinted from *Business Week*, June 29, 1963). On King's praise of Franklin see "Martin" to "Dear C. L.," July 10, 1963, Atlanta, CLFP; *Michigan Chronicle*, August 3, 1963. The march raised more than $33,000; see *Michigan Chronicle*, July 27, 1963.

31. *Michigan Chronicle*, July 13 and 20 and August 17, 1963; Hersey, *The Algiers Motel Incident*, 126; Patterson to "Hy," Thursday [July 11, 1963], Part I, Box 6, folder: Correspondence July 1963 Incoming, NAACP.

32. *Michigan Chronicle*, July 13, 20, and 27 and August 3, 1963; C. Rodgers to anonymous, "Re: demonstration 7/13/63 before 1300 Beaubien," July 15, 1963, Box 4, Folder 1, DCCR; Featherstone Interview, 15; Patterson to "Hy," Thursday [July 11, 1963], Part 1, Box 6, folder: Correspondence, July 1963 Incoming, NAACP; (Reverend) Louis Johnson to Councilman Ed Carry, (copy), n.d. [July 1963], and Reverend Lillia Mae Fate to "Mayor Cavanaugh," July 11, 1963, Detroit, both in Box 88, folder 7, JPC; On Uhuru and Luke Tripp, see Ofield Dukes's interview, "Must Crush White Man," *Michigan Chronicle*, October 19, 1963, and Dukes's two-part opinion column, "Purely Personal," *Michigan Chronicle*, October 19 and 26, 1963.

33. "Race Relations in Detroit: Problems and Prospects," mimeo., n.d. [1964], 6–7, Box 71, DUL. Two years later Samuel Jackson, a federal commissioner with the Equal Employment Opportunity Commission, presented a similar analysis of the national situation before Detroit's Booker T. Washington Business Association; see *Michigan Chronicle*, April 2, 1966.

34. For the Garvey movement in Detroit see Dancy, *Sands against the Wind*, 167–68; Thomas, *Life for Us Is What We Make It*, 194–201; on honoring the last of the Garvey movement see Cleveland Interview, 13–14. On the Nation of Islam see Lincoln, *The Black Muslims in America*, 61–62 and *passim*. On Malcolm X see Henry Interview, 18; DeCaro, *On the Side of My People;* Wood, *Malcolm X;* Perry, *Malcolm*. The quote is from Betty De Ramur, "The New Malcolm Makes Local Debut," *Michigan Chronicle*, April 18, 1964.

35. On the Washington march see Branch, *Pillar of Fire*, 131–36; the text of King's speech is reprinted in Washington, *A Testament of Hope*, 217–20. On the Freedom Now party, see *Amsterdam News*, November 30, 1963; William Worthy, "An All Black Party," *Liberator*, October 1963, 18–19; *Michigan Chronicle*, September 14, October 26, November 2, 1963; *Detroit News*, October 12 and 18, 1963; *Detroit Free Press*, October 12, 1963. The draft platform of the Freedom Now Party can be found in *Liberator*, January 1964, 4–5; Cleage's detailed discussion of its rationale appears in *Illustrated News*, March 9, 1964. See also Ofield Dukes, "Negroes Need More Than a Black Party," *Michigan Chronicle*, November 23, 1963, for a critique of the Freedom Now Party in particular and black nationalism in general. King publicly rejected the Freedom Now Party on a visit to Detroit four months later; see *Michigan Chronicle*, March 28, 1964.

36. The bombing in Birmingham is discussed in Manis, *A Fire You Can't Put Out*, 403–7.

37. Albert B. Cleage, "The Dilemma of Black Leadership," *Illustrated News*, September

16, 1963; "Parents Support School Boycott," *Illustrated News*, September 30, 1963. On the conference see *Michigan Chronicle*, October 12 and 19, 1963; CLF to "The Many Militant Citizens and Civil Rights Leaders," form letter with leaflet announcing the Sunday rally, October 14, 1963, Detroit, Part I, Box 8, folder: Correspondence October 1963 Incoming, NAACP; CLF to Reverend Kelly Miller Smith, September 23, 1963, Detroit, Box 5, Folder 12; Smith to "Dear Frank," October 4, 1963, Cleveland, Ohio, Box 1, folder 13; CLF to Smith, telegram, November 4, 1963, Detroit, Box 5, folder 12, all in KMS; *Detroit Free Press*, October 27, 1963.

38. *Michigan Chronicle*, October 26, 1963.
39. *Illustrated News*, October 28, 1963; Boggs, *Living for Change*, 126–27.
40. *Michigan Chronicle*, November 2 and 9, 1963; see also *Detroit News*, October 28, 1963; *Detroit Free Press*, October 29, 1963.
41. The most complete coverage of both conferences is in *Michigan Chronicle*, November 16, 1963. See also *Detroit News*, November 10 and 11, 1963; *Detroit Free Press*, November 10, 11, and 12, 1963; *Illustrated News*, November 25, 1963; Sterling Gray, "Rev. Albert B. Cleage, Jr.: Architect of a Revolution," *Liberator*, December 1963. A partial transcript (approximately half) of Malcolm X's speech is in Breitman, *Malcolm X Speaks*, esp. 5, 7, 8, 10–14. For insightful critical essays evaluating Malcolm see Als, "Philosopher or Dog?" and Reed, "The Allure of Malcolm X and the Changing Character of Black Politics." Reed directly addresses the "house–field" dichotomy, 228–30.
42. Breitman, *Malcolm X Speaks*, 7, 8, 10; Henry Interview, 21–22; De Ramus, "The New Malcolm Makes Local Debut," *Michigan Chronicle*, April 18, 1964.
43. *Michigan Chronicle*, November 30 and December 21, 1963; February 22, 1964. On the testimonial dinner see *Michigan Chronicle*, February 8 and 29, 1964; for Milton Henry's analysis see *Michigan Chronicle*, February 8, 1964; Dunbar, "The Making of a Militant," 29.
44. For a detailed, contemporary analysis of the political infighting within black Detroit, see Robert Hoyt and Van Sauter, "How Negro Leadership Shifts," *Detroit Free Press*, December 27, 1964. On the 1964 congressional primary and general election see Stepp Interview (2000), 1–7; Featherstone Interview, 9, 15; CLF Interview, October 14, 1977, 63; *Michigan Chronicle*, April 4, June 13 and 27, August 1, 15, and 29, September 5, 12, and 19, October 3, and November 14, 1964; Stovall, *The Growth of Black Elected Officials in the City of Detroit*, 153–56; Titon, "Clarence LaVaughn Franklin," 1039.
45. On the 1964 campaign and the subsequent resignations, see *New York Times*, October 4, 1964; *Michigan Chronicle*, September 26, October 31, November 14 and 28 and December 5, 1964.
46. On Coretta Scott King's visit see *Michigan Chronicle*, November 20 and 27 and December 4 and 18, 1965; on Martin Luther King Jr.'s, *Michigan Chronicle*, October 15 and 22, 1966; on efforts for Selma, *Michigan Chronicle*, February 13 and 20 and April 17, 1965; *National Baptist Voice*, March 1966. Claud Young notes CLF's presence on SCLC's board, Young Interview, 31. On CLF and New Bethel's outreach to the poor, see *Michigan Chronicle*, August 10, 1963; January 2 and July 3, 1965; January 15, 1966; May 20 and November 25, 1967.
47. CLF had minor surgery (ailment unknown) but was in good health; see *Michigan Chronicle*, April 18, 1964. On CLF's easing the demands of preaching see Hooks In-

terview, 21; CLF Interview, November 30, 1977, 177; CLF Interview, May 3, 1978, 202, 224; Kyles Interview, 46.

48. Holley Interview, 17–18; Jasper Williams Interview, 17–18.

49. On the membership decline from the mid-1960s on, see Kincaid Interview, 20–21; Jenkins Interview, 13; Perry Interview, 14; McCoy Interview, 25; Penn Interview, 37–38; Rosenberg, *Can These Bones Live?* 141. See also EF Interview, 57. The break-in was reported in the *Michigan Chronicle*, July 21, 1962.

50. On CLF's daily activities see CLF Interview, November 15, 1977, 150–52; King Interview, 6–7; Thompson Interview, 15; Margaret Branch Interview, 21; Greenleaf Interview, 24–26; Kyles Interview, 17–18. On CLF's relationship with Jesse Jackson see EF Interview, 58–59, 60; Corbett Interview, 22–23; McCoy Interview, 31; Malone Interview, 16; King Interview, 10; *Michigan Chronicle*, July 15, 1967; Miller, *Voice of Deliverance*, 25; Titon, *Give Me This Mountain*, vii (foreword by Jackson).

51. Kirby Interview, 10–11.

52. For CLF's attitude toward reducing his touring see *Detroit News*, September 26, 1977; *Michigan Chronicle*, April 3, 1965; October 8, 1966; on the inaugural, see *Michigan Chronicle*, February 13, 1965; on his anniversaries, *Michigan Chronicle*, May 15, 22, and 29 and June 5, 1965; June 4, 11, 18, and 25, 1966; June 3, 17, and 24 and July 1 and 15, 1967.

53. CLF, federal income tax returns for 1963 and 1964, Michigan income tax returns for 1967 and 1968, and City of Detroit income tax returns for 1967 and 1968, all in CLFP; *Michigan Chronicle*, April 23, 1966. Accounts of his income are very incomplete: a royalty statement from the General Recorded Tape Corporation, dated July 1–December 31, 1974, CLFP, reports royalties of $428.10. GRT purchased Chess Records in January 1969; see Cohodas, *Spinning Blues into Gold*, 292–96.

54. *Michigan Chronicle*, May 1, 1965; Franklin, *Aretha*, 117; CLF to "president Lyndon Baines Johnson," n.d. [1965], unsigned draft, typescript, CLFP; CLF to E. H. Vaughn (U.S. Treasury Department), May 5, 1965, Detroit, and Sheldon S. Cohen to CLF, April 15, 1965, both in CLFP; *Detroit News*, September 26, 1977. This effort to hide income from the IRS was both very American and specifically quite common among black preachers; see Reid, *The Negro Baptist Ministry*, 89.

55. *Michigan Chronicle*, April 23, 30, 1966; McGraw, "Style to Spare," 72–73.

56. *Michigan Chronicle*, October 21, 1967.

57. *Michigan Chronicle*, October 1, 1966. CLF and Sanders Mallory Jr. probably crossed paths in various Detroit nightclubs over the years, but they also shared the same lawyer, Lawrence Massey. See *Michigan Chronicle*, April 23, 1966.

58. On Cleage's development see Cleage, *Black Christian Nationalism, passim;* Wilmore and Cone, *Black Theology*, 67, 68, 251–52, 329–39; on Cleage's nickname see Henry Interview, 2. For Milton Henry's involvement with Malcolm see Henry Interview, 23–24; *Michigan Chronicle*, February 20, 1965; *Detroit Free Press*, February 15, 1965; Parks, "A Time for Martyrs," 316–18. Malcolm's dinner speech is reprinted in Breitman, *Malcolm X Speaks*, 157–77. For a sense of the political distance Malcolm had traveled between 1963 and 1965, compare his five speeches given between December 1964 and February 1965 with his November 1963 speech in Detroit, in Breitman, *Malcolm X Speaks*, 6–14, 105–77.

59. On *NOW!* see Richard Henry to "Dear Rob," May 10, September 5, and November 1,

1966, Detroit, and "R" [Robert F. Williams] to "Dear Milton [Henry]," May 29, 1966, Havana, Cuba, all in Box 1, RFW. On evaluations of the American Communist party and the larger white Left, see Williams to Julian [Mayfield?], December 18, 1963, Habana [Havana]; "Rob" to "Dear Conrad [Lynn]," May 18, 1964, La Habana [Havana]; Mrs. C. L. James to "Dear Robert Williams," June 4, 1964, London; Lynn to Williams, September 7, 1964, New York; Robert F. Williams to the *Toronto Daily Star,* April 5, 1965, La Habana; Robert F. Williams to Henry Wallace, August 2, 1965, La Habana; Williams to Sylvester Leaks, August 2, 1965, La Habana; "Rob" to "Dear Bill" [William Worthy?], April 28, 1966, La Habana; "Richard [Gibson]" to "Dear Rob," March 9, 1967, London—all in Box 1, RFW. On the trip to Cuba see Milton R. Henry to Robert Williams, telegram, January 5, 1966, Detroit, and Milton R. Henry and Laurence G. Henry to "Dear Dr. Castro," January 10, 1966, Mexico City, Mexico, both in Box 1, RFW.

60. On the strike see Federal Bureau of Investigation, "Proposed Nation-wide Strike, 2/13/67, by the United Strike Committee in Support of Powell, Racial Matters," January 25, 1967, 3–4, FBI; leaflet, "Conference: The General Strike as a New Weapon of Struggle," February 13, 1967, GB; *Detroit Free Press,* January 25 and February 14, 1967; *Michigan Chronicle,* January 28 and February 4, 11, 18, and 25, 1967.

61. On the Black Arts conventions in Detroit see *Michigan Chronicle,* July 2, 1966, and July 1, 1967; Smith, *Dancing in the Street,* 191. On Dudley Randall and Broadside Press see Thompson, *Dudley Randall, Broadside Press, and the Black Arts Movement in Detroit.* Powell's unseating is discussed in Hamilton, *Adam Clayton Powell, Jr.,* 13–22, 37–39. On Conyers see *Michigan Chronicle,* March 4, 1967.

62. Perry Interview, 25–26; Henry Interview, 31.

63. Jasper Williams Interview, 13.

64. Corbett Interview, 23–24, 36.

65. *Michigan Chronicle,* July 29, 1967; John Lee Hooker, "The Motor City Is Burning," on Hooker, *Urban Blues.* On the 1967 riot see the National Advisory Commission on Civil Disorders, *Report,* 47–60, 351, 372–73; Fine, *Violence in the Model City;* Hersey, *The Algiers Motel Incident.*

66. For a politically different version of "The Motor City Is Burning," which emphasizes the riot's purported revolutionary potential, see MC5's version on their album *Thunder Express.*

10. Now He Is Down

1. On the growing militancy see interview with Kenneth Cockrell by Sidney Fine, 39–40, 46, 70–71, MHC; interview with Karl Gregory by Sidney Fine, 27–29, 45, MHC; Gregory Interview, 27, 35–41; Hersey, *The Algiers Motel Incident,* 346–48. On Cleage see his columns in the *Michigan Chronicle,* January 6 and 13, 1968; Cleage, "Inner City Parents' Program for Quality Education in Detroit Inner City Schools"; Cleage, "The Death of Fear" and "We Have Become a Black Nation"; Serrin, "Cleage's Alternative." For contemporary overviews of the 1967 violence and its meaning for the city, see Boggs and Boggs, "Detroit: Birth of a Nation," 7–10; Philip Meyer, "The Rioter—and

What Sets Him Apart," *Detroit Free Press*, August 20, 1967; and Meyer's series, "Return to 12th Street," in *Detroit Free Press*, October 27, 28, and 31 and November 1, 1968; Coalition of Black Trade Unionists, *A Review;* Alex Poinsett, "Motor City Makes a Comeback," *Ebony*, April 1978.

2. *Michigan Chronicle*, January 27, March 2 and 30, April 6 and 27, and July 27, 1968; Gregory Interview, 46; Republic of New Africa, *Now We Have a Nation, passim;* Republic of New Africa, "Agenda—Saturday 30 March 1968," and "Declaration of Independence, Approved in Convention, 31 March 1968," all in Box 4, RFW.

3. "Brother Milton R. Henry" to "The Honorable Mao Tse-Tung," March 14, 1968, Detroit, Box 2, RFW.

4. CLF Interview, November 8, 1977, 147; Young, *An Easy Burden*, 444–49; *Commemorative Journal*, 29.

5. CLF Interview, November 8, 1977, 147.

6. Young, *An Easy Burden*, 455–61; Beifuss, *At the River I Stand*, 211–42, 292; Abernathy, *And the Walls Came Tumbling Down*, 417 ff.; Garrow, *Bearing the Cross*, 611–15.

7. The speech is reprinted in Washington, *A Testament of Hope*, 279–86.

8. Young, *An Easy Burden*, 463.

9. Kyles Interview, 55–66; Young, *An Easy Burden*, 464–69; Beifuss, *At the River I Stand*, 290 ff.; Abernathy, *And the Walls Came Tumbling Down*, 439–50.

10. CLF Interview, November 8, 1977, 148.

11. Henry Interview, 25; Sherrill, "We Want Georgia," *passim.* On the creation of the Black Legion and an account of the Republic's deliberations in its first months, see *Ujamaa: News of the Republic* 1, no. 1 (June 15, 1968), Box 4, RFW; *Michigan Chronicle*, June 29, 1968.

12. For the interview with Cecil Franklin see *Michigan Chronicle*, February 3, 1968.

13. For coverage of the campaign in Detroit, see *Michigan Chronicle*, February 10, March 23, April 13, and May 4, 11, 18, and 25, 1968; *Detroit American*, May 14 and 15, 1968; Longworth D. Quinn Jr. (Official Observer, City of Detroit), "Report Concerning Incident Involving Detroit Police Department and Midwest Contingent of Poor People's Campaign," May 14, 1968 (typescript); report of interview of Timothy Chambers by Patrolman Salvatore Palazzolo, May 16, 1968 (typescript); report of interview of Bobby Bass by Detective Richard Redling and Patrolman Reginald Turner, May 20, 1968 (typescript); report of interview of Reverend Cecil Franklin by Detective Richard Redling, May 27, 1968 (typescript); report of interview of Dr. Claud Young by Detective Earl Gray and Patrolman Salvatore Palazzolo, May 29, 1968 (typescript), all in Box 561, folder 1, JPC.

14. Abernathy, *And the Walls Came Tumbling Down*, 494–539; Young, *An Easy Burden*, 477–92; Fager, *Uncertain Resurrection, passim.*

15. Fager, *Uncertain Resurrection*, 102–5; see also CLF, *The Fiery Furnace.* The text is from Daniel 3:17–18 (KJV).

16. Young Interview, 13.

17. On the presidential campaign and George Wallace see *Michigan Chronicle*, May 4, September 21, and November 2, 1968; Malone Interview, 26–29. Marc Stepp was far blunter than Malone about the attitudes of white workers: "How did we not see this when the water's coming through, with the veneer of white liberalism that the labor

movement really doused you with, how was that veneer so thin?" Stepp Interview (1999), 26. On the "Watch" meeting see *Michigan Chronicle,* December 28, 1968.

18. Reverend Richard H. Dixon Jr. to "Brother Franklin," November 21, 1968, Mt. Vernon, New York; International Afro Musical and Cultural Festival, Inc., "Press Release," n.d., Chicago; International Afro Musical and Cultural Festival, Inc., "Board of Directors," n.d.; "Honored Guests," n.d., all in CLFP. The directors included Harry Belafonte, Reuben Gayden, Coretta Scott King, Jesse Jackson, Clara Ward, Roebuck "Pop" Staples, Aretha Franklin, Samuel Billy Kyles, Benjamin Hooks, Nelson Jack Edwards, and Horace Sheffield. See *Michigan Chronicle,* February 15, 1969, for the projected program of the three-day event, "Spectacular '69," then scheduled for the Houston Astrodome.

19. CLF, "Say It Loud, I Am Black and I Am Proud," typescript, CLFP.

20. CLF cited Gladys Knight's 1967 version and not the more recent release by Marvin Gaye, another Motown artist. On the two recordings see Ritz, *Divided Soul,* 122–23. Neither version has the pronoun "I" in the title.

21. CLF, *I Heard It through the Grapevine.* At times in this talking sermon, the power of an alternative vision jangled roughly against CLF's affirmations of such innate black "racial traits" as religiosity, selflessness, loyalty, and simplicity. That he tried to turn these qualities back toward a defense of democratic equality in his conclusion only underscores the conceptual and performative weakness in this effort.

22. CLF, *The Meaning of Black Power,* where he cites Chuck Stone's book *Tell It Like It Is* (1967); Dawson, *Black Visions,* chap. 3. On Detroit's black population in 1970 see Stovall, *The Growth of Black Elected Officials in the City of Detroit,* 6.

23. On CLF's approach in this regard see Gregory Interview, 47; Holley Interview, 12–14; Perry Interview, 27; Young Interview, 21; Kincaid Interview, 18–20.

24. Ralph Williams Interview, 42–44; Henry Interview, 33–34; Lonnie Saunders to Richard V. Marks, "Field Division Report on the March 29, 1969 Shooting at New Bethel Baptist Church and Subsequent Events," April 24, 1969, 1–2, Box 122, folder 36, DCCR; *Detroit Free Press,* March 31 and April 1, 1969; *Detroit News,* March 31 and April 19, 1969; Dunbar, "The Making of a Militant," 30. RNA members believed the two officers were an assassination squad intent on killing Milton Henry; see Lumumba, "Short History of the U.S. War on the R.N.A.," 72–73.

25. Ralph Williams Interview, 45–46; Saunders to Marks, "Field Division Report on the March 29, 1969, Shooting at New Bethel Baptist Church and Subsequent Events," 2–3; CLF Interview, November 8, 1977, 144–45; interview with Brother Imari Obadele in *Muhammad Speaks,* April 25, 1969.

26. Judge George C. Crockett, "Statement," April 3, 1969 (edited typescript), Box 483, folder 2, JPC; interview with George Crockett Jr. by Sidney Fine, 2, MHC; *Detroit Free Press,* March 31 and April 1 and 6, 1969; *Detroit News,* April 1, 4, 6, and 9, 1969; *Michigan Chronicle,* April 12 and 19, 1969.

27. CLF Interview, November 8, 1977, 149; *Detroit News,* March 31, 1969. CLF recounts similar language, but not the reference to Shelby, in *Detroit News,* September 26, 1977.

28. For a devastating analysis of the prejudicial and racially biased coverage by the *Detroit News* of Crockett and the larger event, see Saunders to Marks, "Field Division Report on the March 29, 1969 Shooting at New Bethel Baptist Church and Subsequent

Events," 3–5; "CCR Field Investigation Staff" to "Police–Community Relations Sub-committee," June 13, 1969, 1–2, Box 67, folder 8, DCCR.

29. *Detroit News,* April 1, 1969. The petition ultimately attracted more than two hundred thousand signatures and was widely distributed by white Detroit police officers; see *Detroit Free Press,* May 20, 1969; Detroit Police Officers Association, "God Bless You George!" Box 120, folder 25, NDI. On black Detroit's response see CLF, statement to the press, n.d. [March 31, 1969], Box 185, folder 6, NDI; "Statement of Rev. Ralph Abernathy," n.d. [April 2, 1969], Box 483, folder 1, JPC; *Detroit News,* April 3, 1969; *Detroit Free Press,* April 3, 1969; *Michigan Chronicle,* April 5 and 12, 1969; "CCR Field Investigation Staff" to "Police–Community Relations Subcommittee," 1.

30. *Detroit News,* April 5 and 9, 1969; William Patrick to George Crockett, March 31, 1969, Detroit, Box 483, folder 2, JPC; Law Committee, New Detroit, Inc., "The New Bethel Report: 'The Law on Trial,'" April 1969, Box 67, folder 8, DCCR; Judge George Crockett, "Statement," April 3, 1969, Box 483, folder 2, JPC. For a contemporary portrait see Charles C. Sanders, "Detroit's Rebel Judge Crockett," *Ebony,* August 1969. For an account quite hostile to Crockett see Jacoby, *Someone Else's House,* 244–52.

31. Interview with Crockett by Fine, 37–38. On the League of Revolutionary Workers in Detroit, see the highly partisan discussion by Georgakas and Surkin, *Detroit, I Do Mind Dying.* Although relatively small in number, the black longtime UAW members I interviewed either had no recollection of the league or rejected it outright; see Stepp Interview (1999), 21–22; Jenkins Interview, 11; Todd Interview, 33. Also of interest for its recognition of the UAW's continued resistance to black officials, coupled with strong opposition to the league, is the interview with Robert Battle by Herbert Hill, 83–84, 88, ALUA.

32. *Michigan Chronicle,* February 3, 1968. One minister present at the meeting in Hot Springs, Arkansas, stated as fact that federal agents arrested CLF in Chicago for possession of "$50,000 worth of dope," which required the personal intervention of Joseph H. Jackson to have dismissed. There is no corroborating evidence for this, but it suggests the extent of the rumors CLF's conduct sparked. B. T. Moore Interview, 30–33, 36.

33. *Michigan Chronicle,* June 28, July 5, and December 12, 1969; *Amsterdam News,* May 31 and July 12, 1969; Jasper Williams Interview, 31–32; Receipt, signed by Stanley E. Wise (CLF's tax attorney), July 26, 1972, acknowledging CLF's $10,000 cashier's check for tax penalties, CLFP. See also Wise to CLF, February 3 and 20, 1978, CLFP, for continuing tax difficulties.

34. Robbie McCoy, The Church World, *Michigan Chronicle,* November 1, 1969. On CLF and the rumors of drug use, see Matthews Interview, 43, 45; B. T. Moore Interview, 30–33. On the Detroit response (largely none), see Perry Interview, 32; Stepp Interview (1999), 34–35. Claud Young discussed getting CLF out of the pulpit "when he is high" in Young Interview, 26. The typescript of the mid-1970s version of *Without a Song* is in CLFP. For CLF's recorded comments at James Cleveland's church, see Franklin, *Amazing Grace.*

35. On Richard Henry's resignation see "Brother Imari" to "Brother [Mweusi] Chui (Minister of Defense, RNA), October 13, 1969, Detroit; Milton R. Henry, "Executive Order, RNA," November 12, 1969, Detroit; "Brother Imari" to "Brother Gaidi and Brother Rob," November 21, 1969 (copy), all in Box 2, RFW; *Michigan Chronicle,* No-

vember 22, 1969. For his subsequent career see Dunbar, "The Making of a Militant," 26, 30–31; Lumumba, "Short History of the U.S. War on the R.N.A.," 72–73; Imari Abubakari Obadele, "National Black Elections Held by the Republic of New Africa," 27, 35, 38. On Williams's resignation see Henry Interview, 28; Williams to "Dear Pete & John," n.d. [1969], and Mary Kochiyama to "Dear Brother Rob and Sister Mabel," December 13, 1969, n.p. [New York], both in Box 2, RFW; *Detroit Free Press*, November 27, 1969; *Detroit News*, December 3, 1969.

36. Henry Interview, 34–38, 40–41. On the biblical Saul, see Acts 9:3–19.

37. *New York Times*, February 27, 2000; Boggs, *Living for Change*, esp. chap. 6.

38. Young Interview, 22, 23, 35, 37.

39. Stovall, *The Growth of Black Elected Officials in the City of Detroit*, 6; Rich, *Coleman Young and Detroit Politics*, 92–109; Gale Group, Inc., "George W. Crockett, Jr.," which included the *Time* quote. Young and Crockett both died in 1997.

40. On the accident see *Detroit Free Press*, April 9, 1972; *Detroit News*, April 9, 1972. For Ballard's funeral see *Michigan Chronicle*, February 28 and March 6, 1976; *Detroit Free Press*, February 28, 1976. For McFall's funeral see *Michigan Chronicle*, May 1, 1976. On CLF's illnesses and lack of energy see Hurley Interview, 25; CLF Interview, November 30, 1977, 177, 187; E. L. Branch Interview, 16; Jones Interview, 16–17.

41. Reverend J. W. Evans to CLF, October 12, 1977, Los Angeles, CLFP. On the decline in church membership in these years, see Perry Interview, 14; Penn Interview, 37–38; Kincaid Interview, 20, 21; Jenkins Interview, 13; McCoy Interview, 25; Jasper Williams Interview, 18–19; Rosenberg, *Can These Bones Live?* 141. Compare CLF's text, "From Bones to Destiny," with even the written version of his "Dry Bones in the Valley" to appreciate the seriousness of his decline. The 1970s text is in CLFP; the mid-1950s version is reprinted in Titon, *Give Me This Mountain*, 80–88.

42. Kirby Interview, 21–22, 23; *Michigan Chronicle*, January 29, August 26, and October 7, 1978. On CLF's children see *Michigan Chronicle*, April 10 and August 7, 1976; April 15, 1978; May 19, 1979; *Washington Post*, April 13, 1978.

43. *Detroit News*, September 26, 1977. As a result of Jeff Todd Titon's generosity, his interviews with CLF are used throughout this book.

44. "Featured Minister of the Month," cover, 5–10.

45. E. L. Branch Interview, 15–16.

46. Ibid., 30.

47. *Detroit Free Press*, June 11, 12, 15, and 23 and November 11, 1979; *Michigan Chronicle*, June 16 and 23 and July 7, 1979; *Jet*, June 28, 1979, 13.

48. Young Interview, 43, 45; *Detroit Free Press*, June 12, 1979.

49. Corbett Interview, 27–28; *Detroit Free Press*, June 11, 12, 23, and 30, September 5, November 7, 8, 16, and 21, 1979; June 21, 1980; *Jet*, July 5, 1979; November 29, 1979, 60; July 10, 1980, 30.

50. On the rumors see B. T. Moore Interview, 35; Kyles Interview, 48–49. See also Kirby Interview, 21–22.

51. *Detroit Free Press*, December 4, 1979; *Jet*, December 20, 1979, 56; EF Interview, 54; "Ree" [Aretha Franklin] to "Dear Erma," n.d. [1980], CLFP; Ralph Williams Interview, 32–33; E. L. Branch Interview, 27; Margaret Branch Interview, 20; Jenkins Interview, 16.

52. Harry Brickerson, Chair, Deacon's Board, New Bethel, to Joseph H. Jackson, August 31, 1979, Detroit, Box 11, folder 1970–79, JHJ; *Michigan Chronicle,* October 13, 1979; *Jet,* January 17, 1980, 10; April 17, 1980, 46–47; *Detroit Free Press,* March 25 and 26, 1980; memorandum, "Approximate Weekly and Monthly Expenses," undated [1980–1981], CLFP; New Bethel Baptist Church, *Rev. C. L. Franklin Day;* New Bethel Baptist Church, *Honoring Our Pastor;* Young Interview, 46; CLF Medical Log, December 1979–September 1982; vol. 1: January 10, 1980; vol. 2: February 24 and March 5, 1980; vol. 3: July 16, 1980; vol. 4: November 14 and December 9, 1980, and *passim,* CLFP.

53. CLF Medical Log, pt. 4: April 19, 1981, CLFP.

54. Smith, *In the Shadow of C. L. Franklin,* 27; *Michigan Chronicle,* October 31, 1981; *Detroit Free Press,* September 7, 1981. For recollections of the split see Todd Interview, 27–28; Perry Interview, 33–35; Hall Interview, 17–19; Greenleaf Interview, 38–42; Hurley Interview, 25–27; Rodgers Interview, 16–17; Ralph Williams Interview, 33–38; King Interview, 20–22, 24–25; E. L. Branch Interview, 23–24; Penn Interview, 40; Kincaid Interview, 23–25; Corbett Interview, 28–29; EF Interview, 55–56; Malone Interview, 18–19.

55. *Detroit News,* October 23, 1981; *Detroit Free Press,* October 31, 1981; *Michigan Chronicle,* October 31, 1981; Hall Interview, 17; King Interview, 21.

56. Ralph Williams Interview, 25; New Bethel Baptist Church, *Fifty-fourth Anniversary,* 29; *Michigan Chronicle,* May 1, 1982; *Detroit Free Press,* March 28, 1982. On Smith's selection see *Michigan Chronicle,* June 26, August 14, 21, and 28, and November 6, 1982; Smith, *In the Shadow of C. L. Franklin,* 1–40.

EPILOGUE

1. New Bethel Baptist Church, *In Loving Memory of Rev. Dr. Clarence LaVaughn Franklin,* n.p., CLFP; City of Detroit, "Certificate of Death: Clarence LaVaughn Franklin," CLFP. CLF died at the New Light Nursing Home in Detroit only a few days after he arrived. With the exception of a few months at another nursing home and a few short stays at the hospital, CLF had been cared for at home since he was discharged from Ford Hospital in December 1979. See *Michigan Chronicle,* August 4, 1984.

2. *Michigan Chronicle,* August 4 and 11, 1984.

3. New Bethel Baptist Church, *In Loving Memory of Rev. Dr. Clarence LaVaughn Franklin.*

4. *Michigan Chronicle,* August 11, 1984; *Detroit Free Press,* August 5, 1984.

5. New Bethel Baptist Church, *In Loving Memory of Rev. Dr. Clarence LaVaughn Franklin;* tape of funeral service (partial), CLFP.

6. The reference to Grand Boulevard (West) is to the site of Motown Records headquarters and recording studios.

7. Reverend Jesse Jackson, "Remarks," tape of funeral service (partial), CLFP. For Aretha Franklin's "Never Grow Old," see her album *Aretha's Gospel.*

8. *Michigan Chronicle,* August 11, 1984; *Detroit Free Press,* August 5, 1984; New Bethel Baptist Church, *In Loving Memory of Rev. Dr. Clarence LaVaughn Franklin.*

9. *Michigan Chronicle,* August 11, 1984.

BIBLIOGRAPHY

MANUSCRIPTS

The Clarence LaVaughn Franklin Papers, which I read when they were in the family's possession, are of singular importance for this biography. My deep appreciation to Erma Franklin and her daughter, Sabrina Garrett-Owens, for allowing me to disrupt their lives as I read them at Erma's dining room table. Microfilm copies are now available at the Bentley Historical Library, University of Michigan, Ann Arbor. The following libraries, with their rich and varied collections, were especially important: Archives of Labor and Urban Affairs, Walter P. Reuther Library, Wayne State University, Detroit; the Bentley Historical Library, University of Michigan, Ann Arbor; the Mississippi Valley Collection, Ned R. McWherter Library, University of Memphis, Memphis; and the Southern Baptist Historical Library and Archives, Nashville.

In addition to the manuscript collections listed at the beginning of the notes section, the following were invaluable in providing historical background:

Charles A. Hill Collection, Archives and Labor and Urban Affairs, Walter P. Reuther
    Library, Wayne State University, Detroit
Charles F. Holman Papers, Bentley Historical Library, University of Michigan, Ann Arbor
Civil Rights Congress of Michigan Collection, Archives of Labor and Urban Affairs, Walter
    P. Reuther Library, Wayne State University, Detroit
Charleszetta (Mother) Waddles Papers, Bentley Historical Library, University of Michigan,
    Ann Arbor
Executive Committee Records, Southern Baptist Convention Collection, Southern Baptist
    Historical Library and Archive, Nashville
Junius C. Austin Collection, Chicago Historical Society, Chicago
John Campbell Dancy Papers, Bentley Historical Library, University of Michigan, Ann Arbor
J. Frank Norris Papers, Southern Baptist Historical Library and Archives, Nashville
Leon DeMeunier Papers, Bentley Historical Library, University of Michigan, Ann Arbor
Memphis Blacks Collection, Special Collections, Mississippi Valley Collection, University of
    Memphis Libraries, Memphis
New Bethel Baptist Church Collection, Bentley Historical Library, University of Michigan,
    Ann Arbor
Norman McRae Collection, Archives of Labor and Urban Affairs, Walter P. Reuther Library,
    Wayne State University, Detroit
St. Paul's Missionary Baptist Church File, Bolivar County Library, Cleveland, MS
Richard McGhee Collection, Archives of Labor and Urban Affairs, Walter P. Reuther
    Library, Wayne State University, Detroit
Ralph Rosenfeld Papers, Bentley Historical Library, University of Michigan, Ann Arbor
Shiloh Baptist Church [Detroit] Papers, Bentley Historical Library, University of Michigan,
    Ann Arbor
Walter Sillers Jr. Collection, Delta State University Archives, Cleveland, MS

Interviews

By Author

The original tapes and transcriptions of these interviews are on deposit at the Bentley Historical Library, University of Michigan, Ann Arbor.

Bazemore, Grace. April 15, 2000, Detroit.
Bazemore, Ray. April 15, 2000, Detroit.
Billups, Edward Lee. May 15, 2003, Buffalo.
Black, Alma Hawes. November 10, 2001, Memphis.
_____. December 19, 2001, telephone.
Branch, Margaret. January 28, 1999, Memphis.
Branch, Reverend E. L. April 1, 1999, Detroit.
Buck, Beatrice. April 13, 2000, Detroit.
Carbage, Julia Ann. November 10, 2001, Memphis.

Cleveland, Councilman Clyde. April 13, 2000, Detroit.

Corbett, Brenda. December 5, 1998, Southfield, MI.

_____. August 9, 2000, telephone.

Donelson, Ernest. November 10, 2001, Memphis.

Featherstone, Arthur. November 2, 2000, Detroit.

Franklin, Erma. January 17, 1998, Detroit.

_____. August 9, 2000, telephone.

_____. August 11, 2000, telephone.

_____. November 9, 2001, telephone.

Franklin, Vaughn. March 13, 1999, Mobile, AL.

Fraser, Douglas. June 2, 1999, Detroit.

Greenleaf, Beverli. June 4, 1999, Detroit.

Gregory, Dr. Karl. April 12, 2000, Detroit.

Hall, Milton. October 8, 1998, Detroit.

Henry, Reverend Milton. April 14, 2000, Southfield, MI.

Hentoff, Nat. April 1, 2000, telephone.

Hill, Mary. May 15, 2003, Buffalo.

Holley, Reverend James. June 17, 1998, Detroit.

Hooks, Reverend Benjamin L. January 30, 1999, Memphis.

Hubbard, Nattie. November 10, 2001, Memphis.

Hurley, Hulah Gene. April 14, 2000, Detroit.

James, Reverend Ivory. February 1, 1999, Shaw, MS.

Jenkins, Cneri. March 31, 1999, Detroit.

Johnson, Arthur. April 13, 2000, Detroit.

Jones, Reverend S. L. October 9, 1998, Detroit.

Kelley, Carl Ellan. October 1, 2000, telephone.

Kimble, Reverend J. M. February 2, 1999, Indianola, MS.

Kincaid, Harry. April 1, 1999, Detroit.

King, Carolyn. June 16, 1998, Detroit.

Kirby, Reverend Jerome. April 14, 2000, Detroit.

Kyles, Reverend Samuel Billy. February 4, 1999, Memphis.

Lafayette, Reverend Bernard. January 14, 1999, Nashville.

Lewis, Congressman John. February 3, 2000, Ithaca, NY.

Malone, Wallace. December 3, 1998, Detroit.

Matthews, Reverend David. February 2, 1999, Indianola, MS.

McCoy, Robbie. June 16, 1998, Southfield, MI.

Moore, Lizzie. November 10, 2001, Memphis.

Moore, Reverend B. T., Sr. February 3, 1999, Cleveland, MS.

Moore, Reverend Mary. September 11, 2001, telephone.

_____. November 10, 2001, Memphis.

Moore, Ronald. November 10, 2001, Memphis.

Moseley, Willie Mae. November 10, 2001, Memphis.

Myles, Cleo. February 3, 1999, Cleveland, MS.

Penn, Sylvia. March 31, 1999, Detroit.

Perkins, Myra. December 4, 1998, Detroit.

Perry, Hinken. December 4, 1998, Detroit.

Rodgers, Patricia. December 3, 1998, Detroit.

Rogers, Catherine Hawes. November 10, 2001, Memphis.

Siggers, Semial. November 18, 2000, telephone.

Stephens, Yvonne. April 12, 2000, Detroit.

Stepp, Marc. June 2, 1999, Detroit.

_____. April 12, 2000, Detroit.

Taylor, Reverend Gardner C. May 13, 1999, telephone.

Thompson, Charlie. June 3, 1999, Detroit.

Todd, Willie. October 8, 1998, Detroit.

Williams, Reverend Jasper, Jr. March 12, 1999, Atlanta.

Williams, Ralph. June 4, 1999, Detroit.

Young, Dr. Claud. April 3, 1999, Detroit.

By others

Jeff Todd Titon

Franklin, Rachel. November 13, 1977, Detroit. (Transcript in possession of author.)

Franklin, Reverend Clarence LaVaughn. October 5, 7, 12, 14, and 21 and November 1, 2, 8, 15, and 30, 1977; May 3, 10, and 17, 1978, Detroit. (Transcript in possession of author.)

Deposited in Archives

Delta State University Archives, Cleveland, MS

Goodman, Gladys. Interviewer and date unknown.

Tharpe, Armelda. Interviewed by Annie Hamp, December 11, 1980, Cleveland, MS.

Special Collections, Ned R. McWherter Library, University of Memphis, Memphis

Burkley, Reverend Joseph Lee. Interviewed by Charles W. Crawford, March 17, 1979, Memphis.

Holmes, Reverend W. C. Interviewed by Reverend Randolph Meade Walker, March 23, 1982, Memphis.

Michigan Historical Collections, Bentley Historical Library, University of Michigan, Ann Arbor, Sidney Fine, interviewer

Cockrell, Kenneth. August 26, 1985, Detroit.

Crockett, George, Jr. August 7, 1984, Detroit.

Gregory, Karl. July 12, 1984, Detroit.

Johnson, Arthur. July 23, 1984, Detroit.

Keith, Damon. June 21, 1985, Detroit.

Potts, Reverend Robert. June 4, 1985, Detroit.

Ravitz, Mel. July 26, 1985, Detroit.

Archives of Labor and Urban Affairs, Walter P. Reuther Library, Wayne State University, Detroit

Battle, Robert. Interviewed by Herbert Hill, March 19, 1969, Detroit.

Billups, Joseph. Interviewed by Herbert Hill, Shelton Tappes, and Roberta McBride, October 27, 1967, Detroit.

Coles, Joseph. Interviewed by Jim Keeney and Roberta McBride, July 8, 1970, Detroit.

Crockett, George W., Jr. Interviewed by Herbert Hill, February 2, 1968, Detroit.

Dade, Reverend Malcolm. Interviewed by Jim Keeney and Roberta McBride, September 17, 1969, Detroit.

DiGaetano, Nick. Interviewed by Jim Keeney and Herbert Hill, June 17, 1968, Detroit.

Grigsby, Snow. Interviewed by Roberta McBride, March 12, 1967, Detroit.

Hatcher, Ray. Interviewed by Jim Keeney and Roberta McBride, July 3, 1970, Detroit.

Hill, Reverend Charles. Interviewed by Roberta McBride, May 8, 1967, Detroit.

Macki, Eleanor. Interviewed by Norman McRae, March 26, 1970, Detroit.

McPhaul, Arthur. Interviewed by Norman McRae, April 5, 1970, Detroit.

Robertson, George. Interviewed by Roberta McBride, November [?] 1967, Detroit.

Sheffield, Horace. Interviewed by Herbert Hill and Roberta McBride, July 24, 1968, Detroit.

Whitby, Beulah. Interviewed by Jim Keeney and Roberta McBride, September 16, 1969, Detroit.

DISCOGRAPHY

C. L. FRANKLIN'S RECORDED SERMONS

All Things Work Together for Good to Them That Love God. Battle 6103.

And He Went a Little Farther. Chess LP 64.

———. In Reverend C. L. Franklin, *My Favorite Sermons.* Universal MCAD-21147 (1999).

The Barren Fig Tree. Chess LP 32.

A Bigot Meets Jesus. Jewel LPS 0079.

The Book of Ezekiel. Jewel JCD 3201.

The Challenge of Christmas. Chess LP 48.

Come unto Me, Lazarus. Chess LP 74.

Counting the Cost. Chess LP 29.

The Devil Tempts Jesus. Chess LP 40.

Did Not Our Hearts Burn While He Talked by the Wayside? Battle 6110 (1956). Reissued on Chess LP 50 as *The Journey to Emmaus.*

Dry Bones in the Valley. Chess LP 36.

The Eagle Stirreth Her Nest. Chess LP 21 (ca. 1953).

———. *The Eagle Stirs Her Nest.* Jewel LP 3083.

The Eternity of the Church. Chess LP 37.

Except I Shall See in His Hands the Print of the Nails and Thrust My Hand into His Side. Battle 6102. Reissued on Chess LP 54.

———. In Reverend C. L. Franklin, *Sermons and Hymns.* Universal MCAD-21146 (1999).

The Fiery Furnace. Chess LP 35.

Fishermen, Drop Your Nets. Chess LP 59.

Following Jesus. Chess LP 45 (1955).

The Foolish and the Wise Builders. Chess LP 38.

Fret Not Thyself. Chess LP 79.

Give Me This Mountain. Chess LP 27.

The Golden Calf. Jewel LPS 0049 (ca. 1971).

The Greatest Love Story. Jewel LPS 0076 (ca. 1973).

Hannah, The Ideal Mother. Battle 6112.

Hosea the Prophet and Gomer the Prostitute. Chess LP 44.

How Long Halt Ye between Two Opinions? Battle 6111. Reissued on Chess LP 63.

I Heard It through the Grapevine. Chess LP 73 (ca. 1969).

The Inner Conflict. Chess LP 43.

Jacob Wrestling the Angel. Chess LP 22.

Jesus Met the Woman at the Well. Chess LP 55.

John's Vision of a New Heaven. Chess LP 53.

The Journey to Emmaus. Chess LP 50.

The King, Lord of Hosts. Chess LP 47.

_____. In Reverend C. L. Franklin, *Sermons and Hymns.* Universal MCAD-21146 (1999).

The King of the Jews. Chess LP 25.

Let Your Hair Down. Jewel LPS 0058 (ca. 1971).

Lo, I Am with You Always (The Great Commission). Chess LP 57 (1956).

The Lord's Prayer. Jewel LPS 0068 (ca. 1972).

The Man at the Pool. Chess LP 26.

Man on the Moon. Chess LP 72 (ca. 1969).

The Meaning of Black Power. Chess LP 76 (ca. 1969).

Moses at the Red Sea. Chess LP 19.

Moses Sends Twelve Spies (Promise of Jesus). Chess LP 58 (1956).

My Kingdom Is Not of This World. Chess LP 68.

Nehemiah and the Great Work. Chess LP 39.

Nothing Shall Separate Me from the Love of God. Chess LP 16.

The 100th Psalm (The Lord Is Good). Chess LP 62.

Paul's Hymn of Love. Chess LP 61.

Paul's Mediation on Immortality. Chess LP 56.

The Preacher Who Got Drunk. Chess LP 71.

Pressing On. Chess LP 42 (1955).

_____. In Reverend C. L. Franklin, *Legendary Sermons.* Universal MCAD-21145 (1999).

The Prodigal Son. Chess LP 23 (ca. 1954).

The Project of Making Man. Chess LP 77.

The Rich Man and the Beggar. Chess LP 60.

The Rich Young Ruler. Chess LP 49.

Satan Goes to Prayer Meeting. Jewel LPS 0106.

Silver and Gold Have I None. Chess LP 30.

The Story of Job. Chess LP 34.

Study to Show Thyself to God. Chess LP 41.

There's Danger in a Crowd. Chess LP 66.

This Is My Beloved Son. Chess LP 77.

The Twenty-third Psalm. Chess LP 20.

Two Fishes and Five Loaves of Bread. Chess LP 28.

_____. In Reverend C. L. Franklin, *Legendary Sermons.* Universal MCAD-21145 (1999).

What Is Your Life? Gospel Roots 5003.

What Must I Do to Be Saved? Chess LP 19.

_____. In Reverend C. L. Franklin, *My Favorite Sermons.* Universal MCAD-21147 (1999).

What of the Night? Chess LP 75.

What Think Ye of Jesus? Chess LP 24.

Wheel in the Middle of a Wheel. Chess LP 79.

Why Are Ye So Afraid, O Ye of So Little Faith? Battle 6108. Reissued on Chess LP 70 (1959).

Why Have the Mighty Fallen? Chess LP 67 (ca. 1968).

A Wild Man Meets Jesus. Chess LP 69.

Without a Song. Chess LP 52.

Ye Are the Salt of the Earth. Chess LP 31.

Ye Must Be Born Again. Chess LP 17.

C. L. Franklin's Sermons, Field Recordings by Jeff Todd Titon
(transcripts in possession of author)

"Behold, I Send You Like Sheep into a Pack of Wolves." May 5, 1978, Mt. Zion Baptist Church, Detroit.

"Dives, Lazarus, and the Dogs." October 2, 1977, New Bethel Baptist Church, Detroit.

"The Eternity of the Church." October 2, 1977, Little Rock Baptist Church, Detroit.

"Finding Oneself in a Cave." May 7, 1978, Holy Cross Baptist Church, Detroit.

"Fisherman or Shepherds?" May 7, 1978, New Bethel Baptist Church, Detroit.

"Give Me This Mountain." May 28, 1978, n.p. [New Bethel Baptist Church, Detroit?].

"Jesus at Bethesda." October 16, 1977, Cathedral of Faith, Inkster, MI.

"The Man Who Went to Heaven without Dying." November 7, 1977, New Bethel Baptist Church, Detroit.

"Meeting Jesus in the Dawn." April 30, 1978, New Bethel Baptist Church, Detroit.

"A Mother at the Cross." May 14, 1978, New Bethel Baptist Church, Detroit.

"A Mountain-top Vision." October 30, 1977, New Bethel Baptist Church, Detroit.

"Refusal to the Banquet of God." October 16, 1977, New Bethel Baptist Church, Detroit.

Other Recordings

Battle, Kathleen, and Jessye Norman. *Spirituals in Concerts.* Deutsche Grammophon 429790-2.

Brown, James. *40th Anniversary Collection.* Polydor 31453 3409-2.

Carr, Sister Wynona. *Dragnet for Jesus.* Speciality SPCD-7016-2.

Cliff, Jimmy. *The Harder They Come.* Mango 162-539-202-2.

Cooke, Sam. *Keep Movin' On.* ABKCO 18771-3563-2.

Dorsey, Thomas A. *Precious Lord: The Recordings of the Great Gospel Songs of Thomas A. Dorsey.* Columbia/Legacy CK 57164.

Franklin, Aretha. *Amazing Grace.* Atlantic 2-906-2/0 202 199 (1972).

_____. *Aretha Gospel.* Chess CHD-91521 (1991).

_____. *Aretha Live at Fillmore West.* Rhino R2 71526 (1971).

_____. *Queen of Soul: The Atlantic Recordings.* Rhino 71063, 4 disks (1992).

Franklin, Aretha, and Reverend [C. L.] Franklin. *Never Grow Old.* Creative Sound 3706-2.

Franklin, Erma. *Golden Classics.* Collectibles COL-CD-5453.

Franklin, Reverend C. L. and Aretha Franklin (with the New Bethel Baptist Church Choir). *Only a Look.* Jewel JCD-3059 (1996).

Gates, Reverend J. M. *Complete Recorded Works in Chronological Order. Volume 1: April to September 1926.* Document DOCD-5414 (1995).

_____. *Complete Recorded Works in Chronological Order. Volume 2: September 1926.* Document DOCD-5432 (1996).

Gaye, Marvin. *Marvin Gaye's Greatest Hits.* Motown MDO 5191.

Hastings Street Grease. Vol. 1. Blue Suit BS-110D.

Hastings Street Grease. Vol. 2. Blue Suit BS-111D.

Highway Q.C.'s. *Count Your Blessings.* Charley CPCD 8113.

Hooker, John Lee. *Detroit Blues.* Flyright FLY CD 23 (1987).

_____. *The Legendary Modern Recordings [1948–1954].* Flair/Virgin 72438 39658 2 3 (1993).

_____. *The Unknown John Lee Hooker: 1949 Recordings.* Flyright FLY CD 57.

_____. *Urban Blues.* MCA MCAD-10760 (1993).

Hopkins, Lightin' [Sam Hopkins]. *The Rising Sun Collection.* Just a Memory Records RSCD 0009.

House, Son [Eddie James House]. *Father of the Delta Blues: The Complete 1965 Sessions.* Columbia/Legacy, CZK 48867.

Jackson, Mahalia. *The Apollo Sessions, 1946–1951.* Pride PCD-2-1332 (1994).

_____. *Gospels, Spirituals, and Hymns.* Columbia/Legacy C2K 65594.

Johnson, Robert. *The Complete Recordings.* Columbia C2K 46222.

King, B. B. [Riley B. King]. *King of the Blues. Volume 1, 1946–1966.* MCA MCAD4-10677 (1992).

Lenoir, J. B. *The Parrot Sessions, 1954–5: Vintage Chicago Blues.* Relic 7020.

Malcolm X. *The Malcolm X Story, 7 Speech Set.* Sugar Hill MX 542.

MC5. *Thunder Express.* Jungle Records, Freud CD 71 (1999).

The Meditation Singers. *Good News.* Speciality SPCD-7032-2 (1992).

None but the Righteous: Chess Gospel Greats. Chess (distributed by MCA) MCD 09336/CHD 9336 (1992).

The Pattersonaires. *Book of the Seven Seals.* High Water/HMG 6514.

Patton, Charley. *King of the Delta Blues: The Music of Charlie [sic] Patton.* Yazoo Records 2001.

Rainey, Gertrude "Ma." *The Paramounts Chronologically: 1924–1925, Volume Two.* Black Swan HCD 12002 (1989).

Smith, Bessie. *The Complete Recordings, Vol 1.* Columbia/Legacy C2K 47091.

Staples, Pops [Roebuck Staples]. *Peace to the Neighborhood.* Charisma 07777 86286 2 0.

Steel Pulse. *True Democracy.* Elektra 9 60113-2.

Sykes, Roosevelt. *Roosevelt Sykes Complete Recorded Works: Volume 3, 19 September 1931 to 11 December 1933.* Document DOCD-5118.

Tampa Red [Hudson Woodbridge]. *Tampa Red: The Guitar Wizard.* Columbia/Legacy CK 53235.

Walker, T-Bone [Aaron Thibeaux Walker]. *The Complete Imperial Recordings, 1950–1954.* EMI D 200451.

———. *Stormy Monday.* Laserlight 17 103.

Walk Right In: The Essential Recordings of Memphis Blues. Indigo IGOCD 2038 (1996).

The Clara Ward Singers. *Meetin' Tonight!* Vanguard 145/46-2.

Williams, Marion. *My Soul Looks Back.* Shanachie 6011.

Newspapers and Magazines

Black Church. Boston, 1972–1974.

Buffalo Courier Express. Buffalo, 1942–1947.

Buffalo Criterion. Buffalo, 1943–1945.

Detroit Free Press. Detroit, 1950–1970.

Detroit News. Detroit, 1952–1967.

Ebony. Chicago, 1945–1984.

Illustrated News. Detroit, 1961–1964.

Liberator. New York, 1961–1971.

Memphis World. Memphis, 1943–1945.

Michigan Chronicle. Detroit, 1945–1984.

National Baptist Voice. Nashville, 1940–1985.

Southern Frontier. Atlanta, 1940–1945.

Statistical Survey. Buffalo, 1929–1942.

Government Documents

Buffalo. City Planning Commission. *Buffalo's Population in 1975.* Buffalo, 1949.

Memphis. *Benefits and Opportunities for Colored Citizens of Memphis.* Memphis, n.d. [1945].

U.S. Bureau of the Census. *Special Reports: Religious Bodies: 1906.* Pts. 1 and 2. Washington, DC, 1910.

———. *Religious Bodies: 1916.* 2 vols. Washington, DC, 1919.

———. *Religious Bodies: 1926.* 2 vols. Washington, DC, 1930.

———. *Religious Bodies: 1936.* 2 vols. Washington, DC, 1941.

———. *Thirteenth Census of the United States, Taken in the Year 1910.* Vol. 2, *Population.* Washington, DC, 1913.

———. *Fourteenth Census of the United States, Taken in the Year 1920.* Vol. 3, *Population.* Washington, DC, 1922.

———. *Fifteenth Census of the United States: 1930.* Vol. 3, pt. 1, *Population.* Washington, DC, 1932.

_____. *Negroes in the United States, 1920–1932*. Washington, DC, 1935.

_____. *Sixteenth Census of the United States: 1940*. Vol. 1, *Population: Number of Inhabitants*. Washington, DC, 1943.

_____. *Sixteenth Census of the United States: 1940*. Vol. 2, pts. 4–6, *Population: Characteristics of the Population*. Washington, DC, 1943.

_____. *Sixteenth Census of the United States: 1940*. Vol. 2, pt. 4. *Housing: General Characteristics*. Washington, DC, 1943.

_____. *Sixteenth Census of the United States: 1940*. Vol. 3, pts. 4 and 5, *Population: The Labor Force*. Washington, DC, 1943.

_____. *A Statistical Abstract Supplement: City and County Data Book, 1949*. Washington, DC, 1952.

_____. *Seventeenth Decennial Census of the United States. Census of Housing: 1950*. Vol. 1, pt. 4, *General Characteristics*. Washington, DC, 1953.

_____. *Seventeenth Decennial Census of the United States. Census of the Population: 1950*. Vol. 2, pt. 1 (United States Summary), *Characteristics of the Population*. Washington, DC, 1953.

_____. *Seventeenth Decennial Census of the United States. Census of the Population: 1950*. Vol. 2, pt. 32 (New York), *Characteristics of the Population*. Washington, DC, 1952.

U.S. Commission on Civil Rights. *Hearings Held in Detroit, Michigan, December 14, December 15, 1960*. Washington, DC, 1961.

U.S. Congress. House. Committee on Un-American Activities. *Hearings: Communism in the Detroit Area, March 10, 11, 12 and April 20 and 30, 1952*. 82d Cong., 2d sess., 2 pts. Washington, DC, 1952.

Minutes and Proceedings

Mississippi Baptist State Convention

Proceedings of the Ninety-second Session of the Mississippi Baptist State Convention, Held in Water Valley, Miss., November 18–20, 1930. N.p., n.d.

Proceedings of the Ninety-fourth Session of the Mississippi Baptist State Convention. Held in Gulfport, Miss., Nov. 29–Dec. 1, 1932. N.p., n.d.

Proceedings of the One-Hundredth and First Session (Historically Correct) of the Mississippi Baptist State Convention, Held in Philadelphia, Miss., Nov. 16–18, 1937. N.p., n.d.

Proceedings of the One-Hundredth and Third Session (Historically Correct) of the Mississippi Baptist Convention, Held in Jackson, Miss., Nov. 14–16, 1939. N.p., n.d.

National Baptist Convention

Proceedings of the Fifty-fifth Annual Session of the National Baptist Convention held with the Baptist Churches of New York, New York, September 4–9, 1935. N.p., n.d.

Proceedings of the Fifty-eighth Annual Session of the National Baptist Convention, U.S.A., Inc. Held with the Baptist Churches of St. Louis, Missouri, September 7–11, 1938. N.p., n.d.

Proceedings of the Sixtieth Annual Session of the National Baptist Convention, U.S.A., Inc., Held with the Baptist Churches of Birmingham, Alabama, September 4–9, 1940. N.p., n.d.

Proceedings of the Sixty-first Annual Session of the National Baptist Convention, U.S.A., Inc., Held with the Baptist Churches of Cleveland, Ohio, September 10–14, 1941. N.p., n.d.

Proceedings of the Sixty-second Annual Session of the National Baptist Convention, U.S.A., Inc., Held with the Baptist Churches of Memphis, Tenn., September 9–13, 1942. N.p., n.d.

Proceedings of the Sixty-third Annual Session of the National Baptist Convention, U.S.A., Incorporated, Held with the Baptist Churches of Chicago, Illinois, September 8–12, 1943. N.p., n.d.

Proceedings of the Sixty-fourth Annual Session of the National Baptist Convention, U.S.A., Incorporated, Held with the Baptist Churches of Dallas, Texas, September 6–10, 1944. N.p., n.d.

Proceedings of the Sixty-fifth Annual Session of the National Baptist Convention, U.S.A., Incorporated, Held with the Baptist Churches of Detroit, Michigan, September 5–9, 1945. N.p., n.d.

Proceedings of the Sixty-sixth Annual Session of the National Baptist Convention, U.S.A., Incorporated, Held with the Churches of Atlanta, Georgia, September 4–8, 1946. N.p., n.d.

Proceedings of the Sixty-seventh Annual Session of the National Baptist Convention, U.S.A., Incorporated, Held with the Baptist Churches of Kansas City, Missouri, September 10–14, 1947. N.p., n.d.

Proceedings of the Sixty-eighth Annual Session of the National Baptist Convention, U.S.A., Incorporated, Held with the Baptist Churches of Houston, Texas, September 8–12, 1948. N.p., n.d.

Proceedings of the Sixty-ninth Annual Session of the National Baptist Convention, U.S.A., Inc., Held with the Baptist Churches of Los Angeles, California, September 7–11, 1949. N.p., n.d.

Proceedings of the Seventieth Annual Session of the National Baptist Convention, U.S.A., Inc., Held with the Baptist Churches of Philadelphia, Pennsylvania, September 6–10, 1950. N.p., n.d.

Proceedings of the Seventy-first Annual Session of the National Baptist Convention, U.S.A., Incorporated, Held with the Baptist Churches of Oklahoma City, Oklahoma, September 5–9, 1951. N.p., n.d.

Proceedings of the Seventy-second Annual Session of the National Baptist Convention, U.S.A., Incorporated, Held with the Baptist Churches of Chicago, Illinois, September 10–14, 1952. N.p., n.d.

Record of the Seventy-third Annual Session of the National Baptist Convention, U.S.A., Incorporated and the Woman's Auxiliary, Held with the Baptist Churches of Miami, Florida, September 9–13, 1953. N.p., n.d.

The Record of the Seventy-fourth Annual Session of the National Baptist Convention, U.S.A., Incorporated and the Woman's Auxiliary, Held with the Baptist Churches of Saint Louis, Missouri, September 7–12, 1954. N.p., n.d.

The Record of the Seventy-fifth Annual Session (Diamond Jubilee) of the National Baptist Convention, U.S.A., Incorporated and the Woman's Auxiliary, Held with the Baptist Churches of Memphis, Tennessee, September 7–11, 1955. N.p., n.d.

The Record of the 76th Annual Session of the National Baptist Convention, U.S.A., Incorporated and the Woman's Auxiliary, Held with the Baptist Churches of Denver, Colorado, September 4–9, 1956. N.p., n.d.

The Record of the 77th Annual Session of the National Baptist Convention, U.S.A., Incorporated and the Woman's Auxiliary, Held with the Baptist Churches of Louisville, Kentucky, September 3–8, 1957. N.p., n.d.

The Record of the 78th Annual Session of the National Baptist Convention, U.S.A., Incorporated and the Woman's Auxiliary, Held with the Baptist Churches of Chicago, Illinois, September 9–14, 1958. N.p., n.d.

The Record of the 79th Annual Session of the National Baptist Convention, U.S.A., Incorporated and the Woman's Auxiliary, Held with the Baptist Churches of San Francisco, California, September 9–13, 1959. N.p., n.d.

The Record of the 80th Annual Session of the National Baptist Convention, U.S.A., Incorporated and the Woman's Auxiliary, Held with the Baptist Churches of Philadelphia, Pennsylvania, September 6–11, 1960. N.p., n.d.

The Record of the 81st Annual Session of the National Baptist Convention, U.S.A., Incorporated and the Woman's Auxiliary, Held with the Baptist Churches of Kansas City, Missouri and Kansas City, Kansas, September 5–10, 1961. N.p., n.d.

The Record of the 82nd Annual Session of the National Baptist Convention, U.S.A., Incorporated and the Woman's Auxiliary, Held with the Baptist Churches of Chicago, Illinois, September 5–9, 1962. N.p., n.d.

The Record of the 83rd Annual Session of the National Baptist Convention, U.S.A., Incorporated and the Woman's Auxiliary, Held with the Baptist Churches of Cleveland, Ohio, September 3–8, 1963. N.p., n.d.

The Record of the 84th Annual Session of the National Baptist Convention, U.S.A., Incorporated and the Woman's Auxiliary, Held with the Baptist Churches of Detroit, Michigan, September 8–13, 1964. N.p., n.d.

The Record of the 89th Annual Session of the National Baptist Convention, U.S.A., Incorporated and the Woman's Auxiliary, Held with the Baptist Churches of Kansas City, Missouri, September 9–14, 1969. N.p., n.d.

The Record of the 91st Annual Session of the National Baptist Convention, U.S.A., Incorporated and the Women's Auxiliary, Held with the Baptist Churches of Cleveland, Ohio and Vicinity, September 7–12, 1971. N.p., n.d.

The Financial Record of the 96th Annual Session and Contributions to Boards, Special Funds, etc. of the National Baptist Convention, U.S.A., Incorporated and the Women's Auxiliary, Held with the Baptist Churches of Dallas, Texas and Vicinity, September 7–12, 1976. N.p., n.d.

NATIONAL BAPTIST CONVENTION, WOMAN'S CONVENTION AUXILIARY

First Annual Report of the Woman's Convention, Auxiliary to the National Baptist Convention. N.p., 1901.

26th Annual Report of the Executive Board and Corresponding Secretary of the Woman's Convention Auxiliary to the National Baptist Convention. N.p., n.d.

Report of the Historian of the Woman's Convention Auxiliary to the National Baptist Convention, Chicago, Illinois, August 14–25, 1930. N.p., n.d.

PROGRESSIVE NATIONAL BAPTIST CONVENTION

Minutes of the First Annual Session of the Progressive National Baptist Convention, Inc., held with the Baptist Churches of Philadelphia, Pennsylvania, September 4–9, 1962. N.p., 1962.
Minutes of the Second Annual Session of the Progressive National Baptist Convention, Inc., Held with the Baptist Churches of Detroit, Michigan, September 3–8, 1963. N.p., 1963.

BOOKS AND ARTICLES

Abernathy, Ralph David. *And the Walls Came Tumbling Down: An Autobiography.* New York, 1989.
Adams, Myron E. "The Negro Baptist Churches of Chicago." *Standard,* April 4, 1914, 940–41.
Allen, Ray. *Singing in the Spirit: African-American Sacred Quartets in New York City.* Philadelphia, 1991.
Als, Hilton. "Philosopher or Dog?" In Wood, *Malcolm X,* 86–100.
Anderson, James D. *The Education of Blacks in the South, 1860–1935.* Chapel Hill, 1988.
Anderson, Victor. *Beyond Ontological Blackness: An Essay on African American Religious and Cultural Criticism.* New York, 1995.
Andrews, William L. "The Politics of African-American Ministerial Autobiography from Reconstruction to the 1920s." In Johnson, *African-American Christianity,* 111–33.
Archer, Chalmers, Jr. *Growing Up Black in Rural Mississippi: Memories of a Family, Heritage of a Place.* New York, 1992.
Arnez, Nancy L. "Black Poetry: A Necessary Ingredient for Survival and Liberation." *Journal of Black Studies* 11, no. 1 (September 1980): 3–22.
Babson, Steve. *Working Detroit: The Making of a Union Town.* With Ron Alpern, Dave Elsila, and John Revitte. Detroit, 1986.
Bacote, Reverend Samuel William. *Annual Statistical Report to the National Baptist Convention, Held in the City of Chicago, Illinois, October 25–30, 1905.* Nashville, 1905.
———. ed. *Who's Who among the Colored Baptists of the United States.* New York, 1980. First published in 1913.
Bailey, Ben E. "The Lined-Hymn Tradition in Black Mississippi Churches." *The Black Perspective in Music* 6, no. 1 (Spring 1978): 3–17.
Baldwin, Lewis V. *There Is a Balm in Gilead: The Cultural Roots of Martin Luther King, Jr.* Minneapolis, 1991.
Baptist Ministers Union. *Facts Truthfully Presented Relative to the Differences between the Baptist Ministers Union and the Baptist Pastors' Alliance.* Memphis, n.d.
Barry, John M. *Rising Tide: The Great Mississippi Flood of 1927 and How It Changed America.* New York, 1997.
Bates, Beth Tompkins. "A New Crowd Challenges the Agenda of the Old Guard in the NAACP, 1933–1941." *American Historical Review* 102, no. 2 (April 1997): 340–77.
Bauer, William R. *Open the Door: The Life and Music of Betty Carter.* Ann Arbor, 2002.

Bearden, Romare, and Harry Henderson. *A History of African-American Artists: From 1792 to the Present*. New York, 1993.

Bego, Mark. *Aretha Franklin: The Queen of Soul*. New York, 1989.

Beifuss, Joan Turner. *At the River I Stand: Memphis, the 1968 Strike, and Martin Luther King*. New York, 1989.

Bengston, Dale R. "The Eagle Stirreth Her Nest: Notes on an Afro-American Shamanistic Event." *Journal of Religious Thought* 33, no. 1 (Spring–Summer 1976): 75–86.

Bennett, Robert A. "Biblical Hermeneutics and the Black Preacher." *Journal of the Interdenominational Theological Center* 1, no. 2 (Spring 1974): 38–53.

_____. "Black Experience and the Bible." In Wilmore, *African American Religious Studies*, 129–39.

Berenson, William M., Kirk W. Elifson, and Tandy Tollerson III. "Preachers in Politics: A Study of Political Activism among the Black Ministry." *Journal of Black Studies* 6, no. 4 (June 1976): 373–92.

Berkeley, Kathleen C. *"Like a Plague of Locusts": From an Antebellum Town to a New South City, Memphis, Tennessee, 1850–1880*. New York, 1991.

Bernal, Martin. *Black Athena: The Afroasiatic Roots of Classical Civilization*. New Brunswick, NJ, 1987.

_____. *Black Athena Writes Back: Martin Bernal Responds to His Critics*. Edited by David Chioni Moore. Durham, NC, 2001.

Biles, Roger. *Memphis in the Great Depression*. Knoxville, 1986.

Billingsley, Andrew. *Mighty like a River: The Black Church and Social Reform*. New York, 1999.

Bjorn, Lars. *Before Motown: A History of Jazz in Detroit, 1920–60*. With Jim Gallert. Ann Arbor, 2001.

Boggs, Grace Lee. *Living for Change: An Autobiography*. Minneapolis, 1998.

Boggs, James, and Grace Boggs. "Detroit: Birth of a Nation." *National Guardian*, October 7, 1967, 7–10.

Bontemps, Arna, and Jack Conroy. *They Seek a City*. Garden City, NY, 1945.

Boyd, Jesse Taney. *A Popular History of the Baptists in Mississippi*. Jackson, MS, 1930.

Boyer, Horace Clarence. "Contemporary Gospel." *The Black Perspective in Music* 7, no. 1 (Spring 1979): 5–58.

_____. *The Golden Age of Gospel*. Urbana, IL, 2000. First published in 1995 as *How Sweet the Sound: The Golden Age of Gospel*.

_____. *How Sweet the Sound: The Golden Age of Gospel*. Washington, DC, 1995.

_____. "William Herbert Brewster: The Eloquent Poet." In Reagon, *We'll Understand It Better By and By*, 211–31.

Boykin, Ulysses W. *A Handbook on the Detroit Negro: A Preliminary Edition*. Detroit, 1943.

Boyle, Kevin. "The Kiss: Racial and Gender Conflict in a 1950s Automobile Factory." *Journal of American History* 84, no. 2 (September 1997): 496–523.

Bragg, Rick. *All Over but the Shouting*. New York, 1997.

Branch, Taylor. *Parting the Waters: America in the King Years, 1954–63*. New York, 1988.

_____. *Pillar of Fire: America in the King Years, 1963–65*. New York, 1998.

Breitman, George, ed. *Malcolm X Speaks: Selected Speeches and Statements*. New York, 1965.

Brewster, William Herbert. "Rememberings." In Reagon, *We'll Understand It Better By and By*, 185–209.

Brock, Darla. "Memphis's Nymphs Du Pave: 'The Most Abandoned Women in the World.'"
   The West Tennessee Historical Society Papers 50 (December 1996): 58–69.
Broughton, Viv. *Black Gospel: An Illustrated History of the Gospel Sound.* Dorset, UK, 1985.
Brown, Ruth. *Miss Rhythm: The Autobiography of Ruth Brown, Rhythm and Blues Legend.* With
   Andrew Yule. New York, 1999.
Buffalo League of Women Voters. *1943 Election Bulletin.* Buffalo, 1943.
Bunche, Ralph J. *The Political Status of the Negro in the Age of FDR.* Edited by Dewey W.
   Grantham. Chicago, 1973.
Butler, Arthur, Henry Louis Taylor Jr., and Doo-Ha Ryu. "Work and Black Neighborhood
   Life in Buffalo, 1930–1980." In Taylor, *African Americans and the Rise of Buffalo's Post-
   industrial City,* 2:112–56.
Cantor, Louis. *Wheelin' on Beale: How WDIA-Memphis Became the Nation's First All-Black
   Radio Station and Created the Sound That Changed America.* New York, 1992.
Capeci, Dominic J., Jr. "From Different Liberal Perspectives: Fiorello H. LaGuardia, Adam
   Clayton Powell, Jr., and Civil Rights in New York City, 1941–1943." *Journal of Negro
   History* 62, no. 2 (April 1977):160–73.
_____. *Race Relations in Wartime Detroit: The Sojourner Truth Housing Controversy of 1942.*
   Philadelphia, 1984.
Capeci, Dominic J., Jr., and Martha Wilkerson. *Layered Violence: The Detroit Rioters of 1943.*
   Jackson, MS, 1991.
Capers, Gerald M., Jr. *The Biography of a River Town: Memphis, Its Heroic Age.* Chapel Hill,
   NC, 1939.
Carpenter, Niles. *Nationality, Color, and Economic Opportunity in the City of Buffalo.* Westport,
   CT, 1970. First published in 1927.
Carson, Clayborne. "Martin Luther King, Jr., and the African-American Social Gospel." In
   Johnson, *African-American Christianity,* 159–77. Berkeley, 1994.
_____, ed. *The Papers of Martin Luther King, Jr.* Vol. 1, *Called to Serve: January 1929–June
   1951.* Berkeley, 1992.
_____, ed. *The Papers of Martin Luther King, Jr.* Vol. 2, *Rediscovering Precious Values.*
   Berkeley, 1994.
_____, ed. *The Papers of Martin Luther King, Jr.* Vol. 3, *Birth of a New Age.* Berkeley, 1997.
Cayton, Horace R., and George S. Mitchell. *Black Workers and the New Unions.* Westport,
   CT, 1970. First published in 1939.
Charles, Ray, and David Ritz. *Brother Ray: Ray Charles' Own Story.* New York, 1992. First
   published in 1978.
Childs, John Brown. *The Political Black Minister: A Study in Afro-American Politics and
   Religion.* Boston, 1980.
Church, Annette E., and Roberta Church. *The Robert R. Churches of Memphis: A Father and
   Son Who Achieved in Spite of Race.* Ann Arbor, 1974.
Church, Roberta, and Ronald Walter. *Nineteenth Century Memphis Families of Color.*
   Memphis, 1987.
Clark, Kenneth B. "The Present Dilemma of the Negro." *Journal of Negro History* 53, no. 2
   (January 1968): 1–11.
Clarke, John Henry, ed. *William Styron's Nat Turner: Ten Black Writers Respond.* Boston, 1968.

Cleage, Albert B. *Black Christian Nationalism: New Directions for the Black Church.* New York, 1972.

——. "The Death of Fear." *Negro Digest,* November 1967, 29–31.

——. "Inner City Parents' Program for Quality Education in Detroit Inner City Schools." *Integrated Education,* August/September 1967, 38–45.

——. "We Have Become a Black Nation." *Negro Digest,* January 1969, 30–38.

Cleage, Albert B., and George Breitman. *Myths about Malcolm: Two Views.* New York, 1968.

Clifton, Lucille. *Generations: A Memoir.* New York, 1976.

Coalition of Black Trade Unionists. *A Review: New Detroit and the "(Negro) People," 1967–1977.* Detroit, 1977.

Cobb, James C. *The Most Southern Place on Earth: The Mississippi Delta and the Roots of Regional Identity.* New York, 1992.

Cohen, Lawrence. *Nothing But the Blues: The Music and the Musicians.* New York, 1993.

Cohn, David L. *Where I Was Born and Raised.* Boston, 1948.

Cohodas, Nadine. *Spinning Blues into Gold: The Chess Brothers and the Legendary Chess Records.* New York, 2000.

Collis, John. *The Story of Chess Records.* New York, 1998.

Commemorative Journal: Pilgrimage to Memphis, April 3–5, 1998, Remembering the Man and the Message. N.p., 1998.

Cone, James H. "Black Theology as Liberation Theology." In Wilmore, *African American Religious Studies,* 177–207.

——. *A Black Theology of Liberation.* Philadelphia, 1970.

——. "The Servant Church." In Shelp and Sunderland, *The Pastor as Servant,* 61–80. New York, 1986.

Cooper-Lewter, Nicholas C., and Henry H. Mitchell. *Soul Theology: The Heart of American Black Culture.* San Francisco, 1986.

Coppock, Paul R. *Memphis Memoirs.* Memphis, 1980.

Corlew, Robert E. *Tennessee, a Short History.* 2d ed. Knoxville, 1981.

Counts, Ben. "A Joyful Noise: The Staple Singers." *Tuesday Magazine,* January 1975 (a supplement to the *Detroit Sunday News*), 4–6, 13.

Dalfiume, Richard M. *Desegregation of the U.S. Armed Forces: Fighting on Two Fronts, 1939–1953.* Columbia, MO, 1969.

Dance, Helen Oakley. *Stormy Monday: The T-Bone Walker Story.* Baton Rouge, 1987.

Dancy, John C. *Sand Against the Wind: The Memoirs of John C. Dancy.* Detroit, 1966.

Daniel, Pete. *Deep'n as It Come: The 1927 Mississippi River Flood.* New York, 1977.

——. *Lost Revolutions: The South in the 1950s.* Chapel Hill, 2000.

Davis, Ed. *One Man's Way.* Detroit, 1979.

Davis, Gerald L. *I Got the Word in Me and I Can Sing It, You Know: A Study of the Performed African-American Sermon.* Philadelphia, 1985.

Davis, Stephen. *Bob Marley.* Rev. ed. Rochester, VT, 1990.

Davis, T. J. "A Historical Overview of Black Buffalo: Work, Community, and Protest." In Taylor, *African Americans and the Rise of Buffalo's Post-industrial City,* 2:8–47.

Dawson, Michael C. *Black Visions: The Roots of Contemporary African-American Political Ideologies.* Chicago, 2001.

DeCaro, Louis A., Jr. *On the Side of My People: A Religious Life of Malcolm X.* New York, 1996.

Denby, Charles. *Indignant Heart: A Black Worker's Journal.* Boston, 1978.

Derricotte, Toi. *The Black Notebooks: An Interior Journey.* New York, 1997.

Detroit Commission on Community Relations. *Detroit Area Setting: Population Changes and Characteristics.* Detroit, 1963.

_____. *Detroit Metropolitan Area: Employment and Income by Age, Sex, Color and Residence.* Detroit, 1963.

Detroit Council for Human Rights. *Official Program: Walk to Freedom, with Dr. Martin Luther King, Jr.* N.p. [Detroit], 1963.

Detroit Urban League. *A Profile of the Detroit Negro, 1959–1967.* Rev. ed. Detroit, 1967.

Dickerson, James. *Goin' Back to Memphis: A Century of Blues, Rock 'n' Roll, and Glorious Soul.* New York, 1996.

Dittmer, John. *Local People: The Struggle for Civil Rights in Mississippi.* Urbana, IL, 1994.

Dixie, Quinton Hosford, and Cornel West, eds. *The Courage to Hope: From Black Suffering to Human Redemption.* Boston, 1999.

Dollard, John. *Caste and Class in a Southern Town.* New York, 1949. First published in 1937.

Dorson, Richard M., ed. *Negro Folktales in Michigan.* Cambridge, MA, 1956.

Douglass, Frederick. *My Bondage and My Freedom.* New York, 1968. First published in 1855.

Douglass Alumni Association, Memphis Chapter. *Douglass Heritage: Historical Data Book.* Memphis, 1980.

Doyle, Thomas F. "Gestapo in Memphis." *The Crisis,* May 1941, 152–54, 172–73.

Drake, St. Clair. *The Redemption of Africa and Black Religion.* Chicago, 1970.

Duckett, Alfred. "An Interview with Thomas A. Dorsey." *Black World* 23, no. 9 (July 1974): 4–19.

Dunbar, Ernest. "The Making of a Militant." *Saturday Review,* December 16, 1972, 25–32.

Dyson, Michael Eric. "A Useful Hero." *New York Times Magazine,* January 16, 2000, 13–14.

Early, Gerald. *One Nation Under a Groove: Motown and American Culture.* Hopewell, NJ, 1995.

Easter, Opal V. *Nannie Helen Burroughs.* New York, 1995.

Edwards, David Honeyboy. *The World Don't Owe Me Nothing: The Life and Times of Delta Bluesman Honeyboy Edwards.* Chicago, 1997.

Elbert, Julie. "Black Population Change in Mississippi, 1920–1990." *Southern Studies,* n.s., 6, no. 3 (Fall 1995): 57–65.

Elder, Sean. "Bobby 'Blue' Bland." Brilliant Careers, *Salon,* March 14, 2000, http://www.salon.com/people/bc/2000/03/14/bland/index.html.

Ellison, Ralph. *The Collected Essays of Ralph Ellison.* Edited by John F. Callahan. New York, 1995.

_____. *Invisible Man.* New York, 1981. First published in 1952.

_____. *Juneteenth: A Novel.* Edited by John F. Callahan. New York, 1999.

_____. *Living with Music: Ralph Ellison's Jazz Writings.* Edited by Robert G. O'Meally. New York, 2001.

_____. *Shadow and Act.* New York, 1964.

Embree, Edwin R. *Julius Rosenwald Fund: Review to June 30, 1928.* Chicago, 1928.

_____. *Julius Rosenwald Fund: A Review for the Year.* Chicago, 1930.

_____. *Julius Rosenwald Fund: Review for the Year.* Chicago, 1931.

English, James W. *Handyman of the Lord: The Life and Ministry of the Rev. William Holmes Borders.* New York, 1967.

Escott, Colin. *Good Rockin' Tonight: Sun Records and the Birth of Rock 'n' Roll.* With Martin Hawkins. New York, 1991.

Evans, David. *Big Road Blues: Tradition and Creativity in the Folk Blues.* New York, 1987. First published in 1982.

———. "Goin' Up the Country: Blues in Texas and the Deep South." In Cohen, *Nothing but the Blues,* 33–86.

Fager, Charles. *Uncertain Resurrection: The Poor People's Washington Campaign.* Grand Rapids, MI, 1969.

Fairclough, Adam. "'Being in the Field of Education and Also Being a Negro . . . Seems . . . Tragic': Black Teachers in the Jim Crow South." *Journal of American History* 87, no. 1 (June 2000): 65–91.

Farley, Christopher John. "Soul Sister 2000." *Time,* March 2, 1998, 78.

Farley, Reynolds, Sheldon Danziger, and Harry J. Holzer. *Detroit Divided.* New York, 2000.

Fauntroy, Walter E. "Black Religion and Politics." In Washington, *Black Religion and Public Policy,* 47–57.

"Featured Minister of the Month: Dr. C.L. Franklin, Pastor, The New Bethel Baptist Church, Detroit, Michigan." *Church Magazine* 1, no. 1 (May 1979): 5–10.

Federal Writers Project. *Mississippi: A Guide to the Magnolia State.* New York, 1949. First published in 1938.

———. *Tennessee, a Guide to the State.* New York, 1945. First published in 1939.

Ferris, William. *Blues from the Delta.* New York, 1984. First published in 1978.

Fine, Sidney. *Violence in the Model City: The Cavanaugh Administration, Race Relations, and the Detroit Riot of 1967.* Ann Arbor, 1989.

Fischer, Miles Mark. "The Negro Church and the World War." *Journal of Religion* 5, no. 5 (September 1925): 483–99.

Fitts, Leroy. *A History of Black Baptists.* Nashville, 1985.

Floyd, Samuel A., Jr. *The Power of Black Music: Interpreting Its History from Africa to the United States.* New York, 1995.

Fluker, Walter Earl. "The Failure of Ethical Leadership and the Challenge of Hope." In Fluker, *The Stones That the Builders Rejected,* 1–22.

———, ed. *The Stones That the Builders Rejected: The Development of Ethical Leadership from the Black Church Tradition.* Harrisburg, PA, 1998.

Foner, Eric. *Reconstruction: America's Unfinished Revolution, 1863–1877.* New York, 1988.

Fordham, Monroe. "The Buffalo Cooperative Economic Society, Inc., 1928–1961: A Black Self-Help Organization." *Niagara Frontier* 23, no. 2 (Summer 1976): 41–49.

Frady, Marshall. *Jesse: The Life and Pilgrimage of Jesse Jackson.* New York, 1996.

Franklin, Aretha, and David Ritz. *Aretha: From These Roots.* New York, 1999.

Franklin, V. P., Nancy L. Grant, Harold M. Kletnick, and Genna Rae McNeil, eds. *African Americans and Jews in the Twentieth Century: Studies in Convergence and Conflict.* Columbia, MO, 1998.

Fredrickson, George M. *The Black Image in the White Mind: The Debate on Afro-American Character and Destiny, 1817–1914.* New York, 1972.

Frost, Harlan M. *An Ecumenical Wind in Buffalo: A History of the Local Council of Churches, 1857–1977.* Buffalo, 1977.

Gale Group, Inc., Biography Resource Center. "George W. Crockett, Jr., 1909–1997." http://www.africanpubs.com/Apps/bios/1019CrockettGeorge (2001).

Garland, Phyl. "The Lady Who's the Soul of Soul." *Detroit Sunday News Magazine,* January 11, 1970, 24, 25, 26, 28, 30, 38.

Garrow, David J. *Bearing the Cross: Martin Luther King, Jr., and the Southern Christian Leadership Conference.* New York, 1986.

Georgakas, Dan, and Marvin Surkin. *Detroit, I Do Mind Dying.* Cambridge, MA, 1998. First published in 1975.

George, Luvenia A. "Lucie E. Campbell: Baptist Composer and Educator." *The Black Perspective in Music* 15, no. 1 (Spring 1987): 25 50.

———. "Lucie E. Campbell: Her Nurturing and Expansion of Gospel Music in the National Baptist Convention, U.S.A., Inc." In Reagon, *We'll Understand It Better By and By,* 109–19.

Giddens, Gary. *Riding on a Blue Note: Jazz and American Pop.* New York, 1981.

———. *Satchmo: The Genius of Louis Armstrong.* New York, 2001.

Gilkes, Cheryl Townsend. "The Black Church as a Therapeutic Community: Suggested Areas for Research into the Black Religious Experience." *Journal of the Interdenominational Theological Center* 8, no. 1 (Fall 1980): 29–44.

———. "The Politics of 'Silence': Dual-Sex Political Systems and Women's Traditions of Conflict in African-American Religion." In Johnson, *African-American Christianity,* 80–110.

Goldman, Mark. *High Hopes: The Rise and Decline of Buffalo, New York.* Albany, 1983.

Gordon, Robert. "Bobby 'Blue' Bland." *Rolling Stone,* May 28, 1998, 13.

Gordy, Berry. *To Be Loved: The Music, the Magic, the Memories of Motown. An Autobiography.* New York, 1994.

Goreau, Laurraine. *Just Mahalia, Baby: The Mahalia Jackson Story.* Gretna, LA, 1984. First published in 1975.

Graebner, William. *Coming of Age in Buffalo: Youth and Authority in the Postwar Era.* Philadelphia, 1990.

Gray, Henderson. *History of Monumental Baptist Church, West Philadelphia, Pa.* N.p., 1891.

Greater Shiloh Baptist Church. *The 109th Anniversary Celebration and Homecoming of Greater Shiloh Baptist Church.* Detroit, 1990.

Grossman, James R. *Land of Hope: Chicago, Black Southerners, and the Great Migration.* Chicago, 1989.

Guralnick, Peter. *Last Train to Memphis: The Rise of Elvis Presley.* Boston, 1994.

———. *Lost Highways: Journeys and Arrivals of American Musicians.* Boston, 1999. First published in 1979.

———. *Sweet Soul Music: Rhythm and Blues and the Southern Dream of Freedom.* Boston, 1999. First published in 1986.

Hahn, Harlan. "Black Separatists: Attitudes and Objectives in a Riot-Torn Ghetto." *Journal of Black Studies* 1, no. 1 (September 1970): 35–54.

Haizlip, Shirlee Taylor. *The Sweeter the Juice: A Family Memoir in Black and White.* New York, 1994.

Hamer, Fannie Lou. "To Praise Our Bridges." In *Mississippi Writers: Reflections of Childhood and Youth,* edited by Dorothy Abbott, 2:321–30. Jackson, MS, 1986.

Hamilton, Charles V. *Adam Clayton Powell, Jr.: The Political Biography of an American Dilemma.* New York, 1991.

_____. *The Black Preacher in America.* New York, 1972.

Handy, W. C. *Father of the Blues.* New York, 1970. First published in 1941.

Harkins, John E. *Metropolis of the American Nile: An Illustrated History of Memphis and Shelby County.* Oxford, MS, 1982.

Harrell, David Edwin, Jr., ed. *Varieties of Southern Evangelicism.* Macon, GA, 1981.

Harris, J. William. "Etiquette, Lynching, and Racial Boundaries in Southern History: A Mississippi Example." *American Historical Review* 100, no. 2 (April 1995): 387–410.

Harris, Michael W. *The Rise of Gospel Blues: The Music of Thomas Andrew Dorsey in the Urban Church.* New York, 1992.

Hartigan, John, Jr. *Racial Situations: Class Predicaments of Whiteness in Detroit.* Princeton, 1999.

Hataway, Marsha Perry. "The Development of the Mississippi State Highway System, 1916–1932." *Journal of Mississippi History* 28, no. 4 (November 1966): 286–303.

Hatch, Gary Layne. "Logic in the Black Folk Sermon: The Sermons of Rev. C. L. Franklin." *Journal of Black Studies* 26, no. 3 (January 1996): 227–44.

Hayes, Cedric J., and Robert Laughton. *Gospel Records, 1943–1969: A Black Music Discography. Volume One: A to K.* N.p., 1992.

Heilbut, Anthony. *The Gospel Sound: Good News and Bad Times.* Rev. ed. New York, 1985.

Henderson, Stephen E. "The Blues as Black Poetry." *Callaloo* 16 (October 1982): 22–30.

Hentoff, Nat. "Lester Young." In *A Lester Young Reader,* edited by Lewis Porter, 47–73. Washington, DC, 1991.

Hersey, John. *The Algiers Motel Incident.* New York, 1968.

_____, ed. *Ralph Ellison: A Collection of Critical Essays.* Englewood Cliffs, NJ, 1974.

Herzhaft, Gerard. *Encyclopedia of the Blues.* 2d ed. Fayetteville, AR, 1997.

Hickey, Dennis, and Kenneth C. Wylie. *An Enchanting Darkness: The American Vision of Africa in the Twentieth Century.* East Lansing, MI, 1993.

Higginbotham, Evelyn Brooks. "Rethinking Vernacular Culture: Black Religion and Race Records in the 1920s and 1930s." In Lubiano, *The House That Race Built,* 157–77. New York, 1997.

_____. *Righteous Discontent: The Women's Movement in the Black Baptist Church, 1880–1920.* Cambridge, MA, 1993.

Hirshey, Gerri. *Nowhere to Run: The Story of Soul Music.* New York, 1984.

Holt, Grace Sims. "Stylin' Outta the Black Pulpit." In Kochman, *Rappin' and Stylin' Out,* 189–204.

Honey, Michael Keith. *Black Workers Remember: An Oral History of Segregation, Unionism, and the Freedom Struggle.* Berkeley, 1999.

Hughes, Langston. *Simple's Uncle Sam.* New York, 1965.

Imse, Thomas P. *Metropolitan Buffalo Perspectives: A Pilot Study Report for a Buffalo Metropolitan Area Survey.* Buffalo, 1958.

Jackson, H. C. L. *It Happened in Detroit.* Detroit, 1947.

Jackson, J. H. *A Story of Christian Activism: The History of the National Baptist Convention, U.S.A., Inc.* Nashville, 1980.

_____. *Unholy Shadows and Freedom's Holy Light.* Nashville, 1967.

Jackson, Mahalia. *Movin' On Up.* With Evan McLeod Wylie. New York, 1966.

Jacobson, Matthew Frye. *Whiteness of a Different Color: European Immigrants and the Alchemy of Race.* Cambridge, MA, 1998.

Jacoby, Tamar. *Someone Else's House: America's Unfinished Struggle for Integration.* New York, 1998.

James, Etta, and David Ritz. *Rage to Survive.* New York, 1995.

"James Cleveland: King of Gospel." *Ebony,* November 1968, 74–84.

Jasper, John. "Minority Vote Helped Ruin 'Crump Machine.'" *Washington Afro-American,* August 10, 1948.

Johnson, Charles S. *Growing Up in the Black Belt: Negro Youth in the Rural South.* Washington, DC, 1941.

_____. *Shadow of the Plantation.* Chicago, 1934.

Johnson, Charles S., and associates. *To Stem This Tide: A Survey of Racial Tension Areas in the United States.* Boston, 1943.

Johnson, Eugene J., and Robert D. Russell Jr. *Memphis: An Architectural Guide.* Knoxville, 1990.

Johnson, Paul E., ed. *African-American Christianity. Essays in History.* Berkeley, 1994.

Johnson, T. J., ed. *1943 Year Book and Directory. Containing Reviews of Prominent Negro Men and Women, a Directory of Negro Businesses, Names and Addresses of Thousands of People Engaged in Professions, Government, Work, Industry, Trades, Church and School Work, Together with Important and Interesting Facts about Memphis and the Opportunities It Affords Its Colored Citizens.* Memphis, 1943.

Jones, Arthur C. *Wade in the Water: The Wisdom of the Spirituals.* Maryknoll, NY, 1993.

Jones, Kirk Byron. "An Interview with Gardner C. Taylor, Part 2." *The African-American Pulpit,* Fall 1999, 86–91.

_____. "An Interview with Henry H. Mitchell." *The African-American Pulpit,* Winter 1997–98, 88–93.

Jones, Le Roi [Amiri Baraka]. *Blues People: Negro Music in White America.* New York, 1963.

Joyner, Charles. "'Believer I Know': The Emergence of African-American Christianity." In Johnson, *African-American Christianity: Essays in History,* 18–46.

Kelley, Robin D. G. "'We Are Not What We Seem': Rethinking Black Working-Class Opposition in the Jim Crow South." *Journal of American History* 80, no. 1 (June 1993): 75–112.

King, B. B. *Blues All Around Me: The Autobiography of B. B. King.* With David Ritz. New York, 1996.

King, Reverend Martin Luther, Sr. *Daddy King: An Autobiography.* With Clayton Riley. New York, 1980.

King, Woodie, Jr. "Searching for Brothers Kindred: Rhythm and Blues of the 1950s." *The Black Scholar* 6, no. 3 (November 1974): 19–32.

King, Woodie, Jr., and Earl Anthony. *Black Poets and Prophets: The Theory, Practice, and Esthetics of the Pan-Africanist Revolution.* New York, 1972.

Klinkenborg, Verlyn. *The Last Fine Time.* New York, 1991.

Kluger, Richard. *Simple Justice: The History of* Brown v. Board of Education *and Black America's Struggle for Equality.* New York, 1977.

Kochman, Thomas, ed. *Rappin' and Stylin' Out: Communication in Urban Black America.* Urbana, IL, 1972.

Kornhauser, Arthur. *Detroit as the People See It: A Survey of Attitudes in an Industrial City.* Detroit, 1952.

Kotlowitz, Alex. *The Other Side of the River: A Story of Two Towns, A Death and America's Dilemma.* New York, 1998.

Kramer, John. "The Election of Blacks to City Councils: A 1970 Status Report and a Prolegomenon." *Journal of Black Studies* 1, no. 4 (June 1971): 443–76.

Kraus, Neil. *Race, Neighborhoods, and Community Power: Buffalo Politics, 1934–1997.* Albany, 2000.

"Lady Soul: Singing It Like It Is." *Time,* June 28, 1968, 62–66.

Lawrence Lightfoot, Sara. *Balm in Gilead: Journey of a Healer.* Reading, MA, 1988.

Laymon, Charles M., ed. *The Interpreter's One-Volume Commentary on the Bible.* Nashville, 1971.

Lee, Alfred McClung and Norman Daymond. *Race Riot.* New York, 1943.

Lee, George W. *Beale Street: Where the Blues Began.* College Park, MD, 1969. First published in 1934.

Lefkowitz, Mary R., and Guy MacLean Rogers, eds. *Black Athena Revisited.* Chapel Hill, NC, 1996.

Lesseig, Corey T. "'Out of the Mud': The Good Roads Crusade and Social Change in Twentieth-Century Mississippi." *Journal of Mississippi History* 60, no. 1 (Spring 1998): 51–72.

Lester, James. *Too Marvelous for Words: The Life and Genius of Art Tatum.* New York, 1994.

Levine, Lawrence W. *Black Culture and Black Consciousness: Afro-American Folk Thought from Slavery to Freedom.* New York, 1977.

Lewis, David Levering. *W. E. B. DuBois.* Vol. 2. *The Fight for Equality and the American Century, 1919–1963.* New York, 2000.

Lewis, John. *Walking with the Wind: A Memoir of the Movement.* New York, 1998.

Lichtenstein, Nelson. *The Most Dangerous Man in Detroit: Walter Reuther and the Fate of American Labor.* New York, 1995.

Lincoln, C. Eric. *The Black Muslims in America.* 3d ed. Grand Rapids, MI, 1994.

_____, ed. *The Black Experience in Religion.* New York, 1974.

Lincoln, C. Eric, and Lawrence H. Mamiya. *The Black Church in the African American Experience.* Durham, NC, 1990.

Lischer, Richard. *The Preacher King: Martin Luther King, Jr. and the Word That Moved America.* New York, 1995.

Litwack, Leon F. *Been in the Storm So Long: The Aftermath of Slavery.* New York, 1979.

_____. *Trouble in Mind: Black Southerners in the Age of Jim Crow.* New York, 1998.

Long, Charles H. "Perspectives for a Study of Afro-American Religion in the United States." *History of Religions* 11, no. 1 (August 1971): 54–67.

Lornell, Kip. *"Happy in the Service of the Lord": African-American Sacred Vocal Harmony Quartets in Memphis.* 2d ed. Knoxville, 1995.

Lowry, Eugene L. "Preaching the Great Themes." In *Preaching on the Brink: The Future of Homiletics*, edited by Martha J. Simmons, 57–65. Nashville, 1996.

Lubiano, Wahneema, ed. *The House That Race Built: Black Americans, U.S. Terrain*. New York, 1997.

Luker, Ralph E. "Missions, Institutional Churches, and Settlement Houses: The Black Experience, 1885–1910." *Journal of Negro History* 69, nos. 3 and 4 (Summer/Fall 1984): 101–13.

Lumumba, Chokwe. "Short History of the U.S. War on the R.N.A." *The Black Scholar* 12, no. 1 (January/February 1981): 72–81.

Lutz, Tom, and Susanna Ashton, eds. *These "Colored" United States: African American Essays from the 1920s*. New Brunswick, NJ, 1996.

Lyell, Sir Charles. *A Second Visit to the United States of North America*. 2 vols. 3d ed. London, 1855.

Mabee, Charles. "African Americans and American Biblical Hermeneutics." In Wimbush, *African Americans and the Bible*, 103–10. New York, 2000.

Manis, Andrew M. *A Fire You Can't Put Out: The Civil Rights Life of Birmingham's Reverend Fred Shuttlesworth*. Tuscaloosa, AL, 1999.

Marks, Morton. "Uncovering Ritual Structures in Afro-American Music." In Zaretsky and Leone, *Religious Movements in Contemporary America*, 60–134.

Marsden, George M. *Fundamentalism and American Culture: The Shaping of Twentieth Century Evangelicalism, 1870–1925*. New York, 1980.

Marsh, Charles. *God's Long Summer: Stories of Faith and Civil Rights*. Princeton, 1997.

Mast, Robert H., comp. and ed. *Detroit Lives*. Philadelphia, 1994.

Maultsby, Portia K. "The Impact of Gospel Music on the Secular Music Industry." In Reagon, *We'll Understand It Better By and By*, 19–33.

Mauskopf, Norman, and Randall Kenan. *A Time Not Here: The Mississippi Delta*. Santa Fe, 1996.

Mays, Benjamin E. "The Black Man's Environment and His Minority Status, a Challenge to the Black Church." *The Black Church* 1, no. 1 (1972): 7–16.

———. "A Centennial Commencement Address." *Journal of Religious Thought* 24, no. 2 (1967–68): 4–12.

———. *The Negro's God as Reflected in His Literature*. New York, 1968. First published in 1938.

Mays, Benjamin E., and Joseph William Nicholson. *The Negro's Church*. Salem, NH, 1988. First published in 1933.

McBee, Kurt. "The Memphis Red Sox Stadium: A Social Institution in Memphis' African American Community." *The West Tennessee Historical Society Papers* 49 (December 1995): 149–64.

McBeth, H. Leon. *The Baptist Heritage*. Nashville, 1987.

McCarthy, S. Margaret W. "The Afro-American Sermon and the Blues: Some Parallels." *The Black Perspective in Music* 4, no. 3 (Fall 1976): 269–77.

McDonnell, James R. "The Interview with Olin Wilson: Charter Member, Steelworkers Organizing Committee, Bethlehem Steel Corp., Buffalo, New York." *Afro-Americans in New York Life and History* 21, no. 1 (January 1997): 69–97.

McGraw, Bill. "Style to Spare." *Michigan History Magazine* 84, no. 6 (November/December 2000): 71–77.

McGreevy, John T. *Parish Boundaries: The Catholic Encounter with Race in the Twentieth-Century Urban North.* Chicago, 1996.

McIlwaine, Shields. *Memphis: Down in Dixie.* New York, 1948.

McKee, Margaret, and Fred Chisenhall. *Beale Black and Blue: Life and Music on Black America's Main Street.* Baton Rouge, 1993. First published in 1981.

McKinney, Davene Ross. "This History of Shiloh." In Greater Shiloh Baptist Church, *The 109th Anniversary Celebration and Homecoming,* n.p.

McMillen, Neil R. *Dark Journey: Black Mississippians in the Age of Jim Crow.* Urbana, IL, 1989.

Meier, August, and Elliott Rudwick. *Black Detroit and the Rise of the UAW.* New York, 1979.

———. *CORE: A Study in the Civil Rights Movement, 1942–1968.* New York, 1973.

Mendez, John. "By the Rivers of Babylon (Psalm 137:1–4)." *Black Sacred Music* 7, no. 1 (Spring 1993): 56–61.

Metress, Christopher, ed. *The Lynching of Emmett Till: A Documentary Narrative.* Charlottesville, 2002.

Miller, Keith D. *Voice of Deliverance: The Language of Martin Luther King, Jr. and Its Sources.* New York, 1992.

Miller, Perry, and Thomas H. Johnson. *The Puritans: A Sourcebook of Their Writings.* New York, 1963. First published in 1938.

Miller, William D. *Memphis during the Progressive Era, 1900–1917.* Memphis, 1957.

Mills, Kay. *This Little Light of Mine: The Life of Fannie Lou Hamer.* New York, 1993.

Mission Board of the B. M. and E. Convention of Tennessee. *First Inspirational and Evangelistic Regional Meeting of the Mission Board of the Baptist Missionary and Evangelical Convention of Tennessee. In Session at Progressive Baptist Church, Oct. 4, 5, 6 and 8, 1944.* Memphis, 1944.

Mitchell, Henry H. *Black Belief: Folk Beliefs of Blacks in America and West Africa.* New York, 1975.

———. *Black Preaching: The Recovery of a Powerful Art.* Nashville, 1990.

———. "Two Streams of Tradition." In Lincoln, *The Black Experience in Religion,* 70–75.

Moody, Anne. *Coming of Age in Mississippi.* New York, 1976. First published in 1968.

Moon, Elaine Latzman. *Untold Tales, Unsung Heroes: An Oral History of Detroit's African American Community, 1918–1967.* Detroit, 1994.

Morant, Reverend Jno. J. *Mississippi Minister.* New York, 1958.

Moses, W. H. *The White Peril.* Philadelphia, n.d. [1919].

Mound Bayou Foundation. *Semi-centennial Celebration, July 11–17, 1937. Souvenir Program: The Founding of Mound Bayou, Bolivar County, Mississippi.* N.p., n.d. [1937].

Moyd, Olin P. "Elements in Black Preaching." *Journal of Religious Thought* 30, no. 1 (Spring–Summer 1973): 52–62.

———. *Redemption in Black Theology.* Valley Forge, PA, 1979.

Murray, Albert. *The Omni-Americans: New Perspectives on Black Experience and American Culture.* New York, 1970.

———. *Stomping the Blues.* New York, 1987. First published in 1976.

Murray, Albert, and John F. Callahan, eds. *Trading Twelves: The Selected Letters of Ralph Ellison and Albert Murray*. New York, 2000.

Murray, Charles Shaar. *Boogie Man: The Adventures of John Lee Hooker in the American Twentieth Century*. New York, 2000.

Murray, Florence, ed. *The Negro Handbook, 1944: A Manual of Current Facts, Statistics and General Information Concerning Negroes in the United States*. New York, 1944.

_____. *The Negro Handbook, 1949*. New York, 1949.

Nager, Larry. *Memphis Beat: The Lives and Times of America's Musical Crossroads*. New York, 1998.

The National Advisory Commission on Civil Disorders. *Report of the National Advisory Commission on Civil Disorders*. Washington, DC, 1968.

Neal, Larry. "Any Day Now: Black Art and Black Liberation." In King and Anthony, *Black Poets and Prophets*, 148–65.

_____. "The Ethos of the Blues." *The Black Scholar* 3, no. 10 (Summer 1972): 42–48.

Nelsen, Hart M., and Anne Kusener Nelsen. *Black Churches in the Sixties*. Lexington, KY, 1975.

Nelsen, Hart M., Raytha L. Yokley, and Anne K. Nelsen. *The Black Church in America*. New York, 1971.

New Bethel Baptist Church. *Bidding Farewell to Rev. C. L. Franklin*. Detroit, 1984.

_____. *8th Annual Radio Broadcast Program, April 5, 1959*. Detroit, 1959.

_____. *The Fifteenth Anniversary Program, April 7–13 [1947]*. Detroit, n.d. [1947].

_____. *Fifty-fourth Anniversary of New Bethel Baptist Church, Sunday, March 23, 1986*. Detroit, 1986.

_____. *"Gospel Tribute" for Reverend Clarence LaVaughn Franklin, December 10, 1979*. Detroit, 1979.

_____. *Honoring Our Pastor, Rev. C. L. Franklin, June 3 & 5, 1983*. Detroit, 1983.

_____. *In Loving Memory of Rev. Dr. Clarence LaVaughn Franklin*. Detroit, 1984.

_____. *Rev. C. L. Franklin Day, Sunday June 6, 1982*. Detroit, 1982.

_____. *The Sixteenth Anniversary Program, March 8–14 [1948]*. Detroit, n.d. [1948].

New Bethel Baptist Church and the Progressive Civic League. *Program: Adam Clayton Powell at New Bethel Baptist Church, March 28, 1954*. Detroit, 1954.

Newman, Richard. *Black Power and Black Religion: Essays and Reviews*. West Cornwall, CT, 1987.

Nicholas, Xavier. *Questions of the American Revolution: Conversations with James Boggs*. Atlanta, 1976.

Niles, Lyndrey A. "Rhetorical Characteristics of Traditional Black Preaching." *Journal of Black Studies* 15, no. 1 (September 1984): 41–52.

1901–1951: Gold and Silver Anniversary Honoring Dr. J. C. Austin, 50 Years Preaching the Word, 25 Years, Pastor of Pilgrim Baptist Church. Chicago, n.d. [1951].

Northrup, Herbert R. *Negro Employment in Basic Industry: A Study of Racial Policies in Six Industries*. Philadelphia, 1970.

Oates, Joyce Carol. *them*. New York, 1969.

Obadele, Imari Abubakari. "National Black Elections Held by the Republic of New Africa." *The Black Scholar* 7, no. 2 (October 1975): 27–38.

Oliver, Paul. *The Meaning of the Blues*. New York, 1969.

————. *Songsters and Saints: Vocal Traditions on Race Records.* New York, 1984.

Olivet Baptist Church (Chicago). *In Celebration of Life: A Service of Remembrance for Joseph Harrison Jackson.* Chicago, 1990.

O'Meally, Robert G. "The Black Sermon: Tradition and Art." *Callaloo* 34 (Winter 1988): 198–200.

O'Neal, Jim, and Amy van Singel, eds. *The Voice of the Blues: Classic Interviews from* Living Blues *Magazine.* New York, 2002.

Oshinsky, David M. *"Worse Than Slavery": Parchman Farm and the Ordeal of Jim Crow Justice.* New York, 1996.

Ownby, Ted. *American Dreams in Mississippi: Consumers, Poverty, and Culture, 1830–1998.* Chapel Hill, NC, 1999.

Palmer, Robert. *Deep Blues.* New York, 1982.

Pareles, Jon. "Pops Staples, Patriarch of the Staple Singers, Dies at 85." *New York Times,* December 22, 2000.

Paris, Arthur E. *Black Pentecostalism: Southern Religion in an Urban World.* Amherst, MA, 1982.

Paris, Peter J. *Black Religious Leaders: Conflict in Unity.* Louisville, KY, 1991.

————. "Moral Development for African-American Leadership." In Fluker, *The Stones That the Builders Rejected,* 23–32.

————. *The Social Teaching of the Black Churches.* Philadelphia, 1985.

Parks, Gordon. "A Time for Martyrs." In *Reporting Civil Rights, Part Two: American Journalism, 1963–1973,* 316–21. New York, 2003. First published in *Life,* March 5, 1965.

Parrish, C. H. *National Baptist Statistical Report and Year Book.* Philadelphia, n.d. [1919].

Patterson, Orlando. *Rituals of Blood: Consequences of Slavery in Two American Centuries.* New York, 1998.

Perkins, Reverend Benjamin J. *Rev. Benjamin J. Perkins Answers the Erroneous Statement, Title "A Still Small Voice" Published by a Committee of the Baptist Pastors Alliance and Baptist Women's City Federation of Memphis, Tennessee.* Memphis, n.d.

Perry, Bruce. *Malcolm: The Life of a Man Who Changed Black America.* New York, 1991.

Phillips, Ulrich Bonnell. *American Negro Slavery: A Survey of the Supply, Employment and Control of Negro Labor as Determined by the Plantation Regime.* New York, 1918.

Pinn, Anthony B. *Why, Lord? Suffering and Evil in Black Theology.* New York, 1995.

Pipes, William H. *Say Amen, Brother! Old-Time Negro Preaching: A Study in American Frustration.* New York, 1951.

Polk's Buffalo (Erie County, N.Y.) City Directory, 1946, Including Kenmore. N.p., 1946.

Polk's Memphis (Shelby County, Tenn.) City Directory, 1938. Containing an Alphabetical Directory of Business Concerns and Private Citizens, a Directory of Householders, Occupants of Office Buildings and Other Business Places, Including a Complete Street and Avenue Guide, and Much Information of a Miscellaneous Character; Also a Buyers' Guide and a Complete Classified Business Directory. N.p., 1938.

Polk's Memphis (Shelby County, Tenn.) City Directory, 1939. Containing an Alphabetical Directory of Business Concerns and Private Citizens, a Directory of Householders, Occupants of Office Buildings and Other Business Places, Including a Complete Street and Avenue Guide, and Much Information of a Miscellaneous Character; Also a Buyers' Guide and a Complete Classified Business Directory. N.p., 1939.

Polk's Memphis (Shelby County, Tenn.) City Directory, 1940. Containing an Alphabetical Directory of Business Concerns and Private Citizens, a Directory of Householders, Occupants of Office Buildings and Other Business Places, Including a Complete Street and Avenue Guide, and Much Information of a Miscellaneous Character; Also a Buyers' Guide and a Complete Classified Business Directory. N.p., 1940.

Polk's Memphis (Shelby County, Tenn.) City Directory, 1941. Containing an Alphabetical Directory of Business Concerns and Private Citizens, a Directory of Householders, Occupants of Office Buildings and Other Business Places, Including a Complete Street and Avenue Guide, and Much Information of a Miscellaneous Character; also a Buyers' Guide and a Complete Classified Business Directory. St. Louis, 1941.

Polk's Memphis (Shelby County, Tenn.) City Directory, 1942. Containing an Alphabetical Directory of Business Concerns and Private Citizens, a Directory of Householders, Occupants of Office Buildings and Other Business Places, Including a Complete Street and Avenue Guide; Also a Buyers' Guide and a Complete Classified Business Directory. St. Louis, 1942.

Polk's Memphis (Shelby County, Tenn.) City Directory, 1943. Containing an Alphabetical Directory of Business Concerns and Private Citizens, a Directory of Householders, Occupants of Office Buildings and Other Business Places, Including a Complete Street and Avenue Guide; Also a Buyers' Guide and a Complete Classified Business Directory. St. Louis, 1943.

Polk's Memphis (Shelby County, Tenn.) City Directory, 1945. Containing an Alphabetical Directory of Business Concerns and Private Citizens, a Directory of Householders, Occupants of Office Buildings and Other Business Places, Including a Complete Street and Avenue Guide, and a Postal Unit Guide; Also a Buyers' Guide and a Complete Classified Business Directory. St. Louis, 1945.

Porter, Horace A. *Jazz Country: Ralph Ellison in America.* Iowa City, 2001.

Powdermaker, Hortense. *After Freedom: A Cultural Study of the Deep South.* New York, 1968. First published in 1939.

Powell, Reverend A. Clayton, Sr. *Against the Tide: An Autobiography.* New York, 1938.

Powell, Reverend Adam Clayton, Jr. *Marching Blacks.* New York, 1973. First published in 1945.

"The Preacher with the Golden Voice." *Color* 11, no. 14 (January 1957): 39, 41–42.

Price, Alfred D. "Housing Buffalo's Black Community." In Taylor, *African Americans and the Rise of Buffalo's Post-industrial City,* 2:89–111.

Proctor, Samuel D. "Black Protestants and Public Policy." In Washington, *Black Religion and Public Policy,* 11–19.

_____. *The Substance of Things Hoped For: A Memoir of African-American Faith.* New York, 1995.

Progressive Civic League. *Program: 10th Anniversary Meeting, Congressman Adam Clayton Powell, Speaker, at New Bethel Baptist Church (March 27, 1955).* Detroit, 1955.

Raboteau, Albert J. "African-Americans, Exodus, and the American Israel." In Johnson, *African-American Christianity,* 1–17.

_____. "'The Blood of the Martyrs Is the Seed of Faith': Suffering in the Christianity of American Slaves." In Dixie and West, *The Courage to Hope,* 22–39.

_____. *A Fire in the Bones: Reflections on African-American Religious History.* Boston, 1995.

_____. *Slave Religion: The "Invisible Institution" in the Antebellum South.* New York, 1978.

_____. *A Sorrowful Joy.* New York, 2002.

Radosh, Ronald, and Joyce Milton. *The Rosenberg File: A Search for the Truth.* New York, 1983.

Rampersand, Arnold. *Jackie Robinson: A Biography.* New York, 1997.

Randle, William, Jr. "Black Entertainers on Radio, 1920–1930." *The Black Perspective in Music* 5, no. 1 (Spring 1977): 67–74.

Ray, Sandy F. *Journeying through a Jungle.* Nashville, 1979.

Reagon, Bernice Johnson. "Pioneering African American Gospel Music Composers." In Reagon, *We'll Understand It Better By and By,* 3–18.

_____, ed. *We'll Understand It Better By and By: Pioneering African American Gospel Composers.* Washington, DC, 1992.

Reed, Adolph, Jr. "The Allure of Malcolm X and the Changing Character of Black Politics." In Wood, *Malcolm X,* 203–32.

_____. *The Jesse Jackson Phenomenon: The Crisis of Purpose in Afro-American Politics.* New Haven, 1986.

Reed, Merl E. *Seedtime for the Modern Civil Rights Movement: The President's Committee on Fair Employment Practice, 1941–1946.* Baton Rouge, 1991.

Reid, Ira De A. *The Negro Baptist Ministry: An Analysis of Its Profession, Preparation and Practices. Report on a Survey Conducted by the Joint Survey Commission of the Baptist Inter-convention Committee: The American Baptist Convention; the National Baptist Convention; the Southern Baptist Convention.* Philadelphia, 1952.

Remnick, David. *King of the World: Muhammad Ali and the Rise of an American Hero.* New York, 1998.

The Republic of New Africa. *Freedom: The Eight Strategic Elements Necessary for Success of a Black Nation in America.* Detroit, 1968.

_____. *Now We Have a Nation.* Detroit, n.d. [1968].

Rich, Wilbur C. *Coleman Young and Detroit Politics: From Social Activist to Power Broker.* Detroit, 1989.

Richardson, Jerry and Rob Bowman. "Conversation with B. B. King, 'King of the Blues.'" *The Black Perspective in Music* 17, no. 1 (1989): 135–52.

Ricks, George Robinson. *Some Aspects of the Religious Music of the United States Negro: An Ethnomusicological Study with Special Emphasis on the Gospel Tradition.* New York, 1977.

Ritz, David. *Divided Soul: The Life of Marvin Gaye.* New York, 1991. First published in 1985.

Roberts, J. Deotis, Sr. "A Black Ecclesiology of Involvement." *Journal of Religious Thought* 32, no. 1 (Spring–Summer 1975): 36–46.

_____. *The Prophethood of Black Believers: An African American Political Theology for Ministry.* Louisville, KY, 1994.

Robinson, Smokey. *Smokey: Inside My Life.* With David Ritz. New York, 1989.

Rooks, Charles Shelby. "Toward the Promised Land: An Analysis of the Religious Experience of Black Americans." *The Black Church* 2, no. 1 (1973): 1–48.

Rosenberg, Bruce A. *Can These Bones Live? The Art of the American Folk Preacher.* Rev. ed. Urbana, IL, 1988.

_____. "The Psychology of the Spiritual Sermon." In Zaretsky and Leone, *Religious Movements in Contemporary America,* 135–49.

Rosengarten, Theodore. *All God's Dangers: The Life of Nate Shaw.* New York, 1975.

Ross, Diana. *Secrets of a Sparrow: Memoirs.* New York, 1993.

Rowland, Dunbar. *The Official and Statistical Register of the State of Mississippi, 1924–1928*. New York, n.d.

Salvatore, Nick. *Eugene V. Debs: Citizen and Socialist*. Urbana, IL, 1982.

_____. *We All Got History: The Memory Books of Amos Webber*. New York, 1996.

Sanders, Charles L. "Detroit's Rebel Judge Crockett." *Ebony*, August 1969, 114–16, 118, 120–22, 124.

Savage, Barbara Dianne. *Broadcasting Freedom: Radio, War, and the Politics of Race, 1938–1948*. Chapel Hill, NC, 1999.

_____. "W. E. B. DuBois and 'The Negro Church.'" *Annals of the American Academy of Political and Social Science* 568 (March 2000). 235–49.

Schermerhorn, Jane. "The Unheard Voice of the Negro Woman." *Detroit News Magazine*, October 1, 1967.

Scott, Daryl Michael. *Contempt and Pity: Social Policy and the Image of the Damaged Black Psyche, 1880–1996*. Chapel Hill, NC, 1997.

Second Baptist Church. *Program, Fifth Anniversary of the Pastorate of Robert Lewis Bradby at the Second Baptist Church, Detroit, Michigan, November 7–14, 1915*. N.p., n.d.

Sellers, Cleveland. *The River of No Return: The Autobiography of a Black Militant and the Life and Death of SNCC*. With Robert Terrell. Jackson, MS, 1990.

Sernett, Milton C. *Bound for the Promised Land: African American Religion and the Great Migration*. Durham, NC, 1997.

Serrin, William. "Cleage's Alternative." *The Reporter*, May 30, 1968, 29–30.

Shannon, Samuel. "Tennessee." In *The Black Press in the South, 1865–1979*, edited by Henry Louis Suggs, 313–55. Westport, CT, 1983.

Shaw, Talbert O. "A Tentative Profile of the Black Clergy in Chicago." *Journal of Religious Thought* 30, no. 1 (Spring–Summer, 1975): 39–51.

Shelp, Earl E., and Ronald H. Sunderland, eds. *The Pastor as Servant*. New York, 1986.

Sherrill, Robert. "We Want Georgia, South Carolina, Louisiana, Mississippi and Alabama — Right Now . . . We Also Want Four Hundred Billion Dollars Back Pay." *Esquire*, January 1969, 72–75, 146–148.

Shiloh Baptist Church. *One Hundred Years Pilgrimage of Faith, 1881–1981*. N.p. [Detroit], n.d. [1981].

Shogan, Robert, and Tom Craig. *The Detroit Race Riot: A Study in Violence*. Philadelphia, 1964.

Sigatoos, Robert A. *Cotton Row to Beale Street: A Business History of Memphis*. Memphis, 1979.

Sillers, Florence Warfield, comp. *History of Bolivar County, Mississippi: Its Creation, Pioneer Days and Progress, in the Heart of the Mississippi Delta*. Spartanburg, SC, 1976. First published in 1948.

Silver, Christopher, and John V. Moeser. *The Separate City: Black Communities in the Urban South, 1940–1968*. Lexington, KY, 1995.

Simone, Nina. *I Put a Spell on You: The Autobiography of Nina Simone*. With Stephen Cleary. New York, 1993. First published in 1991.

Sklar, Kathryn Kish. *Catherine Beecher: A Study in American Domesticity*. New Haven, 1973.

Smith, Kelly Miller. *Social Crisis Preaching*. The Lyman Beecher Lectures. Macon, GA, 1984.

Smith, Reverend Robert. *In the Shadow of C. L. Franklin*. N.p., 1995.

Smith, Roland, ed. *The National Baptist Bulletin, 1946*. N.p., n.d.

————, ed. *The National Baptist Bulletin, 1948*. N.p., n.d.

Smith, Suzanne E. *Dancing in the Street: Motown and the Cultural Politics of Detroit*. Cambridge, MA, 1999.

Southall, Geneva. "Black Composers and Religious Music." *The Black Perspective in Music* 2, no. 1 (Spring 1974): 45–50.

Southern, Eileen, comp. "In Retrospect: Letters from W. C. Handy to William Grant Still." *The Black Perspective in Music* 7, no. 2 (Fall 1979): 199–233.

————. "In Retrospect: Letters from W. C. Handy to William Grant Still: Part 2." *The Black Perspective in Music* 8, no. 1 (Spring 1980): 65–119.

Spencer, Jon Michael. *Protest and Praise: Sacred Music of Black Religion*. Minneapolis, 1990.

————. *Sacred Symphony: The Chanted Sermon of the Black Preacher*. Westport, CT, 1987.

————. *Sing a New Song: Liberating Black Hymnody*. Minneapolis, 1995.

Spillers, Hortense J. "Martin Luther King and the Style of the Black Sermon." *The Black Scholar* 3, no. 1 (September 1971): 14–27.

————. "Moving On Down the Line." *American Quarterly* 40, no. 1 (March 1988): 83–109.

Stampp, Kenneth M. *The Peculiar Institution: Slavery in the Ante-bellum South*. New York, 1956.

Stephens, Gregory. *On Racial Frontiers: The New Culture of Frederick Douglass, Ralph Ellison, and Bob Marley*. New York, 1999.

Stevenson, Marshall F., Jr. "African Americans and Jews in Organized Labor: A Case Study of Detroit, 1920–1950." In Franklin et al., *African Americans and Jews in the Twentieth Century*, 237–63.

Stone, Sonja H. "Oral Tradition and Spiritual Drama: The Cultural Mosaic for Black Preaching." *Journal of the Interdenominational Theological Center* 8, no. 1 (Fall 1980): 17–27.

Stovall, A. J. *The Growth of Black Elected Officials in the City of Detroit, 1870–1973*. Lewiston, NY, 1996.

St. Paul Missionary Baptist Church. *A Century with Christ*. Cleveland, MS, 1981.

Stuckey, Sterling. "'My Burden Lightened': Frederick Douglass, the Bible, and Slave Culture." In Wimbush, *African Americans and the Bible*, 251–65. New York, 2000.

Suggs, Henry Lewis, ed. *The Black Press in the South, 1865–1979*. Westport, CT, 1983.

Sugrue, Thomas J. *The Origins of the Urban Crisis: Race and Inequality in Postwar Detroit*. Princeton, 1996.

Sullivan, Patricia. *Days of Hope: Race and Democracy in the New Deal*. Chapel Hill, NC, 1996.

Swain, Jonnie Dee, Jr. "Black Mayors: Urban Decline and the Underclass." *Journal of Black Studies* 24, no. 1 (September 1993): 16–28.

Taft, Michael. *Blues Lyric Poetry*. New York, 1983.

Tallmadge, William. "Blue Notes and Blue Tonality." *The Black Perspective in Music* 12, no. 2 (Fall 1984): 155–65.

Taruskin, Richard. "Music's Dangers and the Case for Control." *New York Times*, December 9, 2001, sec. 2, 1, 36.

Taylor, Gardner C. *How Shall They Preach*. Elgin, IL, 1977.

Taylor, Henry Louis, Jr., ed. *African Americans and the Rise of Buffalo's Post-industrial City, 1940 to Present*. 2 vols. Buffalo, 1990.

_____. "The Theories of William Julius Wilson and the Black Experience in Buffalo, New York." In Taylor, *African Americans and the Rise of Buffalo's Post-industrial City*, 2:66–88.

Taylor, William Banks. *Down on Parchman Farm: The Great Prison in the Mississippi Delta*. Columbus, OH, 1999.

Thelwell, Mike. "Back with the Wind: Mr. Styron and the Reverend Turner." In Clarke, *William Styron's Nat Turner*, 79–91.

Thomas, June Manning. *Redevelopment and Race: Planning a Finer City in Postwar Detroit*. Baltimore, 1997.

Thomas, Latta R. *Biblical Faith and the Black American*. Valley Forge, PA, 1976.

Thomas, Richard W. *Life for Us Is What We Make It: Building Black Community in Detroit, 1915–1945*. Bloomington, IN, 1992.

Thompson, Julius Eric. *Dudley Randall, Broadside Press, and the Black Arts Movement in Detroit, 1960–1995*. Jefferson, NC, 1999.

_____. "Mississippi." In *The Black Press in the South, 1865–1979*, edited by Henry Lewis Suggs, 177–210. Westport, CT, 1983.

_____. "An Urban Voice of the People: The Black Press in Michigan, 1865–1985." In *The Black Press in the Middle West, 1865–1985*, edited by Henry Lewis Suggs, 135–64. Westport, CT, 1996.

Thompson, Patrick H. *The History of Negro Baptists in Mississippi*. Jackson, MS, 1898.

Thurman, Howard. *Jesus and the Disinherited*. New York, 1949.

_____. *The Negro Spiritual Speaks of Life and Death*. New York, 1947.

_____. *With Head and Heart: The Autobiography of Howard Thurman*. New York, 1979.

Tillich, Hannah. *From Time to Time*. New York, 1973.

Titon, Jeff Todd. "Clarence LaVaughn Franklin." In *Encyclopedia of African-American Culture and History*, edited by Jack Salzman, David Lionel Smith, and Cornel West, 2:1038–39. New York, 1996.

_____. *Early Downhome Blues: A Musical and Cultural Analysis*. 2d ed. Chapel Hill, NC, 1994.

_____. *Give Me This Mountain: Life History and Selected Sermons of Reverend C. L. Franklin*. Urbana, IL, 1989.

_____. "Reverend C. L. Franklin: Black American Poet-Preacher." *Folklife Annual*, 1987, 86–105.

Tooze, Sandra B. *Muddy Waters: The Mojo Man*. Toronto, 1997.

Trotter, Joe William. *The Great Migration in Historical Perspective: New Dimensions of Race, Class, and Gender*. Bloomington, IN, 1991.

Trulear, Harold Dean. "The Lord Will Make a Way Somehow: Black Worship and the Afro-American Story." *Journal of the Interdenominational Theological Center* 13, no. 1 (Fall 1985): 87–104.

Tucker, David M. *Black Pastors and Leaders: Memphis, 1819–1972*. Memphis, 1975.

_____. *Lieutenant Lee of Beale Street*. Nashville, 1971.

Turner, William C., Jr. "The Musicality of Black Preaching: A Phenomenology." *Journal of Black Sacred Music* 2, no. 1 (Spring 1988): 21–34.

United Community Services of Metropolitan Detroit. *Population by Race, Metropolitan Detroit Area: 1900–1960*. Detroit, 1963.

Violanti, Anthony. *Miracle in Buffalo: How the Dream of Baseball Revived a City.* New York, 1991.

Walker, Clarence E. *We Can't Go Home Again: An Argument about Afrocentrism.* New York, 2001.

Walker, Randolph Meade. "Dialectic Tensions in T. O. Fuller's Historical Writings." *The West Tennessee Historical Society Papers* 51 (December 1997): 21–34.

Walker, Reverend Charles. "Lucie E. Campbell Williams: A Cultural Biography." In Reagon, *We'll Understand It Better By and By,* 121–38.

_____. "Lucie E. Campbell Williams: A Cultural Biography." In Weisenfeld and Newman, *This Far by Faith,* 56–70.

Walker, Wyatt Tee. *"Somebody's Calling My Name": Black Sacred Music and Social Change.* Valley Forge, PA, 1979.

Walzer, Michael. *The Company of Critics.* New York, 1989.

Ward, Brian. *Just My Soul Responding: Rhythm and Blues, Black Consciousness, and Race Relations.* Berkeley, 1998.

Ward, Hiley H. *Prophet of the Black Nation.* Philadelphia, 1969.

Ward-Royster, Willa, as told to Toni Rose. *How I Got Over: Clara Ward and the World-Famous Ward Singers.* Philadelphia, 1997.

Wartman, Charles J. *Detroit — Ten Years After!* Detroit, 1953.

Washington, James M., ed. *A Testament of Hope: The Essential Writings of Martin Luther King, Jr.* San Francisco, 1986.

Washington, Joseph R., Jr., ed. *Black Religion and Public Policy: Ethical and Historical Perspectives.* N.p., 1978.

_____. "The Peculiar Perils and Promise of Black Folk Religion." In Harrell, *Varieties of Southern Evangelicism,* 59–69.

Watkins, Ralph. "The Marcus Garvey Movement in Buffalo, New York." *Afro-Americans in New York Life and History* 1, no. 1 (January 1977): 37–48.

Weaver, Robert C. *Negro Labor: A National Problem.* Port Washington, NY, 1969. First published in 1946.

Webb, Lillian. "Michaux as Prophet." *Journal of the Interdenominational Theological Center* 8, no. 1 (Fall 1980): 1–16.

Weeks, Linton. *Cleveland: A Centennial History, 1886–1986.* Cleveland, MS, 1985.

Weisenfeld, Judith, and Richard Newman, eds. *This Far by Faith: Readings in African-American Women's Religious Biography.* New York, 1996.

Welding, Pete. "An Interview with Muddy Waters." *The American Folk Music Occasional* 2 (1970): 2–7.

Werner, Craig. *A Change Is Gonna Come: Music, Race and the Soul of America.* New York, 1999.

Wexler, Jerry, and David Ritz. *Rhythm and the Blues: A Life in American Music.* New York, 1993.

Who Started Woman's Day? N.p., 1955.

Widick, B. J. "Black Workers: Double Discontents." In *Auto Work and Its Discontents,* edited by B. J. Widick, 46–52. Baltimore, 1976.

_____. *Detroit: City of Race and Class Violence.* Chicago, 1972.

Wiggins, William H., Jr. "'In the Rapture': The Black Aesthetic and Folk Drama." *Callaloo* 2 (February 1978): 103–11.

Williams, Ethel L. *Biographical Directory of Negro Ministers.* 2d ed. Metuchen, NJ, 1970.

Williams, Lillian Serece. *Strangers in the Land of Paradise: The Creation of an African American Community, Buffalo, New York, 1900–1940.* Bloomington, IN, 1999.

Williams, Mark, and Denise Strub, comp. *Reflections of Bolivar County.* Marceline, MS, 1998.

Williams, Otis. *Temptations.* With Patricia Romanowski. New York, 1988.

Williams, Preston N. "Criteria for Decision-Making for Social Ethics in the Black Community." *Journal of the Interdenominational Theological Center* 1, no. 1 (Fall 1973): 65–79.

Williams, Robert F. "Interview: Robert F. Williams." *The Black Scholar* 1, no. 7 (May 1970): 2–14.

Williams-Jones, Pearl, and Bernice Johnson Reagon, eds. "Conversations: Roberta Martin Singers Roundtable." In Reagon, *We'll Understand It Better By and By,* 287–306.

Wilmore, Gayraud, ed. *African American Religious Studies: An Interdisciplinary Anthology.* Durham, NC, 1989.

_____. *Black Religion and Black Radicalism: An Interpretation of the Religious History of Afro-American People.* Maryknoll, NY, 1983. First published in 1973.

_____. Introduction to Wilmore, *African American Religious Studies,* xi–xxii.

Wilmore, Gayraud, and James H. Cone, eds. *Black Theology: A Documentary History, 1966–1979.* Maryknoll, NY, 1979.

Wilson, Bobby M. "Church Participation: A Social Special Analysis in a Community of Black In-Migrants." *Journal of Black Studies* 10, no. 2 (December 1979): 198–217.

Wilson, Charles Reagan. *Judgment and Grace in Dixie: Southern Faiths from Faulkner to Elvis.* Athens, GA, 1995.

Wilson, Mary. *Dreamgirl: My Life as a Supreme.* New York, 1986.

Wilson, Olly. "The Significance of the Relationship between Afro-American Music and West African Music." *The Black Perspective in Music* 2, no. 1 (Spring 1974): 3–22.

Wilson, Sunnie. *Toast of the Town: The Life and Times of Sunnie Wilson.* With John Cohassey. Detroit, 1998.

Wimbush, Vincent L., ed. *African Americans and the Bible.* New York, 2000.

Wolff, David. *You Send Me: The Life and Times of Sam Cooke.* With S. R. Crain, Clifton White, and G. David Tenenbaum. New York, 1995.

Wood, Joe, ed. *Malcolm X: In Our Own Image.* New York, 1992.

Work, Monroe N., ed. *Negro Year Book: An Annual Encyclopedia of the Negro, 1921–1922.* Tuskegee, AL, 1922.

_____. *Negro Year Book: An Annual Encyclopedia of the Negro, 1931–1932.* Tuskegee, AL, 1931.

_____. *Negro Year Book: An Annual Encyclopedia of the Negro, 1937–1938.* Tuskegee, AL, 1937.

Wright, Richard. *Black Boy (American Hunger).* New York, 1991.

Yearwood, Lennox. "First Shiloh Baptist Church of Buffalo, New York: From Storefront to Major Religious Institution." *Afro-Americans in New York Life and History* 1, no. 1 (January 1977): 81–91.

Young, Al. "Aretha Franklin." Brilliant Careers, *Salon,* August 3, 1999, http://www.salon.com/people/bc/1999/08/03/aretha/index.html.

_____. *Bodies and Soul: Musical Memoirs.* Berkeley, 1981.

Young, Alan. *Woke Me Up This Morning: Black Gospel Singers and the Gospel Life.* Jackson, MS, 1997.

Young, Andrew. *An Easy Burden: The Civil Rights Movement and the Transformation of America.* New York, 1996.

Young, Coleman, and Lonnie Wheeler. *Hard Stuff: The Autobiography of Mayor Coleman Young.* New York, 1994.

Young, Henry J. *Major Black Religious Leaders since 1940.* Nashville, 1979.

Young, Judge J. P., ed. *Standard History of Memphis, Tennessee, from a Study of the Original Sources.* Knoxville, 1912.

Zaretsky, Irving I., and Mark P. Leone, eds. *Religious Movements in Contemporary America.* Princeton, 1974.

Zolten, Jerry. *Great God A'Mighty! The Dixie Hummingbirds: Celebrating the Rise of Soul Gospel Music.* New York, 2003.

Unpublished Work

Dillard, Angela Denise. "From the Reverend Charles A. Hill to the Reverend Albert B. Cleage, Jr.: Change and Continuity in the Patterns of Civil Rights Mobilizations in Detroit, 1935–1967." PhD diss., University of Michigan, 1995.

Fisher, Miles Mark. "The History of the Olivet Baptist Church of Chicago." Masters thesis, University of Chicago, 1922.

Luby, Elliot D. [principal investigator]. "City in Crisis: The People and Their Riot. A Social Psychological Study of the Detroit Uprising and Its Aftermath." Typescript, Detroit, n.d.

Melton, Gloria Brown. "Blacks in Memphis, Tennessee, 1920–1955: A Historical Study." PhD diss., Washington State University, 1982.

Newman, Mark Allen. "Entrepreneurs of Profits and Pride: From Black Appeal to Radio Soul." PhD diss., University of California, Los Angeles, 1986.

Palosaari, Ronald Gerald. "The Image of the Black Minister in the Black Novel from Dunbar to Baldwin." PhD diss., University of Minnesota, 1970.

Spillers, Hortense. "Fabrics of History: Essays on the Black Sermon." PhD diss., Brandeis University, 1974.

INDEX

ABOUT THE AUTHOR

Nick Salvatore is a professor at Cornell University. His two previous books, *Eugene V. Debs* and *We All Got History,* are considered landmark works of biography and have garnered numerous accolades, including a Bancroft Prize.